North Carolina-South Carolina Bible Records

Collected by
Jeannette Holland Austin

HERITAGE BOOKS
2008

HERITAGE BOOKS
AN IMPRINT OF HERITAGE BOOKS, INC.

Books, CDs, and more—Worldwide

For our listing of thousands of titles see our website
at
www.HeritageBooks.com

Published 2008 by
HERITAGE BOOKS, INC.
Publishing Division
100 Railroad Ave. #104
Westminster, Maryland 21157

Copyright © 1988, 1998 Jeannette Holland Austin

All rights reserved. No part of this book may be reproduced or transmitted in any form or by any means, electronic or mechanical, including photocopying, recording or by any information storage and retrieval system without written permission from the author, except for the inclusion of brief quotations in a review.

International Standard Book Number: 978-1-58549-595-5

NOTE TO THE READER

This collection of North Carolina - S. C. Bible records contains an itemized list of the BIRTHS, MARRIAGES, and DEATHS: found in approximately 450 family Bibles.

Many of the records were sent to me over the past twenty years or so by the actual owners, while others I copied from Bibles located in the Georgia State Archives, local libraries, or other genealogical publications or Revolutionary War Pension Applications. The collection spans a period of 1600s to 1900s. It is my express desire that many readers will be helped by this effort, bearing in mind that many of the original owners are now deceased and/or otherwise difficult to locate.

Jeannette Holland Austin

TABLE OF CONTENTS

ABERCROMBIE, James of S. C.	123
ACKER, William H. of S. C.	263-265
ADAMS, Mary Ella of N. C	368-370
ADAMS, George and Sarah of Abbeville, S. C.	286-287
ALEXANDER, Dr. James R. and Dorcas of Mecklenburg Co., N. C., Revolutionary War Soldier	547-548
ALFORD, Green Haywood	504-506
ALLEN, Arva of Abbeville, S. C.	260
ALLISON, Sallie W. of S. C.	113
ANDERSON, John, Revolutionary War Soldier, of S. C.	223-224, 357-358
ANDERSON, James	358-359
ANDERSON, Joshua B. of Edgecombe Co., N. C.	563-564
ARLEDGE-HIGGINS of S. C.	156
ARMSTRONG, Edward of N. C	370-371
ARNOLD, Benjamin, Sr. of S. C.	251-252
ASH, William of S. C., Revolutionary War Soldier	227
BAILEY, Alfred of N. C.	383-384
BAKER, Joseph of Charleston, S. C.	355-356
BAKER, German of N. C.	448-449
BALDRIDGE, Robert of N. C.	463
BALE, John of S. C.	253
BALL-GARRETT of S. C.	274-275
BALL, Jeremiah of Gray Court, S. C.	266-267
BARNES, Bennett of N. C.	412
BARNES of Wilson Co., N. C. near White Oak Swamp	410-411
BARNETT, John H. of Edgefield County, S. C.	331-332
BARNETT, John	46-47
BARNHILL, James of N. C., Revolutionary War Soldier	377-378
BARRON-BYNUM-BAXTER of S. C.	167-169

BARRON, Thomas of S. C.	343-344
BATTLE, Thomas of N. C.	503-504
BELCHER-BISHOP-GREGORY of S. C.	105-106
BELCHER, Elias of S. C.	158-160
BISHOP, Henry Jefferson of S. C.	43-46
BLACK, John J. of N. C.	391-392
BLACKSTOCK, Kindred of S. C.	214-216
BLANTON, Greenberry of N. C.	425
BLASSINGAME, Thomas of S. C.	
BLASSINGAME, Thomas of Anderson Dist., S. C.	290
BLEDSOE, Lewis of Granville Co., N. C., Revolutionary War Soldier	580-581
BODDIE, Nathan of "Rosehill" near Nashville, N. C.	433
BOND, Stephen Findlay of N. C.	389
BOONE, Squire of S. C., Revolutionary War Soldier	351-353
BOYD, William of Chester Dist., S. C., Revolutionary War Soldier	351-352
BRADBURY, Joseph Crency of N. C.	491-493
BRADFORD, John Angel and Mary of S. C., Revolutionary War Soldier	303-304
BRADWELL, Thomas of S. C. (two versions)	194-196, 268-269
BRANNON, John Benjamin of S. C.	70
BRASWELL, Richard and Penelope	551-552
BRETT, Elisha D.	501-502
BRICE-NEWKIRK	526
BRICE, John	403-404
BRIDGER, Edwin B.	548
BRINSON, John L.	429-431
BROCK, Nathaniel	578
BROCK, Thomas Maxwell	578-579
BROCKETT, William	583
BROGDON, John Bagnal	338-341
BROOKS, Elisha of Abbeville, S. C. -	351
BROWN, Jacob	581-582
BROWN, Hamilton Allen	509-510
BROWN, Moses	53-55

Name	Pages
BROWN, Badger L.	398-399
BROWN, John	473-475
BRYAN, John of S. C., Revolutionary War Soldier	282-283, 359-360
BUCHANAN, William of N. C.	231-232, 427-428
BUCHANAN, Benjamin of S. C.	
BUCKHEISTER, John Bellinger, Sr. of S. C.	3-4
BUFFINGTON, Mary of S. C.	224-226
BULL. William H. of Orangeburg, S. C.	281
BUNCH, Jacob K. of N. C.	446-447
BURDEN, William and Drucilla of Newberry District, S. C.	276-277
BYERS, Edward of S. C.	96-97
BYNUM, Gideon of N. C.	552-553
CADDIN, Nancy Ann Dora of S. C.	129-130
CALDWELL, John C. of S. C., Revolutionary War Soldier	360
CALDWELL, John C. of S. C.	108-109
CALLAWAY, Joseph of Rowan Co., N. C.	524-525
CAMPBELL, Richard of N. C., Revolutionary War Soldier	582-583
CANNON, Colonel George Speake of S. C.	314-315
CANNON, Hon. William Henry, Sr. of S. C.	200-201
CANNON, Isaac of S. C.	302
CANNON, William H. of Darlington Co., S. C.	247-249
CARDOZO, David N. of S. C.	318
CARDWELL, David -	131
CARLISLE, James of S. C., Revolutionary War Soldier	360
CARLTON, Lewis and Elizabeth of N. C., Revolutionary War Soldier	556-557
CARROLL, Joseph of S. C., Revolutionary War Soldier	360-361
CARRUTHERS, John H. of N. C.	507
CARSON. John of N. C.	390
CARTER, Jacob of Colleton District, S. C.	133-134
CATER, Irvin of S. C.	250-251
CHANCY, Samuel of N. C.	573
CHANCY, Neill of N. C.	575-576
CHAPPELL, Hicks of S. C., Revolutionary War Soldier	361
CHESTNUT, John, Colonel of S. C.	12-13
CHILDS, Lysander D. of S. C. -	261-262

CLARK, James of Orange Co., N. C.	520-522
CLARK, John of N. C.	290-291
CLARK, Joseph of S. C., Revolutionary War Soldier	362
CLARK, William of S. C.	271
CLARK, Hugh McCrainey of N. C.	371-372
CLAY-COOK of N. C.	408-409
CLEMENTS. William of N. C., Revolutionary War Soldier	377
CLONINGER. Jones Stanhope of N. C.	564-565
COATE, Henry of N. C.	522
COBB, Ann, Mrs. of S. C.	138-141
COBIA, Daniel of S. C.	86
COFFIELD, John of N. C.	484
COLLINS, Moses of S. C.	100-101
COLLINS, Moses of Orangeburg Dist. S. C.	154
CONGER, Stephen of N. C.	464-465
COOKS-SINTON of S. C.	132
COOK, Francis I. of S. C.	237-242
COOPER, Walter Plural of S. C.	59
COOPER, John L. of S. C.	58
CORBIN, Samuel of S. C.	36-37
COX, Esther, Mrs. of S. C.	13-14
COX, David of N. C.	375-376
CRAIG, John Kerr of S. C.	26-29
CRAIN, Stephen of S. C., Revolutionary War Soldier	34-35
CROCKER, Solomon of S. C.	155
CROCKETT, William of N. C.	433-434
CROOM, Jesse of N. C.	549
CRUTCHFIELD, Charles R. of Warren Co., N. C.	527-530
CRUTHIS, James of Randolph Co., N. C.	555
DALLAS, James J. of N. C.	384-385
DANIEL, Jesse of Charleston, S. C.	214-215
DANIELL. Robert of N. C.	431-432
DAVIS, John Maynard of S. C.	350-351
DAVIS, Joshua of S. C.	190-191
DAVIS, Benjamin and Elizabeth of Chatham Co., N. C.	545

Name	Pages
DAWSON, William of S. C.	349-350
DAWSON, S. J. of N. C.	481-482
DELLINGER, Joseph of N. C.	422
DENDY, Leonard Latharo of S. C.	230-231
DERDEN, Mark of S. C.	110-111
DEVANE, Thomas of New Hanover Co., N. C.	463
DEVANE, Thomas of Bladen Co., N. C.	457-458
DEVENY, Aaron of N. C., Revolutionary War. Soldier	520
DICKENSON-THOMAS-POPE of S.C.	60-61
DICKEY, Ebenezer and Mary of Rowan Co., N. C., Revolutionary War Soldier, 2 versions	549-550, 550
DICKINS, Mary Wilson Brown of Person Co., N. C.	536-545
DICKSON, Thomas of Anderson Dist. S. C.	253-259
DIXON, Thomas and Anna of N. C., Revolutionary War Soldier	546
DUDLEY-EATON of N. C.	554
DUNKLIN, James W., M. D. of Hole Swamp, St. Mathew's Parish, Berkley District, S. C.	184-186
DURANT, George of Northumberland Co., Va. & Perquimans Co., N.C.	372-373
DURBOROW, David and Rebecca of N. C.	509
EARLEY of N. C.	386
EBORN, Robert of N. C.	454
EDWARDS, John of S. C.	120-121
EGGER, Andrew of S. C.	64-65
ELLIS, Enoch of S. C.	356-357
EVANS, Zachariah of N. C.	488-490
FARIS-JACKSON of S. C.	91-93
FIELDS, John and Mary of N. C., Revolutionary War Soldier	514
FISHER, Turner of N. C.	470
FITE, Jane C. Abernathy of N. C.	519
FOX, David of S. C.	324-326
FRANKLIN, Elbert	128-129
FREEMAN, John of S. C.	127-128
FREEMAN, David of S. C.	151
FRENCH, James of S. C.	300-301

FRIPP. John E. of S. C.	74-76
GAILLARD, John of S. C.	348-349
GARRISS, Wade of Bertie Co., N. C.	460-462
GIBSON, Prudence of N. C.	523
GIRARDEAU, Revolutionary J. L. of S. C.	287-290
GIST, David C. of S. C.	160-161
GLAZIER, John, Captain of S. C.	186-187
GLEASON, Henry R. of Charleston, S. C.	279
GLOVER, Dr. W. P. of Edgefield Co., S. C.	277-278
GOLDING, Anthony Foster of S. C.	198-199
GORE, William Iredell of S. C.	176-177
GRAY, William of N. C.	436-437
GREEN, Napoleon B. of N. C.	444-445
GRIDER, John and Isabel of N.C., Revolutionary War Soldier	554-555
GRIER, Samuel of Georgetown, S. C.	57-58
GRIFFIN, James of N. C., Revolutionary War Soldier	475
GRIGG, James Hilliard of S.C.	154-155
GUYTON, Moses of Spartanburg Co., S. C.	295
GUYTON, Aaron of S. C., Revolutionary War Soldier	148-149
HABERSHAM, Richard W. of S. C.	249-250
HACKETT, W. J. of S. C.	236-237
HALL, W. L. of N. C.	485-487
HAMLIN, Thomas of S.C.	262, 267
HAMRICK, M. C. of N.C.	425-426
HANEY, Robert of N. C., Revolutionary War Soldier	400-401
HARBIN, Walter of Davie and Rowan Co's, N. C.	419-420
HARDEN, William of S. C.	234-236
HARDY, Samuel of S. C.	271-273
HARRELL, William of Darlington Dist., S. C.	51-52
HARRELL, Levi of N. C.	502
HARRIS, John of Abbeville Co., S. C.	327-328
HARRIS, Robert and Lucy of Rockingham Co., N. C., Rev War Soldier	560-561
HARRISON, Benjamin of Edgefield Co.. S. C.	204-205
HARRIS, George W. of Pitt Co., N. C.	413
HAWKINS, Philemon II of N. C.	485

HEDLESTON, W. D. of S. C.	32-34
HENDERSON, James of S. C.	125
HENDREN, Jesse of N. C.	394-395
HENRY, Joseph of Lincoln Co., N. C.	574
HENRY, Joseph of Buncombe	575
HENRY, Robert and Celia of S. C.	102
HENRY, James of Lincoln Co., N. C.	577
HENSON, Daniel of N. C., Revolutionary War Soldier	467
HERBEMONT, Andre of S. C.	273-274
HICKS, John of N. C., Revolutionary War Soldier ,	378
HICKS, James of N. C.	364-365
HIERS, W. H. of Colleton Co., S. C.	170
HILEY (HIELY), Roland of S. C.	213-214
HOLCOMBE, Hosea H. "Lot" of S. C.	67-69
HOLLAND, William of N. C., Revolutionary War Soldier	402
HOLLAND, Isaac of N. C.	506
HOLLINGSWORTH, Zebedee of Sampson Co., N. C., Revolutionary War Soldier	403
HOOPER, Benjamin Chastain of N. C.	515-516
HOPE, James of S. C.	228-230
HOPE, Hugh Washington of S. C.	228-230
HORN, Joshua L., Jr. of Rocky Mt., N. C.	265, 558-560
HOUSEAL, Johann Adam of S. C.	107-108
HOWARD, John of Edgefield Co., S. C.	293-294
HUGHEY, John of S. C.	37-38
HUGHLETT, William and Mary of Stokes Co., N. C., Revolutionary War Soldier	404-406
HUGUEIN, Abram of Grahamville, S. C.	296-297
HURLEY, William Turner of N. C.	508
HUTCHISON, William F. of S. C.	217-223
INABINET, James Henry Mallard of Orangeburg Co., S. C.	319-324
INARNIT, Jacob of S. C.	341-342
ISBELL, Thomas of Wilkes Co., N. C.	534
ISBELL, Benjamin of Wilkes Co., N. C.	535
IVY, Robert Lucius of Halifax Co., N. C.	479-481

JACKSON. Samuel and Hannah of Stokes Ca., N. C., Revolutionary War Soldier	508
JAMES, Morgan of S. C.	76-78
JAMES, Reuben of S. C.	38
JAMES, Mary of S. C.	344-345
JARNIGAN, Chesley of N. C.	477
JENKINS, Lewis Harris of N. C.	367-368
JESTER, Levi of Edgefield Co., S. C.	280-281
JOHNSON, Gideon of S. C.	227-228
JOHNSON, Isham Peter of N. C.	415-416
JOHNSON-CARTER of N. C.	428-429
JOHNSON-STATON-ARLEDGE of N. C.	386-389
JOHNSON, Ahah of S. C.	243
JOHNSTON, Littleton of N. C.	447-448
JOHNSTON, Daniel of S. C.	141-143
JONES, Mrs. Tignal's Notebook of N. C.	466-467
JONES, Vincent, Sr. of S. C.	22-26
JORDAN, Burrell of Northampton Co., N. C., Revolutionary War Soldier	406-407
KELSICK, William of N. C.	473
KENNEDY, Major of S. C.	157-158
KENNEDY, Andrew of N. C., Revolutionary War Soldier	379
KERR, William of S. C.	334
KIMBROUGH, Mary of N. C.	459-460
KIMZEY, Hamilton of N. C.	477-479
LANCASTER, James of Edgecombe Co., N. C.	516-519
LANE, Jesse and wife, Rhoda Jolly of N. C.	399-401
LANE, Joel of N. C.	476
LANE, Jonathan of N. C.	476
LANE, Charles of N. C.	476
LANG, Mary of S. C.	14-17
LARIMORE, Mary Rebecca Rodgers of S. C.	21-22
LEAGUE, James of S. C.	126-127
LEDBETTER, Isaac of Rutherford Co., N. C.	443-444
LEE, Aron Bridges of S. C.	383
LEE, Aron Bridges of N. C.	165

LEGARE, Elizabeth Hammett of S. C.	242
LEWIS, William of N. C.	381-383
LEWIS, Howell of N. C.	454-456
LILES, Samuel of S. C.	181-182
LOFTIS, Hutson of S. C.	326-327
LONG, James and Margery of Anderson Co., S. C., Revolutionary War Soldier	303-304
LOVETT, Thomas Fenns, Sr. of S. C.	170
LUCAS, Edward P. of S. C.	332-333
LUCAS, Charles D. of Marlboro Co., S. C. of S. C.	316-317
LYNES, George of S. C.	81-84
MARION, Nathaniel of S. C.	100
MARTIN, James of N. C., Revolutionary War Soldier	438-439
MARTIN, John Christian of Charleston, S. C.	171
MARTIN, John of N. C., Revolutionary War Soldier,	437-438
MARTIN, Joseph and Patsy, of N. C., Revolutionary War Soldier	434-435
MARTIN, Joseph of S. C., Revolutionary War Soldier	173-175
MARTIN, Samuel of S. C.	175-176
MARTIN, Thomas of S. C., Revolutionary War Soldier	
MARTIN, David of S. C., Revolutionary War Soldier	171-173
MATTISON, Urius J. of S. C.	203-204
MATTISON, James of S. C.	202-203
MAY, Thomas Jefferson of S. C.	226
MAY, John of Rockingham Co., N. C.	511-512
McCANTS, Jane of S. C.	71-73
McCASKILL, John of S. C.	80-81
McCLENDON, Burrell of S. C.	143
McDONALD, John of Fayetteville, N. C.	580
McDOWELL, John of S. C. (two versions),	56-57, 95
McDOWELL, William of Edgefield Co., S. C.	334-335
McELRATH-SEAY of S. C.	91
McELWEE. James of S. C.	85
McGILL, Hugh of S. C.	199-200
McGILL, Samuel Davis of S. C., son of Roger	202, 206-208
McILVAIN, Sarah of S. C.	4-5

McINTIRE, Andrew of N. C.	531-534
McKIBBEN, Alexander of N. C.	493-494
McKIBBEN, Thomas of N. C.	494-495
McKINLEY, William of S. C.	278-279
McKINNEY, Willis of Rutherford Co., N. C.	423-424
McMILLAN, Malcolm of N. C., Revolutionary War Soldier	393-394
MILLER, John David of S. C.	197-198
MILLER, Jerome of S. C.	47
MILLER, Jacob of N.C.	365-366
MILLER, Andrew of N. C.	472
MILLS, John of S. C., Revolutionary War Soldier	35
MILLS of Camden of S. C.	208-211
MINTON, Silvanus of S. C.	134
MITCHELL-RILEY of S. C.	87-89
MITCHELL, David of N. C., Revolutionary War Soldier	379-380
MITCHELL, Solomon and Nancy of Abbeville Co., S. C., Revolutionary War Soldier	305-306
MOATS, Davis of Newberry Co., S. C.	269-271
MOON, Thomas of N. C.	373-375
MOON, John P. of S. C.	65-66
MOORE, Lemuel C. of N. C.	445-446
MOORE, Stephen of Chatham Co., N. C.	510-511
MOORE-LINDSAY of S. C.	94
MORRIS, Gladys Endell D. of S. C.	265
MOSELEY, Daniel of S. C. (two versions),	205-206, 211-213
MURCHISON, Colin Campbell of S. C.	192-293
MURFF, Randolph S. of S. C.	192-193
MURRAY, John of Grove Hill Plantation, S. C.	217
MYERS-MYRES of S. C.	102-104
NELSON, Robert of Waxhaw, S. C.	29-32
NEWTON, Enoch of Kenansville, Duplin Co., N. C.	551
NOBLE, John, Revolutionary of S. C.	145-146
NORRIS, William Calhoun of S. C.	299-300
NORTH, Edward of S. C.	73-74
OLIFF. John Shears of N. C., Revolutionary War Soldier	471-472
OSBORN, John of N. C.	483

Name	Pages
OSBORN, Jonathan of N. C.	441-442
OSBORN, Jeremiah of N. C.	439-440
OSWALT, Emanuel of S. C.	18-19
OTWELL, John C. of S. C.	66-67
PACE, William of S. C.	244-246
PADGETT, William of Colleton Co., S. C.	181
PALMER, W. P. of N. C.	442-443
PALMER, Thomas Augustus of Stanleyville, N. C.	440-441
PARKER-JENKINS-CRADDOCK of S. C.	1-2
PARKER, Joseph of Edgecombe Co., N. C.	407-408
PEAKE, William I of N. C.	487-488
PEARSON, John of Camden, Fairfield dist., S. C.	285-286
PENDER, Solomon	413-416
PERRY, John Wesley, Jr. of Granville Co., N. C.	420
POOL, James and Ursula of Laurens Co., S. C., Revolutionary War Soldier	301
POPE, Hardy A. and Charity of Robeson Co., N. C., Revolutionary War Soldier	558
PORTER, Phillip of S. C.	193-194
PORTER, James	572-573
POWELL, Britain of N. C., Revolutionary War Soldier	401-402
PRIESTLY, James, Sr. of S. C.	338
PRINCE-FLEMING of S. C.	78-79
PROFFITT, Turner C. of N. C.	500
PROSSER-DARRONS of S. C.	130
RABB, John	188-190
RAINES, James of S. C.	41-43
RANDOLPH, Jesse of Pitt Co., N. C.	192-193, 449-451
RAY, Hosea Holcomb of S. C.	115-116
REECE, Rebekah of S. C.	11-12
REED, Joseph and Isabella of Pickens Co., S. C., Revolutionary War Soldier	304-305
REED, William of S. C.	330-331
REID, George, Capt. of S. C.	244
REID, Joseph of Pickens Co., S. C., Revolutionary War Soldier	292-293

REID, Joseph of S. C.	304-305
RIVERS, William George, Jr. of S. C.	89-90
ROBESON, Noah of N. C.	418
ROBINSON, Clack of N. C.	435-436
ROBINSON, James of S. C.	48-51
ROGERS, Reuben, Sr. of N. C.	561-563
ROLLINS, Jonas of N. C.	426-427
ROSE, John, Revolutionary War Soldier of Surry Co., N. C.	396
ROSS, George, Sr. of S. C.	191-192
ROSS, Noah Webb of S. C.	161-164
RUSSELL, John of N. C.	362-364
SAXON, Lewis of S. C., Revolutionary War Soldier	150
SCRUGGS, Richard of S. C.	134-135
SEYLE, John Henry of S.C.	146-147
SHEARER, Robert Findlay	557
SHEARER, Robert of N. C.	556
SHELNUTT, C. D. of N. C.	495-496
SHERWOOD, Daniel of N. C.	396
SILLS, Samuel Joseph of S. C. (two versions)	114, 345-346
SIMMONS, Benjamin of N. C.	401
SLATTER, Solomon of N. C.	458
SMALL, David of N. C.	468-470
SMITH, O. K. of S. C.	182-183
SMITH, Robert of S. C.	276
SMITH, Stephen, Jr. of Barnwell Dist., S. C.	319-322
SMITH, William D. of S. C.	111-112
SNIDER, William J. of S. C.	9-10
STEPHENS, John of S. C.	10-11
STEPHENS-THAMES of N. C.	417-418
STEPHENSON, Hamilton of N. C.	385-386
STEPHENSON, Hugh W. of S. C.	3
STEPHENSON, John of S. C.	93
STOLL, David of S. C.	298
STRIBLING, Clayton of S. C., Revolutionary War Soldier	36
STROUD, John of S. C.	98-99

Name	Pages
SUDDARTH, Abraham of Sumter Co., N. C.	546-547
SULLIVAN, Jefferson of S. C.	310-314
SUMMERS, John Letton of N. C.	471
SWINSON, Jesse of Brown Marsh Stream, Duplin Co., N. C.	530-531
SWORDS, John, Sr. of S. C.	136-137
TALLEY, Berry, Sr. of Chatham Co., N. C.	392-393
TAYLOR, John and Mary Neely of Mecklenburg Co., N. C.	512
TAYLOR, William Penn of Louisburg, Franklin Co., N. C.	565-567
TERRY, Major Stephen of S. C.	329-330
THOMAS, Etienne of S. C.	291-292
THOMAS, Tristram of Marborough Co., S. C.	346-347
THOMPSON, David Lyon of S. C.	178-180
THOMPSON. Andrew Jackson of S. C.	117-120
TITSHAW, James T. and Fannie Melissa of S. C.	153
TITSHAW, John Stephen of Chester and Edgefield Co's, S. C.	151-153
UZZEL, Elisha of Franklin Co., N. C.	567-568
VAUGHAN, Henry, Sr. of "Cherryvale", Statesburg, Sumter District, S. C.	335-337
VAUGHAN, Henry, Jr. of Cherryvale, Statesburg, Sumter Dist., S. C.	5-7
VENABLES, John of N. C., Revolutionary War Soldier	380-381
VERNER. John, Jr. of Granville Co., N. C.	498-499
WALDRIP, Samuel James of S. C.	8-9
WALKER, John of S. C.	306-308
WALTERS, Elbert Franklin of S. C.	
WARE, William of Fairfield Dist., S. C., Revolutionary War Soldier	354
WARNOCK, John of S. C., Revolutionary War Soldier (two versions),	121-122, 283-285
WATKINS, Lewis of S. C.	353
WATTS, William Dendy of S. C.	308-309
WATTS, William of Richland Co., S. C.	183
WEATHERLY, Joseph of N. C.	451-454
WEBB, Samuel Maurice of N. C.	568-572
WESNER, Henry Philip of S. C.	148

WEST, John B. of N. C.	513-514
WEST, John Littlejohn of S. C.	61-64
WHEELER, John of N. C., Revolutionary War Soldier	397
WHITAKER, Joshua, Sr. of N.C.	483
WHITE, Robert of S. C.	55-56
WHITE, W. F. of S. C.	165-166
WHITENER, Henry, Sr. of N. C.	468
WILEY, William of N. C., Revolutionary War Soldier	397-398
WILEY-HARRIS of S. C.	19-21
WILLIAMS, Moses of S. C., Revolutionary War Soldier	123-124
WOLFE, William C. of N. C.	421
WOOD, Aaron of S.C.	137-138
WOOD, Henry of S.C.	39-40
WOOD, John of Spartanburg Dist., S. C., Revolutionary War Soldier	354-355
WYATT, Elijah of S. C.	196-197
YEATES, James B.	496-498

PARKER-JENKINS-CRADDOCK BIBLE
Barnwell, South Carolina

Moses Boynton, Jr. his daybook, took in the year 1776
Joseph Parker, son of William and Elizabeth, his wife, b. 12/29/1770

Joseph Parker m. Elender Jenkins 1/5/1790

Shadrick Jenkins, Jr., son of Elender Jenkins, b. 2/6/1787

Ashford Parker, son of Joseph Parker, b. 6/22/1791

Mary Parker, daughter of Elender Parker, b. 2/13/1793

William Parker, son of Joseph Parker and Elender, b. 2/16/1795

Elizabeth Parker, daughter of Joseph and Elender Parker, b. 3/28/1797

BIRTHS: of Children of John Craddock:

Salley Craddock 4/3/1769
John Craddock 11/3/1793
David Craddock 2/6/1796
Cornelius Craddock 7/27/1798
Daniel Cargill Craddock 12/19/1803
Charity Craddock, wife of John Craddock, d. 6/20/1804
William Long 1/30/1790
David Long 11/12/1792
Sarah Ann Porter 11/2/1793
Mikel Grimes, son of Lida Porter 8/26/1799

Parker-Craddock-Jenkins Bible continued

BIRTHS: of Children of David Craddock:

John J. Craddock 8/9/1818
Clementine Craddock 8/30/1820

BIRTHS: of Children of David Craddock:

John J. Craddock 8/9/1818
Clementine Craddock 8/30/1820
Salley C. Craddock 3/26/1823
Johnny Norris ---
William Norris b. 11/17/1813
David Norris b. 2/18/1816
Hansford Norris b. 6/15/1820
John P. Craddock b. 8/26/1822
James J. Craddock b. 5/10/1827
Mary S. Craddock b. 2/9/1829
Sarah Rebecca Craddock b. 4/30/1831
John Craddock m. 9/22/1786 and went to housekeeping 10/19/1786

When this you see, Remember me. Signed, John Craddock

Elender Parker, wife of Joseph Parker, d. 6/12/1839 Joseph Parker, her husband, d. 5/7/1848
William Craddock m. Elizabeth 3/28/1826
William Craddock, son of John Craddock and Charity, his wife, b. 2/26/1787

HUGH W. STEPHENSON BIBLE
Owner: A. E. Simpson, San Antonio, Texas

Hugh W. Stephenson b. Ireland 1765, came to America 1772, m. in York Co., S. C. 10/16/1787, moved to Smith Co., Tenn. in 1794, to Maury Co., Tenn. in 1806, to Lawrence Co., Ala. 1819, where he died 1843.

BIRTHS:

Hugh W. Stephenson 1/25/1765
Margaret Stephenson 11/28/1770
Ann Stephenson 7/13/1788
Watson W. Stephenson 10/28/1790
Elizabeth Stephenson 8/13/1792
Polly M. Stephenson 2/9/1795

John C. Stephenson 8/28/1797
Pleasant W. Stephenson 6/9/1800
Hedge L. Stephenson 6/30/1802
Sallie R. Stephenson 8/12/1807
Finis E. Stephenson 11/2/1811

JOHN BELLINGER BUCKHEISTER, SR. BIBLE
Owner: Mrs. Vance R. Bettis
106 Crestfield, Lancaster, S. C. 29720

BIRTHS:

John Bellinger Buckheister, Sr. 3/12/1829
Mary Benson Dillard 1/14/1834

John Bellinger Buckheister, Sr. Bible

John Benson Buckheister 1/3/1853
Mary Bellinger Buckheister 6/8/1854
Warren David Buckheister 6/6/1855
Sallie Elliott Buckheister 10/23/1860
Annie Nation Buckheister 9/15/1864
Edward Hampton Buckheister 10/13/1870

MARRIAGES:

J. B. Buckheister to Mary Benson Dillard 2/28/1852

DEATHS:

John Bellinger Buckheister, Sr. 9/9/1899 Mary Benson Dillard Bockheister 2/1111915

SARAH McILVAIN BIBLE
Owner: Mrs. W. M. Roberts, Savannah, Ga.

Sarah McIlvain Her Book bought in New Castle of Joseph Boyd, price $11.00 about 1820.

BIRTHS:

Sarah McIlvain 6/25/1803
George McIlvain 1/10/1815
John McIlvain 12/9/1804

Sarah McIlvain Bible continued...

Polly McIlvain 1/13/1817
Elizabeth McIlvain 11/12/1806
Jule Ann McIlvain 1019/1819
William McIlvain 7/2/1809
Alexander McIlvain 9/4/1822
James McIlvain 5/1/1812

DEATHS:

James McIlvain 11/1855, aged 43 yrs, 6 mos. 1812 (in pencil)
Mary McIlvain 4/29/1856, aged 70 yrs. 1786 (in pencil)
Mary McIlvaln 1122/1857, aged 40 yrs, 9 days. 1817 (in pencil)
James McIlvain, Sr. 6/7/1837, aged 57 yrs. 1780 (In pencil)
John McIlvain 1/10/1839, aged 34 yrs, 1 mo. 1805 (in pencil)
Sarah McIlvain 3/21/1839, aged 35 yrs, 9 mos. 1804 (in pencil)

HENRY VAUGHAN, JR. BIBLE
Of Cherryvale, Statesburg, Sumter District

MARRIAGES:

Henry Vaughan, Jr. to Margaret Anderson 3/3/1795
John J. Frierson to Julia F. Vaughan 5/1/1817
Henry Vaughan to Emma Rees 3/8/1827
Wentworth F. Rees to Vermeille Vaughan 3/11/1827
Mark Reynolds to Julia V. Rees 6/-/1845
James F. Frierson to Minnie C. Grant 4/29/1856
Mary Chestnut, daughter of James J. and Minnie C. Frierson, 3/23/1857

Henry Vaughn, Jr. Bible continued...

William Grant, son of James J. And Minnie C. Frierson 4/13/1858
Julia Vaughan, daughter of James J. and Minnie C. Frierson 5/7/1859

BIRTHS:

Henry Vaughan, Jr., son of Henry Vaughan, Sr. and Elizabeth, his wife, 9/13/1767 m. Margaret
Anderson. Daughter of John Anderson and Margaret, his wife, b. 2/12/1779.

Henry Vaughan and Margaret, his wife, had issue as follows--

Julia Finetta Vaughan b. 4/20/1796
Mary Margaret Vaughan b. 12/25/1797
Vermeille Vaughan b. 6/28/1809
John Anderson Vaughan b. 3/8/1803
Henry Vaughan b. 3/21/1800

BIRTHS:

John Napoleon, son of John J. and Julia P. Frierson 2/21/1818
Julia Vaughan Rees, daughter of Wentworth F. and Vermeille Rees 10/13/1828
Maria Ford Rees, daughter of Wentworth F. and Vermeille Rees 11/14/1829
James Julian, son of John J. and Julia F. Frierson 1/19/1832
Mary Margaret, daughter of Wentworth F. and Vermeille Rees 4/15/1832

Henry Vaughn, Jr. Bible continued...

Anne Maria Bradford, daughter of John S. and Vermeille Bradford 10/4/1839

DEATHS:

Mary Margaret Vaughan, daughter of Henry and Margaret, 2/1/1814, aged 16 yrs., one month, 6 days

Henry Vaughan, Jr. 3/5/1814, aged 46 yrs., 5 mos., 28 days

John J. Frlerson 11/15/1839, aged 47 yrs., 4 mos., 22 days

Mary Margaret Rees, daughter of Wentworth F. and Vermeille Rees 3/11/1859, aged 26 yrs., 10 mos., 24 days

Anna Maria Bradford, daughter of John S. and Vermeille Bradford 5/1875, aged 36 yrs.

Julia F. Frierson, wife of John J. Frierson, 4/10/1880, aged 80 yrs., 11 mos. 20 days

John N., son of John J. and Julia F. Frierson, 2/19/1887, aged 68 yrs., 11 mos., 29 days

Vermeille Vaughan, wife of John S. Bradford, 9/6/1887, aged 78 yrs., 2 mos., 9 days

James Julian, son of John J. and Julia F. Frierson 8/1/1890
Mary Chestnut Grant (Minnie) Frierson, wife of James Julian Frierson 6/12/1907

SAMUEL JAMES WALDRIP BIBLE
Owner: Mrs. Marie Waldrip Rt. 2, Box 393, Woodruff, S.C. 29388

Samuel James Waldrip m.. Pertima Couch 12/21/1848
Samuel James Waldrip b. 9/22/1820
Pertima Couch b. 4/15/1829

CHILDREN:

Jesse Taylor Waldrip b. 8/17/1849
Henry Jefferson Waldrip b. 5/10/1851
James Albert Waldrip b. 4/15/1853
Margaret Elizabeth Waldrip b. 9/28/1856
John Landrum Waldrip b. 12/1/1859
Ellin Davis Waldrip b. 3/11/1861

Sallie Rochester Waldrip b. 4/29/1863
Samuel Simpson b. 8/4/1865

DEATHS:

Pertima Waldrip 2/27/1866
Sallie Rochester 11/7/1864
James Albert Waldrip 8/25/1853
Samuel James Waldrip m. 8/4/1866 Mary Ellison Campbell (b. 3/7/1836

BIRTHS of THEIR CHILDREN:

Mary Pertima Waldrip 5/11/1867
Thomas Brook Waldrip 4/27/1869

Samuel James Waldrip Bible continued...

Pernecia Victoria Waldrip 7/14/1870
Broadus Ezell Waldrip 5/22/1880

DEATHS:

Pernecia Victoria Waldrip 7/6/1871
Samuel Simpson 9/5/1910
Samuel James 2/3/1902
Mary E. Waldrip 6/23/1908

WILLIAM J. SNIDER BIBLE of Orangeburg District
Owner: Joe V. Hughes, 3548 Old Chamblee-Tucker Rd., 12, Atlanta, Ga. 30340

MARRIAGES:

William J. Snider of Orangeburg, S. C. m. Wilhelmena Farr of Greenville Co., S. C. 6/28/1882 at
Chick Spring by Rev. U. H. Strickland, Pastor, Greenville Baptist Church. Wit: Jennie F. Pierson
W. J. Snider to Jane E. Holland 9/27/1887 by J. U. Elkins

BIRTHS:

William Judson Snider 12/3/1851
William Farr Snider 8/27/1883
Wilhelmena Farr Snider 7/13/1859
Mary Louise Snider 12/1/1884
Earl McKinney Snider 1/12/1875
Jane E. Snider 4/6/1838

DEATHS:

William Farr Snider 9/3/1883
Earl H. Snider 7/21/1902
Wilhelmina Farr Snider 1886
Jane E. Snider 7/26/1904
Mary Louise Snider 1886
William Judson Snider 12/10/1897

JOHN STEPHENS BIBLE
Owner: Mrs. Manning Smith , 2011 S. College Ave., Bryan, Texas

John Stephens m. Sarah Rodgers 12/27/1796

BIRTHS:

Sarah Stephens 11/1771
John Stephens 10/28/1773
Enoch Stephens 10/30/1797
Robert Stephens 10/30/1799
Margaret Stephens 1/9/1809
Reubin Stephens 4/10/1802
John Stephens 11/14/1804
Nancy Stephens 9/19/1807
Sarah Stephens 6/9/1812

W. C. Foster 7/29/1829
C. S. Foster 11//1832
M. P. Foster 2/2/1850
M. A. Foster 6/21/1852
Hawkins Foster 2/17/1854
J. R. Foster 10/12/1855

John Stephens' Bible continued...

Jesse C. Foster 1/26/1857
C. T. Foster 11/7/1859
Zach B. Foster 8/8/1862
J. T. Foster 1//1864

DEATHS:

Elijah Stephens, aged 2 wks, 11/13/1797
Annie Cader Foster Oct. 16 '73
Infant daughter, June 25 `77
John Stephens 4/13/1849
Sarah Stephens 10/2/1852
Margaret Elgin, daughter of John and Sarah Stephens 5/3/1854, aged 44 yrs., 3 mos., 24 days
Infant daughter 7/10/1877, aged 2 wks, 1 day

REBEKAH REECE BIBLE
Owner: A. St. J. Lawton, Charleston, S. C

Rebekah Reece, Her Book. She was b. 7/9/1732
Benjamin Reece m. Rebekah Dixon 5/29/1751
"Our first child was stillborn 12/11/1752"
Mary Reece, daughter of Benjamin and Rebekah Reece b. 2/4/1754

David Stoll m. Rebekah Reece 10/9/1757

Susannah, daughter of David and Rebekah Stoll, b. 7/23/1758

Rebekah Reece Bible continued...

David Dixon Stoll, son of David and Rebekah Stoll, b. 1/23/1762
Gabriel Stoll, son of David and Rebekah Stoll, b. 9/25/1763
Susannah Stoll m. Michael Garvey 8/10/1780
David Dixon Stoll m. Sophia Bourquin 5/6/1782
Sophia Bourquin, daughter of John Lewis and Margaret Bourquin, b. 12/12/1762

COLONEL JOHN CHESTNUT BIBLE

Copied from a record sent by my father, James Chestnut, to his sister, Mrs. Margaret Deas by Sally Chestnut 8/6/1876, Camden. S. C. Transmitted to Harriet Chestnut Stockton by her aunt Sally Chestnut of Bloomsbury, S. C. 5/1889.

John Chestnut b. on Shenandoah in Va. 6/18/1743, his parents from Ireland. He died at Camden 4/1/1818; buried at Knight's Hill. Sarah Cantey his wife, native of S.C., b. 2/15/1753, d. 2/12/1786.

CHILDREN:

Mary Chestnut b. 1/20/1771 d. 1843, Camden, S. C. m. Duncan McRae, native of Scotland and had 8 children, buried at Ouaker Burying Ground, Camden, S. C.

James Chestnut b. 2/19/1773 Camden, S. C. m. Mary Cox, native of Philadelphia who d. Camden 3/13/1864. They had 14 children.

James Chestnut d. Bloomsbury near Camden 3/13/1864. Both are buried at Knight's Hill where 8 of their children are also buried.

Sarah Chestnut b. 12/12/1774 m. John Taylor of Columbia, S. C., had 12 children, d. 6/1851

Harriet Chestnut b. 12/19/1776 d. 9/1831, buried at Knight's Hill

Rebecca Chestnut b. 1/18/1779 d. 11/5/1779

John Chestnut b. 6/3/1783 d. in Charleston of yellow fever 8/16/1799. His remains removed by his brother to knight's Hill, family burial place, after being buried 7 mos. in St. Michael's churchyard, Charleston, S. C.

Margaret Rebecca Chestnut b. 1/24/1789 m. Col. James Deas of Charleston, d. 1874, Mobile, Alabama

MRS. ESTHER COX BIBLE
Owner: James Chestnut Stockton

John Cox, son of William and Catherine Cox, m. Esther Bowes, daughter of Francis and Rachel Bowes 11/16/1760 at Christ Church, Philadelphia, Pa.

Rachel Cox, daughter of John and Esther Cox, b. 11/11/1761
Catherine Cox b. 7/27/1764
Esther Cox b. 9/23/1767
Child, a daughter, stillborn

Mrs. Esther Cox Bible continued...

John Rowes Cox b. 9/5/1770 d. 11/1772, aged 2 yrs, 2 mos.

Mary Cox b. 3/22/1775
Sarah Cox b. 7/10/1779
Elizabeth Cox b. 1/22/1783
John Cox d. 4/28/1793, aged 61 yrs., 7 mos.
Mrs. Esther Cox d. 2/10/1814, aged 73 yrs, 1 mo., 4 days
Note: Mary Cox b. 1775 became wife of James Chestnut of Camden, S. C. 9/20/1796 at Christ Church, Philadelphia.

MARY LANG BIBLE
"Mary Lang" printed on spine of book.

MARRIAGES:

Sally Wyly, daughter of Sam. and Dinah Wyly to William Lang 1775
Thomas and Mary (McRae) Lang to 3/29/1815
Burwell and Sally Boykin to 4/9/1834
Edward and Mary Boykin to 5/4/1841
Samuel Wyly to Dinah Millhouse
Duncan McRae Lang to Mary Honoria Logan 5/30/1853
Samuel Logan Lang to Mary Chestnut Frierson 10/19/1879
Samuel Logan Lang to Louisa Salmond 12/17/1902
Honoria Logan Lang to Lucius Bellenger Phillips 6/22/1912

John Lang d. at Wakefield, England in 1716
Obadiah Lang, his son, d. 1741
Obadiah Lang, son of shove Obadiah Lane, b. 1711 m. 1738

Mary Lang Bible continued...

Elizabeth Wilson, daughter of Joseph Wilson of Barnsley, England.

William Lang, their son, went to S. C. in 1770 and m. Sally Uyly, daughter of Samuel Wyly end Dinah nee Millhouse, his wife.

John Wyly, son of Samuel Wyly and Dilnah (nee Millhouse) his wife was b. Galstown in county of Kildare, Ireland 7/14/1744.
William Wyly. son of same parents, b. same place 4/14/1746
Robert Wyly, son of same parents, b. same place 5/23/1748
Sally Wyly, daughter of same parents, b. Williamsburg Township, S. C. 9/12/1751 Samuel Wyly, son of same parents, b. Fredericksburg Township, Camden District, S. C. 7/18/1756
William Lang, husband of Sally Wyly, b. near Wakefield in Yorkshire, England 2/16/1746

Children of William and Sally Lang:

James Wilson Lang b. 3/10/1776
Samuel Wyly Lang b. 11/4/1782
Elizabeth Lang b. 6/11/1779
John Lang b. 6/3/1785
Hannah Lang b. 5/8/1785
Thomas Lang b. 6/24/1793
William Wyly Lang b. 9/7/1790
Duncan McRae Lang b. 4/21/1817

Sally Wyly Lang, daughter of Thomas and Mary Lang b. 6/10/1815

Mary Lang Bible continued...

William Lang, b. 8/23/1818
Mary Chestnut Lang, b. 2/6/1820
Thomas Lang b. 3/22/1821
William Lang b. 7/17/1822
Marrier McRae Lang b. 12/1/1823
John Chestnut Lang b. 6/8/1825
Edward Brevard Lang h. 11/11/1826
Flora McRae Lang b. 8/17/1828
Septimus Lang b. 6/8/1830
Theodore Lang b. 9/29/1832

Mary Chestnut Phillips, daughter of L. B. and H. L. Phillips b. 12/31/1913

Mary Lang, daughter of Duncan McRae and Mary McRae, b. 10/20/1793
Thomas Lang Boykin b. 2/22/1835
William Hamilton Boykin b. 8/27/1837
Burwell Boykin b. 4/12/1839
John Boykln b. 4/6/1841
Samuel Logan Lang b. 3/7/1854, son of Duncan McRae Lang and Nonorin Logan
Mary Chestnut Frierson b. 3/23/1857
Honoria Logan Lang, daughter of Samuel Logan Lang and Mary Chestnut (nee Frierson) Lang b. 4/30/1884
Mary Honoria Logan b. 2/1/1833 m. Duncan McRae Lang 5/30/1853, and d. 4/30/1855
Logan Lang Phillips, son of L. B. and H. L. Phillips, b. 5/5/1915
Elizabeth Carolina Phillips, daughter of L. B. and H. L. Phillips, b. 8/25/1916

Mary Lang Bible continued...

William Francis Phillips, son of L. B. and H. L. Phillips, b. 11/4/1919
Honoria Logan Phillips, daughter of L. B. and H. L. Phillips, b. 6/19/1922

DEATHS:

Sally Wyly Lang 10/1817
William Lang, her husband, 9/1815
Mary McRae, wife of Thomas Lang, 2/22/1848
William Lang 1/30/1820
William Lang, second son of that name, 8/14/1824
Septimus Lang 6/14/1831
Flora McRae Lang 4/1/1832
Duncan McRae Lang 9/29/1856
Sally Wyly Boykin 5/17/1889
John C. Lang 8/1889 in Philadelphia, Pa.
Thomas Lang 5/13/1861
Harriet McRae Lang 5/18/1892
Theodore Lang 4/18/1896
Mary Chesnut Lang (nee Frierson) 8/25/1901
Samuel Logan Lang 5/4/1905
Louisa Salmond Lang 3/1/1919
Lucius Bellenger Phillips 1/29/1955
Honoria Logan Lang Phillips 5/30/1958

EMANUEL OSWALT BIBLE
Owner: Ernest A. Oswalt, 147 Fairoaks Drive, Jackson, Miss. 39212

BIRTHS:

Emanuel Oswalt 10/15/1818 (Lexington Co., S. C.)
Euhema (Lewis) Oswalt 11/15/1827
Franklin W. Oswalt 8/15/1844
Henry Etter Oswalt 9/1/1857
L. B. Oswalt 7/25/1846
Draden Brooks Oswalt 2/16/1860
Cedicia L. E. Oswalt 10/27/1848
Sary Edney Oswalt 11/8/1862
Sarah E. Oswalt 1/8/1851
Zebulan Zenoah Oswalt 6/26/1865
Nancy Luezer Oswalt 12/13/1852
Ianth M. Oswalt 1131/1866

Samuel Frederick Oswalt 3/26/1855
James Boyd Oswalt 9/29/1870

MARRIAGES:

Emanuel Oswalt and Euphemia, his wife, m. 4/20/1843

DEATHS:

Cedecte Luany Emery Oswalt d. 12/17/1860, aged 12 yrs., 1 mo., 20 days
Ianth Minerva Oswalt 5/20/1892
Reuhama Oswalt 11/10/1892
Emanuel Oswalt 1/24/1897

Emanuel Oswalt Bible continued...

James Boyd Oswalt 8/7/1903
Henry Etta Oswalt Jumper 12/22/1908
Wade Franklin Oswalt 10/1907
Sarah E. Oswalt 3/8/1919

WILEY-HARRIS BIBLE
Owner: Mrs. Jane S. Latta
4805 N. 7th Street, Arlington, Va. 22203

MARRIAGES:

James Wiley to Ann L. Harris 4/18/1824

BIRTHS:

John Gaston 3/25/1818
Alexander Gaston 7/8/1819
Jane Gaston 9/12/1825

Ann L. Harris 11/27/1794
Jane Ann Wiley 5/25/1827
Elizabeth Mary Wiley 8/9/1831

James Wiley 6/4/1794

The ages of negroes:
Amey b. 4/21/1807
John b. 4/19/1852
Juda b. 12/16/1823
Mary b. 6/11/1855
M., a negro boy, b. 5/25/1848
Nelson b. 12/31/1857 Sam b. 7/5/1850
Charles b. 7/12/1861

Wiley-Harris Bible continued...

DEATHS:

Jane Harris 7/8/1826
William Gaston 4/16/1832
John Harris 4/1/1830

Notes: "January 12th 1843 Julius H. Alexander left N. C. 2/4/1843 with a heavy heart. After traveling through the lonesome countrys of N. and S. C. arrived at cousin Simpson's in Loundesville where and when I was very happy to meet with my friends. Signed, Julius H. Alexander."

Notes by C. H. Stone:

James Harris, son of John Harris and Grizzell Steel
Elizabeth Harris, daughter of Col. Robert Harris and Frances Cunningham.
John Harris, son of James and Elizabeth Harris, b. Cabarrus Co., N. C., m. Jane Leslie, daughter of Thomas and Jane Leslie in Abbeville District, S. C. 9/2/1784, Rev. Robert Hall officiating. He d. Abbeville, S. C. 4/1/1830.
Jane Leslie d. 7/8/1826.

This Scott Family Bible belonged to John Harris and was given to his grandson, T. A. Harris, by him. The Ann Harris whose birth 11/27/1794 and marriage to James
Wiley 4/16/1824 are recorded in this Bible, was the daughter of John and Jane Leslie Harris. The Deaths of John and Jane Leslie Harris are also recorded in this Bible.

MARY REBECCA RODGERS LARIMORE BIBLE
Owner: Mrs. Sherry Perkins, 5241 Jacksonville Rd., Ocala, Fla. 32670

Collin Woodbury Larimore 3/27/1819-12/29/1883
Collin Larimore and Eliza Richardson n. 1/12/1854
Eliza Richardson 6/17/1828-6/16/1903
Charles Keen Larimore, son of Collin and Eliza, b. 2/11/1872
Willis Rogers 1/31/1840 in S. C., 5/28/1913 m. Nancy Campbell 6/22/1866
Nancy Campbell 3/25/1834-8/30/1908

Children of Willis and Nancy Campbell Rogers:

James Thomas Rogers 9/29/1867-1/22/1925 m. Bertie Johnson 11/6/1895
Robert Simeon Rogers 12/11/1868-3/6/1904 m. Telutha Johnson 2/16/1897

Jeremiah Foster Rogers b. 5/15/1870 m. Fannie King 11/3/1897
Fannie B. Rogers 8/3/1871-8/20/1872
Eli Oscar Rogers 9/23/1872-10/25/1873
Mary Rebecca Rogers 8/24/1874 Zion, S. C.-11/9/1953 m. Charles Keen Larimore, Zion, S. C.

William Capers Rogers b. 2/16/1876 m. Mary Eloise Owens 12/12/1912

Charles Keen Larimore of Brittona Neck, S. C. m. Mary Rebecca Rogers of Zion, S. C. 1/31/1894 at the house of the bride by Rev. T. D. Moody. Witnesses: J. V. Rogers, Martha S. Higgins

Mary Rebecca Rodgers Larimore Bible continued...

Children of Charles and Mary Larimore (all b. Marion Co., S. C.):

Rufus Maxey Larimore b. 6/29/1897
Leon Grady Larlmore b. 3/14/1899 m. Amanda Hall Hunt 11/13/1919
Lila Mona Larimore b. 6/27/1900 m. Ist Solomon Bryant 2/5/1915, 2nd, Melons Hall 6/2/1917
Simeon Giles Larimore b. 9/25/1901
Bessie Alma Larimore b. 8/4/1904
Capers Elmo Larimore b. 1/21/1907

Elsie Lorine Larimore b. 4/27/1910 m. William Henry Cave 3/12/1927, d. 12/31/1967
Mary Louise Larimore b. 2/10/1913 m. Hood Dennis Perkins 12/23/1934

VINCENT JONES, SR. BIBLE
Owner: Mrs. Thomas J. Bruister, Rt. 1, Box 166, Del Acres, Tutwiler, Miss. 38963

Bennett Greer d. 7/1/1936
Jesse Greer 6/22/1827-2/1904
J. Wallace Greer d. 8/1909
Isaiah Greer d. 12/1911
Ellen Thompson Greer d. 9/1921
Little Ray or Roy Thompson d. 4/1914
Eunice Thompson Brister d. 2/1920
Ollion Guess d. 9/30/1921

Vincent Jones, Sr. Bible continued...

Martha Ann Greer Meal d. 8/1917
Calvin Brister d. 8/1917
Mrs. Calvin Brister d. 7/1915

Sallie Greer d. 2/3/1903
Floyd Greer d. 4/1917
Charles Greer d. 8/1917
Mae Greer Smith Schmid d. 7/29/1914
Mae Greer Price d. 7/1920
George C. Greer d. 5/24/1929
Vida Thompson d. 12/24/1928
Sillar Thompson 4/9/1878-10/29/1941
Monroe Greer 4/20/1851-7/26/1923
Sallie Greer 5/8/1855-2/10/1902
Jim Greer 1874-1925
George C. Greer b. 11/22/1869
Chaney Greer 3/5/1868-10/18/1935

Malcolm Hardy Reeves b. 10/14/1903

Floyd Clark 9/17/1861-3/27/1913
Mollie or Mary E. Clark b. 1863

Cooper Raiford 11/10/1893-11/30/1924

MARRIAGES:

Benjamin Brister to Sinthy Jones 12/10/1835
Aaron Davls to Drucilla Jones 12/9/1840
Daniel Asbury Jones to Jane Sorrels 4/11/1841

Vincent Jones, Sr. Bible continued...

Andrew V. Jones to Phariby Hickman 11/4/1841
Elizabeth Jones 11/24/1844
Granny Pat Jones 12/11/1841
Zachariah Jones to Emily Sorrels 7/24/1845

John A. Greer to Margaret Jones 2/8/1849
Amos Greer to Dolly Jones 11/8/1854
Joseph McClendon to Phebe Jones 3/4/1862
Thomson Busby to Emily Jones 12/18/1860

BIRTHS:

Sinthy Jones 8/7/1818
Martha Ann Jones 1/28/1842
Daniel Asbury Jones 1/20/1820
James William Jones 4/4/1844
Zachariah Jones 8/14/1821
Ira Vassus Brister 3/8/1847
Andrew Vastine Jones 11/24/1822
Dolly Louise Brister 9/22/1850
Drucilla Jones 10/4/1824
Vinson Vastine Brister 12/23/1836
Elizabeth Jones 6/13/1826
Pheby Jones 5/15/1828
Jane Brister 11/19/1839
Vincent Jones 3/22/1830
Sinthy - 9/--
Margaret Jones 2/2/1832
William Benson Davis 2/3/1842
Dolly Jones 12/27/1833

Vincent Jones, Sr. Bible continued...

Amanda Jones 6/22/1842
Nancy Jones 7/22/1836
Vinson Grier Jones 8/11/1842
Bennet Jones 3/13/1838
William Andrew Jones 10/2/1844
Emily Jones 1/16/1840
---Davis b. 7/4/1844

DEATHS:

Vinson Jones 9/9/1832
Jane Jones 6/4/1897
Nancy Jones 9/9/1937
Katherine Greer Felder 2/--

James William Jones 11/24/1846
Dolly Jane Greer 9/1894
Bennet Jones 9/4/1850
D. C. Greer 4/20/1908
Vinson Jones, Sr. 8/1/1860
Aunt Pat Bailey 4/1917
Graham Sue Vinson Jones 5/26/1837
Andrew V. Jones 10/26/1861
Zachariah Jones 9/18/1862
Daniel Asberry Jr. 9/3/1883
Phebe McClendon 10/9/1881
Dolly Jones 11/24/1862
John A. Greer 10/5/1822-3/3/1892
Margaret Jones Greer 3/3/1832-5/11/1897
Victoria Greer Guy 10/22/1856-9/11/1920

Vincent Jones, Sr. Bible continued...

George W. Guy 5/26/1852-8/6/1922
W. Linus Reeves 8/25/1921-8/25/1924
Malcolm Hardy Reeves 11/18/1919
Martha Davis Greer 5/27/1832-7/20/1922
Polly Greer McComb 9/9/1833-8/1915

JOHN KERR CRAIG BIBLE
Owner: John B. Craig 8207 Grayledge Drive, Austin, Texas 78753

MARRIAGES:

John Kerr Craig to Aletha Keziah Barry 8/3/1841
Richard Albert Barry Craig to Ida Martin Stribling Nelson 1/4/1879
John Simeon M. Price to Margaret Elizabeth Craig 12/5/1867
James Leroy Craig to Ella Virginia Owens 12/10/1873
R. T. Davis to Mary Cordelia Craig 2/8/1876
Alonzo Franklin Craig, to Grisselda P. Pierce 12/4/1879
John Andrew Knox Craig to Anny Gorden 9/21/1887
John Stribline Craig to Frances Elizabeth Smith 2/10/1909
John R. Craig to Bonnie Lee Almon 1/28/1933
Charles Weldon Craig to Camille Pruett Hoffman di Curtoni 10/31/1908
Richard William Craig to Jessie Wilkerson 3/30/1913
Billie Gene Craig to Dorothy D. Abbott 6/25/1948
Dr. John Almon Craig to Dr. Toni Funicella 3/18/1972
Charles Michael Craig to Debra Funicella 6/25/1977

John Kerr Craig Bible continued...

BIRTHS:

John Kerr Craig 1/28/1817 and wife Aletha Keziah Barry 1/13/1824

THEIR CHILDREN:

Richard Albert Barry Craig 10/3/1842
Mary Cordelia Craig 11/20/1853
Margaret Elizabeth Craig 4/8/1844
Rosanna Alice Craig 11/28/1855
Nancy Amanda Craig 7/17/1846
John Andrew Knox Craig 8/12/1858
James Leroy Craig 10/12/1848
William Luther Craig 2/5/1860
Alonzo Franklin Craig 2/18/1851

John Stribling Craig 10/19/1884, son of Richard A. B. Craig and Ida Stribling Craig.

Children of John Stribling Craig and Frances Smith Craig:

John B. Craig 1/18/1911
Charles Weldon Craig 10/20/1917

Children of John B. Craig and Bonnie Lee Craig:

John Almon Craig 2/2/1941 Charles Michael Craig 6/18/1947

John Kerr Craig Bible continued...

Children of Charles W. Craig and Camille P. Craig:

Travis Stribling Craig 11/13/1953
Stuart Hoffman Craig 11/14/1956

Children of Richard A. B. Craig and Ida Stribling Craig:

Minnie Alice Craig (Parham) 10/9/1881
Richard William Craig 6/14/1888
Billie Gene Craig, son of Richard William Craig and Jessie W Craig - no date
Michael Lynn Craig, son of Billie Gene Craig and Dorothy Craig, 9/23/1953
Bryan Keith Craig, son of Billie Gene Craig end Dorothy Craig, 12/11/1959

Thomas Clarkston Craig b. 1/8---

DEATHS:

Nancy Amanda Craig 8/1/1883
Agnes Craig 11/16/1857
Mary Cordella Craig 116/1888
James D. Craig 1/19/1859
Aletha Keziah Barry Craig 5/1/1892
Richard Barry 5/23/1858
John Kerr Craig 12/21/1892
Mary M. Nelson 10/22/1859
John Stribling Craig 3/30/1955

John Kerr Craig Bible continued...

William A. Craig 4/14/1871
Richard William Craig; 1/25/1962
Ida Stribling Craig 1/11/1940
Jessie Wilkerson Craig 1/13/1962
Richard Albert Barry Craig 9/2/1925
Frances Elizabeth Smith Craig 8/3/1971
Daniel Milbourn Nelson 6/14/1860
A. F. Craig 7/20/1864, killed in battle of Confederate Army at Atlanta. Ga.

James D. Craig b. 9/25/1785
Agnes Craig, b. 11/15/1810?
James D. Craig and Agnes Grier m. 1/16/1810
Alexander Craig b. 1/22/18-
James G. Craig b. 10/31/1810
Martha Amanda Craig b. 10/28/1812
William Alexander Greer Craig b. 11/8/1814
John Kerr Craig, b. 1/28/1817
Mary Matilda Craig b. 5/19/1819
Margaret Lucinda Craig b. 9/22/1824

ROBERT NELSON BIBLE of Waxhaw

Robert Nelson to Elizabeth Moore 2/21/1811
Daniel Milbourn Nelson to Mary Matilda Craig 2/2/1837
William Alvah Nelson to Sarah Davis 2/2/1837
Margaret Aseneth Nelson to Robert C. Davis 9/7/1847
Hannah Harriet Nelson to Robert Davis Montgomery 11/4/1839

Robert Nelson Bible continued...

Jonathan A. Nelson to Margaret Moore 8/17/1846
Martha M. Nelson to John G. Moore 7/15/1845
John Nesbet Nelson to Martha Isabella Alexander 11/18/1852
Robert Thomas Nelson to Sarah Harriet Alexander 11/17/1856

BIRTHS:

Mary Montgomery 7/7/1774
Daniel Milbourn Nelson 12/10/1811
Daniel Nelson 6/9/1756
Sarah Montgomery 2/25/1776
James Alex Nelson 10/15/1813
Robert Thomas Nelson 2/19/1829
Jonathan Montgomery 2/22/1778
William Alvah Nelson 12/13/1815
Margaret Nelson 10/1756
Robert Nelson 9/19/1782
Hannah Harriet Nelson 3/12/1818
James Moore Nelson 4/14/1831
James Nelson 8/5/1784
Margaret Asenath Nelson 5/5/1821
Martha Nelson 1/8/1791
Elizabeth Nelson 9/20/1786
Jonathan Alex Nelson 2/12/1823
John Nesbit Nelson 12/19/1826
Hannah Nelson 9/9/1788
Martha Malinda Nelson 10/17/1824

Mary M. Nelson, wife of Daniel M. Nelson, b. 5/19/1819
Sarah Nelson, wife of William A. Nelson, b. 9/10/1819

Robert Nelson Bible continued...

Robert Nelson b. 9/19/1782
Elizabeth Nelson, his wife, b. 12/17/1788

DEATHS:

Daniel Nelson 5/8/1806
James Alex Nelson 6/13/1815
Margaret Nelson 7/7/1840
Elizabeth Nelson 12/25/1825
James H. Nelson 12/27/1848
Elizabeth Nelson 1/30/1853

Robert Nelson 11/25/1839
John Nesbit Nelson 4/23/1856
John Nesbit Nelson 4/23/1856, 29 yrs, 4 mos., 4 da
Mary M. Nelson, wife of D. M. Nelson, d. 10/22/1859
L. M. Nelson 6/14/1860
James Calvin G. Nelson, son of Daniel M. Nelson and Mary M. Nelson. d. 3/22/1861
Robert Watt Nelson 1/21/1844-10/8/1877
Ida Martin Stribling Nelson 12/8/1856-1/11/1940?
Mary Lucinda Nelson b. 8/26/1876
John Stribling Craig b. 10/19/1884
Robert Miriam Nelson 4/1/1878-12/13/1878
Minnie Alice Craig b. 10/9/1881
Robert Watt Nelson m. Ida Stribling 1/6/1875
R. W. Nelson d. 10/8/1877
R. A. B. Craig and Ida M. Nelson m. 1/21/1879
Robert Lee McCamant and Mary Lucinda Nelson .. 2/7/189-at Campbell, Texas

Robert Nelson Bible continued...

John Calvin Greer Nelson d. 3/23/1861, Neshoba Co., Miss.
James D. Craig 12/25/1785-11/9/1859
Agnes Greer Craig 11/25/1789-11/16/1857
James D. Craig m. Agnes Greer 1/10/1810
James G. Craig b. 10/31/1810
William Alexander Craig b. 11/8/1814
Amelia Craig b. 10/25/1812
John Kerr Craig b. 1/28/1817 (R. A. B. Craig's father)
Aletha Keziah Craig d. 5/1/1892
Mary Matilda Craig Nelson b. 5/19/1819 (R. W. Nelson's mother)
Margaret Lucinda Craig b .9/22/1820

Thomas Clarkston Craig b. 1/1824
Alexander Franklin Craig b. 11/22/1825
Aletha Keziah Barry b. 11/3/1824 m. John Kerr Craig 8/3/1841
Richard Albert Barry Craig 10/3/1842-9/29/1925 John Kerr Craig d. 12/21/1892
Mary Matilda Craig m.Daniel Milbourn Nelson d. 6/14/1860

W. D. HEDLESTON BIBLE
Owner: William Barlow Hedleston
Ft. Lauderdale, Fla.

BIRTHS:

Jane P. Hedleston 9/15/1818
Sarah Jane Hedleston 8/6/1853
John James Hedleston 7/17/1820

W. D. Hedleston Bible continued...

Elizabeth Hedleston 5/6/1881
William Davis Hedleston 2/22/1822
Ann Agnes Hedleston 7/15/1849
John Presley Hedleston 8/10/1851
Ann Susannah Ulmer 8/3/1825

Jefferson Davis Hedleston 11/18--
William Davis Hedleston 10/5/1879
Samuel Barlow Hedleston 8/24/1883
Maggie Lou Hedleston 6/18/1890
Annie Gertrude Hedleston 1/12/18--
Ernestine Sutton Hedleston, daughter of William C. and Allis Hedleston, 10/8/1881

MARRIAGES:

William Davis Hedleston to Ann Susannah Ulmer 4/9/1846
William Charles Hedleston to Allie Gertrude Brannen 9/7/1878
Samuel Barlow Hedleston to Susie Edna Hedges 1/24/1904
Glendine Elizabeth Hedleston to Mooney Alphonso Strouse 10/12/1921
William Barlow Hedleston to Debbie Ions Durrence 5/7/1932
Edna Mae Hedleston to Redic L. DeLoach 7/4/1936

DEATHS:

John James Hedleston 9/11/1851, age 31 yrs., 1 mo., 24 days
Mary Agnes Hedleston 6/11/1854, aged 4 yrs., 10 mos., 26 days
John Presley Hedleston 6/13/1854, aged 2 yrs., 10 mos, 3 days
William Davis Hedleston 11/10/1879, aged 57, 7 mos, 18 days

W. D. Hedleston Bible continued...

Ann Susannah Hedleston 1/11/1880, aged 54 yrs.,
William Davis Hedleston, son of William C. and Allie Hedleston, 5/26/1880, aged 7 mos, 21 days
Willie C. Hedleston 3/8/1890
Maggie Lou Hedleston 6128/1890
Infant bnby of Samuel Barlow Hedleston and Susie Edna Hedleston 8/6/1912-8/8/1912
Nettie Lou Hedleston, daughter of Samuel and Susie, 5/13/1925
Herbert Nathaniel Hedleston 12/8/1926

BIRTHS:

Glendine Elizabeth Hedleston 2/16/1905
Willie Barlow Hedleston 7/13/1906
Mattie Lou Hedleston 12/17/1908
Herbert Nathanlel Hedleston 9/19/1910
Edna Mae Hedleston 9/23/1915

STEPHEN CRAIN BIBLE
From: Revolutionary War Pension #W9823

BIRTHS:

Sarah Crain 6/26/1785
Stephen Crain 7/24/1795
James Crain 5/2/1792
William Crain 12/4/1789
Mary Crain 4/16/1798

Stephen Crain Bible continued...

Isaac Crain 2/18/1801

Note: Stephen Crain made application dtd 4/611832, aged 73 yrs., Chester Co., S. C., stating he was b. in Va. at Fleets Point, on mouth of Little Wecommoco River. 4/4/1846 Hugh McLure, Chesterfield District, S. C., testified that he was son-in-law and exr of LWT of Mary Crain, widow of Stephen and that Stephen Crain m. Mary Brinkley 9/9/1784 (she d. 6/18/1845). Stephen Crain b. 3/29/1834.

JOHN MILLS BIBLE
From: Rev. War Pension #W9191

Thomas Sumter Mills 3/8/1783-1/1832
Robert Mills 10/31/1184-10/5/1785
Robert Mills 12/27/1786-1/1842
Mary Mills b. 4/30/1789
John Mills 12/21/1791-1/31/1826
Alexander Feagon Mills 11/9/1794-7/19/1797

Note: Mary Mills, widow, stated that she n. 5/21/1782 Chester Dist. S. C. and was Mary Gill before she m. John Mills. That John Mills d. 3/19/1795. Mary d. 1/29/1841. 6/30/1806

Alexander Pagan of Chester District, S. C. applied for pension due his wife, Mary as only surviving child of John Mills.

CLAYTON STRIBLING BIBLE
From: His Revolutionary War Pension Application 8W6208

BIRTHS: of Children of Clayton and Molly Stribling:

Thomas Stribling 11/9/1788 Lucy Stribling 18/1799

John Beckham Stribling 1/24/1790
Mary Leak Stribling 8/10/1805
Elisabeth Henderson Stribling 10/10/1793
Samuel Henderson Stribling 2/1795
Fanny Martin Stribling 11/23/1803
Nancy Kinchelow Stribling 2/15/1807
Clayton Stribling 1/9/1962-3/11/1831 m. Molly 11/11/1787

Molly b. 1/10/1768
Fanny Martin Strlbling d. 1/12/1836, aged 33 yrs., 1 mo., 20 days

Note: Application of Mary Stribllng. wid. of Brown's Creek, Union District, S. C., 10/22/1840, aged 72 yrs., stated she m. Clayton Stribling 11/11/1787 who d. 3/11/1836, Neshoba Co., Miss 31/1841
Mary Stribling lately removed from Union District S. C. because most of her children had moved west.

SAMUEL CORBIN BIBLE
Calhoun Co. Museum, Sr, Matthews, S. C.

Samuel P. Corbin n. 3/15/1827
Murray Susanah Corbin 4/1/1828-6/18/1829, dau of Samuel P.

Samuel Corbin Bible continued...

Corbin & Caroline Corbin, his wife
R. D. Rucker m. Margaret Rucker, his wife, 6/12/1828
"Our ancestors sailed from Ireland on the 23rd November and James Seawright dyed the 12th of December following on sea.

John Seawright d. 11/6/1807
Jane Ellison d. 3/20/1817
Elizabeth Chambly d. 6/6/1798
Susanah Corbin d. 10/9/1814
Elizabeth Corbin b. 12/27/1771
Samuel Corbin 2/15/1774-12/27/1822
--llender Corbln b. 9/4/1777
Margaret Rucker b. 3/5/1804
Margaret Stivender d. 4/23/1885
Lucious d. 1/31/1820
Mrs. Ocain d. 3/22/1820 ----d. 1/19/1820
Samuel Senn Corbin 7/1/1823-8/22/18--, son of Samuel and
Hannah Mary O. Rucker b. 5/8/1829
Wesley Asbury Rucker b. 9/13/18--
William P. Corbin b. -/10/--
David Rucker 3/8/1801-6/19/1858

JOHN HUGHEY BIBLE
Owner: Shirley C. Thompson , Rt. 2, Box 218, Chesnee, S. C.

BIRTHS:

John Hughey 5/24/1792
Maryan Hughey 9/7/1832

John Hughey Bible continued...

Maryan Hughey 12/15/16/1805
Martha Jane Hughey 9/7/1832
Nancy Hughey 4/20/1827
Rebecca Hughey 9/25/1835
Harland Hughey 9/1111828
Milly M. Hughey 7/23/1837
William Hughey 7/29/1850
Susan Hughey 5/7/1839
Charles Hebron Hughey 2/24/1842

Livingston Green Hughey 2/25/1844

DEATHS:

Nancy Hughey 23/26/1831
William Hughey 12/14/1861
C. H. Hughey 10/31/1844
Harland Hughey 5/2/1863
L. G. Hughey 1845
Mary Hughey 1/5/1894
Sally Nolen 8/7/1853
Susan Bishop 4/8/1895
John Nolen 11/11/1858
Tex Anner Bishop 3/25/1867

REUBEN JAMES BIBLE

Owner: Mrs. Earline Lancaster Dendy, Woodland, Miss. 39776

Reuben James is son of Charles James
Reuben James. Sr. 12/21/1805-8/16/1845
Kitty James (nee Lancaster) 3/2/1809-3/18/1857
Milas Milford James b. 9/13/1833
John Luther James b. 1/6/1832
William Lancaster James b. 9/11/1833
Manervy Adaline James b. 10/27/1836
Alfred Javan James b. 8/1/1839
Albert Franklin James 5/6/1842-9/4/1842
Walker Manning James b. 2/24/1844
Reuben Joseph James b. 4/5/1846
Absalom Lancaster b. 1/28/1779
Nancy Lancaster (nee Simmons) b. 2/12/1784

HENRY WOOD BIBLE

Spartanburg Herald-Journal, Spartanburg, S.C., 5/2/1923:

"Bible in family from Revolution. Henry Wood's Book is still read by descendants, by P. H. Pike, Staff Correspondent.

Greer, April 20th. The Bible owned by Henry Wood, Revolutionary Soldier and Methodist Preacher and constantly brought by him to the little log Meeting House that was the predecessor of the present Wood's Chapel Methodist Church 3 miles below the City of Reidvllle Road is now in possession of David H. Smith, descendant of Henry Wood. It is an Interesting Volume of Holy

Writ printed In Birmingham, England by N. Borden and T. Appleby In 1770.

The volume is of large size about 12 x 22 print exceedingly clear and bold and old timey in type used. The book is hound by and in buckskin. It contains all the books of the Old and New Testaments and the Apochryphe."

Henry Wood b. 12/16/1756
Elizabeth Wood, his wife, b. 12/19/1759

Ann Wood, daughter of Henry and Elizabeth, b. 8/29/1778
John Wood b. 8/12/1780
Elizabeth Nash Wood b. 5/27/1787
Mary Wood b. 9/3/1784
Henry Wood b. 7/19/1786
Daniel Wood b. 7/29/1789
Charity Wood b. 3/27/1791
James Wood b. 1111011792
Lotty Wood b. 4/26/1795
Mahala Wood b. 6/17/1797
Isham Wood b. 6/31/1799

Martha O. Wood, mother of J. Terry Wood, was daughter of Isham Wood

Mr. Wood is a prominent businessman of Greer, S. C.

JAMES RAINES BIBLE
Owner: Mary N. Mills, P. O. Box 281, Chesnee, S. C. 29323

James Raines'and his wife m. 1/26/1823 Rebecca Raines m. Alin E. Page -- /29/1846 Robert C. Raines and his wife m. /13/1849 William Raines and his wife d. 2/24/1856

BIRTHS:

James F. Raines 9/10/1805
Robert C. Raines 10/17/1826
Margaret Raines 11/25/1805
William Raines 9/19/1830
Rebecca A. Raines 1/13/1824
Clerinda P. Raines 2/4/1833
Mary M. Raines 10/17/1826
James E. Raines 12/18/1834
Marget N. E. Raines 10/8/1840
Joseph R. Raines 1/2/1837
Nathaniel W. Raines -1/21/1843

John T. Raines 12/1/1839
Christopher C. Raines 7/13/1842 (b. Polk Co., N. C.)
Marget N. E. Christopher 6/14/1859
Leander J. C. Christopher 12/1/1862
J. E. Raines 12/18/1835
Arkansas Raines 5/19/1876
S. J. Raines 4/15/1848

Walter Raines 5/20/1881
Christopher C. Raines 3/6/1873

James Raines' Bible continued...

James Raines 3/23/1888
J. E. Raines and wife m. 3/5/1870 E. E. Putman and wife, 10/8/1986
J. J. Raines and wife m. 12/17/1911 Nellie J. Raines b. 6/22/1914
Walter Raines b. 2/1/1917
Frank Coleman Raines b. 7/6/1925 (owner of Bible)
James Joseph Raines 3/23/1888-7/5/1955

DEATHS:

Marget Nancy Elizabeth Christopher 8/1/1865
Rebecca A. Page 9/3/1865
Elizabeth Emaline Page 1/24/1870
N. W. Raines 8/2/1865
Marget Raines 1/23/1870
James E. Raines 1117/189
Sarah J. Raines 8/24/1913
Joseph Raines 7/5/1955
William Raines 8----
Mary Raines 2/26/1835
John T. Raines 12/8/1838
James Christopher 11/29/1839
James W. Raines 11/13/1851, aged 14 mos
Marget Allis Raines 7/5/1865
Marget Nancy Elizabeth Raines 3/1/1859
Joseph R. Raines 9/10/1862
Leander M. Christopher 10/12/1862
James Pritchard Shatana 12/13/1862
Viny Sary Ann Raines 7/7/1865

James Raines' Bible continued...

William Robert Christopher Hutcherson 7/24/1865

Notes: James Joseph Raines d. age 67 10/1928, at his home, Lynn, N. C., a native of Polk Co.

HENRY JEFFERSON BISHOP BIBLE
Owner: Miss Evie Bishop, Valley Falls, S. C.

BIRTHS:

H. J. Bishop 10/I/1820
Martha E. Bishop 2/16/1871
Eliza L. Bishop 10/13/1817
Marzie Lee Nora Bishop 12/16/1881
Tusarah Bishop 7/27/1845
Isaac Neuron Bishop 8/5/1889
Eliza Jane Bishop 3/23/1849
Mary E. Bishop 8/31/1883

Henry Simpson Bishop 11/5/1851
Elijah Defate Bishop 6/ 14/1886
John Jeff Bishop 1/31/1854
Henry Jeff Bishop - -18/1876?
Mary Bishop 5/4/1856
William Trolinger 9/15/1866
Edith Abigail Bishop 9/2/1918
John H. Trolinger 6/13/1870
Alburpha Bishop 1/28/1858

Henry Jefferson Bishop Bible...

Nancy Terlula Trolinger 4/24/1872
Cleveland Bishop 1/19/1859
Jesse Lee Bishop 1/14/1867
James Alms Bishop 8/17/1891
Talithalums Bishop 7/11/1894

MARRIAGES:

H. J. Bishop to Eliza Williams 10/24/1844 by Rev. T. J. Rollins
H. J. Bishop, 2nd, to Mrs. Julie Trolinger 2/20/1885 by William H. White. J. P.
L. J. Bishop to Martha Nix 11/13/1878
William H. Nix to M. E. Chapman 9/3/1818 or 1819
M. L. Bishop to W. D. Seay 10/8/1819
Mary Elizabeth Bishop to Belcon Seay 11/22/1903

BIRTHS:

Dean Durant Seay 10/8/1900
Robert Elbe Seay 6/13/1902-10/30/1902
Mary Abigail Seay 9/17/1903
Mattie Kate Seay 3/15/1905
N. A. Nix 6/8/1840
Elijah Nix 9/17/1884
Elizabeth Seay 3/9/1907
H. J. Bishop's wife, Eliza. and his children. Died 8/24/1884:

Henry Jefferson Bishop Bible...

DEATHS:

Liza Jane Bishop 5/15/1871 L. or Tusnrah Bishop 5/17/1876
Mary Elizabeth Bishop 6/17/1858
Henry Simpson Bishop 3/13/1889
Henry Bishop, father of H. J. Bishop, d. 7/22/1865, aged 90 yrs.. 5 mos., 13 days
Martha J. Bishop, mother of H. J. Bishop, d. 4/10/1862, aged 82 yrs., 14 days
H. J. Bishop. son of Henry Bishop, d. 2/21/1888

Albertha Bishop. daughter of H. J. Bishop, d. 1/1/1898
Mary Bishop m. Belton Seay 11/22/1903
Elijah Nix d. 2/27/1911

Cleveland Columbus Phillips Seay b. 10/31/1909
Bertha Lee Seay b. 5/4/1909
William Cleveland Seay b. 10/8/1916

Mary Elizabeth Seay b. 3/9/1907
H. J. Bishop, son of Henry. d. 12/31/1898 (given earlier as 1/1/1893)
Robert Clee Seay d. 10/30/1902
N. A. Nix 6/8/1840-6/31/1902
Elijah Nix b. 9/17/1834
Mattie Kate Seay b. 3/15/1905
Elijah D. Nix d. 6/16/1909
Cleveland Columbus Phillips Seay b. 10/31/1909
Henry Jeff Bishop m. Eunice Seay 9/13/1919
Isaac N. Bishop m. Bessie Reeves 7/4/1914

Henry Jefferson Bishop Bible...

Dean Seay n. Eunice Wingo 1/1/1919
Grover Cleveland Bishop d. 4/29/1932, aged 72 yrs., 5 mos., 20 days
Jane N. Bishop d. 5/29/1947
James E. Bishop, Sr., d. 9/30/1947
Callie B. Sherbert d. 2/24/1934
Elijah I. or A. Bishop d. 2/9/1955
Beauford G. Bishop d. 9/27/1960
Henry Jeff Bishop d. 3/22/1966
Mary Elizabeth Bishop d. 5/25/1927, parents, H. J. Bishop and Eunice Seay

JOHN BARNETT BIBLE
Owner: Frank C. Raines, Lynn. N. C.

This family is buried At Landrum, S. C. City Cemetery

Anna Barnett m. Jack Foster 12/5/1910

Anna Foster d. 7/3/1945, aged 52 yrs.
Alice Foster b. 12/15/1919
Florence Barnett m. Jack Mayfield 9/8/1912
Vance Suttle m. Addie Barnett 2/23/1913
John Foster b. 12/22/1914
Patti Mayfield b. 7/30/1913 d. 8/---
John Barnett b. -20/189-
Willie Barnett d. 10/23/1913
Ray Barnett 7/22/1906-9/15/1907
Peter Barnett b. 10/6/1909

John Barnett Bible continued...

John Barnett m. Emma Henson 3/1891
Anner May Barnett b. 12/25/1891
A. Evin Barnett b. 7/22/1893

Florence Eller Barnett b. 7/2/1895
Willie E. Barnett b. 6/28/1897
Jesse C. Barnett 4/18/1902-9/29/1904
Emma Barnett b. 1/10/1871 Will Barnett b. 1913

JEROME MILLER BIBLE
Owner: Mrs. Hazel Cape, Rt. 4, Box 774, Union, S. C.

BIRTHS:

Jerome Miller 5/26/1777
Thomas R. Miller 1/26/1814
John Miller 7/27/1803
Mary Miller 1/10/1791
Rebecca Miller 12/17/1816
Mary Mahala Miller --/22/1818
William Miller 2/23/1807
Jerome A. Miller 8/23/1823
Elizabeth Miller 6/23/1808
Albus Miller 3/26/1826
Jonas T. Miller 3/8/1831
Selena Miller 9/24/1811
Mary Miller 7/14/1829

JAMES ROBINSON BIBLE

James Robinson b. 9/2/1807 S. C., baptized by Rev. Alexander Porter, the son of William Robinson and Eliza Ann Boggs. 7/19/1837 in Ala. He m. Eliza Ann Bonner, daughter of William Bonner and Ann Lee Joel, b. 4/19/1817 In Abbeville, S. C., baptized by Rev. Robert Irwin.

MARRIAGES:

James Robinson to Eliza A. Bonner 7/19/1837 by Rev. James P. Pressly
Robert Davidson to Mary Susannah Robinson 7/21/1858 by James N. Henderson
Walker Y. Davidson to Ann Eliza Robinson 5/11/1859 by Rev. Modrell
William Wire Bonner Robinson to Mary S. Irvine 5/14/1873 by Rev. Reed
Irvine H. Bonner to Rebecca Jane Robinson 12/8/1875 by Rev. T. J. Bonner
James P. Robinson to Mary F. McCracken 11/17/1874 by Rev. Groves
Tom H. Robinson to Mary C. Bonner 1/8/1882 by Rev. T. J. Bonner
Oliver Y. Bonner to Sallie H. Robinson 12/20/1883 by T. J. Bonner
John L. Bonner to Elizabeth Boggs Robinson 10/6/1881 by T. J. Bonner

BIRTHS:

James Robinson, son of William and Elizabeth Robinson, 9/2/1807

James Robinson Bible continued...

Eliza Ann Robinson. daughter of William and Ann L. Bonner 4/19/1817
Mary Susannah Robinson, 1st daughter of James and Eliza A. Robinson 4/2/1839.
Ann Eliza Robinson. A daughter of James and Eliza A. Robinson, 11/12/1840
Infant son, 3rd child and 1st son of James and Eliza A. Robinson 5/12/1843. baptized by Rev. Joseph McCrary 7/1/1843, on second Centennry of Assembly of Westminster Divines

Willlam Wirt Bonner Robinson, 2nd son and 5th child of James and Elian A. Robinson, 2/26/1845, baptized by Rev. David Pressly 4/27/1845

Margaret Joel Robinson, 4th daughter and 6th child of James and Eliza A. Robinson. 9/26/1847, baptized by Rev. John Miller 12/3/1849

James Pressly Robinson, 3rd son and 8th child of James and Eliza A. Robinson, 10/9/1852, baptized by Rev. John Miller 7/31/1853 John Lee Rohinson,

4th son and 10th child of James and Eliza A. Robinson, 12/5/1855, baptized by Rev. T. J. Bonner 9/2/1860
Samuel Robinson, 5th son and 11th child of James and Eliza A. Robinson, 1/13/1858-6/10/1859, aged 1 yr., 4 mos., 27 days
Thomas Harvey and Sarah Hope Robinson, son and daughter 5/3/1860. 12th and 13th children of James and Eliza A. Robinson baptized 9/2/1860

James Robinson Bible continued...

DEATHS:

Infant son 5/14/1842, buried Ramburg burying ground, Wilcox Co. Alabama. Survived a few moments.

Samuel Robinson 6/10/1859, 1 yr., 4 mos., 27 days. buried at family cem, Freestone Co., Texas

Margaret Joel Robinson 7/28/1864, aged 16, 10 mos., 2 days, buried beside of her bro., Samuel, family cemetery.

Martha Campbell Robinson 7/8/1865, 16 yrs., 1 mo., 17 days, bur. beside sis and bro.

Rebecca Jane Bonner 11/2/1920, Fairfield, Tx.

Thomas Harvey 1/16/1925, buried Corsicana.
Elizabeth Boggs Bonnet 10/9/1921

James Robinson 4/16/1888, family graveyard, Freestone Co., Texas

Eliza A. Robinson 5/19/L897, buried family burying ground, Freestone Co., Texas

Eliza Davidson 1883, buried Davidson family graveyard, Navarro Co. Texas

James Robinson Bible continued...

Mary S. Davidson 10/10/1911, bur. Eureka Church, Navarro Co., Texas

William Wirt Bonner Robinson 11/28/1913 Corsicana, buried at Eureka Church, Navarro Co. Texas

James Pressley Robinson 11/30/1918, buried at Fairfield, Texas

WILLIAM HARRELL BIBLE
Of Darlington District, S. C.
Owner: Mrs. Rudolph Fletcher, Live Oak, Fla.

BIRTHS:

William Harrell, son of John and Sarah, 5/15/1822 Altina Jane, his wife, 6/29/1822

Sarah Rebecca Ann Harrell 1/5/1842
Handy Altina Harrell 4/1/1864
William Osker Harrell 8/22/1843
John Riley Harrell 8/12/1866
Zedun Bentrice Harrell 1/22/1898
L. E. Maud Harrell 4/22/1888
Hartwell Spain Harrell 5/23/1845
Mary Elenor Harrell L123/1846
Eliza Elizabeth Harrell 5/12/1849
Marthy Mazell Harrell 12/17/1850
Nancy Henraetter Harrell 5/31/1853

Roxalaney Jane Harrell 5/12/1856
Harriett Laura Tabitha Harrell 2/28/1862
Maxie Alexander Harrell 4/21/1867

BIRTHS: of Rebecca Riley's Children

William Jasper Riley 1/78/1842
Ira Draton Riley 9/20/1849
Annie Bessie Carter 10/27/1885
Lula Carter 6/13/1892
John Henry Harrell 8/9/1889
Silas Tafford Harrell 4/17/1893
William Edward Harrell 10/4/1891
Liley Hay Harrell 3/23/1895

MARRIAGES:

William Harrell to Altina J. Riley 11/29/1840
Martha Mozell 12/4/1866 to ---

DEATHS:

William Osker Harrell 4/22/1844
Mary Elender Harrell 2/8/1875
Handy Altina Harrell 10/1/1864
Altina Jane Harrell 9/15/1875
William Harrell 2/15/1872
Sarah Riley 11/11/1853
Silas Tafford Harrell 11/29/1917
Harriett Laura Tabitha Harrell 1/21/1902
Maxie Alexander Harrell 10/10/1939
Nancy Henrietta Harrell 12/16/1857
William Edward Harrell 12/10/1957, Veterans hospital, Lake City, Fla., bur Pine Grove Cemetery

MOSES BROWN BIBLE
Owner: Marcus Roddy, Duncan, S. C.

MARRIAGES:

First Generation Joseph Brown to Abigail Hills

Moses Brown, son of Joseph and Susannah, both of Newbury, to Mary, daughter of Caleb and Hannah Kimball, both of Newbury 11/20/1794

BIRTHS and names of THEIR CHILDREN:

Susannah M. Brown 3/17/1797-9/29/1831
Moses Brown Jr. 5/27/1799-10/7/1839
Sophie Brown 2/6/1801-10124/1864
Mary Brown 1/1/1803-9/17/1803
Mary Brown 6/28/1804-9/19/1889
Hannah Brown 5/30/1806-10/17/1810
Abigail Brown 12/22/1808-2/16/1879
Joseph Brown 1/6/1811-7/5/1831
Ellen Ann, wife of Moses Brown, d. 9/6/1863
Joseph Brown, father of above Moses Brown, d. 1/15/1810, aged 80 yrs. 8 mos.
Mary Brown, wife of above Moses Brown, d. 8/14/1831, aged 64 yrs.

DEATHS:

Mrs. Mary, relict of Abner Chase 6/29/1828, aged 92 yrs.
Samuel Pillsbury 4/1/1836, aged 2 yrs.
Elizabeth, relict of Samuel Pillsbury, aged 63 yrs.

Moses Brown Bible continued...

Moses S. Brown 5/9/1923 aged 84 yrs., 4 mos.
Eliza Florence. daughter of Moses S. Brown and Hannah E. Brown

Sarah Armesbury 6/23/1862, d. 7/4/1863
Mary L., daughter of Moses S. Brown and Hannah E., 2/2/1860-7/15/1863
Moses S., son of Moses S. Brown and Hannah E., 6/24/1864-4/21/18--

BIRTHS:

Mrs. Mary, relict of Abner Chase, was Ist female baptized in Merrimac River
Moses S. Brown, son of Moses, 1/7/1839
Hannah E., wife of Moses S. Brown, 2/20/1838, was m. at West Newbury 1/8/1859

Obituaries:

"BROWN--in this city Dec. 8th at 11 Fifth Avenue, Hannah E. Brown, wife of Moses S. Brown, aged 84 yrs., 9 mos, 18 days. ... Burial in Church Street cemetery, Merrimac....private. (dated 1922)"

"Miss Mary Abbie Hoyt, a resident of this town d. Newburyport on Saturday at age of 74 yrs.

Miss Hoyt has been in poor health for some time and closed her home here awhile ago and went to Newburyport where she was

Moses Brown Bible continued...

cared for. She leaves no near relatives, only several cousins who reside out of town. Miss Hoyt had many friends here and she was a member of the All Saints Church....

Funeral services for Hannah E. Brown were held at the home, 11 Fifth Avenue....Mrs. Brown was a native of Marblehead Neck, b. 2/20/1838, later lived in West Newbury and Bradford. She m. 1/8/1859 Moses S. Brown who survives her. She leaves besides her husband, two sisters, Mrs. Susan Salkins of Bradford and Mrs. Emily Willis of West Newbury; two nephews, Barley G. Keeler and William H. Dixon, both of this city; and two nieces, Miss Josephine Keeler and Mrs. Minnie Bradley, W. Newbury.

ROBERT WHITE BIBLE
Owner: Lorene Barnett P. O. Box 292, Greer, S. C. 29652

Robert White 2/9/1743-11/21/1843.

His CHILDREN:

BIRTHS:

William White 11/11/1829-11/23/1876
John White 2/8/1778
Susan White 4/12/1780-4/12/1851
Jane White 3/28/1782-
Robert White, Jr. 3/16/1784
Stephen White 4/28/1786-
Mary White 9/7/1788-

Robert White Bible continued...

Tillman White 3/15/1791
Elizabeth White 1/9/1793-3/13/1835
Charles White 9/20/1800
Benjamin White 9/20/1800

Robert White, Jr. b. 3/16/1784, his children:

Susan C. White 6/30/1812
Paley D. White 5/4/1814-12/16/1853
Mildred M. White 9/2/1815-7/4/1818
Nancy N. White 8/20/1817
James U. White 5/6/1819-10/30/1843

Jessie T. White 5/27/1821
Thomas T. White 5/6/1823
Robert E. White 2/28/1825
Calvin A. White 2/20/1827
Charles White 6/5/1829-7/21/1863
Lewis R. White 2/21/1835

JOHN McDOWELL BIBLE
Owner: Mrs. Mary Sue Keith
Rt. 1, Jonesville, S. C.

MARRIAGES:

D. H. Miller to Mary M. Mayes 12/17/1874, Rev. A. A. James

John McDowell Bible continued...

BIRTHS:

John McDowell, Sr. 8/12/1759 Glenmuluon Co., Antrim, Ireland

Mary McDowell 8/3/1790 Glenmuluon Co., Antrim, Ireland
David McDowell 3/31/1793 Glenmuluon Co., Antrim, Ireland
John McDowell Jr. 11/3/1795 Union District
David H. Miller 10/22/1853
Mary M. Miller 7/24/1851
Hannah Elizabeth Miller 9/7/1877
Mary Dorcus Miller 11/8/1885

DEATHS:

William Black 3/10/1829, aged 39 yrs.
Henry McDowell 9/7/1833, aged 35 yrs.
Jones T. Miller 3/8/1831

SAMUEL GRIER BIBLE
Of Georgetown, S. C.
Owner: Mrs. Lorene B. Barnett, Greer, S. C.

Samuel Grier 5/1/1792-4/26/1871 m. Harriet Elizabeth Varien? 12/25/1812.

THEIR CHILDREN:

James Martha Grier b. -17/1813

Samuel Grier Bible continued...

Samuel Grier Jr. b. 6/5/1815
Ebenezer Grier b. 8/6/1817
Mary Jane Grier b. 8/7/1820 m. 10/24/1837
Robert H. Collins who d. 1/29/1856, aged 43 yrs.
Judith Grier b. 10/21/1824
Elizabeth Grier 12/30/1827-7/28/1834
Thomas William Grier 2/27/1832-8/18/1886
George Benjamin Grier b. 2/7/1834

Ann Grier b. 3/13/1840 m. Ist Bennie Rawls, Sr., 2nd, Daniel Peal Daniel Bath Grier b. 7/25/1845

Samuel B. Grier b. 12/9/1857
Mary Prudence Peal b. 8/2/1867
John Henry Peal b. 3/20/1870-d. infant Daniel Merry Peal b. 6/9/1875

JOHN L. COOPER BIBLE

Annie Belle Frye Cooper, daughter of John Pinkney Frye and Tennessee Arkansas Smith
Walter P. Cooper 1/12/1908

John L. Cooper, Sr. d. 1/1/1907, buried Bethlehem Baptist Church, Roebuck, S. C. beside Emma Cooper Holland.

WALTER PLURAL COOPER BIBLE
Owner: Mary N. Hills, Chesnee, S. C.

Walter Plural Cooper 4/19/1883-1/6/1959, buried Dewberry Cemetery, Cowpens, S. C., m. 1/12/1908

Annie Belle Frye 3/26/1888-1944, buried Dewberry Cemetery
Leon Cooper b. 9/26/1909 m. 3/12/1926 Kathleen Brock
Lillie Grace Cooper b. 9/2/1911 m. 3/4/1932 Reuben Banks
Elmer Reid Cooper b. 2/18/1914 m. 10/18/1932 Jessie Derrick

Ruth Kathlyn Cooper b. 12/31/1915 m. 8/17/1932 Paul James Emery

J. P. Cooper b. 4/2/1918 m. Ist 2/6/1937 Winnie Cox, 2nd, Helen Reeder
Myrtle Sarah Cooper b. 10124/1919 m. 12/6/1937 Clarence Mitchell, d. 2/1957
Eugene Clarence Cooper b. 9/17/1921 m. 4/15/1942 Evelyn White
Thelma (Ted) Aline Cooper b. 10/21/1923 m. 1st, Petty, 2nd 8/7/1941 Tommy Waddell, a Blind Minister, also now decd

Gwendolyn Anne Emery b. 2/9/1957 Charleston, S. C.
Cecil Bernard Emery, Jr. b. 6/6/1958 Spartanburg, S. C.
Baby Boy Emery b. and d. 4/1959 Spartanburg, S. C.
Baby Boy Emery b. and d. 4/1960 Spertanburg, S. C.
Kimberly Diane Emery b. 10/24/1961 Spartanburg, S. C.
Cecil B. Emery, Jr. m. Debra Key Morrow

DICKENSON-THOMAS-POPE BIBLE
Owner: Mary N. Hills, Box 281, Chesnee, S. C. 29323

Jacob Dickenson Family Bible Record received from Jane Fore, Adams, Tennessee, aged 81 in 1959 when obtained.

Jacob Dickenson m. Mourning Thomas
George Wimberly, half bro. to Jacob Dickenson, m. Charity Thomas, her sister
Mother of Jacob and George was Sarah Fort

Anne Fort's gg grandfather was losleh Fort who settled in Edgecombe Co., N. C. 1792 and resided 50 miles from Nashville

BIRTHS: of children of John and Elizabeth Thomas

John Thomas 1710- --
Martha Thomas 179/1719
Mary Thomas 8/18/1712
Susannah Thomas 2/26/1721
Christian Thomas 3/14/1715
Jacob Thomas 11/4/1923
Elizabeth Thomas 1/14/1717
Micajah Thomas 2/13/1725

DEATHS:

Joseph Thomas 4/25/1758
Mary Crudups 8/22/1775
Micajah Thomas 12/14/1760
Mourning Wimberly 3/17/1781

Dickenson-Thomas-Pope Bible continued...

BIRTHS:

Priscilla Horn, daughter of William and Mary Horn, b. 5/20/1762
Mary Pope, daughter of Solomon and Susannah, 4/13/1766
Elizabeth, daughter of Solomon and Susannah, 9/13/1767
Mourning Pope, daughter of Solomon and Susannah, 6/9/1769
Solomon Pope. son of Sampson Pope and Susannah, 3/11/1741
Elijah Pope, son of Sampson Pope and Susannah, 9/10/1743
Jacob Pope, son of Sampson Pope and Susannah. 2/29/1744
Henry Pope. son of Sampson Pope and Susannah, 5/10/1746

JOHN LITTLEJOHN WEST BIBLE
Owner: Mrs. Joyce Williams, Rt. I, Pauline, S. C.

DEATHS:

Bryan Cornelius West 12/21/1970
John Littlejohn West to Martha Susan Ann McWhirter m. 12/20/1864
William C. West to Lula West 6/10/1888
Charles N. West to Sarah N. Lancaster 2/25/1894

BIRTHS:

Rachel West 5/21/1769
Caty Cunningham 12/7/1786

John Littlejohn West Bible continued...

Elizabeth West 9/1/1790
Dorcas Haselwood 4/10/1766
Cassander West 10/17/1797
Lancaster Haselwood 2/14/1768
Benjamin T. West 10/19/1803
Cora West 11/14/1904
Solomon West 10/19/1803
Carrie West 10/11/1901
Lety West 10/19/1806
Francis West 11/1/1907

DEATHS:

Rachel West 5/26/1842
Lancaster Haselwood 9/18/1854
Mary Cunningham 10/3/1862
Elizabeth Dukes 11/26/1872
Dorcas Haselwood 6/11/1849

BIRTHS:

William West
Isaac West 5/19/1823
Jasper West 9/3/1821
Rhoda West 4/23/1795
Nancy West 3/2/1825
John Littlejohn West 10/11/1836
Thomas Jefferson West 6/13/1815
Mesina West 2/28/1828
Selena West 11/4/1819

John Littlejohn West Bible continued...

Seborn West 11/30/1816
Mitchell West 2/3/1830
William Carson West 5/12/1834

DEATHS:

William West 6/12/1876
Isaac West 8/5/1864
Rhoday West 7/9/1861
Nancy Williams 8/20/1853
T. J. West 8/8/1863
Mitchell West 12/29/1899
Seborn West 10/14/1889
Jasper West 8/26/1873
William Carson West 3/9/1899
Selena McArthur 5/17/1888

Polly West, wife of William C. West, 3/6/1863
John Littlejohn West 7/25/1903

BIRTHS:

John Littlejohn West 10/11/1836
Isabel West 10/26/1896
Charles Norris West 7/6/1869
Martha Susan Ann West 10/29/1845
Landy` Porter West 12/28/1898
Charles Marion West 6/4/1903
Annie Bernard 1/26/1902
William Carroll West 9/12/1866

John Littlejohn West Bible continued...

Uncle Lester McWhirter 2/23/1855-8/28/1906

DEATHS:

John Littlejohn West 7/25/1903-
Forest Littlejohn 11/2/1956
Martha Susan Ann West 3/26/1925
William Perrian West 1/8/1957
Charlie Norris West 10/16/1931
Lula Adella West 3/22/1958
William Carroll West 9/24/1938
Charles Nation West 7/6/1963
Sarah Nettie L. West 2/12/1954
Annie Bernard West 3/22/1971

ANDREW EGGER BIBLE
Owner: Mrs. Lorene Barnett
P. O. Box 292, Greer, S. C. 29652

BIRTHS:

Andrew Egger 3/12/1762
Ann Egger b. 6/24/1769 m. 11/23/1786
Elizabeth Orr Egger 1/6/1788
Ann Hubbard Egger 7/15/1796
Ursley Holland Egger 3/4/1790
Moses Bond Egger 11/11/1798
Mary Egger 2/7/1792

Andrew Egger Bible continued...

John Egger 4/7/1802-4/7/1802
Mary Egger 6/28/1794
Rhoda Egger 1/27/1803
Lovice Egger 6/11/1805-9/6/1807
Alexander Ramsay Egger 8/31/1807-9/9/1807
Lemuel William Egger 9/13/1808
Sally Egger 4/28/1811

JOHN P. MOON BIBLE
Owner: Mrs. Annie Noon Turner Kendrlcks

John P. Moon m. Agnes Barnett 1/18/1844

BIRTHS:

John P. Moon 12/15/1822
Rebecca Adaline Moon 10/21/1848
Agnes M. Moon 4/14/1827
Louisa Jones Moon 8/12/1850
Frances Jane Moon 12/11/1844
John Walker Moon 1/1/1855
Elinder Angaline Moon 7/8/1846
Malinda Caroline Moon 2/29/1852
Susan Elizabeth Moon 12/24/1856
Thomas Henry Moon 2/24/1864
James Randal Moon 9/2/1859
Sintha Moon 9/22/1865
Narcissa Moon 7/18/1861
William H. Moon 6/29/1868

John P. Moon Bible continued...

DEATHS:

Malinda Caroline Moon 1/13/1859, aged 6 yrs., 10 mos., 13 days
Rebecca Moon 1/4/1863, aged 14 yrs., 2 mos., 14 days
Thomas Henry Moon 11/16/1864, aged 8 mos. 23 days
William Henry Moon 9/2/1914, aged 46 yrs., 2 mos. 6 days

JOHN C. OTWELL BIBLE

BIRTHS: of Children of John C. Otwell and Sarah, his wife

George H. Otwell 4/10/1858-- -

Sarah El Otwell 17113/1842
Charles G. Otwell 4/22/1862
Mary J. Otwell -/12/1848
Obed. J. Otwell 10122/1835
Amelia C. Otwell 5/17/1852
Watson T. Otwell 2/26/1838
John H. Otwell 10/2/1850
William W. Otwell 618/1838
Mathew C. Otwell 4/20/1853
Alexandria B. Otwell 12/17/1845

DEATHS:

Obed. Otwell 1/28/1834, aged 52 yrs.
Mary Otwell, wife of above man, 10/22/1850, aged 72 yrs.

John C. Otwell Bible continued...

John H. Otwell 6/22/1851, aged 8 mos. 20 days
Sally Otwell 9/26/1870, wife of John C. Otwell
John C. Otwell 7/21/1877 Watson T. Otwell 2/19/1888
Obad. J. Otwell 2/25/1906
William W. Otwell 11/5/1906

HOSEA H. "LOT" HOLCOMBE BIBLE
Owner: Horace Hamilton, Rt. 6, Emmet, Ark.

Hosea H. Holcombe 7/20/1780-7/31/1841. Union District, S. C. Died Jefferson Co., Ala., 120 miles from home, aged 61 yrs, 11 days.

Cassandra (Casey) Jackson 3/31/1780-2/10/1848, Lafayette Co., Miss., 67 yrs., 10 mos.,11 days
Hosea H. Holcombe baptised 9/5/1800.
Hosea H. Holcombe was licensed to preach 4/16/1803 as Baptist minister. He was ordained 8/17/1805 Union District, S. C.

BIRTHS: of CHILDREN:

Darius Holcombe 4/11/1802
Harmon C. Holcombe 6/15/1814
Alva J. Holcombe 6/28/1804
Martha R. Holcombe 2/4/1816
Tartan Holcombe 3/6/1805
Son b. 6 d. 11/7/1817
Teresa Holcombe 4/1/1808

Hosea H. "Lot" Holcombe Bible continued...

John R. Holcombe 4/15/1820
Eudocia Holcombe 10/30/1809
Daughter 9/3/1822
Daughter born and died 5/7/1811
Frances H. S. M. Holcombe 3/22/1824
William Holcombe 5/11/1812 Mecklenburg, S. C.

MARRIAGES:

Hosea H. Holcombe to Casey Jackson 617/1801 Union District, S. C.
Darius J. Holcombe to Rebecca Barger 7/31/1825
Tarton P. Holcombe to Rhoda D. Mundine 12/20/1827
Thomas M. Holcombe to Rebecca Jones 11/2/1827
Thomas M. Holcombe to Nancy L. Moreland 11/25/1847
Teresa Holcombe to William Hunt 6/5/1825
Eudocia Holcombe to James Rockett 2/24/1831
W. H. Holcombe to Emaline D. Yeager 11/27/1834
W. H. Holcombe to Martha Finley 9/26/1836
Harmon C. Holcombe to Susan McAdams 1/4/1838
Martha R. Holcombe to W. Bunch 12/21/1837

John B. Holcombe to Dolly McAdams 3/1/1840
Dr. A. S. Holcombe to Mary T. Rockett 4/12/1838

DEATHS:

Rebecca Jones Holcombe 9/14/1842 One son d. 9/13/1842

Hosea H. "Lot" Holcombe Bible continued...

Thomas N. Holcombe 12/15/1848, aged 42 yrs., 7 mos., 28 days
Harriet N. Holcombe 9/13/1842 Mary Ann Francis 11/24/1839

Birth of first child of Thomas Jefferson Purtle and wife, Frances Cassandra Holcombe - John Thomas Purtle b. 12/13/1871.

BIRTHS: of Children of Thomas M. Holcombe and Rebecca Jones

Nancy Holcombe 8/8/1828
Harriet N. Holcombe 9/26/1831-9/13/1842
One daughter born and died 9/22/1833
Martha Ann Hasseltine 4/28/1835
William Henry Holcombe 8/13/1837

MARRIAGES:

Nancy E. Holcombe to Jesse McCoulter 2/1845

Thomas M. Holcombe to Nancy. Moreland. There was only one child born to this union,

Frances Cassandra 8/29/1848 who m. Thomas Jefferson Purtle.

JOHN BENJAMIN BRANNON BIBLE

John Benjamin Brannon m. Laura Mickey Joanna Bruce
12/1/1870

Family Records

John Benjamln Brannon b. 2/2/1853 Kershaw, S. C. d. 3/30/1908 m. 12/1/1870

Laura Mickey Joanna Bruce b. 10/11/1853 Kershaw, S. C. d. 11/16/1928 n. 12/1/1870
Joseph Monroe Brannon b. 12/14/1871 Kershaw, S. C. d. 7/22/1942 m. 1/9/1901
John Wesley Lee Brannon b. 8/13/1873 Kershaw, S. C. m. 1/1/1896 Francis Marion Brannon b.
9/4/1875 Kershaw, S. C. d. 6/1/1930 d. 11/8/1902
William Manson Brannon b. 2/19/1877 Kershaw, S. C. d. 3/1937 m. 4/18/1906
Lois Alice Brannon b. 8/16/1879 Kershaw, S. C. d. 11/6/1888
Daisy Rosalie Brannon b.
3/28/1881 Kershaw, S. C. d. 9/13/1951
Mildred Arlivia Brannon b. 5/18/1885 Kershaw. S. C. d. 3/28/1924 m. 9/15/1908
O. Murray Brannon b. 7/15/1890 Kershaw, S. C. m. 6/10/1920
Alice Belle Brnnnon b. 7/15/1890 Kershav, S. C. m. 6/10/1920
James Bruce Brannon b.
3/24/1894 Pave, Ga. d. 10/16/1959 m. 8/15/1915

Robert Columbus Brannon b. 8/29/1897 Pave, Ga. d. 2/7/1930 m. 10/23/1925

JANE McCANTS BIBLE
Owner: Mrs. George Erwin, Athens, Ga. 30601

BIRTHS:

Jane McCants, daughter of Nathaniel and Elizabeth Gautier McCants, 9/12/1779 St. John's Parish, Charleston Dist., S. C.
James McCants, husband and first cousin of Jane McCants, 6/10/1784 S. C.
Robert James Pembrook McCants, son of James and Jane McCants, 10/13/1812 S. C.
Allen Gautier McCants, son of Robert James Pembrook McCants and Caroline Elizabeth Allen
McCants 12/3/1835 Abbeville Dist., S. C. Victoria Jane McCants, same parents, 9/14/1837.
Abbeville, S. C. Amanda Louisa McCants, same parents, 5/30/1840 Chambers Co., Ala.
Lois Anna Rebecca McCants, same parents, 9/30/1842, Chambers Co., Ala.
John James Clay McCants same parents, 3/10/1844, Chambers Co., Ala.
Robert George Alexander Nathaniel McCants, same parents, 4/2/1850, Chambers Co., Ala.
Buena Vista McCants, daughter of Robert George Alexander Nathaniel McCants and Pristine Cherokee
Taylor McCants, 4/3/1873 Mobile, Ala. Allen Gautier McCants, same parents, 8/20/1875, Spring Hill, near Mobile, Ala.
Samuel Inman McCants, same parents. 1/28/1878, Mobile, Ala.
John Showell Allen 9/19/1788 Mecklenburg Co., Va.
Caroline Elizabeth Allen, daughter of John Showell Allen and Ruth LInton Allen, and wife of Robert James Pembrook McCants, 3/23/1815, Abbeville Dist., S. C.

Jane McCants' Bible continued...

Pristine Cherokee Taylor, daughter of John T. and Nancy Curry Taylor and wife of Robert George
Alexander Nathaniel McCants, 3/1/1855, Mobile, Ala.

MARRIAGES:

James McCants to his 1st cousin Jane McCants, daughter of Nathanlel McCants 2/21/1805 S. C.
John Showell Allen to Ruth Linton, daughter of Esquire Samuel Linton at county estate of Esquire
Samuel Linton "Mt. Pleasant" in Abbeville List., S. C. 6/1814
Robert James Pembrook McCants to Caroline Elizabeth Allen, daughter of John Showell Allen and
Ruth Linton Allen 10/9/1834 Abbeville Dist., S. C.
Showell Allen to Ruth Linton Allen 10/9/183- Abbeville, S. C.
Robert George Alexander Nathaniel McCants to Pristine Cherokee Taylor, daughter of John T. and Nancy Curry Taylor, 6/5/1872, in Government Street, Mobile, Ala.
Buena Vista McCants to Joseph E. Dixon 4/5/1899, Christ Church, Tuscaloosa, Ala.
Samuel Inman McCants to Jessie Corine Hedge 4/15/1903, Meridian, Miss.

DEATHS:

James McCants father of Nathaniel McCants 1771, S. C.
Nathaniel McCants, son of James
McCants, 1816, St. John's Parish, Charleston, S. C.
James McCants, husband of Jane McCants 2/28/1816 S. C.

Jane McCants' Bible continued...

John Showell Allen 2/5/1855 Chambers Co., Ala.
Ruth Linton Allen, wife of John Showell Allen,
2/4/1835,Abbeville, S. C.
Robert James Pembrook McCants 9/21/1849
Caroline Elizabeth Allen, wife of Robert James Pembrook McCants, 10/12/1886

EDWARD NORTH BIBLE
Owner: Beaufort Armory Museum, Beaufort, S. C.

Grant to Edward North with Record of BIRTHS: and DEATHS::
"Edward North, 714 acres - 1514 - recorded."

Edward North m. Susannah Cook 7/29/1720.

BIRTHS of THEIR CHILDREN:

Dead son 1/19/1721
Elizabeth North 1/29/1728
Edward North 1/15/1726
John North 2/1/1722
William North 1/9/1730
Ann North 12/21/1724
Joshua North

DEATHS:

Mrs. Susanna North 11/21/1733

Edward North Bible:

William North 2/21/1738
Miss Ann North 5/4/1735
Joshua North

JOHN E. FRIPP BIBLE
Owner: Beaufort Arsenal Museum, Beaufort, S. C.

BIRTHS: of Children of John E. and Isabella Phoebe Fripp

Mary Rosa Fripp 12/7/1853, baptised by Rev. Dr. McIleran, sponsors: Edgar and Eliza Fripp

Julian Jenkins Fripp 12/15/1855, baptized by Rev. Dr. McElleran; sponsors: D. P. Jenkins and A. L. Jenkins at St. Helena Island Florence Amanda Fripp 3/7/--, baptized in Grahamville by Rev. Wigfall.

Edgar Walter Fripp 7/16/1857, baptized by Rev. Mr. Johnson, at St. Helena Island
Daniel Perry Fripp 12/24/1860, baptized in Grahamville by Rev.Wigfall; sponsors: C. A. and M. E. Chisum
Thomas Screven Fripp 11/24/186-, baptized in Grahamville by Rev. Wigfall; sponsors: W. P. Fripp.

Ella Rosalie Fripp ---, baptized by Rev. Bellinger; sponsor: E. L. Fripp.
Eliza Emily Fripp 9/15/1867, baptized by Rev. Bellinger; sponsors: Ellen Louisa Fripp and William P. Fripp.

John E. Fripp Bible, contd...

Charles Benjamin Fripp 3/23/1870, baptized by Rev. Bellinger; sponsor: William P. Fripp.
Robert Lee Fripp 4/13/1872, baptized by Rev. Bellinger; sponsors: William P. Fripp and E. L. Fripp.
Alice Louisa Fripp 9/17/1875, baptized by Rev. Bellinger; sponsors: Martha S. Fripp and ----.

DEATHS:

Mary Rosa Fripp 8/22/1854
Florence Amanda Fripp 7/17/1867
Ella Rosalie Fripp 10128/1880, aged 16 yrs., I mo., 12 days.
Note: Obituary notice of John E. Fripp glued in Bible, died 5/22/1906, eldest son of late William B. Fripp of St. helena Island, and was b. on that island 75 yrs. ago....in 1853 he m. Miss Isabel Jenkins....

MARRIAGES:

Martha M. Fripp to Thomas Philson 118/1824 Charleston, S. C.
William B. Fripp to Eliza Chaplin 10/14/1824 by Rev. Philip Mathew

John Ervin Fripp to Isabella Phebe Jenkins 1/1/1853 at Pendoall Church by Rev. D. McElleran.
Thomas Fripp to Ellen Louisa Chisolm 4/21/1853 on John's Island by Rev. Hale.
William P. Fripp to Martha Sarah Fripp 6/5/1856 at St. Helenaville by Rev. D. McElleran.

BIRTHS:

Paul Fripp, son of John, 12/8/1737-3/7/1800, aged 63 yrs.
William B. Fripp, son of Paul and Amelia, 2/18/1792
Eliza Chaplin, daughter of John and Mary, 12/1/1796
Mary Emily Fripp, son of William B. and Eliza, 5/10/1826, baptised by Rev. P. Mathews.
William Augustus Fripp, son of William and Eliza, 4/5/1828, d. 6/2/, aged 2 mos., 3 days.

Thomas Benjamin Fripp, son of William and Eliza, 6/24/1829, baptized by Rev. Joseph Walker.

John Edwin Fripp, son of William and Eliza, 11/28/1831, baptized by Rev. O. McElkeran.

DEATHS:

Thomas A. Philson b. 3/23/1825, 11 days. Francls S. Philson 10/25/1826-9/10/1831
Mary Rosa Fripp 8/22/18541
Florence Amanda Fripp 7/17/1867

MORGAN JAMES BIBLE

BIRTHS: of Children of Morgan and Mary James

Benjamin James 9/8/1713   Aaron James 874/1717
Martha James 12/24/1714   Hannah James 9/18/1718
Thomas James 3/17/1715/1716   Jonathan James 12/19/1722
----C. Evans 12/25/1814

Morgan James Bible continued...

Note: LWT of Morgan James of Newton, Chester Co., Pa. Deceased, 1/14/1737 names wife, Mary and CHILDREN: Margaret Lewis. Joseph James, "all my children by first and second wives"; names kinsman, Samuel Lewis and friend, Thomas Thomas of Radnor, both of Chester Co., Pa., exrs. Descendants removed to Darlington, S. C.

Daniel Murchison, son of John, b. Isle of Skye, Scotland, 1759. With his father, a brother and a sister, he came to Montgomery Co., N. C. in 1777. He d. Kershaw Co., S. C. 10/13/1843. Margaret McCaskill, daughter of John HcCaskill and Catherine Campbell, b. In Montgomery Co., N. C. in 1770. She d. Kershaw Co., S. C. 7/30/1847.

Children of Daniel and Margaret Murchison

Alexander Murchison 1794-8/10/1860 Montgomery Co., N. C.
Nancy Murchison 6/22/1795-1/9/1880 Montgomery Co., N. C.
John Murchison 4/28/1799-9/14/1872 Montgomery Co., N. C.
Daniel Murchison 1802-10/7/1822 Montgomery Co., N. C.
Margaret Murchison 4/4/1804 Montgonery Co., N. C.-d. Kershaw Co., S. C.
Kenneth Murchison 4/14/1806 Montgomery Co., N. C.-4/11/1845 Orangeburg Co., S. C.
Mary Murchison 1/24/1808 Montgomery Co., N. C.-5/1/1884 Kershaw Co., S. C.
Isabella Murchison 8/28/1809 Montgomery Co., N. C.-8/15/1885 Kershaw Co., S. C.
Samuel Murchison 5/6/1811 Montgomery Co., N. C.

John E. Murchison 12/22/1812 Montgomery Co., N. C.-8/17/1836
Susan? Colin Campbell Murchison 10/7/1815 Montgomery Co., N. C.10.28/1889 Independence, Kansas

Granddau., Caroline V. Ewan
My mother - Regina Catharine Murchison (3rd daughter of Colin Campbell Murchison) m. William I. Ewan, a Virginian, in 1873.

PRINCE-FLEMING BIBLE
Owner: Mrs. Morett Fleming, Anderson, S. C.

BIRTHS:

Jonathan Prince 2/12/1787
Margaret L. Prince 9/7/1851
Milly Prince 1789
Sarah C. Clark 1/18/1830
Rebecca Prince 2/8/1812
George Taler 4/8/1854
Edward Prince 3/7/1814
George Marvin Fleming 12/13/1844
Hudson Prince 5/23/1818
Martha Bell 5/17/1844
George W. Prince 6/10/1825
Belinda Catherine Fleming 4/26/1849
Catharine Prince 10/1/1820
Calhoun Fleming 12/15/1875 ---- 1/23/1846
William Prince 11/7/1827
Samuel Mathew Fleming 4/2/1853
Jonathan Prince, Jr. 10/14/1816

Prince-Fleming Bible continued...

Barbara Atlas Fleming 2/6/1867
W. A. Fleming 9/7/1818
Mary Emily Fleming 2/11/1860
Nancy Y. Fischarde 6/10/1821
Sary Jane Fleming 1/3/1863

MARRIAGES:

Jonathan to Milly Prince 1/10/1811 Hugh M. Prince 3/2/1845
Rebecca W. Prince to W. A. Fleming 10/20/1842
Nancy Y. Fischarde to W. A. Fleming 1/22/1852

DEATHS:

Rebecca W. Fleming 8/27/1851
Wm Anderson Fleming 8/23/1885
Jonathan Prince. Jr. 2/25/1817
Barbara Atlas Fleming 12/7/1876
Edward Prince 5/28/1834
Mary Emily Fleming 11/18/1888
Cuetan W. Prince 11/23/1843

Sarah Jane Fleming 6/18/1895
Melba? Prince 7/19/1835, In his 46th yr.
Belinda Catherine Fleming 7/1/1864

JOHN McCASKILL BIBLE
Owner: Mrs. R C. Reames, Bishopville, S. C

MARRIAGES:

John McCaskill to Florah McCaskill 10/13/1783
Alexander McCaskill to Margaret Murchison 9/18/1838
S. P. Murchison to Mary McCaskill 9/18/1838
Margaret McCaskill to Samuel Webb 8/10/1849
S. P. Murchison to Isabell Webb 3/16/1849
S. L. A. Murchison to James Smith 5/23/1876

BIRTHS: of Children of John and Florah McCaskill

Murdoch McCaskill 7/11/1784-
Daniel Mc Caskill 12/30 /1788
Alexander McCaskill 8/21/1786
Catherine McCaskill 3/5/1791

BIRTHS: of Children of Daniel and Margaret Murchison

Margaret McCaskill Murchison 4/4/1804
S. P. Murchison b. 5/6/1811 m. Mary McCaskill 9/18/1838

BIRTHS: of Children of S. P. and Mary Murchison Allen

Alexander Murchison 10/12/1839 Sarah Isabel Murchison 1/19/1841
Margaret Jane Murchison 4/5/1842 Daniel Peter Columbus Murchison 2/9/1844
Mary Murchison 11/19/1845

John McCaskill Bible continued...

BIRTHS: of Children of S. P. and Isabel Murchison

Catherine Ann Murchison 5/23/1853 John Wesley Murchison 7/4/1856
Christian Eliza Murchison 4/13/1859

DEATHS:

Catharine McCaskill 3/4/
Margaret 9/8/1857
John McCaskill 10/30/1845
S. P. Murchison 10/8/1857
Alexander McCaskill 11/11/1846
Daniel Murchison 10/13/1843
Margaret Murchison, wife of Daniel, 7/30/1847
Sarah Isabel Murchison 10/8/1857
Mary Murchison, wife of S. P. Murchison, 5/29/1847

GEORGE LYNES BIBLE

Owner: Mrs. Julia Johnson Britton 472 St. Andrews Blvd., Charleston, S. C. 29407

Toney b. 2/23/1817 San Children age
Lency confind a girl name Betsy 7/9/1872

DEATHS:

W. H. Walling 10/23/1898
Ellie E. Blizzard 3/6/1922

George Lynes' Bible continued...

Annie B. Lynes 3/14/1938
J. H. Lynes 11/24/1898
Hay B. Walling 2/22/1918
J. Florrie Walling 3/28/1916
E. H. Guyton 12/28/1898
Annie V. Sylvia 9/22/1920
R. W. Haynes 11/12/1907
George Lynes 7/3/1901
S. E. Blizzard 3/10/1923
Rebecca S. Sims 2/11/1938
Ann Lynes, Dick's wife, 7/21/1904
A. J. Glen 5/20/1924

MARRIAGES:

George Lynes to Elizabeth Whitfield 8/27/1829
J. E. Blizzard of N. C. to Ellie E. Glen at Fox Bank 7/8/1891 by Rev. Samuel Lynes. (Fox Bank located in Berkley Co., S. C. between entrance of Cypress Gardens on Hwy 52 and 17-A near Baptist Church called Groomsville, orig. called Old Bethlehem Church).
E. H. Lynes to N. H. Guyton 4/17/1850 by Rev. S. Lynes at Comingtee, Cooper River
Richard Lynes to Anna E. Sanders 9/20/1871 at Grooms.
Samuel Lynes to Cathrine G. Dennis of Charleston 3/2/1875 by Rev. L. C. Tebeau at Lucknow
Plantation, Sav Back Riv, S. C. Richard Lynes to Annie Elizabeth Sanders 9/20/1871 Groomsville

George Lynes' Bible continued...

BIRTHS

Christiana Lynes 11/16/1830 at Exeter Plantation
Eliza, delivered a girl child but died in a few minutes 5/22/1834
Elizabeth H. Lynes 8/1/1835 at Savannah at Judge Cheves Pine Land
George J. Lynes 12/13/1837, Judge Cheves Plantation, Savannah Riv.
Mather Ann Lynes 10/1/1839 at Fife Genl. Hamilton's Plantation, Savannah Back River
Eliza 12/12/1840 confined at John R. Williamson, Esq. Swamp Plantation, Savannah River, with
a girl named Emely Lynes.

Eliza 9/16/1842 confined a girl at Mr. John R. Williamson's Swamp Place, Union Creek, S. C.
Eliza 7/16/1844 confined a boy child named Robert Lynes, Comingtee Cooper River
Eliza 1/29/1846 confined a girlnamed Adelaide J. Lynes at Comingtee Plantation
Eliza 10/24/1847 confined a girl named Rebecca at Comingtee
Eliza 8/17/1849 confined a girl named Ann at Comingtee Plantation
Eliza 12/8/1850 confined a boy named John Henry at Comingtee.
Eliza 6/29/1852 confined a boy named Samuel
Eliza 8/31/1853 was delivered with a boy named Richard at Fox Bank
R. W. Haynes b. at Fox Bank 8/26/1858
Cathrine G. Lynes 11/25/1876 confined a boy named James Conner Lynes at Fox Bank Plantation

George Lynes' Bible continued...

DEATHS

Christiana Lynes 9/5/1831 at Blessing
Martha Ann Lynes 12/14/1840 on Savannah River at John P. (or R.) Williamson's Swamp Place.
My dear baby d. with lockjaw 9/22/1842 at Mr. Williamson's Place My dear Robert, croup
1/24/1845, Comingtee Plantation, Cooper Riv. 10/24/1847 -- (blank)
My old father, Samuel Lynes, 3/30/1845, aged 70 yrs. at Fox Bank
My bro., George Lynes 10/14/1848 at Grumesbelle
My mother-in-law d. in Grumesville 6/8/1853
Sarah J. Lynes 1/23/1855, my bro.'s wife, at Kibbleswork?
My bro., George Lynes, 7/3/1901?
Mrs. Eliza Donaly 3/6/1849
Christian C. Rough 9/9/1862 in Va.
A. J. Glen --
Mrs. Elizabeth Lynes 3/26/1880, Fox Bank Plantation, S. C., aged 66 yrs., 3 mos., 20 days
Our dear father, George Lynes, 4/23/1870
Our bro., J. H. Lynes, 11/24/1898 at Fox Bank

Our sister, Mrs. H. E. Guyton, 12/28/1898, at Oakley.

JAMES McELWEE BIBLE,
Rev. War Pension W9553

BIRTHS

Ann McElwee 4/1/1795
Ross McElwee 7/9/1812
Rhoda McElwee 6/8/1808
James McElwee 9/17/1802
Elizabeth McElwee 10/1/1817
Abner McElwee 1/6/1814
Dan McElwee 5/2/1806

MARRIAGES

Ann McElwee to Josiah Henry, 1822, York Dist, S. C.
Rhoda McElwee to John Givens 5/14/1840, Pike Co., Mo.

Note: James McElwee applied for pension from Pike Co., Mo., stating he was b. 8/19/1758 VA, lived York Dist., S. C., removed 3/1832 to Pike Co., Mo. m. Abbevllle, S. C. 1793, Rhoda Black b. 3/1777. Soldier died 1/13/1834. Widow applied for pension 4/27/1848, Pike Co., Mo. She d. 8/23/1848.
Surviving children: Dan, James, Rose, Abner, Elizabeth, Henry and Rhoda Givens.

DANIEL COBIA BIBLE

Owner: Julia LaFar, 24 Montaigue St., Charleston, S. C.

BIRTHS

Daniel Cobia 12/18/1714.

His Children:

Francis Cobia 6/11/1757
Daniel Cobia 1758
John Cobia 1705
Mary Cobia 1760
Christiana Elizabeth (Speidel), wife of Francis J. Cobia, b.2/15/1759

Their Children:

Daniel Cobia 1/12/1775
Col. Francis Joseph Cobin 4/4/1787
Elizabeth Cobia 8/2/1778
Ann Cobia 10/4/1781
Sarah Cobia 1/21/1790
Mary Cobia 3/3/1784
William Henry Cobia 2/5/1794
Henry Cobia 1805. His wife, Ann M., 1804
Anne Flutter Cobia 9/8/1791 in London, England

Barbara Christine Bates 1/24/1754

MITCHELL-RILEY BIBLE
Owner: Lamar Riley
361 Beachcomer Dr., Lynn Haven, Fla.

"My good will I bear to my children I have this Holy Book at my decease-to my daughter, Sarah
Riley and heirs...not to be sold on any acct.... Signed- J. B. Mitchell 4/13/1834. Ann Mitchell, the Grandmother."

John B. Mitchell 1/22/1759-6/5/1842
Ann Mitchell, his wife 2/1757-2/5/1840, buried Riley's graveyard
William Mitchell 11/7/1782-
John Mitchell 5/27/1784-9/3/1827
Margaret Mitchell 1/25/1786-3/15/1825
Martha Me. G. Mitchell 11/27/1788-6/17/1795
Sara Mitchell 8/7/1790-
Mary Mitchell 3/1/1792-5/27/1814
Lani Mitchell 7/7/1795-1019/1822

Children's MARRIAGES

William Wilson Mitchell to Genny (Jane) Bamer 9/17/1804
John Mitchell to Margaret Whitman 12/21/1808 Margaret Mitchell to James Cromley 3/1/1806
Mary Mitchell to Jacob Whitman 9/4/1813 Sara Mitchell to William Riley 1/18/1816

John Cromley, son of James and Margaret, 11/27/1800-3/3/1807
Samuel Cromley 1/10/1809-
Irah Cromley 11/27/1813
James R. Cromley 10/9/1811-

Mitchell-Riley Bible continued...

Children of John and Margaret Cromley

Catey Cromley 11/24/1809-
Dead Child 10/17/1815
William Cromley 11/10/1811-
Anne Cromley 1/10/1818
Christly Cromley 3/10/1813-
John B. Cromley 11/19/1820-

Children of William and Sarah Riley

John Riley 10/1/1816-
William F. Riley 10/21/1824-
Anne Riley 4/9/1818-
Sarah Riley 6/22/1827
Rebecca Riley 10/14/1819-4/12/1830
James H. Riley 12/20/1830
Rachel Riley 11/24/1822-5/28/1839
Susan C. Riley 11/22/1833-
Rosa Anna Riley 11/22/1833-

DEATHS

Susan C. Riley 6/17/1856
Rosa Anna Riley 1/20/1897

MARRIAGES

William Wilson Mitchell to Jane Bamer 9/14/1804

Mitchell-Riley Bible continued...

BIRTHS of Their Children

Eli Mitchell 9/11/1805 -
John Wesley Mitchell 4/14/1820
Mary Ann Mitchell 4/9/1808
Susa Mitchell 6/14/1814
Helena Mitchell 11/27/1811
William Wells Mitchell 3/15/1823
Zachariah Mitchell 1/24/1817

"I give and bequeath this Holy Bible to my grandson, Eli Mitchell, son or my elder son, William W. Mitchell, for him, his heirs forever not to be sold out of the family. Witness my hand. 9/8/1823. J. B. Mitchell."

"I allow and give this Bible to my daughter, Sarah Riley." The LWT found loose in Bible of John B. Mitchell of Edgefield District, S. C. names daughter Sarah Riley, executrix, 8/4/1841.

WILLIAM GEORGE RIVERS, JR. BIBLE
Owner: Mrs. Emily F. Rivers 7 Rutledge Ave., Charleston, S. C.

William George Rivers, Jr. 11/10/1879 Augusta, Ga.-2/28/1943 Charleston, S. C.
Emily Frances Leggett 7/3/1884 Greenvllle, Pitt Co., N. C. 1/21/1966 Charleston, S. C.

William George Rivers, Jr. continued...

Their Children:

William Sinclair Rivers b. 9/22/1902 Dorchester, S. C. m. 1/24/1936 Reba Gladys Stone

Brandwell Cozart Rivers b. 10/15/1905 Charleston, S. C. m. 11/8/1933 Ruth Gissell Latson

John Randolph Rivers b. 12/14/1908 Charleston, S. C. m. 2/20/1924 Eva Lavon Spell

Mamie Rivers b. 8/24/1910 Charleston, S. C. d. 12/12/1913

Mabel Rivers b. 8/24/1910-2/1913 Charleston, S. C.

Tresse Al Wilder Rivers b. 4/15/1914 Charleston, S. C. m 1/24/1936 Harold Lamar McLaws

Ashley Grey Rivers b. 2/19/1916 Charleston m. 1937 Evelyn Whitson

Evora Janet Rivers b. 5/14/1918 Charleston, S. C. m. 6/15/1936 Russell Henry Teuscher

Sopha Neal Rivers b. 11/2/1919 Charleston, S. C. d. 2/29/1920
Benjamin Lafayette Rivers b. 11/2/1919 Charleston, S. C. m. 9/7/1941 Vivian Ella Lewis
Sopha Serfaniel Rivers b. 9/18/1921 Charleston m. Harriett Shuler O'Hagan
Lacurkias Rivers 6/7/1923-2/4/1924 Charleston, S. C.

McELRATH-SEAY BIBLE
Owner: Dean Rathbone Rt. 1, Box 178, Clyde, N. C. 28721

BIRTHS

Sarah Maria Seay 2/28/1827
John McElrath 3/21/1827

Their Children:

James Matthew 9/20/1852
Margaret Lula 11/4/1858
Wilmath C. 9/17/1853
Nancy Jane 10/5/1859
William Joseph 4/18/1855
John Augustus 7/25/1863

FARIS-JACKSON BIBLE

Dan, a boy, b. 11/9/1856
James F. Jackson m. Emily C. Sizemore 1/10/1851

BIRTHS of Children of Robert Faris and Dorcas, his wife

Sarah Faris 9/5/1772
Rachel Faris 9/8/1780
James Faris 3/28/1774
Dorcas Faris 3/10/1783
Margaret Faris 4/29/1776
Robert Faris 11/28/1784
Isabella Faris 6/24/1778
Elizabeth Faris 5/18/1785

Faris-Jackson Bible continued...

DEATHS

Alphonso Jackson 1017/1879
John F. Jackson 10/22/1962
Robert Mayes 1120/1855
Joannah Jackson 8/25/186-
Dorcas Mayes 9/22/1855
Dorcas, wife of William Jackson, 5/31/1846, aged 63 yrs., 2 mos., 21 days
William Jackson 11/22/1783-8/1/1869, an Elder in North Pacolet Church 35 yrs.
William Jackson and Dorcas, his wife, m. 2/28/1804.

BIRTHS of Their Children

Betsy Faris-Jackson 9/25/1806
James F. Jackson 5/18/1815
Joannah A. Jackson 8/2/1808
Eupheny A. Jackson 5/29/1817
Dorcas A. Jackson 5/26/1810
Alfonses A. Jackson 10/31/1819
William Jackson 1/13/1812
Robert Jackson 1/13/1812
Joseph Hillhouse Jackson 6/23/1822
Margret Minerva Jackson 6/24/1827

Negro Childrens BIRTHS:

Lyda, a girl, 8/1830
Prince, a boy, 9/13/1853

Faris-Jackson Bible continued...

Sara, a girl, 2/1837
Luis, a boy, 11/15/1854
Jane, a girl, 8/1845
Martha, a girl, 1/31/1855
Charles Columbus, a boy, 7/22/1849
Suzanna, a negro girl, 5/1860   Moses, a negro boy, 5/27/1862
Marchel, a negro boy, 5/4/1864
Lucy, a girl, 5/10/1864 Curtis, a boy, 10/10/1864
Elizabeth, a negro girl, 6/18/1862

JOHN STEPHENSON BIBLE

BIRTHS

John Stephenson 8/16/1785
Darkus M. Stephenson 4/13/1813
Eleaner Stephenson 5/10/1787
Robert B. Stephenson 12/9/1815
Jane Stephenson 3/12/1807
John H. Stephenson 2/27/1819
Marey Stephenson 11/20/1808
James G. Stephenson 8/24/1821
Elizabeth C. Stephenson 11/5/1910
Samuel T. Stephenson 3/16/1825

DEATHS

Eleanor Stephenson 12/5/1845 John Stephenson 12/10/1845
James G. Stephenson 3/21/1875

MOORE-LINDSAY BIBLE
Owner: Mrs. J. Palmer Williams, McConnells, S. C.

Rest of entries inscribed in her Bible by Clarissa (Moore) Lindsay, wife of Philip Williams Lindsay of York Co., S. C. nest of persons are buried at Bethesda Presbyterian Church.

Jamie Moore b. 10/8/1785
Elizabeth Marion Moore, his wife, b. 12/5/1788. They were m.1/28/1808

BIRTHS

John Edwin Augustus Moore 4/17/1855
Our little babe 10/4/1852 Nadaline Marion Moore 12/7/1859

DEATHS

Elizabeth Marion Moore, my mother, 1829
My dearly beloved father, 1/31/1857
Grandmother Moore 8/18/1859
My little daughter 11/3/1860
My beloved brother, John M. Moore, 3/5/1885
My beloved brother, J. W. Moore, 1/3/1888, aged 78 yrs.
My beloved brother, J. P. Moore, 4/8/1888. aged 67 yrs.
My beloved sister, Emma Katharine Hemphill. 9/6/1892
My dear husband, Philip W. Lindsay, 5/20/1897
My beloved and only sister, J. Adeline Williams, 5/2/1904
My dear and only child, Johnie E. A. Lindsay, 11/10/1874
Philip W. Lindsay m. Clarissa Moore 12/16/1851

JOHN McDOWELL BIBLE
Owner: Mrs. Mary Sue Keith, Rt. 1, Jonesvllle, S. C.

MARRIAGES

D. H. Miller to Mary H. Mayes 12/17/1874 by Rev. A. A. James

BIRTHS

John McDowell, Sr. 8/12/1759 at Glenmelllon County Antrim, Ireland
Mary McDowell 8/3/1790 at Glenmellion County Antrim, Ireland
David McDowell 3/31/1793 at Glenmellion County Antrim, Ireland
John McDowell, Jr. 11/3/1795 Union Dist., S. C.
David H. Miller 10/22/1853
Mary M. Miller 7/24/1851
Hannah Elizabeth Miller 9/7/1877
Mary Dorcas Miller 11/8/1885

DEATHS

William Black 3/10/1829, aged 39 yrs.
Henry McDowell 9/7/1833, aged 35 yrs.

EDWARD BYERS BIBLE

"Edward Byers, his Book." "Samuel G. Brown's Book, 1838."
Edward Byers and Martha Alexander m. 5/4/1786

BIRTHS

Edward Byers 12/5/1761
William Walton Byers 11/6/1788
Samuel Baldwin Byers 2/22/1787
Ison Davis Byers 1/3/1793
Joseph Alexander Byers 11/28/1790
Edward Byers m. Elizabeth Byers 8/16/1796
Benjamin Byers 4/27/1799
Martha Adalina Byers 9/6/1801
Edward Byers m. Mary Chambers 5/10/1804
James C. Byers 3/27/1805
Adam Meek Byers 5/11/1809
Elizabeth Byers 1/30/1807
Mary Margaret Byers 11/14/1812 m. 3/6/1834 to Joseph B. Clinton, 2nd, 10/23/1838 to S. G. Brown
Edmund Rutter Chambers 3/18/1799
Edward B. Clinton 12/4/1834
Mary Elizabeth Brown 9/5/1839

Eliza Ann Brown 9/5/1839
John Alonzo Brown 12/13/1840
Mary Margaret Lyle 2/15/1826
Jane Byers Lyle 6/3/1832
Elizabeth Narcissa Lyle 12/12/1827
Edward Byers Lyle 7/29/1834
Joseph Banks Lyle 11/6/1829

Edward Byers Bible continued...

Martha Adaline Lyle 4/5/1837
Samuel Sesostris Brown 12/22/1842
James Chambers Brown 3/8/1849
Margaret Eugenia Brown 6/5/1845-11/22/1918
Sophia Adalaide Brown 5/4/1847-5/24/1879
Laura Iantha Medora Brown 3/24/1851-1/22/1895
Samuel Myers Deal 8/6/1874-1907
Augusta Moore Deal 12/12/1876-1950
Eli Morrison Russell 7/3/1877
Sarah Ada Russell 9/19/1879
James Lyle m. Elizabeth Byers 11/25/1824
Mary Byers 10/6/1773
Elizabeth Brown 4/12/1774
Paralee Pennsylvania and Cemira Carolina Lyle 7/27/1839
James Lyle 4/1/1797-11/13/1840
Samuel G. Brown 2/7/1814
John Alonzo Brown 4/28/1809
James Gordon 2/12/1769

DEATHS

Edward Byers 3/13/1832
Ison Davis Byers 5/2/1794
Martha Byers 9/11/1794
Elizabeth Byers 10/8/1803
William Walton Byers 11/7/1794
Mary Byers 6/3/1849
Elizabeth Brown 2/1/1809

JOHN STROUD BIBLE
Owner: Bernal M. Meador, Kansas City, Mo.

BIRTHS

John Stroud 12/19/1758
Joshua Stroud 1/6/1781
Mary Stoud 11/29/1760
James Stroud 2/5/1790
James Stroud 4/26/1763
John Megs 2/2/1788
Elizabeth Stroud 3/30/1765

Rebekah Stroud 6/12/1790
Isom Stroud 6/27/1768

James Stroud 4/15/1792
Patty Stroud 2/25/1770
William Stroud 2/12/1795
Caty Stroud 8/7/1771
Caty Stroud 2/22/1797
Joseph Stroud 5/5/1776
Joseph Stroud 3/26/1799
Jesse Stroud 8/29/1778
John Prewit Young, son of John Young and Raney, his wife,
Washington Rice 10/9/1815
John Lee 7/3/1803
Gardiner Lee 12/15/1783
Elizabeth Lee 10/8/1804
Montgomery Stroud, son of James, 3/13/1816
John Haun Stroud 5/15/1818
Adam Stroud 6/6/1820

John Stroud Bible continued...

Susanah Stroud 10/12/1822
Margaret Stroud 2/10/1825
Emma Line Stroud 12/29/1827
Clarissa Stroud 12/12/1829-2/11/1892
James Chant Stroud 9/29/1840-7/5/1919
Robert Hardin Stroud 5/31/1838
William Stroud 10/7/1840
Martha Stroud 9/8/1841
William Stroud 1/30/1843
Sarah Elizabeth Coon 8/21/1855
George Coon 7/1/1855

MARRIAGES

John Stroud to 9/28/1837
Montgomery Stroud to 8/28/1840
William Coon to E. Stroud 12/16/1852
James Stroud to Elizabeth Haun, his wife 6/18/1815

DEATHS

Joshua Stroud 11/29/1783 William Stroud 9/1/1798
Elizabeth Stroud, wife of James Stroud, 9/24/1795-11/4/1870

NATHANIEL MARION BIBLE
"Nathaniel Marion, his Book, bought 2/18/1817"

BIRTHS of His Children

Elizabeth Mary Wickham Marion 1/14/1812
John Samuel Marion 9/27/1813
Louisa Charlotte Marion 3/111816
Nathaniel Peter Marion 2/19/1820, Lebanon, Abbeville, S. C.

MOSES COLLINS BIBLE
Owner: S. D. Collins, Jr., Jackson, Miss.

S. C., Winton Co., William Willis of New York m. Susana Toney, but now she is called William Willis' wife, Susana Willis. "Hannah Burnam was my mother's name. William Willis, a sailor from the Lost seas, Jeremiah William, (Willis) a squire, 1789 Moses Collins m. 8/6/1774 Hanah Collins b. 12/10/1754

BIRTHS of Children of Moses Collins and Hanah, his wife

Susannah Collins 5/16/1775
Henry Collins 10/8/1785
Ann Collins 1/31/1777
Sarah Collins 10/9/1787
Joseph Collins 3/31/1779
Rebecca Collins 12/27/1789
Moses Collins, Jr. 7/16/1781
Alice Collins 10/27/1792
Hannah Collins 8/22/1783

Moses Collins Bible continued...

Joshua Collins 1794
Seaborn Collins 1/22/1796
Lemuel P. Collins 2/25/1817
Rhesa Hatcher 9/19/1810

BIRTHS of Children of Seaborn Collins and Mary May, his wife

Joseph Collins, Jr. 8/1817
Elizabeth Collins 2/3/1827
Moses Collins 2/6/1819
Mary Collins 12/1/1828
Etheldred Collins 10/7/1820
Lucinda Collins 7/5/1831
Seaborn Davis Collins 3/12/1825
Wiley Harris Collins 12/15/1833
Joshua Greenberry Collins 11/24/1822
James Richardson Collins 4/7/1836

DEATHS

Henry Collins 4/23/1793
Moses Collins, Sr. 1/29/1816

ROBERT AND CELIA FIELDS HENRY BIBLE

Robert Henry m. Celia Fields 4/24/1795

BIRTHS of Their Children

Mary Henry 5/12/1786
Liza Henry 4/22/1800
Lydia Henry 2/5/1788
Robert Henry 9/2/1803
Loucey Henry 11/26/1789
Jane Henry 10/31/1806
Nancey Henry 12/24/1791
Celia Henry 11/30/1809
Joel Henry 11/27/1793
Mutual (dau) 5/8/1813
William Henry 4/24/1796
Theophilus Henry 7/3/1816
Temperance Henry 4/16/1798

MYERS-MYRES BIBLE
Owner: William F. Myers, Elizabethton, Tenn.

John Myres b. 7/17/1759
Isabel Myres b. 7/18/1766

MARRIAGES

John Myres to Isabel 1/13/1791
George Myers to Leodicia, (daughter of Joseph and Sophia Goodwin Conwell). 7/9/1822

Myers-Myres Bible continued...

John Myers to Unity Evans 6/10/1830
John David Myers to Maggie T. Johnson 1/22/1886
Frank Floyd Gann to Pearl Ethel Myers 12/29/1925

BIRTHS of Children of John and Isabel Myres

Their first son 8/16/1792-8/1792
John Myres 3/3/1799
Molly Myres 8/14/1794
Elizabeth Myres 5/25/1801
George Myres 12/3/1796
Sarah Myres 2/11/1803
John David Myers 6/8/1840
Pearl Ethel Myres 4/9/1888
Marget T. Myres 3/16/1845
Jense Julien 8/15/1778
Adaline Julien 7/16/1813
Elizabeth Julien 9/16/1777
Peter Julien 3/28/1817
Mary Julien 1/25/1803
Ruth Julien 5/3/1820
Precious Julien 9/13/1808
Susannah Julien 12/17/1810
Yates C. Myers 4/8/1823
Mary Ann E. Myers 5/15/1832
Isable W. Myers 5/10/1826

Myers-Myres Bible continued...

DEATHS

John Myres 6/1/1804, interred in burying ground on Bush River.
Molly Young 8/24/1822 (daughter of John and Isabel Myers)

Isabel Myers 8/5/1833
John David Myers 3/30/1821
Margaret Turner Burdine, wife of J. D. Myers 7/29/1831
Jesse Julien 1/20/1826
Isaac Evans 5/13/1823 (par. of Unity Evans, wife Elizabeth
Evans 1/19/1835 (of John Myers, Jr.
Sarah Ann I. Myers, daughter of John and Unity Myers,
9/15/1826 Mary Elizabeth Myers, daughter of
John and Unity Myers. 5/30/1840 John Myers 9/27/1844
(Spartanburg Dist., S. C.)
Unity Lamb 9/13/1895
Eliza Myers Mason 3/18/1924

BIRTHS of Children of John and Unity Myers

Sarah Ann Isabellah Myers 8/2/1831
Eliza Eveline Myers 5/10/1833
George McDuffy Myers 1/25/1835
Second Son 12/11/1836-12/29/1836
Mary Elizabeth Myers 3/27/1838
John David Myers 6/8/1840
Margaret Caroline Myers 7/8/1842-1842
Isaac Newton Myers 9/14/1844 (Spartanburg Dist., S. C.)
Emma Victoria Lamb, daughter of William and Unity Lamb, b.
11/8/1850 Margaret Burdine, wife of
John David Myers, b. 3/16/1845
   Note: Spelling - Myres and Myers as appears in Bible.

BELCHER-BISHOP-GREGORY BIBLE
Owner: Ott Gregory, Spartanburg, S. C.

BIRTHS

Elias Belcher 3/3/1846
Thomas Belcher 3/25/1876
Polly Ann C. Bishop 1/29/1849
Tennessee Belcher 6/16/1878
Arrela T. Belcher 9/1/1866
Posey Belcher 2/8/1881
Carrie T. Belcher 12/11/1868
Roa Delia Belcher 6/26/1883
Mary E. Belcher 3/27/1871
Joseph Elias Belcher 6/13/1887
Johnie Belcher 8/1/1873

Garibaldi Gregory, son of J. A. and J. C. Gregory, 10/6/1867
Rowland Montague Gregory 8/15/1869
Minnie Hettie Lee Gregory 6/1/1872
Ottis Grady Gregory 1/17/1890
Wells Reicher 9/18/1895
Ottis Grady Gregory, Jr. 12/11/1915
Paul James Gregory 9/3/1919
Sarah Francis Gregory 11/15/1924
Bobby E. Gregory 7/3/1936
James Donald Gregory 6/30/1947

Michael David Gregory 11/10/1948
Paul Franklin Gregory 9/26/1950

MARRIAGES

Elias Belcher to Polly Ann C. Bishop 8/22/1865
Baldia Gregory to Arrela T. Belcher 3/4/1888
Rowland Montague Gregory to Carrie T. Belcher 4/22/1888

Ottis Grady Gregory to Ella Agnes Greet 12/16/1909
F. H. Parris to Carrie Gregory 9/18/1915
Ottis Grady Gregory, Jr. to Madeline Solesby 10/12/1935
Ottis Grady Gregory to Mary------ 3/29/1942
Paul James Gregory and Irene Allison Solesbee 3/2/1946

DEATHS

Tennessee Belcher 10/8/1881, aged 3 yrs, 3 mos., 22 days
Koa Delia Belcher 3/6/1895
Sallie Stephens 12/25/1906
Arrelia T. Gregory 6/7/1902
Elias Belcher 8/17/1899
Garibaldi Gregory 8/14/1897
Juda Caroline Gregory 4/20/1897
James A. Gregory 8/20/1880
Rowland Montague Gregory 5/15/1912
Sarah Frances Gregory 5/19/1926
Polly Ann Belcher 4/29/1936
Carrle T. Belcher Gregory Parris 6/23/1943
Mary Lillian ----- Gregory 11/15/1943?
Ottis Grady Gregory Sr. 6/1/1951
Posey Belcher 7/22/1950
Ottis Grady Gregory, Sr., 6/1/1951

JOHANN ADAM HOUSEAL BIBLE
Owner: Wessels Library, Newberry College, Newberry, S. C.

Lewis Coon b. 9/24/1761 S. C., Amelia Township, and was partly raised at the Congaree in Camden District. August 29, 1784, his hand and pen.

Robert Creswell Sligh b. 10/19/1819, his sponsors in baptism were George Eigleberger and Rosen Catharine, his wife, by birth summer.

Note: The following written In German (translated to English) Johann Adam Hausihl, his Bible, 11/29/1794

4/30/1795 Johann Adam Hausihl took as his wife Maria Magdalena Summer 11/27/1799 Rosinna Catharine b., her sponors, George Michael Eigelberger and his wife,
Rosinn Cathrina, Minister, as above.
5/3/1808 Johann George H., sponsors Johan Benedict Nayer and his wife, Eva Margreta.
Minister, F. J. Wallern.
5/28/1776 Casper Coon m. Elizabeth, his wife

5/13/1811 Johann Adam b., sponsors J. Benedict Mayer and Maria Margreta, widow of Mr.
John Adam Summer.
Mary Elizabeth Houseal b. 12/15/1815, sponsors in baptism, Rev. Frederic Joseph Wallern and
his wife, Mary Urshel, by birth and Eigelberger.
John Adam Housenl, Esq., d. 3/24/1816, 42 yrs., 5 mos, 23 days.

Johann Adam Houseal Bible continued...

William Lockhart Rawls m. Rose Cathrine Houseal by Rev. Frederick Joseph Wallern 5/29/1817.
Solomon Sligh m. Mary Magdalene Housel by Rev. Frederic Joseph Wallern 10/2/1817.
Solomon Sligh d. 5/4/1825, aged 29 yrs, 4 mos., 29 days.
Elizabeth Coon, her Holy Bible, left to her by her Executors 4/14/1783.
Rose Cathrine Rawls d. 8/12/1821, aged 21 yrs, 15 days.
John Adam Houseal d. 1/29/1826, aged 14 yrs, 8 mos., 16 days.
Robert Creswell Sligh d. 2/22/1826, aged 6 yrs, 4 mos. 3 days.
David Counts m. Mary Elizabeth Houseal 11/13/1832
Robert C. Boyd m. Mary Magdalena Sligh 5/13/1838
John C. Houseal m. Elizabeth Ridlehuber 2/17/1831

JOHN C. CALDWELL BIBLE
Owner: Miss Edna Daniel
1423 Reidville Rd., Spartanburg, S. C. 29301

BIRTHS

John C. Caldwell 5/21/1797
Margaret M. Caldwell 6/4/1827
Laney Caldwell 9/26/1796
Sarah A. Caldwell 6/19/1829
W . A. Caldwell 6/18/1822
Samuel A. Caldwell 12/21/1831
Mary C. Caldwell 11/29/1823
Laney A. Caldwell 10/4/1834
Andrew P. Caldwell 10/12/1825

John C. Caldwell Bible continued...

MARRIAGES

John C. Caldwell to Laney Coan 118/1821
D. M. Brice to Mary C. Caldwell 2/10/1841
Thomas P. High to Sarah A. Caldwell 12/21/1848
Andrew P. Caldwell to Barbery A. Bomar 3/8/1849
Benjamin M. High to Margaret M. Caldwell 3/8/1855
Samuel A. Caldwell to Francis C. Bomar 4/5/1855
William B. Bomar to Laney A. Caldwell 12/22/1851

DEATHS

Andrew P. Caldwell 7/3/1864, City of Richmond, Va., aged 39 yrs.

J. C. Caldwell 7/18/1871, aged 75 yrs.

Laney Caldwell 1/17/1878, aged 82 yrs.

W. A. Caldwell 1/24/1892, aged 70 yrs.

Margaret M. C. High 3/23/1897, aged 70 yrs

Mary C. Brice 1/27/1882, aged 74 yrs., 2 mos.

William Caldwell 4/2/1840, aged 80 yrs.

Margaret Caldwell 10/22/1863, aged 87 yrs.

Adolphus L. Brice 9/4/1907, aged 55 yrs., 4 mos.

MARK DERDEN BIBLE
Owner: Wilma D. Spengler
San Antonio, Texas

MARRIAGES

Mark Derden to Dorothy Hill 6/14/1817
Elijah B. Derden to Jane Baker 3/25/1844
H. D. Richardson to Sarah A. Derden 12/24/1843

BIRTHS

Mark Derden 7/24/1791
Dorothy, his wife, 12/8/1798

Their Children:

Elijah Dobbit Derden 2/14/1818
John Marcus Derden 4/10/1831
Temperance Hill Derden 9/5/1819
George Washington Derden 12/3/1821
Sarah Ann Derden 9/21/1834
James Patterson Derden 3/29/1826
Martha Harris Derden 1/15/1823
Andrew Jackson Derden 8/21/1837
Amy Lizabeth Derden 2/18/1827
Mary Emma Derden 6/10/1839

James Marcus, son of Horace Davis and Sarah Richardson, 3/27/1845
John M. Derden 2/8/1845
George W. Derden 3/10/1849
J. W. Derden, son of George W. and Matilda Derden 5/18/1875

Mark Derden continued...

DEATHS

John Marcus Derden 10/12/1843, aged 12 yrs., 6 mos., 2 days.
Sarah Ann Richardson, daughter of M.

Mark Derden and Dorothy, his wife, 8/7/1845, aged 23 yrs., 7 mos., 7 days.
Mark Derden 9/16/1854, aged 63 yrs.

WILLIAM D. SMITH'S BIBLE
Mrs. Alma Cope, Gray, S. C.

DEATHS

Mary A. Harriet 12/12/1812-7/14/1862
W. M. Ginn 8/23/1870
Jacob A. Smith 9/18/1871, aged 17 yrs., 8 mos., 6 days
Cherry Ginn 12/23/1871
Mother: Darcas Ginn 10/22/1888
Sary Ann Ginn 11/10/1888
William Bowers 9/17/1888

J. W. Tuten killed himself ---/16/1888
Tamp Rowell 9/22/1888

William D. Smith Bible continued...

DEATHS of my Father and mother

William D. Smith 10/24/1836
Ann Smith 9/5/1841
Charles B. Smith --
Grandmother Sarah Smith 8/2/1848 Urias M. Smith 8/14/1852
Alford J. Ginn 8/20/1852
Uncle George Sanders 1/16/1836 Samuel Sanders 7/10/1795-
4/14/1861 Grandmother Mary
Sanders 8/6/1832 William H. Crosby 7/30/1836

BIRTHS

George H. Smith 10/26/1820 Lucretia Smith, his wife, 9/9/1826

BIRTHS of Their Children:

Urias H. Smith 9/17/1849
Piasl Calvin Smith 10/10/1956
Charles H. Smith 8/4/1851
Mary E. Smith 12/1/1858
Jacob A. Smith 1/12/1854
Lost one 1/15/1861
Jacob Phillips m. Mary Ginn 10/9/1866
Jane Conneler, daughter of Jacob and Mary Phillips b. 3/2/1863
Miles Ginn d. 1/3/1887

SALLIE W. ALLISON BIBLE
Of York Co., Hickory Grove, S. C.

Hugh Allison landed In America 9/13/1735, aged 22 yrs., 3/7/1799

MARRIAGES:

Robert Allison, Esquire, age 25, to Sarah Turner, age 24, 7/15/1779

BIRTHS: of Children of Robert and Sarah Allison

Martha Allison 2/23/1782
Catherine Allison 1/18/1792
Hugh Allison 11/13/1783
Sarah Allison 6/7/1794
Thomas Allison 3/7/1786
Robert Turner Allison 8/17/1798
Margaret Allison 1/27/1788

DEATHS:

Robert Allison, Esquire 6/29/1827
Hugh Allison 7/22/1849
Sarah Turner Allison 3/4/1841
Thomas Allison ---
Martha Allison Cain 6/29/1860
Margaret Allison Henry --
Catherine Allison Henry 9/21/1867
Dr. Robert Turner Allison 10/21/1882

SAMUEL JOSEPH SILLS BIBLE
Owner: Thomas Kees Maxwell

Samuel Joseph Sills b. 1773/1774 m. 1794 Jane M. Heard b. 1/23/1777 in Pittsylvania Co., Va.

BIRTHS: of THEIR CHILDREN:

James Monroe Sills 9/13/1794 Laurens Co., S. C.
Abigail Sills 7/2/1797 Laurens Co., S. C.
Elizabeth Sills 3/26/1799 Abbeville Co., S. C.
John Sills 10/29/1801 Abbeville Co., S. C.
Tabitha Sills 5/12/1804 Abbeville Co., S. C.
Nancy Sills 6/27/1807 Abbeville Co., S. C.
Samuel Joseph Sills Jr. 10/23/1812 Abbeville Co.. S. C. m. 4/8/1857 to Susannah Cliburn in

Lawrence Co., Miss. Benjamin Sills 11/28/1814 Abbeville Co., S. C.
Jane H. Sills 1/4/1817 Abbeville Co., S. C.
Thomas Kees Maxwell 11/2/1836 Lawrence Co., Miss.

DEATHS:

Jane Sills 3/29/1889 Monticello, Miss.

HOSEA HOLCOMB RAY BIBLE
Of Union Co., S. C.
Owner: Hugh Edwin Ray, Jr., Corinth, Miss.

BIRTHS:

Hosea Holcomb Ray 9/30/1776
Mary Lamb 12/25/1777
Hosea Ray m. Mary Lamb 1/20/1796

THEIR CHILDREN:

Adah Delilah Ray 1/1/1797
Robert Ray 2/27/1809
Ambrose Ray 10/17/1798
Willis Ray 4/16/1811
Homer Thomas Ray 1/7/1800
Irena Ray 5/3/1814
Carrolton Ray 11/15/1802
Wm Martindale Ray 3/3/1817
Spencer Ray 3/2/1805
Jesse Ray 8/6/1821
Elijah Ray 2/6/1807
William H. Ray 9/25/1831
Jane Ray 3/18/1811

DEATHS:

Robert Ray 9/20/1832
Ambrose Ray 10/10/1849
Willis Ray 1832
Spencer Ray 4/11/1849

Hosea Holcomb Ray Bible continued...

Irena Ray 1836
Mary Lamb, wife of Hosea Ray, 11/4/1856

MARRIAGES:

Hosea Ray to Mary Lamb 1/20/1796
Thomas Ray to Sarah 18--
Judith Ray to James Gibbs ---
Ambrose Ray to Mary Garrett 2/2/1819
Carrolton Ray to Janet Scott Martin 9/25/1823
Robert Ray to Jane Browning 1829
Thomas Ray to Matilda Norman 183-
Jesse Ray to Sarah Hill 12/8/1842

ANDREW JACKSON THOMPSON BIBLE
Owner: Mary Eugenie Thompson Powell, Willis, Texas

BIRTHS:

Jane Lenoir, father of Sarah Lenoir, 10/5/1743 Brunswick Co., Va., d. in S. C.
Martha Lenoir, his wife David Thompson 9/1772
Sarah Lenoir, daughter of Isaac and Martha Lenoir, 1772

James Middleton Lenoir, son of Sarah Lenoir and --- Lenoir, a cousin, 2/16/1796
William Vance Thompson, son of David and Sarah Lenoir Thompson, 11/18/1805
Andrew Jackson Thompson, son of David end Sarah Lenoir Thompson, 5/28/1816 Sumter Co., S. C., moved to Catawba, Ala. In 1820, then to Walker Co., Tx. in 1853.

Andrew Jackson Thompson Bible continued...

Mary Elizabeth Tabb, Ist wife of A. J. Thompson, 12/10/1817 Meckenburg Co., Va. m. 12/18/1838

Mary Ann Gillespie, daughter of John Gillespie and Jean McMillian, 2nd wife of A. J. Thompson, 9/18/1844, Madison, Indiana

BIRTHS: of Children of A. J. Thompson and wife, Mary Elizabeth Tabb

Melville Edward Thompson 4/24/1846 Alabama
Sarah Josephine Thompson 2/18/1848 Alabama
Eudora Lucy Thompson 11/11/1850 Alabama
John Tabb Thompson 3/10/1854, Waverly, Tx.
Walter Jackson Thompson 3/9/1856, Waverly, Tx.
Albert Crenshaw Thompson 8/2/1858, Waverly, Tx.

BIRTHS: of Children of A. J. Thompson and 2nd wife, Mary Anna Gillespie

Robert Andrew Thompson 7/11/1869, Waverly, Tx.
Jane Gillespie Thompson 6/15/1871, Waverly, Tx.
Gideon Phillips Thompson 11/27/1873, New Waverly, Tx.
Anna Lillia Thompson 2/12/1876, New Waverly, Tx.
Susan Fly Thompson 10/3/1878, New Waverly, Tx.
Frank Lenoir Thompson 6/19/1881, New Waverly, Tx.

Andrew Jackson Thompson Bible continued...

DEATHS:

David Thompson 11/22/1821
Sarah Lenoir Thompson 11/30/1843 in Alabama
James Middleton Lenoir ---
William Vance Thompson 6/5/1839
Andew Jackson Thompson 1/20/1897, New Waverly, Walker Co., Tx.
Mary Elizabeth Tabb Thompson 3/13/1860, New Waverly, Tx.
Mary Anna Gillespie Thompson 4/18/1908, Houston, Tx.
Mary Eugenia Thompson Powell 12/24/1935, Willis. Tx.
Melville Edward Thompson 7/11/1912, Amarillo, Tx.
Sarah Josephine Thompson Patrick Paddock 12/19/1980, Willis, Tx.
Eudora Lucy Thompson Bass Paddock 1/10/1930, Houston, Tx.
John Tabb Thompson 10/19/1901. Willis, Tx.
Walter Jackson Thompson 4/13/1926
Albert Crenshaw Thompson 7/20/1867, Willis, Tx
Anna Lillia Thompson Traylor 12/11/1927, Houston, Tx.
Frank Lenoir Thompson 2/27/1925, Mazatlan, Sinoloa, Mexico
Robert Andrew Thompson 5/29/1941

MARRIAGES:

David Thompson to Sarah Lenoir 10/2/1803 Sumter Co., S. C.
William Vance Thompson to Jane Hall 12/22/1825, Alabama
Andrew Jackson Thompson to Mary Elizabeth Tabb 12/18/183--. Alabama
Mary Eugenia Thompson to Dr. W. P. Powell 1/1/1863, Waverly, Tx.

Andrew Jackson Thompson Bible continued...

Sarah Josephine Thompson to J. H. Patrlck 12/14/1865, Waverly, Tx.
Sarah Josephine Thompson Patrick 2nd to Thomas J. Paddock, Phelps, Tx.
Eudora Lucy Thompson to Dr. Richard Bass in Willis, Tx.
Walter Jackson Thompson
Thomas J. Paddock, Willis, Tx., ca 1892
Andrew Jackson Thompson, 2nd to Mary Anna Gillespie 7/10/1866, Waverly, Tx.
Jane Gillespie Thompson to Frank L. Sewell 12/3/1891 New Waverly, Tx.
Susan Fly Thompsoo to George A. Byers 10/3/1895 New Waverly, Tx.
Robert Andrew Thompson to Evelyn Dickson 12/21/1897 Cleburne, Tx.
Anna Lillia Thompson to John R. Traylor 12/2/1897 Waverly, Tx.
Frank Lenoir Thompson to Maria ---
Letter written "to the children and grandchildren of Andrew Jackson Thompson" by R. A. Thompson in 1937:

Children of Mary Eugenia Thompson and W. P. Powell

Mary Eugenia Thompson 4/22/1844-12/24/1935 m. Dr. W. P. Powell 12/12/1835-11/5/1915.
William Edward Powell 1863 - decd 1937
Marion Granville Powell 1866 - decd 1937
Mary Eugene Powell 1869 - decd 1937

Carrie Jones Powell --- decd 1937
James Moore Powell 1870-1872

Andrew Jackson Thompson Bible continued...

Albert Crenshaw Powell 1872-decd 1937
Josie Arvie Powell 1874-decd 1937 Walter Tabb Powell 1876-decd 1937
Emma Christian Powell 1878-decd 1937
James Abercrombie Powell -- died young
Minnie Jackson Powell 1883 - decd 1937, Willis, Tx.
Clara Travis Powell 1886-decd 1937, Odessa, Tx.

JOHN EDWARDS BIBLE

Owner: Mrs. Hazel Arnold MacIvor 2481 Eaten Gate Rd., Lake Orion, Mich. 48035

BIRTHS: of Children of John Edwards and Henrietta, his wife

Betty Edwards 3/25/175?-
Mary Edwards 4/1/1760
Joseph Edwards 2/1/1754
Thomas Edwards 4/10/1762
John Edwards 7/5/1757
Sarah Edwards 3/14/1765
Martin Edwards
William Edwards 2/10/1767
Joseph Edwards

A List of BIRTHS: of Children of Joseph and Mary Edwards

John Edwards 1/27/1776
William Edwards 6/20/1785
Sally Edwards 12/17/177-
Polley Edwards 12/14/1787

John Edwards Bible Continued...

Joseph Edwards 1/1/1781
Thomas Edwards 5/20/1791
Sanford Edwards 2/17/1783
James Edwards 9/20/1794

JAMES CARLISLE BIBLE
From: Rev. War Pension #W8583

BIRTHS:

James Carlisle 5/23/1763
Margaret Carlisle 6/27/1762

THEIR CHILDREN:

John Carlisle 5/18/1782
William Carlisle 5/19/1797
Frances Carlisle 12/15/1786
Samuel Carlisle 6/16/1799
Ann Carlisle 6/8/1789
Margaret Carlisle 11/9/1800
James Carlisle 2/9/1791
Isaac Carlisle 2/4/1805
Agnes Carlisle 2/2/1793
Robert E. Carlisle 12/26/1808
Martha Carlisle 6/23/1795

Note: Soldier applied for pension 10/21/1835, aged 72 from Abbeville Dist., S. C., served with his brother, Lt. Francis Carlisle, etc. Margaret Carlisle, widow, applied 8128/1845, stating that she m. James Carlisle 9/1783 and that he d. 4/9/1842. 9/14/1849 Frances Carlisle states she m. her late husband, John Carlisle (eldest child of James and Margaret) 2/19/1821 as shown by leaf from Bible kept by her late husband and written by her father, Ethl Tucker.

JOHN WARNOCK BIBLE
From: Rev. War Pension #W22515

BIRTHS:

Mary Warnock 1/29/1787
Margaret Warnock 2/1/1797
Jane Warnock 1/4/1789
Fanny Warnock 6/28/1799
Elizabeth Warnock 1/11/1791
Annie Warnock 8/25/1801
Eleanor Warnock 10/14/1792
John Warnock 11/17/1803
Robert Warnock 11/20/1794
James Warnock 2/15/1806
Betsy Warnock 3/5/1808

Note: Soldier applied for pension 3/14/1833, Anderson District, S. C., stating he was b. in Ireland, came to America in 1774 when 17 yrs. old landed in Delaware. Mrs. Eleanor Warnock, Anderson Dist., S. C., 2/10/1845, aged 77 on Sept. 3d last, stated she lived in York Dist. during war, is daughter of Robert Dowdle, m. John Warnock in Abbevllle Dist., S. C. 5/28/1842.

JAMES ABERCROMBIE BIBLE
Owner: G. Troy Jones, Laurens, S. C.

James Abercrombie m. Elizabeth.

MARRIAGES: of THEIR CHILDREN:

Mary Abercrombie to William O'Daniel
Isabella Abercrombie to Josiah Blackwell
Rebecca Abercrombie to Gabriel Jewell
Susannah Abercrombie to --- Matthews.
Margaret Abercromble to Richard Blackwell
Elizabeth Abercrombie to --- Andrews
James Abercrombie to Cynthia. Son, James
Step-son, Archibald McDaniel (1750-1825) to Edith Pinson; son, Pinson McDaniel

MOSES WILLIAMS BIBLE
From: Rev. War Pension #W9013

Moses Williams 1/8/1761-12/31/1821 m. Martha Faulk 1780. She d. 5/10/1838, Chester Dist., S. C. Only surviving CHILDREN: James R. and Esther Williams.

BIRTHS: of THEIR CHILDREN:

James R. Willlams 11/1/1783-
Aaron Williams 12/12/1789
Margaret Williams 9/19/1785
Esther Williams 8/18/1792
John Williams 1127/1788

Moses Williams Bible continued...

Eleanor Williams 1/8/1794
Noami Williams b. 12/18/1794 d. 10/30/17851

Others:

William Williams 3/15/1753
Sarah Williams 6/8/1774
Rebekah Williams 5/6/1757
Noami L. Williams 1/9/1778
Moses Williams 1/8/1761
Jane Williams 10/2/1781
Aaron Williams 5/8/1763
John M. Lockert 11/2/1809
Marget Williams 12/1/1765
James R. Locket 11/2/1809
John Williams 7/18/1768
Susanna Williams 4/27/1772

Note: James R. Williams, son of Moses and Martha Williams, applied 4/4/1846 for pension due his decd mother, wid. of Moses Williams.

Elzey Williams states that he is nephew of
James R. Williams, Tombsville, York Dist., S. C., and refers to his Aunt Esther.

JAMES HENDERSON BIBLE
Owner: G. Troy Jones, Laurens, S. C.

James Henderson d. 9/2/1836 m. Rebecca Wells who d. 2/17/1833.

THEIR CHILDREN:

William F. Henderson 6/7/1794-8/23/1876 m. Eleanor Boyd 10/12/1796-8/4/1878

John H. Henderson 8/3/1796-7/25/1858 m. Lucinda Moore 12/30/1798-10/6/1888

Ruth Henderson b. 12/24/1798 m. 1st Aaron Wells, 2nd J. H.

Calder Mastin Henderson 11/18/1802-2/10/1871 m. 1st Elizabeth Brock 3/10/1806-4/4/1843, 2nd, Lucinda Pinson.

James C. Henderson 12/15/1804-2/23/1866 m. Mary Ann Burton 7/11/1814-7/8/1857

Rebecca Henderson b. 3/2/1806 m. Henry Williams.
Nancy Henderson b. 5/29/1808 m. Elihu Pinson.
Drury Hampton Henderson b. 5/8/1810 m. Celia Puller.
Lucinda Henderson 5/8/1812-2/13/1892 m. Gabriel Pinson Henderson 8/31/1812-7/17/1890.

Hugh Lee Henderson 12/27/1815-11/21/1854 m. Sarah Davenport
Sarah Davenport 11/3/1819-11/18/1892.

JAMES LEAGUE BIBLE
Owner: G. Troy Jones, Laurens, S. C.

James League 1725-3/4/1813
Mary, his wife, d. 11/5/1817

BIRTHS: of Their Children

Benjamin League 2/21/1755 -
Elijah League   12/28/1766
Joshua League 5/18/1756
Elisha League 5/17/1769
Oney League 1/8/1758
Usilla League 1013/1771
Joab League 5/5/1759
Candace League 7/24/1773
George League 10/6/1761
Rachel League   7/3/1776
Drusilla League 4/14/1763
Isham League 2/16/1780
Lucy League 3/8/1765
Anna League 5/10/1782
Joel League 7/11/1783-7/7/1857

Note: Joel League m. Mary Holt (4/14/1791-1/18/1857) and both came from Amelia Co., Va. To Greenville Co., S. C. abt 1830.

BIRTHS: of Children of Joel League and Mary Holt

Nathan League 6/10/1810
Harriett League 8/22/1821
Archer League 4/22/1812
Edward League 9/4/1823

James League Bible continued...

Robert League 7/27/1813
William League 3/14/1825
George B. League 11/29/1814
Mary League 11/21/1826-5/1/1906
Elizabeth League 9/20/1816
Berry League 7/23/1828
Jane P. League 4/22/1818
Nancy League 7/21/1830
Joshua League 8/26/1819
Casander League 3/25/1832
Sallie League 2/22/1834

Mary League m. W. B. Jones 1813-1893

JOHN FREEMAN BIBLE
Owner: Anna Belle Freeman Sullivan

John Freeman b. 10/29/1781 m. Nancy W. b. 5/23/1787.

BIRTHS: of THEIR CHILDREN:

Polly T. Freeman 1/11/1808 -
Henry Freeman 10/30/1819
Betty Baulden Freeman 1/11/1808
Elmira Amanda Freeman
Roberson Freeman 9/19/1821
Roberson Freeman 11/30/1810
Permelia Freeman 1/11/1813
Edith Arabella Freeman 1/29/1825

John Freeman Bible continued...

Winfield Freeman 9/28/1814
John Forsythe Smith Freeman 9/6/1826
Martha Ann Freeman 2/24/1816
Aveline Augusta Freeman 12/16/1817
Roberson Freeman m. 10/12/1839
Susan Emily Childs, Jones Co., Ga., d. 9/18/1866 (Columbia Co., Ark.)

THEIR CHILDREN:

Mary Elizabeth Freeman 1/21/1841-9/26/1926
William Henry Freeman 6/7/1842-1/16/1900
Eugenia Frances Freeman 6/12/1844-
John Holland Freeman 1/29/1846-2/15/1913
Nannie A. Freeman 9/14/1848-
Sarah E. Freeman 12/2/1850-
James Hiram Freeman 9/14/1852-
Susan Alice Freeman 12/10/1854-
Thomas Edwin Freeman 5/5/1857-12/111933
Arabella Myriam Freeman 11/25/1859
Martha Lelia Freeman 5/4/1862-11/2/1928
Roberson Camilla Freeman 2/16/1865-

ELBERT FRANKLIN WALTERS BIBLE

Elbert Franklin Walters 2/6/1839-6/1/1865
Martha Frances Walters 10/24/1861-7/8/1866
George Franklin Walters 8/27/1865-7/31/1891
Marion Howard 3/1/1819-8/30/1881

Elbert Franklin Walters Bible continued...

George Howard, husband of Marion Howard, d. 9/30/1853
Spencer Claborn Howard d. 7/18/1845
Mrs. L. A. Dwight d. 2/4/1887 Mrs. C. H. Parke 3/19/1864-d. 9/8/1904
Sarah Jane Dwight d. 10/19/1916 William Dwight d. 8/4/---

NANCY ANN DORA CADDIN BIBLE
Owner: J.W. Caddin, 2714 Edenwood, Austin, Tx

Redmon Caddin 1801-1867 m. 10/9/1848
Catherine Bayling 1822-3/15/1861, daughter of John Bayling

THEIR CHILDREN:

Redmond Ausley Caddin 10/1/1850 Barnwell Co., S. C.-6/7/1920 Birmingham, Ala., bur. Oak Hill Cemetery, m. Sarah M. Ravanna
Nancy Ann Dora Caddin 10/29/1851 Barnwell Co. S. C. - 8/25/1920 Langley, Aiken Co.. S. C., m. 1/20/1864, A. D.
Nelson Edward Baker Caddin b. 1/19/1853 Barnwell Co., S. C.
John Wesley Caddin 1/24/1856 Barnwell Co., S. C.-5/6/1928 Augusta, Ga., bur. Westvlew Cem., Augusta m. Mary G. Moseley

Catherine Caddin 7/29/1858 Barnwell Co., S. C. m. Jutson Love

James Jackson Caddin 10/29/1860 Barnwell Co., S. C.-5/14/1923 Miami, Dade Co., Fla., bur. Levels Baptist Church Cemetery, Aiken, S. C. m. Lucy Elizabeth Moseley

Nancy Ann Dora Caddin Bible continued...

Richard David Caddin 5/5/1863 Barnwell Co., S. C.-6/29/1913 Augusta, Ga., bur. Westview Cem., Augusta, Ga. m. Amanda Watkins

PROSSER-DARRONS BIBLE
Owner: Dr. Edward Cardwell, Columbia, S. C.

BIRTHS: of Children of William Prosser and Elizabeth Otey

Otey Prosser 1/20/1761 -
Rebecca Prosser 11/3/1768
Mary Prosser 9/25/1762
John Prosser 2/17/1771
Susan Prosser 7/17/1781
Elizabeth Prosser 9/14/1764
George Prosser 4/2/1773
Ann Prosser 9/5/1766

DEATHS:

Francis Richard Strobia 2/28/1813
Ann Darrons 7/6/1805, daughter of William and Elizabeth Prosser, m. 4/27/1786 John Darrons (he d. 1/6/1814)
Mary, daughter of John and Ann Darrons, 10/4/1787
Elizabeth Otey Darrons b. 7/10/1787 m. 11/16/1806 John Ligon Cook, daughter of John and Ann Darrons

Note: Richmond, Va. is written on one of older pages, and family states these pages were brought from Virginia

DAVID CARDWELL BIBLE
Owner: Dr. Edward Cardwell, Columbia, S. C.

David Cardwell m. 6/12/1873 Anna Cook Sinton b. 8/9/1848

THEIR CHILDREN:

Infant daughter, born and died 12/31/1874 Columbia, S. C.
David Cardwell b. 6/3/1876 Richmond, Va. m. 6/22/1904 Alexa Wylie McLure
Edward Sinton Cardwell b. 1/12/1879 in Columbia, S. C., m. 6/23/1908 Josephine Randolph Withers
Thomas Davant Cardwell b. 8/23/1881 m. 9/12/1912 Nancy Berry Edwards
Virginia Cook Cardwell b. 2/15/1886 in Columbia, S. C. m. 6/12/1911 Frank M. Durham

BIRTHS: of Grandchildren

Jane Sinton Cardwell 4/20/1904, dau,of David Edward Sinton Cardwell

11/14/1909, son of Edward Frances Livingston Cardwell

4/7/1911, daughter of Edward David Withers Cardwell

9/17/1912, son of Edward Josephine Randolph Cardwell

9/29/1914, daughter of Edward Francis Marion Durham, Jr.

2/1/1913, son of Virginia

Anna Sinton Durham 7/13/1916, daughter of Virginia

COOK-SINTON BIBLE
Owner: Dr. Edward Cardwell, Columbia, S. C.

Edward Cook m. 8/23/1782 Sarah Castlen (she d. 1/2/1784)
John Ligon Cook, son of Edward and Sarah, 11/16/1783-4/23/1836
Elizabeth Otey Darrons, daughter of John and Ann Darrons, b. 7/10/1787 m. 11/16/1806
John Ligon Cook
Ann Martha Cook, dau., 6/16/1808-7/17/1811
John Henry Cook 1120/1810-2/6/1852
Sarah Ann Cook 12/19/1811-7/17/1839 m. 10/6/1836
John E. Laughton Francis Strobia Cook 2/2/1813-9/1/1834
Elizabeth Darrans Cook 3/29/1815-10/20/1872

Edward Bocksins Cook b. 8/22/1817
Oliver Cook 8/29/1819-7/2/1820
Maria Virginia Cook 7/17/1821-10/8/1884 m. 6/12/1845
Edward Sinton
William Prosser Cook 8/7/1823-8/27/1849
Charles Cook 8/111825-8/10/1825
Mary Susan Cook 8/5/1827-1/6/1831
Emily Jane Cook b. 12/7/1829 m. 1/21/1851
Alexander Sterling
Sarah Elizabeth Sinton, grdau., b. 5/16/1846 m. 11/4/1884
Samuel Sinton
Anna Cook Sinton, granddaughter, b. 8/9/1848 m. 6/12/1873
David Cardwell Samuel Sinton, son of William and Rebecca C., d. 3/3/1913, Richmond, Va.

JACOB CARTER BIBLE Of Colleton Dist., S. C.

Jacob Carter m. Miss W. C. King 3/23/1834
J. Williams Carter, son of Jacob and Wilhelmenia King Carter, to Laura Julia Smith, daughter of
John and Valeria Elmer Smith, 12/2/1910

BIRTHS:

Jacob Carter 12/18/1828   -W. C. Carter, his wife, 7/1833

BIRTHS: of THEIR CHILDREN:

Lewis Carter 8/9/1855
Conrad Carter 7/17/1864
Elizabeth Carter 6/18/1857
Adam D. Carter 6/21/1866
Margaret O. Carter 11123/1858
Mattie S. Carter 1/1/1868
Thomas Carter 6/23/1860
J. William Carter 11/8/1869
Anna D. Carter 9/27/1861
N. Lula Carter 7/4/1872
Lucy Carter 7/8/1863
Jacob H. A. Carter 2/9/1875

BIRTHS: of Children of J. Williams Carter and Laura Smith

J. Williams Carter Jr. 9/20/1914
Leonard David Carter 3/16/1922
Ronald St. Clair Carter 10/7/1916

Jacob Carter Bible continued...

DEATHS:

William Carter Sr. 4/1/1863
Adam D. Carter 10118/1867
Margaret Carter, his wife, 3/14/1855
Conrad Carter 7/17/1863
Lewis Carter, son of Jacob, 9/15/1868
Jacob Carter 8/19/1883
Thomas Carter 11/1/1868

RICHARD HARRIET SCRUGGS BIBLE
Owner: Martha Sue Scruggs Cooper
1904 112 Williams St., Valdosta, Ga.

MARRIAGES

Margaret Horne b. 11/28/1839 Richard Scruggs b. 9/18/1820
Richard Scruggs to Margaret Horne 2/12/1861

BIRTHS of Their Children

John Goldwire Scruggs 11/15/1861
Charles G. Scruggs 6/19/1871
Lilly Scruggs 2/17/1863
Beulah Scruggs 2/12/1874
Susan E. Scruggs 1/9/1865
Margaret Scruggs 11/20/1876
Thomas Sutton Scruggs 1/13/1867

Richard Harriett Scruggs Bible continued...

Kate Young Scruggs 12/9/1878
Francis Scruggs 3/17/1869
Richard Lawson Scruggs 9/27/1881

DEATHS

Kate Scruggs 9/1/1884
Susan E. Scruggs 10/6/1908
Richard Scruggs 2/4/1897
Margaret Scruggs 8/17/1911
Margaret Horne Scruggs 9/16/1937
Franklin Scruggs 7/16/1944
John Goldwire Scruggs 12/9/1934

Children of R. L. and Ira Casey Scruggs:

Infant son 6/4/1908
Wm Richard Scruggs 10/9/1912
Hazel Elizabeth Scruggs 7/13/1911
Richd Lawson Scruggs 9/28/1960

BIRTHS of Children of Richard L. Scruggs and Ira Casey

Infant son 6/4/1908
Ralph Leon Scruggs 10/15/1919

Hazel Eliz Scruggs 6/15/1909
Martha Sue Scruggs 5/13/1926
Wm Richard Scruggs 6/21/1912
Glenn Allen Scruggs 10/16/1916
James Frederick Scruggs 1/26/1914

JOHN SWORDS, SR. BIBLE
Owner: Ken B. Waites P. O. Box 356,
Birmlngham, Ala. 35294

BIRTHS

John Swords Sr. 3/19/1755
James Swaney Swords 6/20/1787
Eleanor Swords 6/9/1754
Elizabeth Swords 1/30/1789
John Swaney 1/21/1766
Ruthy Swords 11/21/1790
Robert Swaney 3/26/1775
Esther Swords 3/15/1792
Nathaniel Swaney 9/1/1777
Mary Swords 10/21/1793
William Swaney 3/19/1783
John Swords 5/13/1795
Isabella Swords 4/10/1784
Jonathan Swords 12/31/1796
Dorcas Swords 10/24/1785
Andrew Swords 7/28/1799

MARRIAGES

John Swords to Eleanor Swaney 4/24/1782

DEATHS

Robert Swaney 1/7/1791
Mary Morris 3/30/1841
Elizabeth Swords 5/19/1824
William Swords 1/30/1794

John Swords, Sr. Bible continued...

James Moor 12/9/1823
John Swords, Sr. 9/28/1834
James Swaney Swords 6/16/1796
Eleanor Swaney Swords 5/3/1841

AARON WOOD BIBLE
From: Rev. War Pension #W6566

Aaron Wood m. Dorotha 5/28/1778.

BIRTHS of Their Children

Matthew Wood 5/9/1779
Candis Wood 8/31/1794
Stephen Wood 10/21/1781
Barzilia Wood 9/23/1797
 Joseph Wood 8/13/1783
Fanney Wood 2/5/1800
Rezen Wood 11/6/1785
 ----- Wood 4/3/1802
Rebecca Wood 12/17/1787
     ----- Wood 12/20/1804
 Patsy Wood 4/2/1790
---lia Wood 6/3/1807

Elizabeth Wood 5/17/1792

Aaron Wood Bible continued...

BIRTHS of Children of Aaron and Matilda Mayhew Wood

Achsah Wood 5/28/1830
Matilda Wood 2/3/1834 Martha Wood 4/29/1832
Note: Aaron Wood applied for pension 10/17/1832, York District, S. C., stating he was b. 1757 Loudoun Co., Va., and removed to Hnlifax Co., N. C. with his parents, while still a boy. Enlisted 6/1776 while living with relatives In Maryland. Soldier d. 7/19/1834 York District, S. C.

Widow, Matilda Wood, applied for pension 4/24/1853, aged 55 yrs., York District, S. C., stating she was
Matilda Mayhew, daughter of Charity Mayhew when she married a.soldier 7/21/1824 by Joseph McKenzie in York District. S. C., and that she is the second wife. Rezen Mayhew of York District, S. C., aged 56, 11/7/1853, states that Matilda is his sister. Widow's son-in-lew, H. A. Wallace, was alive in 1856.

MRS. ANN COBB BIBLE
Owner: Mrs. Frank Beaird   Rt. 3, Box 9, Centre, Ala. 35960

*On flyleaf: "Presented to Mrs. Ann Cobb by her brother, William Choice, Greenvllle, S. C., Ist of
January 1849."*

BIRTHS

William Choice 1/30/1756
Mary, his wife, 2/10/1768

Mrs. Ann Cobb Bible continued...

Tully Choice 12/18/1787
Cyrus Choice 10/18/1799
Ann Choice 7/30/1790
Aralintha Choice 7/20/1802
Mary Choice 7/7/1792
Sophia Choice 10/29/1805
John Choice 10/11/1793
Josiah Choice 3/28/1808
William Choice 10/4/1796
Jefferson Choice 4/29/1811
Thomas J. Cobb 2/25/1834
Mary H. Cobb 12/23/1815
Amanda Cobb 1/18/1825
William C. Cobb 6/1/1817
Tulley Cobb 11/13/1828
John D. Cobb 12/21/1819
Samuel Cobb 8/26/1830
Josiah Cobb 9/21/1821
Ransom H. Cobb 8/25/1832
Lovicy Cobb 8/16/1823

MARRIAGES

William Choice to Mary McDonald 5/11/1786
Wade H. Lokey to Alice Horn 2/25/1886

DEATHS

William Emley Lokey 7/16/1888
Sheppie A. Lokey 10/25/1902
M. A. Wood 12/10/1894

Mrs. Ann Cobb Bible continued...

BIRTHS

Wade Lokey 7/6/1860
Allce S. Horn b. 12/20/1863 Smith Co., Va. d. 10/21/1941

William Earley Lokey 1/1/1887
Burt C. Lokey 2/25/1898
Mary E. S. Lokey 4/1/1889
Shepie A. Lokey 8/29/1902
Mackey Lokey 5/17/1893
Emily Mae Lokey 2/13/1907
Samuel B. Lokey 8/1/1895
Early Lokey 6/16/1817

DEATHS

Mary Choice 8/2/1792
Samuel Cobb 6/17/1855
John Choice 9/2/1842
John D. Cobb 8/1/1862
William Choice, father, 9/30/1843
Ransom M. Cobb 2/26/1868
Mary, the mother, 10/6/1848
Sarah Cobb 9/2/1824
Sophia Fowler 7/30/1829
Nancy Cobb 2/26/1868
Mary M. Lokey 4/9/1887
Sallie Lokey 8/16/1870

Mrs. Ann Cobb Bible continued...

Samuel Cobb 6/17/1855
Eliza A. Lokey 8/20/1862
Thalia Bradley Cokey 5/24/1862
Mary C. Lokey Elder 12/21/1905

William T. Lokey was mortally wounded 5/15th, 5 days
William C. Cobb 3/6/1865, aged 47 yrs., 9 mos. died 6/2/1864
William Horn 3/4/1910
Sarah E. Horn 12/20/1905
Eliza A. Lokey 8/2/1849
Thalia B. Lokey 10/5/1853
Emily C. Lokey 7/29/1851
Early W. H. Lokey 7/6/1860
Joseph Early O'Neal 8/9/1855
Amanda O'Neal 9/5/1860
Mary E. O'Neal 12/12/1856
Georgia A. M. O'Neal 3/7/1859

DANIEL JOHNSTON BIBLE
Owner: Mrs. Lillie Johnston Rogers   Sulphur, Oklahoma

BIRTHS

Daniel Johnston 2/11/1784-6/12/1835
Mary T. Johnston 3/9/1818
Margarett Johnston 7/21/1785
Margarett G. Johnston 3/11/1820
H. R. Johnston 2/6/1808
R. C. Johnston 2/10/1811

Daniel Johnston Bible continued...

J. D. Johnston 5/22/1822
Sarah Johnston 11/15/1812
Hannah Johnston 1/5/1825
Elizabeth S. Johnston 7/18/1815
Eliza Johnston 2/21/1827

DEATHS

Daniel Johnston 6/12/1835
Mary J. Reeves 10/14/1856
Margaret Morgan 9/26/1852
James D. Johnston 11/5/1856
Sarah Bradwell 6/24/1840
Joseph P. Johnston 7/1850
Elizabeth Burton 7/24/1840
Eliza Cook 1/20/1855
R. C. Johnston 10/8/1872
Hannah Irena Johnston b. and d. 4/15/1854, daughter of R. C. Johnston
Henderson R. Johnston b. and d. 4/28/1855
Annalisa Johnston b. and d. 5/21/1857
Daniel J. Johnston 3/2/1868
Myra Johnston 10/20/1872

BIRTHS

R. C. Johnston 2/13/1811
Mariah W. Johnston 2/18/1822
James J. Johnston 4/9/1840
William Johnston 4/6/1842

Daniel Johnston Bible continued...

Margaret Elizabeth Johnston 5/9/1844
Daniel J. Johnston 11/21/1846
Joseph R. Johnston 2/13/1849
Mary M. Johnston 5/23/1857
Hannah Irena Johnston 4/12/1854
Reuben J. D. Johnston 4/26/1861
Sarah L. Johnston 8/25/1862
Omy L. Johnston 9/28/1864
Margareta Johnston 10/6/1870

BURRELL McCLENDON BIBLE

Burrell McClendon b. 12/5/1802 in S. C. m. Nancy Crumb b. 3/5/1804 in Ga.

BIRTHS of Their Children

James McClendon 5/5/1821
Judy Lee McClendon 3/28/1835
Sarah McClendon 12/23/1823
Patsey McClendon 11/17/1837
Elizabeth McClendon 2/7/1825
Burwell McClendon 3/16/1840
Mary NcClendon 5/13/1826
Ellender I. McClendon 7/16/1844
Susan McClendon ---
William McClendon 7/5/1846
John McClendon 7/4/1829
Lewis McClendon 7/7/1830
Nancy Mariam McClendon 2/13/1833 (m. Rubin Washburn)
Anderson McClendon 10/9/1860

SILVANUS MINTON BIBLE
Owner: Dennis C. Minton, Jacksonville, Fla.

BIRTHS

Silvanus Minton 8/27/1791
Mary Minton 4/10/1788
Reuben R. Minton 5/11/1814
Silvanus Moody Minton 11/5/1827
Rebeccah L. Minton 11/14/1817
Sarah Ann Minton 11/5/1827
John M. Minton 9/4/1819
Joseph Alphred Minton 1/6/1829
Hannah E. Minton 1/28/1821
Martha Miles Minton 3/11/1831
Mary Ann Minton 4/23/1823
Harriett Good Minton 3/11/1831
Sidney R. Minton 12/29/1824
Francis Marion Minton 11/25/1840
James Madison Minton 6/1/1834
David Hampton Minton 5/15/1843
Thomas Allen Minton 4/23/1836
Edward Priestly Minton 2/1/1847
Nancy Jane Minton 3/12/1838
Sarah Matilda Minton 2/23/1849

DEATHS

Silvanus Moody Minton 10/8/1839 Silvanus Minton 11/10/1880
Mary Minton, wife of Sllvanus, 11/16/1827

MARRIAGES
Silvanus Minton to Mary Morris 4/8/1813 Silvanus Minton to Janie Quails 2/12/1828

REV. JOHN NOBLE BIBLE
Owner: Mrs. Robert Noble, Rt. 1, Attalla, Ala.

Rev. John Noble b. Spartanburg District, S. C., d. at age of 87 yrs. m. Sarah Holloway of Spartanburg, S. C.

BIRTHS of Children

Nancy Noble m. Thomas Logan, S. C.
John Baptist Noble
William Noble 12/2/1815-10/29/1866
Bennett Noble
Betsy Noble a. Madison Hendrix
Eliza Noble m. Job Miller
Patsy Noble m. Eliza Scillman and Hiram Nalms, d. 4/22/1909, Alabama City, Ala.
Allen Avery b. 10/26/1805 Tenn. d. 1-1/2 miles SW of Attalla, Ala. Sarah McBrayer b. 9/2/1809
William Noble b. 12/2/1815 Spartanburg, S. C. m. Luvena Avery b. 8/27/1838 Centerville, Ala. m. 2nd, Margaret Atklns.

Children:

John Camp Noble b. 12/10/1845 m. Sallie B. Pickens
Adolphus Avery Noble b. 2/13/1848
Francis Elizabeth Noble b. 11/15/1850
Rufus Bennett Noble b. 5/3/1853
William Noble, Jr. b. 5/14/1855 m. Claudie Bentley Madison Noble b. 7/1/1858

BIRTHS of Children of William Noble by 2nd marriage

Sarah J. P. Noble 3/8/1863
Ellen E. J. Noble 5/1/1865

Rev. John Noble Bible continued...

MARRIAGES

Madison Noble to Nannie Florence Talton 8/22/1906 at Avery. Ala. by P. W. Gilbreath, J. P.
Robert H. Noble to Jewell McDaniel 6/7/1930, by Rev. W. F. Tullls

JOHN HENRY SEYLE BIBLE
Owner: Sanford Branch LaFar, Savannah, Ga.

MARRIAGES

John Henry Seyle of Charleston, S. C. to Miss Eliza Bolles Haupt of Savannah, Ga. 5/16/1833
John Frederick Seyle of Charleston, S. C. to Catherine Elizabeth Patterson of Charleston, S. C., 10/20/1859
Allred W. Stevens to Mary Lavinder Seyle 4/10/1862, both of Charleston, S. C.
John F. LaFar of Chacleston, S. C. to Margaret U. Seyle of Charleston, S. C. 10/6/1870
Charles Y. Richardson to Susannah U. Seyle 4/10/1872, both of Charleston, S. C.
Samuel H. Seyle of Charleston, S. C. to Laura Elizabeth Collins of Savannah, Ga., 12/21/1873
William J. Seyle of Charleston to Mary F. Miller, 12/16/1879

BIRTHS

John Henry Seyle b. Charleston 9/10/1806
Eliza Bolles Haupt, wife of John Henry Seyle, 10/7/1810

John Henry Seyle Bible continued...

Savannah John Frederick Seyle 12/30/1834 Charleston, S. C.
Samuel Henry Seyle 8/11/1837 Charleston, S. C.
Mary Lavinder Seyle 5/2/1840 Charleston, S. C.
Rebecka Eliza Seyle 7/3/1842 Charleston, S. C.
William Jackson Seyle 9/17/1844 Charleston, S. C.
Margaret Will Seyle 3/8/1848 Charleston, S. C.
Susannah Wesner Seyle 3/22/1851 Charleston, S. C.
Maria Edgerton Seyle 1/18/1854 Charleston, S. C.

DEATHS

Maria Edgerton Seyle 8/31/1855, aged 1 yr., 7 .os., 13 days
Eliza Bolles Seyle 10/15/1860, aged 50 yrs., 8 days
William Jackson Seyle 1/27/1882, aged 38 yrs., 2 mos., 10 days

Margaret Will Seyle LaFar 4/1/1918 Savannah, Ga.
Henry Hamilton LaFar 2/26/1918 Savannah, Ga.

Charles Henry Richardson 12/17/1927 Savannah, Ga.
Susannah Wesner Seyle Richardson 1/4/1910 Savannah, Ga.

Rebecca Eliza Seyle 3/20/1904, buried Charleston, S. C.
Laura Collins Seyle 2/9/1927
Samuel Henry Seyle 2/13/1888
Mary Lavinder Seyle Stevens 1/15/1889 Charleston, S. C.

John Henry Seyle 2/14/1891, buried Charleston, S. C.
John Frederick Seyle 1/26/1906 Charleston, S. C.
Mary F. Miller Seyle 4/14/1933 Charleston, S. C.

HENRY PHILIP WESNER BIBLE
Owner: Mrs. Sanford Branch LaFar, Savannah, Ga

BIRTHS

Henry Philip Wesner 1755 m. Barbery in 1781.

Their Children:

Henry Philip Wesner 1/16/1782
Frederick Wesner 1/14/1788
Mary Susannah Wesner 7/27/1785
Margaret Wesner 1790

DEATHS

Henry Philip Wesner before 1798
Mary Susannah Wesner 5/28/1856
Frederick Wesner 3/1/1818
Seyle Barbery Wesner 10/1/1798
Henry Philip Wesner 3/27/1818

AARON GUYTON BIBLE
From: Rev. War Pension #WZ1237

BIRTHS

Aaron Guyton 10/27/1761
Margaret McCurdy 12/1773 m. 10/6/1789

Their Children:

Mary Guyton 12/15/1791
Robert Guyton 11/21/1802

Aaron Guyton Bible continued...

Aaron W. Guyton 11/22/1808
Hannah Guyton 12/18/1793
Joseph Guyton 4/14/1805
Katherine Guyton 8/22/1798
Elizabeth Guyton 11/7/1795
Margaret V. Guyton 1/7/1807

MARRIAGES

Jane Guyton 12/31/1800

DEATHS

Katherine Smith 9/28/1796
Jane Guyton, daughter of Aaron and Margaret, 8/30/1802

Note: Aaron Guyton applied for pension 1/1/1833, Anderson District, S. C., stating he was b. 10/27/1761 Baltimore, Maryland. lived 96th District during war. Soldier d. 6/30/1841.

Widow applied for pension 12/29/1853 stating she a. 10/611789, by Abraham Smith, magistrate of York District. S. C.

She was alive 9/25/1860, Anderson District, S. C. Joseph Guyton, Union District, S. C., 11/24/1845, stated his elder bro., Aaron Guyton m. Margaret McCurdy 10/1789 and that he was not at wedding.

LEWIS SAXON BIBLE
From: Rev. War Pension

BIRTHS

Lewis Saxon 12/10/1765-1/14/1831
Sally, wife of Alexander Saxon. 2/1/1767-8/12/1792
Clarissa Saxon 12/19/1787-12/16/1837
Charles Saxon 2/7/1790-
Louisa Saxon 8/2/1791-
David Saxon 11/29/1794

Polly Saxon 10/23/1796-
Hugh Saxon 10/8/1798-
Allen Saxon 6/4/1800-2/23/1822
Joshua Saxon 11/29/1801-
Lydall P. Saxon 4/15/1803-
Tabitha Saxon 7/2/1804-11/11/1833
Susannah Saxon 12/14/1805-
Samuel Saxon 9/25/1807-1/15/1831
Harriette Saxon 5/20/1809-6/16/1826
Lewis Saxon 12/14/1810-8/20/1811

Note: Widow's Pension, Mrs. Sally McNeese. Soldier was b. 12/10/1765, lived Ninety-Six District, S. C. during war. Her maiden name was Sally Allen and she m. Lewis Saxon 2/1/1787.

Soldier d. 10/31/1813, then she m. 2nd, Robert McNeese, 1816, who d. 1/7/1840.

DAVID FREEMAN BIBLE
Owner: Mrs. Alexander Langford , Orlando, Fla.

BIRTHS

David Freeman 9/20/1804 S. C.
Jacob Elbert Freeman 8/16/1850
Mary Elender Rivers 9/1/1825
John Fraser Freeman 12/5/1855
James Albert Freeman 4/26/1848.
Mary Elizabeth Freeman 10/7/1853 killed during Civil War

DEATHS

David Freeman 2/20/1863
Jacob Elbert Freeman 6/24/1892
Mary Elender Rivers Freeman 1/1/1861
John Fraser Freeman 4/14/1922
Mary Elizabeth Freeman Langford 9/1930

JOHN STEPHEN TITSHAW BIBLE
of Chester and Edgefield Co.'s, S. C.
Owner: Wilson Titshaw

BIRTHS

Stephen Titshaw Jr. 9/15/1797-9/26/1875
Elizabeth Titshaw 11/7/1797-8/1848
Niles A. Titshaw 12/23/1821 m. Emily I. Clegg 12/5/1852
Anderson Harrison Titshaw 9/24/1823-9/11/1888 m. Mary Ann Cronick 10/20/1846
John Sampson Titshaw 12/30/1825-1/13/1907 m. Lucinda S. Thompson 1/13/1853

John Stephen Titshaw Bible continued...

Isaac E. Titshaw 12/5/1829 m. Sarah Reed 9/24/1848, moved to Ala. Alexander Wilson
Columbus
Titshaw 11/13/1833 m. Mrs. Serena Pirkle Wheeler 11/19/1867
Serena Pirkle Titshaw 8/31/1836-10/8/1903
Wilson Titshaw d. 11/6/1915

S. W. and Mary Titshaw, ch. of Sheriff Titshaw, d. 3/6/1879
Meley (Mary) Titshaw d. 6/25/1879, wife of Sheriff Titshaw
Mary Titshaw 1/12/1883-1/12/1889, daughter of Manley Titshaw
Emma Cintha Titshaw d. 1/2/1835
Cornella A. Titshaw 6/26/1837 m. John J. Wilkins 10/16/1859, son of Samuel M. Wilkins
Rosina Tishaw----Florida

Stephen Titshaw Jr. m. 2nd Elizabeth Tacky 10/23/1849, had sons
Manley H. and Sheriff Titshaw.

L. V. C. Titshaw appointed guardian of Sheriff Titshaw, orphan of Stephen Titshaw, Jr., decd,
12/11/1875

L. C. Titshaw m. 2nd Fannie M. Lyle 3/5/1904
Sheriff Titshaw m. Mary Strange 9/14/1876 by Rev. J. W. Davis
Manley O. Titshaw m. Calvina
Strange 7/26/1877, Rev. J. U. Davis John Wilson Titshaw 8/27/1868 m. Sarah Jane Tuggle 1/13/1895 by Rev. R. F. Sloan

John Stephen Titshaw Bible continued...

Lewis Columbus Titshaw 6/30/1870 m. Lillie Greeson 12/17/1891 by Rev. J. Frank Jackson
James Tyler Titshaw 9/21/1871 m. Fannie Melissa Titshaw 9/21/1890
L. Wilson Titshaw, Pvt., Co. C., 9th Regt., Ga. Inf., Col. E. R.Goulding, Walton Co.
L. W. C. Titshaw and wife m. 8/12/1900, Methodist Church, by Rev. J. L. Hall

JAMES T. AND FANNIE MELISSA TITSHAW BIBLE

Fannie Melissa Titshaw b. 5/10/1868, daughter of John Sampson and Lucinda Thompson Titshaw

BIRTHS of Children of James T. and Fannie Melissa Titshaw

James Omer Titshaw 2/14/1892 -
Carl Shaw Titshaw 12/2/1905
Ara Frances Titshaw 9/28/1892
James Tyler Titshsw 2/1/1908-3/6/1908
Ezra Tyler Titshaw 5/10/1896
Grady Wilson Titshaw 6/30/1901
Erie Sampson Titshaw 9/28/1899
Maude Myrtle Titshaw 10/2/1910
Serene Titshaw 6/6/1903-2/6/1904

MOSES COLLINS
Of Orangeburg District, S. C.
Owner: Seaborn Collins, Yazoo City, Mississippi

Published in Edinburg In 1771
Moses Collins m. 8/6/1774
Hannah Collins b. 12/10/1754

BIRTHS

Susannah Collins 5/16/1775
Henry Collins 10/8/1785
Ann Collins 1/31/1777
Sarah Collins 10/9/1787
Joseph Collins 3/31/1779
Rebecca Collins 12/27/1789
Moses Collins Jr. 7/16/1781
Ailsey Collins 10/27/17-
Hannah Collins 8/22/1783
Seaborn Collins 1776

JAMES HILLIARD GRIGG BIBLE
Owner: Louise Brown Heffner
7456 Centauri Rd., Jackson, Fla. 32210

James Hilllard Grigg m. Mary Jane Powell 10/28/1869

BIRTHS

James Hilliard Grigg 1/23/1847-819/1912
Mary Jane Powell 7/19/1853-6/23/1906
Cynthia Lenorah Grigg 2/15/1871

James Hilliard Grigg Bible continued...

Parmonnos Elverson Grigg 8/22/1872
Williard Sisero Grigg 2/6/1874
Lily Cornelia Grigg 12/1/1875
Eslcy Vann Grigg 1/27/1878
Marinda Leonria Grigg 10/19/1879
Burton Crage Grigg 12/9/1881
Alonso (Tanso) Roland Grigg, 11/18/1884
Joseph Jonah Grigg 3/9/1887
William Pinkney Grlgg 2/6/1889
Thomas Clingman Grigg 6/13/1891
Note: William Pinkney Grigg's surname changed to "Gregg"

SOLOMON CROCKER BIBLE
Owner: Faye Berry Emory

BIRTHS of Children of Solomon and Susannah Crocker

William Crocker 1/2/1781
James Crocker 11/18/1795
Dorcas Crocker 8/9/1783
Nancy Crocker 3/25/1797
Rhoda Crocker 1/11/1785
Arthur Crocker 8/8/1799
Patsey Crocker 2/14/1787
John Crocker 7/9/1803
Polley Crocker 4/23/1790
Susannah Crocker 10/30/1805
Betsey Crocker 4/15/1793
Susannah, their mother, was b. 12/19/1762 *(Written on back of page)*
James Arthur Crocker
South Carolina, Spartanburgh January the 23, 1800

ARLEDGE-HIGGINS BIBLE
Owner: Grace Arledge Berry, Spartenburg, S. C.

BIRTHS

Theodocia Leah Higgins 3/11/1866
Eliza Ann Higgins 7/8/1872
John Butler Higgins 3/2/1868
Harriet Jennie Higgins Wilbur 12/22/1876
Yates Higgins 1/14/1871
Horace Arledge m. Magnolia Ramsey Wilson 4/14/1951, 2d wife
J. S. Higgins
Israel Arledge
Etelka Williams d. 8/11/1914
Credy Williams, only child of Eleika, b. 9/1911
Israel Arledge 1/15/1884
Etelka Arledge 11/23/1885
Harriet Arledge 11/22/1889
Glenn Arledge 8/27/1893
Elsworth Nun Arledge b. 5/1/1896
Jennie Grace Arledge b. 2/2/1900
Butler Patterson b. 8/21/1903
Annie Dorcas Arledge b. 6/22/1908
Edith O'Delt b. 9/7/1891

MARRIAGES

Horace Volney Arledge to Edith O'Dell 2/28/1912
Howard Williams to Etelka Arledge 11/22/1910
Israel Clement Arledge to Core Outs 11/28/1912
H. P. Arledge to Theodocia Higgins 11/2/1882
James Wakefield of Abbeville Co. to Elvira S. Clinkscales of Anderson Co., at res. of bride's
father, by Rev. W. A. Hedges, 11/30/1871

Arledge-Higgins Bible continued...

E. L. Clark to Miss Bettie N. Crosby, 2nd daughter of David Crosby, Esq., all of Anderson, S. C., 12/13/1871 by Rev. J. Scott Murray
Miss Julia Werner, late of Pendleton, S. C. d. at Greenvllle C. H., in her 29th yr.

MAJOR KENNEDY'S BIBLE
Owner: Cecile Henry Irwin, Chester, S. C.
printed in Belfast, Ireland in 1746

"Given to me the 11th Aug. 1923 by Mrs. S. E. Babcock tie belonged to her grandfather, John Kennedy to give to posterity. J. K. Henry."

Notations In margins:

John Kennedy, Richard Kennedy, George Kennedy's hair, Mary Ann K., and Catherine Kennedy's hair

BIRTHS

Ann 6/9/1750
Agness 3/1/--
John Foster –
Wil. 10/2/1756
Catrin 10/9/1753
Margaret 1/2/1763
?Hope 8/9/1774
John 10/16/1755

Major Kennedy's Bible continued...

Robert 8/28/1770
Janet 5/27/1767
James 5/28/1765
Mary 7/11/1759

ELIAS BELCHER BIBLE
Owner: Ott Gregory   Spartanburg, S. C.

BIRTHS

Elias Belcher 3/3/1846
Thomas Belcher 3/25/1876
Pollyann C. Bishop 1/29/1849
Tennessee Belcher 6/16/1878
Arrella T. Belcher 9/1/1866
Posey Belcher 2/8/1881
Carrie T. Belcher 12/1/1868
Roa Della Belcher 6/26/1883
Mary E. Belcher 3/27/L871
Joseph Elias Belcher 6/13/1887
Johnie Belcher 8/1/1873
Garibaldi Gregory, son of J. A. and J. C. Gregory, 10/6/1867
Rowland Montague Gregory 8/15/1869
Minnie Hettie Lee Gregory 6/1/1872
Ottis Grady Gregory 1/17/1890
Wells Belcher Gregory 9/18/1895
Ottis Grady Gregory Jr. 12/11/1915
Paul James Gregory 9/3/1919
Sarah Francis Gregory 11/15/1924

Elias Belcher Bible continued...

Bobby E. Gregory 7/3/1936
James Donald Gregory 6/30/1947
Michael David Gregory 11/10/1948
Paul Franklin Gregory 9/26/1950

MARRIAGES

Elias Belcher to Pollyann C. Bishop 8/22/1865
Baldin Gregory to Arrela T. Belcher 3/4/1888
Rolland Montague Gregory to Carrie T. Belcher 4/22/1888
Ottis Grady Gregory to Ella Agnes Greer 12/16/1909
F. H. Parrls to Carrie Gregory 9/18/1915
Ottis Grady Gregory Jr. to Madeline Soleby 10/12/1935
Ottis Grady Gregory to Mary ---- 3/29/1942

Paul James Gregory to Irene Allison Solesbee 3/2/1946

DEATHS

Tennessee Belcher 101811881, aged 3 yrs, 3 mos., 22 days
Roa Delia Belcher 3/6/1895 Sallie Stephens 12/25/1906

Arrelia T. Gregory 6/7/1902
Elias Belcher 8/17/1899
Garibaldi Gregory 8/14/1897
Jude Caroline Gregory 4/20/1897
James A. Gregory 8/20/1880
Rolin Montague Gregory 5/15/1912
Sarah Francis Gregory 5/19/1926
Pollyann Belcher 10/16/1935

Elias Belcher Bible continued...

John Belcher 4/29/1936
Carrie T. Belcher Gregory Parris 6/23/1943
Mary Lillian ---- Gregory 11/15/1943
Ottis Grady Gregory Sr. 6/1/1951
Posey Belcher 7/22/1950
Ottis Grady Gregory Sr. 6/1/1951

DAVID C. GIST BIBLE
From: S. C. Supreme Court, April Term 1918
P. 22-24, Gist et al vs. W. H. Gist, et al

BIRTHS

Annie Belle Gist 7/23/1897
Vivian Gist 5/3/1906
Alice Victoria Gist 6/13/1904
Mary Elizabeth Gist 2/27/1899
Lillian Estelle Gist 9/29/1907
Inez Gist 1/10/1903
Lavinia Katherine Gist 4/19/1901
Addie Eloise Gist 9/10/1910
Thomas Monroe Gist 9/7/1912

DEATHS

Alice Victoria Gist 10/1/1905
Lillian Estelle Gist 11/26/1907
Thomas Monroe Gist 12/31/1913

David C. Gist Bible continued...

Ellen Douglas Gist 4/27/1867-7/4/1870, 3 yrs, 3 mos., 7 days
Laura Lavinia Gist b. 11/111868, 48 yrs., 7 mos., 17 days
William Henry Gist b. 12/19/1869, 47 5 mos. 17 days
David Jesse Gist 7/12/1871-8/29/1879, age 8 yrs.; 1 mo, 17 days
Mary Elizabeth Gist 4/7/1873-11/10/1873, 7 mos., 3 days
Richard Valerius Gist b. 9/8/1875, 41 yrs., 9 mos., 8 days
Sadie Isabel Gist b. 1/5/1881, 36 yrs., 9 mos.. 10 days
Clarence Calhoun Gist and Carrie Clemintina Gist b. 10/6/1882
Carrie Clementing Gist d., 34 yrs, 9 mos. 10 days
Clarence Calhoun Gist 5/23/1907, 24 yrs 7 mos., 17 days
Mary Ann Eugenia Jones 9/19/1847-7/21/1885, 37 yrs, 10 mos, 2 days
David C. Gist 1845-9/9/1915, aged 70 yrs.
David C. Gist and Mary Ann Eugenia Jones m. 3/13/1866 - lived together until death of Mary A.
E. Jones Gist 7/21/1885, 19 yrs. 4 mos., 8 days

NOAH WEBB ROSS BIBLE

Sallie Ross Book 1816

Front cover: E. J. Ross founded Church, Corinth, S. C. 8/11; baptised 8/13/1865. Noah Webb

Ross joined Baptist Church, New Prospect 8/12/186.1 Back cover: E. J. Ross joined Baptist
Church at Corinth, S. C. 8/11/1863. Moses C. Ross left home for

Noah Webb Ross Bible continued...

the Amy 8/1861 and was killed 8/29/1862 at Manassas. A. M. Ross joined the Baptist Church at Sandy Plains 8/28/1883. Mrs. G. P. Hamrick. George A. Ross.

MARRIAGES

Moses Ross to Rachel Bookout 9/10/1818   Osborne Ross to Faster Bookout 5/1/1843
Moses C. Ross to Mary Crowder 7/26/1855   Perry Ross to Margaret L. Morrison 10/11/1860
Noah W. Ross to N. R. Harmon 1/8/1891

BIRTHS

Moses Ross 4/16/1785
Moses C. Ross 11/3/1835
Rachel Ross 5/15/1904
Easter L. Ross 6/26/1837
Osborne Ross 5/3/1823
Julia Ann Ross 2/14/1841
Eliza Ross 7/7/1828
Noah V. Ross 10121/1843
Perry Ross 11/18/1831
Margaret C. Ross 7/3/1846

DEATHS

Osborne Ross 5/5/1863 (In Military Hospital, Goldsboro, N. C.)
Moses C. Ross 8/29/1862 (Killed at 2nd Battle of Manasses, Va.)
Margaret Caroline Ross 4/29/1864

Noah Webb Ross Bible continued...

Perry Ross 7/17/1905
Julia Ann Ross 12/7/1869
Rachel Ross 4/29/1863
Eliza Ross 3/8/1871

BIRTHS

Reuben Jacob Forest Ross 10/7/1891
James Harlan Ross 6/10/1913
Lettie Ula Belle Ross 8/1/1897
Fred Ramsey Ross 1/6/1914
Ada Maude Matina Ross 5/22/1900
Annie Louise Ross
John Lester Crowell Ross 6/10/1913
Mattie Ruth Ross 12/19/1920
R. I. Harmon 1/20/1840
M R. Harmon 8/24/1877
C. M. Harmon 5/6/1849
M.G. Harmon 12/16/1880
N. R. Harmon 4/8/1867
G. A. Harmon 12/22/1869
P. Harmon 2/18/1885
C. S. E. Harmon 12/22/1870

Jacob Harmon 11/13/1890
S. C. Harmon 12/28/1885
A. H. Harmon 5/5/1873
J. H. Harmon 9/8/1875

Noah Webb Ross Bible continued...

MARRIAGES

N. W. Ross to N. R. Harmon 1/8/1891
G. A. Heavnee to S. E. Harmon 11/15/1891 Belle Ross to Tom Ramsey 4/6/1917
Maude Ross to James Jenkins 12/27/1918 Forest Ross to John Cline 9/3/1911

DEATHS

C. N. Harmon 5/4/1886
D. R. L. Harmon 2/27/1919
M. G. Harmon 8/31/1882
Ada P. Taylor 11/30/1920

BIRTHS

James Harlan Ross 6/15/1922
James Conrad Ramsey 1/21/1912
Fred Ramsey Ross 1/6/1914
Dorothy Irene Jenklns 11/1/1920
Cecil Ross Jenkins 8/7/1919
Mattie Ruth Ross 12/19/1920

ARON BRIDGES LEE BIBLE
Owner: Roy Lee, Rt. 3, Shelby, N. C.

Aron Bridges Lee 1/3/1874-8/30/1904
Elizabeth Black 6/1/1878-5/2/1935, wife of Aron Bridges Lee

Children:

Hatcher Lee 11/2/1896-1/9/1974 m. 10/19/1919 Lennie Dobbins 3/2/1901-1/18/1941
Evie Lee b. 3/6/1899 (living 1983), m. 11/12/1916 J. J. Campbell Roy Lee 5/19/1901-6/19/1982 m. 12/16/1926 Tillie Green

W. F. WHITE BIBLE
Owner: Marjorie White Vaughn, Rt. 8, Inman, S. C.

MARRIAGES

W. F. White to Eva P. Foster 11/1/1903
Dud Lowe to Carrie White 2/19/1927
Boyce White to Myrtle Hamrick 7/12/1930
Broadus Hawklns to Mary White 4/18/1931
Paul White to Ada Lee Parris 9/23/1931
Ralph White to Pauline Home 10/14/1940
Marjorie White to L. E. Vaughn 3/27/1954
Mildred White to Marshall Perkins 4/5/1957
Wallace and Phyllis White 6/23/1961

W. F. White Bible continued...

BIRTHS

W. F. White 2/16/1883
Joseph Miller Hawkins 4/10/1934
Eva P. White 2/16/1885
Marjorie Ethel White 9/3/1934
William Boyce White 10111/1904
Betty Lee White 6/23/1932
Mary Anne White -1/9/1906
Marian Elizabeth White 3/19/1934
Cnrrie Ruth White 3/11/1911
Marsha Lynn Perkins 11/6/1960
William Rnlph White 4/5/1921
Mildred Pauline White 7/11/1937
Carrie Roberta Lowe 10/11/1929
William Boyce Lowe 10/6/1939
Hazel Lorene White 4/6/1931
Wallace Franklin White 1/22/1942
Dudley Thomas Lowe 9/27/1932
Franie Charmayne 12/4/1961

DEATHS

Hazel Lorene White 1/9/1933
William Boyce White 11/15/1976
Mrs. Eva Foster White 4/11/1952
Mrs. Eva d. age of 67
William F. White 12/18/1958
Will White d. age of 76
Mary Ann White Hammet 10/27/1957
Boyce White d. age of 72
Marlene Vaughan 12/26/1964
Mary White d. age 51

BARRON-BYNUM-BAXTER BIBLE
Owner: Union Co. Museum Union Co. Historical Society

MARRIAGES

S. D. Barton of York Co. to L. A. Bynum of York Co., S. C. 12/15/1874 at Rock Hill, S. C., by Rev. Mr. Watson
Sam Elmer Barton to Kathleen Pix 8/8/1916 by Rev. E. S. Jones at the home of her parents
P. D. Barron to Mrs. Caroline Dendy by Rev. Pressley at home of her father, Dr. Wideman in Due West, S. C., 7/5/1917
John G. Barton to Mary Allen 1/3/1899 by Rev. O. J. Jones at the 2nd Pres. Manse
Glenmore B. Barton to Mary Louise Hunter 12/24/1900 at home of bride by Rev. Leon Pressley

BIRTHS

Mary J. Barton 1/27/1840
Preston DeKalb Barron 8/4/1877
S. D. Barton 1/31/1847
Samuel Preston Barron 9/1/1921
Philo Conner Barton 4/27/1879
L. A. Barton 11/29/1846
Benjamin Glenmore Barron 6/13/1881
Mary Locke Barron 12/17/1901
Allen D. Barron 4/12/1904
Samuel Elma Barron 10/13/1883
John Grey Pressley Barron 4/23/1906
Lucy Rebecca Barton 9/13/1917
Grey B. Barton 5/8/1876
Elma Kathleen Barton 8/29/1919

Barron-Bynum-Baxter Bible continued...

DEATHS

Eliza E. A. Barton 3/25/1881
S. D. Barton 10/30/1885
Philo Conner Barton 8/3/1881, aged 2 yrs., 3 mos., 6 days

Mary J. Grier 9/21/1881
John Barton 5/27/1882
Sam Pressley Barron Jessia Hix Barron b.--
Mary Locke Barton m. Dibbie Rukenbaker 4/18/1923
Lillie Mary Locke Rukenbaker b. 3/9/1924
Louise Barron m. Townsend Freeman 12/21/1924

BIRTHS and MARRIAGES

James Bynum 3/21/1821
Cynthia L. Bynum 9/26/1821
James Bynum to Cynthia L. Moore, daughter of James and Sophia Moore, near Ebenezer, York Co., S. C., 1/8/1846 by Rev. P. E. Bishop
Elma Bynum to D. L. Black 4/7/1886 by Rev. J. S. White
Florida Bynum to C. B. Butts 10/1887 by Rev. J. S. White, assisted by Rev. Bells.

BIRTHS

L. A. Bynum 11/29/1846
L. S. Bynum 4/29/1857
E. J. Bynum 10/23/1848
Florida Bynum 12/17/1860
Mary S. Bynum 6/5/1851

Barron-Bynum-Baxter Bible continued...

DEATHS

Leon Sumpter Bynum 12/21/1887
Mary Sophia Bynum 11/26/1916
Mrs. C. L. Bynum 1/24/1903
Florida Betts 5/12/1899
Mrs. Elma Bynum Black 1/25/1917
James Bynum 2/22/1897
Glenmore Benjamin Barron 5/18/1931
Mrs. Lucy Anna Bynum Barron 10/15/1933

Andrew Barter 3rd had following children:

John H. Baxter 3/2/1785-11/18/1810 in Mississippi Territory
James Baxter b. 1786
Thomas N. Baxter 1787-1844 m- Mary Wiley 1815. She was b.11/25/1798-d. 1869
Andrew Baxter 1790-1793
Cynthia Baxter 1792-1793
Eliza Thomson b. 1796

Mary Baxter d. 9/10/1846
Eli H. b. 1778
Richard 1801-1807
Mary Laird b. 1794 m. William Green Springer 1808

THOMAS FENNS LOVETT, SR. BIBLE
Owner: Mary Helen Mobley Kitchen
Rt. 1, Box 412, Palm Harbor, Fla.

Thomas Fenns Lovett, Sr. b. 8/22/1771 South Carolina-d. 4/9/1830 m. Rebecca Bonnell 9/16/1774-7/30/1848 (daughter of Anthony Bonell 8/3/1743-11/19/1804)
Thomas F. Lovett, Jr. b. 9/30/1792 on Beaverdam Creek Nancy Lovett, his wife, b. 4/1/1799

BIRTHS of Children of Thomas F. and Nancy Lovett
Rebecca Lovett 11/16/1816 Goshen
Mary McKinny Lovett 1/18/1819 Mobley's Pond
Martha Crawford Lovett 2/22/1821 Pine Thicket
John Forbes Lovett 4/3/1823 Pine Thicket
Candace Lovett 7/29/1825
Elizabeth Lovett 12/30/1828
Thomas F. Lovett Jr. 8/3/1832
Berrien M. Lovett 1/3/1835
Louisiana Lovett 4/4/1838
William Henry Lovett 10/15/1840

W. H. HIERS BIBLE Of Colleton Co., S. C.

BIRTHS

Julia Elizaheth Hiers 2/23/1849
Wm Abraham Hiers 5/18/1855
Cornelia Ellot Hiers 2/24/1851
Joseph Abraham Hiers 5/18/1855
Wade Hampton Hiers 4/9/1853
Rote 7/23/1871 by W. H. Hiers, 98 yrs. old, Colleton Co., S. C.

JOHN CHRISTIAN MARTIN BIBLE
Of Charleston, South Carolina
Owner: Mrs. Erma Martin Couch, Luthersville, Georgia

John Christian Martin 7/2/1786-1/24/1835 m. 2/24/1808 Ann Catherine Norman 11/19/1786-3/1869

Their Children:

Thirsa Ann Martin 11/15/1808-8/24/1887 m. Joseph Absalom Williams
Elizabeth Martin 6/24/1810-8/28/1810
Henry Martin 8/5/1811-9/22/1887 m. Susan Ligan Molmen 10/17/1839
Jane Ropers Martin 8/9/1813-10/3/1888 m. William Harrison Wright 10/2/1840
Mariah Martin b. 12/19/1815 m. 3/6/-- John Adam Summers
Benjamin Monroe Martin 4/8/1818-6/15/1900 m. Mary Ann Kobb
John Christian Martin II 3/10/1820-3/1111908 m. Emily Bates 12/27/1847
Mary Margaret Martin 9/8/1823-9/7/1880 m. Reuben Whitten Keith 8/1838
Nicholas Martin 5/16/1825-2/21/1910 m. Elizabeth Wright 12/23/1858
Albert Martin 11/24/1826-3/17/1895 m. Martha Ann Walker 12/23/1856
Elizabeth Martin (named after a sister who d. in Infancy) 6/13/1829-10/31/1861 m. Benjamin Wortham 6/27/1844
Francis Marion Martin 7/1831-6/16/1928 m. Molly Braswell

DAVID MARTIN BIBLE
From: Rev. War Pension 8W9533

BIRTHS

Robert Martin 10/25/1791
William Aiken Martin 4/1801
James Martin 7/1793
Mary Martin 6/13/1803
David Martin 12/7/1795
Jean Meek Martin 9/18/1806
Elizabeth Reed Martin 11/25/1797
John Martin 4/1808
Rebeccah Martin 4/1799
Margaret Martin 9/16/1810
Edward Martin 2/14/1812

MARRIAGES

Elizabeth R. Martin to J. T Peden 9/12/1815
James Martin to Jean Peden 8/19/1817
Reheccah Martin to William Templeton 10/7/1819
David Martin to Agnes Teague
Margaret Martin to R. A. R. Hallum 4/23/1829
Robert Martin to Milburry Serena Daniel 9/18/1828
Mary Martin to John McClintock 2/4/1830
David Martin b. in Ireland
Margaret Martin b. Ireland - d. 9/7/1847
David Martin m. Margaret Aiken 12/29/1790
"No. 1 Aug.? Martin was b. June the 4 1847"

David Martin Bible, continued...

Note: William A. Martin, son of Mrs. Margaret Martin (d. 6/7/1847 aged 75 or 76) of David Martin who d. in 1812, applied for pension 1849, Fairfield Dist., S. C., Winnsboro. In 1852 the only living children of David to Margaret--William A., Robert, Elizabeth Peden, Mary McClintock, wife of John, Jane M. Smith Margaret Hallums. In 1850 Mrs. Mary Martin, sister of Margaret, said she was present at marriage of David and Margaret Martin in 1789.

JOSEPH MARTIN BIBLE
From: Rev. War Pension 186950

BIRTHS

Rachel Rawling 1/--
Joel Martin 1/2/1793
Rebecca Martin 8/12/1816, daughter of Joel Josiah Martin 10/31/1795
Daniel Martin 5/18/1786
Nancy Martin 9/5/1797
Joseph Martin 5/16/1787
Jerusha Licuzen Martin 1/10/1800 (or 1810)
James Martin 1/30/1789
Benjamin Martin 3/11/1792
John H. Martin 6/18/1811
Zadeyadlin Martin 12/14/1815
Elizabeth Martin 2/9/1800
Martin Martin 12/26/1814/15

Joseph Martin Bible continued...

James M. Martin 5/24/1813
Joseph Martin 2/24/1816/18, son of Daniel

Ages of Josiah Martin and Lovice, his wife

Eliza Rebiah Martin 3/31/1817
Nancy Martin 8/1/1819
John Theodore Brunson Martin 9/16/1821
Note: Joseph Martin applied for pension 12/6/1831, Richland Co.. S. C., Joannah Martin, wid., applied 12/26/1848, sd co. Joseph d. 4/24/1833. Joannah d. 1852. Children: David. Joseph, James. Thomas, Benjamin, Joel, Josiah, Nancy and Jerusha Martin. In 1852, son. Joel E.
Martin, made claim. In 1853, son, Daniel Martin, apptd H. G. McCutchen his atty.

Absalom Martin, his hand and pen

BIRTHS

Joab Martin 12/10/1819 or 1809
Sabre Martin 5/13/1759   Thomas Martin 5/18/1756

Ages of Their Children

William Martin 12/17/1776 -
John Martin 2/27/1784
Thomas Martin 12/12/1778
Elizabeth Martin 1/20/1787
John Martin 8/24/1781-3/16/1783
Valentine Martin 3/15/1790

Joseph Martin Bible continued...

Tinney Martin, daughter of Josiah and Elizabeth, 12/7/1825
Thomas Martin Sr. d. 5/13/1835, aged 80 yrs, 2 days Sarah Martin b. 2/8/180

Ages of Absalom Martin's Children

Joab Martin 12/10/1819 -
Josiah Martin 2/22/1824

Paley S. Martin 5/28/1821
Sabra A. Martin 11/30/1825
Valentine Martin 12/16/1822
Syrene B. Martin 3/4/---

Note: Thomas Martin applied for pension from York Dist., S. C., aged 76 yrs., b. 5/11/1756 Brunswick Co., Va. Lived In Chatham Co. N. C. when entered service; moved York Co. after war. Sabra Martin, wid., applied at York Dist., S. C., stating she m. soldier 3/1776 and that he d. 5/10/1835.

SAMUEL MARTIN BIBLE
Owner: Marine Andrews Rt. 1, 11308 Elm Drive
Hernando, Miss. 38632

Liser Jane Weldon d. 7/7/1837
Samuel Martin b. 7/24/1834

Liser Jane Weldon m. Samuel Martin 8/3/1854

Samuel Martin Bible continued...

BIRTHS

Henry Benjamin Martin 10/2/1855
Toliver Hison Martin 1/17/18--
Samuel Wilborn Martin 10/12/1860
Georgia Anner Zilpha Jane Martin 2/4/1863
William Jerryl Martin 3/8/1865
Shug Martin 10/3/1867
Joseph Frankling Martin 9/11/1868
Louts Fountain Martin 10/8/1870
Cary Idorah Martin 6/30/1872
Newton Claudius Martin 6/7/1874
Shug Martin d. 10/6/1867

WILLIAM IREDELL GORE BIBLE
Owner: B. Otis Prince, Columbia, S. C.

William Iredell Gore 12/25/1829-6/27/1903, son of William Henry
Gore and Edith Inman, 0. 6/8/1854 at Little River S. C., to
Rachel Ann Litchfield. 9/19/1833-
4/2/1914, daughter of Y. L. B. Litchfield and Mary Lewis

BIRTHS of Children of William I. Gore and Rachel A.

Julia Gore 5/14/1855 Darlington, S. C.
Victoria Gore 12/24/1856 at Little River, S. C.
Albert Gore 6/26/1858 at Little River, S. C.
Georgia Gore 2/18/1862 at Little River, S. C.
Fred Elias Owen, son of Elias Keith Owen and Sophia Hooper,

William Iredell Gore Bible continued...

b. Owego, N. Y. 3/25/1857 and m. in Wilmington, N. C. 4/24/1890
Virginia Gore b. at Little River, S. C. 12/24/1856, daughter of William Iredell Gore and Rachel Ann Litchfield. Their dau: Julia Gore Owen 11/21/1894-5/18/1896
"Red Elias Owen's mother, Sophia Cynthia Hooper, is a descendant of a signer of the Declaration of Independence."
Albert Gore, son of William Iredell Gore and Rachel Ann Litchfleld, b. 6/26/1858 at Little River, S. C. and m. at St. James Church, Wilmington, N. C. 12/27/1881 to Bessie Ledford. He d. 1/24/1895 and was bur. at Oakdale Cemetery, Wilmington, N.C.

BIRTHS of Children of Albert and Bessie Gore

Bessie Ledford Gore 1/24/1883
Thurber Gore 8/18/1887
Albert Gore, Jr. 1/8/1885
Milton Burr Gore 1/31/1889
William Iredell Core 4/9/1886
Mile Corbitt Gore 8/16/1890-5/15/1891

DAVID LYON THOMPSON BIBLE
"Purchased 1832 by David Lyon Thomson"

MARRIAGES

David Lyon Thomson to Christianna Margaretha Houseal in Beaufort, S. C., 5/31/1833, by Rev. D. Blythewood

David Lyon Thompson Bible continued...

John Mouseal Thomson, son of David L. and Christianna M. Thomson to Eugenia Eliza Purse in Barnwell Co., S. C. 5/31/1833

Anna Margaretta Thomson, daughter of David L. and C. M. Thomson to Stephen Smith Furse of
Barnwell Co., S. C., by Rev. James Walker. 7/10/1867 in Beaufort, S. C.
William Thomson, son of D. L. and C. M. Thomson to Anne Ellen Purse in Barnwell Co., S. C. 4/7/1868

Elspeth Lyon Thomson, daughter of D. L. and C. M. Thomson to James G. Garnett 9/11/1872

James Thomson, son of D. L. and C. M. Thomson to Addie Thomson at Blackville, S. C. 10/28/1870 by R. T., minister.
Robert Thomson, son of D. L. and C. H. Thomson, at Stonehaven, Scotland, 8/13/1872 to Margaret A. W. Crockett, by Rev. Watt

BIRTHS

David Lyon Thomson, eldest son of John and Elspeth Thomson, 10/14/1804 Stonehaven,NB.
Christianna Margaretha Houseal, daughter of John Bernard Houseal, M. 0. and Mary Talbird, his
wife, 2/19/1811 at High Park near Coosawahatchie, Beaufort District, S. C.

Children of David and Christianna H. Thomson
Mary Thomson 10/17/1834-10/19/1834 in Charleston, S. C.

David Lyon Thompson Bible continued...

Mary Talbird Thomson 8/7/1836 Beaufort, S. C.
John Houseal Thomson 11/14/1837 Beaufort, S. C.
David Lyon Thomson 7/16/1839 Beaufort, S. C.
William Thomson 1/18/1841 Beaufort, S. C.
Elspeth Lyon Thornson 10/10/1842 Beaufort, S. C.
Robert Thomson 1/14/1846 Beaufort. S. C.
Anne Margaretta Thomson 8/3/1847 Beaufort, S. C.
James Thomson 10/28/1848 Beaufort. S. C.
Chrlstianna Crawford Thomson 8/26/1860 Beaufort, S. C.
Bernard Helchlor Thomson 2/6/1853 Beaufort, S. C.

Children of Robert Thomson and wife, Margaret Crockett Thomson

Euphemia J. Thomson 10/10th Camden, S. C. - 10/20/1876 Augusta, Ga.
James C. Thomson 7/13/1876 Augusta, Ga.
Christianna B. Thomson 11/13/1878
Robert R. Thomson 2/23/1881
Margaret W. Thomson 9/18/1882
Emilie A. Thomson 12/31/1886
David L. Thomson 12/29/1889

DEATHS

Mary Thomson, Ist child of D. L. and C. H. Thomson, 0/19/1834 in Charleston, S. C.
Mary Talbird Thomson, 2nd child of D. L. and C. M. Thomson, 11/13/1838

David Lyon Thompson Bible continued...

In Beaufort, S. C. Mary Talbird, mother of C. N. Thomson and grandmother of D. L. and C. M. Thomson children, 10/19/1840 in Beaufort, S. C. Christianna Crawford Thomson, 10th child of I. and C. M. Thomson, 9/1/1851 Beaufort, S. C.
John Houseal Thomson, 3rd child of D. L. and C. M. Thomson, fell in Battle of Manasses in Va. 8/30/1862. David Lyon Thomson,
4th child of D. L. and C. M. Thomson, 10/27/1866 in Beaufort, S. C. at res. of his father.
William Thomson, 5th child; D. L. and C. M. Thomson. 5/23/1869 In Barnwell Co., near Martin,

S. C. David Lyon Thomson, eldest son of John and Elspeth Thomson, 6/4/1870, in Beaufort,
S.C., 65 yrs., 7 mos., 21 days Christianna Margaretta, wife of David L. Thomson. 4/24/1875,
Aiken, S. C., 64 yrs., 2 mos., 5 days, res. of Robert Thomson Bernard Melchior Thomson, 11th
child of D. L. and C. M. Thomson, 8/6/1880, Martin, Barnwell Co., S. C., son. of Stephen S.
Furse.James Thomson, 9th child of D.I and C. M. Thomson, 10/25/1898 in Blackville, S. C.,
aged 49 yrs., 11 mos., 27 days. Elspeth Lyon Thomson, 6th child of D. L. and C. M.
Thomson, 3/1928 in Savannah, Ga., aged 81 yrs., 7 mos., bur. Bonaventure, Savannah, Ga.
Margaret Ann Walton. wife of Robert Thomson Furse, 3/18/1928 in Savannah, Ga.. bur. in
Bonaventure, Savannah, Ga.
"D. L. Thomson landed in Savannah, Ga. 8 May and in Beaufort, S. C. on 12 May 1821"

WILLIAM PADGETT BIBLE
Of Colleton Co., South Carolina
Owner: B. B. Padgett, Andalusia, Ala.

William Padgett 10/28/1782-1/3/1843 m. Elizabeth 3/17/1803
Elizabeth, wife of William Padgett 5/15/1790-10/3/1856

BIRTHS of Their Children (all b. S. C.)

James Padgett 5/12/1804 m. Carolina Ward
Levina Padgett 10/23/1807
Anna Padgett 9/1/1805 m. 8/7/1828 John Teel

William Padgett 5/28/1811 m. Nancy ---
Martha Padgett 1/18/1818 m. Simeon Ward
Wiley Padget 10/18/1813
Ira Padgett 3/8/1816-9/9/1821

Henry Padgett 8/18/1820 m. Anna Diamond
Elijah Padgett 2/15/1823 m. Anna --
Elizabeth Padgett 5/17/1825-1/4/1850

SAMUEL LILES BIBLE

BIRTHS of Children of Samuel and Susannah Liles

Daniel H. Liles 1/3/1820
Abraham Liles 3/10/1830
Telitha O. J. Liles 9/17/1822
Narcissa Liles 1832
William M. Liles 4/20/1824

Micah Liles 1/28/1824
Obediah Liles 7/7/1826
George W. Liles 6/10/1836
Amanda K. Liles 7/1828
Judith M. Liles 1/1/1838

Samuel, son of John (Rev. War Soldier) and Nancy (Howard) Liles b. 5/8/1795 m. 2/2/1819
Susannah---

O. K. SMITH BIBLE
Owner: Mrs. Jo Parris Bishop
2909 Highland Ave., So.,
Apt. 911, Birmingham, Ala. 35205

O. K. Smith m. Nancy C. Peer 12/12/1844

BIRTHS

O. K. Smith 2/8/1824
Joseph E. Smith 12/28/1858
Nancy Caroline Smith 5/12/1827
Eliza J. Smith 12/10/1845
Martha Rebecca Elizabeth Smith 7/11/1861
Benjamin C. Smith 2/6/1850
William P. Smith 3/26/1847
Emma Lovenia Smith 1/18/1863
Nancy Annah Smith 2/26/1849
Sarah Emiline Smith 1/7/1865
Lula C. Smith 2/5/1867
James Franklin Smith 1/8/1855
Mary Frances Smith 3/8/1853
Charlie M. Smith 11/8/1869

Owen K. Smith 9/4/1871
Sara E. Smith 4/21/1873
Margaret Palestine Smith 12/2/1856

DEATHS

William P. Smith 12/17/1856, aged 1 yrs.
Nancy C. Smith 3/17/1907
Nancy Peer Smith 3/17/1907

WILLIAM WATTS BIBLE
Richland County Libary, Columbia, South Carolina

William Watts b- Ireland in 1768, and his wife Jane Thompson b. Ireland In 1768

BIRTHS of Their Children

Martha Watts 1792 m. Hugh Bell John Watts
Charles Watts m. Nancy A. Martin
Nancy Ann Kincaid Margaret Watts m. Thomas Ware
James Watts m. Margaret Bell
William Watts m. Nancy A. Martin
Charles Watts m. Mary Wyatt
Martin Jane Watts m. David Hamiter
Thomas Watts m Harriet Candy.
Jonathan Rabb m. Nancy Chappell and she was b.1824
William Estes b. 1773 m. Susanna Jaggers
Stephen Gibson Sr. m. in 1784 to Martha Pope

JAMES W. DUNKLIN, M. D. BIBLE
Of 4-Hole Swamp, St. Mathev's Parish,
Near Boneau, Berkley District, S. C.
Owner: Mrs. Douglas Earl Kirk
105 Valley Creek Church Rd., Selma, Ala. 36701

MARRIAGES

James W. Dunklin to Ann R. Clayton 4/6/1832, Lexington, Ky.
Hugh S. Paisley to Mary E. Dunklin 1/6/1856
Edward C. Dunklin to Mary A. Hardy 3/19/1857
William H. Pierce to Florence Dunklin 9/17/1867
Charles P. Dunklin to Angie E. Rives 12/15/1878
C. P. Dunklin To Alice E. Hardy 12/20/1877
T. N. Dudley to Berta D. Pierce 8/16/1885
Mary Camilla Pierce to S. B. Cowling 5/1/1887
Edna Faust Pierce to D. K. Love 3/20/1906

BIRTHS

James Washington, son of William and Anne Dunklin, 9/5/1805, Greenville District, S. C.
Ann Rebecca, daughter of Edward and Rachel Clayton, 8/21/1812, in Dover, Delaware

Children of James and Rebecca Clayton

Edward Clayton 6/23/1833 -Virgil James Clayton 9/26/1841

Mary Clayton 1/10/1835
Frances Temperance Clayton 6/28/1839
Florence Clayton 10/16/1845
William Herbert Clayton 3/6/1837
Charles Polk Clayton 11/18/-

Children of Edward and Mary Dunklin

Freemen Hardy Dunklin 6/9/1861
Mary Paisley Dunklin 10130/1865
Edward Clayton Dunklin 4/28/1863
Rebecca Clayton Dunklin 9/30/1869

Children of William and Florence Pierce

Herberta Pierce 11/21/1868
James Augustus Pierce 4/4/1876
Mary Camilla Pierce 3/6/1871
W. Harry Pierce 8/31/1878
Maude Pierce 12/12/1872
Edna Faust Pierce 7/20/1886

Children of Charles and Angie Dunklin

Claudia Dunklin 11/4/189
Charles Raymond Dunklin 9/6/1871
James Herbert Dunklin 10/11/1873
Angie L. Dunklin 11/12/1875-8/24/1880
Oscar Leonard Dunklin 6/29/1881
Charles Elbert Dunklin 1/23/1879-3/18/1879, aged 2 mos.
Willie Clayton Dunklin 1/28/1880-10/1/1880, aged 8 mos., 2 days

Children of Herberta and I. N. Dudley

Florence Doling Dudley 8/7/1886
Willa Pierce Dudley 9/24/1896
Willie Nell Dudley 4/27/1888
Anne Faust Dudley 9/6/1898

Frank Gordon Dudley 2/24/1890
Julia Myrtle Dudley 9/30/1901
John Augustus Dudley 10/24/1893-1/16/1901

DEATHS

William Herbert Dunklin lost at Battle of Chancellorsville, Va. on morning of 5/3/1863
J. W. Dunklln 10/9/1872
Frances Temperance Dunklin 5/8/1840
A. R. (Ann Rebecca) Dunklln 3/21/1883
E. C. Dunklin Sr. 112/1900 in Florida
Mary Paisley 2/1902
Florence D. Pierce 11/27/1925
William H. Pierce 10/19/1920
Charles P. Dunklin 12/1920
T. N. Dudley 8/23/1910
James W. Dunklin, Jr. 7/21/1863
Mary Paisley Dunklin 11/1/1865
Charles Raymond Dunklin 7/23/1874
John Augustus, son of Herberta and T. N. Dudley, 11/6/1901
Frank Gordon, son of Herberta and T. N. Dudley, 9/16/1954
Wills Pierce, son of Herberta and T. N. Dudley, 10/5/1859
Willie Nell, daughter of Herberta and T. N. Dudley, 9/24/1963
Herberta (Dudley) Mitchell 8/16/1969
Angie R. Dunklin, wife of C. P. Dunklin, 5/17/1877
James Augustus, son of W. H. and F. D. Pierce, 2/8/1878

CAPT. JOHN GLAZIER BIBLE
Richland County Library, Columbia, South Carolina

John Glazier b. 3/9/1755 and his wife, Elizabeth Edwards b. 9/5/1759

Capt. John Glazier Bible continued...

BIRTHS of Our Children

Elizabeth Edwards Glazier 4/4/1782
Rebecca Glazier 12/15/1791
Nancy Glazier 6/2/1785
Renthea Glazier 7/27/1793
Mary Glazier 11/2/1787

MARRIAGES

Elizabeth E. Glazier to Arthur Yarborough, 1804
Nancy Glazier to Nathaniel Holley, 1806
Renthea Glazier to John Rabb 2/2/1808
Rebecca Glazier to William May 5/1811

DEATHS

Capt. John Glazier 12/14/1831
Rebecca May 12/8/1832
Elizabeth E. Glazier 1/20/1840
Renthea Rabb 2/22/1852
Elizabeth E. Yarborough 1822

JOHN RABB BIBLE
Richland County Library, Columbia, SC

John Rabb b. 1/6/1781, son of James Rabb and Hannah Barnett

Renthea Glazier b. 7/17/1793, daughter of John Glazier and Elizabeth Edwards

John Rabb Bible continued...

John Rabb m. Renthea Glazier 2/2/1808

BIRTHS of Children of John and Renthea Rabb

Elizabeth Edwards Rabb 5/6/1809
William Rabb 2/4/1817
Harriet Rabb 4/16/1815
James Bell Rabb 6/17/1810
Sarah A. Rabb 2/2/1820

Robert Rabb 4/26/1822
Martha C. Rabb 5/26/1818
Patience Rabb 12/30/1811
John Glazier Rabb 10/1/1813
Louise Rabb 7/26/1823 m. 1849 --- Kinard
Mary E. Rabb 7/5/1825 m. Elisha Ragsdale
Calvin W. Rabb 10/15/1829 m. Malissa King
Thomas U. Rabb 7/6/1833 m. Keziah Robinson
Joel Rabb 6/17/1836 m. 1/14/1848 Charity Crosby
Elizabeth E. Rabb to Thurston Crumpton, 1832
Patience Rabb to Daniel Dansby, 1836
Harriett Rabb to James Montgomery, 1841
Martha C. Rabb to John Holley
Sarah A. Rabb to William English, removed to Starkville, Miss.
Robert Rabb to Susan Proctor, 1846
John Glazier Rabb b. 10/1/1813 to Nancy Kincaid Watts 3/12/1840

John Rabb Bible continued...

BIRTHS of Children of John Glazier Rabb and Nancy

John Watts Rabb 3/24/1841
Edwin Belzer Rabb 7/27/1850
Killed--Gaines Mill 5/30/1872
Jessie Mary Rabb 5/1/1853
James Kincaid Watts Rabb 9/26/1843
Horace Rabb 5/27/1855
William Clarence Rabb 3/10/1846
Nina Rabb 2/6/1858
Virginia Rabb 5/27/1848-5/13/1858
Charles Kincaid Rabb 2/12/1860

DEATHS

John Glazier Rabb 2/26/1872
Jessie M. Miller 12/17/1903
Nancy K. Watts. wife of John G. Rabb 4/11/1900
William Clarence Rabb 8/28/1929
Charles Kincaid Rabb 3/24/1917
Kate Henderson Rabb 6/5/1908
Lily Provence. wife of Charles K. Rabb. 3/28/1932

MARRIAGES

James Kincaid Rabb to Kate Henderson of Laurens Co., S. C., 1/5/1865
William Clarence Rabb to Mary Holley, 1871
Jessie Mary Rabb to Rev. W. H. Miller 4/17/1879
Horace Rabb to Mary Jefferson Walker 1/10/1873

John Rabb Bible continued...

Charles K. Rabb to Lily Provence 12/4/1879
Nina Rabb to Warren P. Castles 11/2/1892

DEATHS

John Rabb, son of James and Hannah Rabb, 10/1/1844
Renthea Glazier Rabb 2/22/1858
John Bell Rabb 8/29/1841
John Glazier Rabb 2/26/1872
William Rabb 9/25/1839
Calvin Rabb 8/8/1864

JOSHUA DAVIS BIBLE
Owner: Mrs. James A. Mackey
Oak Hill Apts, 0-4, 11411
Columbia Pike, Silver Springs, Maryland

Joshua Davis 11/4/1787-8/31/1859, aged 72 yrs, 10 mos.
Esther (Gamble) Monford Davis 6/1/1788-6/5/1876, aged 87 yrs.

Joshua Davis m. Esther (Gamble) Monford 4/29/1814

BIRTHS

Ann Johnson Monford, daughter of John Monford and Esther, his wife, 2/12/1811-9/1821
Henry Jefferson Davis 2/12/1816-1/13/1875

Joshua Davis Bible continued...

Sarah Elizabeth Davis 5/22/1818-7/1823
Martha Lucinda Davis 12/28/1820
Thomas Allen Davis 3/16/1822-10/2/1831
Ann Elizabeth Davis 4/17/1827
William Booker Wright Davis 3/26/1830
Daniel G. Smith m. Martha L. (Lucinda) Davis 12/21/1837
Henry Jefferson Davis m. Mary A. G. (Ann Graves) Wood 1/25/1844
Esther Eliza Davis. daughter of Henry Jefferson and Mary A. G. Davis, b. 12/13/1850

Jesse Wood m. Anne E. (Elizabeth) Davis 2/20/1845

BIRTHS of Children of Jesse and Anne E. Wood

Martha Josephine Wood 5/7/1847
Thomas Jefferson Wood 6/7/1849
William Davis m. Zentippe Wood 1/10/1859
Bettie Gamble, daughter of Zantippe and William Davis b. 10/16/1859

GEORGE ROSS, SR. BIBLE
DAR, Nancy Anderson Chapter, Lubbock, Tx.

George Ross m. 10/12/1769 Isabella Montgomery

BIRTHS of Their Children (all b. S. C.)

Maryland Jane Ross 12/1/1771
Catherine Ross 10/10/1782
Margaret Ross 6/12/1775

George Ross, Sr. Bible continued...

George Ross 11/11/1776
John Ross 10/29/1784
Rebecca Ross 2/15/1777
George Ross 11/22/1778
Isabella Montgomery Ross 2/16/1753-6/2/1833
James Ross 8/23/1780-4/1785

MARRIAGES

Jane Ross to Humphrey Hunter
Margaret Ross to Thomas Patton 12/6/1792
Catherine Ross to James Davis 6/27/1799
Rebecca Ross to John Kennedy -/19/1795
George Ross (Jr.) to Sophia Elmore 5/31/1816
John Ross to Betty (Elizabeth) Ferguson 3/15/1810
Sophia Elmore (wife of George Ross, Jr.) b. 10/18/1794

RANDOLPH S. MURFF
Owner: Miss Jo Ballentine
Ware Shoals. South Carolina

BIRTHS of Children of Randolph S. and Caroline Gaines Murff

Caty C. Murff 1/10/1809 - Malinda Murft 10/25/1812
Wyly Murff 11/30/1809?

Randolph S. Murff m. Elizabeth Hannan 2/28/1816

Randolph S. Murff continued...

BIRTHS of Children of Randolph S. And Elizabeth Murff

Helena-Murff 2/28/1817 -
John Randolph Murff 8/2/1826
Waldemar Murff 8/31/1818
Elizabeth Martha Manson Murff
Minus Hillery Murff 6/8/1820 7/5/1828
Uriah Hilton Murff 11/21/1821
Washington Murff 8/30/1830
Malachi Andrew Murff 12/18/1823
Margaret Murff 12/15/1832
Randolph S. Murff b. 12/2/1784 (father of above 12 children)

PHILLIP PORTER BIBLE
Owner: Mrs. John Brock, Pickens, S. C.

Phillip Porter b. 7/1/1764
Mary Smith, wife of Philip Porter, b. 1769

BIRTHS of Their Children

Elizabeth Porter 2/25/1784 -
John Porter 3/20/1796
Hugh Porter 2/14/1786
Joseph Porter 6/2/1798
Rebecca Porter 2/25/1788
Baziel Smith Porter 9/2/1801
William Porter 2/20/1790

Phillip Porter Bible continued...

Job Porter 4/8/1804
James Porter 3/20/1792
Thomas Porter 12/2/1807
Martha (Patsy) Porter 4/5/1794
Mary Ann Porter 2/12/1814

THOMAS BRADWELL BIBLE
Owner: Mrs. Annie Campbell Bradwell, Bainbridge, Georgia

Thomas Bradwell, father of Dr. Daniel Bradwell, b. 3-mi. of Charleston, S. C., d.
9/1857 Charleston, S. C. Wife, Catharine Durr, d. 1859 Charleston. S. C.
Dr. Daniel Bradwell b. 9/5/1800 Cotton Dist., Mathews Parish, 10 mi. of Pond Bluff, on
Plantation of Gen. Francls Marion on Santee River, d. 2/22/1881 Statesville, N. C.
Louis Phillip Taylor Bradwell b. Gadsden Co., Fln. 1/6/1847
James Sumter Bradwell b. Gadsden Co., Fla. 3/7/1849
Jane McCutcheon Gordon b. 8/22/1806 Williamsburg Dist., S. C.
Mary Catharine Bradwell h. 12/30/1829 Kingstree, S. C.
Matilda Caroline Bradwell b. 11/8/1841 on B. River, Williamsburg Dist., S. C.

Emily Angeline Bradwell b. 12/30/1833 Knoxville, La.
Thomas Maclon Bradwell b. 2/5/1836 Houston Co., Ga.
Alexander Moultry Bradwell b. 11/7/1838 Houston Co., Ga.
Eleanor Jane Barnwell b. 7/25/1841 Houston Co., Ga.
Isaac Gordon Bradwell b. 3/15/1843 Houston Co., Ga.

Thomas Bradwell Bible continued...

MARRIAGES

Daniel Bradwell to Jane McCutcheon Gordon 11113/1828
Daniel Bradwell to Mrs. Mary N. Baker 7/20/1858
Daniel Bradwell to Mrs. Isabella Watts 5/16/1871 Statesville, Iredell Co., N. C.
Moselle M. Griffin to James Sumter Bradwell 7/6/1875. Annie Eleanor Campbell to James Sumter Bradwell 10/6/1910
Leiler Remelle Bradwell to W. W. Palmer 7/21/1897
Irene Gordon Bradwell to Arthur Franklin Paramore 10/25/1898

BIRTHS of Grandchildren

Francis Orland Bradwell, 1st b. of Moselle M. Griffin Bradwell James Sumter Bradwell 10/2/1876-6. same day
Irene Gordon Bradwell, 2nd daughter of Moselle M. Griffin and James Sumter Bradwell, 4/10/1878
Lelle Ramelle Mos. 11/6/1879
Herbert Durr Bradwell 10/20/1885-12/28/1885
Moselle M. Griffin and James Sumter Bradwell 10/2/1898 in Bainbrldge, Ga.
Marion Gordon Bradwell, son of Annie Eleanor Campbell and James Sumter Bradwell, 3/5/1911 in Bainbridge, Ga.

DEATHS

Jane McCutcheon Gordon 9/20/1857, aged 51 yes. She lived with her husband 29 yrs.
Thomas Bradwell 9/1857, Charleston Dist., S. C., within 3 miles of his place of birth

Thomas Bradwell Bible continued...

Catharine Durr, wife of Thomas Bradwell, d. same place as her husband in 1859
Louis Philip Taylor Bradwell 2/26/1912 at Ft. Myers, Fla.
Dr. Daniel Bradwell 2/22/1881 in Statesville, N. C., aged 80 yrs., 3 mos., 17 days
Mary Catherine Bradwell, consort of Thomas Scott, 4/30/1884
Moselle M. Griffin, wife of James Sumter Bradwell, 6/1/1899
V. W. Palmer, husband of Leila Ramelle Bradwell, 2/7/1901
James Sumter Bradwell 2/6/1921

ELIJAH WYATT BIBLE
Owner: Miss Willie Wystt (decd), Nation. Alabama

Elijah Wyatt, son of William, b. 2/2/1774 Prince William Co., Va.-d. Anderson Co., S. C.
2/18/1858 m. 9/15/1793 Fairfax Co.,
Mary Grigsby Foster b. 5/3/1773 Fairfax Co., Va.-d. Anderson Co., S. C. 3/5/1858

BIRTHS of Their Children

Eliza Wyatt 3/7/1796-1/11/1882 m. 10/28/1817 William Mattison
Edna Esther Wyatt 12/20/1798-8/1651 m. 11/24/1817 Ephraim Mitchell
James Feater Wyatt 5/1/1801-3/10/1868 m. 6/30/1821 Nancy Rosamond Pyles
William Newton Wyatt 8/29/1803-3/10/1868 m. 2/26/1840 Eliza Miller
Redmond Grigsby Wyatt 5/22/1806-10/17/1857 m. 9/15/1829

Elijah Wyatt Bible continued...

Elizabeth Dunn Richey m. 9/30/1842 Eleanor Ann Seawright
Mildred Lunni Wyatt 8/16/1808-11/15/1893 m. 8/31/1844 Abner Cox (his 2nd wife)
Susan Cecile Wyatt 5/3/1811-9/10/1851 m. 7/30/1833
Elias Key Harriet Wyatt 3/15/1914-6/17/1874 m. 11/7/1839 John Mauldin
Malinda Wyatt 9/20/1817-10/27/1887 m. 2/8/1838 Hugh C. Alexander

JOHN DAVID MILLER BIBLE
Owner: Mrs. E. D. Young, 6170 Eastshore Drive, Columbia, South Carolina

John David Miller m. 10/25/1779 Jane Righton, daughter of McCulley Righton
John David Miller, son of John David and Jane Miller, b. 7/30/1780, d. same day
John David Miller m. Anne Bounetheau 8/10/1872, daughter of Peter Bounetheau

BIRTHS of Children of John David and Anne Miller

Peter Bounetheau Miller 8/2?T1783-9/6/1783, aged 15 days
James Anderson Miller 12/12/1784
John David Miller 6/8/1786-12/7/1791, aged 5 yrs., 6 pea. Anne
Judith Miller 2/2/1788
Samuel Stuit Miller 2/13/1790
Mary Magdalene Grimball Miller 4/20/1793

John David Miller Bible continued...

Rachel Alexander Miller 12/29/1794
John Bounetheau Miller 12/15/1796
Maria Juliana Miller 8/17/1798

ANTHONY FOSTER GOLDING BIBLE

Owner: Mrs. Charles H. Duke, 2411 Monroe Sr., Columbia, S. C.

Anthony F. Golding, son of Anthony Golding by his 2nd wife, Isabella Reid, m. Caroline Matilda Brown, daughter of Jacob Roberts Brown and his wife, Chrlstini Neely of Newberry Co., S. C.

BIRTHS

Anthony Foster Golding 8/10/1791
Caroline Matilda Brown 12/11/1793

Their Children:

Marquis Lafayette Golding 7/17/1817
Clementina Brown Golding 12/25/1818
Sallie Morgan Golding 2/1/1821
Christina Neely Golding 3/3/1823
John Reid Golding 12/30/1824
Henry Laurens Golding 2/11/1827
Thomas Willis Golding 12/20/1829
Nancy Campbell Golding 8/14/1831
John Brown Golding 11/2/1833

Robert Cunningham Golding 11/11/1835
Caroline Matilda Elizabeth Golding 11/18/1837
Pamela Cunningham Golding 11/16/1839

DEATHS

Isabella Golding, my mother, 6/21/1822
Thomas Wadsworth Golding, my brother, 2/1/1822
John Reid Golding, my brother, 7/16/1824
Rachel, my sister, wife of Samuel Caldwell, 7/18/1826

DEATHS of Children

Marquis Lafayette Golding 11/4/1826
Sallie Morgan Golding 9/14/1824
John Reid Golding 9/10/1830
Nanny Campbell Golding 1/14/1833
Thomas Willis Golding 1/18/1835
Henry Laurens Golding 2/3/1850
Christina Neely Golding "Our Little Kitty" 8/22/1846

John Brown Golding 8/28/1860
Caroline H. E. Smith Colton 11/18/1900
Pamela C. Fogarty 6/2/1914

HUGH McGILL BIBLE

"Hugh McGill, the father of the McGill family in Williamsburg Co., S. C. was married to Sarah Gordon 10th June 1732 and departed this life 30 June 1857 in the 50th year of his age and was married 23 years to Sarah Gordon, his wife."

BIRTHS of Children of Hugh and Sarah McGill

Hugh McGill Bible continued...

John McGill 4/1/1734
Roger McGill 8/28/1742
Mary McGill 1/20/1738
James McGill 10/28/1744
Jean McGill 9/12/1740
Samuel McGill 9/12/1747
Sarah McGill 8/15/1750
Sarah Dicky d. 12/24/1759, aged 49 yrs.

HON. WILLIAM HENRY CANNON, SR. BIBLE
Owner: Mrs. Walter Gregg, Wallace, S. C.

BIRTHS

William H. Cannon Sr. 4/25/1783
Sarah Ann Cannon, wife of William H. Cannon, 12/28/1787

BIRTHS of Children of William H. and Sarah Ann Cannon

William H. Cannon 4/24/1783
Jane Cannon 4/25/1784-8/9/1793
Susanna Wilson Cannon 3/26/1786-8/23/1793
Hugh E. Cannon 9/4/1787
George James Cannon 2/6/1789-8/23/1793
Mary Cannon 11/26/1791
Elizabeth Cannon 6/30/1790-6/20/1791
Sarah Cannon 10/5/1793-1/12/1793
Robert Augustus Cannon 2/17/1795-1/23/1798

Hon. William Henry Cannon, Sr. Bible continued...

John Julius Cannon 10/19/1796-9/15/1822

BIRTHS of Children of Henry Cannon and Susanna Cherry, wid. Of George Cherry. They m. 8/14/1798 by Rev. E. Pugh Cherry

Susan Morville Cannon 1/16/1800
Augustus Swan Cannon 12/31/1801
Sarah Ann Cannon, wife of William H. Cannon, 9/23/1824
William H. Cannon, Sr. 12/2/1843

MARRIAGES

William H. Cannon to Sarah Ann McTyer 5/13/1804 by Rev. James Coleman
Joseph A. Jolly to Susan N. Cannon 1/15/1823
William H. Cannon to Ann Sanders, wid. of Jordan Sanders, 6/21/1825 by Rev. Campbell
Simon Connell to Mary Cannon, daughter of Henry Cannon, 10/10/1805
Hugh E. Cannon to Ann Muldow 10/5/1809
James Brown to Susanna W. Cannon 3/17/1819
John J. Cannon to Ann --- 2/1821

SAMUEL D. McGILL BIBLE

Roger McGill, son of Hugh McGill and Elizabeth Wesbury. m. 2/23/1767

BIRTHS of Children

Hugh McGill 12/30/1767
Burr McGill 2/23/1777-d.y.
Jean McGill 9/8/1769
John McGill 1/2/1779
Mary McGill 1/7/1783
Martha McGill 8/8/1771
Samuel McGill 2/25/1781
Mary McGill 5/29/1773-d.y.
Elizabeth McGill, wife of Roger McGill, d. 7/24/1787 in child bed of two sons and they departed the same day

JAMES MATTISON BIBLE
Andrea Files, Columbia, S. C.

James Mattison 8/20/1762-7/3/1849
His wife - Frances Wyatt 12/23/1767-2/2/1840

BIRTHS of Their Children

William Mattison 8/21/1788-1/12/ 1873-m. Elizabeth Acker
Presley Mattison 10/27/1789-11/2/1801
Malinda Mattison 1/19/1793-d. Case Co., Ga. m. Thomas Townsend

James Mattison Bible continued...

Elizabeth Mattison 5/22/1794 m. Asbury Carpenter
Lettice Nicoll Mattison 1/2/1796-6/5/1856 m. Matthew Gambrell
James Mattison, Jr.12/4/1797-4/11/1837 m. Mary King Stark
Anna Mariah Mattison 8/30/1799-10/15/1883 m. William Smith, son of Nimrod and Lettice Wyatt Smith
Mary Mattison 1/18/1801-8/11/1884 m. Joseph Elvire Cox
Mahala Mattison 9/27/1802-1/2/1806
Abner Mattison 4/24/1804-5/10/1805
Mahala Mattison 8/4/1806-5/11/1879 m. James Gambrell
Daniel Mattison 11/9/1807-9/13/1869 m. Anne Southerland

Wyatt Mattison 10/19/1809-5/8/1878 m. Nancy Clement
    On scrap of paper:
Lettice N. Mattison m. 5/11/1815 Matthew Gambrell
James Gambrell d. 4/3/1886
Joseph Elvira Cox, son of Elizabeth Davis and Reuben Cox, 12/29/1799-12/5/1883 m. 11/21/1822 to Mary Mattison

URIUS J. MATTISON BIBLE
Owner: Thomas J. Chatworthy, Honea Path, South Carolina

Urius Jackson Mattison b. 7/24/1820-8. near Richmond. Va. 8/13/1864 in Confederate Army, m. 10/27/1842 at Honea Path, S. C. to - Sarah Maulding 12/17/1820-7/5/1909, daughter of Elizabeth Symmes and Benjamin Maulding

BIRTHS of Children of Urius and Sarah Mattison

Margaret Elizabeth Mattison 9120/1843-1/20/1926 .. 12/6/1859

Thomas John Chatworthy, Sr.
William Mattison 10/27/1844-8/30/1849
Wyatt Maulding Mattison 8/3/1846-8/5/1846
Mary F. Mattison 6/11/1847-11/14/1890 m. 11/27/1870
Warren S. Fleming

Ann Paralee Mattison 6/10/1850-5/15/1933 m. 8/24/1890
Herion Ephraim Mitchell, m. 2d J. Polk Cox
William Robert Mattison 1/8/1852-7/16/1927 m. · 2/8/1874
Ella Angeline Brock
Savanna Eudora Mattison 11/1/1854-4/8/1865
James Lawrence Mattison 2/15/1857-5/27/1868
Gabriel Walter Mattison 6/15/1859-11/10/1926
Benjamin Newton Mattison 7/11/1861-8/5/1887

BENJAMIN HARRISON BIBLE of Edgefield Co.
Owner: Mrs. Douglas Smith, 3185 Lenox Rd., Atlanta, Ga.
Benjamin m. Mary Harrison 12/11/1794 Edgefield Co., S. C.

BIRTHS

Benjamin Harrison 2/12/1769
Mary "Polly" Harrison, his wife, 3/31/1777 m. 12/11/1794

Their Children:

John Harrison 1/12/1797
Nancy Harrison 4/10/1808
Heartwell Harrison 7/19/1799
James Henry Harrison 8/23/1819
Polly Harrison 5/28/1811

Benjamin Harrison Bible continued...

Edmund Harrison 12/18/1801
Benjamin Harrison 2/9/1815
Steuart Harrison 7/15/1804

DEATHS

Benjamin Harrison, Gent., 9/19/1829, aged 60 yrs.
Mary Harrison, wife of Benjamin, 5/8/1854, aged 77 yrs.
Stewart Harrison, son of Mary and Benjamin, 9/18/1854
E. W. Hnrrison, son of Mary and Benjamin, 9/29/1830
Heartwell Harrison, son of Mary and Benjamin, 5/24/1856
He was b. in Edgefield Dist., S. C., d. in Macon Co., Ala.

DANIEL MOSELEY BIBLE

BIRTHS

Daniel Moseley 3/16/1787
Amelia Moseley 7/26/1821
Mary Moseley 9/14/1791
--id Moseley -12/1824
Hampton Moseley 1/2/1811
Harriett Moseley 6/23/1813
Dandridge Moseley 9/19/1826
Mildred Moseley 4/10/1819
Thomas R. Moseley 3/29/1830
John W. Batte 11/16/1870
Augustus Moseley 4/7/181-
John Moseley 1/5/1832

Daniel Moseley Bible continued...

Richard Moseley 4/8/1817

James Henry Batte 1/1837

MARRIAGES

Daniel Moseley to Mary Copeland 3/6/1809
Edward L. Batte to Amelia Moseley 2/25/1836

DEATHS

Hampton Moseley 10/12/1817
Wade Moseley 2/8/1870
Sally Moseley, wife of ----Moseley -/3/1847
Thomas Moseley 2/10/1870
Armentia Jeters, daughter of Daniel and Sally Moseley, 1/12/1849
Polly Jeters, wife of G. Jeters, 1/26/1848
James Batte 10/2/1890
Daniel Moseley 5/12/185-, aged 69 yrs., 1 mo., 26 days

SAMUEL DAVIS McGILL BIBLE

Samuel McGill, son of Roger McGill, m. Mary Ann Sanders 4/21/1806

BIRTHS of Their Children

Elizabeth Amelia McGill 8/12/1807

Samuel Davis McGill Bible continued...

John Sanders McGill 11/2/1808-d.y.
Jennet Louisa McGill 1/17/1810
Samuel Gadsden McGill 1/21/1812-d.y.
Drucilla McGill 2/12/1813-d.y.
Mary McCottry McGill 10/7/1814
Jane Caroline McGill 3/1816
Sidney Spencer McGill 1/14/1824
Martha Emeline McGill 10/22/1817-d.y.
Samuel Davis McGill 2/12/1819
William Wilson McGill 3/5/1821-d.y.
Mary Ann Sanders McGill 6/22/1822

Amanda M. McGill 1/3/1826-d.y.
Minto Witherspoon McGill 2/26/1828
Elizabeth Amelia McGill m. J. T. Scott 4/27/1826. They moved to Arkansas 1860. Mr. Scott died on the way.

Jennet Louisa McGill m. L. J. Snowden 6/6/1826 and d. in child bed 3/5/1827, bur. In Indiiantown Church Yard.
Mary McCottry McGill m. J. G. Burgess 4/24/1834. Her husband d. in 1855 and In 1866 - she moved to Arkansas.
Jane Caroline McGill m. W. R. Scott 4/24/1834. After her husband's death she moved to Arkansas and d. 1863.
Samuel Davis McGill m. L. E. Pressley 3/14/1844 and is only direct descendant living in this county.
Mary Ann Sanders McGill m. A. J. Murphy 12/13/1843. After her let husband's death she again married and died in Arkansas.

Sidney Spencer McGill m. M. E. Duke 7/25/1844, d. at his place on Cedar Swamp 7/24/1848, bur. Indiantovn Church Yard.

Samuel Davis McGill Bible continued...

Minto Witherspoon McGill m. S. E. McIntosh 12/21/1848, moved to Arkansas in 1857 and is parent of 10 children. Of those who died young:
Samuel Gadson McGill 10/3/1814, bur. in Indiantown Grave Yard
Martha Emeline McGill 9/29/1819, bur. in Indlantown Grave Yard
Drucilla McGill 9/10/1823, in her 11th yrs., bur. Indiantown Graveyard.
Amanda M. McGill 12/13/1826 in her Ist yr., bur. IndianTown Graveyard.
William Wilson McGill 9/21/1831 in his 11th yr., bur. lndiantown Grave Yard
Mary Ann McGill, wife of Samuel McGill and mother of above 14 children, b. at Muddy Creek 12/12/1785-8. 5/7/1850, bur. Indiantown Church Yard.

MILLS BIBLE of Camden
Owner: Mrs. Laurens T. Mills
Camden, South Carolina

Richard Baker 2/5/1732/3-10/4/1769
Mary Stol 3/15/1733/4-3/4/1796
Richard Baker m. Mary Stol 12/12/1754 by Rev. Mr. Clarke

BIRTHS of Children of Richard and Mary Baker

Richard Baker 12/10/1755
Mary Baker 1/29/1760

Mills Bible continued...

Sarah Baker 2/12/1757, baptised by Rev. Mr. Robert Smith.
Sureties: Sarah Baker,
Susannah Sommers, Christopher Rodgers
Edward North b. 3/20/1747 m. Sarah Baker 3/4/1776 by Rev. Mr.Oliver Hart in Eutaw

BIRTHS of Children of Edward and Sarah North

Edward Washington North 5/15/1778, baptised 11/13/1778 by Rev. Mr. Charles Frederick
Moereau at St. Michael's Church, Charleston. Sureties: Mrs. Alice Baker, John Baker, Edward Trescott

George Tucker North 7/6/1779, baptised 11/24/1779 by Rev. Mr. Charles Frederick Morreau at home). Sureties: Sarah and Edward North, Capt. David Burch of Bermuda. George T. North d. 7/10/1780

Richard Baker North 12/26/1780, baptised by Rev. Mr. Robert Smith 1/15/1782 at Philadelphia

John Laurens North 9/30/1782 in Philadelphia, baptised at same place by Rev. Mr. Robert Smith
Sarah Tucker North 6/16/1784
Mary Elizabeth North 12/29/1786
Tucker North 9/15/1790, baptized privately by Rev. Henry Purcell

Daughter of Edward and Sarah North b. dead 12/6/1792

Mills Bible continued...

Edward North d. 8/21/1798, aged 51 yrs.. 5 mos., 1 day
Sarah North, wife of Edward North, 7/26/1797, aged 40 yrs., 5 mos, 14 days

MARRIAGES

Edward Washington North to Mrs. Jane Caroline Parker 3/11/1802 in Georgia
John Laurens North to Eliea Elliott Drayton 12/31/1805 by Rev. Edward Jenklns at Mrs. Fosters, Ring Street
Dr. Edward Darrell Smith to Sarah Tucker 11/11/1802 by Rev. Mr. Hollingshead
Eliza Jane Smith, daughter of Edward and Sara Smith, b. 8/17/1806
Benjamin Smith b.7/25/1776 m. Mary Elizabeth North 1/2/1806 by Rev. Mr. Hollingshead

BIRTHS of Children of Benjamin and Mary Elizabeth Smith

Edward North Smith 10/19/1806-10/23/1806
Sarah North Smith 3/20/1808, christened 4/17/1808 by Rev. Dr. J. S. Keith
Mary Elizabeth Smith, wife of Benjamin Smith, d. 12/27/1809, aged 23 yrs.
William C. Smith m. Sarah North, daughter of Benjamin and Mary E., 5/11/1826 at Rustlchelle, Pendleton, by Rev. Anthony U. Rose

Mills Bible continued...

BIRTHS of Children of William C. and Sarah Smith

Mary Eliza North Smith 4/4/1827 in Georgetown, S. C.
Our little son 4/2/1828-d. a few hrs. after in Pendleton, S. C.
Benjamin Savage Smith 7/26/1830 Pendleton-d. there 7/15/1831

Alice Elliott Drayton Smith 10/2/1831 Pendleton,S. C.
John Laurens North Smith 11/29/1833 at Rivoll, Pendleton
William Cuttine Smith 7/8/1835-9/4/1836
William Cuttine Smith 1/20/1837
Sarah Edith Ann Smith 12/29/1839
Benjamin Savage Smith 4/2/1841
Emily Hayne Smith 5/22/1843
Stephen Mazyck Wilson m. Elizabeth Sarah Vinson Smith at Rivoli in Anderson Dist., S. C. 1/15/1845 by Rev. Mr. Pearce
William Wilson Mills m.Sarah Edith Ann Smith at Rusticello in Anderson Dist., S.C. 12/23/1868 by Rev. J. B. Edgar D.D.

DANIEL MOSELEY BIBLE

BIRTHS

Daniel Moseley 3/11/1787
Sarah Moseley, wife of Daniel Moseley, 9/14/1791
Wade C. Moseley 11/2/1824
Lurena Moseley, wife of Wade C. Moseley, 8/31/1828
Sallie Moseley 10/19/18-3

Daniel Moseley Bible continued...

Thomas P. John Martin Moseley 1/24/1847
Julia Carlisle Moseley 8/1/1848
Charlotte I. Moseley 12/3/1849
Sarah Elizabeth Moseley 1/11/1852
-urlean Olivia Moseley 10/18/1855
Sam--- 5/1875
Samuel ---5/6/1840
Katie Louis 8/14/--
Daniel Eugene Moseley 4/1511857

Addie Harriet 2/28/1859
Luriah Moseley 5/28/1860
Carrie T. Moseley 2/9/1862
Jessie Eva Moseley 5/16/18-3
L----ade Moseley 3/--65

MARRIAGES

Daniel Moseley to Sarah Copeland 3/6/1809
Wade C. Moseley to Lurene Moseley 4/6/1848

DEATHS

Sarah Moseley, wife of Daniel Moseley 12/3/1847
Polly Jeters, wife of George W. Jeters, 1/26/1848
Arminta Jeters, wife of E. A. Jeters, 1/12/1849
Daniel Moseley 5/12/1856
Hampton Moseley 10/28/1817
Elizabeth Phillip, wife of George Phillips, 8/17/1857
Julia C. Moseley 9/22/1849

Daniel Moseley Bible continued...

Luriah Moseley 11/27/1860
Thomas P. J. M. Moseley 12/31/1862
Wade C. Moseley 2/8/--
Daniel Moseley 5/1881

ROLAND HILEY, Ft. Valley, Ga.

BIRTHS

Anna Sophia Hiley 4/17/1787
Mary Magdalene Hiley 10/4/1795
Barbary Hiley 4/26/1789
John Hiley 7/27/1794
Nancy Hiley 3/9/1819
Thomas Hiley 3/20/1797
Elizabeth Hiley 1/8/1792
Cathrine Hiley 3/8/1799

From Hollingshead Bible:

Ann Sophia Hiley 4/17/1787-3/7/1867 m. 1804 William Holllnshead of Richland Dist., S. C. (d. 2/20/1842)

Their issue:

Eliza Hiley 11/7/1805
Frances Emma Hiley 12/7/1814

Roland Hiley continued...

James Samuel Hiley 1/24/1807
Lavinia Adelaide Hiley 7/2/1816
Mary Caroline Hiley 12/16/1808
John Thomas Hiley 6139/1818
Martha Sophia Hiley 5/7/1810
Anderson Jacob Hiley 6/4/1810
Mary H. Hiley 3/10/1823
William Hiley 3/12/1812
Ann Elizabeth Hiley 7/31/1813
Rebecca Caroline Hiley 3/18/1826

Note: spelling changes from Hiely to Hily

JESSE DANIEL BIBLE of Charleston, S. C.

BIRTHS of Children of Jesse Daniel and Fannie Nelson Daniel

John Daniel 12/18/ 1791-d. inf. Ellyson Anderson Daniel 1/17/1797
Jane Anderson Daniel 7/5/1793 A. Montague Daniel 5/6/1808
Eliz. Anderson Daniel 1/18/1795 m. Pleasant Daniel
Charlotte Stith Daniel 6/30/1803 m. William H. Nelson
Jane Mickelborough Daniel 9/1/1807
Matilda A. Daniel 8/9/1811 m. Charles Daniel

BIRTHS of Children of Charlotte Stith Daniel and William H. Nelson

Jesse Daniel Bible continued...

Jesse Daniel Nelson 1/31/1829
Eliza J. Nelson 2/2/1830 m. Robert Nelson
James B. Daniel 1/25/1832 m. Ist, Elizabeth Green, 2nd, Margaret Jones, 3rd, Frances E.Johnson
Frances E. B. Nelson 1/29/1834 m. John P. Bush
Harvey G. Nelson 6/22/1839 m. Annette Huet

KINDRID BLACKSTOCK BIBLE
Owner: Mrs. Clara Blackstock Morgan

MARRIAGES

Kindrid Blackstock to Sarah Cooper 7/2/1843
V. H. Byns to Nancy Blackstock 3/11/1860
James Blackstock to Malinda Core 7/18/1874
William Blackstock to Sallie Hodges 12/27/1875

Henry Williams to Susan Blackstock 3/3/1862 or 1865
A. N. Elliott to Loucinda Blackstock 11/3/1864
James A. Clegg to Fannie Blackstock 4/23/1865
John P. Dawson to Mirah (Martha) Blackstock 7/12/1868

BIRTHS

Kindrid Blackstock 11/10/1817
Sarah Cooper, wife of K. Blackstock, 9/6/1628
Susana Blackstock 7/16/1844
William B. Blackstock 6/24/1827

Kindrid Blackstock Bible continued...

Francis Blackstock 12/26/1845
Elizabeth Blackstock 7/22/1859
Lucinda Blackstock 11/25/1847
Nancy Blackstock 1/24/1850
Daniel Blackstock 2/1/1862
Henry Blackstock 12/4/1864
Martha Blackstock 2/29/1852
Andrew L. Williams 9/17/1865
James Blackstock 7/19/1854

DEATHS

Kindred Blackstock 9/4/1880, aged 62 yrs., 6 mos., Claiborne, La.
Daniel Blackstock 2/6/1862, aged 6 days
Elizabeth Blackstock 11/9/1862, aged 3 yrs, 3 mos., 18 days
John L. Blackstock b. 10/15/1869
John L. Blackstock m. Elvira Bell 10/13/1880

Children of John L. and Elvira Blackstock:

Effie Blackstock 7/26/1890-1941 m. Roscoe Dendy
Floyd Blackstock 4/19/1891
Leroy Blackstock 3/26/1894
Kennie Blackstock 7/16/1898
Lizzie Mae Blackstock 11/2/1900
Nola Blackstock 10/9/1902
Ona Blackstock 2/22/1907
John Blackstock 5/1/1910
Clara Blackstock 4/23/1915
James Blackstock 3/23/1917-11/1917

JOHN MURRAY BIBLE of Grove Hill Plantation
Sumpter Co., SC

John Murray b. near Edinburgh, Scotland 1/21/1760-d. 11/23/1815 Sumpter Co., S. C. m. his 2nd wife, Elizabeth Nelson 9/21/1767-11/15/1833 m. 9/15/1791

John, eldest son of John and Elizabeth Murray, 1792-1793 John, second son of John and Elizabeth Murray, 1793-1794 Samuel John, third son of John and Elizabeth Murray, 6/23/1794-7/26/1850

WILLIAM F. HUTCHISON BIBLE
Owner: Mrs. Irvie R. Fonts, Lakeland, Florida

W. P. Hutchison's Bible bought fro. the Rev. William Walker in 1847
Martha Clymph b. 9/30/1800
John Ruff 1794 John and Martha Ruff m. 1/30/1816

BIRTHS of Children of John and Martha Ruff

Martha Ruff 2/11/1819
George W. C. Ruff 10/20/1834
David Franklin Ruff 2/4/1821
Francis M. Ruff 9/1/1837
Mary Ann Ruff 9/11/1823
Henry F. Benson Ruff 8/9/1839
John Lemuel Ruff 11/1/1825
Sarah Victoria Ruff 1/30/1841

William F. Hutchison Bible continued...

John Holmes Ruff 9/12/1828
Samual A. Coke Ruff 9/1/1843
Thomas J. Ruff 3/2/1831

William Franklin Hutchison 5/30/1822
Mary Ann Ruff 9/11/1823

Children of William F. and Mary Ann Hutchison:

Joseph Fletcher Hutchison 2/21/1846
Rebecca Frances Hutchison 11/7/1848
William Carvosson Hutchison 3/18/1850
Sonora Benicia Hutchison 8/10/1852
John Maxamilian and Martha Lydia Hutchison 2/22/1855
Mary Ann Hutchison 10/27/1857
Jefferson Hutchison 10/15/1861
Sarah Elizabeth Hutchison 4/16/1864
Mittie A. Perdue 1/27/1872
Jefferson Perdue, son of Jefferson D. and Mittie A. Hutchison, 8/17/1896

Thomas Ardus Perdue, son of above, 6/29/1898
Joseph Walter Perdue, son of above, 12/24/1913

MARRIAGES

William Franklin Hutchison to Mary Ann Ruff 12/10/1844
Henry Narcum to Rebecca F. Hutchison 11/24/1867
Joseph F. Hutchison to Mary Kerce 5/2/1869
Ebenezer Odom to Rebecca F. Marcum 11/5/1872

William F. Hutchison Bible continued...

William C. Hutchison to Mary V. Watkin 10/24/1872
Daniel A. Robertson to Sonora B. Hutchison 12/17/1879
Murry J. Sweat to Sarah E. Hutchison 1/29/1883
Benjamin Carpenter to Martha L. Hutchison 6/3/1886
Jefferson Davis Hutchison to Mittie A. Perdue 12/30/1894

DEATHS

John Maxamillian Hutchison, son of W. F. and M. A., 3/11/1855, aged 17 days
Mary Ann Hutchison, wife of W. F., 12/14/1880, aged 57 yrs., 3 mos. 3 days
Rebecca F. Odom, wife of E. N. Odom and daughter of W. F. and M. A. Hutchison, 3/20/1887, aged 39 yrs, 3 mos., 3 days
William Franklin Hutchison 2/7/1893, aged 70 yrs. 8 mos., 8 days William Carvosson, son of W. F. and Mary A. Hutchison, 5/16/1902, aged 52 yrs.. 1 mo., 28 days
Joseph Fletcher Hutchison, son of W. F. and Mary A., 11/7/1924,aged 7 yrs.. 10 mos., 27 days
Sonora Robertson, wife of D. A. and daughter of William F. and Mary A. Hutchison, 9/24/1927, aged 75 yrs., 1 mo., 14 days
Jefferson Davis Hutchison, son of V. F. and Mary A. 10/30/1934,aged 73 yrs., 15 days
Martha I. Carpenter (Mattie) wife of Benjamin F. Carpenter and daughter of W. F. and M. A. Hutchinson, 8/13/1938, aged 83 yrs., 5 mos., 21 days Newspaper Clippings In Bible:
"Mary Jane Chipley was been Abbeville County, S. C., March 29th, 1849....DIed July 19, 1875...

William F. Hutchison Bible continued...

"Emily Philpot died Aug. 15, in the 44th year of her age. Z.eaves husband, Joseph Philpot and seven children.....Member of M. E. Church (Edgefield Co.)

"Memoriam. Hardy H. Quillian. son of I. W. and Eliza Quillian, died at his father's residence Jan. 18, 1887, age 25 years, 11 mos.. 20 days. Born Lumpkin Co. (Dahlonega) Georgia, Jan. 28, 1856. Removed to Whitfield County with his parents when young. Member Methodist Church...."
"Irvin Hutchison, son of Maximillian and Lydia Hutchison, was born in Newberry District, S. C., Nov. 26, 1811. Died in Abbeville District, Dec. 4, 1871. Joined Methodist Church in his 14th years...."

"Memoriam. Died: William H. McDowell, leaves widowed mother. Born in Barnesville, Ga. On the 22 July 1871 being next to the youngest of 6 sons. United with the Baptist Church April 12, 1887.

Baptised by Dr. R. J. Willingham Date of Death: 29 Dec. 1895."
"Hutchison. Died at Turkey Creek, Hillsborough Co., Fin. Feb. 7, '93, Bro. William Franklin Hutchison. Born Abbevllle, S. C., May 30, 1822. Married Mary Ann Ruff, Dec. 10 '44.
Member Methodist Church tor 57 years. (Obituary written by A. Brown).

"Quillian: Miss Mary Quillian, member of a pioneer family of Whitfield County (Georgia) died Sat. morning after long illness. Buried at Quillian Cemetery. Funeral held at Pleasant Grove

William F. Hutchison Bible continued...

Methodist Church. Deceased was lifelong member....Daughter of Lewis (Quillian and Eliza (Hutchinson) Quillian; born In the Old Mint House at Dahlonega, where her father was government mint master. Came to Whltfield Co. with er parents over 70 years ago when Just a Child over 5 yrs. of age and has continuously lived here since that time. Her parents were brother and sister to Mr. and Mrs. Milligan P. Quillian, deed, and relatives constitute one of the largest families in the section. Laster member of her immediate family; only one member of the Milligan P. Quillian family remains. Survived by nieces and nephews: Henry I. Brooker, Mrs. Emma Wolfe, Whitfield Co.; Mrs. Elizabech Stonecipher and Mrs. Nelle Trippe, Texas; Mrs. Kate Rudolph and Mrs. Beulah Thompson of Atlanta; Clem M. Brooker, Columbus, Ohio; Mrs. Mary Day Quillian of Florida." "M. Hutchison died 26 of July of typhoid dysentary in his 69th year. Was a methodist about 32 years, embracing religion at Old Tabernacle in Abbeville Dist., S. C. .... leaves wife and children...

Joseph Fletcher Hutchison 2/21/1846 Mary Cathron Kerce 3/13/1844

BIRTHS of Children of Joseph F. and Mary C. Hutchison

Mary Christianah Hutchison 4/12/1870
William Richard Hutchison 4/2/1872
Samuel Peter Hutchison 2/1876
Martha Eliddier Hutchison 3/24/1881
Dolpheus Franklin and Dolpheus Sophia Hutchinson 3/19/1874
Sarah Jane Elizabeth Hutchison 1/30/1875

William F. Hutchison Bible continued...

BIRTHS of Children of Eras. S. and Mary C. Roberts

Fabian Malone Roberts 12/4/1898 Big Bend, Hillsboro Co., Fla
Bavarin Kabira Roberts 2/4/1900 Big Bend, Hillsboro Co., Fla.
Joy Olmutz Roberts 1/5/1905 Big Bend, Hillsboro Co., Fla.
Adeal Kremlin Roberts 11/22/1907 Lee Co., Fla.
Khiron Euca Roberts 5/9/1910 Haines City, Fla.

BIRTHS of Children of William R. and Mary E. Hutchinson

William Vearl Hutchison 5/31/1903 Haines City, Fla.
Bessie May Hutchison 1/18/1905 Haines City, Fla.
Lucy Elizabeth Hutchison 9/21/1906 Haines City, Fla.
Willie Geneva Hutchison 5/8/1910 Haines City, Fla.
Joseph Wesley Hutchison 5/17/1913 Haines City, Fla.

MARRIAGES

Joseph F. Hutchison to Mary C. Kerce 5/2/1869
Jesse G. Tillman to Dolpheus S. Hutchison 5/17/1893
Erasmus S. Roberts to Mary C. Hutchison 1/12/1898
Joseph F. Hutchison to Sarah A. Kerce 10/14/1918

DEATHS

Mary Elizabeth Hutchison, wife of William R., 11/24/1915, aged 36 yrs., 6 mos., 6 days
Bessie May Hutchison 1/31/1907, aged 2 yrs., 13 days
Mary Cathron Hutchison 2/14/1918, aged 73 yrs., 11 mos., 1 day

William F. Hutchison Bible continued...

Mary Christiana Roberts 3/1/1919, need 48 yrs., 10 mos., 8 days
Joseph Fletcher Hutchison 1/17/1924
William Vearl Hutchison 7/26/1973
William Richard Hutchinson 6/11/1943

JOHN ANDERSON BIBLE
Microfilm-Ga. State Archives

BIRTHS

John Anderson 2/2/1794 m. 11/27/1817
David C. Anderson 3/13/1827
Harriet Anderson 3/12/1818
Moses Anderson 11/13/1829
James Anderson 10/12/1819
Edmond W. Anderson 10/30/1831
Martha Anderson 3/20/1821
Josiah Eldridg Anderson
John F. Anderson 11/16/1822 1/1/1834
Mariah Anderson 3/13/1866
William C. Anderson 9/14/1824
Jasper V. Anderson 6/1/1836
Elizabeth Anderson 3/13/1838
John Anderson 2/2/1794-12/2/1876

David C. Anderson 3/13/1827-11/11/1899, 72 yrs., 7 mos., 28 days

Jincy A. Anderson 5/14/1831-9/27/1900, 69 yrs., 4 mos., 13 days
Dennis Anderson 1/1864

MARY BUFFINGTON BIBLE
Owner: Mrs. Daniel, Eastman, Ga.

Thomas Gordon, son of John and Elizabeth Gordon, b. 12/21/1758 in Spotsylvania Co., Va.
Mary Buffington, daughter of Joseph and Mary (Few) Buffington b.1/1/1760 in Chester Co., Pa.
Thomas Gordon m. Mary Buffington 1777. Spartanburgh Co., S. C.

BIRTHS of Their Children

John Few Gordon 11/1777 Liberty Iron Works on Lawson's Fork, S. C. , M. N. Lindsey
Joseph Roy Gordon 4/17/1779 Swan Pond on Yadkin River-d. 1800
Charles Gordon 7/17/1780-1850 m. Dorcas Bryan d. 1825 Gwinnett Co., removed Walker Co.
Samuel Gordon 3/16/1782 Swan Pond on Yadkin River-d. 1841
George Aston Gordon 2/16/179- Fairforrest In 96 Dist., S. C.-d. 12/21/1841, bur. Gwinnett Co., Ga., m. Susan Bulloch 1793-1856
Alexander Gordon 11/16/1785-11/28/1789, b. Michety Creek, Spartanburg Co., S. C., d. Fair Forrest. He was burned to death
William Gordon 8/16/1787 Spartanburg Co., S.C.-5/23/1852 Gwinnett Co.,Ga. m. Martha Baker

Mary Buffington Bible continued...

Mary Gordon 1/10/1789 Michety Creek, Spartanburg Co., S. C. m. Allan Powell
Elizabeth Gordon 2/3/1791 m. Almon Powell
Thomas Few Gordon 4/6/1793-1850 m. Lavinia Powell, removed to Walker Co., Ga.
Few Gordon 1/17/1797 Oglethorpe Co., Clouds Cr.-12/1/1857 Gwinnett Co. m. Clarissa Herdin
Buffington Gordon 1/17/1797-11/25/1799
James Gordon 6/11/1801-1863 m. Sarah A. Lord 1804-1858, removed fr Gwinnett to Walker Co.
Few Gordon, son of Thomas Gordon and Mary Buffington, m. Clarissa Few Gordon, Hardin, dau. of Lt. Henry Hardin & Sarah Cook, daughter of Benjamin Cook & Effy Fletcher, in 1820.

BIRTHS of Children of Few and Clarissa Gordon

Dr. James M. Gordon 4/21/1821-9/18/1854 m. Miss Alexander of Lawrenceville, Ga.
William M. Gordon 4/15/1823-5/22/1852 m. Patty Hector. No issue.
Mary B. Gordon 7/17/1825-11/11/1902 n. Mr. Hisaw. No issue.
John Fletcher Gordon 1/29/1828-7/26 1898 m. Polly Sanders (removed to TX, had large family)

Thomas J. Gordon 10/8/1832-1/10/1834
Sarah Cook Gordon 11/3/1835-9/18/1885 m. 11/14/1852 Wilburn Rauseller Wells
Marquis de Lafayette Gordon 6/15/1831-4/2/1874 m. Kate Maltbie, Lawrenceville, Ga.
Alonzo Gordon 3/23/1840-1862

Mary Buffington Bible continued...

Georgianna Gordon .. Samuel Newton Martin, son of Abraham Martin of Walker Co., Ga.

Missouri Gordon 1/15/1845-6/1923 m. John William Johnson (Issue:
Lois Johnson Aycock; Luticia Wells Johnson, Sarah Cook Gordon Wells, Few Gordon, Thomas Gordon and John Gordon)

THOMAS JEFFERSON MAY
May Family Newsletter 8/1969

Thomas J. May b. S. C.-d. 1858 m. Eliza James h. S. C.-d. 1849

BIRTHS of Their Children

Dorethea Ann Francis May 4/25/1838 m. 1858 Elihu Barksdale
William F. May m. 1853 Lucinda C. McCrary; he d. 1862
Martha Catherine May 1840-1904 m. 1884 to W. D. Johnson
John Perry May 1846-4/1928
James Franklin Elmore May 4/21/1849-1927 m. 1875 Sarah Jane Shell
Eliza Rebecca May 1857-

WILLIAM ASH BIBLE
From: Rev. War Pension #WS645

William Ash b. Pa.-d. 10/15/1831 Franklin Co., Ga.
Wife, Anne Fleming b. 1764 Pa.-d. 9/18/1854 Franklin Co., Ga.
m. 4/8/1783 York Dist., S. C.

BIRTHS of Children of William Ash

John Ash 11/30/1~3 m. Margaret Newton
Alexander Fleming Ash 3/5/1785 m. Elizabeth McCracken
James Ash 10/24/1786 m. Nancy Martin
Dovey Ash 3/18/1789 m. Thomas Mays
William Ash, Jr. 1/26/1791 m. Martha Strange
Jennet Ash 1/21/1793 m. James S. Fleming
Robert Rutherford Ash 5/31/1795
Mary Hunter Ash 3/6/1798 m. Richmond Hammonds
Elizabeth Ash 12/26/1800 m. Louis Thomas
Elijah McWhorter Ash 11/20/1802-d. infancy
Isabella P. Ash 10/29/1804
Rachel Ash 10/29/1804 m. Edward Mayes

GIDEON JOHNSON BIBLE

Gideon Johnson b. 11/7/1728 Spartanburg, S. C.
Ursula Deatherage, Gideon's wife, b. 2/16/1734 Spartanburg, S. C.
William Weakley Johnson, son of Gideon Johnson, Jr. and Mary de Graffenreid, b.10/10/1807

Gideon Johnson Bible continued...

Sarah Alston, wife of William Weakley Johnson, b. 10/3/1810
William Weakley Johnson, Jr., son of William W. and Sarah Alston Johnson, b. 6/12/1835
Frances Anne Vanderslice, wife of William Weakley Johnson, Jr., b. 12/2/1840, Nolensville, Tenn.

Their dau:

Mary de Graffenreid Johnson b. 12/3/1868 Nolensville, Tenn.
Mary de Graffenreid Johnson m. Robert Anderson Williams (b. 12/4/1866 Nolensville, Tenn.)

JAMES HOPE BIBLE
Owner: Mrs. Mary Darwin Hope
623 Grant St., S. E., Atlanta, Ga.

Great-great grandfather, James Hope, b. 12/28/1732 in England m. 1776 Ellen DeMoss in York, Pa.

Ellen DeMoss b. 1742 France-d. S. C. 1814

BIRTHS

James Hope 4/13/1769 York, Pa - :d. 8/30th York, S. C.
Catherine Hope 8/12/1771 Hartford, Md.
John Hope 12/4/1773 Hartford, Md.
Adam Hope 1/5/1776 Lincoln, N. C.
Isaac Hope, great-grandson, 4/13/1790 York, S. C.
Jane Barron, great-grandma, 11/13/1764-11/30/1841

James Hope Bible continued...

Great Aunts and Uncles:

Agnes Hope 8/12/1800
Pamela Hope 10/5/1802
Ellen DeMoss Hope 11/1/1805
James Maddison and Jane Maddison Hope 1/2/1809-11/25/1874 Lucinda Powell Hope 11/27/1910-11/25/1874 (daughter of John Powell end Rachel Darwin)
J. Albertus Hope 9/13/1829
Jane Amanda Hope 8/11/1831-9/2/1882
J. William Preston Hope 1/21/1833-7/8/1890
Russell La Hatte 9/19/1834-11/3/1881
Lucinda Calista 5/8/1836 Rachel Pamela 12/29/1937
Davis McDonough 7/4/1840-1010/1864 at Richnond, Va.
Isaac Meek Hope 4/26/1842-5/6/1864 Florence, S. C.

BIRTHS

Sylvanun Amazi 2/18/1844-7/27/1848
Syntha Selena 9/18/1845-6/12/1852
Julius Amazi 6/18/1848
Hugh Washington Hope 9/4/1850-2/13/1890
Robert Peyton Hope 8/6/1853-11/3/1855
Celena Mary Ellen 12/13/1855

MARRIAGES

Robert Stevenson to Jane Barron 12/3/1784
James Hope to Jane Stevenson 9/19/1799 (great grandfather)

James Hope Bible continued...

B. F. King to Pamela Hope 7/18/1824 (great aunt)
N. W. King to Ellen D. Hope 7/8/1824 (great aunt)
J. D. Robinson to Agnes Hope 2/16/1826 (great aunt)
James M. Hope to Lucinda Powell 12/4/1828 (grandfather)
J. H. Kind to Jane Hope 12/11/1828 (great aunt)
J. W. P. Hope to M. L. Wylie 8/9/1858
J. Albertus Hope to E. Whitesides 8/30/1865
R. L. Hope to M. M. Neeland 1/2/1868
Julius A. Hope to A. Ferguson 1/8/1868
R. A. Gilfillian to Pamela Hope 10/11/1830
J. Powell Hope to Rachel Barron 2/4/1806

LEONARD LATHARO DENDY BIBLE
Owner: Bob Dendy, Photo Dept., Atlanta Constitution, Atlanta, Ga. Microfilm-Ga. State Archives

MARRIAGES

Leonard Latharo Dendy to Minnie Almedia Walker at Boiling Springs, S. C. 12/22/1891.
Witnesses: Mr. and Mrs. M. M. Walker and family; Mr. and Mrs. J. E. Kell, by Rev. W. T. Smith
Nathaniel Walker Dendy to Christine Coskrey 10/26/1915 (div. 1942)
Eugene Lemand to Ethel I.. Boswell 12/22/1923 (diy.)
Nathaniel Walker Jr. to Beatrice Ann Smith 9/24/1942 (div. 9/26/1944)
Nathaniel Walker Sr. to Ida Blanche McBee 9/23/1923

Leonard Latharo Dendy Bible continued...

BIRTHS

Nathaniel Walker 9/23/1892
Jan Clyde Dendy 10/20/1903
Eugene Leonard Dendy 12/17/1897

Grandchildren

Nathaniel Walker Jr. 12/21/1918

Children of Eugene Leonard:

Harvey Eugene Dendy 12/1/1924
Bobby Gerald Dendy 6/3/1930
Martha Ann Dendy 2/13/1927

DEATHS

Jan Clyde Dendy 3/17/1919
Minnie A. Dendy 7/24/1956
Nathaniel Walker 7/14/1958
Leonard Latharo Dendy 6/27/1925

BENJAMIN BUCHANAN BIBLE

BIRTHS

Firstborn, abt 1779
Anna Buchanan 11/16/1787
William Buchanan 4/27/1789

Leonard Latharo Dendy Bible continued...

Sara Buchanan 6/13/1792
John Wood Buchanan 11/16/1790 m. Mary Suber
George Buchanan 5/17/1795
James Buchanan 9/3/1793 m. Teresa Clay
Susannah Buchanan 1/11/1801
Thomason Buchanan 7/31/1802
Benjamin Buchanan, Jr. 2/16/1797 m. Mrs. Gray
Silas Brooks Buchanan 4/22/1799 m. Candus Riley Jones
Mary Elizabeth Buchanan 12/15/1800
Micajah Buchanan 9/29/1804 m. Sara Hamilton Alewine
Jessie Buchanan 4/11/1814

WILLIAM HARDEN BIBLE

William Harden of Edgefield, S. C. m Mary Ann Sharpe of Edgefield, S. C., 10/3/1853.
Witnesses: Quincy Price, Jane Johnson

On back of this - Number of Confederate Badge 82566

BIRTHS

William Harden 1/31/1832 Barnwell Co., S. C.
Mary Ann Price Sharpe Harden 2/23/1826 Barnwell Co., S. C.
Opelia Sharpe 9/27/1845 Barnwell Co., S. C.
John Hansford Sharpe 9/1/1847 Edgefield Co., S. C.
William LaFayette Harden 7/1/1854 Edgefield Co., S. C.

William Harden Bible continued...

Thomas Jefferson Harden 5/1/1859 Edgefield Co., S. C.
Frances Elizabeth Harden 2/15/1862 Edgefield Co., S. C.
Nancy Ann Harden 7/25/1869 Edgefield Co., S. C.

DEATHS

Mary Ann Ellis 11/4/1865 Augusta, Ga.-8/17/1866
Elizabeth Sharp 8/27/1867 Augusta, Ga. - 7/17/1868
R. S. Cobb b. 12/28/1872
Thomas Jefferson Harden 5/19/1860
"Sacred to the memory of our Mother who was born on the 8th day of August in the year
of our Lord 187- (1807) and departed this life on the 14th day of May In the year of our
Lord 1878 Francis   pr----, her age and death recorded."
Johnie Sharp 3/9/1881
John Morris of Aiken, S. C. m. 12/23/1880 Francis Harden of Vaucluse, Aiken Co., S. C.,
John H. Sharp m. Annie Loyd 8/4/1869 by Rev. J. S. Hard

BIRTHS

Anne Loyd 1/23/1848 --
Nancy Ann Catherine Stephenson
Alice Sharp 8/30/1871
G. W. Sharp 6/28/1876
Correy Allice Harden 1/12/1877
Mary Amedia Harden 10/20/1880 at Vaucluse, S. C.
Areldia Ann Cobb, daughter of Samuel and Ophelia Cobb of Langley, S. C., 4/25/1881, Langley, S. C.

William Harden Bible continued...

Nancy Ann Catherine Stevenson 1/23/1847
Clyde Thomas Stevenson 12/25/1848
George Washington Stevenson 4/4/1850
Martha Stevenson 10/8/1852
   ---Sharp --/30/--

Johnie Sharp 11/3/1880 Pearl Sharp 12/21/1886
Tyler Edward Sharp 1/28/1890-8/12/1893
Johnie Herbet Martin 3/19/1907
Eddie Lee Sharpe, son of C. W. Sharpe and Annie Sharpe, 6/3/1896 Erma Beatrice Sharpe, dau. of G. W. and Annie Sharpe, 9/19/1898 Annie Davis, wife of G. W. Sharpe, 12/28/1876
Katherine Martin Streppe d. 12/9/1948
Mary Amedia Harden d. 7/30/1883, aged 2 yrs, 9 mos., 10 days

The Birth of My Grandchildren. William Harden.

"My dear wife was 59 yrs., 7 mos., 24 days old when she departed this life....9/13/1885"
Augusta, Ga., James Edward Harden b. 7/17/1883, son of M. D. Harden and Nancy.

MARRIAGES

Johnnie Martin to Louise Clark 11/21/1924 by Rev. Thomas Walker
M. A. Kirkland to Alice Sharp 3/22/1893 by Rev. N. G. Jack's, Augusta, Ga.
W. Sharp to Annie Davis 10/29/1883 by Rev. N. G. Jack's, Augusta, Ga.

William Harden Bible continued...

W. N. Martin to Pearl Sharp 6/23/1901 by T. B. Stredson
Jack Dodgen to Dorris D---- 7/19/1949
Bernice Leora Martin to Fred Dodge 2/1/1926 in Lake City, Fla. by Rev. M. Jameson, Pastor of the First Church of Florida

DEATHS

John H. Sharpe 11/1906
Mrs. Anni Sharpe 6/17/1918
Mrs. Alie Kirkland 4/6/1919
George Sharpe 6/27/1929
W. E. Martin Sr. 12/5/1945, husband of Pearl Sharpe Martin

BIRTHS

Bernice Leoria Martin 3/19/1907
Katherine Virginia Martin 11/18/1914
---Martln 3/12/1911
William Elbert Martin Jr. 1/4/1917
Allen Hansford Martin 1/26/1913
William Elbert Martin 7/29/18--
William Elbert Martin 7/29/1882
Katie Bell Ramsey 6/18/1890
Annie Lee Ramsey 1/20/1892
Carrle Elizabeth Ramsey 9/29/1894
Effie Meal Ramsey 1/21/1896
Johnnie Herbert Martin, Jr., son of Louise and Johnnle Martin, 4/20/1926
William Anderson Dodgen, son of Bernice and Fred Dodgen, 11/11/1926

William Harden Bible continued...

George Washington Dodgen, son of Bernice and Fred Dodgen, 1/18/1929
Jack Allen Dodgen, son of Mr. and Mrs. F. J. Dodgen, 3/12/1931
Doris Martin 11/2/1928
Herman Hughes 7/14/1921
Jack Hughes 7/14/1921
Pearl Dennis 9/22/1932, daughter of Katherine Martin Dennis
Allen Hansford Steppe 8/13/1943, son of Katherine Martin Steppe

W. J. HACKETT BIBLE
Owner: Mrs. I. H. Kinnett
160 Belvedere Dr., Macon, Ga. 31204

MARRIAGES

W. J. Hackett to Minnie S. Adams, both of Edgefield Co., S. C.,2/15/1877 by Rev. Mr. Alexander
W. W. Hackett to Isabel Dendy 11/15/1899
Frederick T. Field to Lillie Fuller Hackett 1/14/1914
Isabel Wright Hackett to Donovan DeWitt Kinnett 6124/1925
Mary Isabel Kinnett to Malcolm Davis 8/---
Donovan DeWitt Kinnett to Ann Hodges 11/1955, Oconee, Ga.

BIRTHS

William Julian Hackett 12/17/1853 Minnie Savannah Adams 2/9/1855

W. J. Hackett Bible continued...

William Wright Hackett 2/28/1878 Augustus Griffin Hackett 11/9/1880
Lillie Fuller Hackett 6/30/1889 Edgar Sheppard Hackett 5/22/1892

DEATHS

Edgar Sheppard Hackett 5/30/1892
William Julian Hackett 2/1011910, aged 57 yrs.
Augustus Griffin Hackett, son of William J. and Minnie S. Hackett, 3/10/1919, aged 39 yrs.
William Wright Hackett 12/1/1961
Mary Isabel Dendy Hackett 2/5/1959
Donovan DeWitt Kinnett 6/16/1939

FRANCIS COOK I. BIBLE

Francis Cook, from his father, 1818 Robert Byers m. Susanne Robinson 5/30/1756

BIRTHS of Their Children

Henry Byers 9/30/1758
Margaret Byers 1/25/1761
Joseph Byers 10/31/1762-9/11/1763
Joseph Byers 11/23/1764-1/30/1765
Robert Byers 7/25/1766
Susanna Byers 8/20/1769-9/13/1770

Francis I. Cook Bible continued...

Susannah Byers Sr. d. 10/31/1770, aged 35 yrs., and was 14 yrs. married woman and had three sons and three daus.
Joseph Milligan m. Margaret Byers 3/16/1777

BIRTHS of Their Children

Robert Milligan 4/8/1778-5/6/1778
Susannah Milligan 7/22/1779-2/24/1817
Robert Milligan 10/3/1781-1/3/1785
Margaret Milligan 4/9/1784-10125/1786
Rachel Milligan 3/9/1787-12/3/1861
Elizabeth Milligan 9/15/1790-5/26/1868
Mary Byers Milligan 11/13/1792-12/10/1862
Margaret Milligan 2/7/1802-11/10/1861
Jane Milligan 3/6/1795-11/26/1860
Joseph Milligan 1/29/1800
Susanna Milligan was the wife of John Ellison and mother of Margaret Milligen Ellison, the wife of Rev. Francis Cook
William Cook Sr. b. 3/4/1757 m. Jemima Flake 4/1782

BIRTHS of Their Children (Children of the Ist wife)

James Cook 3/8/1783
William Cook 6/27/1793
William Cook 2/15/1790
Samuel Cook 4/6/1786
John J. Cook 2/10/1796
Francis Cook 2/17/1798

Francis I. Cook Bible continued...

William Cook Sr. m. Miss Mary Brock 4/1805

BIRTHS of Their Children

Mary Cook 11/1806
Isaac Cook 9/13/1813
Jemima S. Cook 1/17/1812
Benjamin Cook 3/4/1807
Robert Cook 11/1815
Henry S. Cook 11/7/1810
Sarah Jemima Cook 1/2/1817

DEATHS

William Cook, Sr. 8/12/1827
Samuel Cook 9/27/1810
Jemima Cook 7/15/1804
William Cook 8/17/1809
Mary Cook 1/30/1817
Henry S. Cook, son of William and Mary Cook, 11/7/1847
James Cook, son of William and Jemima Cook,

MARRIAGES

Francis Cook to Elizabeth Heath Massey 3/11/1819 by Rev. Isaac Smith
Francis Cook to Margaret Milligan Ellison 6/25/1828 by Rev. Robert Adams in Fairfield Dist., S. C.

Children of above:

Francis I. Cook Bible continued...

John Ellison Cook m. Miss Frazer of Alabama
William Francis Cook m. Miss Richards of Macon, Ga.

Samuel K. Cook m. Miss Elder of Barnesville, Ga.
J. O. A. Cook m. Miss Frazer of Alabama
Margaret J. Cook m. Robert McEvoy of Macon, Ga.
Julia Cook m. James H. Smith of Culloden, Ga.
Susan E. Cook m. J. T. Jelks of Alabama
Francis Cook, son of William and Jemima, b. 2/17/1798, abt 6 miles from Camden, S. C.
Margaret Milligan Cook, daughter of John and Susannah Ellison, b.2/6/1808, Charleston, S. C.

BIRTHS of Children of Francis and Elizabeth H. Cook

Henry Massey Cook 1/17/1820, baptised by Rev. Whitman C. Hall
Sarah Jemima Flake Cook 11/1/1821
Francis Asbury Cook 5/12/1823, baptised by Rev. Reuben Tucker 12/23/1823
William Thomas Cook 6/17/1825, baptised by Rev. Henry Bass 10/16/1825
Susan Elizabeth Cook 5/16/1829, baptised by Rev. William H. Kennedy 2/21/1830
John Ellison Cook 12/6/1830, baptised by Rev. Samuel M. Capers
William Francis Cook 11/20/1832, baptised 4/1833, Rev. W. H. Ellison
Sarah Jane Cook 12/2/1834, baptised by Rev. Willis O. Matthews 7/21/1835

Francis I. Cook Bible continued...

Samuel Kennedy Cook 10/10/1836, baptised 4/20/1837 by Rev. W. H. Ellison
James Osgood Andrew Cook 8/23/1838, baptised 11/11/1838 by Rev.W. H. Ellison
Margaret Jane Cook 8/31/1840, baptised by Rev. William H. Ellison 9/22/1840
Julia Blending Cook 8/5/1842, baptised by Rev. L. C. Harrison 9/1841
Robert Dunlap Cook 10/31/1844, baptised by Rev. C. O. Johnson 6/17/1846
Susan Elizabeth Cook 6/20/1848, baptised 9/21/1848 by Rev. V. W. Robinson
Winfield Leonard Davis Cook, son of Francis and M. M. Cook, 6/21/1850

DEATHS

Sarah Jemimah Flake Cook, daughter of Francis and Elizabeth H., 6/10/1822
Francis Asbury Cook, son of Francis and Elizabeth H., 8/20/1824, Waxhaws, Lancaster District, S. C., bur. in family burial ground at Thomas Carlton's.
William Thomas Cook, son of Francis and Elizabeth H., 10/9/1826, aged 16 yrs., 3 mos., 32 days, bur. Camden, S. C.
Elizabeth H. Cook, wife of Francis, 7/18/1827
Sarah Jane Cook, daughter of Francis and Margaret M., 8/7/1835, aged 8 mos.. 5 days, bur. Mt. Zion, Harris Co., Ga.
Susan Elizabeth Cook, daughter of Francis and Margaret M., 8/5/1847, bur. graveyard at Culloden

Francis I. Cook Bible continued...

Robert Dunlap Cook who was blind from his brith and otherwise afflicted died at his grandfather's in Talbot Co. 9/3/1847. Bur. in graveyard at Culloden, Ga.
Winfield Leonard Davis Cook, son of Francis and Margaret M., 9/15/1855, bur. Graveyard in Culloden, Ga.

Henry Massey Cook, son of Francis and Elizabeth H., 9/30/1870, bur. near Pensacola, Fla.
Margaret Milligan Cook, wife of Rev. Francis Cook, 8/1/1871, bur. in cemetery at Marietta
Rev. Francis Cook 5/10/1872 at Marietta Ga., buried beside wife

ELIZABETH HAMMETT LEGARE BIBLE
Owner: Mrs. S. T. Whitaker, Columbus, Georgia

Thomas Isaac P. Legare 1791-1821
Isaac Legare III
Isaac Legare II/2/1754-3/17/1788
Mary Legare 5/22/1760
Ed Mortimer Legare m. --- Hammett 1823
Martha Whildon b. 3/27/1714
Elizabeth Hammett Legare 1826 Charleston, S. C.
Isaac Legare II m. Mary Player 1790-1802
Isaac Legare m. 1755 Susannah White b. 1740
A. B. Waters b. 3/12/1858 Charleston, S. C.
Elizabeth Hammett Legare m. A. B. Waters

AHAH JOHNSON BIBLE
Owner: Elizabeth Marlow, Monticello, Georgia

BIRTHS

Ahah Johnson 10/14/1810 Newbury Dist.. S. C.
Lucretia Davenport Johnson 1/25/1811 Newbury Dist., S. C.
John H. Johnson 9/17/1825
William F. Johnson 11/22/1840
Greene P. Johnson 9/14/1827
Lucy A. Johnson 12/29/1842
Louise Johnson 9/20/1830
Fannie E. Johnson 11/18/1853
Leussie E. Johnson 5/15/1846
Sarah J. Johnson 3/29/1833
Mary F. Johnson 4/15/1833
Elizabeth G. Johnson 6/4/1850

MARRIAGES

Louise Johnson to Henry Colbert 12/16/1852
Mary Frances Johnson to Thomas G. King 12/16/1852
Sarah Jane Johnson to Marcus De Lafayette Simmons 11/18/1852
Martin Ann Johnson to Lafayette F. Roquemore 9/19/1860
Laussie Emmeline Johnson to Thomas W. Pritchett 12/12/1865

DEATHS

John H. Johnson 1827
Fannie Emma Johnson 9/18/1862
Greene Berry Johnson 9/13/1846
William Floyd Johnson 9/10/1881, bur. Greenbriar River in Va

CAPT. GEORGE REID BIBLE
Owner: Raymond M. Bell, State College, Pa.

Capt. George Reid b. 12/23/1719 Ireland m. Abigail Leger, b. France-d. Abbeville, S. C. 11/3/1786

Children:

Rosa Reid m. Malor John Rowie
Ann (Nancy) Reid b. 12/25/1747 .. 1/12/1769 Capt. William Raskin, Jr. Margaret Reid m. Ist
Hugh Reid 2nd William Cauder Baskin Samuel Reid m. Caroline Thomson
Alexander Reid
Joseph (Lieut.) b. 6/5/1756 Va. m. Isabella Baskin

WILLIAM PACE BIBLE
Owner: Mrs. B. E. Bell, Atlanta, Georgia

MARRIAGES

William and Polly Pace to 6/6/1793, aged 20 yrs.

Elizabeth Pace, daughter of above William and Polly, to 8/22/1811 to Zeno Weddington, aged 17 yrs., 4 mos.
Polly, our dau., 8/26/1818 to Hundy May, age 22 yrs., 21 days
William Pace. our son, 4/3/1833 to Susan Slaughter, age 24 yrs., 2 mos., 19 days

William Pace Bible continued...

Stephen Pace, our son, 7/10/1827 to Polly Ardis, age 25 yrs.
Lucy Pace, our daughter 11/6/1828 to James Burt. age 22 yrs., 28 days
Clement Pace, our son, 4/7/1830 to Polly Crouch, age 29 yrs., 9 mos., 28 days
Catherine Pace, our dau., 6/29/1870 to John May, age 25 yrs., 9 mos., 24 days, at Moody Mays, S. C., Pendleton Dist.
William Pace, our son, the 2nd time 6/21/1831 to Tabitha Moles, age 33 yrs. lacking 24 days
Elkana Pace, our son, 10/29/1835 to Nancy Burt, age 20 yrs., 9 sos., 27 days
John Pace, our son, 2/5/1A36 to Columby or Sarah Ardis, age 26 yrs., 1 mo., 27 days
Nancy Pace, son William's dau., 9/16/1847 to William May of Ala.

BIRTHS

William Pace, son of Stephen and Catherine, 6/6/1773
Polly Pace, my wife (daughter of William and Lucy May) 10/28/1770

BIRTHS of Children of William and Polly Pace Elizabeth Pace 4/29/1794

Catherine Pace 9/5/1804
Polly Pace 8/5/1796
Lucy Pace 10/9/1806
William Pace 7/15/1798
John Pace 12/7/1809

William Pace Bible continued...

Clement Pace 7/11/1800
Elkanah Pace 1/23/1815
Stephen Pace 7/11/1802

BIRTHS of Children of Elkanah and Nancy Pace

William Henry Pace 9/4/1837
Mary Havilah M. Pace 6/14/1849
James Pace 3/8/1840
Elkanah Stephen Olin Pace 3/24/1856
Americus Martial Pace 10/11/1843

DEATHS

Catherine Pace, wife of Stephen, my father, 11/24/1813
Stephen Pace, my father: 11/12/1822
Susan Pace, son William's wife, 7/22/1870
Lucy Birt, our dau., 6/1/1840. Her little son d. 5/30th, aged 2 days, 4 hours
Nancy Pace, William's dau., 8/8/1853 in Alabama
Americus Martial Pace 11/11/1844
Clement Pace 1/14/1865, son of William Pace, Sr.
Elkanah Pace 8/18/1867, son of William Pace, Sr. and Nancy (Mary)

WILLIAM H. CANNON of Darlington

MARRIAGES

William H. Cannon to Sarah Ann McTyer 5/13/1804 by Rev. James Coleman
Joseph A. Jolly to Susanna W. Cannon 7/15/1823
William H. Cannon to Ann Sanders, widow of Jordan Sanders, 6/26/1825 by Rev. Rob. Campbell
Simon C. Muldrow to Louisa A. Cannon 11/1826
Charles B. Howard to Amelia M. Cannon 8/1828
Simon Connett to Mary Cannon, daughter of Henry Cannon, 10/10/1805
Hugh E. Cannon to Ann Muldrow 10/5/1809
James Brown to Susanna M. Cannon 3/17/1819
John J. Cannon to Ann Shova Pawley 1/1821

BIRTHS of Children of William H. and S. A. Cannon

Mary Ervin Cannon 4/10/1805-
Son 12/23/1815, lived 9 days
Susanna Williams Cannon 6126/1807
Sarah Ann Cannon 1/18/1817
Louisa Adaline Cannon 1/3/1809
Elizabeth Jane Cannon 2/10/1819
Amelia Melvina Cannon 8/4/1810
Robert Rasha Cannon 6/12/1822
William Henry Cannon 7/28/1812

William H. Cannon Bible continued...

BIRTHS

John Julius Cannon, son of John Julius and Ann S. Cannon, 1/22/1823

William H. Cannon, Sr. 4/25/1783-12/2/1843
Sarah Ann Cannon, wife of William H. Cannon, 12/28/1787-9/23/1824

Children of Henry and Mary Cannon:

William H. Cannon 4/25/1783
Samuel Cannon 8/23/1784-8/9/1793
Susanna Wilson Cannon 3/26/1786-8/14/1793
Hugh E. Cannon 9/4/1787
George James Cannon 2/6/1789-8/23/1793
Elizabeth Cannon 6/30/1790-6/20/1791
Mary Cannon 11/26/1791
Sarah Cannon 10/5/1793-11/2/1793
Robert Augustus Cannon 2/17/1795-1/23/1798
John Julius Cannon 10/19/1796-9/15/1822

Children of Henry Cannon and Susannah Cherry, wid. of George Cherry. They m. 8/14/1798 by Rev. E. Pugh:

Susanna Monselle Cannon 1/16/1800
Augustus Devan Cannon 12/31/1801- -/20/1817

DEATHS of Children of William H. and Sarah Ann Cannon

William Pace Bible continued...

Mary Ervin Cannon 10/27/1820 -
John J. Cannon 9/15/1822
Sarah Ann Cannon 1/23/1823
Augustus D. Cannon 10/20/1817

RICHARD W. HABERSHAM BIBLE
DAR Records, Ga. State Archives

MARRIAGES

Richard W. Habersham to Sarah H. Elliott only daughter of Barnard Elliott, Esq. of Port Royal Island, S. C., by Rev Galen Hicks 5/18/1808.
Richard W. Habersham to Martha I. Mathewes 6/23/1836 in Habersham Co., 4th dau of J. R. (John Raven) Mathewes of S. C. by Alonzo Church, D. D., President of Franklin College

Edward M. Habersham to Emily Jones Miller of Beech Island, S. C., daughter of Margaret Smith Miller and Edward Jonathan Meyer Miller, 11/25/1876 by Rev. J. G. Richards, Presbyterian Church of Liberty Hill., S. C., uncle of the bride

Annie Righton Habersham to Louis Morris Magid, daughter of Edward M. Habersham and Emily Jones Miller Habersham, by Rev. Francis Brome, Rector of Christ Episcopal Church at home in Savannah, Ga., 1/21/1908

BIRTHS of Children of Richard W. and Sarah Habersham

Richard W. Habersham Bible continued...

Richard Wiley-Habersham 2/11/1812, Beaufort, S. C.
Barnard Elliott Habersham 9/20/1814, Beaufort, S. C.
Catherine Esther Habersham 10/18/1816, ---bel Dist., S. C.
James Habersham 3/20/1818-7/2/1818
John Bolton Habersham 4/6/1820-4/19/1820
Stephen Elliott Habersham 10/1/1821, Beaufort, S. C.
Sarah Georgia Habersham 11/7/1823. Savannah, Ga.
Alexander Wylly Habersham 8/2/1826, Mt. Pleasant, Sing, Sing, NY
Francis Bolton Habersham 3/22/1828. Savannah, Ga.

DEATHS

Richard U. Habersham at Azalea, Habersham Co., Ga., 12/2/1842, aged 56 yrs. At the time member of Congress from this State.

IRVIN CATER BIBLE
Owner: Charles F. Cater, Quitman, Georgia

MARRIAGES

Thomas W. Anderson to Mrs. Catherine (Johnson) Cater daughter of Richard Johnson, 11/2/1827, Barnwell Oistrlct, S. C., by Rev. Duncan

BIRTHS of Their Children

Richard Cater 1828
Samuel F. Cater 6/26/1829
Sarah May Cater 11/15/1830

Irvin Cater Bible continued...

Margaret Elizabeth Cater 8/13/1833
William Francis Cater 8/22/1832
Caroline and Catherine Cater (tuins) 9/20/1836

DEATHS

Catherine Anderson, consort of Thomas W. Anderson, 10/6/1836
Thomas W. Anderson 8/8/1845

BENJAMIN ARNOLD, SR. BIBLE
Owner: William Sullivan, Gray Court, South Carolina

Benjamin Arnold, Sr. b. Bedford Co., Va. 1719-d. Greenville Co., S. C.. 12/1797
Ann Hendricks Arnold d. 1806

BIRTHS

William Arnold 1756
Temperance Arnold 1764
Edward Arnold 1760
Thomas Arnold 1767
Charity Arnold 1761
Edmund Arnold 1768
Hendricks Arnold 1763
Benjamin Arnold 7/30/1769
Kezziah Camp Arnold, wife of Benjamin Arnold, Jr., 5/20/1777
Alston Arnold 6/23/1804
Martin Arnold 9/9/1809

Benjamin Arnold, Sr. Bible continued...

Benjamin Arnold 1/22/1818
Temperance Hamilton Arnold 3/8/1801
Winifred Washington Arnold 11/20/1802
Ann Hendricks Arnold 7/10/1797
Sarah Arnold 6/8/1799
Malinda Arnold 12/25/1805

MARRIAGES

Charity Arnold to Capt. George Martin
Temperance Arnold to Thomas Hamilton
Hendricks Arnold to Mary Tiere
John Arnold to Jane Woodson
Thomas Arnold to Polly Boylston
Benjamin Arnold to Kezziah Camp
Ann Hendricks Arnold to Dr. John Sullivan
Sarah Arnold to Abijah Pinson
Temperance Hamilton Arnold to Joseph Sullivan
Malinda Arnold to William Arnold
Alston Arnold to Nancy Thomason
Winifred Washington Arnold to Benjamin Camp 12/1828
Martin Arnold to Abigail Belling
Benjamin Arnold to Mary McDavid

DEATHS

Benjamin Arnold 11/1/1858, aged 89 yrs.

JOHN BALE BIBLE
Owner: Judge John Bale, Rome, Ga.

BIRTHS

John Bale, London, England 12/15/1795-1/4/1864 Floyd Co., Ga.
Malinda Mason, South Carolina

William Mason, South Carolina (father of Malinda Mason)
John Bale m. Malinda Mason 1822 in Greenville, S. C.

Their Children:

Caroline Emeline Bale 1824 Greenville, S. C.-8/20/1893 m. J. T. Stewart
Matilda Moore Bale 1826, Greenville, S. C.
James Alfred Bale 1828-12/15/1900 m. 4/12/1866 Naomi Shropshire
Amanda Bale 1830, Greenville, S. C.

THOMAS DICKSON of Anderson District
Owner: Thomas Eugene Dickson
153-20 41st Ave., Flushing, Cong Island, N.Y.

John Dickson, the 1st son of Thomas Dickson of County Down, Ireland. b. 8/1/1769
Elizabeth Franks b. 8/16/1777
John Dickson m. Elizabeth Franks 2/25/1794

BIRTHS of Children of John and Elizabeth Dickson

Thomas Dickson Bible continued...

Sarah Dickson 12/17/1794
Thomas Dickson 3/20/1799
Michael Dickson 2/9/1797
Janetta Montgomery Ramsey of Augusta Co., Va., 5/10/1799
Michael Dickson of Abbeville District. S. C. m. Janetta Montgomery Rawsey 9/6/1821

BIRTHS of Children of Michael and Janetta Dickson

Jane Eliza Dickson 8/17/1821-
James Remey Dickson 5/21/1826
Sarah Ann Dickson 2/14/1824
John Franks Dickson 2/18/1828
Sarah Dickson m. Jacob Belotte 5/12/1819
Thomas Dickson m. Nancy Young Scott, both of Abbeville District, S. C., 1/6/1829

BIRTHS of Children of Thomas and Nancy Y. Dickson

Mary Montgomery Dickson 11/16/1829
Elizabeth Eugenia Dickson 1/11/1832
William Scott Dickson 3/12/1833
Henry Franks Dickson 5/5/1834
Sarah Antoinette Dickson 12/5/1836
John Miller Dickson 10/11/1839
Florence Scott Dickson 4/26/1844
Lucius Clark Dickson 10/13/1847
Thomas Eugene Dickson 6/26/1852
Martha Eula Dickson 8/31/1854
Samuel R. McElroy m. Mary Montgomery Dickson of Anderson District, S. C. 11/24/1853

Thomas Dickson Bible continued...

BIRTHS of Children of Samuel R. and Mary H. McElroy

William H. McElroy 7/24/1854
James D. McElroy 7/24/1856
Sarah Antoinette McElroy 9/29/1858
Martha Ellen McElroy 3/10/1861
Samuel M. McElroy 10/4/1863
James T. Steele m. Sarah Antoinette Dickson of Anderson District, S. C. 12/4/1856
Sarah Antoinette Steele, our granddau., b. 1/5/1858

MARRIAGES

Henry Franks Dickson, son o f Thomas and Nancy S. Dickson, to Ruth J. Cannon of Anderson Co., S. C., 12/29/1859
Thomas Eugene Dickson, son of Thomas and Nancy S. Dickson to Mary Elsie Jones of Anderson Co., S. C., 12/9/1874
Michael Calvin Dickson, son of Thomas and Nancy S. Dickson of Anderson Co., to Annie Adelaide Gilkerson of Laurens Co., S. C., 11/30/1875
J. L. Gilkerson of Laurens Co., S. C. to Sarah Antoinette McElroy 2/21/1877
W. H. McElroy 12/21/1876 to ---
U. L. Milam of Greenville Co., S. C. to Martha Ellen McElroy 5/3/1881
James V. McElroy to Carrie Watkins 11/24/1891, all of Anderson Co., S. C.
George W. Russell To Florence Scott Dickson 11/15/1892

BIRTHS of Children of Thomas E. and Elsie J. Dickson

Thomas Dickson Bible continued...

Henry Franks Dickson 10/3/1875
Inez-Sadler Dickson 5/7/1880
Christine Jones Dickson 1/11/1878
Thomas Eugene Dickson 2/21/1893
Mary Scott, daughter of Michael Calvin and Annie Dickson, b. 7/3/1877

Thomas Paul Dickson. son of above, b. 12/6/1879
John Calhoun Dickson
Nancy Eugenia Dickson
Michael Calvin Dickson

DEATHS

Jane Eliza, 1st daughter of Michael and Janetta M. Dickson, 9/17/1823
Elizabeth Eugenia, 2nd daughter of Thomas and Nancy S. Dickson, 3/10/1832
Elizabeth Dickson, our Mother, 11/27/1832
John Dickson, our Father, 5/1/1849
William Scott Dickson, our 1st son, 5/5/1833
Sarah Belotte, our sister, 1/25/1851
John Miller Dickson, our 3rd son, 12/18/1839

Samuel R. McElroy 9/25/1864
Lucius Clark Dickson, our 5th son, 10/15/1851
Thomas and Antoinette Steele
Sarah Antoinette Steele, our 3rd dau., 1/6/1858
Mary M. Dickson McElroy 3/28/1910
Rev. Michael Dickson 3/16/1874, aged 78 yrs

Thomas Dickson Bible continued...

Sarah Antoinette Steele, our granddau., 8/10/1858, daughter of James
Mrs. Mary Miller Scott 12/19/1872, aged 84 yrs.
Nancy Young Scott, wife of Thomas Dickson. 10/10/1887
Nancy Eugenia, 2nd daughter of Michael C. and Addie C. Dickson, 8/26/1891
Henry Franks Dickson, Ist son of Thomas E. and Ella Jones Dickson, 9/5/1892
Thomas Dickson, our Father, 1/20/1892, aged 93 yrs.
Thomas Eugene Dickson, our 6th son, son of Thomas and Nancy Scott Dickson, 5/5/1914, aged 62 yrs.
William Scott, soldier in the Revolutionary War, 12/3/1761-6/19/1830, Anderson Co., S. C.
Mary Miller Scott, widow of William Scott, b. 4/2/1790. 5 mi. north of Abbeville Co., S. C.
Nancy Young Scott, daughter of William and Mary of Abbeville District, S. C., b. 11/1/1810

Partial List of Slaves and Ages:

Johneston 9/1822
Banister 1/23/1840
Albert 8/15/1840-8/4/1904
Mary 2/1825
Ann 2/15/1837
Elmirah 2/6/1827
Nanny 10/12/1817-6/5/1838
Stephny 3/5/1841
Catherine 5/12/1824
John 9/12/1842

Thomas Dickson Bible continued...

Isaac 4/15/1836
Garison 9/30/1842
Angerona 2/22/1838
Sam 1/6/1843
Jackson 4/3/1840
Emily 3/1823
Lucinda 4/5-10/4/1846
Sally 12/17/1850-9/11/1851
Frances 7/17/1844-11/2/1845
Oliver 12/17/1844-3/11/--
Major Randal 11/5/1851
Dallas 2/6/1845
Edmon 1/10/1851-9/1/1851
Susan 12/4/1853
Cornelius 2/26/1846
Ellen 5/8/1852-2/20/1853
Eliza 12/29/1827
Ferry 4/11/1846
Caroline 6/5/1852
Cecelia 10/15/1845
Cubit 11/24/1845
Franks 5/1/1854-4/14/1856
Brena 5/4/1847-12/29/1847
Hariet 6/16/1846
Andy 9/21/1854-3/8/1856
Joseph 11/3/1854-3/25/1856
Agusta 1/19/1847-12/31/1847
Anderson 10/15/1854-3/25/1856
Jane 6/10/1848
Miles 3/8/1856

Thomas Dickson Bible continued...

Joseph Linton 4/6/1858
Lucy 2/21/1848
James 4/19/1856
Napoleon 5/10/1848
Rutter 10/27/1848
Jerry 7/1/1857-6/5/18--
Sophia 11/5/1848-11/20/1920
Robert 4/3/1858
Tolivar 1/8/1861
Ferasure 9/23/1849
Fanny 7/4/1859
Peter 12/26/1860
George 12/27/1849 (alive in 1934)
Holacy 8/18/1859
Louise 12/23/1864
Allen 12/1858
Nannie 5/7/1861
Lizzie 10/11/1860
Henrietta 6/18/1860-7/12/1889
Martha 6/30/1863
Esther 12/14/1863

"Susan Robinson cooked many years for Thomas Dickson's family. Susan's children are: Noll Sharp Robinson b. 5/21/1885 and Guy Hartwell Robinson b. 5/7/1887

ARVA ALLEN BIBLE of Abbeville Co.

Owner: Mrs. Leon Wilson, 400 Hillcrest Ave., Macon, Ga.
Arva Allen m. Polly Clarke 8/1/1786 Mecklenburg Co., Va.,

BIRTHS

John Showell Allen 7/19/1787 Mecklenburg Co., Va.
Bannister Allen 10/13/1788 Pittsylvania Co., Va.
Charlotte Allen 2/2/1794 South Carolina
Nancy Allen 3/17/1797 South Carolina
Thompson Allen 12/22/1802 South Carolina
Leroy Allen 7/20/1806 Abbeville Co., S. C.

LYSANDER D. CHILDS BIBLE

Owner: Mrs. David Wallace Robinson, 2230 Taylor St. Columbia, S. C.

MARRIAGES

Lysander D. Chllds to Nancy Harriet Hoke 6/11/1843
William Guion Childs to Alice E. Gibbes 9/2/1872
Lysander D. Childs, Jr. to Mary E. Spring 7/13/1881
David Augustus Childs to Mary E. Gibbes 7/15/1884
Edith Childs to David U. Robinson 2/11/1897
R. W. Gibbes to Caroline E. Cuignard 12/20/1827
Nancy Childs to O. Frank Hart 1/1/1902
Alice Childs to James B. Urquhart 12/22/1903
Elizabeth Childs to John M. Cantey 9/2/1902
Mary T. Chllds to C. Pinckney Seabrook 6/11/1911
Eugenia T. Childs to J. R. Westmoreland 3/25/1913
Robert G. Childs to Frances Sams
Ellen Childs to Jack Reigel (not In Bible)
William Childs Robinson to Mary McConkey 6/22/1921, Salem, Va.

Lysander C. Childs Bible continued...

Henry Burton Robinson to Lyda Carter Studatert 4/22/1930
Raleigh
David U. Robinson, Jr. to Elizabeth Mason Gibbes 1/21/1933
Edith Courtenay Robinson to Henry Garad Schwartz 9/13/1935

BIRTHS

Lysander O. Childs 12/17/1813
Nannie Childs 4/3/1877
R. W. Gibbes 6/8/1809
Nannie H. Hoke 9/6/1823
Wm Gibbes Childs 3/9/1879
Hoke Childs 9/6/1888

John Eben Childs 8/1844
Alice Childs 5/14/1881
Caroline E. Guignard 4/14/1811
William Guion Childs 10/2/1850
Elizabeth Childs 7/15/1884
Mary Thomas Childs 5/7/1891
Lysanders D. Childs Jr. 7/6/1855
Eugenia Talley Childs 3/4/1886
Alice E. Gibbes 6/11/1853
Ellen Hoke Childs 4/18/1894
Eben Allston Childs 6/9/1873
Robert Gibbes Childs 2/3/1897
Edith Childs 3/21/1875
John Ball to Sarah Martin 3/23/1857

Lysander C. Childs Bible continued...

BIRTHS

Martin Ball 5/13/1838
Mattie I. Ball 4/28/1870
Francis Permelia Anil 11/28/1842
Elan Sophia Ball 1/23/1877
Simeon P. Ball 1/30/1844
Florence C. Ball 10/30/1878
Huldah Ball 7/11/1847
John Minyard Ball 2/11/1881
Samuel Ball 4/5/1859
Walter Jeremiah Ball 4/19/1883

THOMAS HAMLIN BIBLE
Owner: Rev. J. L. Giradeau, S. C.

Thomas Hamlin, son of Thomas, b. 1/17/1794
Mary Moore, daughter of Phillip, b. 2/6/1799

Their Children:

Harriet Moore Hamlin
Nicholas Cobia Hamlin 6/26/1827
Philip Moore Hamlin 5/1825
James Hibben Hamlin
Penelope Sarah Hamlin 2/12/1829 m. 6/24/1849 John Hamlin
Ann Cobia Hamlin m. Samuel J. Blackwell

WILLIAM H. ACKER BIBLE
DAR Bible Collection Georgia State Archives

BIRTHS

Grandpa William H. Acker 6/7/1824 Anderson Co., S. C.
Mary C. Acker 12/22/1827
Sue Acker 11/12/1853
Ella Acker 10/14/1859
H. H. Acker 11/7/1851

Willie Acker 1/8/1861
P. B. Acker
Guy H. Norris 1/12/1876
Marion F. Norris 4/25/1882
Mamie M. Norris 3/25/1878
Ophelia C. Norris 2/2/1883
Pearl S. Norris 0/29/1880
Joicey Moore 5/7/1854
Guy Hammond Norris Jr. 5/25/1911
Baxter Andrew Norris 5/3/1918
Rachel Norris 11/9/1912
Mary Cornelia Norris 9/10/1921
Francis Reuben Norris 6/21/1914
John Ewing Norris 2/28/1924
James Rufus Norris 4/23/1916
Wade Benjamin Norris 7/7/1926

MARRIAGES

William H. Acker to Mary C. Hammond 12/4/1845
Sue Acker to F. M. Norris 5/9/1875

William H. Acker Bible continued...

H. H. Acker to Joicey Moore 10/24/1876
Wade Drake to Mamie Norris 9/22/1902
Guy Hammond Norrls to Ophelia Clinkscales at home of bride's mother in Anderson, S. C., 6/8/1910, by Dr. Charles M. Boyd. Pastor of the A. R. P. Church, assisted by Rev. M. R. Kirkpatrick of Seneca, S. C.

BIRTHS

Florence Sue Drake 6/28/1903
Thomas Franklin Drake 6/5/1907

DEATHS

My Mother, Sue C. Norris, 8/28/1883
My Father, Frank M. Norris 8/17/1886

William H. Acker 2/19/1862
Mary C. Acker 6/20/1883
Ella Acker 7/21/1883
Guy Hammond Norris, Jr. 8/7/1911
Ann Eliza Cox 4/30/1840
Cary Spencer Cox 8/5/1852
Martha Griggs Cox 3/6/1842
Hattie Graham Cox 9/12/1854
Orren D. Rountree Cox 6/19/1844
Benjamin Lee Cox 10/9/1860

MARRIAGES

Frances E. Cox 1/19/1853 to Ambrose Hutcherson

William H. Acker Bible continued...

Ann Eliza Cox to Joseph C. Head
Mary Mildred Cox to Jessie J. Whitaker
Martha Griggs Cox to Turner L. Green
Willis C. Cox to Mary T. Gullatte 1/12/1871
Joseph Edwin Cox to Calista Alberta Hilley 3/4/1874
Emery Taylor Cox to Lucy Green 2/5/1880
Hattie Graham Cox to George W. Collier
Benjamin L. Cox to Emma Hanson 1885

GLADYS ENDELL D. MORRIS BIBLE
Owner: Mrs. P. K. Morris, S. C.

Gladys Endell D. Morris b. 10/27/1898 m. 1/12/1927 Frederick Keating Morris b. 10/3/1881 S. C.
Frederick Keating Morris, Jr. b. 2/25/1928
Carolyn Gladys Morris b. 3/23/1932

HUGH WASHINGTON HOPE BIBLE
Owner: Mrs. Mary Darvin Hope, 623 Grant St., S. E., Atlanta, Ga.

Hugh Washington Hope m. Mollie Darwin 11/1/1877, both of Yorkville, res.of P.B. Darwin
Their Children:

Clarence Bland Hope 12/12/1879-9/13/1881
James Lindsay Hope 12/29/1881-8/5/1899
Ethel Hope 7/17/1886
William Asbury Hope 7/19/1887-10/30/1906

Claude Hutchins m. Ethel Hope 11/23/1908
Child: Mary Lalagi Hutchins 11/4/1909

JEREMIAH BALL'S BIBLE of Gray Court

BIRTHS

Sally Ball 5/8/1804
John Ball 10/19/1816
Harris Ball 1/14/1814
Stephen Ball 5/28/1805
Minyard Ball 2/28/1817
Elizabeth Ball 7/19/1807
Jesse Ball 6/27/1821
Nancy Ball 1019/1809
Mary Driscilla Ball 12/18/1825
Fanny Ball 4/25/1812

Young Jeremiah Ball 12/25/1826

DEATHS

Jeremiah Ball 2/7/1856, 79 yrs.
Martin M. Ball 8/7/1861
Sarah Ball 11/25/1854
Mary Ball 2/24/1862
Huldey Ball 6/23/1898   John Bell 5/16/1893

MARRIAGES

John Ball to Huldah Madden 5/10/1855
Joseph Rabb to Huldah Ball 1/19/--
Simeon P. Ball to Malinda Bramlett 7/24/1866
Samuel H. Ball to Martha J. Hopkins 2/10/1876

John Ball to Sarah Martin 3/23/1857

BIRTHS

Martin Ball 5/13/1838
Mattie I. Ball 4/28/1870
Francis Permelia Anil 11/28/1842
Ella Sophia Ball 1/23/1877
Simeon P. Ball 1/30/1844
Florence C. Ball 10/30/1878
Huldah Ball 7/11/1847
John Minyard Ball 2/11/1881
Samuel Ball 4/5/1859
Walter Jeremiah Ball 4/19/1883

THOMAS HAMLIN BIBLE
Owner: Rev. J. L. Giradeau, S. C.

Thomas Hamlin, son of Thomas, b. 1/17/1794
Mary Moore, daughter of Phillip, b. 2/6/1799

Their Children:

Harriet Moore Hamlin
Philip Moore Hamlin 5/1825
Nicholas Cobia Hamlin 6/26/1827
John Hamlin
Penelope Sarah Hamlin 2/12/1829 m. 6/24/1849
James Hibben Hamlin
Ann Cobia Hamlin m. Samuel J. Blackwell

THOMAS BRADWELL BIBLE
Owner: Mrs. Annie Bradwell, Edge, Georgia

Thomas Bradwell, father of Dr. Daniel Bradwell, b. 3 miles of Charleston, S. C. 9/1857 m. Catharine Durr b. 1859, Charleston

BIRTHS

Dr. Daniel Bradwell 9/5/1800 Cotton Dist., Mathew Parish on Plantation of Gen. Francis Marion on Santee River-
2/22/1881,Statesville, North Carolina
Louis Phillip Taylor Bradwell 1/6/1847-d. Gadsden Co., Fla.
James Sumter Bradwell 3/7/1849-Gadsden Co., Fla.
Mary Catharine Bradwell 12/30/1829, Kingtree, North Carolina
Jane McCutcheon Gordon 8/22/1806 Williamsburg Dist., S. C.
Matilda Caroline Bradwell 11/8/1831 on Broad River, Williamsburg
Emlly Angeline Bradwell 12/30/1833 Knoxville, La.
Thomas Marion Bradwell 2/5/1836 Houston Co., Ga.
Alexander Mountry Bradwell 11/7/1838 Houston Co., Ga.
Elenor Jane Gordon Bradwell 7/25/1841 Houston Co., Ga.
Isaac Gordon Bradwell 3/15/1843 Houston Co., Ga.

MARRIAGES

Daniel Bradwell to Jane McCutchen Gordon 11/13/1828
Daniel Bradwell to Mrs. Isabella Watts 5/16/1871 Statesville, Iredell Co., N. C.
Daniel Bradwell to Mrs. Mary N. Baker 7/20/1858
James Sumter Bradwell to Moselle M. Griffin 7/6/1875
James Sumter Bradwell to Annia Eleanor Campbell 10/6/1910
Leila Ramelle Bradwell to W. W. Palmer 7/21/1897
Irene Gordon Bradwell to Arthur Francis Passmore 10126/1898

Thomas Bradwell Bible continued...

Francis Orland Bradwell, child of Moselle M. Griffin and James Sumter Bradwell, 10/2/1876-d. same day
Irene Gordon Bradwell, daughter of Moselle M. Griffin and James Sumter Bradwell, b. 4/10/1878
Leila Ramelle Bradwell b. 11/16/1979

Herbert Burr Bradwell 10/20/1885-12/28/1885
Marion Gordon Bradwell b. 3/5/1911
Harriet Ramelle Bradwell b. 10/2/1898

DEATHS

Jane McCutchen Gordon 9/20/1837, aged 51 yrs.
Thomas Bradwell 9/1857 in Charleston District, S. C.
Catharine Durr 1859 Charleston District, S. C.
Louise Philip Taylor Bradwell 2/26/1912 Ft. Myers, Fla.
Dr. Daniel Bradwell 2/22/1881, Statesville, N. C., aged 80 yrs.

Mary Catharine Bradwell 4/30/1884
Moselle M. Griffin 6/1/1899
W. W. Palmer 2/7/1901
James Sumter Bradwell 2/6/1921

DAVID MOATS BIBLE of Newberry
Owner: William Moats, Poulan, Georgia

David Moats b. Virginia; his parents moved when he was quite young, to Newberry, S. C.
Where he lived until he died. His wife, Martha Ann Coggins, b. Newberry, S. C.

David Moats' Bible continued...

BIRTHS

David Moats 3/2/1811
Martha Ann Goggins Moats, wife of David Moats, 5/29/1818

BIRTHS of Children of David and Martha Moats

Ann H. Moats 4/2/1842 -- -
Jennie W. Moats 6/22/1855
Charlie H. Moats 8/29/1843
Henrietta Moats 2/13/1858
Martha Clemmit Moats 2/7/1847
William B. Moates 11/5/1859
Henry J. Moats 8/2/1852
Arthur Moats 6/15/1862-d.y.
Cary J. Moats 1/23/1886
Martha Lou Moats 10/19/1888
Cary Johnston, Ist husband of Martha Clemnit Moats, 5/12/1825

MARRIAGES

Martha Clemmit Moats to Cary Johnston 4/3/1866
Henry Moats to Lucretia Johnston 9/27/1876
Alice Elizabeth Moats to Ben West 2/16/1896
Henrietta Moats to James McKittrick 9/21/1897
William B. Moats to Adds Johnston 12/30/1884
Fannie Johnston to Frank Spearman 2/3/1892
J. Gillian Johnston to Sue Alma Guy 11/28/1900

David Moats' Bible continued...

DEATHS

Ann H. Moats 1/10/1862
Charlie H. Moats 9/4/1848
Martha Ann Moats, wife of David Moats, 8/27/1868
David Moats 4/2/1896
Cary Johnston, husband of Martha Clemmit Moats, 4/5/1885
Martha Clemmit Moats Johnston, Sr. (lst wife of Cary Johnston, 2nd Wife of Jesse Genn), 1/1929

WILLIAM CLARK BIBLE
Owner: W. S. Ervin Clarkesville, Georgia

MARRIAGES

William Clark of Virginia to Mary Goodwin of South Carolina 2/19/1792

John Clark to Millie Hooner
Oliver Clark to Betty Trimmer of South Carolina
Sevier Clark to Ely Ingram
William Clark 4/1757-6/4/1843

Ruth Goodwin Clark 3/14/1767-12/1/1852

John Clark 11/5/1792
Oliver Clark 10/9/1794
Sevier Clark 9/11/1797

SAMUEL HARDY BIBLE
Owner: Frank Epps
Greenville, South Carolina

MARRIAGES

Samuel Hardy to Elizabeth Hardy 4/7/1782
Martha Hardy, daughter of Samuel and Elizabeth, to John H. Ragsdale 12/25/1798
Henrietta Marie Hardy, daughter of Samuel and Elizabeth, to William Epps 4/9/1805
Susannah, daughter of Samuel and Elizabeth Hardy, to John Jennings 6/29/1813
Mary Hardy, daughter of Samuel and Elizabeth, to Daniel Epps 11/19/1812

BIRTHS

Samuel Hardy 3/7/1764
Henrietta Marie Hardy 5/5/1785
Elizabeth L. Epps 2/8/1813
Elizabeth Hardy 7/18/1762
Susannah Hardy 12/5/1787
Francis H. Epps 10/24/1816

Martha Hardy 4/18/1783
Mary Hardy 12/5/1791
Louis T. M. Epps 4/25/1823
Samuel N. Ragsdale 1/8/1800
John W. Ragsdale 12/25/1809
Samuel M. Epps 10/9/1820
William M. Ragsdale 3/4/1802

Samuel Hardy Bible continued...

Susannah Regsdale 11/8/1811
Elizabeth A. Epps 1/12/1808
James H. Ragsdale 1/4/1804
Mary C. C. Ragsdale 3/9/1814
John Epps 3/27/1805
Laura H. W. Epps 1/2/1814
Harriet M. Epps 2/2/1813
Sarah Ann Epps 8/20/1818
James N. Epps 8/15/1815
Peter G. Epps 5/5/1815
Susannah M. Epps 8/30/1818
George J. T. Epps 1/19/1817

DEATHS

Martha Ragsdale 11/18/1818
John H. Ragsdale 10/8/1822
James H. Ragsdale 8/12/1822

Susannah E. Epps 7/1/1814
Harriet W. Epps 6/18/1813
George J. T. Epps 9/22/1818

Louisa H. W. Epps 9/30/1814
Daniel Epps 9/10/1834

Mary Epps 7/9/1818
Susannah H. Epps 9/9/1816

ANDRE HERBEMONT BIBLE
Owner: Mrs. David W. Robinson
Columbia, South Carolina

Andre Herbemont m. Marguerite de Barotte (ca 1690)
Michel Herbemont, son of Andre and Marguerite m. 1729 Claire Antoinette Genevive de Bardot (she was b. 1700)
George Laurent Herbemont, son of Michel and Claire, b. 1741 m. Elizabeth Camus

Andre Herbemont Bible continued...

Nicholas Michel Laurent Herbemont, son of George and Elizabeth, 1/29/1771-6/3/1838 m. Victoere Euprosine Garcon in 1791 in N. Y.
Alexander Herbemont,son of Nicholas and Victoire, b.1/8/1792 m. 9/20/1827 Martha Davis Bay

Alexander Herbemont, son of Alexander and Martha, b. 7/10/1828
Alexander Herbemont,Sr.having been apptd U. S. Consul to Genoa, left Columbia, SC 7/26/1851 and reached Genoa latter part of Sept. following. At Genoa.

Alexander Herbemont Jr. m. Clara Isabella Fraser, daughter of John Fraser of Cherleston, S. C., 1/29/1855

Clara Isabella, their dau., b. Genoa 8/29/1856
Alexander Herbemont Jr. d. Liverpool, England 9/12/1857, Interred in St. James Cemetery in that City. The family consisting of Alexander Herbemont and Martha, his wife, Clara Isabella Herbemont, the widow of Alexander Herbemont, Jr., decd, and Clara Isabella, their infant child, returned to Columbia on 11/22/1858

BALL-GARRETT BIBLE
Owner: S. M. Ball, Gray Court, S. C.

BIRTHS

Ambrose Garrett 3/33/1798
Frances Garrett 5/26/1821
Joseph Martin Garrett 4/19/1825
Nancy Delong 1/2/1799

Ball-Garrett Bible continued...

Elizabeth Garrett 6/25/1825
Reuben Garrett 3/4/1819
Manervy Garrett 6/21/1817

Ambrose Garrett was son of Nicholas Garrett and grandson of Edward Garrett.

John Ball m. Sarah Martin 3/25/1857

BIRTHS

Martin Ball 5/13/1838
Simeon Ball 1130/1844
Francis Parmely Ball 11/28/1842

Huldy Ball 7/11/1847

BIRTHS of Children of Jeremiah Ball

Sally Ball 5/8/1804
Harris Ball 1/1814
Fanny Ball 4/15/1811
Stephen Ball 5/8/1801
Minyard Ball 2/28/-
Jeremiah Ball 12/25/1826
Elizabeth Ball 7/19/1807
Jesse Ball 6/27/1821
Nancy Ball 10/9/1809
Mary Priscilla Ball 12/18/1823

ROBERT SMITH BIBLE
Of Winnsboro, Fairfield District

Robert Smith 2/20/1760 Ireland (son of Hughy Smith)

BIRTHS of Children

Hugh A. Smith 11/27/1787
Elizabeth Smith 7/4/1789-2/6/1858 (m. Francis James Torbet in South Carolina)
Jane Smith 5/19/1792
Robert Wilson Smith 3/10/1794 (m. Jane Rowe In South Carolina)
Anne Adair Smith 8/15/1796
Mary A. Smith 12/14/1798-6/15/1888
David Smith 9/16/1801 (m. Eliza Lovern 2/18/1836 Butts Co.. Ga.)
Rosannah Smith 5/4/1804 (m. 3/18/1830 Isaiah Wise, Butts Co.)
Wilson Smith 4/23/1806
William Smith 6/12/1808
Margaret Smith 12/1011810 (m. Robert P. Coleman 3/1/1832)
Nancy Smith (m. Robert Harvey)

WILLIAM AND DRUCILLA BURDEN BIBLE
Of Newberry District
Owner: W. L. Jarrell, Round Oak, Georgia

William Burden. son of Thomas and Mary Burden, m. Drucilla 2/16/1784-10/6/1820

BIRTHS of Their Children

Thomas Liles Burden 1/25/1809 Newberry District

William and Drucilla Burden Bible continued...

Sarah Burden 1811
Lucinda Burden 1812
Nancy Burden 1815

William Burden m. 2nd 1/22/1822 Milly Liles

BIRTHS of Children of William and Milly Burden

Sisley Burden 1/22/1925
James Burden 1830
Lathy Burden 1/18/1833
William Burden 1/8/1836 (father of Thomas)

Note: The History of Jones County (Georgia), p. 599, contains more complete record.

DR. W. P. GLOVER BIBLE of Edgefield, S. C.
Owner: Mrs. Lula Glover Lowe Clinton Rd., Macon, Georgia

Julius N. Glover - killed in youth at battle of Jan Jacinto,Texas 8/26/1836. He was the brother of: Nathaniel Seth Glover
Temperance Towles Glover b. Edgefield District-d. 7/9/1840, the first wife of Wiley Glover
William Towles d. 9/17/1846
Wiley Glover b. Edgefield District near Little Saluda River in 1791-d. 4/26/1852
Elizabeth Glover d. 9/5/1852, 2d wife of Wiley Glover and mother of John T. and Allen A. Glover
John T. Glover b. 7/5/1843
Allen A. Glover 6/28/1846

Dr. W. B. Glover Bible continued...

John Towles Sr. b. 3/24/1772-d. 11/27/1852
John Towles Jr. b. 1833
Nathaniel Seth Glover 5/11/1813 Edgefield District, near Little Saluda River-1/26/1889
Caroline N. Finney Glover 2/.7/1816-10/14/1881
Henry W. Glover 10/7/1835-wounded Oct. 15th, d. 10/20/1864 Richmond, Virginia
Julius Jefferson Glover 5/22/1838-4/14/1881
Temperance Mary J. Glover 5/26/18-- - 9/26/1913
John Jackson Glover 1/14/1849-8/9/1883, drowned in Ocmulgee River
Nancy A. E. Glover 1/13/1851-6/19/1873, wife of James Middlebrooks
Washington Pierce Glover b. 3/7/1853
Henry Finney d. 5/24/1849
Nancy Finney 1795-3/8/1864, wife of Henry Finney

WILLIAM McKINLEY BIBLE
Owner: Guy McKinley, Milledgeville, Georgia

William McKinley 8/10/1744-4/22/1798
Mary Beatty 6/25/1756-12/14/1808

Children:

Enter Barksdale McKinley 10/13/1772-2/28/1808

Elizabeth Montgomery McKinley 1/16/1775-3/3/--
John Wilson McKinley 9/1/1777
Archibald Carlisle McKinley 9/9/1779
James Betty McKinley 2/22/1782
Mary Ansley McKinley 2/26/1784-10/1828

William McKinley Bible continued...

William Harris McKinley 6/23/1787-10/10/1793
Robert Mecklin McKinley 8/25/1790
Jane Moseley McKinley 9/9/1792

HENRY GLEASON BIBLE of Charleston
Owner: Mrs. Ernest M. Witte, Charleston, S. C.

BIRTHS

Henry B. Gleason 6/27/1804. Hartford, Conn
A daughter born and died 9/21/1833
Elizabeth P. Milnor 4/27/1814, Enston, Pa
Mary Dick Gleason 8/17/1834 Charleston, SC
Harris Hall Gleason 12/27/1832 Charleston, S. C.

A son, b. D. 10/8/1836, Charleston, S. C.
Anna Milnor Gleason 10/21/1837 Charleston, S. C.
Sarah Potter Gleason 7/11/1840 Charleston, S. C.
Frances Parker Gleason 4/20/1843 Charleston, S. C.
John Cleaveland Gleason 11/1845 Charleston, S. C.

MARRIAGES

Henry Bull Gleason to Elizabeth Paul Milnor 3/3/1830 in City of Charleston, by Rev. Dr. McDowal

DEATHS

Harris Hall Gleason 1/31/1833 Charleston, S. C., aged 5 weeks
Elizabeth Gleason 1/10/1836 Charleston, S. C., aged 10 days

LEVI JESTER BIBLE of Edgefield Co.
DAR Records, GA State Archives

Levi Jester 1760 Edgefield Co., S. C. - 6/17/1841
Rayannah Frazier Jester, wife of Levi Jester, 1765-6/14/1850 m. Edgefield, S. C. 1787

BIRTHS of Their Children

John Jester 3/26/1788 William Jester 2/22/1790 James Jester 4/20/1792 Sara Jester 12/17/1793
Levi Jester 1/2/1796 Nancy Jester 2/4/1798 Mary Jester 1/20/1800 Levi Dickey Jester 1/16/1802
Henry Jester 3/4/1804 Twin.Benjamin Jester 3/4/1804
Abner Jester 2/22/1806 Razannah Jester 1808

Note: Levi Jester was son of William Jester who came from Scotland to Virginia, then to Edgefield, S. C., then Butts Co., Ga. Where parents and children are buried
Abner Jester m. 1838 Lucretia Angeline Foster

BIRTHS of Children of Abner and Lucretia Jester

James Jester 1840
Levi Jester 1842
Nancy Jester 1844
Anne Jester 1847
William Jester d. Infancy
Mary Jester d. Infancy
Mary Jane or Polly 2/23/1851
Harrison Foster Jester 6/8/1849
Harrison Foster Jester d. 10/21/1875 m. 11/14/1871
Jane Caroline Stirman b. 4/3/1849

Levi Jester Bible continued...

BIRTHS of Children of Harrison Foster and Jane Jester

Rosa Lee Jester 1/23/1873
Allie Mae Jester 5/14/1874-2/15/1901
Ellis Fleming Huddleston b. 8/31/1869 m.12//24/1893 Rosa Jester, b. 1873
William Harrison Phinazee b. 9/6/1869 m. 12/27/1892 Allie Mae Jester

WILLIAM H. BULL BIBLE Of Orangeburg County
DAR Records, Ga State Archives

MARRIAGES

William H. Bull of Orangeburg, South Carolina to Elizabeth F. Way of Orangeburg County 7/7/1870, by E. I. Pennington

BIRTHS

William James Bull 5/16/1871
Lula Rebecca Bull 6/15/1878
Jessie Daisy Bull 3/21/1875
Minnie Gertrude Bull 8/26/1872
Izard Wittie Bull 8/18/1884

DEATHS

Minnie Gertrude Bull 8/23/1876
William James Bull 12/6/1903
William Henry Bull 2/20/1891
Lula Rebecca Bull 5/18/1887
Elizabeth Frances Bull 3/31/1924

BROWN BRYAN BIBLE Of Cheraw District
Owner: Mrs.I. L. Hendren, Athens, Georgia

MARRIAGES

Brown Bryan to Martha A. V. Smith 1/8/1824
Maria Louisa to J. F. Pegues 6/4/1845
Rosa Jane Bryan to James C. Medlin 10/8/1850
Joseph F. Renard to Julia B. Bryan 5/7/1857 by Rev. J. R. Pickett
H. F. Bryan to A. J. Wilson 7/12/1860 by Rev. J. Bostick
W. B. Wilkins to L. M. Bryan 11/16/1865 by Rev. S. B. Wilkins
Thomas M. Bryan to Mise S. F. Moris 11/14/1866 by Rev. Overton at Union Point,Ga.

BIRTHS

Maria Louisa Sparks Bryan 11/18/1825
Mary Frances Bryan 2/21/1828
Rosanna Jane Bryan 7/2/1830
William Drayton Bryan 5/10/1833
Julia Brown Bryan 5/21/1836

Thomas Marion Bryan 3/26/1839
Lucille Van Cleve Smith Bryan 6/27/1841
Little Pepues 6/6/1846
Francis Henry Pegues 12/7/1848
Annie Louisa Pegues 6/4/1851
John Julian, son of W. B. and Lucille Wilkins, 9/7/1866
Mary Rosa Wilson 8/19/1867 near Little Rock, nation Dist., S. C.
William Thomas Bryan 8/23/1867 at Union Point, Georgia
Willie Thomas Wilkins 3/23/1869
Lula Martha, Ist daughter of T. H. and S. F. Bryan, 7/8/1869 at Union Point, Georgia

Brown Bryan Bible continued...

Robert Francis, 2nd son of T. M. and S. F. Bryan, 2/12/1872 at Union Point, Georgia
Brown Bryan 1/13/1797
Martha A. V. Smith, his wife, 3/25/1805
James Lewis Harrell 12/8/1822

DEATHS

John Smith 6/23/1832
Mrs. Martha Smith 7/1/1834. aged 73 yrs.
6/23/1844 I lost a dear little boy
10/27/1845 I lost a second son
Brown Bryan 1/19/1854, aged 88 yrs.
Annie Louise Pegues 12/1854
Thomas A.Bryan, bro. of Brown Bryan, 10/3/1854, aged ca 38 yrs,City of Charleston, SC.
Lizzie Pegues 6/20/1847
Francis Henry Pegues 9/12/1854
Mrs. Julia Renard 6/23/1858 at Charleston, S. C., aged 22 yrs, 1 mo., 2 days
William D. Bryan 1871 in Union Point, Georgia at home of her brother. aged 38 yrs

JOHN WARNOCK BIBLE
DAR Records, Ga. State Archives

John Warnock 1757 Ireland-5/28/1842 m. 6/21/1786 Abbeville . S. C. Elenor Dowdle, District 9/3/1767-9/11/1850, the daughter of Robert Dowdle.

John Warnock Bible continued...

BIRTHS of Their Children

Mary Warnock 1/29/1787 m. Adam Todd
Jane Warnock 1/4/1789 m. Solomon Gees
Elizabeth Warnock 11/1/1791 m. William Gillilah Elenor
Warnock 10/18/1792 m. John Reid
Robert Warnock 11/20/1794 m. Lucretia
Frances Warnock 6/28/1799 m. George Telford
Margaret Warnock 2/1/1797 m. 1st Samuel Baker, 2nd, Thomas Hill
Anna Warnock 8/25/1801 m. Samuel R. McFall
John Warnock 11/17/1803 m. Mary Warnock
James Warnock 2/15/1805-d. infancy
Rebecca Warnock 3/5/1808 m. Mr. Hamilton

Samuel Robertson McFall 3/6/1803, Anderson Co., S. C., son of John McFall (b. Antrim Co., Ireland) and Mary Norris
Anna Warnock 8/25/1801 Anderson Co., S. C.
Samuel McFall m. Anna Warnock 1823
Samuel McFall killed in War between the States 6/27/1862
Anna Warnock McFall d. 9/1/1873

BIRTHS of Children of Samuel and Anna McFall

John Cater McFall 10/5/1825
Rachel Amanda McFall 1/16/1836
Margaret Jane McFall 10/28/1826
Sarah Cinderella McFall 12/1/1837
Mary Elizabeth McFall 3/1/1828
Aletha Caroline McFall 4/17/1840
Rebecca Ann McFall 4/25/1830
Samuel Newton Whitmill McFall 2/10/1842

John Warnock Bible continued...

Elenor Frances McFall 3/12/1832
Martha Cornelia McFall 12/18/1843
Julia Emily McFall 10/8/1833

MARRIAGES and DEATHS of Children of Samuel Robertson McFall and Anna Warnock McFall

John Cater McFall never married, d. 1/10/1878
Margaret Jane McFall never married, d. 4/8/1871
Mary Elizabeth McFall m. Dr. L. B. Johnson, d. 7/31/1909
Rebecca Ann McFall m. William Hunter, d. 2/17/1896
Elenor Frances McFall m. William E. McDowell d. 5/1910
Julia Emily McFall m. John Coleman Neville, d. 8/13/1855
Rachel Amanda McFall m. Josiah Freeman Auld, d. 2/23/1822
Sarah Cinderella McFall m. Robert A. Gilmer, d. 5/16/1915
Aletha Caroline McFall m. James Alex Ballenger, d. 3/29/1925
Samuel Newton Whitmill McFall never married, d..7/1/1862
Martha Cornelia McFall m. John Birdsey Pickett, d. 12/30/1925

JOHN PEARSON BIBLE of Camden, Fairfield District
Records, John Houston Chapter, DAR, Georgia State Archives

John Pearson m. 4/25/1742 Mary Raiford, daughter of Philip Raiford and his wife, Martha

Their Children:

John Pearson 5/30/1743-10/25/1817 m. 5/21/1765 Sarah Raiford
Philip Peter Pearson m. 4/13/1783 Mary Butler
Mary Ann Pearson m. 10/16/1764 Thomas Bond

John Pearson Bible continued...

Martha Pearson 11/7/1754-ca 1796) in S. C. m. Capt. John Cook
Rachel Pearson m. Henry Hancock

Philip Pearson, son of John and Mary, b. 4/13/1783 Mary Butler, daughter of Francis and Ann Butler

BIRTHS of Their Children

Philip Edward Pearson 5/7/1786 -
Mary Ann Peason 12/22/1799
George Butler Pearson 6/29/1788
Joel Erskine Pearson 9/18/1802
John Weston Pearson 9/20/1792
Martha Christian Pearaon 3/3/1803
Robert Raiford Pearson 2/22/1795
Isaac Kirkland Pearson 10/26/1797

MARRIAGES

Philip Edward Pearson to Rachel Younge (moved Ala., then Texas)
Mary Ann Pearson to Rev. Joseph Holmes
Martha Christian Pearson to Major William Taylor

GEORGE AND SARAH ADAMS BIBLE of Abbeville
DAR Records, Ga. State Archives

BIRTHS of Children of John and Olive Adams

John Arch Adams 4/11/1845
James Nealy Adams 12/25/1859
Nancy Olive Adams 12/2/1846
John Wisdom Adams 10/9/1813

George and Sarah Adams Bible continued...

Sarah Elizabeth Adams 5/26/1848
Olive Welch Adams 4/8/1821
Benjamin Franklin Adams 2/28/1850
William Sims Adams 11/8/1837
Charley Gillum Adams 11/28/1851
Martha Newberry Adams 1/3/1839
Jesse Arrington Adams 11/28/1853
Margaret Susan Adams 6/3/1840
Leonard Hamilton Adams 9/30/1855
Lucinda Holland Adams 8/26/1841
Zachariah Taylor Adams 9/12/1857
Mary Retincey Adams 11125/1842

DEATHS

Mary Retincey Adams 9/28/1928
William Sims Adams - duringwar of smallpox
  Note: George and Sarah Proctor Adams emigrated from Scotland to Abbeville. South Carolina. George Adams was Lieutenant in the Continental Army and hero in the Battle of Ninety-Six. John Adams m. Olive in 1836. Neither were related and both were from S. C. They reared 14 children, two of whom lived over 80 and 84 yrs.

REV. J. L. GIRARDEAU BIBLE
DAR Records, Ga. State Archives

John Girardeau, son of Isaac Girardeau and Mary Westcoat, b. 3/1/1756 Liberty Co., Ga.   m. 3/20/1783 (bro. of William, settled in South Carolina.)
John Bohun Girardeau, son of John and Eleanor Dashvood Girardeau b. St. Paul's Perish, Colleton Co., S. C., 10127/1798

Rev. J. L. Girardeau Bible continued...

Claudia Hearne Girardeau, wife of John Bohun Girardeau, b. James Island, Charleston Co., S. C., 3/17/1801, the daughter of Edward and Margaret Freer

BIRTHS of Children of John B. and Claudia H. Girardeau

John L. Girardeau 11/14/1825 James Island, S.-C. m. 1/24/1849 Sarah P. Hamlin
Emily Margaret Girardeau 11/24/1826 James Island, S. C. m. Francis L. Wilkinson
Thomas Jefferson Girardeau 1/21/1828 James Island, S. C.
Edward Freer Girardeau 9/13/1829 James Island, S. C.-d. infancy
Claudia Mary Girardeau 4/27/1831 James Island, S. C. m. James Legare

Edward Freer Girardeau II, b. 11/28/1832 James Island. S. C., d. 9/9/1885 Adams Run, Colleton Co., S. C.

BIRTHS of Children of Rev. John L. and P. Sarah Girardeau

Susan King Girardeau 12/23/1849 Adams Run, S. C.
Thomas Hamlin Girardeau 4/3/1851
Edward Hearne Girardeau 9/13/1852
John Rohun Girardeau 1/3/1854 Charleston, S. C.
Edward Freer Girardeau 12/24/1855 Charleston, S. C.
Claude Hearne Girardeau 12/5/1857 Charleston S. C.
Sarah DuPre Girardeau 10/3/1859 Charleston, S. C.
Hannah Moore Girardeau 5/1/1861
William Richmond Girardeau 12/7/1866
John Bohun Girardeau m. 6/23/1897 Emmie Trice, Thomaston, Ga.

Rev. J. L. Girardeau Bible continued...

John Bohun, son of J. B. and Emmie Girardeau, b. 2/3/1899 Thomaston, Ga.
Evelyn Lee, daughter of J. B. and Emmie Girardeau, b. 10/16/1900
Richard Bohun, son of J. B. and Emmie Girardeau, b. 6/3/1904

DEATHS

John Girardeau, son of Isaac, 4/14/1837 James Island, S. C.
Eleanor D., wife of John Girardeau, 12/1842 Charleston, S. C.
John Bohun Girardeau, son of John and Eleanor D., 1/16/1852 Beech Island, Edgefield, S.C.
Claudia Hearne Girardeau, wife of John Girardeau, 6/21/1833 Ft. Johnson, James Island, S.C.
Edward Freer, son of John H. and Claudia H. Girardeau, 9/13/1830 James Island, S. C.. his birthday, age 1 yr.
Edward Freer Girardeau II, son of John B. & Claudia H., 9/9/1855, Adams Run SC., age 22.
John Bohun Girardeau, son of John B. and Mary F., 7/30/1852, aged 14 yrs.
Thomas Hsmlin Girardeau, son of Rev.J. L. & P.S., 6/18/1852, Adams Run, SC., 1 yr., 2 mo.
Edward Hearne Girardeau, son of Rev. J. L. and P. S., 10/3/1852
Hannah Moore Girardeau, dau of Rev. J. L. and P. S., 9/8/1862

Sarah DuPre Webb, daughter of Rev. J. L. and P. S. Girardeau and wife of Rev. R. A. Webb, 4/18/1881, Columbia, S. C., bur. Elmwood Cemetery.
Sarah Elizabeth Webb. inf. daughter of Rev. R. A. and S. D. Webb ---
Rev. John L. Girardeau, D. D., L. L. D., 6/23/1898 at 1018 Lumber St.. Columbia, S. C.

Rev. J. L. Girardeau Bible continued...

John Bohun Girardeau, son of J. B. and Emmie, 9/24/1899,Thomaston, aged 7 mos., 22 das

Note: John Girardeau, son of Pierre and Catharine Girardeau, b.Tremont, Province (now Vendes) France, was the Hugenot ancestor of the family in America. Catherine's maiden name was Lariene.

THOMAS BLASSINGAME BIBLE of Anderson District
Southern Lineages, P. 288

BIRTHS

Polly Ann Blassingame 5/23/1797
Samuel Easley Blasingame and Thomas, sons of Thomas and Nancy
Easley Blassingame, 5/20/1799
Robert Easley Blassingame 9/3/1801
Elizabeth Blassingame 10/29/1804
Obedience Blasingame 7/2/1806
James Blassingame 5/10/1808-d. young

JOHN CLARK BIBLE
Owner: W. H. Ivy
Covington, Georgia

Father - John Clark 11/19/1780 South Carolina-11/27/1870
Mother - Susan Parks 2/24/1796 South Carolina-8/5/1880

BIRTHS of Their Children

Dr. C. J. Clark 10/17/1816 S. C. m. 1855

John Clark Bible continued...

Thomas E. Clark 2/21/1818 S. C.
Avalin Clark 9/30/1819-1846 S. C.
Matilda Clark 3/20/1821-1825 S. C.
Nancy A. Clark 12/30/1822 S. C.-7/2/1889
Elvica A. Clark 12/11/1823 S. C

H. I. Clark 5/24/1825 S. C.
Mary L. Clark 3/21/1827 S. C.

Martha S. Clark 3/21/1827 S. C.
Harriet Clark 10/8/1827 S. C.
John P. Clark 1015/1830 Newton Co., Ga.
Emily J. Clark 5/24/1831 Jasper Co., Ga., m. Ist 1851, 2nd, 1868
Julia P. Clark 6/18/1833 Jasper Co., Ga.-1865
Albert Clark 8/26/1835-1835 Jasper Co., Ga.
Eliza M. Clark 1/17/1837-1837 Jasper Co., Ga.
Henry T. Clark 5/2/1838 Jasper Co., Ga.-1861
Elmira Clark 3/8/1841 Jasper Co., Ga.
Robert U. Clark 2/1/1845 Jasper Co., Ga.

ETIENNE THOMAS' BIBLE
Owner: Mrs. Mike Powell, Newnan, Georgia

A French Edition

J. F. Ostervald, pastor Neuchatel
Nouvelle Edition, revue. corrigee and augmentee
A Neufehatel de 1'Imprimerie D'Abraham Boyne at Compagnie.
HDCCXLIV (1746)
This March 15. 1938 - Mary G. Jones
(Across from Page VIII, the names are written In French)

Etienne Thomas'Bible continued...

BIRTHS

Stephen Thomas, 8/19/1750 atymit -came over to Carolina 4/12/1764
Marie Frezil, his wife, 12/25/1752 at St. Palsis, a village in Xalntage. a province of above Kingdom-d. 10/13/1808, aged 56 yrs.,m. 5/8/1774
Mary Thomas, their Ist, 7/16/1775 at Charleston,.S. C.
James Thomas, their 2nd, 5/5/1777 Charleston, S. C.-d. 2/27/1785
John Thomas, their 3rd, 1/24/1782 Charleston, S. C.
Susanne Thomas, their 4th, 6/24/1784 Charleston, S. C.
Ann Thomas, their 5th, 12/16/1785 Charleston, S. C.
Jeane Thomas, their 6th, 5/27/1788 Charleston, S. C.-d. 5/10/1789
Samuel Joseph Thomas, their 7th, 3/10/1791 Charleston, S. C.
Stephen (Etienne) Thomas, their 8th, 11/13/1792 Charleston, S. C.

Bible brought from France by the Frezil and Thomas families, Hugenots, to Charleston, South Carolina 4/19/1764.

JOSEPH REID BIBLE
From: Rev. War Pension

BIRTHS

Margaret Reid 12/26/1792
Isabella Reid 5/22/1796
Thomas Baskin Reid 1/12/1787
Rose Reid 5/3/1799
Joseph Reid, Jr. 3/5/1789

Joseph Reid Bible continued...

Samuel Reid 2/25/1802
Mary (Polly) Reid 5/16/1791
Sara Hartgrove Reid 9/25/1804
Elizabeth Reid 5/13/1793

Note: Joseph Reid 6/5/1756-10/10/1828, bur. 7 miles from Seneca, South Carolina. He m. 2/28/1782 Isabella Baskin b. 10/15/1760. Joseph Reid served as a Lieutenant.

JOHN HOWARD BIBLE of Edgefield Co.
Owner: Mrs. Roberta Howard Videtto
1252 - 15th St., Augusta, Georgia

John Howard 8/23/1756 Granville Co., N. C.-1832
Margaret Fudge, b. Edgefield Co., S. C. (now Aiken Co.)-d. 1834 m. John Howard 1793 in Edgefield District, S. C.

BIRTHS

William Sanders Howard, Sr., son of John, 11/18/1792 Edgefield Co., S. C.-12/1/1885
Ann Thorn 1/28/1804 Edgefield Co., S. C.-1858
William Sanders Howard, Jr. 3/20/1833 Edgcfield Co., S. C. 4/20/1913-

Georgia V. Walker 5/3/1840 Edgefield Co., S. C.-2/21/1903 m. 12/6/1856 William S. Howard, Jr.
Roberta Howard 1/6/1876 Aiken Co., S. C. m. 11/21/1891 Robert James Videtto, Augusta, Georgia
Robert James Videtto 2/18/1866 Burke Co., Ga.-11/2/1924 Augusta, Georgia

John Howard Bible continued...

Roberta Howard Videtto 6/16/1901 Augusta, Georgia..
6/16/1923 Henry Allen Robinson

BIRTHS of Grandchildren of Mrs. Roberta Howard Videtto

Anne Videtto Robinson 7/27/1927 Augusta, Ga.
Henry Allen Robinson 2/6/1930 Augusta, Ga.
Tallulah Bell Howard 8/11/L867 Aiken Co., S. C.-2/4/1920 Augusta, Ga. m. John Robert Key 12/8/1886, McCormick, S. C.
John Robert Key 12/26/1856 Hones Path, S. C.-5/6/1912 Augusta, Georgia
Vivian Key 10/31/1896 Richmond Co., Georgia-
Georgia Walker Key 8/22/1899 Augusta, Georgia m. 6/15/1922 Neil Robert Jones
Neil Robert Jones b. 11/25/1895 Mazeppa, Minnesota
Virginia Key Jones b. 5/5/1925 Augusta, Georgia

Carol David Jones b. 11/11/1926 Elko, Nevada

Notes: Charnel Hightower Thorn, great-grandfather of Mrs. Roberta Howard Videtto, b. Buncombe Co., N. C.-d. Gwfnnett Co., Ga. (near Lawrenceville, Rev. War Soldier. John Howard was Rev. Soldier, fought for seven years. William Sanders Howard, Sr. served In War of 1812 as Sgt. In Capt. John Miller's Co., Youngblood's Regt., S. C. Militia.

MOSES GUYTON BIBLE
Of Spartanburg County
Owner: Helen Bishop, Eastman, Georgia

Moses Guyton b. 10/27/1758 France-d. Spartanburg, S. C. 1807 m. 1782 to Tabitha Saxon 12/10/1764-2/10/1811

BIRTHS of Their Children

John Guyton 2/5/1784-12/29/1855
Joseph Guyton 9/12/1795
Judith Guyton 3/22/1786
Sarah Guyton 8/24/1797-7/27/1849
Hannah Guyton 6/29/1788
Moses Guyton 9/4/1799-12/12/1870
Mary Guyton 4/4/1791
Tabitha Guyton 8/11/1801-2/1811
Charles Guyton 9/6/1793
Elizabeth Guyton 11/25/1803
Moses Guyton b. 9/4/1799 m. 10/24/1829 Mary Ann Love 2/18/1811- 5/3/1895

BIRTHS of Their Children

Tabitha Jane Guyton 12/6/1830
Mary Elizabeth Guyton 7/7/1833
Sarah Caroline Guyton 5/4/1836-12/29/1855
Margaret Love Guyton 2/7/1839
Augusta Helen Guyton 5/7/1841
Emma Saxton Guyton 8/24/1843
Moses Guyton 8/30/1846
Julia Elmira Guyton 10/17/1849
Amos Charles Guyton 9/3/1852
John Guyton 3/31/1855-12/29/1855

ABRAM HUGUEIN BIBLE Of Grahamville
Owner: Adelaide H. Colcock, McPhersonville, South Carolina

Berry Pitman Gillison b. 6/10/1743 in Warwick, Mass. or Province of Maine and m. 1/8/1770 Elizabeth Bethson who was b. 12/12/1750

Children of Derry Pitman Gillison and Elizabeth Bethson

Mary Gillison 12/21/1770-12/28/1770
Thomas Charles Gillison 2/27/1772-6/4/1825 m. 12/4/1794
Molsey Gillison 1/19/1775-9/1780
Joseph Gillison 4/1/1777-1/11/1777
Elizabeth Gillison 4/28/1779-12/1798 m. 2/7/1798

David William Gillison 12/30/1782-5/1815 m. 8/4/1806
Anna Gillison 7/14/1784-1/25/1854 m. 4/9/1801
Sarah Gillison 7/14/1784, twin-9/14/--
Susannah ---
Mary Drayton ---
Rebecca Gillison 12/12/1750 m. 1/8/1770
Berry Gillison 6/10/1743-2/3/1819

MARRIAGES

Abram and Anna Huguenin 4/9/1801
Julius G. Huguenin 1/31/1827 to Theodora O. Gaillerd
W. F. Colcock to Sarah Rebecca Huguenin 1/22/1829, eldest daughter of Abram and Anna
J. G. Huguenin to Eliza L. Horrall 12/26/1833
Cornelius M. Huguenin to Adelaide M. Barksdale 11/23/1837
W. F. Colcock to Emmaline L. Huguenin 3/16/1838

Abram Huguein Bible continued...

BIRTHS

Julius Gillison Huguenin 12/10/1806
Sarah Rebecca Huguenin 12/4/1808
Thomas E. Huguenin 12/19/1811-6/8/1812
Daughter, 7/1821
Lawrence A. Huguenin 7/8/1814-7/14/1816
Cornelius Macdonough Huguenin 2/21/1817
Emaline Lucia Huguenin 9/20/1819
Daughter, 1/14/182-, lived a few hours
Abram Huguenin 8/13/1826-6/6/1827
Julia Theodora Huguenin 9/1/1828 (child of J. G. and Theodora)
Abraham and Theodora Huguenin 9/20/1830 (twins of J. G. and Theodora)
Anna Serena Huguenin 9/6/1838, daughter of Cornelius and Adelaide
Abraham Huguenin 10/5/1838, son of Julius and Louisiana

DEATHS

Sarah Rebecca, wife of W. F. Colcock, 7/1/1829 at Gillisonville, aged 21 yrs.
Mrs. Theodora O. Huguenin 1115/1831 at Gillisonville
Julia Theodora Huguenin 8/26/1838, Woodlawn near Grahamville, SC., wife of Julius G. Huguenin
Capt. Abraham Huguenin 4/11/1846, aged 68 yrs.
Mrs. Elizabeth V. McLaws, on 7th inst., in 55th yr., consort of James McLaws, Augusta, eldest dau. of David and Sarah Huguenin of St. Luke's Parish, SC
Anna Maria Huguenin 1/25/1854 in Charleston, 69 yrs. old.

DAVID STOLL BIBLE
Owner: A. St. J. Lawton, Charleston, South Carolina

David Stoll (grandson of Jacob and Catherine Stoll who came from Purysburg, S. C. in 1732 with a colony of Huguenots under Col. John Fury)

Rebekah Reece, her Book, b. 7/9/1732
Benjamin Reece m. Rebekah Dixon 5/29/1751
Our 1st Child was stillborn 12/11/1752
Mary Reece b. 2/4/1754
David Stoll m. Rebekah Reece 10/9/1757

Children of David and Rebekah Stoll

Susannah Stoll 7/23/1758
David Dixon Stoll 1/23/1762 m. Sophia Bourquin 5/6/1782
Gabriel Stoll 9/25/1763
Susannah Stoll m. Michael Garvey 8/10/1780

BIRTHS

Sophia Bourquin, daughter of John Lewis and Margaret, 12/12/1762
Rebekah Sophia Stoll, daughter of David Dixon and Sophia Stoll, 2/19/1782
Elizabeth Stoll, daughter of David Dixon and Sophia Stoll, 11/12/1784
Susannah Garvey Stoll 5/14/1786
John Lewis Bourquin Stoll 11/30/1788-9/23/1789
Louisa Bourquin Stoll 4/14/1794 Beaufort, South Carolina

WILLIAM CALHOUN NORRIS BIBLE
Owner: Mrs. John J. Coker Anderson, South Carolina

MARRIAGES

John Thompson to Mary Haile 10/2/1804
Dr. William Calhoun Norris to Elvira Thompson 5/8/1823
Elliott Monroe Keith to Mary Rebecca Norris 1/16/1845 by Rev. David Humphries
Thomas Hamlin Anderson to Eugenia Rachel Norris 10/10/1846 by Rev. William Carlisle
Dr. John Thompson Norris to Lucinda Jane Gilder 12/24/1852
Dr. John Thompson Norris to Elizabeth Heneretta Halfacre 12/23/1863 by Rev. Boyd

BIRTHS

John Thompson 7/13/1769
Mary Haile 12/29/1783

Dr. William Calhoun Norris 1/1/1796
Elvira Thompson 8/18/1805
Dr. John Thompson Norris 4/14/1824
Rachel Eugenia Norris 2/18/1826
Mary Rebecca Norris 7/15/1828
James Edward Anderson 7/27/1847
Dr. William Calhoun Norris Jr. 9/24/1830
Flora Cornelia Keith 6/22/1849
John Bon'jon Anderson 10/11/1849
Virginia Elvira Keith 10/2/1851
Mary Valira Anderson 7/11/1852
James Gilder Norris 1/12/1853
Calhoun William Keith 1/13/1854
Mary Tabitha Norris 7/1857

William Calhoun Norris Bible continued...

William Norris Anderson 5/27/1855
Elvira Eugenia Anderson 4/26/1857
Elizabeth Mary Keith 6/21/1857
Fanny Claudia Norris 9/19/1859
Wilson Abney Norris 4/8/1861

Elliott Monroe Keith 9/27/1862
Leila Jane Norris 10/1864
John Thompson Norris, Jr. 1867
Ada Hamlin Anderson 10/3/1866 (now Mrs. John J. Coker)

DEATHS

Dr. William Calhoun Norris 11/4/1830
John Thompson 12/19/1849
Mary Thompson 12/1857
Lucinda Norris 10/1861
Dr. William Calhoun Norris, Jr. 7/10/1862

JAMES FRENCH BIBLE
P. 35, v. xxxVr, No. 1 Natl Gen. Soc. Qtly

James French b. 6/19/1788 m. 8/1813 Eleanor Shanks b. 6/22/1794

BIRTHS of Their Children

Lewis P. French 8/30/1814-1876
Sallie French 4/29/1817-2/3/1919
Moses T. French 5/29/1819

Love Ann French 4/14/1821-10/1881

James French Bible continued...

Ashabel J. (Zale) French 2/14/1824-1912
Eleanor Jane French 11/24/1825
Lafford Berry French 11/20/1827
Elizabeth R. French 1/6/1830
William Doss French 3/15/1832
Joseph Taylor French 1/23/1834
Ruth Sylvania French 3/15/1837-3/28/1859

JAMES AND URSULA POOL BIBLE
Of Laurens County From: Rev. War Pension W9233

James Pool 4/5/1756 Hawkins Co., Va. - 7/29/1839
Ursula b. 1/1/1762 m. 7/11/1782 Mecklenburg Co., Va.

BIRTHS of Children

Rebekah Pool 4/22/1783
Gabriel Pool 11/9/1793
C--- Pool 1/18/1785

Betsey Pool 11/6/1796
William Pool 2/21/1787
John Pool 7/16/1799
Salley Pool 3/9/1789
James Pool Jr. 3/15/1804
Polley Pool 6/23/1791

Note: James Pool applied for pension 10/15/1832 from Laurens Co., S. C., later Ursula. widow, applied 2/22/1845.

ISAAC CANNON BIBLE
Owner: Mrs. Mason L. Copeland Laurens. South Carolina

BIRTHS

Isaac Cannon 6/8/1759-8/9/1808
Alsey Cannon, Ist dau., 2/24/1785
William Cannon, Ist son, 11/19/1786-6/24/1857
Samuel Cannon, 4th son, 2/3/1796-1/1/1827
Richard Speake Cannon, 2nd son, 10/11/1788-1/31/1844
Mary Cannon, 2nd dau., 12/5/1790-3/22/1855
David Cannon, 3rd son, 10/23/1793-10/22/1869
Hezekiah S. Cannon, 5th son, 6/1/1798
Sarah Cannon, 3rd dau., 9/9/1800-9/13/1804
Isaac Pennington Cannon, 6th son, 10/11/1802
George Speake Cannon, 7th son. 8/14/1806

JAMES AND MARGERY LONG BIBLE Of Anderson
From: Rev. War Pension W509

BIRTHS

Elizabeth Long 7/25/1777
Henry Long 8/22/1787
James Long 4/16/1785
Ezekiel Long ---
John Anderson Long 8/22/1787
Margery Long---
Mathew Long 12/29/1780
Ann Long 3/28/1790
Mary Long 5/14/1782
William and George Long ---

George and Margery Long Bible continued...

Note: -- Margery Long, widow, applied for pension 2/19/1846. Anderson, S. C., aged 88, stating she m. James Long 9/1775 by Dr. Dellahme, a magistrate In Abbeville, S. C. her maiden name was Margery Thomas (Thomson or Thompson) of Pendleton Dist., S. C. James Long had a bro., Henry. They moved from Abbeville to Tenn. for abt 5 yrs.. during which her daughterPolly and son, James, were born, then moved to Pendleton District,lived 56 yrs. Margery d. 3/13/1846, leaving surviving children: Mathew Long Mary Tippin, wid. of George, Cherokee Co., Ga.; John A. Long of Jackson Co., Ga.; Ezekiel Long of Anderson District. S. C. (admr Margery Long who m. David Gorteny); George Long of Henry Co. Ga.; William Long of Anderson Dist., S. C.; and Anna Herrion m. James Herrion, Anderson Dist., S. C.)

JOHN ANGEL AND MARY BRADFORD BIBLE
From: Rev. War Pension IR1127

John Angel Bradford b. Va. 9/16/1764-d. near Sumterville, S. C. 12/5/1829

Mary Mitchell, his wife, b. on Black River, Sumter Co.. S. C. 8/20/1768-8, 5/19/1818

Frances Bradford 3/16/1789-3/22/1845
Middleton Bradford 1/6/1794
Winfret Bradford 1/7/1792-5/26/1849
Susan Bradford 12/15/1795, d. age 3
Hariot Bradford 12/26/1797, d. age 11
William Wade Bradford b. 5/4/1804
John Mitchell Bradford 3/24/1802-1/17/1841, Miss.
Robert Rivets Bradford 1/1/1807-12/14/1839, La.

John Angel and Mary Bradford Bible continued...

Nathaniel Bradford b. 3/8/1809
Mary Ann Mercy b. 7/2/1812

Note: Nathaniel Bradford, admr and son of Mary Bradford, widow, applied for pension 7/4/1859, Sumter Dist., S. C.
Mary Bradford, widow of John A., d. 5/19/1848 and left Children:
Nathaniel Middleton and William Wade, Mary Ann Mercy and Winfret.

JOSEPH AND ISABELLA REED BIBLE Of Pickens County
From: Rev. War pension W9249

Joseph Reed Sr. 6/5/1756-10/10/1828 Pickens, S. C. .. 2/28/1782
Isabella Baskin, his wife, b. 10/18/1760

BIRTHS of Their Children

Margaret Reed 12/26/1782
Elizabeth Reed 11/13/1793
George Reed (before 1792)
Thomas Baskin Reed 1/12/1787
Isabella Reed 5/22/1796
Samuel Reed 2/25/1802
Joseph Reed Jr. 3/15/1789
Rose Reed 5/3/1799
Mary Reed 5/16/1791
Sarah Hartgrove Reed 9/25/1804

Joseph and Isabella Reed Bible continued...

Note: Isabella Reed, widow, applied for pension 1/9/1844 Pickens, S. C., stating she m. Joseph Reed 2/28/1782 as Isabella Baskin. During war she resided with her mother, a widow, on the Rocky River Abbeville, S. C.; 1792 moved to Pendleton Dist. Her uncle, William Baskin, mentioned. 12/30/1844 Elizabeth Thompson testified that she was half-sister of Isabella and was m. 3/26/1787.

SOLOMON AND NANCY MITCHELL BIBLE
Of Abbeville District From: Rev. War Pension W181

BIRTHS

Stephen Mitchell 12/25/1788
Robert Mitchell 1/18/1801
Elizabeth Mitchell 10/6/1810
Rebecca Mitchell 11/26/1789
Morris Mitchell 7/7/1803
Polly or Mary.Mitchell 4/4/1798
Lewis Mitchell 11/24/1791
Nancy Mitchell 10/29/1804
Greenberry Mitchell 12/28/1793
Richard Mitchell 7/18/1806
Jesse Mitchell 5/16/1796
Susannah Mitchell 5/18/1808

Note: Solomon Mitchell applied for pension 9/7/1833, Hawkins Co.,Tenn., stating he was born Granville, N. C. 1759, son of Robert and Jane (or Taner) Mitchell. Nancy Mitchell, widow, applied for pension 7/19/1845, Hawkins Co., Tenn., aged 83,

Solomon and Nancy Mitchell Bible continued...

stating she m. 5/1797 in home of John Simms in Abbeville Dist., S. C. by George Anderson in presence of John Simms. his wife Ann, and his bro., George. The next day John and George Simms end their sister, Sarah, went with her and her husband to her mother-in-law's Taner Mitchell, widow of Robert Mitchell. In 1794 Solomon and Nancy Mitchell moved from Abbeville, S. C. to Hawkins Co., Tenn.

JOHN WALKER BIBLE
Owner: Edward Eugene Simpson, RFD, Wareshoals, South Carolina (1936)

MARRIAGES

John Walker to Leah Holcombe 12/6/1810
James Walker to Caroline Shaw 3/4/1847
Berriman Walker to Catherine Clardy 9/10/1839
Phebe Walker to W. F. Holt 11/16/1854
Mahala Walker to Joseph B. Simmons 2/18/1841
Mary Walker to Pleasant Shaw 8/18/1850
Sarah Walker to James Simpson 12/31/1857

BIRTHS

John Walker 6/17/1789
Leah Holcombe, wife of John Walker, 12/10/1792

Ages of John and Leah Walker's Children

Berriman Walker 11/16/1811
8th child 12/5/1825 never md.
Elizabeth Walker 8/24/1813

John Walker Bible continued...

Leah Walker 12/7/1827
Mary Walker 7/24/1815
Nancy Caroline Walker 8/3/1829
John H. Walker 3/30/1817
Phebe Walker 8/19/1831
Mahala Walker 1/20/1819
Sarah Walker 9/5/1833
James Walker 10/31/1821
Moses H. Walker 10/16/1823

Leah Elizabeth Holt, our granddau., 10/28/1855
Pheby Caroline Holt, our granddau., 11/19/1858
Joseph Pleasant Simmons, our grandson, 11/12/1859

DEATHS

The 8th child and 5th son of John and Leah Walker 11/19/1826
Moses H. Walker, 7th child, 10/21/1844

Berriman Walker, 1et child, 9/26/1855
James Walker, 6th child, 7/19/1857
Pheobe Bolt, 11th child, 11/26/1854
Mahala Simmons, 5th child, 11/19/1859
Leah Walker, wife of John, 1/4/1869. her maiden name was Leah Holcombe-decd 1/4/1869
John Walker 11/9/1873
Elizabeth Gaines, 2nd child, 1/7/1886
John Walker, 4th child, 5/26/1887
Mary Miller, third child, 6/1/1888
Nancy Caroline Walker 11/17/1895
Leah Walker 11/16/1907

John Walker Bible continued...

BIRTHS

John W. Simpson 1/23/1859
Leah E. Simpson 9/14/1866
William H. Simpson 1/18/1862
Charles U. Simpson 6/6/1869
James W. Simpson 4/11/1864
Edward E. Sinpson 1/29/1874

DEATHS

Sarah Walker Simpson, wife of James Simpson and 12th child of John and Leah Walker, 7/11/1912
James W. Simpson 1/22/1936

John W. Simpson 5/13/1929
William H. Simpson 9/30/1929
Leah F. Simpson 12/12/1866

WILLIAM DENDY WATTS BIBLE
Owner: Mrs. Mason L. Copeland Laurens, South Carolina

BIRTHS

William O. Watts 8/22/1800
Susan Speake Cannon 11/28/1820
Susan C. Young 8/16/1812

W. D. Watts m. S. C. Young 10/2/1828
W. D. Watts m. S. S. Cannon 2/11/1837
W. D. and S. C. Watts had three children
Nancy Dendy Watts 4/2/1830-7/15/1834

William Dendy Watts Bible continued...

Phoebe Augusta Watts 7/14/1832-7/11/1833
William Augustus Watts 8/5/1834-8/5/1836
John William Watts 3/17/1839
Beaufort Watts Ball 1803-1902
Laurens Hayne Watts 7/28/1841
William Hills Watts 2/20/1850
Susan Young Watts 11/24/1843
Arah Newberry Watts 3/11/1852
Lucy Nancy Watts 11/22/1845
James Dunklin Watts 7/15/1854
Eliza Henrietta Watts 2/6/1848
Rhoda Belle Watts 1/11/1858 m. 1867

DEATHS

W. D. Watts 7/10/1861 William Watts 6/30/1856
J. V. Watts 9/24/-- A. N. Watts 6/28/1856

BIRTHS

Eliza Kynnion Watts 12/14/1792 (m. Vaughan)
Braxton Watts 1/23/1795
Richard Watts 4/8/1797
Louisa Watts 5/30/1799
Narcissa Watts 5/29/1801 m. 1829 John Ball (1800-1834)
John Pollard Watts 5/18/1803

Cornelia Watts 6/25/1805
Elvira Watts 8/26/1807
Peggy Watts 10/17/1809
John Watts d. 10/13/1812, aged 48 yrs.

JEFFERSON SULLIVAN BIBLE
Owner: Mrs. Sara S. Ervin, Ware Shoals, South Carolina

(Older records made by Mary Charlton Sullivan, b. Va. 6/1/1722- 8. S. C. 12/20/1837)

Owen Sullivan b. 1/1770- Lunenburg Co., Va .m. Margaret Hughlett
(Hewlett) and had children: James, Owen, Pleasant, Charles and Margaret
Margaret Hughlett, wife of Owen Sullivan, b. 3/170-
Pleasant Sullivan b. 8/15/1757
Mary Charlton b. 6/1/1772- in Goochland Co., Va.
Charles Sullivan b. 4/2/1728 on Twltty's Creek, Charlotte Co.,Va. m. widow, Mary
Charlton Johnson and removed to S. C. near beginning of old Rev. War.
Issue: Moses, Sara Margaret, Hewlett, Stephen, Clayborne
Clayborne Sullivan b. 12/1/1772, went to Kentucky
Hewlett Sullivan b. 12/28/1763
Mary Dunklin Sullivan, consort of Hewlett above, b. 2/17/1771 and they had Issue: 8 sons, 4 daus as follows:

Dunklin Sullivan 2/27/1791
George Washington Sullivan 9/27/1809
John C. Sullivan 1/18/1793
Hewlett Sullivan 4/28/1801
Jane Sullivan 9/21/1798
Charles Pinckney Sullivan 10/3/1811
Frances Sullivan 12/28/1803
Mary Sullivan 10/31/1813
Elizabeth Sullivan 10128/1805
James M. Sullivan 3/11/1816

Jefferson Sullivan Bible continued...

Thos. Jefferson Sullivan 9/28/1801
Joseph P. Sullivan 6/17/1796

Joseph Dunklin, father of Mary who m. Hughlett Sullivan, b. in England, came to Berkley Dist., S. C., served in Old Rev. War

BIRTHS

Mary Sullivan, daughter of Moses, 12/25/1785
John Hewlett Sullivan 3/8/1821
Benjamin Sullivan 10/8/1822
Keziah Sullivan 5/29/1824
Mary Anne Sullivan 4/7/1826
Clarissa Sullivan 3/8/1828
Milton A. Sullivan 6/5/1829
Joseph Sullivan 5/20/1831
William Dunklin Sullivan 4/19/1838
Temperance Sullivan 11/6/1835
Charles Pleasant Sullivan 2/10/1841

Mary Henrietta Sullivan 7/11/1836
Frances Elizabeth Sullivan 4/12/1839
Adelaide Sullivan 8/18/1841
Sarah Cureton Sullivan 4/7/1844
John Dunklin Sullivan 2/22/1847
Claudia Caroline Sullivan 9/15/1849
Thomas Jefferson Sullivan 12/24/1853
Charles Pascal Sullivan 6/11/1859

MARRIAGES

Charly Sullivan, Bachelor, and Mary Charlton Johnson, widow,

Jefferson Sullivan Bible continued...

Hewlett Sullivan and Mary Dunklin 12/19/1787
Dr. John C. Sullivan and Ann H. Arnold 2/4/1823, Greenville Co.
Joseph P. Sullivan and Temperance H. Arnold 4/30/1820
George W. Sullivan and Jane Washington Brooks of Edgefield 1/14/1836
T. Jefferson Sullivan & Sarah Moon Cureton 9/12/1833,of Greenville Co.,by J. Dueast
Miss Addie J. Sullivan to Pascal D. Buff of Greenville Dist. by C. B. Stewart

Miss M. Hettie Sullivan, eldest daughter of late Thomas J. Sullivan of Laurens to Capt. C. M. Perkins of Greenville 8/23/1866
Miss Sallie C. Sullivan to L. T. Mahaffey 6/18/1868, all of Laurens Co.
Miss Fannie A. Sullivan to Cept. J. W. Goodgoin 2/19/1880 by C.B. Stewart
J. D.Sullivan of Laurens to Miss Ellen Clinkscales,Abbeville 5/15/1873
Miss Claudia C. Sullivan to Augustus Huff of Greenville Co. 10/16/1877 by J. B. Traywick
Charles M. Sullivan to Miss Arrah Watts of Laurens 12/24/1882 by J. Y. Fair
Capt. William m. Harriet G. Humbert 10/23/1864 at Mt. Bethel Methodist Church
Thomas J. Sullivan, 2nd, to Felicia A. Sullivan at Tumbling Shoals, 11/11/1884

DEATHS

John Sullivan of Virginia, soldier. 169-
Owen Sullivan of Virginia 176-

Jefferson Sullivan Bible continued...

Charly Sullivan at his plantation "The Grove" in Greenville Dist., S. C. 11/3/1808.

He was soldier in Old Rev. War in S. C.Mary Charlton Sullivan, consort of Charles Sullivan, 12/20/1837, 115 yrs. old. She was known as Granny-in-the-Bed

Moses Sullivan 1810 at Lebanon
Hughlett Sullivan 7/11/1830 at his summer home, Lickville, Greenville Dist. He raised Co. Rangers in Old Rev. War in S. C.
Mary Dunklin Sullivan 6/12/1850, aged 79 yrs, and left large family of sons and daus.
Mary Sullivan Scott Interred at Sullivan graveyard 3/27/1855
Robert Scott 1873, aged 101 yrs.
Joel Ferguson of the Jackson War
Peter Ragsdale of 6th Va. inf. in old Rev., consort of Sallie Charlton, 1805
Samuel Moore, consort of Jane Sullivan
Dunklin Sullivan, eldest son of late Capt. Hewlett Sullivan,12/1837, on the Bench in Ala.

Joseph Pinckney Sullivan 10/20/1849 in City of Charleston, S. C.
Francis Sullivan Calhoun 5/8/1837
Sarah Smith, consort of Hon. Charles P. Sullivan of Laurens,12/30/1845
Elizabeth Sullivan Pinson 9/5/1847 near Culbertson's nill
Sarah Mimms Sullivan, consort of Dr. James Sullivan, 9/28/1856
Jane Washington Brooks Sullivan 2/1/1855
Dr. John C. Sullivan 4/14/1864, old age
James M. Latimer, Esq. 10/16/1865, consort of Mary Sullivan

Jefferson Sullivan Bible continued...

Capt. Milton A. Sullivan of the Confederate War 2/19/1865 in hospital in Columbia, S. C. when Sherman burned the city
T. Jefferson Sullivan. Esq. 1/13/1866 at his home, Mt. Bethel
Mary Mayberry Sullivan, consort of Judge Dunklin Sullivan, 8/2/1872 in Alabama
Dr. James N. Sullivan, youngest son of Capt. Hewlett & Mary Sullivan 4/9/1875 at Warthen
Charles P. Sullivan, Esq. of Laurens, 7/27/1876
Sarah Rutledge Cureton Sullivan, consort of T. Jeff Sullivan, 12/17/1882, old age
Mary Sullivan Latimer 2/10/1883
Hewlett Sullivan, 2nd, 5/30/1887 of old age, bachelor
George W. Sullivan Esq. 12/19/1887 at his home, Charlton Hall, Laurens Co., S. C.
Temperance Sullivan, wid. of Joseph P. Sullivan of Tumblin Shoals, 9/25/1857
Harriett Humbert Sullivan 8/27/1868
Capt. William D. Sullivan 9/2/1931
Thomas J. Sullivan, 2nd, 11/5/1923 at Mt. Bethel

COLONEL GEORGE SPEAKE CANNON BIBLE
Owner: Mrs. Mason L. Copeland, Laurens, South Carolina

BIRTHS

George Speake Cannon 8/14/1806
Elizabeth Jane Cannon, 4th dau., 6/18/1842
Sarah Smith Cannon, wife, 6/10/1814
George Dallas Cannon, 2nd son, 8/2/1844
Mary Louisa Cannon, Ist dau., 8/2/1834

Colonel George Speake Cannon Bible continued...

Richard Speake Cannon, 3rd son, 12/13/1845
William Smith Cannon, Ist son, 4/19/1836
Sarah Abigail Cannon, 5th dau., 1/25/1849
Martha Ann Cannon, 2nd dau., 6/4/1838
Angeline Cannon, 3rd dau., 4/14/1840

MARRIAGES

George Speake Cannon to Sarah Smith 12/21/1832
Mary Louisa Cannon to Jared Smith Johnson 8/9/1852
Martha Ann Cannon to Spencer L. Glascow 3/18/1856
William Smith Cannon to Texana C. Sligh 10/5/1860
Angeline Cannon to C. W. I. Spearman 5/1/1861
Elizabeth Jane Cannon to Thompson Conner 10/5/1865
Sarah A. Cannon to William C. Sligh 11/18/1869

DEATHS

George Speake Cannon 11/16/1888
Sarah Cannon 7/13/1895
Mary Louisa Johnson 7/21/1917
William Smith Cannon 11/11/1868 (effects of wounds)
Martha Ann Glascow 2/20/1892
Angeline Spearman 3/4/1875
Elizabeth Jane Conner 12/12/1915
George Dallas Cannon 10/19/1864 (killed Strasburg, Va.)
Richard Speake Cannon 3/24/1064 (from wounds, Va.)

CHARLES D. LUCAS of Marlboro County

BIRTHS

Charles D. Lucas 6/30/1771
William Lucas 4/22/1814
Nancy B. Lucas 4/18/1826
Mary Lucas 9/10/1786
Uriah Lucas 9/17/1816
John Lucas 2/22/1812
Thomas Lucas 10/11/1803
Mary Lucas 1/2/1819-7/6/1913
Dorcas Lucas 11/14/1810
Elizabeth Lucas 10/29/1806
Jane Caroline Lucas 9/20/1820
Mary Holliman 9/12/1837

Lorenzo Lucas 3/18/1821
Maryan Nancy McCoy 3/28/1844
Lorenzo Lucas m. Margaret 1/17/1856
William James Lucas b. 11/17/1856

Nancy B. Lucas d. 1/19/1853
Mary Jane Lucas b. 6/8/1859
Margaret Lucas b. 7/23/1855
John Lucas d. 9/27/1894
Charles D. Lucas d. 5/31/1853
Charles D. Lucas d. 6/30/1863 at Ringgold, Ga.
Mary Lucas d. 1/21/1867
Elizabeth Jane Lucas d. 8/20/1867
Jane Lucas d. 9/14/1877
Lorenzo Lucas and Margaret Lucas was baptised 9/17/1859
John Lucas 2/2/1812-9/27/1894
Jane Lucas 10/26/1818-9/14/1877

Charles D. Lucas Bible continued...

Lorenzo Lucas 5/1/1837-3/16/1917, aged 79 yrs., 11 mos., 6 days
William Marion Lucas 2/21/1939-

Maryan Frances Lucas 7/2/1841-
Charles Daniel Lucas 7/14/1843-
Elizabeth Jane Lucas 7/21/1845-
Jesse Ludlen Lucas 7/27/1850-6/16/1852
John Hasten Lucas 6/3/1848-4/20/1939
Silas Watts Lucas 12/26/1852-1/13/1931
Amanda Emily Lucas 6/3/1856-6/29/1929
John Thomas Lucas 2/26/1862-
Henry Martin 11/--
Mary Lucas 7/20/1842
Monica Lucas 3/10/1844
Holley Elizabeth Lucas 11/5/1846
Alfred Lucas 4/28/1845
Louisa Lucas 3/11/1849
Manervey Rosan Lucas 12/23/1850
Margret An Feline Lucas 6/9/1852
Sarah Frances Lucas 2/5/1854
Silns W. Lucas 12/26/1852-1/13/1935, aged 82 yrs., 17 days
James T. Lucas 10/12/1876
Purvey F. Lucas 8/24/1878
Murray L. Lucas 5/28/1880
Jeritta H. Lucas 3/20/1883
Jennie Ann Lucas 8/16/1885
Marthy Allis Lucas 5/1/1858-2/12/1877
John Marion Lucas d. 3/13/1901

DAVID N. CARDOZO BIBLE
Owner: Alice Landrum, Galveston, Texas

David N. Cardozo 8/29/1753-7/13/1835, in 83rd yr. of age wife, Leah, 4/8/1765-7/10/1780
Wife, Sarah, 6/12/1766-10/25/1853, aged 87 yrs., 4 mos., 13 days

BIRTHS of Children

Sarah Cardozo 1/12/1780
Jacob Cardozo 6/17/1786
Frances Cardozo 1/27/1788-10/5/1849, in 62nd yr.
Judith Cardozo 8/3/1790-2/25/1854, in 65th yr.
Isaac N. Cordozo 3/2/1793-8/18/1853, aged 62
Rachel Cordozo 6/16/1795-d. Savannah, Ga. 2/14/1860, in 65th yr. m. 4/11/1821 Charleston, S. C., Abraham (Mendez) Seixas Leah Cordozo 7/6/1797-7/9/1802
Aaron Cordozo 2/18/1802-9/2/1804, aged 2 yrs., 7 mos.
David Cordozo 2/1/1804-2/23/1804
Sarah Levy, together with daus., Frances and Olivia, d. 10/9/1837, lost in steamer Home on her passage from New York to Charleston
Abraham (Mendez) Seixas h. 1/22/1786 NY-d. 8/28/1834 Charleston,S. C., wife, Rachel Cardozo

BIRTHS of Their Children

David Cordozo Seixas 1/30/1823 Richmond, Va.
Virginia Zipporah Seixas b. 9/3/1824 Charleston, S. C. m.12/22/1847, Moses S. Cohen
Benjamin Seixas b. 6/20/1826 Charleston, S. C.-d. 1/22/1828
James Madison Seixas b. 7/20/1829 Charleston, S. C.
Miriam Seixas b. 3/15/1834 Charleston, S. C.-d. 11/9/1837

STEPHEN SMITH, JR. BIBLE Of Barnwell District
Owner: Mrs. Robert Walton, Augusta, Georgia

Capt. Joseph Vince d. 2/19/1811
Mrs. Elizabeth Robison d. 7/9/1830

Mrs. Lucy Vince d. 9/17/1830, aged 73 yrs.
Stephen Smith Jr. 1/17/1776 Burke Co., Ga.-7/21/1840, bur. Near Steel Creek, S. C. m. 12/5/1799 Barnwell District, S. C.
Judith Vince, wife of Stephen Smith, Jr. b. Barnwell District, S.C.- d. 11/12/1857, bur. near old Dunbar place, beside husband

BIRTHS of Children of Stephen Smith Jr. and Judith

Thomas Bonaparte Smith 9/6/1800 Barnwell Dist., S. C.-d. age of 66
Martha Smith 10/3/1802 Barnwell Dist., S. C. (m. 1/1829 John H. Lafitts).
James Vince Smith 5/16/1805 near Augusta, Ga.-7/1/1811, aged 6 yrs., 1 mo., 15 days in
Burke Co., Ga.
Lucy Eleanor Smith 7/23/1807 Burke Co., Ga.-11/17/1883 (m. Francis)
Finklin Dunbar, son of George Robison Dunbar and Mary Pickling
Dunbar. Lucy. Eleanor Smith Dunbar and Maj. Francis Fickling Dunbar are bur. in Boyd Place burying ground-the home plantation of George Robison Dunbar)
Sarah Elizabeth Smith 5/25/1809 Burke Co., Ga. (2nd wife of James Jennings Wilson)
Ann Vince Smith 2/18/1811 Burke Co., Ga.
Catherine Barnes Smith 10/31/1812 Burke Co., Ga.

Stephen Smith, Jr. Bible continued...

Lovisa Robison Smith 8/14/1814 Barnwell Dist., S. C. (m. Edward Furse)
Mary Louisa Smith 7/2/1816-8/1816
Stephen Smith 7/1/1817 Barnwell Dist., S. C.
Joseph Smith 7/24/1819 at Silver Bluff, Edgefield Dist., S. C.
Julia Arabella Smith 9/1/1821 Edgefield Dist., S. C. (m. James Purse)
Ann Millege Smith 4/18/1823 Barnwell Dist., S. C. (m. James T. Bothwell of Augusta, Ga.)
Susan George Smith 10/15/1824 Barnwell Dist., S. C.
Eliza Carey Smith 4/4/1826 Barnwell Dist., SC (m. Winchester M. Graham. She d. 1867)
Barbara Scriven Smith 5/6/1828 Barnwell Dist., S. C.

DEATHS

Lovisa Robison Furse 2/29/1848
Ann Milledge Bothwell 8/1861
Martha Lafitte 12/27/1863
Thomas B. Smith 1/22/1866
Eliza Carey Smith Graham 12/27/1869
Sarah Elizabeth Wilson 1877
Lucy Eleanor Dunbar 11/17/1883
Julia A. Furse 5/17/1894
Capt. Joseph Vince 2/19/1811, aged 67 yrs.
Stephen Smith Sr. 10/17/1788
Elizabeth Smith 8/14/1788
Robert Hankinson 8/21/1788
Thomas Filput Sr. 6/11/1789
Martha Smith 8/4/1799
Eleanor Collins 5/15/1813
Sarah Galphin 1/15/1802

Stephen Smith, Jr. Bible continued...

St. Collins 11/11/181-
Ann Lark 11/19/1802
James Vince Smith, aged 6
Stephen Smith, Jr.
Judith Vince Smith ---

Miscellaneous

James Furse Collins, son of George W. Collins and Susan Ann, 3/6/1820-6/10/1820
Stephen Smith, Sr. d. 10/17/1788 (bur. near Ellenton) m. Martha
Newman (d. 8/4/1799 Barnwell Dist., S. C.)

Children of Stephen and Martha Smith

Sarah Smith d. 11/5/1802 (m. Thomas Galphin)
Henrietta Smith b. 2/15/1784 (m. Lark Robison)
Eleanor Smith d. 5/15/1813 m. Stephen Collins
Elizabeth Smith 1/12/1786-8/14/1788
Stephen Smith, Jr. d. 7/21/1840

Children of Stephen and Eleanor Smith Collins

George W. Collins b. 3/17/1791 m. 11/21/1818 Susan Ann Furse, dau.
of James and Martha, by Rev. William B. Willard
Barbara Collins b. 3/24/1793
Martha Collins b. 1/23/1795 m. 6/23/1814 James Lambright, by Rev.J. W. Wilson

Stephen Smith, Jr. Bible continued...

Augusta Chronicle, Augusta, Ga., November 20, 1820

"Departed this life at the residence of her father Mr. James Furse in Barnwell District, S. C. on Tues. the 10th inst. in the 19th year of her age, Mrs. Susan Ann Collins, wife of George W. Collins, formerly of this place."

George W. Collins (d. 10/14/1836 Lover Three Runs, Barnwell District) m. 2nd, 9/14/1826, Lucy Jerusha Gillett 8/7/1810-12/29/1871, daughter of Dr. Elijah Gillett of Barnwell Dist., S. C. and his wife, Elizabeth Scarborough. Five children by this marriage. She m. 2nd, 1/28/1838, Barnett M. Enicks and had five more children.

JAMES HENRY MALLARD INABINET BIBLE
Of Orangeburg County Owner: Mrs. David H. Gillam
1436 Cue St., N. W., Orangeburg, S. C.

James Henry Mallard Inabinet 1838-6/9/1890, bur. Limestone Churchyard, m. 11/10/1870 Annie Walsh. They had 8 children. Annie Walsh 10/6/1848-12/12/1902, bur. Limestone Churchyard, was daughter of Thomas P. Walsh and Rebecca Leysath

BIRTHS of Children

J. Preston Inabinet 8/7/1871 m. Pearlie Whetstone 11/2/1897
William L. Inabinet 3/13/1873 m. Lula Robinson 1/25/1905
Adria R. Inabinet 9/9/1875 m. William R. Knotts 11/30/1901
Mary E. Inabinet 12/29/1877 m. Frank L. Knotts 11/25/1903
John O. R. Inabinet 9/9/1880-11/5/1881
J. H. Kennerly Inabinet 5/26/1882 m. E. Byrd Goff 12/9/1908

James Henry Mallard Inabinet Bible continued.....

Emanuel P. Inabinet 11/19/1884 m. Lula B. Browning 4/23/1909
Earle A. Inabinet 1/13/1888 m. Pearle E. Robinson 7/9/1914-3/2/1956, bur. Limestone Churchyard, Orangeburg Co., S. C.

Note: Some Descendants of James Henry Mallard Inabinet and Annie Walsh
Earl Alva Inabinet 1113/1888-3/2/1956 bur. Limestone Courtyard m.
7/9/1914 Pearl Edith Drucilla Robinson. They had 6 children
Earl Alva Inabinet Jr. b. 1127/1915 m. 2/28/1936 Juanite McCall who was b. 1/5/1918. Issue:
Nancy Carole Inabinet b.12/21/1937 m. James Arthur Miller 10/11/1961
(children: James Michael Miller b. 5/1962 and Charles Christian Miller b. 11/1964);
Alva Juanita Inabinet b. 10/16/1940 m.1/20/1959 Jesse Owen Allen III (children: Charlotte
Renee Allen b. 9/26/1961 and Garrett Allen b.1/17/1964); Sarah Frances Inabinet
b. 12/1947 m. 1964 Rodney Beard; and Barbara Lynn Inabinet b 8/25/1961.

Pearl Edith Inabinet b. 9/18/1918 m. 2/25/1940 David H. Gillam,Jr. Children: David Earl
Gillam b. 11/19/1941 m. 8/22/1964 Harriett Smith (son, Kenneth David Gillam b.
8/20/1965) and Edith Elaine Gillam b. 6/23/1952
Marian Durham Inabinet b. 6/4/1920 m. 8/25/1949 Arthur W. Wade, decd. 12/17/1963. Child: Mary Beth Wade b. 12/14/1962
Harriett Stack Inabinet b. 4/12/1922 m. 4/18/1946 William J. T. McEachern.

James Henry Mallard Inabinet Bible continued...

Children:

Linda Faye McEachern b. 1/17/1948 and Peggy Marian McEachern b. 10/10/1960
Mary Cornelia Inabinet b. 1/2111926 m. 3/12/1949 George Harmon Culler II. Child: Mary
Ann Culler b. 2/23/1952
James Henry Mallard Inabinet b. 9/20/1928 a. 10/31/1953 Alice Moore. Children: Mark Rennerly Inabinet b. 8/27/1955. Pamela Durr
Inabinet b. 6/1/1959 and James Mallard Inabinet, Jr. b. 7/6/1961

Note: Name spelled "Inabnit" in Bible.

DAVID FOX BIBLE
Owner: Georgianna Catonnet, Augusta, Ga. (Probably decd)

BIRTHS of David and Elizabeth Fox

David Fox 9/2/1720-12/11/1766
Ann Fox 12/11/1733-11/16/1783
Mary Fox 4/1/1722
Margaret Fox 6/29/1736-2/2/1779
John Fox 2/28/1723-2/3/1786
Benjamin Fox 3/23/1738-1/7/1773
Joseph Fox 9/29/1725-12/4/1754
Richard Fox 4/23/1741-3/12/1772
Elizabeth Fox 10/15/1727-9/21/1741
James Fox 4/23/1743-11/9/1773
William Fox 12/26/1729-2/3/1783

David Fox Bible continued...

George Fox 4/7/1746-10/31/1788
Jonathan Fox 12/29/1731
George Fox m. Jane Gotue 5/29/1766

BIRTHS of Children of Benjamin and Ann Fox

Ann Fox 12/18/1753
Elizabeth Fox 11/14/1765
Mary Fox 5/9/1763
Benjamin Fox 9/24/1770
Catherine, wife of David Fox, d. 1766

Elizabeth, daughter of George Fox and Jane, his wife, 9/16/1767-10/29/1794
Jane, daughter of George and Jane Fox, 5/18/1769-9/8/1770
Roger Cameron d. 11/7/1788
James Pace d. 4/22/1782

Notes from "My Father's Old Bible Records" by George Twiggs Jackson, son of William and Anne Eliza Fox Jackson
Mrs. Mary Fox d. 4/14/1848 near Berzelia, Ga.
Amelia, daughter of Benjamin and Mary Fox, b. 8/1/1787
Benjamin, son of Benjamin and Mary Fox
Richard, son of Benjamin and Mary Fox
Ann Eliza, daughter of Benjamin and Mary Fox, b. 6/8/1793 m. William Jackson.

Children of William and Ann Eliza Jackson

Samuel Jackson
George T. Jackson
John K. Jackson

David Fox Bible continued...

William Jackson
Mary Ann Jackson

Mary Ann Jackson m. Benjamin F. Verdery

Notes from Historical Collections of the Ga. Chapters NSDAR, Vol. 2, Page 64: Mrs. Mary
Fox, widow of Benjamin Pox, d. near Irerzelia, Ga., 4/14/1848. They were parents of Anne
Eliza Fox Jackson. Her maiden name is unknown, but the Mrs. Ann Urquhart whose death Is
recorded in the Jackaon Bible Record was sister of Mrs. Mary Fox. Mrs. Urquhart In her Will
refers to Mrs. Mary Fox as her sister, and to Ann E. Jackson as her niece.

HUTSON LOFTIS BIBLE
Owner: H. A. Carlisle
P. O. Box 112, Lowndesville, South Carolina 29659

MARRIAGES

Hutson Loftis to Jane H. Black 12/23/1847 Hutson Loftis to Sarah Gilliam 6/8/1854

BIRTHS

Hutson Loftis 12/23/1825
Jane M. Loftis 6/6/1826-7/18/1853
William P. Loftis 11/14/1848
Elizabeth M. Loftis 10/23/1850-12/10/1929
James T. Loftis 1/12/1853

Hutson Loftis Bible continued...

Sarah L. Gilliam Loftis 2/15/1837
H. A. Loftis 8/28/1862
Luther B. Loftis 8/21/1857

Mary M. Loftis 1/17/1868
John L. Loftis 12/14/1859
C. V. Loftis 6/27/1873

(next page)

James W. Loftis 12/10/1870
Maggie B. Loftis 9/30/1886
Sarah R. E. Loftis 10/4/1882
Mattie M. Loftis 9/23/1888
George W. McNair 1/23/1862-11/12/1934
Arthur Murray McNair 2/28/1882
Ada Leala May
McNair 4/22/1888 Mrs. Arthur McNair d. 2/9/1924

JOHN HARRIS BIBLE of Abbeville District

MARRIAGES

James Wiley to Ann L. Harris 4/18/1824

BIRTHS

John Gaston 3/25/1818
James Wiley 6/4/1794
Alexander Gaston 7/8/1819
Ann L. Harris 11/27/1794

John Harris Bible continued...

Anne Gaston 9/12/1825
Elizabeth Mary Wiley 8/9/1831

The Ages of Negroes

Amey 4/21/1807
John 4/19/1852
Juda 12/16/1823
Mary 6/11/1855
M. (boy) 5/25/1848
Nelson 12/31/1857
Sam 7/5/1850
Charles 7/12/1861

DEATHS

Jane Harris 7/8/1826
William Gaston 4/16/1832
John Harris 4/1/1830

"January 12th A. D. 1843. Julius H. Alexander left North Carolina on the 4 day of February in 1843 with heavy heart.

After traveling through the lonesome countys of North and South Carolina arrived at cousin Simpson's in Loundesville where and when I was very happy to meet with my friends." /s/ Julius H. Alexander

MAJOR STEPHEN TERRY BIBLE

"Departed this life on his fern about four niles from Atlanta on the 15th of November, 1866, Major Stephen Terry, one of the earliest settlers of the city and one of her nest respected citizens. (Apparently the Lakewood Park area)

Major Terry was born in Chester District, S. C., August 10, 1788, and was consequently at the time of his death in the 79ch year of his Age, retaining to the last the faculties of his naturally strong mind, and much of the energy which characterized his young manhood.

On July 4, 1809 he was married in Fairfield District, S. C. to Miss Elizabeth H. Hill, and in 1826 removed to DeKalb Co., Ga. He had the misfortune to lose his wife on Dec. 3, 1838, but in the same year he joined the Methodist Church, of which he remained a firm and consistent member. In uniting with the church he followed the examples and teachings of his youth. His father, John Terry, having joined with the Methodists in 1774.

In 1843 Major Terry settled in Atlanta, which was then an unimportant depot known as Marthasville...He was a contractor for the Monroe (now Macon 5 Western) and Georgia Railways, and the builder of the original "Washingtonton Hall" one of the first, if not the first, hotel built in the city..../s/A Friend."

Stephen Terry d. 12/19/1769 in Chester Co., S. C. m. Ist Sarah who d. 5/4/1765. His 2nd wife was Mrs. Susannah Stover who d. 1785

William Terry, son of Stephen and Sarah, b. 8/8/1750 in Va., and was father of Stephen D., John, Rowland, Anna, Joseph Minter, Elizabeth and Mariah Terry.

Major Stephen Terry Bible continued...

John Terry, son of Stephen and Sarah, 4/27/1752-4/12/1834 in Chester District, S. C. His Ist wife was Sarah Sely who d. 5/20/1788. 2nd wife was Priscilla Stokes whop he m. 12/21/1779.By Sarah, John was father of Jeremiah Sely Terry 2/7/1778-1/8/1823 Abbeville, S C

Priscilla Stokes Terry was the mother of his remaining children: Benjamin, Thomas, John W., and Major Stephen, Sarah Patterson, Elizabeth and William

Elizabeth Terry, daughter of Stephen and Sarah, m. William Ham.
Benjamin Terry, son of Stephen and Sarah, 9/22/1755-1/16/1831 Abbeville District, S. C.

Sarah Terry, daughter of Stephen and Sarah, m. William Morris, Revolutionary War Soldier

WILLIAM REED BIBLE
Owner: Laura McClain Mallon, South Carolina (decd)

William Reed 5/8/1756-7/9/1840
Frances Reed, his wife, 9/12/1760-6/7/1836

BIRTHS

Abel Reed 11/26/1777
Charlotte Reed 4/4/1787
Rebecca Reed 11/7/1781-2/15/1830
Jesse Reed 1/25/1791
Daniel Reed 6/10/1783
Asa Reed 1/14/1793
Mary Reed 1/3/1785

William Reed Bible continued...

Susannah Reed 2/3/1795
Daniel Reed 6/10/1783-1/22/1865
Rebecca Reed 2/11/1796-10/24/1869
Francis Reed 12/14/1815-decd
Milford Reed 7/30/1817-7/25/1818
John L. Reed 9/24/1818-7/37/1877
Kezziah Reed 12/15/1819-4/1895
William B. Reed 4/24/1821-2/5/1894
Sarah Reed 1/24/1823-2/5/1894
Nancy O. Reed 2/23/1824-3/15/1908
Joshua Reed 10/30/1825-9/25/1906
Jesse Reed 7/19/1827-9/20/1862
Leasy Reed 3/4/1829
Rebecca Reed 1/7/1831
Lorrah Reed 3/28/1833-8/20/1856
Silas Reed 3/28/1836-10/29/1861

Daniel R. Reed 11/18/1838
Levi Reed 2/9/1797
Francis Reed 2/6/1801

Keziah Reed 1/29/1799
William Reed 3/8/1804

JOHN H. BURNETT BIBLE
Of Edgefield County
NSDAR Library, Washington, D. C.

BIRTHS

John H. Burnett 6/16/1858
Wm C. Burnett 2/6/1866

John H. Burnett Bible continued...

Mary Jane Burnett 8/29/1861
James A. Burnett 3/27/1868
Susan F. Burnett 8/10/1863

MARRIAGES

John H. Burnett to Hattie M. Giles
Mary J. Burnett to C. M. Phifer 10/4/1883
Susie F. Burnett to Joe J. McDowell 12/5/1894

DEATHS

Susan A. Burnett 6/11/1850
William E. Bearden was killed 9/17/1862 in Maryland, Battle of Sharpsburg

On backside of page:

"W. C. Burnett was not married. He lived the life of a happy bachelor."

EDWARD P. LUCAS BIBLE
Owner: Mrs. R. H. Wilder, Orlando, Florida

BIRTHS

Emmie V. Lucas, daughter of Edward P. and Sarah J., 12/27/1865
Eddie R. Lucas daughter of Edward P. and Sarah J., 8/25/1869
Emmie V. Bass, daughter of Dr. J. L. and Emie V., 5/4/1888 Willacoochee, Georgia

Edward P. Lucas Bible continued...

Enmie Inez Bass, daughter of W. L. and E. R., 3/23/1887 at Kingstree

Natalie Bass, daughter of W. L. and E. R., 11/27/1890, Lake City, South Carolina
Sallie G. Bass, daughter of W. L. and E. R., 3/8/1892, Lake City, South Carolina

Gretchen Bass, daughter of W. L. end E. R., 3/3/1896, Lake City, South Carolina

MARRIAGES

Edward P. Lucas to Sarah J. Brown 16J23/1863, Charleston, S. C.
Eddie R. Lucas to W. L. Bass 6/16/1896, Kingstree, S. C.
Emmie V. Lucas to Dr. J. L. Bass 5/23/1887, Kingstree, S. C.

DEATHS

Emmie Bass, daughter of Dr. J. L. and Emmie Y., 5/4/1888 at Willacoochee, Ga.
Emmie Inez Bass, daughter of W. L. and E. R., 8/29/1887, Kingstree, South Carolina
Natalie Bass, daughter of W. L. and E. R., 1/2/1891, Adel, Ga., both buried at Baptist graveyard, Kingstree, South Carolina
Eddie R. Bass, wife of W. L. Base, 8/13/1919, Tampa, Florida
William Leonidas Bass 1/31/1920. Lake City, South Carolina
Mrs. S. J. Lucas 10/3/1902, Lake City, South Carolina
Mrs. Emma P. Brown, grandmother of Mrs. E. R. and E. V. Bass, 8/12/1900 at Lake City, SC
Dr. J. L. Bass, Lake City, South Carolina

WILLIAM KERR BIBLE
Owner: Mrs. H. Grady Wright
Apt. 1102, Christopher Towers, 1805 Devine Sr., Columbia, S. C.

MARRIAGES

William Kerr to Dulcena Frances Mobley 8/31/1858

BIRTHS

James Harold Kerr 8/23/1859
Elizabeth Jane Kerr 7/22/1865
Fanny Drucilla Kerr 6/7/1861
John Robert Kerr 1/13/1869
William Mobley Kerr 3/18/1863
Henry Richard Kerr 9/23/187-

DEATHS

James Kerr 5/14/1862
William M. Kerr, son of William and D. F. Kerr, 6/1864, ca 1 yr, 3 mos. old
John R. Kerr 12/20/1869, 11 mos, 7 days old
William Kerr 5/21/1898
James Harold Kerr 1901

Mrs. D. E. Kerr, wife of William Kerr, 9/22/1925

WILLIAM McDOWELL BIBLE of Edgefield Co.
Owner: Mrs. J. T. McDowell
8 Marshall Road, Greenwood, South Carolina

BIRTHS of Children of William and Elizabeth McDowell

William McDowell Bible continued...

Elizabeth McDowell. Jr. 11/20/1815
Daniel McDowell 4/11/1827
Francis McDowell 3/6/1817
Wister McDowell 3/11/1830
James Talbert McDowell 10/28/1818
Georgia Ann McDowell 2/23/1833
Shennel McDowell 9/22/1820
Benjamin McDowell 4/17/1827 (twin)
Kitish McDowell 8/18/1822
Savannah McDowell 11/10/1835
George B. McDowell 2/20/1825
Lucintha McDowell 7/6/1838

Note: John McDowell b. Ireland in 1763, came to America with his parents; settled in Pa.ca 1770.

Later, he came with Wright Nicholson to Edgefield Co., S. C., After Rev. War, he m. Wright Nicholson's dau., in 1788. Their child - William McDowell - b.8/30/1789. John McDowell mysteriously disappeared in 1789 or 1790 and was never heard of William McDowell m. Elizabeth Ouzts in 1814, the only daughter of Peter Ouzts. (She had 12 bros)

HENRY VAUGHAN BIBLE
Of "Cherryvale", Statesburg, Sumter District
Owner: Mrs. Mary Britton 221 Hasell St., Sumter, S. C. 29150

MARRIAGES

Henry Vaughan, Jr. to Margaret Anderson 3/3/1795
John J. Frierson to Julia F. Vaughan 5/1/1817

Henry Vaughan Bible continued...

Henry Vaughan to Emma Rees 3/8/1827
Wentworth F. Rees to Vermeille Vaughan 3/11/1827
Mack Reynolds to Julia V. Rees 6/1845
James J. Frierson to Minnie C. Grant 4/29/1856

BIRTHS of Children of James J. and Minnie C. Frierson

Mary Chestnut Frierson 3/23/1857
William Grant Frierson 4/13/1858
Julia Vaughan Frierson 5/7/1859

BIRTHS

Henry Vaughan, Jr., son of Henry Vaughan, Sr. and Elizabeth. 9/13/1767 m. Margaret Anderson, daughter of John and Margaret Anderson, b. 2/1779

BIRTHS of Children of Henry Vaughan and Margaret

Julia Finetta Vaughan 4/20/1796
John Anderson Vaughan 3/8/1803
Mary Margaret Vaughan 12/25/1797
Vermeille Vaughan 6/28/1809
Henry Vaughan 3/31/1800

BIRTHS of Children of John J. and Julia F. Frierson

John Napoleon Frierson 2/21/1818
James Julian Frierson 1/19/1832

BIRTHS of Children of Wentworth F. and Vermeille Rees

Henry Vaughan Bible continued...

Julia Vaughan Rees 10/13/1828
Mary Margaret Rees 4/15/1832
Maria Ford Rees 11/14/1829
Anna Maria Bradford, daughter of John S. and Vermeille Bradford, b.10/4/1839

DEATHS

Mary Margaret Vaughan, daughter of Henry and Margaret, 2/1/1814, aged 16 yrs, 1 mo., 6 days
Henry Vaughan, Jr. 3/5/1814, aged 46 yrs., 5 mos., 20 days
Margaret Vaughan, wife of Henry, Sr., 6/18/1832, aged 53 yrs., 4 mos., 6 days
John J. Frierson 11/15/1839, aged 47 yrs., 4 mos., 22 days
Mary Margaret Rees, daughter of Wentworth F. and Vermeille Rees, 3/11/1859, aged 26 yrs, 10 mos, 24 days
Anna Maria Bradford, daughter of John S. and Vermeille Bradford, 5/1875, aged 36 yrs
Julia F. Frierson, wife of John J., 4/10/1880, aged 83 yrs, 11 mos., 22 days
John N., son of John J. and Julia F. Frierson, 2/19/1887, aged 68 yrs, 11 mos., 29 days
Vermeille Vaughan, wife of John S. Bradford, 9/6/1887, aged 78 yrs, 2 mos., 9 days
James Julian, son of John J. and Julia F. Frierson, 8/1/1890
Mary Chestnut Grant (Minnie) Frierson, wife of James Julian Frierson, 6/12/1907

JAMES PRIESTLY, SR. BIBLE
Owner: Mrs. U. C. Moreow Jacksonville, Texas

BIRTHS of Children by 1st Marriage

James Priestly 4/10/1817
Eliza Ann Ragsdale Priestly 9/11/1819, South Carolina

John Nimrod Priestly 7/11/1839

William Plylander Priestly 2/27/1841
Edward Leonadas Priestly 1/26/1843
James Polk Priestly 12/1/1844
Samuel Baxter Priestly 2/11/1848
Ann Iserbeller Priestly 11/11/1849
Mary Eliza Priestly 2/10/1852
Martha Elizabeth Priestly 1/10/1854
Harriet Chapel Priestly 2/2/1856
Frances Montgomery Priestly 5/17/1858
Louisa Josephine Priestly 9/29/1860

JOHN BAGNAL BROGDON of Sumter Co.

BIRTHS

John B. Brogdon 1/10/1815

Elizabeth P. Brogdon 12/1/1819

Their Children:

Malle Demetrius Brogdon 10/2/1839-8/26/1846
Joel Davis Brogdon 11/18/1841-6/29/1862, 20 yrs, 7 mos., 11 days, on battlefield, Richmond, Va.

John Bagnal Brogdon Bible continued...

Anna Leonora Brogdon 6/22/1843
Mary Amanda Brogdon 4/14/1845
Harriet Rebecca Brogdon 7/25/1847
John Ingram Brogdon 5/21/1849
William Turner Brogdon 11/19/1850
Susan Frances Brogdon 12/111855-7/21/1884
Jane Adelaide Brogdon 2/25/1857
Margaret Eudora Brogdon 10/29/1858
Alice Cornelia Brogdon 2/24/1860
Joel Thomas Brogdon 6/6/1862
Sally Melvina Brogdon 12/15/1867

MARRIAGES

John B. Brogdon to Amanda Davis 2/1837
John R Brogdon to Elizabeth P. Davis 1/9/1839
Michael J. Blackwell to Anna L. Brogdon 12/22/1859 by H. Graham
John Ingram Brogdon of Sumter Co., S. C. to Susan Rebecca McDonald of Williamsburg Co., SC., 5/28/1868 at Mr. S. W. Davis' by Rev. W. H. Mahony

BIRTHS

John Ingram Brogdon 5/21/1849
Susan Rebecca McDonald 1/22/1850
Jake Brogdon 10/15/1892

Samuel McDonald Brogdon 7/11/1869
Wm Graham Brogdon 4/19/1877
Infant daughter 10/16/1870
Addie Inez Brogdon 7/28/1879

John Bagnal Brogdon Bible continued...

Esther Lillian Brogdon 9/2/1871
Geo. Albertus Brogdon 2/13/1882
Harriet Elizabeth Brogdon 3/13/1873
Julius Leon Brogdon 4/20/1883

John Bagnal Brogdon 12/9/1874
Cecil Eugene Brogdon 4/21/1889
Joel Edwin Brogdon 3/10/1876
Sue Brogdon 5/15/1890

DEATHS

Infant daughter 10/16/1870
Susan Brogdon Wells 8/28/1929, aged 39 yrs.
William Graham Brogdon 6/28/1877
Harriet Elizabeth Brogdon 11/7/1836
Samuel McDonald Brogdon 9/21/1882, aged 13 yrs., 2 mos., 10 days
Addie Inez White 7/25/1913, 34 yrs. old   Lou Bounds 3/24/1912
Bertha Lawrence Brogdon 10/1918
Joel Edwin Brogdon 10/24/1923, aged 47 yrs.
John Ingram Brogdon 11/28/1923, aged 74 yrs.
John Bagnall Brogdon 6/12/1937 at his res., Harvin Station, Clarendon Co., South Carolina
Julius Leon Brogdon 5/20/1938 at his res., Sumter Co., South Carolina, aged 55 yrs.

MARRIAGES

Esther Lillian Brogdon to Theodore C. Proctor 1/18/1893
John Ragnal Brogdon to L. Eudora McFaddin 2/5/1896

John Bagnal Brogdon Bible continued...

Joel Edwin Brogdon to Lou Bounds 12/23/1898
Addie Inez Brogdon to James Darby White 11/2/1899
George Albertus Brogdon to Bertha Irene Lawrence 12/26/1906
Susie Brogdon to Frank A. Wells 4/6/1910
Cecil Eugene Brogdon to Ethel Lawrence 11/19/1911
Julius Leon Brogdon to Estelle Moore 6/24/1914
Joel Edwin Brogdon to Mary Alice Michaux 8/11/1914
Jake Brogdon to Louise Mann 6/25/1915

JACOB INABNIT BIBLE
Owner: Frank H. Inabnit, Orangeburg, S. C.

BIRTHS

Jacob Inabnit 1/5/1787
Ann Mary Wolfe 10/1/1803

BIRTHS of Children of Jacob and Elizabeth Inabnit

Mary Inabnit 1/18/1811
John Inabnit 11/25/1813
Ann Caroline Inabnit 1/20/1816
Sarah Elizabeth Inabnit 2/20/1818
Drucilla Colson Inabnit 3/12/1820

BIRTHS of Children of Jacob and Ann M. Inabnit

Hilliard Jacob Malachi Inabnit 3/1/1824
Rachel Olivia Inabnit 3/26/1829
Derrell George Washington Inabnit 4/16/1826
Anna Matilda Inabnit 6/1/1831
Jane Rebecca Inabnit 9/12/1833

Jacob Inabnit Bible continued...

Elkanah Emory Inabnit 11/4/1935
James Henry Mallard Inabnit 1/15/1838
Malinda Emily Inabnit 4/11/1840

MARRIAGES

Jacob Inabnit to Elizabeth Golson 6/i1/1810
Jacob Inabnit to Ann Mary Wolfe 5/15/1823
Jane Inabnit to William H. Ehney 10/29/1856
Anna M. Inabnit to W. L. Ehney 4/8/1857

DEATHS

Elizabeth Inabnit, wife of Jacob, 5/9/1820, funeral preached by William Whetsone
Ann Caroline Inabnit, daughter of Jacob & Elizabeth, 10/2/1836
Jacob Inabnit 9/17/1840
Derrell G. W. Inabnit 2/1879
Ann M. Inabnit 9/21/1880
Emery E. Inabnit 5/31/1881
J. H. Mallard Inabnit 6/9/1890
Hilliard Jacob Malachi Inabnit 11/28/1895

BIRTHS

Ann Susan, daughter of W. H. and J. R. Ehney and granddaughter of Ann M. Inabnit, 1/6/1858
Carrie Diana, daughter of W. L. and Anna M. Ehney and granddaughter of A. M. Inabnit, 2/4/1858
Talula Emma Ehney, daughter of William and Jane, 12/6/1859
George Marion Ehney, son of William and Jane, 9/9/1860
Stacy Houser Inabnit, son of Jacob H. and Mary Ann, 2/111861
Jacob Preston Inabnit, son of Mallard and Annie, 8/7/1871

THOMAS BARRON BIBLE
Owner: Mrs. W. F. Martin
2292 Nelson, Memphis, Tenn. 38104

Ancestors
Archibel (Archibald) Barron b. 1733
Elizabeth Ingram, his wife, b. 1735

Note: They are bur. in Ebenezer Presbyterian Cemetery, Rock Hill, South Carolina)

Thomas Barron m. Mary Neely 5/24/1838

BIRTHS

Thomas Barron 3/21/1817
Mary L. Barron 1/23/1847
Mary N. Barron 12/2/1817
W. M. Barron 7/27/1849
W. I. Barron 4/30/1839
Thomas A. Barron 10/24/1852
S. L. Barron 3/16/1844

William Barton 8/24/1774
Fannie (Stewart) Barron 3/11/1775, both bur. Ebenezer Cemetery, Rock Hill, South Carolina

BIRTHS of Children of William and Fannie Barron

Margaret Barton 712/1799
William Barron 1/1/1801
Eliza Barron 10/17/1803
Jane Barron 3/29/1805
Barron 7/5/1807

Mary Barron 8/13/1809
John Barron 3/19/1811
S. D. Barron 11/22/1814
Rebecca Barron A. E.

Thomas Barron Bible continued...

DEATHS

Rebecca M. Curry 6/2/1844
Caroline Porter 5/20/1846
Mary N. Barron 3/20/1863
J. T. Barton 12/2/1863 in Yorkville, South Carolina
N. H. Walker 5/2/1870
W. H. Barron 6/24/1877

Mary E. Barron 10/27/1870
Margaret Fewell 1/10/1878
Elmer Barron 2/9/1879

Alexander Fewell 4/4/1882
Livy Barron 1897
Eliza Barron 3/25/1881
John Barton 5/26/1882
Harriet Hancock 9/8/1882
William Barton 6/11/1871
Mary A. Barron 12/21/1884
Mary L. Ivy 8/5/1887
A. I. Barron 8/27/1887
Iola Ivy 2/26/1897

MARY JAMES' BIBLE
Found and contributed to Houston, Texas Library

BIRTHS

Mary James 2/10/1799
William James 1/9/1818
Nancy James 10/10/1801

Mary James' Bible continued...

H. G. James 1/22/1822
Rebecca James 8/30/1802
Joseph F. James 9/6/1830
John James 5/11/1804
Sarah C. James 4/1832 in Union Dist., SC
Sarah James 4/14/1806
Drury James 11/6/1808
L. A. James 8/1827
Martha James 12/31/1810
Mary E. James 8/1828
Thomas James 12/6/1812
Lucinda James 1829
Elizabeth James 5/31/1815
Susannah James 6/26/1817
Ela A. James, daughter of J. F. James and Georgia A. James, 2/24/1877
Edgar Boyt James 9/22/1878 in Pennington, Trinity Co., Texas

Note: Mary James identified as wife of Willis Fowler

SAMUEL JOSEPH SILLS' BIBLE
Owner: Thomas Kees Maxwell, Monticello, Mississippi

Samuel Joseph Sills b. 1773/1774 m. 1794 Jane M. Heard b. 1/23/1777 In Pittsylvania Co., Virginia

BIRTHS of Their Children

James Monroe Sills 9/11/1796-in Laurens Co., S. C.
Abigail Sills 7/2/1797 in Laurens Co., S. C.
Elizabeth Sills 3/26/1799 In Abbeville Co., S. C.

Samuel Joseph Sills Bible continued...

John Sills 10/29/1801 in Abbeville Co., S. C.
Tabitha Sills 5/12/1804 in Abbeville Co., S. C.

Nancy Sills 6/27/1807 in Abbeville Co., S. C.
Samuel Joseph Sills, Jr. 10/23/1812 in Abbeville Co., S. C. m.
4/8/1857 to Susannah Cliburn in Lawrence Co., Mississippi
Benjamin Sills 11/28/1814 in Abbeville Co., S. C.
Jane M. Sills 1/4/1817 in Abbeville Co., S. C. m. Thomas Kees
Maxwell 11/2/1836 in Lawrence Co. Miss. Jane d. 3/29/1889
Monticello, Mississippi

TRISTRAM THOMAS' BIBLE of Marlborough Co.
Owner: Arthur Caraway
2765 Oak Ridge Lane East Point, Ga. 30044

MARRIAGES

Tristram Thomas to Mary (2nd) 12/27/1780
Joseph Thomas to Susannah 1/16/1793
T. H. Thomas to Mary 12/17/1837
Joseph Thomas, son of Phil Thomas, 8/28/1770-8/3/1841

Ages of Joseph and Susannah Thomas' Children

Tristram Thomas 8/7/1795-9/16/1816
James Thomas 1/7/1798-7/1836
Elizabeth Thomas 2/14/1800-8/11/1821
Sarah Thomas 2/26/1802
Mary Thomas 7/5/1805-9/30/1844
William Thomas 8/28/1807-9/30/1844
John Clothier Thomas 2/12/1810-8/12/1821
Josiah Thomas 4/2/1814-6/1844

Tristram Thomas' Bible continued...

Tristram Thomas 9/3/1816-7/20/1857, aged 41 yrs.
Tristram Thomas, son of Stephen, 7/28/1752-9/3/1817
Mary Hollingsworth, now wife of Tristram Thomas, 1/6/1751-1/15/1817, aged 66 yrs., 9 days, 38 yrs. a member of the Baptist Church of Christ

BIRTHS of Tristram and Mary Thomas' Children

Elizabeth Thomas 12/25/1781
John Thomas 3/18/1784
Sarah Thomas 9/26/1786-10/26/--
Tristram H. Thomas 5/8/1789
James Clothier Thomas 7/10/1792

BIRTHS of Tristram and Ann Thomas' Children

Robert Thomas 6/10/1775
Susannah Thomas 9/10/1777-4/9/1841
Philip Thomas 10/15/1779
David Harry, son of David Harry and Mary, his wife, b. 7/1770

BIRTHS of Children of T. H. Thomas' Children

George Augustus Thomas 9/22/1839-1/16/1903
Narcissa Elizabeth Thomas 5/8/1842-6/18/1850
Martha Ann Thomas 7/27/1845-7/2/1928
Joseph D. Thomas 5/30/1849-9/22/1863
Narcissa Elizabeth Thomas 4/25/1852-4/9/1922
Cornelia Jane Thomas 3/9/1855-9/12/1932

Note: Tristram Thomas b. 7/28/1752 Maryland, was Capt., Major and Colonel during Rev. War; afterwards Brig. General of Marlborough District.

JOHN GAILLARD BIBLE

On flyleaf: "Mrs. E. Gaillard to her son, John, 1793"

BIRTHS

John Cordes, Sr. 1718-7/13/1756
Catherine Cordes, wife of John, 11/10/1724-8/5/1805
Theo. Gaillard 9/3/1737-5/26/1805
Ellinor Cordes 5/23/1744-10/31/1808 m. 6/7/1764 Thee. Gaillard

Their Children:

James Gaillard 9/5/1765-9/14/1765
Elizabeth Gaillard 10/13/1766
Theodore Gaillard 1/6/1768
John Gaillard 10/16/1769
Samuel Gaillard 11/13/1770
Serre Gaillard 12/26/1771-8/23/1772
Ellinor Serre Gaillard 12/26/1771-8/23/1772
Henrietta Catherine Gaillard 9/6/1774
Bartholomew Gaillard 4/24/1776
Thomas Gaillard 6/7/1778
Peter Gaillard 10/2/1782
David Gaillard 6/26/1786

Samuel and Thomas left Charleston 9/18/1795;were lost upon their voyage to West Indies.

David d. 7/26/1801, landing in Charleston Habor.
John E. 3/1807
Peter d. 9/4/1813

John Gaillard Bible continued...

Elizabeth m. Theodore Gourdin
John m. Harriet Lord
Theodore m. Martha Doughty
Henrietta m. Joseph Sanford Barker
Bartholomew m. Rebecca Cheppelle Doughty
Peter m. Rebecca Weyman Foster

Theodore Gourdin m. Elizabeth Gaillard 10/20/1785

BIRTHS of Their Children

Elizabeth Gourdin 9/25/1786
Ellinor Gourdin 1/7/1789
Theodore Lewis Gourdin 5/1/1790
Hester Gourdin 8/8/1791
Henrietta Gourdin 3/17/1794
Peter Gaillard Gourdin 11/4/1795
Samuel Thomas Gourdin 4/3/1797
Robert Marion Gourdin 3/10/1799
John Gaillard Keith 3/10/1801
Hamilton Courturier Gourdin 12/20/1802-1/12/1809
Elizabeth m. Peter Galliard, son of Peter
Henrietta m. Doctor James Ravenel, son of Daniel, 10110/1812

WILLIAM DAWSON BIBLE

William Dawson m. 12/29/1802 Caroline Prioleau by Rev. Mr. Frost

BIRTHS

Joanna Dawson 7/28/1804, baptised 8/26/1804 by Rev. Mr. Jenkins

William Dawson Bible continued...

William Alfred Dawson 7/15/1806, baptised 8/11/1806 by Rev. Mr. Bowen
Samuel Prioleau Dawson 9/30/1808, baptised 10/30/1808 by Rev. Mr. Simons
Catherine Cordes Dawson 5/4/1811, baptised 3/10/1812 by Rev. Mr. Mills
John Cordes Dawson 10/6/1813, baptised 9/16/1818 by Rev. Mr.Dalcho

William Dawson d. 3/27/1822, bur. at Back River.
Joanna Dawson m. Augustus T. Gaillard 9/29/1824 by Rev. Mr. Alston Gibbes
Caroline
Ellen
Catherine Cordes Dawson m. Elias Ball, M. D., 11/26/1829 by Rev. Mr. Francis F. Rutledge

Carolina Dawson b. in City Philadelphia durin g the Rev. War 7/15/1782, christened by Bishop
White of Pa. and named Carolina in testimony of the regard her mother bore to her Native State, she being banished at that time. She d. 5/1/1870, aged 87 yrs., 9 mos., 15 days, bur. Back River 5/5th.

JOHN MAYNARD DAVIS' BIBLE

Frances Davis d. 9/17/1796, aged 67 yrs., bur. St. Phillips Church, new churchyard
Hannah Baker (her dau.) d. in Charleston 11/1798, bur. near her mother
Ann Moore d. 7/29/1790

John Maynard Davis Bible continued...

Ann Bower (Elizabeth) d. Charleston 8/20/1800
Joseph Moore d. Charleston 9/17/1813
Catherine Ireson Davis d. 1/12/1811
Cordelia Strobel d. 6/25/1813
John Maynard Davis d. 5/27/1827, aged 71 yrs., 13 days

John Maynard Davis m. Mary Eliza Moncrief in Charleston, S. C. by Rev. George Buist of Presbyterian Church 9/26/1793

BIRTHS

Thomas Davis Baker 7/20/1794 in Exeter Great Britain
Catherine Ireson Davis 2/14/1792 in London (adopted daughter of J. M. and M. E. Davis)
Cordelia Strobel, daughter of Martin and Eliza Strobel, b. Charleston, S. C. 9/1/1810
R. H. Steobel m. Amelia Davis 12/12/1844 by Rev. John Bechmann, Charleston, S. C.

BIRTHS of Children of R. H. and Amelia Strobel

Mary Eliza-Strobel 5/9/1848 - -Arthur Merkley Strober 1/31/1852

WILLIAM BOYD BIBLE of Chester District, S. C.
From: Rev. War Pension W5845

BIRTHS of Children of William and Keziah Boyd
Nancy Boyd 3/5/1796 m. 4/18/1816 William Wylie
Hugh M. Boyd 6/9/1802

William Boyd Bible continued...

Note: William Boyd b. Ireland 1766, came to Charleston, S. C. in 1771 *or* 1772 and settled in Craven Co., which was later Chester District, S. C. He m. in Chester Dist., S. C. 1/1794 to Kezlah Porter and was allowed a pension 10/24/1832. Soldier d. 1/18/1838, Chester District, S. C. His widow, Keziah, applied for pension 12/23/L852, aged 80 yrs., DeKalb Co., Ga.

ELISHA BROOKS' BIBLE
Of Abbeville District, S. C. From: Rev. Pension W9741

BIRTHS of Children of Elisha and Nancy Brooks

Obediah Brooks d.infancy
Betsy Brooks 1797/8
John Wesley Brooks 2/18/1790
Stanmore Brooks
Matilda Brooks 1791
William Butler Brooks
Lavina Brooks 1793

Note: Elisha Brooks m. 1/12/1786 in Edgefield District, S. C., Nancy Butler (b. 9/22/1765). He d. 11/3/1804 in S. C. Widow, Nancy, applied for pension 6/1845, Abbeville District, S. C. (alive 1852). She and her husband had eight children.

SQUIRE BOONE BIBLE
From: Rev. War Pension W8372

BIRTHS of Children of Squire and Anna Boone

Thomas Boone 12/24/1785 -
Ira Boone 12117/1799

Squire Boone Bible continued...

Susanna Boone 1/28/1787
Isaiah Boone 3/7/1802-8/23/1835
Lucy Boone 10/15/1792-10/18/1828
Daidamia Boone 8/11/1804-8/1826
Cinthia Ann Boone 5/11/1795
Higgason Grubbs Boone 10/23/1806
Samuel Boone 9/2/1797-5/29/1835
Levi Boone 12/8/1808
Squire Boone 9/2/1797-7/26/1836
Nancy Boone 12/24/1811/12

Polly Boone 1/27/1814

Note: Squire Boone, son of Samuel Boone, and nephew of Daniel Boone, b. 10/13/1760. Drafted in Camden List., S. C., m. 9/1/1784 In Fayette C., Ky., Anna Grubbs (h. 6/23/1766). Soldier d. 6/28/1817. Anna Boone, widow, applied for pension 10/28/1839, Todd Co., Ky. She had 15 children.

LEWIS WATKINS' BIBLE
Owner: Mrs. Jenny Futral
Rt. 3, Box 378, Franklin, Georgia 30217

Lewis Watkins b. 9/25/1810 (Laurens Co., S. C.-d. 11/28/1867, Heard Co., Ga. m. Peninah Henry b. 2/23/1814

BIRTHS of Children

Othello J. Watkins 5/29/1831 - Sarah J. Watkins 1/25/1836
William N. Watkins 8/4/1833 (m. 5/12/1862 Nancy Jane Dink Wood)

WILLIAM WARE BIBLE of Fairfield District
From: Rev. War Pension IW8969

BIRTHS of Children of William and Priscilla Ware Priscilla

Priscilla Ware 9/1/1793
Angelina Ware 5/17 1803

Thomas Cooke Ware 3/9/1796
Adeline Ware 9/8/1807
Sarah Aedy Ware 3/9/1798
Francis Asbury Ware 9/28/1811
Francis Asbury Ware m. Eliza Jane Bell 4/2/1835

BIRTHS of Children of Francis Asbury and Eliza Jane Ware Priscilla Ware

Priscilla Ware 4/13/1836
Hugh Bell Ware 12/5/1838
4/18/1842

Martha Watt Ware 11/2/1840
William Thomas Ware

Note: William Ware applied for pension 8/18/1821, Richland District, S. C., .. 8/14/1791 Priscilla (b. 7/23/1764). Soldier d. 3/28/1833. Widow, Priscilla, applied for pension 11/20/1843, Fairfield District, S. C.

JOHN WOOD BIBLE of Spartanburg District
From: Rev. War Pension #W902R

BIRTHS of Children of John and Elizabeth Wood

William Wood 11/22/1783-7/15/1792
Patsey Ruckner Wood 5/13/1802
Nancy Wood 11/5/1786

John Wood Bible continued...

Constantine Wood 9/25/1805
James Edmund Wood 12/1787
Salley Anderson Wood 10/19/1807
John Wood 12/27/1789
Patsy Bush Wood 9/23/1812
Stony Wood 2/24/1792
William Bush Wood 6/10/1814
Robert Wood 4/8/1794
Keziah Wood 3/15/1811
Robertson Wood 3/16/1796
Gracy Wood 4/18/1813
Rebecca Wood 4/10/1798
Nancy Wood 3/5/1815
Elizabeth Wood 4/16/1800
James Edmund Wood 12/22/1816

Salley Anderson Wood d. aged 4 yrs., abt. 7 mos.

Note: John Wood b. 9/1/1798 King and Queen Co., Va.; in 1797 removed Spartanburg Dist.,SC
where applied for pension 9/8/1812;d. 6/20/1838. John Wood m. 2/13/1783 Halifax Co., Va.,
Elizabeth Bruce (b. 1/1/1764). Widow, Elizabeth, applied pension 9/9/1839, Spartanburg Dist., SC.

JOSEPH BAKER BIBLE of Charleston, SC.
Rev War Pension W9713

BIRTHS

Elizabeth Mary Baker 8/13/1789
Lois Baker 9/3/1803

Joseph Baker Bible continued...

William N. Baker 2/22/1792
John Baker 12/16/1804
Anna Mariah Baker 4/29/1796
Edward Bonneace Baker
Joseph Baker 7/22/1798 11/15/1806
Thomas Jefferson Baker 11/27/1799
Robert Little Baker 10/14/1807

Note: Mary Baker, widow of Joseph Baker applied for pension 8/5/1844, aged 74 yrs., Charleston, S. C. She d. 5/11/1845, only surviving children being: Elizabeth Mary Toomer, William H. Baker, Ann M. Baker, John G. Baker, Edward B. Baker and Robert L. Baker. Testimony of Mrs. Sarah Johnson who was present at marriage of Mrs. Mary Baker to Joseph Baker at house of Mrs Thomas Bennett, the aunt of Mrs. Mary Baker, in Charleston, S.C. 9/25/1788, by Rev. MacCauley of Presbyterian Church. Joseph Baker, house carpenter, d.1826.

REV. ENOCH ELLIS BIBLE
Owner: Mrs. R. L. Creighton, Coronado, California

MARRIAGES

Enoch Ellis to Statia Atkins 6/8/1837
Martha Ann H. Ellis to M. V. Cleavland 9/6/1854

Phebie Caroline F. Ellis to Robert S. Monroe 6/28/1866
Frances Louise Ellis to Isaac D. Melton 12/27/1866
Rosa Amanda Ellis to Reuben D. Crump 5/16/1867
Little Ednie Ellis to Julius C. Coleman 7/6/1869
Sarah Malinda Ellis to John R. Riggs 7/7/1869

Enoch Ellis Bible continued...

Augusta P. Ellis to Julius S. Tomlin 12/25/1881
Nora B. Ellis to J. V. Potter 7/25/1882

BIRTHS

Enoch Ellis 6/18/1814
Statia Ellis 3/27/1822
Roda Amanda
R. A. Ellis 10/31/1843
Martha Ann Hicks Ellis 12/16/1839
Mary Adeline Ellis 2/13/1842
Sarah Malinda Ellis 12/20/1851
Augusta Fair Ellis 6/21/1860
Lizzie Ednie Ellis 7/13/1854
Nora Bell Ellis 3/21/1863
George Dyer Ellis 4/3/1857

DEATHS

Mary Adaline Ellis 12/14/1842
Enoch Ellis 9/2/1885
George Dyer Ellis 10/24/1861
Statia Ellis 1/8/1887

JOHN ANDERSON BIBLE
From: Rev. War Pension W884

BIRTHS of Children of John and Ann Anderson

Benjamin Anderson 10/13/1782 -
Isaac Anderson 17/7/1796
John Anderson 3/10/1787

John Anderson Bible continued...

Summerfield Anderson 12/1/1798
Robert B. Anderson 1/26/1789
Beriman D. Anderson 11/29/1801
George Anderson 2/14/1791
Baylis E. Anderson 11/7/1802
Oliver Anderson 3/27/1792
Merium Anderson 1/21/1805
William P. Anderson 3/16/1794

Summerfield Anderson m. 7/10/1816

Note: John Anderson was b. 7/30/1758 Frederick Co., Va., After the war he moved to S. C., then Ky., then Davidson Co., Tenn.

JAMES ANDERSON BIBLE of Chester Dist.
From.: Rev. War Pension 809699

BIRTHS of Children of James and Jane Anderson

William Anderson 7/12//1784
David Anderson C~22/1798
Elizabeth Anderson 11/6/1785
Robert Anderson 10/18/1800
Marey Anderson 12/2/1787
Amos Anderson 10/23/1802
James Anderson 8/14/1789
Samuel Anderson 3/27/1805
John Anderson 6118/1791
Jannet Anderson 6/1111808
Sarah Anderson 2/15/1795

James Anderson Bible continued...

Note: James Anderson b. in Ireland in 1759. Enlisted from Craven Co., S. C. Applied for pension 10/23/1832, Chester District, S. C.
He m. 3/27/1783 Jane Hetherington who d. 10/10/1843 Chester Dist., S. C.

JOHN BRYAN BIBLE
From: Rev. War Pension W8388

BIRTHS

Edward Ball Simons, son of Lydia Ball and Edward Simons, baptised 1/5/1774
by Rev. Robert Purcel, surities: E. Ball, B.Simons, Mrs. Catherine Simons, 12/3/1773-9/25/1775, bur. at Pompion Hill Chapel

BIRTHS of Children of John and Lydia Simons Bryan

Elizabeth Bryant 3/4/1784, baptised 6/1784 by Rev. Robert Smith
John Bryan 7/18/1791, baptised 8/29/1791 by Rev. Robert Smith

Note: John Bryan d. 11/10/1803, aged 50 yrs., 11 mos., Interred at Pompion Hill Chapel on 11/21/1803. He m. Mrs. Lydia Simons, widow, on 2/2/1783 by Rev. Edward Ellington, Rector of Episcopal Church of St. James, Goose Creek, near Charleston, S. C. The marriage took place at house of Benjamin Simons, his plantation "Middleburg" on Cooper River, St. Thomas' Parish, in Charleston, S. C. Mrs. Lydia Simons was Lydia Ball, daughter of Elias and Lydia Ball. She m. Edward Simons

John Bryan Bible continued...

10/17/1771. Testimony of John Bryan, aged 52, res. of Charleston, S. C. 8/24/1843 that he was the son and only child of Lydia Bryan, decd., who was widow of John Bryan, decd. Lydia Ball Simons Bryan d. Charleston 1/29/1843.

JOHN CALDWELL BIBLE
From: Rev. War Pension #8580

BIRTHS of Children of John and Elender Caldwell

Wiley Caldwell 9/1783-5/20/1828 m. Jesse McMeans

George Caldwell 10/26/1794
Joshua Caldwell 4/5/1790
Jane Caldwell 2/--
Margaret Cameron Caldwell 1/13/1797 m. M. McMeans.

Note: John Caldwell was b. Waxhaw District, N. C. 2/19/1762. Enlisted from Lancaster District, S. C. Applied for pension 4/3/1833, Chester District, S. C. Soldier m. 1787 Ellender Fallas who was b. 8/16/1762. She had two children by former marriage, Ann and Elizabeth. Widow resided in York Dist., S. C. in 1847; d. 4/7/1848 at house of Isaac Holcomb, husband of Ann Fallas Holcomb.

JOSEPH CARROLL BIBLE
From: Rev. War Pension W9778

BIRTHS of Children of Joseph and Martha Carroll

Samuel Carroll 1772   -
Joseph Carroll 9/15!1781

Joseph Carroll Bible continued...

Elizabeth Carroll 10/4/1774
John Carroll 2/2/1784
Je--et Carroll 11/6/1776
Henry Carroll 6/19/1789
Sarah Carroll 3/20/1778
Isabella Carroll

Note: Joseph Carroll, son of Joseph of York Dist., S. C.. m. 2/28/1771 Martha Swancy (Swansey). He d. 2/17/1803. Widow, Martha, applied for pension 1/26/1846, York District, S. C.

HICKS CHAPPELL BIBLE
From: Rev. War Pension W22758

BIRTHS of Children of Hicks and Elizabeth Chappell

John Joel Chappell 1/19/1781
William Chappell 6/12/1783-9/1/1783
Howell Chappell 2/3/1785-9/19/1785
Joseph Henry Chappell 10/13/1786
Polly Ellen Chappell 12/17/1788-10/26/1790
Robert Chappell, bro. to Hicks, d. 6/14/1798
Dewellen Threewits (bro. to Elizabeth) d. 8/2/1796

Note: Hicks Chappell was b. 3/5/1757 in Brunswick Co., Va., in 1764 moved with father to Richland Dist., S. C. Applied for pension 3/13/1833. He d. 4/11/1836. Hicks Chappel m. 6/14/1780
Elizabeth Threewits (d. 7/4/1841)

JOSEPH CLARK BIBLE
From: Rev. War Pension WB608

BIRTHS of Children of Joseph and Ruth Clark

Rebecca T. Clark 2/15/1790
Margaret Clark 10/11/1800
Mary Clark 11/26/1792-6/2/1795
James A. Clark 12/18/1802
William A. Clark 5/25/1794
Josiah D. Clark 5/1/1805
Susanah Clark 4/8/1797
Elijah Clark 5/20/1810
Josiah G. Clark d. 8/5/1805
Elijah C. Clark 9/2/1837

Note: Mrs. Ruth Clark, widow of soldier, Joseph Clark (his brother, Benjamin Clark, also served as Rev. War Soldier), aged 79, Giles Co., Tenn.
Joseph Clark m. Ruth Alexander in Mecklenburg Co., N. C. 4/2/1789.

JOHN RUSSELL BIBLE
Owner: Mrs. Pauline McConnell
Box 44, Hiawassee, Ga.

John Russell b. 5/20/1803 Rutherford Co., N. C., son of George Russell, Jr. b. 1772 Va. and Rhoda Reavis b. 1769 in Northampton Co., N. C. George and Rhoda d. Carnden, Co., Mo. after 1850 census was taken. George Russell's parents were George Russell, Sr. b. Ca 1734 in County Antrim, Ireland d. ca 1780 at Russell's Station, Rutherford Co., N. C. and his wife, Mrs. Mary Underwood Whiteside, widow of John Whiteside, Sr.

John Russell Bible continued...

Nancy Dickey b. 1/18/1804 N. C., daughter of George Dickey b. 4/26/1776, d. 9/15/1842, and wife of Hannah Steel Taylor, daughter of Joshua Taylor and Hannah Steel. The Dickey family settled in Cherokee, N. C.

BIRTHS

John Russell 5/20/1803
George W. Russell 4/19/1828
Nancy Russell, wife of John Russell, 1/18/1804
Jane Amanda Russell, dau., 9/11/1830
Hannah Adaline Russell 3/10/1832
Martha Russell 5/9/1834
Albert Burton Russell, son of John Russell, 7/19/1836
Aminta Matilda Russell 4/13/1838
John Harrison Russell 10/2/1839
Andrew Dacia Russell 8/26/1843
Mira Louisa Russell 5/26/1845

MARRIAGES

Andrew Davis: Russell to A. Phiny Stroud (Nancy Triphena Stroud)
11/21/1865, Borned to: (Andrew and A. Phiny Russell)
Oily Haseltine Russell, dau., 12/3/1866
Samantha Ellen Russell, dau., 11/9/1868
Loucinda Adline Russell, dau., 5/15/1870
Esteline Mary Russell, dau., 3/1/1873
Maggie Seavina Russell, dau., 5/21/1875
John Burton Russell, son, 1/12/1883

John Russell Bible continued...

DEATHS

Aminta Martha Russell 1/14/1851
Nancy Russell 8/22/1859 (w. of John Russell, Sr.)
Martha Wood, daughter of John and Nancy Russell, 4/5/1861
John H. Russell 5/15/1881
John Russell (Sr.) 4/5/1883, age 79 yrs., 10 mos., 15 days
Mim Louisa Kimsey, daughter of John and Nancy Russell, 2/16/1893
Jane Amanda Brown, wife of G. W. (George W.) Brown and daughter of
John and Nancy Russell 1/4/1904
Carrie Virginia (Penland) Russell b. 7/2/1879
D. C. Russell, son, b. 3/30/1909
Carl Ferris Russell, son, 9/16/1912
James Frank Russell, son, 3/31/1920

DEATHS

D. C. Russell 4/1/1909
Carl Ferris Russell 12/1954

Carrie Virginia Russell 5/25/1947
John Burton Russell 2/19/1966
Carrie Virginia, wife of John Burton Russell

JAMES HICKS BIBLE
Owner: Gladys Gibson, Box 51354
OSC Lafayette, La. 70505

James Hicks, son of Jonathan and Nancy Hicks, b. 8/17/1803, Buncombe Co., N. C.

James Hicks Bible continued...

Mary Addington, daughter of William and Delilah Addington, b. 3/30/1802 Newberry Dist

James and Martha Hicks m. 8/1/1822, Buncombe Co., N. C.

Children of James and Martha Hicks:

BIRTHS

Mary A. D. Hicks 7/9/1827, Buncombe Co., N. C.
Naomi Hicks 1/28/1825, Macon Co., N. C.
William Nú Hicks 3/29/1827, Habersham Co., Ga.
Elizabeth Jane Hicks 2/11/1829, Macon Co., N. C.
John D. Hicks 1/12/1830, Tuscaloosa, Ala.
Harvy K. Hicks 8/5/1832, Tuscaloosa, Ala.
James Tú Hicks 1/16/1835, Tuscaloosa, Ala.
Hardy D. Hicks 5/23/1837 Tuscaloosa, Ala.
Martha E. Hicks 7/27/1839, Tuscaloosa, Ala.

JACOB MILLER BIBLE
Owner: Mrs. Harry J. Clark 180 Oronwyn St. Southern Pines, N. C.

BIRTHS

Jacob C. Miller 11/4/1809
Samuel N. Miller 1/26/1812
Emma Miller 7/18/1814
Stephen H. Miller 4/9/1817
Sarah E. Miller 9/1819
Emma P. Miller 8/26/1822
John W. Miller 10/29/1824

Francis C. Miller 10/16/1828
Margaret C. Miller 9/10/1830
Jane L. Miller 11/14/1832
Laura A. Miller 12/21/1834
Edward B. Miller 11/26/1836
Jacob Miller, Sr. 12/9/1784

Jacob Miller Bible continued...

Edward R. Miller 11/19/1826
Sarah Clastrier Miller 11/12/1794

MARRIAGES

Jacob Miller and Sarah Clastrier 12/31//1808
Jacob C. Miller and Mary Jane Manno (or Marino) 12/31/1832 in Trinity Church, by Dr. William Capers
Stephen N. Miller and Jane Barter (or Barton) Fraser 12/24/1839 by Rev. Samuel E. Norton in Bishopville, Sumter District, S. C.
John Brown and Emma P. Miller 5/5/1842 by Rev. John H. Honour at her father's residence on Vanderhorst Street
Louis Webb and Margaret C. Miller 10/2/1851 by Rev. Samuel K. Cox in M. P. Church
John William Miller and Ellen Margaret Evans 4/16/1857
Francis C. Miller and Theodora Robins m. by Dr. Lynch at father's res. Market St.

DEATHS

Emma Miller 1/18/1816
J. Claudius Miller 4/3/1875
Edward R. Miller 10/15/1829
Dr. Stephen H. Miller 6/29/1890
Laura A. Miller 3/13/1837
Sarah Clastrier Miller 9/14/1850
Samuel D. Miller 6/23/1858
Jacob Miller 11/17/1850
Jane L. Miller 6/20/1873, Bishopville, S. C.

LEWIS JENKINS' BIBLE
Owner: Mrs. Tom Lolley, 310 Cherry St.
Oxford, N. C. 27565

Mrs. Mary Petty's Bible. Presented by her lost one who sleeps in a soldier's grave.

BIRTHS

Lewis Harris Jenkins 4/18/1840
Mary A. Nunelee 10/3/1828
Walter F. Nunelee 12/29/1830
William D. Nunelee 1/24/1833
J. A. Nunelee 1/29/1838

S. E. Nunelee 5/5/1841
R. C. Nunelee 12/10/1843
W. F. Nunelee 11l13/1847
B. M. Nunelee 4/24/1835

DEATHS

W. D. Nunelee 12/5/1835
Loucinda Nunelee 5/6/1850
John A. Nunelee m. Mary C. Jenkins 12/4/1860
John A. Nunelee d. 9/18/1863
Thomas Bartow Nunelee b. 10/6/1861
James M. T. Petty m. Mary C. Nunelee 4/4/1867

J. M. T. Petty b. 1/12/1826
Mary C. Petty b. 3/6/1838
Lewis Walter Petty b. 3/23/1868
Mary C. Petty d. 10/31/1878
J. M. T. Petty d. 8/28/1883
John Thomas (Bartow) Nunnelee and Ida Jane Raley m. 12/31/1891 by Elder J. P. Nail

Their children:

Lewis Jenkins Bible continued...

John Ervin Nunnelee b. 9/21/1892
William Asa Nunnelee b. 6/17/1894
Bryant Huhbard Nunnelee b. 10/7/1897
Mary Sarah Nunnelee b. 8/29/1899

Note: Spelling of surname as appears in Bible

MARY ELLA ADAMS BIBLE
Owner: Mrs. Marjorie Haley Stewart 410 Melrose Ave. Vicksburg. Miss. 39180

BIRTHS

Samuel David Adams, son of Abigail Leopard and Alfred Adams, 12/11/1841
Mary Jane McRae, daughter of Sarah McLeod and Moses Branson McRae, 6/18/1843

BIRTHS of Children of Samuel David and Mary Jane Adams

Charlie Adams 10/1862
Nattie Adams 9/3/1870
John McLeod Adams 3/5/1865
Walter Branson Adams 12/7/1873
Katie Adams 3/5/1865
Nona Belle Adams 1876
Thomas Alfred Adams 2/4/1867
Mary Ella Adams 11/6/1884
Maude Eliza Adams 4/10/1868

Mary Ella Adams Bible continued...

DEATHS

Alfred Adams 2/1880
Abigail 11/10/1884
Samuel David Adams, son of Alfred and Abigail Adams, 11/30/1904
Mary Jane Adams, dau of Moses Branson McRae and Sarah McLeod McRae 8/23/1905
Sarah McLeod was b. in N. C.
Moses Branson McRae was b. in N. C

Alfred and Abigail Adams were natives of Selma, Ala.
Thomas Alfred Adams, son of Samuel David and Mary Jane Adams, 1/24/1851
Katie Adams Curtisú 12/27/1955

Walter Branson Adams 4/1945
Winston Adams b. 12/26/1889 d. 10/1964
Robert Kent Curtis d. abt 3/1954
James W. Curtis d. abt 3/1961
Nettie Adams 1/7/1967, aged 96 yrs, 4 mos.

Samuel David and Mary Jane Adams are buried in Utica Cemetery, Utica, Miss.
Alfred Adams and Abigail Leopard Adams are buried in Bear Creek
Cemetery, 8 miles east of Utica, Miss. on Hwy 27.
Nona Bell Adams buried beside her grandparents, Alfred and Abigail Adams in Bear Creek Cemetery. Died age 3 years.
Mary Ella Adams Haley d. 11/7/1968. Buried in Bear CreekCemetery.

Mary Ella Adams Bible continued...

Clarence Trenton Haley d. 1/6/1975. Buried in Bear Creek Cemetery beside his beloved Mary.

EDWARD ARMSTRONG BIBLE
Owner: Mrs. Pauline Armstrong
Rocky Point, N. C. 28457

Mary, wife of Edward Armstrong, daughter of Isham and Barbara Shuffield, b. 7/7/1778
Richard James-Armstrong, son, b. 9/19/1876, son of Thomas James Armstrong and Alice.
Thomas James Armstrong, son of Thomas James Armstrong and Annie, b. 8/3/1887
Dawson T. Armstrong b. 9/7/1856
Sarah Isabella Armstrong b. 9/9/1860
William Freeman Armstrong b. 7/12/1862
Samuel Horton Armstrong b. 9/12/1865
Edward Hall Armstrong b. 5/10/1841
Thomas James Armstrong b. 1/12/1851
Wilson Alderman Armstrong b. 2/20/1854
Mary Armstrong, wife of Edward Armstrong, d. 4/20/1826
Edward Armstrong d. 10/5/1827
Martha Ann Armstrong, daughter of T. J. Armstrong, d. 12/31/1858
Thomas James Armstrong d. 9/1011877
William Freeman Armstrong d. 8/18/1866
Wilson Alderman Armstrong d. 8/16/1866
Samuel Horton Armstrong d. 2/9/1866
Martha Jane Armstrong, daughter of John Freeman and Sarah Horton, d.10/23/1865
Mary Elizabeth Everitt, wife of David K. F. Everitt, d.11/19/1867
Huldah Armstrong, wife of T. J., d. 10/1/1872

Edward Armstrong Bible continued...

Sarah Isabella Hold d. 12/17/1887
Ella P. Barry d. 6/1874
Annie E. Durham d. 9/10/1909
Thomas J. Armstrong d. 4/8/1917

Edward Armstrong, son of John and Barbara Armstrong, b. 3/17/1768
T. J. Armstrong and Martha Jane Freeman m. 6/23/1859
T. J. Armstrong and Hulda Moore, relict of late George I. Moore m. 11/23/1865
Mary Eliza Armstrong and David Kendrick Futch Everitt were m.
T. J. Armstrong Rod m. Alice Bourdeaux 11/18/1872
Mary Eliza Armstrong, daughter of Thomas James Armstrong b. 10/14/1838

HUGH McCRAINEY CLARK BIBLE

MARRIAGES

Hugh Clark b. 10/23/1809 in Cumberland Co., N. C.
Cinthia M. Clark was b. 3/15/1818 in Jackson Co., Ga.

BIRTHS

David Alexander Clark 9/7/1840
Marthy Jane Clark 5/12/1850
Joel Erwin Clark 9/7/1842
James Crawford Clark 6/13/1853
Sarah Anne Margaret Clark 5/27/1844
Catherine Me. Clark 4/11/1856
Mary Stuart Clark 7/21/1846
Diedmiah B. Clark 9/23/1858

Hugh McCrainey Clark Bible continued...

Cinthia Mourning Clark 8/26/1848

DEATHS

Joel E. Clark 2/20/1843
Miss Mourning Clark 5/28/1928
D. Alexander Clark 7/27/1850
D. A. Clark 4/21/1952
James Crawford Clark 3/23/1910

GEORGE DURANT BIBLE
Of Northumberland Co.. Va. and Perquimans Co., N. C.
Owner: University of North Carolina

George Durant b. 4/1682
John Durant d. 1/15/1699
Sarah Stevens d. 8/16/1717, age 49 yrs.
Ann Durant d. 1/22/1694
Hagar Durant d. 1/14/1723
George Durant d. 9/12/1730
Elizabeth Clayton d. 1/14/1730
Sarah Durant d. 3/29/1695
Mary Durant d. 5/1698
John Ratcliff, son of Thomas and Ann, his wife, b. 8/9/1711
Mary Reed, wife of Christian Reed, d. 12/10/1746, 28 yrs., 8 days
Christian Reed and wife, Mary, gave the Bible to William Reed(their eldest son)
Ann Durant, daughter of George and Sarah, b. 7/8/1714
John Durant b. 9/13/1716
John Durant d. 10/8/1721

George Durant Bible continued...

Mary and Sarah Durant (twins) b. 12/2/1718
Elizabeth b. 3/12/1720
George Durant b. 8/20/1723
Ann Durant b. 1/10/1689
Elizabeth Durant b. 1/28/1692
Sarah Durant b. 3/29/1695
Mary Durant b. 5/19/1698
William Reed, son of Christian and Mary, his wife, b. 10112/1740
Penelope Reed, daughter of Tulle Wllliems and Elizabeth, his wife, b. 11/12/1745
William Reed and Penelope Williams were m. 9/10/1761
Ann Reed, daughter of William and Penelope b. 11/20/1764
Joseph Reed d. 5/7/1765
Rebecca Reed, daughter of William Reed and Alice, his wife, b. 6/29/1794
Rebecca Reed and Joseph Sutton m. 7/31/1810; she d. 12/28/1815. Leaving infant.
Richard Reed, son of Wilson Francis, b. 10/7/1817

Frances Reed d. 11/12/1817
Wilson Reed, his Book, 1/1/1800, given to him by his father. William Reed, his Bible
given to him by his father, Christian Reed, and he will give it to his daughter, Rebecca.

THOMAS MOON BIBLE
Owner: Mrs. Louenna Kirkpatrick
Franklin, Indiana

BIRTHS

Thomas Moon, son of John Moon and Mary, his wife, 10/25/1742
James Moon 10/5/1745
Elizabeth Moon 3/23/1748
Joseph Moon 3/20/1750
Jemmy Moon 10/4/1752
John Moon 11/4/1755
Johnney Moon 5/26/1759
Rachel Moon 1/26/176-
Joseph Moon and Ann, his wife, m. 4/13/1772
Daniel Moon   b. 4/27/1773
Samuel Moon b. 4/17/1781
Mary Moon b.   1/30/1775
Joseph Moon b. 7/19/1783
William Moon   b. 1/25/1777
John Moon b. 11/4/1785
Grace Moon b. 1/26/1779
Jesse Moon b. 1/30/1788

John Moon and Sary, his wife, m. 8/22/1780
Lawrence Moon b. 10/28/1781

Elizabeth Moon b. 10/20/1783
William Moon h. 9/29/1785
John Moon b. 1/18/1788
Joseph Moon b. 12/15/1789

Thomas and Leucrecher Moon m. 12/26/1719

Thomas Moon Bible continued...

Sara Moon b. 7/7/1772
Thomas Moon b. 10/5/1779
John Moon b. 2/19/1774
Elizabeth Moon b. 10/17/1780
Jesse Moon b. 2/24/1776
Edom Moon b. 12/26/1782
Carey Moon b. 3/7/1778
Leucrecher Moon b. 4/18/1785

DAVID COX BIBLE

David Cox his Book bought of Thomas L. Cowan of Salisbury, N. C.
Rowan Co. 4/25/1818. price of this Book 2 pounds, 10 shillings.

Israel Cox b. -/25/-
Mary Quick b. 7/26/--
Israel Cox and Mary Quick .. 7/3/1765
David Cox b. 8/27/1766
Ephralm Cox b. 2/19/1769
Benjamin Cox b. 2/12/1771 d. 8/5/1784
Moses Cox b. Sept. between 25th and 26th, 1773
Susannah Cox b. 12/16/1778
Frederick Ezell h. 7/2/1782
Phebe Ezell b. 12/11/1784
Israel Cox b. 9/27/1790
William Cox b. 4/5/1792
Benjamin Cox b. 10/30/1794
Mark Cox b. 5/23/1797
Susannah Cox b. 12/25/1799
Charles C. Cox b. 5/5/1802
Mary Cox b. 8/2/1804

David Cox Bible continued...

Martha Cole b. 9/22/1764
Martha Cox d. 10/17/1821

David Cox and Magdelene Loop m. 10/28/1824
Magdalene Waggoner b. 12/18/1778
Charles C. Cox, Doctor, d. 9/25/1828

Benjamin Cox d. 5/27/1838
Susannah Shemwell d. 8/3/1839
David Cox, Sr. d. 6/15/1840
David Cox, Jr., son of Benjamin and Sarah Cox, b. 1/16/1814
--aniel Cox, a son of Benjamin and Sarah Cox, b. 6/11/1815
Ally Cox, daughter of Benjamin and Sarah Cox, b. 1/1/1817
Mary Cox, daughter of Benjamin and Sarah Cox, b. 11/11/1820
William Cox, son of Benjamin and Sarah Cox, b. 11/30/1822
Frederick Ezell b. 1753 d. 6/18/1825
Frederick Ezell m. Mary Cox 1780
Mary Ezell d. 8/22/1829
Ephraim Cox, Sr. d. 6/3/1771

Jacob Lopp and Magdalene Waggoner m. 10/16/1794
Elizabeth Lopp b. 9/19/1795
John Lopp b. 2/25/1797
Susannah Lopp b. 2/25/1799
Jacob Lopp b. 11/28/1800
Catherine Lopp b. 1/16/1805
David Lopp b. 3/21/1803
Mary Lopp b. 7/6/1808
Magdalene Nyfong b. 7/30/1817
Emly Nyfong b. 7/30/1817
David Lopp d. 1/9/1838
Jacob Lopp d. 7/29/1840

WILLIAM CLEMENTS' BIBLE

Included in his Revolutionary War Pension R2042 Application
Application of widow, Elizabeth Clements, Wake Co., N. C.,
3/1/1845, aged 80 yrs.,
states that William Clements d. 3/4/1835 and that they were married before
General Wallis was at Hillsborough, N. C.

Woodson Clements b. 9/2/1785 m. 1/24/1805 Kesiah Durkin

BIRTHS

Baldy Nichols 7/7/1805
Lucco Nichols 12/28/1834
Arrenia Nichols 3/7/1808
W. Nichols 11/18/1839
Dudley Nichols 10/23/1828
Archibald Nichols 12/22/1843
Susan Ann Nichols 9/18/1831

Baldy Nichols m. Arrenia Clements 4/11/1825

JAMES BARNHILL BIBLE
From: Rev. War Pension W3751

BIRTHS

James Barnhill 10/10/1756
William Barnhill 6/9/1800
Susan Harper 3/16/1769
Susan Barnhill 10/21/1802
Robert Barnhill 2/1/1781
Nancy Barnhill 11/26/1804

James Barnhill Bible continued...

Elizabeth Barnhill 8/27/1791
James Barnhlll 3/6/1807
Calvin Barnhill 11126/1794
Ellen Barnhlll 2/25/1809
John Barnhill 8/24/1797
Eliza Barnhill 9/22/1812- 2/8/1817

Note: The widow of James Barnhill, Susan, aged 70, made her application dtd 5/21/1839, Oconee Co., N. C., stating that she m. James Barnhill 1788 and that he d. 3/25/1825.

JOHN HICKS' BIBLE
From: Rev. War Pension W4695

BIRTHS of Children of John and Elizabeth Hicks

Fanney Hicks 4/9/1787
Polley Hicks 9/29/1789
Larkin W. Hicks 9/29/1789
Sarcy Hicks 2/18/1795
Elizabeth Hicks 2/23/1809

Anna Hicks 3/14/1798
Joseph Hicks 2/6/1801
John Hicks 11/20/1803
Alexander Hicks 6/20/1806
David W. Hicks 10/18/1814

Note: Elizabeth Hicks, widow of John Hicks, made her application for pension in Person Co., N. C. dtd 3/17/1843, aged 73 yrs. stating that she m. her husband 12/1785 and that he d. 4/25/1824.

ANDREW KENNEDY BIBLE
From: His Revolutionary War Pension Application W161

BIRTHS

Peggy Kennedy 11/16/1787
Polly Kennedy 6/2/1797
Ginsey Kennedy 6/1/1790
Nancy Kennedy 9/27/1799
Esther Kennedy 12/25/1792
Alexander Kennedy 1/5/1801
Arthur Kennedy 1/25/1794
Betsy Kennedy 8/25/1804

Note: Andrew Kennedy's application dtd 11/25/1821, Rowan Co., N.C., lived Blount Co., Tenn. in 1820. Soldier d. 5/5/1834. He was m. in Rowan Co., N. C. to Rachal Penny 11/17/1784. The widow applied for pension 1/5/1839, aged 78, Blount Co.. Tenn. She d.10/23/1845, survived by children: Esther Rhea, Polly Means, Nancy Kennedy and Alexander Kennedy.

DAVID MITCHELL BIBLE
From: Rev. War Pension W7460

BIRTHS
John Mitchell 4/28/1783
Jane Mitchell 5/10/1791
William Mitchell 5/5/1785
Francis Mitchell 9/26/1795
David Mitchell 4/2/1787-7/15/1841
Anderson Mitchell 3/19/1798
Samuel Mitchell 3/19/1798
Robert Mitchell 3/1/1789

David Mitchell Bible continued...

Elizabeth Mitchell 11/30/1802

Note: The Application of Ann Mitchell, widow, dtd 3/20/1843,Carswell Co., N. C., aged 81, states that she m. David Mitchell 6/13/1782 and that her husband d. 8/30/1831. William Mitchell of Rutherford Co., Tenn. testified on 7/6/1843, aged 78, that he served in war with his brother, David Mitchell of Caswell Co. and attended the wedding of his brother to Ann Anderson, at the residence of her father, William Anderson.

JOHN VENABLES BIBLE
From: Rev. War Pension W18220

John Venables b. 9/1/1762
Mary Curry b. 6/25/1762
The above were m. 12/23/1783.

BIRTHS of Children

Richard Venables 2/14/1885
Sally Venables 3/12/1795
Jesse Venables 5/14/1787
Mary Venables 11/30/1797
Betsey Venables 11/21/1789
Rebecca Venables 6/2/1800
William Venables 6/24/1792
John Venables 6/2/1803
Malcolm Venables 7/29/1805

Notes: Margaret Venables, wife of William and mother of William, Rebecca and John, d. 11/23/1774. William Venables, husband of Margaret and father of William, Rebecca and John, d.

12/22/1815. William Venables, bro. of John, d. 6/8/1823, aged 62 yrs., 8 mos. 23 days. Ursuly Venables, wife of shove named WilliamVenables, d. 12/2/1830. Rebecca Stelle d. 6/10/1829, aged 69, 8 mos. 27 days. John Venables application dtd Stokes Co., 9/10/1833, aged 11, states he was b. Frederick Co., Va. 9/1/1762 and that In 1780 be was living with his Uncle Richard Venables in Lincoln Co., N. C.

WILLIAM LEWIS BIBLE
Owner: Mrs. C. T. Carmichael
12418E St. Andrew Drive, Sun City, Az. 85351

"Erasmus Ware left for the War 7/11/1861."
"G. W. Ware left in the Army 5/20/1862."

BIRTHS

William Lewis 10/4/1777
Lotspeich Lewis 7/22/1805
Ann Lewis 1/10/1784
Elizabeth Lewis 1/10/1808
Syntha Lewis 10/23/1803
Ann Lewis 8/4/1810
William F. Lewis 8/23/1812
Martial B. Lewis 2/7/1826
Lewellen Lewis 8/12/1814
William E. Chiam 12/23/1821
Milton Lewis 8/19/1817
Elisha W. Chism 2/9/1824
Abigail Lewis 2/12/1823
Willis L. Vaughn 7/31/1831
Martha Lewis 6/23/1820
Elizabeth Ware 1/10/1808

William Lewis Bible continued...

George W. Ware 7/7/1811-11/1864
Virginia Ware 7/27/1839-8/4/1842
Cornelius Ware Taylor 11/1/1841-1915
Erasmus Ware 5/18/1843-10/18/1861
Olivia Ware Gunnels 3/26/1845-5/27/1937
Alutia Ware Tinnon 5/22/1847-/14/1934

DEATHS

Martha Lewis 8/21/1823
Ann Lewis 7/8/1859
Ann Vaughn 8/10/1831
Adella Ware Murphy ---
Willis L. Vaughan 119/1832
Andrew J. Lewis 1/16/1857
William Lewis 11/25/1840
Lotspeich Lewis 12/28/1850
Estella Gunnells 11/29/1950
G. M. Gunnels b. 12/23/1878
Electra Guniiels 12/10/1876-11/9/1950
George W. Murphy b. 7/29/1871
Rachel M. Murphy b. 2/19/1873
Abner J. Murphy 10/14/1874-5/6/1875
E. N. Gunnels 2/5/1881-11/17/1938
Mary E. Gunnels b. 1883
Charles O. Gunnels 5/19/1887-6/6/1889

On Inside front page: Now belonging to Mrs. Frank Brooks, Bryson,Texas:

Joe H. Brooks m. M. Octavia Tinnin
Joe H. Brooks b. 12/6/1875

William Lewis Bible...

M. Octavia Tinnin b. 12/13/1874 m. 6/7/1898 before Joe Fort, P. C. of Bluffdale Circuit in presence of Edward McDonald Doss, b. 7/24/1866.

ARON BRIDGES LEE BIBLE
Owner: Roy Lee, Rt. 3, Shelby, N. C.

Aron Bridges Lee 1/3/1874-8/30/1904
Elizabeth Black 6/1/1878-5/2/1935, Wife of Aron. Lee

Their Children:

Hatcher Lee 11/2/1896-1/9/1974 m. Lennie Dobbins 10/19/1919 (3/2/1901-1/18/1941)
Evie Lee 5/19/1901-6/19/1982 m. Tillie Green

Note: Aron Bridges Lee was son of William Wallace Lee and Sarah Ann Hamrick and grandson of William O. Lee and Harriet Adeline Bridges (paternal) and "Racking" Billy Hamrick (maternal).

ALFRED BAILEY BIBLE

Alfred Bailey m. Nancy Carpenter 8/16/1873, Rutherford Co., N. C. by Willie Freemen, Esq. Wits: Nancy Bailey, Duffie Freeman

Alfred Bailey 5/16/1853-12/31/1918
Nancy P. Bailey 9/20/1853-7/13/1930
Marinthis L. Bailey 9/7/1874-7/26/1915
Susan B. Bailey 3/28/1876-11/5/1914

Alfred Bailey Bible continued...

Loretta Bailey 11/25/1877-8/14/1914
John T. Bailey 9/28/1879-7/25/1955
Baylus C. Bailey 5/23/1881-4/18/1959
Mary C. Bailey 11/17/1882-10/5/1928
Theodocia Eú Bailey 2/21/1884-11/14/1912
Amelia T. Bailey 1/15/1886-6/1/1887

Arthur A. Bailey 1/7/1888-12/5/1937
Nancy E. Bailey 1/7/1888-1/28/1888
Emma L. Bailey 1/21/1890-6/4/1891
Mattie B. Bailey 11/16/1891-3/21/1910
Rosa A. Bailey 1/12/1893 -
E. Thurlo Bailey 1/26/1895-6/20/1950
Minnie M. Bailey 1/30/1896-9/10/1947
Grace M. Wilkie 8/4/1908 -

JAMES J. DALLAS BIBLE
Owner: Frank Hobley, Jr., Danville, Va

James J. Dallas b. Pittsylvania Co., Va. 1818 and moved to Rockingham Co., N. C. in 1856 where he d. in 1894 and is buried near Eden, N. C.

BIRTHS

Cora Ella Dallas 10/30/1862
Mary D. Dallas 8/1830
Sarah S. Dalles 10/28/1843
James J. Dallas 11/18/1818
Thomas G. Dallas 1/7/1849-10/21/1850
James J. Dallas m. Mary D. Suttle (or Settle) 3/1848

James J. Dallas Bible continued...

DEATHS

Andrew S. J. Dallas 8/27/1866
James Blair 5/28/1840
Polly Blair 3/18/1831
Henrietta Dallas 9/17/1868
Sarah S. Dallas 3/21/1853
Francis Smith Dallas 1/12/1870

BIRTHS

James Blalr 3/27/1775
John F. Blair 1/1/1804
Polly Blair 4/29/1776
James J. Dallas 11/18/1818
Nancy Booker 12/24/1796
Robert W. Dallas 10/5/1820
Sally Dallas 2/8/1799
Milton K. Dallas 3/27/1825
Drury Blair 3/20/1801
Mary J. Dallas 11/18/1822-5/1824

HAMILTON STEPHENSON BIBLE
Owner: Lorene B. Barnett, Greer, S. C.

Hamilton Stephenson 2/22/1796-4/23/1886 m. 3/27/1823 Mary McCullough, 5/23/1805-9/23/1884.

BIRTHS of Children:

Robert S. Stephenson 2/4/1824
Edward M. Stephenson 7/26/1838

Hamilton Stephenson Bible continued...

William J. Stephenson 12/1/1825
Samuel T. Stephenaon 2/5/1841
David L. Stephenson 9/2/1827
Infant Stephenson 1/20/1843

Jane Stephenson 4/14/1831
Samuel E. Stephenson 9/1/1846
James H. Stephenson 4/7/1834-1/1882
Abigale K. Stephenson 3/21/1836
Mary Elizabeth Stephenson 8/25/1844

EARLEY BIBLE
Owner: Perry Earley McEntire
King Street, Spindale, N. C

Temperance Earley d. 1/28/1881
L. S. Cole b. 2/11/1879
R. W. Earley d. 5/4/1899
L. O. Earley b. 8/28/1881
George Lee Earley d. 4/14/1816
Robert W. Earley

JOHNSON, STATON, ARLEDGE BIBLE
Owner: Bailey Meredith Johnson
Horse Shoe, N. C.

Handwritten notes by Mrs. Johnson in 1981, aged 89.

John S. Johnson 1/4/1854-6/17/1937, his father, Leonard Johnson, mother, Matilda Dalton. Leonard Johnson died and later Matilda m. Mr. Summey

Johnson, Staton, Arledge Bible continued....

Mary Johnson, sister of John S. Johnson, m. Billy Henderson,Green River Cove, abt 15 miles from Saluda, N. C. Betty Johnson, sister of John S. Johnson, m. Jasper Henderson, a bro. of Billy Henderson. Dick Johnson, bro. of John S. Johnson, m. Ist nandy Lankford, 2nd, Miss Figgins, Campobello, S. C.
John S. Johnson m. 1st Eveline Staton in 1875, 2nd, Clementine Arledge.
John S. Johnson and L. Eveline Staton were m. at S. C. line near her father's home 12/5/1875 in presence of M. M. Staton, Alice Pace and others. Signed, Rev. James Blythe.
Eveline Staton, wife of John S. Johnson 2/15/1858-3/24/1892. daughter of Thomas Staton and Elizabeth Capps. Walton Staton m. Eliza Thompson, their son, Thomas Staton m. Elizabeth Capps.
John S. Johnson, 2nd wife, Clementine Arledge 9/16/1859-5/19/1951 m. 3/12/1893 by Rev. J. B. Arledge, Saluda, N. C.

BIRTHS of Their children

Annie Bell Johnson 2/11/1894 Saluda, N. C., Registered Nurse,never married. Died Golet C. Johnson 4/6/1894, Saluda, N. C., never married

Ola Kathaleen Johnson 2/22/1897
John Patterson Johnson 7/14/1899, Saluda, N. C. m. 4/13/1890
Baton Rouge, La to Bernice Hutson. He d. 3/20/1952. Children: Evelyn and John P. Johnson, Jr.

Bailey Meredith Johnson 12/27/1901, Saluda, N. C. never married.

Johnson, Staton, Arledge Bible continued....

Nelle May Johnson 8/14/1903, Saluda, N. C. m. 1st Joseph Edward Ethoffer, 2d Dr. Robert C. Fuller, Asheville, N. C. Son, Edward J. Fuller m. Lillian and had three children-Edward, Diane and one other.

BIRTHS of Children of John S. Johnson and Eveline Staton

Infant son, b. & d. 1876
Elizabeth Johnson 10/15/1877
Wm Luther Johnson 1/10/1888
Oleva Johnson 3/31/1890
Thomas Furman Johnson 6/12/1886
Saloma Loma Johnson 6/6/1880
Leaner Johnson 5/18/1884
Lilly Johnson 3/12/1882
Evelyn Johnson 2/29/1892

Elizabeth Johnson m. John Rhodes 1872-1929, buried Tryon Cemetery, Tryon, N. C.- had three children: Jesse, Viola, Melvin

Jesse Rhodes b. 12/9/1900 m. Stella Streadwick, their dau., Jenelle Rhodes b. 6/7/1923 m. Roy Dalton
Viola Rhodes b. 7/28/1898 m. Dewey Lewis 4/6/1919, one son, George Lewis, b. 3/7/1920 m. Frances Walker 2/26/1943, Rocky Mount, N. C.

Children of Thomas Staton and Elizabeth Capps Staton:

Alice Staton m. John Pace
Loma Staton m. Toll Roberson
Mont Staton m. Jen McCalf
Adlyn Staton m. Harmon Pace

Johnson, Staton, Arledge Bible continued....

Margie Staton m. Willie Pace
Jesse Staton m. Rose Pace

U. Grant Staton m. Viola Torrence 1st and Billy ? 2nd
Eveline Staton m. John S. Johnson
Melvina m. Joe Alphonse Newman

STEPHEN FINDLEY BOND BIBLE
Owner: Mrs. Raymond Bostick
6914 Scotadale Drive, San Antonio, Tx. 78209

Ann Eliza Bond 2/26/1864-2/15/1926
William Leon Bond 12/18/1865-1/15/1903 buried Nexia City Cemetery
Mary Bell Bond 12/11/1867-2/18/1868
James McCarver Bond 11/9/1869-6/2/1925
Charles Stanhope Bond 6/24/1873-3/13/1947
Mary Adah Bond b. 9/25/1875
Stephen Homer Bond 7/8/1876-12/6/1956
Guy Hamilton Bond 10/6/1880-1/22/1948
Lizzie Kate Bond 2/15/1883-8/27/1892
S. F. Bond m. M. Kate McCarver 11/23/1862
S. F. Bond 7/10/1834-6/14/1913

Mahaly Katherine Bond
Anne McCarver d. 4/1868
C. C. McCarver d. 1/21/1859
William Pitt McCarver d. 9/23/1862, Confederate Soldier

JOHN CARSON BIBLE
Owner: Mrs. L. K. Rush, Rt. 1, LeCompte, La. 71346

John Carson b. 6/26/1773. Elizabeth Smith, wife of John Carson, b. 5/6/1773
John Carson m. Elizabeth Smith 8/25/1796. Their Children:

BIRTHS

James Carson 7/4/1797
Robert Carson 11/8/1807
Elizabeth S. Carson 12/9/1798
Mary Hennery Carson 2/14/1809
William Carson 9/19/1800
Sarah Isabella Carson 6/1/1811
Mary Carson 7/25/1802
Elmina Carson 4/15/1813
John E. Carson 4/25/1804
Charles Edwd Carson 11/5/1815
Selina Carson 4/25/1804

DEATHS

James Carson 9/18/1797
Elmina Carson 8/13/1816
Robert S. Carson 1886
Mary Carson 8/13/1803
Charles Edwd Carson 9/14/1819
Selena Carson 9/17/1877
Thomas Carson 9/1/1820
John Edward Carson 1/1/1880
Sarah Isabella Carson, wife of A. Dolsheimer 5/11/1853
Elizabeth S. Carson, widow of Henry P. F. Robertson 11/1/1826

JOHN J. BLACK BIBLE
Owner: Charles Black
809 Lucia Road, Stanley, N. C.

James Black, son of William Black, 7/11/1792-10/4/1855
Susana, his wife, b. 2/25/1785 (Susann Allen)
James Black m. Susana Allen 10/16/1807. Their Children:

BIRTHS

William Black 8/20/1808
Thomas P. Black 12/30/1816
Mary Ann Black 5/25/1825
Vincent Black 1/29/1809
John J. Black 9/12/1819
Susana Black 9/20/1813
    J. S. Black 6/9/1811
    Elizabeth Black 12/1822
William M. Black, Jr. m. Ann Nixon 3/15/1829 Isador Black b. 2/9/1858
John J. Black b. 9/12/1821 m. Nancy Cody 10/20/1833, 2nd wife

BIRTHS of Children

James Solomon (Gus) Black 12/23/1826
Catherine Mary Black 4/13/1849
Malinda Jerusia Black 1/4/1854
Susanah Victoria Black 8/14/1855

Wade Will Black 5/22/1857
Docia T. Black 3/15/1866
Samuel Thomas Black 1/9/1861
Flora A. Black 8/16/1868

John J. Black Bible continued...

Martha Frances Sardenia Black 3/2/1864
Nancy J. Black 12/29/1870
Isodor Eugenia Priscilla Black 2/19/1858

MARRIAGES

John J. Black to Catherine Stroup 10/1/1845
John J. Black to 2nd wife, Nancy Cody, 11/30/1851
Edward K. Edwards b. 6/11/1877
Rufus E. Lowe b. 5/25/1873
Orla Alson b. Black b. 9/23/1874

DEATHS

Catherine Black 4/13/1849
N. or J. Black 7/11/1871
James S. Black 2/23/1886
 Cathertne Hansel 7/3/1881
   J. Black 11/5/1895
   Jerusha Parker --/13/1884
 Isodor Eugenia Black 6/25/1883
Nancy Black 4/9/1912
S. Victoria Black 4/6/1926

BERRY TALLEY, SR. BIBLE of Chatham Co., N. C.
Owner: William D. Storey 6718 Beaver Ct., Midland, Ga. 31820

MARRIAGES

Berry Talley Sr. 1/14/1805
Alex Talley 5/22/1834
Polly P. Talley 5/3/1838

Berry Talley, Sr. Bible continued...

Polly Talley 11/2/1806
Rebecca A. Talley 2/12/1836
Winnie S. Talley 5/2/1840
William A. Talley 7/1/1824
Wiley M. Talley 7/11/1826
Nancy P. Talley 2/12/1842
John W. Talley 11/18/1828
Charles B. Talley 8/10/1852
Ann Talley 4/2/1848
Sarah D. Talley 11/1/1830
James K. Talley 11/14/1844
Elizabeth P. Talley 2/9/1832

MALCOLM McMILLAN BIBLE
Ref: Rev. War Pension WC4201

Malcolm McMillan was the son of Edward McMillan and Jean Huie of Fayetteville, N. C. Pension application of Joanna Jacobs McMillan, wife of Malcolm, aged 91 in 1872 living in Boone Co., Ark Malcolm McMillan d. 6/14/1837 Carroll Co., Ark. m. 12/1803.

BIRTHS

Edward McMillan 9/2/1804
Henry McMillan 12/19/1814
Joanna McMillan 8/17/1819
John McMillan 3/10/1806

Joseph McMillan 7/31/1817
Josiah McMillan 6/9/1821
Robert McMillan 9/30/1807

Malcolm McMillan Bible continued...

Jason McMillan 8/9/1823
Jane McMillan 3/2/1810
William McMillan 5/3/1811
Malcolm McMillan 2/14/1813

JESSE HENDREN BIBLE
Owner: Mrs. R. Ivey Moore N. Wilkesboro, N. C.

Jesse Hendren b. 2/13/1829 Wilkes Co., N. C. d. 3/29/1869 m. 6/5/1851 Rebecca Emily Parlier, 2/23/1835-7/6/1916 Wilkes Co, NC.

BIRTHS of Their Children-

Rebecca Emily Hendren 7/20/1852
Theodosia Marie Hendren 5/21/1864
Louisa Jane Hendren 5/3/1854
Andrew G. Hendren 12/5/1863-9/4/1937
Mary Elizabeth Hendren 1/17/1859
William Rufus Hendren 1/30/1862-6/15/1939
Andrew G. Hendren m. 11/5/1891
Eugenia B. Hilliard, 1874-10/13/1920.

BIRTHS of Their Children:

Effie Leola Hendren 9/15/1892
Ruby Thelma Hendren 1/3/1904
Rufus Luther Hendren 12/31/1893
Pearl Eugenia Hendren 12/8/1906
Naomi Hendren 10/23/1895
Chas Bradford Hendren 9/21/1911

Jesse Hendren Bible continued...

Russell Blaine Hendren 12/29/1897
Mable Rebecca Hendren 8/5/1914
Della May Hendeen 9/23/1899
Clyde Elizabeth Hendren 1918-1922
Freda Emily Hendren 9/24/1902

MARRIAGES

Thomas Campbell to Louisa J. Hendren 9/25/1872
A. G. Hendren to Genie Hilliard 11/5/1891
J. H. McLeon to Mary Elizabeth Hendren 1/17/1877
R. L. Miller to Rebecca E. Hendren 12/6/1876

BIRTHS

Cora Antonia Miller 9/22/1877
Hannibal Edger Miller 2/13/1883
Stella Augusta Miller 3/13/1880
Ernest Sherwood McLean 10/13/1881
Nora T. Hendren 9/10/1880
Jesse Van Dora Hendren 3/28/1886
Anna Saloma McLean 10/15/1877
Jesse Ezra McLean 12/2/1883

DEATHS

Ruby T. (Hendren) Benfield 1924
Delia H. Hendren Blevins 1957
L. H. Hendren 7/3/1932
Luther Hendren 12/29/1959

DANIEL SHERWOOD BIBLE
Owner: Dr. Benjamin Sherwood Hawywood
Riverside, California

Daniel Sherwood b. 5/20/1749 d. 3/18/1838, aged almost 89, Guilford C. H., N. C.
Frances Lynthycum. wife of Daniel Sherwood, b. 11/30/1749 d. 5/4/1806, aged 56 yrs.

JOHN ROSE BIBLE
From: Rev. War Pension W18,824

BIRTHS of Children of John Rose and Rachel Sparks

Ann Rose 11/27/1774
John Rose 12/11/1787
Milley Rose 3/8/1776
Elizabeth Rose 1/19/1790
Patience Rose 3/4/1778
Asa Rose 7/23/1792
Rachel Rose 17B1
Thomas Rose 12/11/1796
William Rose 7/2/1785
Benjamin Rose 4/14/1799

Note: Soldier applied for pension 8/6/1832, Surry Co., Va; He was b. 1750, Southampton Co., Va.; 6/1772 he m. Rachel, dau.of William Sparks in Surry Co. Soldier d. 4/23/1843. Widow received pension 1843, aged 89, then resident of Surry Co., N. C. 11/24/1843
Sterling Rose, aged 85, father of John Rose, and Nancy Rose, aged 85, wife of Sterling Rose, lived Wilkes Co., N. C.

JOHN WHEELER BIBLE
From: Rev. War pension WB999

BIRTHS of Children of John Wheeler and Susanna Clark

Henry Wheeler 11/16/1870
Benjamin Wheeler 3/22/1791
James Wheeler 10/16/1782
Polly Wheeler 7/28/1793
John Wheeler 12/9/1784
Matilda Wheeler 4/15/1798

Mary Ann Wheeler 12/25/1786
Isaac Wheeler 6/25/1800
Sally Wheeler 5/10/1789
Susan Wheeler 3/11/1804

Note: Soldier applied for pension 5/6/1833, Livingston Co., Ky; aged 76 yrs., b. Prince Edward Co., Va., Co.1776 moved from Surry to the Holston, John Wheeler
Susanna Clark 12/15/1779 ater father's plantation, Kendrick's Ct. neat Long Isl. On Holstein, Greene Co., N. C. Susanna was b. 7/21/1761, daughter of Henry Clark (b. 10/8/1732) and Sarah Jones (b. 7/26/1737).

WILLIAM WILEY BIBLE
From: Rev. War Pension W10,002

BIRTHS

Abener Wiley 12/25/1789
William Wiley 12/18/1796
Shannon Wiley 1/4/1791
Isaiah Wiley 3/23/1801

William Wiley Bible continued...

Samuel Wiley 2/24/1793
Alfred Wiley 3/18/1803

Note: Soldier applied for pension 11/12/1832, Hendricks Co.,Ind; he was b. 1760 Guilford Co.; 1830 removed to Ohio, then Indiana. Soldier d. Hendricks Co., Ind. 10/12/1838. Widow's pension to Ann Wiley 11/13/1843, aged 72 Hendricks S. C. She (Ann Shannon) m. soldier 1/4/1789 Guilford Co., signed James Shannon.

BADGER L. BROWN BIBLE
Owner: Mrs. Mary Lyles, Wilson, N. C.

Badger L. Brown b. 6/30/1792 Wayne Co., N. C., wife. Nancy, b. 1/6/1778, Wayne Co., on Walnut Creek, d. 3/7/1861, daughter of Nancy Brown.
Dorcas Smith b. 1/27/1809 Greene Co., N. C.

BIRTHS of Children of Badger L. and Nancy Brown

Elizabeth Brown 12/6/1811
James Brown 8/23/1822
Dempsey Brown 8/4/1816
Rebecca Brown 3/25/1824
Zora B. Brown 10/30/1817
Michael Brown 4/11/1826
Mary Ann Maria Brown 4/18/1819
George E. Brown 4/9/1834
Henry Brown 5/18/1827-11/16/1854 Hanover Co., NC

BIRTHS of Children of Mary Brown and grandchildren of B. L. and Nancy Brown:

Michael James Brown 4/23/1846
John Henry Brown 10/23/1850

JESSE LANE BIBLE
Owner: Mrs. Neal Hetzler, Kensington, Ga. 30727

Jesse Lane b. 6/12/1772
Rhoda Jolly Lane b. 12/17/1787

BIRTHS of Their Children

Sarah Sophia Lane 3/18/1811
Rhoda Caroline Lane 12/9/1821
Lorena Winaford Lane 12/3/1812
Sharlotte Ann Lane 4/.23/1824
Elizabeth Francina Lane 1/14/1815
Almeda Malvina Lane 3/28/1826
Emily Ann Lane 6/10/1817
Adelia Manerva Lane 3/21/1829
William Robertson Lane 10/9/1819
Julia Artimissa Lane 9/12/1831

MARRIAGES

Jesse Lane to Rhoda Jolly 5/1810
William Ezzard to Sarah S. Lane 1/7/1830
William F. Chewning to Lorena W. Lane 1831
F. J. Jones to Elizabeth F. Lane 12/14/1834
Jeremiah Perry to Emily Ann Lane 4/30/1835
William R. Lane to H. A. Allan 7/2/1850

William W. Hinton to Rhoda C. Lane 4/24/1838
Alfred Blevins Taylor b. 2/15/1897
Leroy W. Napier to Sharlotte A. Lane 2/12/1841
William J. Jones to Julia A. Lane 7/15/1847
William B. Taylor to Almeda M. Lane 5/6/1841
Robert Thomas Taylor b. 11/26/1898
Joseph T. McConnell to Adelia M. Lane 3/4/1851
Tom P. Taylor to Dora Foster 11/13/1895

ROBERT HANEY BIBLE
From: Rev. War Pension 184563

BIRTHS of Children of Robert and Elizabeth Haney

John Haney 11/24/1781
Rebecca Haney 5/9/1797
Salley Haney 11/19/1783
Syntha Haney 5/17/1799
Nancy Haney 1/10/1785
William Haney 6/11/1801
Timothy Haney 4/14/1787
Betheney Haney 7/8/1803
Elizabeth Haney 5/14/1789
Thomas B. Haney 8/17/1806
Robert Haney 7/30/1792
Washington Haney 12/30/1808
Mary Haney 2/2/1795
Celia 7/--
Timothy Haney 2/13/1819
 Mary An Bobbins 7/17/1839
Drusilla Haney 8/28/18--
Lidemia Haney 1/17/1829

Robert Haney Bible continued...

Note: Robert Haney m. 1789 Elizabeth Bailey, Union District,S. C. In 1846, she applied for pension from. Polk Co., Tenn., 86. She died Polk Co., Tenn. 2/10/1850

BENJAMIN SIMMONS BIBLE
Owner: Mrs. P. M. Utley, Wake Forest, N. C.

Benjamin Simmons b. 10/4/1751 m. Annie Alexander 1767-7/1846. Their son, Lockey Simmons b. 4/14/1796 Montgomery Co., N. C. d.1/23/1880

Wake Forest m.12/21/1826 Mary Lundy Pennington 1/12/1809-7/11/1834.

BIRTHS of Their children

Nancy Ann Simmons 1/29/1838
Calvin Jones Simmons 1/30/1829
William Gaston Simmons 3/4/1830 m. Mary Elizabeth Foote b. 9/2/1833 Warren Co., N. C. d. 4.14.1917 Gainesville, Ga.
Walter Alexander Simmons 10/19/1831
Benjamin Franklin Simmons 2/5/1834

BRITAIN POWELL BIBLE
From: Rev. War Pension W4768

BIRTHS of Children of Britain and Mary Powell

Elijah Powell 10/4/1786
Milly Powell 1/29/1788

Britain Powell Bible continued...

Britain Devan Powell, son of Elisha and Mary, 10/19/1810
Polly Powell 11/15/---

Note: Britain Powell applied for pension from Duplin Co., N. C. 11/23/1832, abt 92 yrs.. he was b. in Va. abt 1740. Mary Powell, widow, applied 7/3/1841 Duplin Co., N. C., aged 81, says me m. 5/10/1784, husband d. 10/13/1838 Duplin Co., N. C. Her statement 9/21/1844, aged 85, states she m. 5/10/1786 in New Hanover Co., N. C. by Thomas Devane, Esq. 12/19/1845 Jesse Lee of New Hanover stated he knew Britain and Mary Powell's children: Elisha, Isaac, Jacob, Milly and Jolcey (Mary). Isaac Newton testified that Milly Powell m. Joel Johnson; Molsey (Mary) m. James Bland.

WILLIAM HOLLAND BIBLE
From: Rev. War Pension W4688

BIRTHS

William Holland 5/22/1783
Isaac Holland 6/3/1786
Matilda Holland 12/25/1784
Susannah Holland 1/11/1788

Note: William Holland applied for pension 9/10/1832, Rutherford Co., N. C., stating he was b. abt 1747 in Pa., enlisted in Mecklenburg Co., N. C. He He substituted his bro., Mathew Holland, to finish one term. William Holland 9/19/1837. Widow, Margaret Holland, applied for pension 6/28/1842, aged 76. She m. William in 1781.

ZEBEDEE HOLLINGSWORTH BIBLE
From: Rev. War Pension W5301

BIRTHS of Children of Zebulon and Elizabeth Hollingsworth

Eve Hollingsworth 6/10/1786
Polly Hollingsworth 471791
Jenny Hollingsworth 9/21/1788
Anny Hollingsworth 1/13/1799

Note: Zebedee Hollingsworth applied for pension 11/20/1833, Sampson Co., N. C. He m. Elizabeth 1/1784. She was b. 2/27/1767. Soldier d. 4/22/1836.

JOHN BRICE BIBLE
Owner: Harriet Newkirk, Willard, N. C.

BIRTHS

John Brice 1/3/1765
Joseph Brice 6/27/1769
George Brice 7/4/1768
Abraham Newkirk 6/15/1754
Ann Brosard. daughter of John Penny and Ann, his wife, 1/6/1716
Elisabeth Neson, daughter of Ann Brosard, 12/27/1742
Mary Ann Brosard, daughter of Peter Andrus Brosard and Ann, 11/21/1749
Peter Andrus Brosard, son of Peter Andrus Brosard and Ann, 11/20/1756-d. 5/26/1773
Mary Ann Newkirk, wife of Abraham Newkirk, 11/21/1749

Their Children:

John Brice Bible continued...

Penny Newkirk 6/30/1785
Mary Ann Newkirk 10/22/1787
Rachel Newkirk, wife of Abraham Newkirk, 7/30/1767
Joseph and Timothy Newkirk 11/20/1791
Bryan Newkirk 6/5/1794
Ann Jane Newkirk 5/5/1796
Abraham Newkirk, Jr., 2/20/1798
Benjamin Rhodes Newkirk 4/3/1801
Jacob Felix Newkirk 8/26/1807
Henry John Thomas Newkirk 6/12/1804
Henry Newkirk, son of Tobias Newkirk, 1/10/1750

WILLIAM HUGHLETT BIBLE
From: Rev. War Pension W4996

BIRTHS

William Thrift Hughlett, father, 11/11/1757   Mary Tate, mother, 5/15/1764

Their Children:

John Hughlett 6/3/1785
Robert Hughlett 4/3/1798
Mary Hughlett, twin, 3/16/1788
Sally Winifred Hughlett 8/29/1801
Elizabeth Hughlett, twin, 3/16/1788
Peter Morgan Hughlett 2/11/1807
Ann Hughlett 5/27/1790
Eunice B. Hughlett 1/12/1817
William Hardy Hughlett 6/30/1793
Thomas Tate Hughlett 3/11/1796

William Hughlett Bible continued...

Thomas Arterbery 3/19/1806
Elizabeth Arterberry 4/17/1813
Benjamin H. Arterberry 1/23/1831
Wilson C. Arterberry 12/30/1839
Benjamin F. Arterberry 10/11/1832
Nancy A. Arterberry 4/12/1842
William F. Arterberry 5/27/1834
Lucinda B. Arterberry 1/15/1845
Moses A. Arterberry 12/11/1837
Mary L. Arterberry 2/21/1847
Martha R. Arterberry 8/6/1850

MARRIAGES

William T. Hughlett, father, to Mary Tate, 7/1/1784
John Hughlett, bro., to Christennah Shouse 1/15/1805 --
1/1827 to Elizabeth Maybry
  Mary Hughlett to Elizabeth Hughlett, twin sisters, 8/16/1807
Mary to Thomas F. Sumner and Elizabeth to Gen. Samuel Wilson.
Mary m. 2nd to Rev. Thomas D. Porter 7/23/1820
Ann Hughlett, sister, to Harvey Johns 12/25/1805, 2nd to Col. James McColgan
William M. Hughlett, bro., 4/16/1818 to Polly McCraw
Robert Hughlett, bro., to Elizabeth McCraw 6/3/1819
Sally Winefred Hughlett to Dr. William Chilton 3/25/1819
Peter Morgan Hughlett to Eunice B. White 11/26/1834

DEATHS

William Thrift Hughlett, my father, 1/16/1827, aged 70, Centreville, Hickman Co., Tenn.
Thomas Tate Hughlett, my bro., 8/9/1815

William Hughlett Bible continued...

Thomas E. Sumner. my bro-in-law, 7/21/1819, aged 50.
Gen. Samuel Wilson. my bro-in-law, was murdered 3/25/1831
Elizabeth Wilson, my sister. 1/3/1835
Sally Winefred Chilton, my sister, 5/22/1837
Peter Morgan Hughlett 7/8/1837, Texas
Thomas D. Porter, my bro-in-law, 7/10/1837, Texas
Mary Hughlett 9/21/1843, aged 80, Tonpkinsville, Monroe Co., Ky.

Note: Anna (or Nancy) McColgan, wid. of Col. James McColran, maiden name Ann Hughlett, only surviving child of William Hughlett and Mary Tate Hughlett, applied for pension 10/25/1852, aged 62, Jackson Co., Tenn. She stated that her father was b. 11/11/1757, was member of NC Gen. Assembly in 1797, served 12 yrs. in NC Senate and State Legislature from Stokes Co.

BURREL JORDAN BIBLE
of Northampton County
From: Rev. War Pension W29726

BIRTHS of Children of Burrell and Mary Jordan

Mary Jordan 2/6/1755 -- Burrel Jordan 9/15/1757
John Jordan 5/8/1756
Wineford Jordan, daughter of George Jordan and wife of John Jordan, 9/9/1763

John Jordan m. Wineford 2/19/1786.

Their Children:

Burrel Jordan Bible continued...

Britian Jordan 6/18/1787
Burwell Jordan 9/30/1800
Green H. Jordan 4/26/1789
John Jordan 4/16/1800
Priscella Jordan 8/17/1791
Mary Jordan 7/2/1804
Patience Jordan 9/22/1793

"Be it enacted by the Senate and House of Representatives of the United States of America in Congress assembled, That the Secretary of the Interior be, and he is hereby, authorized and directed to place on the pension-roll the name of Mrs. Mary Newton, the daughter and only surviving heir of John Jordan, of the Continental Line, in the war of the Revolution and to pay her at the rate of twelve dollars per month from and after the passage of this act. Approved, March 2, 1889."
"This claimant is a relative of and lives with Hen. Henry H. Carlton of Athens, Ga."

Note: Wineford Jordan applied for pension from Washington Co., Ga., aged 84 yrs., 10/3/1846, stating that she is widow of John Jordan, and was married to him in the house of George Jordan her father's house in Northampton Co., Va. by Lauvern Smith.

JOSEPH PARKER BIBLE of Edgecombe Co.
Owner: Mrs. Rom B. Parker, Sr., Enfield, N. C.

Joseph Parker b. 1/18/1761
Joseph Parker 5/8/1822
James Harvey Parker, son of Joe and Temperance (Holt), 1/10/1823-6/16/1899

Joseph Parker Bible continued...

Mary C. Scott, daughter of Mrs. Rebecca M. Scott, d. 6/11/1863, aged 65 yrs.

James Harvey Parker m. on 12/21/1841
Mary C. Scott (1/26/1819- 8/13/1902). Their Children:

James William Fletcher Parker b. 11/6/1842
Mary Jane Parker 10/29/1849
Cornelia Ann Mitchell 10/20/1843-4/6/1878
Sam Watts Parker b. 6/3/1847

Sam Watts Parker b. 5/3/1847
Infant son 12/13/1850-44/29/1851
William Rebecca Parker b. 9/26/1852

CLAY-COOK BIBLE
Owner: Mrs. Walter Williams, Russellville, KY

BIRTHS

Archer Clay 2/26/1780
Elizabeth High 12/20/1785
They were m. in Virginia 12/23/1807.

Children:

Maria A. Clay 10/24/1808	Docie W. Clay 3/31/1820
Sarah B. Clay 5/20/1810	Charity H. Clay 8/30/1822
Mary Ann Clay 12/9/1811	John W. Clay 9/15/1825

Mary Ann Clay, daughter of Archer and Elizabeth Clay, b. 12/9/1811 Va.

Clay-Cook Bible....

Jesse Cook, son of Jacob Cook and Elizabeth Rabb Cook, b. 7/27/1790 in North Carolina. They m. 7/29/1829 Wilson Co., Tenn.

BIRTHS of Children of Jesse and Mary Ann Cook

Elizabeth T. Cook-1830
John F. Cook 1837
Jacob Newton Cook 4/15/1832
James L. Cook 1843
Martha P. Cook 1834
Jacob N. Cook, b. 4/15/1832, son of Jesse and Mary Ann Clay Cook
Ellen Elizabeth Barton b. 5/13/1840, daughter of Rev. Rutherford Barton and Ary Matilda Thomas.

BIRTHS of Children of Jacob N. and Ellen Cook

James A. Cook 10/21/1861
Naomi Cook 9/28/1871
Amy Leona Cook 11/25/1864
Elizabeth Cook 8/27/1873
Mary I. Cook 10/28/1867
Ella Newton Cook 7/30/1880
Adah Cook 1/15/1870

BARNES BIBLE
Of Wilson Co., near White Oak Swamp
Owner: Mrs. Mary H. Forbes, Wilson, N. C.

Sherod 1804
George 5/1843
Mary 9/9/1847
Clary 1/1818
Sherod 5/16/1843
Jones 9/16/1849
Venas 8/1818
Sary 7/1/1848
Gerret 5/--
Berry 1822
Peter 9/5/1845
Blount 1/22/--
Lewis 4/1826
George 2/29/---
Dina 2/15/--

Julia 7/1826
Mima 5/9/1847
Rebecca 1/16/185-
Pen 1829
Ann 6/13/1847
Ann 2/26/185-
Eacy 5/1835
Feriby 7/15/1847
Marina 3/31/1845-
Carolina 1840
Aaron 7/1847
Frank 6/5/185-
Sam 12/13/1839

Barnes Bible continued...

Fanney 1848
Jarmon 8/28/185-

Joe 5/4/1841
Ned 1848
Mariah 4/20/1853
Frances 1843
Tom 5/6/1849
Jane 5/6/1853
George 2/13/1839
Isaac 6/26/1849
Harry 7/10/1855
Hannah 7/10/1855
Hector 1856
Warren 1857
Mike 3/4/1857
Arch 3/18/1857
Mary 10/27/1860
Ann 4/30/1861
Rose 5/17/1861
Harriet 8/10/1862
Jane 12/26/1864
Giles 7/16/1865
Mariam 9/16/1865

BENNETT BARNES BIBLE
Owner: Miss Essie Bunn, Rocky Mount, N. C.

Bennett Barnes d. 4/5/1857 Nash Co., N. C.

BIRTHS of his slaves:

Martha 3/8/1829
Martha Frances 1/1/1840
William 9/14/1846
Sylva 8/25/1844
Frances 1/28/1833
Joe 2/28/1860
Sam Perry 12/3/1862
Henry 7/15/1862
Washington, son of Prissy, 1/15/1831
Mary Elizabeth 2/24/1851
George Washington 6/3/1848
William Henry 8/23/1854
Lucy 1/6/1833
Prissy 7/30/1856
Toney 11/4/1851
Laura 1857
Louisa 3/1859
John 3/29/1853
Alfie 1861
Florence 10/18/1855
Sarah 1/26/1858
Joshua 2/21/1860
Rosa 5/12/1863

GEORGE W. HARRIS BIBLE of Pitt Co.
Owner: Mrs. Francis I. Denny, Wilson, N. C.

George W. Harris 9/12/1817-5/14/1888 m. Pernetta Thigpen (11/5/1819-4/13/1880), then wid. of William Smith (d. 1/9/1841) on 2/13/1849.

BIRTHS of Slaves:

Daniel 11/6/1845
Turner 4/5/1851
Pennina 7/7/1847
Harry 3/19/1853
Alford 3/1849
Mariah 5/8/1855

SOLOMON PENDER'S BIBLE
Owner: Paul Pender, Lansing, MI 48823

Solomon Pender 5/22/1783-9/8/1852, son of John and Nancy (White) Pender of Edgecombe Co., N. C. m. Mary Batts (4/26/1789-10/10/1825), daughter of Capt. Joseph Batts, Edgecombe Co., N. C. on 12/17/1807.

BIRTHS of Slaves:

Peter 1782-sold
Rachel 3/1814
Isaac 1829-sold
Dinah 3/1789
Ilander 1782
Frank, Dallas
Lewis 1/1830
Jane 1/1816

Solomon Pender's Bible continued...

Patty 3/1786
Dick (yelloe) 1815
John 11/25/1830
Hannah 4/8/1832
Ned 1768
Charles 10/1815
Elijah 1/1/1831-
sold Robert 11/23/1833
Abby 1/2/1820
Mary 4/20/1833
Harriet 4/4/1852
Hannah 4/8/1835
Winney 1/1827
Julia 4/1837
Maria 12/15/1835
Marina 4/11/1834
Joe 1808
Betty 7/1818
Mike 3/1836
Eliza 1808
Anna 7/1849
Nancy 3/1836
Fanny
Monroe 12/25/1851
Agnes 1808
William 8/1852
Henry 12/15/1837
Julia 4/1837
Kitty 1824
Dicey 8/1820
Martha 1838
Amanda 7/1838

Solomon Pender's Bible continued...

William 8/1852
Tom 1838
George 9/7/1839
Lasarus 7/11/1839
Turner 9/16/1849
Richmond 3/1841
Dinah 2/1840
Bunny 1827-1886
Adaline 11/5/1851
Daniel 1824
Matthew 12/23/1857
Charles 8/9/1859
Dick (Black) 1809
Harriet 11/1824
Hilliard 3/1/1812
Mary Baly 1/1852
Willis 2/1829
Julius 3/6/1842
Sucky 12/17/1854
Deborah 2/1814

ISHAM PETER JOHNSON BIBLE
Owner: Rev. Thomas Bradley Johnson

BIRTHS

Isham Peter 9/27/1830, son of Thomas and Joycy (Bookout) Johnson
Margaret M. Johnson 10/1/1841 (Isham's Ist wife, Margaret Kemp)

Isham Peter Johnson Bible continued...

Mary Ann Johnson 3/8/1828 (Isham's 2nd wife, Mary A. A. Couch)
Jessie Lawrence Johnson 11/28/1857, (son by 1st wife)
Neucie Sylvania Johnson 1/28/1860 (daughter by 1st wife)
Thomas Bradley Johnson 8/14/1865 son by 2nd wife)
Martha Ann Melissa Johnson 8/2/1868 (daughter by 2nd wife)
Samuel Henry Johnson 2/1/1862 (son by 2nd wife)
Lawrence Johnson, son of Thomas, 7/20/1827
A. S. Craven to Neucie Sylvania Johnson 9/9/1883
W. H. Mann to M. M. (Martha Ann Melissa) Johnson 12/17/1888

DEATHS

Margaret M. Johnson 4/29/1860-
Samuel Henry Johnson 3/15/1862
Mary Ann Johnson 10/15/1882
Malissa M. Mann 11/9/1895
Isham Johnson 11/24/1910
Rev. Thomas B. Johnson 6/2/1943
Lawrence Johnson, son of Thomas Johnson 11/5/1849   Thomas Johnson 8/14/1865
J. L. (Jesse Lawrence) Johnson 10/20/1932   Martha Ann Lisa Johnson 8/2/1867
Mary Virginia Conley Johnson, wife of Rev. Thomas Bradley Johnson, 6/4/1954
Mary A. Johnson b. 3/8/1828 m. Isham Johnson 1/6/1860
Lawrence Johnson, son of Thomas, 7/20/1827-11/5/1849
William H. Mann m. Martha A. M. Johnson 12/19/1888

STEPHENS-THAMES BIBLE
Owner: Elsie David
Clio, South Carolina

John Thames, son of John Thames and Nancy, his wife, 9/10/1803- 8/30/1860
Martha Ann Thames, daughter of above and Sarah, his wife, b. 7/19/1831
Sarah Rebecca Thames, dau. of above, d. 9/7/1862
Polly Thames, wife of above, d. 5/20/1868
Eliza Jane Wright, wife of J. T. Wright, d. 3/22/1849

John Stephens, son of Hardy and Jemima, his wife, b. 5/2/1767
Zelphia? Stevens, daughter of John Stevens and Mary, b. 3/21/1788

BIRTHS of Children of John and Mary Stevens

William Stevens 4/20/1789
John Stevens 5/17/1794
Drusella Stevens 4/17/1791
James Stevens 6/1/1800
Surthoma? Stevens -/20/1792
Sally Stevens 12/30/1801
Hardy Stevens 1794
Mary Stevens 7/28/1803
Sabre Stevens 12/19/1795
Tistoni Stevens 3/6/1805
Willoughby Stevens 1/5/1807
John Stevens, son of John and Mary, his wife, b. 1798
William S. Cooper b. 1/6/1810
Floziel b. 8/4/1743
Betty b. 3/7/1839
John Stephens d. 8/4/1829

Stephen Thames Bible continued...

Mary Stephens d. 9/22/1831
Amanda Stephens 9/2/1831
W. D. Stephens m. Martha Ann Thames 3/24/1850

BIRTHS of Children of W. D. and Martha Ann Stephens
John W. Stephens 1/1/1851
Mary Eliza Stephens 9/10/1852
Sarah D. Stephens 5/8/1854
Willoughby D. Stephens 5/10/1856
William Ann Stephens 8/5/1858
David Augustus Stephens 6/4/1860
Hardy Henry Stephens 4/12/1862
Ella Cornelia Stephens 8/3/1872
Joseph A. McArthur Stephens 9/2/1864
Martha Ann Thames Stephens 2/9/1867
Sabra Underwood Stephens 5/31/1869
D. Stephens m. Amanda Riddle 9/13/1877 by Malcolm McIver
Hardy Henry Stephens d. 10/19/1936
W. D. Stephens, husband of M. A. Stephens, d. 2/24/1886

NOAH ROBESON

James Robason, son of Henry and Martha, d. 10/4/1811

BIRTHS of Children of James

Cloanna Robeson 5/6/1769 - - Martha Robeson 2/3/1780
Luke Robeson 5/26/1772   Milley Robeson 6/2/1784
Mary Robeson 10/3/1773   Anna Robeson 11/3/1786
Henry Robeson 2/12/1775   Harmon Robeson 5/31/1789
John Robnson 12/8/1777   Noah Robeson 12/24/1790
Chloe Robeson, daughter of James and Milley, his wife, 4/9/1814

WALTER HARBIN BIBLE of Davie and Rowan Counties

Walter Harbin, son of Allen C. Harbin 8/27/1787
Easter Harbin, daughter of Walter Etchison, 5/1011789

BIRTHS of Walter and Easter Harbin's Children:

Lydia Harbin 6/12/1810
Nancy Harbin 9/15/1820
Allen C. Harbin -/10/1815
Frances Harbin 2/22/1823
Elizabeth Harbin 5/19/1818
Caswell Harbin 4/20/1825
Cosmodore P. Harbin 2/14/1818
Matilda A. Harbin 8/13/1827
Jackson Harbin -/14/1818
Sarah A. M. Harbin 10/9/1829

MARRIAGES

Walter Harbin to Easter Etcherson 8/27/1809
Lydia Harbin to Jacob Sain 10/15/1827
Frances Harbin to John Nevis 4/14/1846
Elizabeth Harbin to William A. Taylor 11/12/1835
Allen Harbin to Elizabeth Hamiline 12/20/1836
Lydia Sain to Wylie B. Nash, the 2nd time, 4/14/1845
Nancy Harbin to John B. Nash 5/15/1845

DEATHS

Jackson Harbin, son of Walter and Easter
Walter Harbin 2/3/1834
Jacob Sain 2/14/1834
Elizabeth Harbin, wife of A. C., 8/1837

Walter Harbin Bible continued...

Matilda A. H. Harbin, daughter of Walter and Easter, 10/11/1855
Allen C. Harbin, son of 1st above, 7/21/1844
Lydia Nash, wife of W. B. Nash, daughter of Ist above, 1/13/1844
Commodore e. Harbin, son of above, 6/20/1849
Easter Harbin, wife of Walter, 11/9/1851

Note: Walter Etchison b. Charles Co., Md., moved Fanquier Co., Va. and Rowan Co., N. C. before 1878

JOHN WESLEY PERRY, JR. BIBLE of Granville Co.

BIRTHS

John W. Perry Jr. 5/4/1808
Willie Perry 2/26/1899
Frances Perry 9/17/1895
Frances A. Hotley 6/29/1873

Roy Arnold Perry 6/18/1901
Nellie May Perry 9/24/1896
Eddie Pendleton Perry 3/2/1891
Eunice Lee Perry 7/9/1903
Ethel Motley Perry 10/3/1909
Maude Ellen Perry 12/10/1892
Cleo Clifford Perry 6/18/1900
Elsie Marie Perry 3/8/1909
Charley Wesley Perry 5/26/1894
Earl Franklin Perry 6/22/1907
Infant sons of John

WILLIAM C. WOLFE BIBLE

MARRIAGES

William C. and P. L. Wolfe 9/20/1855
D. J. Grigg and N. E. Wolfe 12/5/1880
Jefferson Beauregard Wolfe and Ernma Mary McGill 7/30/1889

BIRTHS

W. C. Wolfe 12/4/1833
John C. Wolfe 11/27/1904
Nancy Ellen Wolfe 4/7/1957
Phebe L. Wolfe 6/9/1833
Mary P. Wolfe 11/11/1911
Mary L. Wolfe 4/10/1866
Marshall L. Wolfe Jr. 6/11/1947
Sary G. Jane Wolfe 2/25/1859
Jefferson Beaureguard Wolfe 6/28/1861
A. Ere Wole 10/17/1868
William Ivey Wolfe 10/15/1870
Sanford Robert Wolfe 10/31/1876
Larance Marchel Wolfe 10/18/1879

DEATHS

Jacob Wolfe 12/11/1865
Nancy Wolfe 1/27/1876
George Lee 7/17/1875
Jefferson Beauregard Wolfe 6/19/1902
Sanford Robert Wolfe 3/16/1927
Phoebe L. Wolfe 8/4/1915, aged 78 yrs., 1 mo., 25 days
William Cathey Wolfe 5/9/1917-d. suddenly In Shelby, N. C.
A. Era Wolfe 3/5/1936
Sarah Jane Wolfe 2/23/1945

JOSEPH DELLINGER BIBLE

MARRIAGES

Joseph Dellinger to Margaret S. E. Wacaster 11/20/1873
Violet Robene Dellinger to Abner Franklin Carpenter 3/9/1905

BIRTHS

Joseph Dellinger 7/4/1847
Barbara Jezebel Dellinger 6/8/1874
Margaret Sarah Elizabeth Dellinger 10/26/1851
Lillen Florence Dellinger 10/22/1876
Violet Rebena Dellinger 9/15/1878
Franklin P. Dellinger 8/3/1880
George Levi Dellinger 9/28/1882
Marcius Wesley Dellinger 11/3/1884
Cleveland Odell Dellinger 3/11/1887
Lucy Clementine Dellinger 8/22/1889

DEATHS

Barbara Jezebel Dellinger 6/1/1875
Joseph Dellinger 1/13/1934
Inf. daughter 2/20/1892
Bettie Dellinger 3/14/1908
Franklin P. Dellinger 1/25/1954
Margaret Sarah Elizabeth Dellinger 2/15/1908

Memoranda

Mary Ann Dellinger b. 2/20/1892
Inf. Daughter b. 2/20/1892
James Buran Dellinger b. 10/19/1918

WILLIS A. McKINNEY BIBLE of Rutherford

Willis A. McKinney of Rutherford, N. C. m. Biddy S. McDaniel of Rutherford, N. C. on 10/4/1860 at J. B. McDaniel's by Elder Dove
Pannel. Wit: J. B. McDaniel and G. W. Lookadoo

BIRTHS

Willis A. McKinney 5/10/1836
Biddy S. McKinney 2/3/1844
Martha A. McKinney 9/9/1861
A. L. Hamrick 10/4/1893
M. L. Hamrick 11/23/1858
E. O. Hamrick 9/8/1896
M. S. Hamrick 2/3/1883
R. Z. Hamrick 12/6/1900

A. Hamrick 11/7/1884
G. E. Hamrick 5/17/1904

W. C. Hamrick 12/9/1886
N. C. Hamrlck 6/17/1908
N. O. Hamrick 10/10/1888
Oma Jane Hamrick 10130/1909
E. E. Hamrick 6/6/1891
Abbie D. Hamrick 4/9/1912

MARRIAGES

M. T.. Hamrick to H. A. McKinney 1882
W. O. Hamrick to N. S. Hamrick 11/7/1900
M. L. Hamrick to Johnie Hamrick 8/2/1906
George M. Self to Ollie Hamrick 11/8/1907

Willis A. McKinney Bible continued...

Grove Hamrick to Ellie Hamrick 3/28/1909
M. L. Hamrick to Susan Webb 1/1/1914
Charlie Hill to Ockie Hemrick 8/19/1914
Cicero Tate to Oaky Hamrick 11/30/1921
A. L. Hamrick to Thelma Austin 9/21/1920
G. M. Self 7/20/1889-4/18/1959

DEATHS

Willis A. McKinney 7/13/1863 at Battle of Falling Water
Biddy S. McKinney 8/16/1898
Siley C. Hamrick 11/19/1882
Amelia Hamrick 1/17/1905
Johnnie Hamrick 5/5/1913
Abbie Dean Hamrick 6/11/1913, age 1 yr., 2 mos.
A. L. Hamrick 11/1/1920
Martin Luther Hamrick 5/29/1934

Susan E. Hamrick 10/4/1948
Octavia Hamrick Hill ---
A. L. Hamrick 10/25/1955
Mary Susan Hamrick 4/9/1962
Susan Faye Webb Hamrick 10/4/1948
N. C. Hamrick 2/12/1980
Oaky R. Hamrick Tate 4/27/1978

GREENBERRY BLANTON

BIRTHS

Greenberry Blanton 3/10/1869
Ida May Blanton 7/18/19--

Mary Blanton 2/18/1879
Huston Lee Blanton 2/9/1920
Axem Fready Blanton 7/30/1891
Jacob Deva? Blanton 8/26/1901
James Ody Blanton 6/27/1893
Carl Green Blanton 7/20/1903
Flora Lenora Blanton 7/20/1898
Kenon Shilet Blanton 4/11/1906
Ira Bull Blanton 12/8/1899
Veola Lorene Blanton 2/9/1908
Agness Alene Blanton -/4/1911
Andrew Pinky Blanton 12/5/1909
Mendel Cletous Blanton 9/19/1914

M. C. HAMRICK BIBLE

BIRTHS

Martin Colver Hamrick 9/3/1856
Isom Clinton Hamrick 10/11/1882
Mattie Priscilla Hamrick 2/17/1856
Grover Cleveland Hamrick 5/9/1888
James W. Hamrick 6/3/1874
Ezra C. Hamrick 10/5/1891
Thomas Frank Hamrick 6/4/1876
Francis Ann Hamrick 11/22/1895

M. C. Hamrick Bible continued...

William Edgar Hamrick 8/22/1880
W. W. Hamrick 1/1/1910
Frances E. Owens 2/2/1818
Wiley D. Owens 3/4/1841
Andrew Owens 9/16/1836
Sarah J. Owens 10/19/1844
Mary E. Owens 1129/1839
Isom W. Owens 1/16/1816

DEATHS

Isom Owens 4/24/1890
Caroline Owens 2/19/1901
Frances E. Owens 9/6/1860
Maria E. Blanton 2/6/1902
Elizabeth Owens 7/8/1872
W. C. Hamrick 9/3/1856-5/2/1908

JONAS ROLLINS BIBLE

Jonas Rollins 1/4/1795
Malley Rolllns 7/29/1831
Mary Rollins 3/18/1801
James J. E. Rollins 11/10/1833
Martha Jane Rollins 1/24/1820
Doctor O. Rollins 12/24/1835
O. D. Rollins 9/25/1822
Noah J.Rollins 8/2/1838
Rebecca Rollins 9/14/1824
Mary A.Rollins 12/20/1840
John E. Rollins 1/24/1827

Jonas Rollins Bible continued...

Julian Rollins 12/9/1842
George W. Rollins 12/7/1828
Lawson R. Rollins 7/30/1846
Rebecca A. Greene 9/16/1848
J. W. Greene 5/24/1857
L. R. Wall 5/22/1860
L. M. Rollins b. 3/4/1842

Jonas Rollins m. Mary Allison 3/18/1819
D. O. Rollins m. Letty Margaret Wall 2/19/1871

BIRTHS of Children of George W. Greene and Martha Jane Rollins

Jefferson Greene 3/24/1857-   Ellen E. Greene ---
Rebecca A. Greene 9/16/1848   Noah J. Greene---

WILLIAM BUCHANAN BIBLE
Owner: Mrs. Naomi Sparks, Estatoe, N. C.

Arthur Buchanan, son of James and Isabella Buchanan, b. 1/24/1743 m. Mary Boswell on 1/24/1762

BIRTHS of Children of Arthur and Mary Boswell Buchanan

Benedictor Buchanan 8/29/1770
James Buchanan 8/23/1770
William Buchanan 8/23/1765
Annie Buchanan (2d) 11/7/1779
Annie Buchanan 3/9/1769
James Buchanan (2d) 12/14/1780
William Buchanan m. Elizabeth Jones 4/16/1793

William Buchanan Bible continued...

BIRTHS of Children of William and Elizabeth Jones Buchanan

Mary J. Buchanan 10/21/1794
Patsy Buchanan 1/31/1808
George B. Buchanan 11/26/1795
Sally Buchanan 8/3/1806
Leonard Buchanan 10/24/1809
Elizabeth Buchanan 3/6/1797
Clement Buchanan 8/15/1811
William Buchanan 11/18/1800
Lewis Buchanan 2/21/1813
Annie Buchanan 3/7/1802
Nancy Buchanan 11/1/1814
John Buchanan 5/16/1803
Ruth Buchanan 10/9/1816
Arthur Buchanan 11/16/1804
Joseph Alexander Buchanan 7/7/1818

JOHNSON-CARTER BIBLE
Owner: Mrs. Arthur L. Johnson, DAR
Alexander Martin Chapter, NC

BIRTHS

Michael Johnson 1/17/1781
Abbott Carter 6/14/1814
Mary Phillips Johnson, his wife, Elizabeth Phillips Johnson 12/24/1819
Abbott Carter m. Elizabeth P. Johnson 4/8/1837

Johnson-Carter Bible continued...

BIRTHS

George Friend Carter 5/11/1839
Alice Loring Carter 6/8/1849
Gardiner Fieoths Carter 12/6/1840
Albert Freeman Carter 1/15/1855
Elmer Abbott Carter 6/10/1843
William D. Carter 6/14/1857
Pauline Augusta Carter 9/5/1846

DEATHS

Michael Johnson 5/11/1849, aged 68 yrs., 4 mos.
Mary Phillips Johnson, his wife, 9/18/1880
Elizabeth Phillips Johnson 11/16/1880
Elmer Abbott Carter 9/29/1894
Pauline Augusta Carter 1/13/1913

JOHN L. BRINSON BIBLE
Owner: Mrs. Oliver Dixon, Grantsboro, N. C.

John L. Brinson m. Stativa Brinson 11/23/1837

BIRTHS of Their Children

Susannah Slade Brinson 1/22/1839 Mary Smith Brinson 5/9/1841
Charles Brinson m. Elizabeth 5/19/1839
Elizabeth d. 7/5/1846
Sarah L. Brinson, daughter of Charles Brinson and Nora, his wife, b. 8/18/1854

John L. Brinson Bible continued...

Elder James Brinson, Preacher of Gospel of the Newlight Baptist Faith and order b. 2/5/1730, d. as we suppose in 1796
And all of these offspring of the Brinson Family wrote in this book are from him.
Asa Brinson d. 9/6/1836

Smith Brinson d. 10/17/1839
Silas Brinson d. 9/22/1841
Mathew Brinson d. 9/10/1847
Mathew Brinson 4/9/1758-7/24/1832
Elizabeth, his wife, was supposed to be between 50 and 60 yrs. of age when she d. in 1826.
Daniel Brinson, son of same, 11/9/1795-10/17/1826--which both of these decd at one time.
James Brinson, son of same, 1/30/1798-2/11/1817
Persia Brlnson, daughter of same, we suppose was b. 1791. She died age 6 mos.
Asa Brinson b. 1/10/1788, baptised 9/10/1825 by Elder Biggs, the new light preacher.
Matthew Brinson b. 5/10/1783
Mrs. Meaty Brinson d. 2/22/1877, aged 91 yrs, 2 mos.. 18 days

Silas Brinson b. 10/28/1789
Charles Brinson d. 8/4/1884
Asa Brinson b. 1/10/1788
Mary Brinson b. 12/4/1785

BIRTHS of Children of Asa and Mary Brinson

Charles Brinson 1/18/1813
Smith Brinson 9/10/1820
Stativa Brinson 8/5/1818
Elizabeth Brinson 1/14/1826
Daniel Brinson 9/5/1827

John L. Brinson Bible continued...

BIRTHS of Children of Charles and Elizabeth Brinson

Elizabeth Brinson 3/13/1840
Luvenia Brinson 12/20/1845
John Smith Brinson 11/13/1842
Elizabeth Brinson d. 2/5/1832
John. Brinson d. 9/1/1862
Elizabeth Fanning b. 1/7/1803

ROBERT DANIELL BIBLE
Owner: R. G. Daniell, Metter, Ga.

BIRTHS

William Daniell 11/25/1743 New Hanover Co., N. C.

Mary Daniell 3/11/1770
Ollive Daniell 2/15/1815
Rachel Daniell 7/31/1789
Masters H. Daniell 12/27/1802
Josiah Daniell 2/26/1792
Clarissa Daniell 12/29/1804
Susannah Daniell 6/8/1794
Alfred Daniell 2/17/1807
Jeremiah M. Daniell 1/18/1797
Stephen Daniell 2/4/1809
Eleanor Daniell 2/19/1799
Moses Daniell 5/4/1810
Deaton Daniell 3/8/1801
Robert Daniell 2/2/1813
Marian Fuller 4/29/1821
Rachel Crow 2/10/1779

Robert Daniell Bible continued...

BIRTHS of Children of William and Rachel Daniell

William Daniell 1767 - -
Rebecca Daniell 7/17/1779
Elizabeth Daniell 3/16/1769
Isaac Daniell 10/13/1781
Mary Daniell 2/22/1772
George Daniell 9/17/1783
Nathaniel Daniell 3/18/1774

Note by W. F. Daniel: This Bible Record does not include the following children of William Daniell's Ist wife, Rachel, as follows:
Sarah Daniell 5/22/1762 twin who m. James Irwin
James Daniell, R.W.S., 5/22/1762 who m. Rebecca Stephens
Thomas Daniell, R.W.S., 1765 who m. Patsy Smith
James Daniell who m. Sarah Nixon
Robert Daniell m. Naomi (Burnett) Daniel 8/11/1836

BIRTHS of Children of Robert and Naomi Daniell

Martha Ann Daniell 9/25/1837-
William P. Daniell 2/5/1841
Olive Ann Daniell 6/14/1839
Catharine F. Daniell 4/13/1843

BIRTHS

Green B. Daniell 9/29/1845
John S. Daniell 2/4/1852
George L. Daniell 1/14/1848
Pinkney Y. Daniell 10/24/1856
Robert P. Daniell 2/3/1850

NATHAN BODDIE of "Rosehill" near Nashville, N. C.
Owner: Mrs. Anna Boddie Bunn

Chloe Crudup, wife of Nathan Boddie 1745-9/16/1781
Nathan Boddie 12/7/1797-
Children b. Nash Co., N. C.
Bennett Boddie 9/9/1763 m. Sarah Smith
Elijah Boddie 1765 m. Elizabeth Taylor
Temperance Boddie 1767 m. Col. Jeremlah Perry
George Boddie 11/19/1769 m. Ist Susannah Parham Hill, 2d, Lucy Williams
Mary Boddie 3/24/1771 m. Joshua Perry
Basheba Boddie 8/10/1773-3/1782

Elizabeth Boddie 4/10/1776 m. Capt. John Perry
Mourning Boddie 2/25/1778 m. James Hilliard

WILLIAM CROCKETT BIBLE

BIRTHS

William Crockett 11/14/1786-11/1/1806
Agnes Crockett 12/7/1779-2/23/1834 m. 1/10/1899
John Miles Smith 9/1836 Newton Co., Ga., near Conyers-2/20/1907,383 Central Ave
Martha Jane Saunders Smith 10/8/1838-10/20/1921
Francis Lee Smith 8/26/1868
Lula Jane Smith 1870
Sanders Egleston Smith 9/25/1871
Martha Ann Smith 7/28/1873-3/17/1910 m. E. C. Maddox 12/19/1906

William Crockett Bible continued...

Edward Steward Smith 1/29/1876-6/17/1893
McMichael Lafayette Smith 10/6/1881

Ist Generation, Captain Richardson Smith, b. London England in 1741-fought as
Captain in the Revolutionary war, supposed to died in Rockingham, N. C.
2nd - Capt. Dill Smith (son), Capt., in N. C. Guards, d. Henry Co. ca 1864
3rd - John Smith b. Rockingham Co., N. C.
4th - John Miles Smith b. Newton Co., Ga. 1831
5th - McMichael Lafayette Smith 10/6/1881 Henry Co.
Francis Maddox b. 4/4/1908
Newborn baby 3/15/1910-3/18/1910, bur. in coffin with mother
Martha Jane Sanders m. John M. Smith 8/18/1867
Newspaper clipping in Bible: "Mrs. Martha J. Smith: The friends of Mrs. Martha J. Smith, Sanders E. Smith, P. L. Smith, Mr. and Mrs. J. L. Smith of Jacksonville, Fla., Mr. and Mrs. E. C. Maddox, Dr. and Mrs. F. P. Smith and family, Mrs. A. C. Smith,Mrs. E. L. McMillan and family are invited to attend funeral of Mrs. Martha Smith....Oct. 22, 1921...Interment will be at McDonough, Ga....Mrs. Martha J. Smith, 83 yrs., of age, died at the residence ...at Clarkston, Ga. She is survived by three sons,Sanders E.I F. L. and M. L. Smith, and one daughter, Mrs. E. C.Maddox....

JOSEPH MARTIN BIBLE
From: Rev. War Pension W9532

BIRTHS of Children of Stephen and Patsy Martin

Stephen Martin 11/28/1779   Joseph Martin 9/7/1792

Joseph Martin Bible continued...

Susanna Martin 5/8/1787
Mourning Martin 8/1/1789

Thomas Martin 5/26/1795
Patsy Martin 5/27/1798

Note: Patsey Martin applied for pension 2/26/1839, Rockingham Co., N. C., aged 78 or 79, wid. of Joseph Martin who d. in Henry Co.. Va. They m. abt 18 mos. before close of war at Loudoun Co., Va., then moved to Pittsylvania Co.,Va. when they had one child.

Stephen Martin (now lives in Patrick Co., Va., age 25.) They moved to Halifax Co., Va. Then to Hugh Warre River in N. C. where last child was born. Joseph Martin d. 2/14/1832 Henry Co., Va.Children: Stephen, Susanna, Mourning and Joseph lived in Patrick Co., Va. In 1839; Thomas lived somehwere in the west. Petsy lived In Rockingham Co., N. C. (m. John Perdue).

CLACK ROBINSON BIBLE
Virginia State Archives

Clack Robinson and Eleanor Young, his wife, m. 10/11/1809

BIRTHS

Clack Robinson 6/2/1777
Eleanor Robinson 10/11/1786
Sarah Ann Robinson 12/22/1811
Rowena T. F. Robinson 4/21/1818
Mary C. Robison 9/22/1813
William E. Robinson 4/8/1820
Lucy R. Robinson 7/23/1815
Allen Y. Robinson 12/30/1821

DEATHS

Eleanor A. Robinson 1/11/1823
Mary C. Robinson 8/11/1825
Clack Robinson m. Ann Johnston 10/1/1828 at Lebanon, near Norfolk

BIRTHS

Mary Carolina Ann Robinson 9/8/1829 Virginia Robinson 10/14/1833
John Burrell Robinson 7/13/1831
Clack Robinson d. 11/30/1843, aged 67 yrs.
Martha Virginia B. Robinson 10/7/1844

WILLIAM GRAY BIB1E
Owner: Mrs. Arthur L. Johnson
High Point, North Carolina

MARRIAGES

William Gray to Emily 1/24/1821
Emiline Gray to Seneca Mahan 9/1838

BIRTHS

William Gray 3/15/1794
Emily, his wife, 2/3/1802
Emiline Gray 5/14/1822
Jessica Gray 8/21/1830
Alonzo William Gray 11/23/1823
Francis Ve Gray 9/30/1832
Tereno Erastus Gray 6/4/1825

William Gray Bible continued...

Harriet Gray 4/13/1835
Henry Childs Gray 3/18/1827
Emma Jane Gray 6/7/1838
Joseph Gates Gray 12/29/1828
Emily Ann Gray 12/9/1841

DEATHS

Tereno Erastus Gray 8/9/1827
William Gray 6/5/1849
Emma Jane Gray 2/14/1840
Emily A. Gray 4/9/1863
Joseph G. Gray 2/11/1845

JOHN MARTIN BIBLE
From: Rev. War Pension W4722

BIRTHS of Children of John and Nancy Martin

Mary Coalman Martin 4/23/1785 - --
John Martin 5/5/1800
Elizabeth Martin 2/5/1787
George Martin 10/30/1802
James Martin 3/20/1789
Thomas Martin 1/18/1805
Joseph Martin 2/21/17--
William Gilliam Martin 8/26/1809
Ginney Martin 6/26/1797

John Martin Bible continued...

Note: Deposition of Thomas Shipp 8/28/1840 Stokes Co., N. C. that he served in militia with John Martin whose sister is Nancy Martin, the latter marrying in his house in 1784. Nancy Martin applied for pension 11/24/1840 Stokes Co., N. C., wid. of John (d. 4/5/1823 Stokes Co., N. C.), aged 77; she m. 6/1784 in Surry Co., N. C. John Martin, by Micajah Clarke

JAMES MARTIN
From: Rev. War Pension R6968

BIRTHS of Children of James and Rachel Martin

William Martin 12/24/1786 Chatham Co., N. C. m. Nancy Rucker,daughter of George Rucker and Catherine, his wife, 5/29/1817. She was b. 8/31/1794
Archibald Martin 1/25/1789-9/15/1817
Andrew Martin 12/30/1790
Nancey Martin 11/30/1792
James Martin 1/20/1795

Micajah Martin 5/21/1797
Salley Martin 3/28/1800
James Martin Sr. m. Catherine Wheeler (or Wheeling) 4/16/1929
James Martin, son of Zachariah and Rebecah, his wife, 1/20/1760 and m. Rachel Heden, daughter of John Headen and Sarey. his wife, 12/23/1785. She was b. 12/8/1767

Note: James Martin applied for pension 6/7/1832 from Franklin Co., Ga., aged 77 yrs., stating he was b. Chatham Co., N. C. where he enlisted and moved from thereto Franklin Co., Ga. 7/16/1853 Rachel Martin applied for pension,

Franklin Co., Ga. widow, aged 87 yrs. old, on 12/8th last (1852), stating she m. her husband In Chatham Co., N. C. 12/23/1785 by Richard Cannon and was 19 yrs. old at the time - maiden name, Rachel Heding ---Heden, Heding, Headen spellings in these papers---

JEREMIAH OSBORN BIBLE
Owner: Samuel Osborn, N. C.

Jeremiah Osborn 1720-1772 m. Annie Blyth b. 3/27/1771

BIRTHS of Their Children

Nancy Osborn 8/13/1794 m. Jerry Wood
Ruth Osborn 11/18/1795
Mary Osborn 9/6/1797
John Osborn 3/18/1803
Jessie Osborn 8/27/1799 m. Ann Johnson 4/18/1822
Rebecca Osborn 1/24/1805-10/1862 m. Henry Lyons
Jane Osborn 1/19/1809
Champion Osborn 1/30/1807
John Osborn 10/27/1770 m. Jane Claypool in 1790
Jane Claypool 2/18/1769-1834
John Osborn d. 11/2/1849, bur. near Asheville, N. C.

BIRTHS of Children of John and Jane Osborn

Newman Osborn 2/9/1791 m. Elizabeth Hester
Margaret Osborn 9/3/1793 m. George Allen
Sarah Osborn 9/21/1794-9/10/1816 m. Henry Hayes
Eleanor Osborn 4/23/1798-4/5/1866 m. Nathan Drake
Mary Osborn 4/23/1800-1/25/1866 m. William Heifren
Jeremiah Osborn 4/15/1802 m. Rebecca Fletcher 1/25/1829

Jeremiah Osborn Bible continued...

John Osborn 3/30/1804
Jonathan Osborn 1/19/1809 m. Harriet Grady 1/19/1832

Ann Osborn 1/13/1801? m. 12/20/1835 John G. Hightower
Jane Osborn 10/8/1813 m. 8/11/-- John Orr

THOMAS AUGUSTUS PALMER BIBLE
Stanleyville, North Carolina

BIRTHS

George Daniel Palmer 7/19/1866
Hannah B. Palmer 5/31/1813
Sarah Virginia Palmer 5/5/1869
Mary Adelaide Reed Palmer 8/31/1867
James Edwin Palmer 5/26/1871
Thomas J. Palmer 9/17/1873
Martha Gertrude Palmer 6/9/1892
William P. Palmer 11/1/1811
George D. Palmer Jr. 12/26/1895

MARRIAGES

Thomas A. Palmer b. 1/30/1839 to 7/12/1865 Julia A. b. 4/2/1842
George D. Palmer to Addie Reed 8/31/1891
Sarah Virginia Palmer to Edgar Freeman Eddins 2/19/1889

DEATHS

James E. Palmer 2/28/1872
George D. Palmer Jr., son of George and Addie, 10/6/1899

Thomas Augustus Palmer Bible continued...

Addie Reed Palmer 7/28/1904
Martha Gertrude Palmer 2/13/1912
George Daniel Palmer 2/10/1939
Thomas J. Palmer 1/24/1951
Thomas A. Palmer 7/16/1873
Julia A. Palmer 9/28/1873
William P. Palmer 2/19/1881
Hannah R. Palmer 3/22/1895
Sarah Virginia Palmer Eddins 6/22/1965

JONATHAN OSBORN BIBLE
Bainbridge, Ga. DAR

Jonathan Osborn, 9th child of John, b. 10/27/1770, d. in Buncombe Co., N. C., in home of his son, Jonathan Osborn in 1834 Jonathan Osborn b. near Asheville, N. C. 1/19/1809-d. in Texas 11/19/1877 m. Harriett Sammons Grady b. 5/26/1815 Buncombe Co., N. C., d. 1/2/1902, daughter of Henry Grady and Leah King.

Jonathan Osborn m. Harriett Sammons Grady 1/17/1832 Buncombe Co., N. C

BIRTHS of Children of Jonathan and Harriett Osborn

Henry Grady Osborn b. Asheville, N. C. 10/27/1833 d. Parker Co.,Tx. 1/27/1917 m. 1st 10/9/1859 Mary Cox, 2nd, Fannie Powell John Griffin Osborn b. Asheville, N. C. 12/7/1834 d. Parker Co.,Tx. 8/30/1893 m. Ailsey Gober Leah King Osborn b. Asheville, N. C. 4/3/1836 d. Commerce, Ga. 2/16/1912 m. 1/14/1855 Andrew Jackson West 6/15/1836-4/29/1891 Turnerville, Ga., son of John B. West who d. 1872 Joshua Caleb

Jonathan Osborne Bible continued...

Osborn b. Asheville, N. C. 2/3/1838 d. in C.S.A.1862, 12th Regt., Hagerstown William Augustus Osborn b. 4/18/1840 Gilmer Co., Ga., drowned in Mt. Town Creek 3/13/1847, aged 7 yrs. Mary Jane Osborn b. Gilmer Co., Ga. 11/19/1842, d. Parker Co.,Tx. 1/8/1917, m. 10/15/1863 John Humphrey George Sammons Osborn b. Gilmer Co., Ga. 1/4/1848, d. Parker Co.,Tx m. 5/23/1868 Keziah Pruett, daughter of John Pruett, Commerce, Ga. Harriet Elizabeth Osborn b. Gilmer Co., Ga. 2/7/1856, d. 1/10/1874, unmd.

W. P. PALMER BIBLE
Stanley, North Carolina

BIRTHS

W. P. Palmer 5/26/1854
Willie Eugene Palmer 8/17/1883 Martha Palmer 12/20/1784
E. L. Palmer 9/15/1855
Charley Reny Palmer 5/13/1886
James Palmer 1/27/1786
Freddie Lee Palmer 5/5/1879
Wilbur Lucius Palmer 5/8/1890

Their Children:

Lucy Palmer 6/9/1808
Edward P. Smith Palmer 12/27/1833
Mary Palmer 11/17/1809
James Daniel Palmer 9/1831
William Palmer 11/1/1810
William J. Love Palmer 8/3/1847
Marthen Palmer 6/1/1815

W. P. Palmer Bible continued...

W. P. Palmer Jr. 5/26/1854
Elizabeth Palmer 8/7/1817
Ella L. Palmer 9/15/1855
Serbeann Palmer 3/3/1819
Freddie Lee Palmer 5/5/1859
Seardl Palmer 4/4/1821
G.? Palmer 7/19/1866
Margaret Palmer 4/8/1824
Hannah B. Palmer 5/31/1813

DEATHS

Lucy Palmer 8/24/1814
James Palmer -/21/1873
William Palmer 2/19/1881
Elizabeth Palmer 11/20/1827
Martha Palmer 7/18/1879
Serbeana Palmer 3/16/1823

ISAAC LEDBETTER BIBLE of Rutherford County
Owner: James P. T. Goodbread Rt. 1, Box 285
Cleveland, Ohio 74020

Isaac Ledbetter 7/2/1796-7/10/1837, son of Richard Ledbetter and Nancy Ann Johnson, m. Rutherford Co., N. C. 1817 Sarah Bradley 12/18/1798-8/27/1837, daughter of Sarah Goodbread and Rev. War Soldier, George Walton Bradley

Maternal Grandparents: Catherine and Phillip Goodbread, Sr.
Paternal Grandparents: John Bradley, Sr. and 2nd wife, Mary Ledbetter

Isaac Ledbetter Bible continued...

BIRTHS of Children of Isaac and Sarah Ledbetter

John Ledbetter 8/15/1818 m. Margaret Heath Ann Ledhetter 6/26/1824 m. William Mills
Richard Ledbetter 7/17/1819 m. Elizabeth Bean
Joseph Ledbetter 1/10/1827 m. Jane Sitton
Jonathan Ledbetter 10/13/1820 m. Amanda Jones
James Ledbetter 11/24/1821 m. Rebecca Covington
Isaac Ledbetter 2/27/1823 a. Elizabeth Espy
Nancy Ledbetter 10114/1825 m. John Clark
Elizabeth Ledbetter 2/24/1828 m. Ambrose Sitton
Alfred Webb Ledbetter 6/15/1829 m. Rachel Bryson
Silas Ledbetter 8/28/1831

Infant 7/15/1830
Ozias Denton Ledbetter 9/30/1832 m. Remedy Jones
Ephraim Ledbetter 12/6/1833 m. Mary Rice, 2nd, Isabella Hollis
"7/10/1837, at noon, Isaac Ledbetter returned to his home hot and tired from a hunting trip and drank too much cool water. He died few minutes later, leaving Sarah pregnant. 48 days later, Sarah, too, died."

NAPOLEON B. GREEN BIBLE
Owner: Napoleon Bonapart Green Arty
Marietta, Georgia

Napoleon B. Green b. 8/20/1816 Rutherfordton, N. C., son of William and Jane Green, d. 12/8/1873 Marietta, Ga. m. 5/30/1837 Clotilda Adams
b. 7/22/1822 Mississippi, daughter of John Adams and Lois Newcomb, d. 11/4/1892

Napoleon B. Green continued...

BIRTHS of Children of Napoleon B. and Clotilda Green

Byron Bonapart-Green 7/16/1844-10/6/1855 Marietta, Ga
Lois Josephine Green -/13/1846 m. 2/7/1887 George H. Grimling Marietta, Ga.
Julia Jane Green 2/24/1849-7/31/1919
DeWitt Oscar Green 3/3/1855 m. 8/19/1880 (5 mi from Spring Hill, Ala.), d. 11/18/1914 Marietta

LEMUEL C. MOORE BIBLE
Owner: Mrs. T. L. Spangler Jackson, Mississippi

MARRIAGES

Lemuel C. Moore to Margaret W. Dauge 1015/1817 in Elizabeth City, N. C.
John McMorine to Martha Sawyer in Camden Co., N. C.
Lemuel C. Moore, Jr. to Marion McNorine 2/8/1860 in Elizabeth City, N. C.

BIRTHS

Lemuel C. Moore, Jr., son of Lemuel C. and Margaret W. Moore, 5/28/1828 in Elizabeth City, N. C.
Marion McMorine, daughter of John and Martha McMorine, 12/4/1832 in Elizabeth City, N. C.

Children of Lemuel C. and Marion Moore:

Charles McMorine Moore 8/4/1861 Vicksburg, Mississippi
James Moore 4/17/1863 Oxford, North Carolina
Edward Martin Moore 11/27/1867 Vicksburg, Mississippi

Lemuel C. Moore Bible continued...

DEATHS

Margaret W. Moore, wife of Lemuel C. Moore, 2/1836 in Elizabeth City, N. C
John McMorine 3/4/1842 in Elizabeth City, N. C.
Martha McMorine, wife of John McMorine, 11/1/1854 In Portland, Maine
James, son of Lemuel C. and Marion Moore, 9/16/1864, aged 17 mos.. in Brandon, Mississippi
Charles McMorine, son of Lemuel C. and Nation Moore, 7/29/1865, aged 4 yrs., less 6 days, near Brandon, Mississippi
Marion McMorine, wife of Lemuel C. Moore, 11/30/1868, Vicksburg, Mississippi, aged 35 yrs.

JACOB K. BUNCH BIBLE
Owner: Mrs. Frances Schafer

Jacob K. Bunch, son of Mary and Willis Bunch, b. 12/6/1796 in Gates Co., N. C.
Sarah Hobbs, daughter of Thomas and Sarah Hobbs, b. 1/25/1802 in Gates Co., N. C. (Sarah m. Ist Kedar Hurdle 10/2/1822 and had a dau., Nancy)
Nancy Hurdle, daughter of Kedar and Sarah Hurdle, b. 3/10/1824

BIRTHS of Children of Jacob K. and Sarah Bunch

Gilbert H. Bunch-8/4/1826
Americus Bunch 10113/1828
Elijah Bunch 2/13/1831
Thomas Jefferson Bunch 6/14/1833
Jacob Bunch 8/28/1835

Jacob K. Bunch Bible continued...

Joseph Alexander Bunch 8/1/1837
Benjamin Franklin Bunch 8/25/1839
Mary Jane Bunch 9/20/1841-9/22/1841
John Bunch 11/3/1842
Margaret Melissa Bunch 10/26/1945-12/14/1862
Andrew Jackson Bunch 2/12/1848

LITTLETON JOHNSTON BIBLE
Owner: Mrs. Myrtle Andrea Roberts RFD 82, Taylors, South Carolina

Littleton Johnston b. 2/18/1761 Granville Co., N. C. d. 7/7/1842 Jasper Co., Ga. m. Ist 1/4/1781   Lucy Childs 1/30/1756-6/9/1826
Littleton Johnston m. 2nd Mrs. Sarah Durbin 1/12/1828

BIRTHS of Children of Littleton and Lucy Johnston

John Chew Johnston 3/17/1782 Orange Co., N. C.-7/18/1792
Larkin Johnston 9/13/1783 Orange Co., N. C.-5/12/1834 Monroe Co., Ga. m. 6/29/1803 Sally Underwood
Elizabeth Johnston 4/26/1785 Caswell Co., N. C. m. 5/7/1803 Wiley Thornton
William Johnston 1/19/1787 Granville Co., N. C. m. 11/7/1805 Elbert Co., Ga. to Sarah Grizel (Grizelle)
Thomas Johnston 2/5/1789 N. C.-9/17/1848 Ga. m. 1/18/1816 Peggy C. Gaines, Elbert Co., Ga.
Margaret C. Gaines, wife of Thomas Johnson 12/22/1798-12/8/1847
Nathan Johnston 6/27/1790 Person Co., N. C. m. 3/19/1812 Biddy Thornton in Jasper Co., Ga.

Littleton Johnston Bible continued...

John Johnston 10/14/1793 Person Co., N. C.-7/14/1844 Jasper Co.,Ga.
Frankey Johnston 3/18/1793 Person Co., N. C. m. 6/2/1808 Joseph Henderson

GERMAN BAKER BIBLE
Owner: William DeKay Baker 1333 Park St., Beaumont, Texas

German Baker b. 6/7/1792 Halifax Co., N. C. m. at home of Col. Newton Cannon, Williamson Co., Tennessee, d. 6/9/1875 Cochran, Mississippi m. 12/24/1820 Mary Keyser 7/24/1798-9/6/1852

German Baker Jr. 12/4/1836-6/27/1837
Charles Keyser Baker 7/11/1831-1/23/1857
James Denton Baker 12/4/1836-4/7/1924
Felix Walker Baker 6/22/1838-7/7/1921 m. 2/6/1861 Anna Elizabeth Young 12/27/1843-3/24/1928
William Rucker Baker 5/4/1835-
Mary Elizabeth Baker 2/22/1843-11/14/1814 m. William Gillum

BIRTHS of Children of Felix Walker and Anna E. Baker

Mary Etta Baker 10/10/1862 m. 4/11/1883 J. D. Fogg
Reese Henderson Baker 8/20/1864-8/30/1864
Alice Reedy Baker 9/9/1865 a. 4/26/1893 Joseph H. Malone
German Clyde Malone 4/7/1904 (grandchild)
Samuel Walker Malone 11/4/1905 (grandchild)
Fowler Reed Malone 7/11/1907 (grandchild)
Henry Roland Baker 5/20/1870
Charles Edward Baker 12/31/1872-9/17/1877
Rebecca Bowen Baker 8/14/1875 m. 1/16/1901 P. B. Marshall

German Baker Bible continued...

Jim Ella Baker 1/13/1878-11/1/1903 m. 2/7/1900 Clyde Tarver
German Baker 4/20/1870-2/10/1920

JESSE RANDOLPH of Pitt Co.
Owner: Lucille Randolph Lane
Greenville, North Carolina

BIRTHS

John Eborn, son of Henry, 1750   Elizabeth 7/14/1790
Arcadia Foreman, daughter of Joshua and Rebecca, 2/8/1754
Zachariah F. 12/13/1717   Benjamin Foreman 4/13/1794

Children of Benjamin and Lucille Eliza Eborn:

Eliza Ann Eborn 12/18/1818 John Robert Eborn 10/1/1820
Harriet Ann Elizabeth Eborn 12/12/1821
Lydia Olive Eborn 12/1/1825
William Benjamin Eborn 12/8/1828
Thaddeus Caleb Eborn 11/24/1833
Theodore Eborn 9/8/1836
Lucille Eliza Eborn 2/22/1844
Benjamin F. Eborn to Lucille Eliza Lanier 2/24/1818
Eliza Ann Louisa Eborn to Louis G. Little 5/3/1838
Lydia Olive Eborn to John Randolph 4/26/1849
Eborn and Mary, 12/23/1851
John Robert Eborn to Mrs. Margaret Ann Jordan, daughter of John B.
Robert Lanier to Edith Pearce 4/5/1792
William Clarke to Louisa P. Lanier 9/29/1814
Robert F. Lanier to Elizabeth Mary Ann Campbell 2/14/1826

Jesse Randolph Bible continued...

James H. Hartmouth to Lydia Lanier 11/8/1825
John Cherry to Lovinda R. Lanier 10/30/1827
James L. Clarke to Martha A. Lanler 7/1/1828
Warren Kennedy to Harriette A. Lanier 11/17/1833
William A. Lanier to Letitia Grimes 1/24/1839

BIRTHS

Robert Lanier, Sr., son of William and Martha, 6/30/1763
Edith, daughter of Lazarus and Elizabeth Pearce, 7/2/1772

Children of Robert and Edith Lanier:

Leucy Lanier 8/23/1793
Lowenda R. Lanier 10/24/1804
Lydia L. Lanier 6/29/1806
Lothenis Lanier 10/12/1795
Martha H. Lanier 1/1/1813
Robert F. Lanier 9/8/1802
Louisa P. Lanier 12/24/1797
Wm Alexander and Harriette Ann Lanier 8/4/1817

DEATHS

Harriette Ann Elizabeth Eborn 2/27/1843, 21 yrs, 2 mos., 10 days
Martha Ann Eborn
Thaddeus Caleb Eborn 9/27/1844, aged 10 yrs, 11 mos., 3 days
Lydia Olive, wife of John Randolph, daughter of Benjamin F. and Luella Eliza, his wife, 10120/1849, interred Baptist Church, Greenville

Jesse Randolph Bible continued...

Lucille Eliza Eborn, wife of Benjamin F., 6/19/1850, aged 50 yrs., 2 mos., 23 days, interred in Baptist Church, Greenville
William Benjamin Eborn, son of Benjamin F. and Lucille Eliza, 1862
John Robert Eborn, son of Benjamin F. Eborn and his wife, Lucille Eliza, 1/22/1895, Yeatsville, N. C., aged 74 yrs., 3 mos., 21 days
Elizabeth Pearce, wife of Lazarus Pearce, d. 1/19/1785
Lazarus Pearce d. 3/3/1800, aged 75 yrs.
Rhody Pearce d. 2/21/1785
Lazarus Pearce, son of Lazarus and Elizabeth Pearce, 12/10/1802

JOSEPH WEATHERLY BIBLE
Owner: Leslie Hall, San Antonio, Tx

Joseph Weatherley to Resina Anderson 8/7/1800 John McKibben to Elizabeth ---
Henry Shrader to Mary F. Weatherley 4/6/1820   Moses L. Barr to Nancy Herding 3/8/1832
Joseph Herding to Nancy Weatherley 12/14/18--A.H. Weatherley to Martha Glaze 1/30/1837

F A.Weatherley to Elizabeth Obanion 8/30/183 Jas A Weatherley to Agnes Childress 6/24/1832
Jesse R. Weatherley to Lucinda Jane Hughs 3/8/1842
Joseph P. Weatherley Jr. to Ellen Price Patterson 1/1/1852
Benjamin Franklin Weatherley to Sarah Elizabeth King 12/28/1852
Benjamin Franklin Weatherley to Mrs. Sarah Jane Boyd 6/12/1878

Joseph Weatherly Bible continued...

BIRTHS

Joseph Weatherley 10/8/1774
Rezina Anderson 1/20/1782, daughter of James Anderson and Rachel Johnson who m. Tyrrell Co., N. C., 12/23/1772.

Their children:
Mary F. Weatherley 10/22/1801
Francis A. Weatherley 9/8/1813
Nancy Weatherley 11/19/1803
Isaac J. Weatherley 7/9/1816
James A. Weatherley 10117/1805
Jesse R. Weatherley 3/9/1818
Asa A. Weatherley 9/2/1807
Elizabeth Weatherley 5/19/1820
John P. Weatherley 8/26/1809
Frankling Weatherley 8/10/1822
William N. Weatherley 9/20/1811
Joseph Weatherley Jr. 3/22/1825
Katharine Shrader 1/30/1821
James Asa Clark Shrader 8/8/1834
John W. Shrader 1/6/1823
Jackson Van Buran Shrader 3/4/1837
Mary A. R. Shrader 9/31/1824
Isaac Chancery Shrader 4/4/1839
Henry H. Shrader 2/24/1828
Charles T. Harding 4/1011821
Thomas W. Shrader 5/21/1830
Mary Harding 5/16/1825
Rachel Shrader 11/3/1827
Julia Harding 1/23/1828
George Washington Shrader 7/25/1832

Joseph Weatherly Bible continued...

Retina Ann Barr 2/14/1833
Joseph William Barr 7/5/1834
Robert Emmet McKibbin 7/28/1839
Charles Holland Weatherley, son of J. A. and Agnes, 9/28/1834
Joseph H. Weatherley, son of J. A. and Agnes, 4/21/1833
Thomas Jefferson Weatherley, son of F. A. and Elizabeth, 9/31/1838
Julia Ann Levinia Weatherley, daughter of F. A. & Elizabeth, 3/12/1842
Joseph Morgan Weatherley, son of A. H. and Martha, 8/29/1843
Mary Eliza Weatherley, daughter of James A. and Agnes, 11/16/1843
----Amelia, daughter of James and Agnes Weatherley, --1/6/--
---Benjnmin Weatherley, son of F. A. and Elizabeth, 4/19/1840
Rezina Jane McKibbin 12/6/18-7
Joseph William McKibbin 3/15/1842.

DEATHS: -

Katharine Shrader 6/25/1822
Rachel Shrader 3/23/1827 Joseph Harding 3/41/1828
Nancy Barr 10/4/18--, aged 30 yrs., 10 mos., 15 days
Isaac J. Weatherley 9/27/1836
John Benjamin Weatherley 9/3/1841
John P. Weatherley 7/20/1838, son of Retina and Joseph Sr.
Charles T. Harding 9/17/1825
Retina Jane McKibben 11/5/1841
Jesse R. Weatherley 5/12/1867
Joseph Weatherley Sr. 6/1/1852
Retina, consort of Joseph Weatherley Sr., 79 yrs., 8 mos., 19 days
Robert Emmet McKibben 6/20/1840
Amelia Swain 11/4/1843 Benton Co., Ala.

Joseph Weatherly Bible continued...

Mary McKibben 9/183--
Joseph Swain 11/10/1842 Jackson Co., Ga

ROBERT EBORN BIBLE
Owner: Mrs. J. Lawrence Jones
1209 Selwyn Ave., Charlotte, N. C.

BIRTHS

Nancy Olive Eborn, daughter of Robert Boyd Eborn and Arcadia F. E. Satchwell, 7/9/1843
Robert and F. Arcardia Eborn m. 8/16/1827 by Thomas Barrow, Esq.
John Eborn 11/20/1828
Eliza Eborn 5/28/1834
Mary Ann Eborn 2/14/1832
Arcadia Eborn 9/17/1839-9/7/1843

HOWELL LEWIS BIBLE

MARRIAGES

Howell Lewis to Ellen H. Pollard 9/26/1795
Betty Washington Lewis to Joseph Lovell 2/19/1818
Ellen Joel Lewis to Robert Steele 1/21/1819
Frances Fielding Lewis to Humphrey Brooke Gwathmey 6/27/1822
Virginia Lewis to Robert A. Hereford 1/6/1825
Howell Lewis to Emily G. Burch 1/14/1831
George Lewis to Mrs. Eliza MacLean 10/3/1833
John E. Lewis to Mary M. Drinan 9/15/1840
Martha E. Steele, their granddau., to Joseph Perkins 10/25/1841

Howell Lewis Bible continued...

Lawrence Lewis to Mary Ferguson 2/8/1843
Ellen Joel Gwathmey to James K. Caskie 5/27/1844

William Steele to Fannie DeLaney 8/20/1845
Lawrence Lewis to Mary E. Reynolds 3/14/1853

BIRTHS of Children of Howell and Ellen Lewis

Robert Pollard Lewis 10/13/1798
Howell Lewis 7/10/1808
Virginia Lewis 9/13/1806
George Lewis 7/26/1800
Mary Ball Lewis 1/22/1810
Jane Lewis 2/11/1805
Ellen Joel Lewis 1/28/1802
John Edward Lewis 11/5/1811
Frances Fielding Lewis 2/11/1805
Lawrence Lewis 12/15/1813
Henry Daingerfield Lewis 1/14/1815
Betty Washington Lewis 10/14/1796
Alfred Lewis Lovell, our grandson, 12/27/1818

Martha Ellen Steele, our granddau, 7/5/1821
Richard Channing Moore Lovell, grandson, 3/23/1822
Howell Lewis Steele, grandson, 12/31/1822
William Steele. our grandson, 12/12/1819
William Gaston Gwathmey, grandson, 4/2/1823
Ellen Lewis, their granddau., 7/18/1834
Robert McAney Steele, grandson, 12/28/1824
Ellen Joel Gwathmey, granddau., 9/25/1824
Betty Washington Steele 12/10/1825
Howell Lewis Lovell, grandson, 7/9/1974

Joseph Weatherly Bible continued...

Robert Hereford Jr. 7/17/1827
Brook Gwathmey Hereford 12/16/1829
Mary Mason Bronaugh Hereford 1/25/1832
George Lewis, their grandson, 10/27/1832
Janette Lewis, their granddaughter7/2/1837
Harold Lewis, their grandson,1/14/1839
George Baylis Lewis, their grandson, 9/14/1842

DEATHS

Jane 2/21/1805
Mary Rall 2/2/1810
Howell Lewis Sr. 12/26th, aged 52 yrs., 14 days
Col. Joseph Lovell 11/25/1835
Mrs. Joel Pollard, wife of Robert, 9/17/1839, 80 yrs., 24 days
Robert Pollard 10/10/1842, aged 87 yrs.

Alfred L. Lovell 9/6/1842, aged 21 yrs.
Virginia Hereford, daughter of Howell and Ellen, 8/29/1843, 36 yrs.
Eliza M.Lewis,wife of George Lewis, 9/20/1843 George Lewis 12/3/1843, 43 yrs.,4 mos., 8 das
Bette Lewis, daughter of George & Eliza, 12/14/1843, 6 yrs., 4 mos.
Robert M. Steele Jr. 7/14/1844 Charleston, Ka., 19 yrs., 6 mos.
Mary Lewis, wife of L. Lewis, 12/24/1845
Robert Pollard Lewis 1/4/1853, aged 54 yrs., 2 mos., 22 days
Lowell Lewis Steele 12/26/1850, aged 28 yrs, Ophir, California
William Gaston Gwathmey 8/5/1852, aged 29 yrs., 4 mos.
H. B. Gwathmey 10/22/1857, aged 59 yrs.
Augustus Dana Lewis, son of Howell, 2/10/1853, 19 yrs., 3 mos.

THOMAS DEVANE BIBLE of Bladen Co.

Thomas DeVane Sr. 1700-1760
Thomas DeVane 7/15/1762-7/27/1831
Nellie H. Stewart 3/24/1771-1/1845

BIRTHS of Children of Thomas and Nellie DeVane

Stewart DeVane 9/29/1793-3/18/1861
Ireton C. DeVane 3/23/1795-3/15/1851
Patrick Stewart DeVane 1/7/1797
Rufus DeVane 9/22/1798-7/5/1865
Mary Jane DeVane 1/15/1801-2/15/1801
Elizabeth DeVane 2/24/1809
William King DeVane 4/12/185-3/26/1846
Franklin DeVane 4/12/1807-1/21/1837
Thomas DeVane 1/27/1803-10/11/1847

MARRIAGES

Thomas DeVane to Nellie Stewart 1790
William King DeVane to Margaret Fennel 4/14/1822
James Stewart DeVane to Cornelia Dickson 10/20/1860

BIRTHS

James Stewart DeVane, son of William King DeVane and Margaret DeVane, 8/21/1826
Margaret Fennell DeVane 7/11/1807
Cornelia Dickson DeVane 5/20/1842

Children of James and Cornelia DeVane:

Thomas DeVane Bible continued...

James Dickson DeVane 8/21/1861 Burrell DeVane 10/1/1870
Stuart James DeVane 11/11/1875

DEATHS

Margaret Dennell DeVane 11/10/1870, aged 53 yrs.
James Stewart DeVane 1/13/1897 at 71 yrs.
Cornelia Dickson DeVane 10/1/1898

Burrell DeVane 7/6/1915
James Dickson DeVane 9/3/1924
Stuart James DeVane 8/10/1930

SOLOMON SLATTER BIBLE
Owner: Mrs. Lucius Hill, Chaplain DAR,
Dorothy Walton Chapter, Dawson, Ga

Solomon Slatter, Ist. 7/22/1699-1/24/1749 near Scotland Neck, S. C. (just off hwy near Old Trinity Church)
Solomon Slatter, Jr. 6/14/1733-5/21/1789 m. 1/2/1764 Mary Whitmel, daughter of Col. Thomas Whitmel, Jr. and Elizabeth West, daughter of Thomas West and Mattha Blount and Elizabeth Davis; John Blount was the son of Capt. James Blount who settled near Edenton, N. C. at Mulberry Hill

MARY KIMBROUGH BIBLE
Owner: Duke Cheek
Mocksville, North Carolina

BIRTHS

Mary Kimbrough 4/10/1742
Anna Kimhrough, daughter of Marmeduke and Mary, 10/27/1761
George Kimbrough 11/3/1764
Goldman Kimbrough 6/1/1766
Orinon Kimbrough 1/30/1768
George Kimbrough m. 2/29/1786
Catey Kimbrough, wife of George Kimbrough, 2/2/1763
Marmaduke Kimbrough, son of George and Catey Kimbrough, 6/29/1786
Sarah Kimbrough 2/19/1788-12/28/1789
George Kimbrough 11/12/1790-4/21/1823
Catey Kimbrough 10/20/1792
Anne Kimbrough 2/18/1795
Mary Kimbrough 10/29/1797
Ormon Kimbrough 12/5/1800
John William Kimbrough 9/13/1803
Rebecca Kimbrough 3/8/1806

DEATHS

My wife, Catherine Kimbrough, 10/29/1828, aged 65 yrs. the 2d of Feb. last
and we had been m. 42 yrs. Feb. last. She was bur.10/31/1828....George Kimbrough
George Kimbrough 5/18/1846, aged 81 yrs.
Ormon Kimbrough 5/12/1844, aged 44 yrs.
William S. Jones m. Ann Kimbrough 10/17/1815

Mary Kimbrough Bible continued...

Sally A. C. Jones 8/15/1816
George K. Jones 7/26/1819
Polly K. Jones 12/20/1822
Rebecca K. Jones 4/7/1824
Elizabeth P. Jones 6/17/1827
John Kimbrough m. Amy Joyner 6/27/1837
Their son, George Marmaduke Kimbrough, 6/2/1838

John Anderson Young Kimbrough 11/23/1839
Ormon Harison Kimbrough 1/20/1841-1/22/1841
William Nathaniel Kimbrough 10/12/1842
Lewis William Kimbrough, son of John and Amy, 4/7/1844
James Gimerson Kimbrough 4/30/1846-2/16/1847

WADE GARRISS BIBLE of Bertie Co.
Owner: Miss Frances Garriss, Lewiston, N. C.

BIRTHS

Wade H. Garriss 1/28/1803   Salley Garriss 1/28/1806
Mary Jane Garriss 10/26/1827   Littlebury Garriss 5/8/1831
John Whitfield Garriss 12/27/1828 --L. C. Garriss' father
Levenia An Garriss 2/26/1833
William S. Garriss 9/18/1834-Portsmouth abt 1910
Sarah An Rebecker Garriss 2/20/1836-Edenton abt 1905
Elizabeth Frances Garriss 9/1/1838-Ports.outh 1925
Anny Thomas Garriss 11/7/1839-died young
Harriet T. Garris 12/22/1840-1856
Patrick Henry Garris 12/19/1842

Wade N. Garriss to Salley Stephenson 1/11/1821
Mary Jane Garriss 3/26/1846

Wade Garriss Bible continued...

John W. Garriss 5/22/1851
S. B. Garriss to Louisa T. 2/28/1856
Sarah R. Garriss 5/20/1858
Wade N. Garriss to Mary Jordan 9/8/1857

BIRTHS

Simon Rebecker, daughter of Mary Garriss, 7/20/1858 m. DeLoatch
Mary J. Garriss (or Molly), daughter of Mary, 10/18/1859 m. Mitchell James Henry Garriss 1/28/1865-died y. Andrew J. Garriss 10/21/1863-1884
Miss Willie R. Garriss 4/27/1870 m. Dr. Daniels of Winton

DEATHS

Levenia An Garrias 10/31/1855
Harriet An Garriss 2/14/1856
Henry P. Garriss 2/15/1856
George W. Garriss 10/1/1865
L. B. Garriss 3/17/1874
John W. Garriss 4/19/1876
Sally Garriss, wife of Wade H. Garriss, 2/19/1856
Wade H. Garriss 9/14/1871
Rebecca Garriss 7/14/1872

BIRTHS

John Pembroke Harrell 6/22/1878-4/76/1885, aged 56 yrs., 9 mos., 24 days
Jack 1838
Margaret 6/1/1844

Wade Garriss Bible continued...

Wade H. D. Dallas Garriss 3/19/1844-Lewiston 1905
George Washington Garriss 5/2/1846
Daniel Webster Garriss 8/24/1847-about 1920
Martha's children, Sidney, 8/27/1864
Margaret's children
Sallie John Harrell 8/11/1863
Henry, 9/8/1859   Poley 7/19/1864
Paul Wade Harrell 12/28/1869
Lucey 8/11/1862

                    Ann's children (slaves)

Hawkins 1/8/1860
Lender 4/24/1863
L. C. Garriss 5/21/1852—
John W. Garriss' children
    F. Garriss 3/31/1853—
    John W. Garriss' children
M. L. Garriss 6/29/1857-d.—
John W. Garriss' children
N. L. Garriss 6/29/1857-d.—
John W. Garriss' children

John W. Garriss m. Margaret B. Garriss 5/22/1851
John F. Garriss 3/31/1854-USN 9/1877 Portsmouth, Va.
Mary Turner Garriss 1/25/1857

THOMAS DEVANE BIBLE of New Hanover Co.
Owner: Claude Lee DeVane Plant City, Florida

BIRTHS

Thomas DeVane 1700 (France)-1781, New Hanover Co., N. C.
John DeVane, Sr. 1740 New Hanover Co., N. C.
John DeVane, Jr. ca 1760 New Hanover Co., N. C.
Benjamin DeVane 1796 Bladen Co., N. C.
Franklin E. DeVane 1835 Lowndes Co., Ga.
Clause Lee DeVane 1897 Plant City, Fla.
George Albert DeVane, Sr. 1856 Madison Co., Fla.

ROBERT BALDRIDGE BIBLE
Owner: Hugh Baldridge, Milan, MO

"John Baldridge, father of the children whose ages and names are hereafter given, was born in Orange County, NC 23rd day of June 1775. Sarah Baldridge, wife of John Baldridge, whose maiden name was Sarah Clark, was born Caswell, NC some 4-5 years after her husband."

BIRTHS:

Robert Baldridge 9/18/1802
Lucinda Baldridge-d. when young
Polly Baldridge 2/23/1805
John Baldridge 2/2/1817
Wilson Baldridge 6/18/1807
Nancy S. Baldridge 10123/1820
Catherlne Baldridge-d. when young
Sarah J. Baldridge 10/20/1823
Daniel Baldridge 11/1/1812
James A. J. Baldridge 5/1/1825

STEPHEN CONGER'S BIBLE

David Conger 9/7/1760
Elizabeth Ayres 9/22/1764
David Conger m. Elizabeth Ayres 9/20/1781

BIRTHS of Children:

Abijah Conger 5/4/1782 - Betsey Conger 3/27/1793-1/22/1796
Stephen Conger 10/14/1783
Polly Conger 1/19/1796?
John Conger 1/29/1785
Abbe J. Conger 12/25/1797-11/5/1798
Sally Conger 10/23/1786
Betsey Conger 10/1/1799
Anne Conger 8/23/1788
Emily Conger 12/13/1801
Phebe Conger 3/29/1790
Delia Conger 7/13/180-
Zenas Conger 3/27/1793
Cyntha Conger 9/18/1805

Ira Seymour Jr. to Betsy Morehouse 12/25/1800, being 22 yrs. old, she being 18
Evelina Seymour to Ezra Parker 2/17/1825
Ruth B. Seymour to Samuel W. Foster 2/23/1829
Frances D. Seymour to Theodore Foster 7/8/1832
Evelina Parker to Samuel Nichols 10/23/1832
Alma Janett Seymour to Dwight C. Foster 6/8/1833
Joseph W. Seymour to Lydia Foster 1/25/1835
Cornelia Seymour to Dwight C. Foster 11/1/1843
Claudius B. Seymour to Harriette N. Hoskins 6/25/1846
Evelina Seymour 9/22/1801
Joseph W. Seymour 3/1/1811

Stephen Conger Bible continued...

Francis D. Seymour 6/9/1804
Urania Smith Seymour 8/1/1813
Cornelia Seymour 4/17/1806
Alma Janette Seymour 3/9/1816
Ruth B. Seymour 11/6/1808
Claudius B. Seymour 11/13/1821

Helen May Parker 3/24/1826
Orin Ezra Parker 9/9/1827
Edward Foster 5/12/1838
Lydia Foster 5/30/1845
Lydia Foster 7/23/1840
Mary Foster 2/2/1848

DEATHS:

Joseph W. Seymour 5/6/1840, aged 29 yrs. Esra Parker drowned 6/15/1828
Alma Janett Foster 1/11/1843, aged 26 yrs., 10 mos.
Betsy Seymour 2/17/1844, aged 60 yrs., 8 mos., 17 days
Dwight C. Foster 8/12/1852, aged 43 yrs., 7 mos.
Lydia Foster 7/20/1842, aged 2 yrs. Ira Seymour 2/11/1861, aged 82 yrs, 2 mos.
Evelina Nichols 7/30/1868, aged 65 yrs. Ruth B. Foster 3/24/1870, aged 60 yrs.
Helen M. Parker 5/25/1848, aged 22 yrs. Samuel Nichols 3/30/1845

MRS. TIGNAL JONES NOTEBOOK (HIGH-JONES)
Owner: Mrs. G. P. Herndon, Jr.,
Darien, Connecticut

BIRTHS

Alsey High 1/5/1758
Agnes High 12/29/1759

Alsey High m. Agnes Martin 2/24/1780

BIRTHS of Children of Alsey and Agnes High

Fanney Martin High-T/8/1782
Elizabeth Ann High 5/6/1793
Martin High 12/5/1783
Delilah Hawkins High 10/4/1795
Scriven High 10/5/1785
Patsey Brandy High 12/19/1798
Solomon High 7/23/1787
Ruth Terrell High 10/9/1802
Amelia Mitchel High 7/23/1789
Candes Scriven High 8/20/1805
John Terrell High 6/22/1791
Tignal Jones m. Amelia M. High 1/25/1825

BIRTHS of Children of Tignal and Amelia Jones

Winkler R. Jones 8/10/1826
Robert Smith Jones 3/11/1830
John Pride Jones 2/27/1828

Mrs. Tignal Jones Bible continued...

DEATHS

John Terrell High 8/13/1810
Alsey High 11/27/1822
Agnes High 9/5/1824
Ruth T. Hunter 9/21/1829
Robert Smith Jones 11/22/1831
Tignal Jones 3/31/1830, aged 61 yrs., 4 mos., 23 days
Amelia Mitchel Jones, wife of Tignal Jones, 6/4/1864, aged 74 yrs., 10 mos., II days

DANIEL HENSON BIBLE
From: Rev. War Pension W3991

Daniel Henson b. 8/17/1764 Culpepper Co., Va.- d. 1/1/1843 Haywood Co., N. C. m. 7/1788 Fariba Pool in Anson Co., N. C. (She d. 1851)

BIRTHS of Their Children

Lloyd Henson 12/27/1789
Absalom Henson 10/17/1790
12/28/1798

Alton Henson 1/20/17957
Aaron Henson

Wiley Henson 8/20/1793
Charlotte Henson 5/14/1805
Charlotte Henson m. Rev. William Alfred Cobb

HENRY WHITENER, SR. BIBLE

Henry Whitener, Sr. b. Cobury, Saxony, Germany 10/9/1719 d. Lincoln Co., N. C. 7/31/1792 m. Catherlne Mull, b. Pa. 5/24/1733 -d. Lincoln Co., N. C. 8/20/1804

BIRTHS of Their Children

Daniel Whitener 1751 m. Elizabeth Wilfong
(Capt.) Henry Whitener 1752 m. Catherine Schell
Abram Whitener 1754 (killed at Battle of Kings Mountain, N. C.)
Barbara Whitener 1756 m. John Kellinger
Mary Ann Whitener 1755 m. Lightfoot Williams
Catherine Whitener 1757 m. John Mull
Elizabeth Whitener 1764 m. Henry Summerow
Molly Whitener 1770 m. Jesse Robinson

DAVID SMALL BIBLE
Owner: Mrs. W. E. Bond Clement Hall Farm
Edenton, North Carolina

BIRTHS

D. Small 11/13/1796   Martha Small 8/14/1796
James Bond 2/14/1760   Mary Bond 5/30/1767

Children of James and Mary Bond:

Edm. Bond 12/18/1792   Winefred Bond 12/18/1800
Richard Bond 9/21/1794   Nancy Bond 5/18/1803
Lewis Baker Bond 9/17/1798
Elizabeth Bond 12/21/1805

David Small Bible continued...

DEATHS

James Bond 2/1/1812
Richard, their son, 10/15/1895
Mary, his wife, 8/1831
Richard H. Small m. Jane E. Small 6/12/1856

BIRTHS of Children of Richard H. Small and Jane

Richard T. Small 1/3/1831
William B. Small 3/31/1830
Jane E. Small 1/27/1829
Mary F. Frances Small 3/31/1831
Richard H. Small 8/30/1857
D. Small m. Martha 5/25/1828

BIRTHS of Children of D. and Martha Small

Jane E. Small 1/27/1829 ---
David A. Small 12/1011833
William B. Small 3/31/1830
Edmond B. Small 4/20/1835
Mary F. Frances Small 3/31/1831
Thomas M. Small 2/12/1837

DEATHS

Mary F. Small, daughter of D. and Martha Small, 8/31/1835
Martha Small, wid. of David, 10/29/1845
William B. Small 8/26/1854
Edmund B. Small 7/26/1862
David A. Small 2/28/186-

David Small Bible continued...

Thomas M. Small, the last scion of his family tree, 8/9/1909 in Edenton, N. C., aged 72 yrs., 6 mos.
Fanny Reed, daughter of Richard and Winifred Hoskins, 1011817
Richard Hoskins 1/17/1922, aged 49 yrs., 7 mos.
Elizabeth Bond 7/21/--
James, their son, 8/26/1802
Baker Bond 10/17/1825, aged 27 yrs.
Edmund Bond 1014/1826, aged 34 yrs
James Bond m. Mary Hoskins 10/8/1787

TURNER FISHER BIBLE
Owner: Forrest Letton, Paris, Ky

BIRTHS

Turner Fisher 6/12/1792 Ann Richards 6/27/1799
Turner Fisher m. Ann Richards 3/22/1821
Thomas Edwin Fisher 9/22/1822-4/9/1823
Turner Franklin Fisher 5/21/1824
Martha Elizabeth Fisher 8/31/1828

Oscar Fisher 8/1/1833-7/23/1834
Martha Letton b. 10/3/1792
My father, William Fisher, d. 7/7/1834 Turner Fisher m. Martha Letton 9/12/1811

Martha Fisher, wife of Turner Fisher, d. 8/7/1820
Ann Fisher, wife of Turner Fisher, d. 8/29/1831

JOHN LETTON SUMMERS' BIBLE
Owner: Mrs. J. H. Letton, Valrico, Fla.

John Letton Summers 5/12/1764-6/15/1802, son of Grace Letton and Benjamine Summers, m. 2/22/1789 Anna Maria Letton, 1/17/1767- 12/18/1843, daughter of Michael and Mary Willett Letton.

BIRTHS of Their Children

Benjamine Summers 2/9/1790-4/23/1790
Michael S. Summers 2/9/1791-same day
Caleb Letton Summers 2/27/1797-1/29/1798
Leah Summers 2/20/1792-1/23/1842 m. 4/7/1818 Horace Willson
Mary Letton Summers b. 24/1795-8/7/1812 m. 11/28/1811 Charles H.Crabbe
Anna Maria Summers 2/8/1799-5/1/1874 m. Benjnmine Stoddard Forrest
Rheubin Summers 4/11/1801-12/29/1866 m. 1/14/1830 Susan W Johnson.

JOHN SHEARS OLLIFF BIBLE
From: Rev. War Pension 187788

John Shears Olliff b. 1752 Duplin Co., North Carolina
His wife, Johannah Jackson, b. 1755 North Carolina m. 1786

BIRTHS of Their Children

John Shears Oliff, Jr. 1792 m. Elizabeth Fitzpatrick 3/30/1815
Benjamin Shears Olliff 1/23/1794 m. Elizabeth Turner 9/24/1815
Joseph Olliff 4/18/1798 m. Rebecca Donaldson 1819

John Shears Oliff Bible continued...

Susannah Olliff m. Jordan Brooks
Elizabeth Olliff m. William Stanford
Mary (Polly) Olliff m. Allen Robinson 1/17/1822

ANDREW MILLER BIBLE
Owner: Mrs. E. M. Miller St. Petersburg, Florida

Andrew Miller b. 7/20/1734 Glasgow, Scotland d. 9/24/1784 Charleston, S. C. m. 3/1/1763 Elizabeth Blount in Edenton, N. C.

BIRTHS

James Miller 5/8/1765-d. single
Charles Worth Miller 3/29/1767
Elizabeth Miller 2/13/1769 m. Ist John Piper 12/14/1782, 2nd, Norman McLeod
Richard Cauley Miller 12/12/1790 m. 8/13/1796 Jane Johnson
Marry Miller 1/15/1772-9/7/1773
Mary Clayton Miller 4/4/1774 m. 5/7/1799 William Taylor
Alexander Miller Taylor 8/22/1800
Elizabeth Ann Taylor 6/23/1802 m. 12/6/1821 Robert Morris Goodwyn
Elizabeth Miller 2/13/1769 N. C. m. 12/14/1782 John Piper in Charleston, S. C. - John Piper d. 11/27/1790
Elizabeth Miller Piper m. in Savannah, Ga., Norman McLeod 1/20/1798
Murdock B. McLeod 10/7/1801
Norman William McLeod 7/25/1805
Andrew (William) Miller 6/14/1809, had children:
Norman McLeod 8/2/1830, Savannah, Ga.
Elizabeth McLeod 9/9/1835, Savannah, Ga.

WILLIAM KELSICK BIBLE
Owner: Mrs. Mary Thomas Evens Asbell
Edenton, North Carolina

William Kelsick m. Levina Skinner 2/2/1833

BIRTHS

Rosanah Lane, daughter of William Lane and Elizabeth Lane, his wife, 9/9/1846
Penelope Standin 11/25/1843
Lavenia Standin 1/2/1846
John R. Kelsick, son of William Kelsick and Levina Kelsick, his wife, 3/22/1834
William H. Skinner, son of Harvey and Harriet Skinner, his wife, 1/30/1848
Lucille H.. Speight 2/28/1872

JOHN BROWN BIBLE
Owner: Mrs. Hugh Thomas Brown
N. Wilkesboro, North Carolina

John Brown b. Derry Co., Ireland, 10/31/1738-8. Wilkes Co., NC
Jane McDowell, his wife, b. Lancaster Co.. Pa. 9/25/1750-d. 10/28/1838 m. 12/19/1770

BIRTHS of Their Children

James Brown 12/1/1771 Lancaster Co., Pa.
William Brown 1/11/1774 Wilkes Co., NC
Elizabeth Brown 12/4/1776 Wilkes Co., N. C.
Ann Brown 10/10/1782 Wilkes Co., N. C.

Alexander Brown 10/30/1778 Wilkes Co., N. C.

John Brown Bible continued...

John Brown 10/20/1780 Wilkes Co., N. C.
Hugh Brown 10/4/1784 Wilkes Co., N. C.
Hamilton Brown 9/30/1786 Wilkes Co., N. C.
Thomas Brown 9/26/1788 Wilkes Co., N. C.
Margaret Brown 9/20/1790 Wilkes Co., N. C.
Allen Brown 7/26/1793 Wilkes Co., N. C.
Richard Ransom Gwyn b. Gloucester Co., Va. 9/26/1765-6/8/1822 m. 12/4/1789
Martha Lenoir, his wife, b. Kershaw Dist., S. C. 9/16/1769

BIRTHS of Their Children

James Gwyn 3/28/179G Wilkes Co., N. C.
Lorenzo Gwyn
Peyton Gwyn
Sarah Gwyn 10/6/1798 Wilkes Co., N. C. m. Ist Nathaniel Gordon
10/7/1830, 2nd, Hamilton Brown
Caroline Gwyn m. Harvey Gordon
Children of Sarah Gwyn and her 2nd husband, Major Hamilton Brown:
Capt. Hugh Thomas Brown h. Wilkes Co., N. C.
Colonel Hamilton Allen Brown 9/25/1837

MARRIAGES

John Brown to Jane McDowell 12/19/1770
Richard Ransom Gwyn to Martha Lenoir 12/4/1789
Thomas Lenoir to Selina Avery
James Gwyn, Sr. To Amelia Lenoir 1789

John Brown Bible continued...

DEATHS

Richard Ransom Gwyn 6/8/1822 Wilkes Co., N. C.

Martha Lenoir, his wife
Amelia Gwyn
James Gwyn, Jr. 9/11/1888 Wilkes Co., N. C.
Hamilton Brown 3/27/1870
Hugh Thomas Brown killed at Battle of Oakes Hill on Wilson Creek, Mo., 8/10/1861
James B. Gordon (son of Nathanial Gordon and Sarah Gwyn), 5/18/1864 in Richmond, Va. of wounds received in battle
Mary Lenoir Brown 9/22/1877

Hamilton Allen Brown 4/9/1917
Amelia Selina Gwyn Brown 12/13/1918

JAMES GRIFFIN BIBLE
Owner: Rev. War Pension RW7586

James Griffin 10/23/1766 Edgecombe Co., N. C.-12/19/1836 Irwin Co., Ga. m. 4/1/1780 Sarah Lodge

BIRTHS of Their Children

Noah Griffin 6/7/1783 m. Priscilla Hall
Joshua Griffin 3/22/1785 m. Elizabeth Bradford
Thomas Griffin 12/4/1787 m. Nancy Hall
Rhoda Griffin 10/11/1790 m. John Hall
Shadrack Griffin 10112/1792 m. Nancy Bradford
Solomon Griffin 10/20/1794
Elizabeth Griffin 7/28/1803 m. William Bradford

JOEL LANE BIBLE
Owner: Marshall DeLancey Haywood
Raleigh, North Carolina

Joel Lane m. Martha Hinton 12/9/1762. She d. 9/9/1771

BIRTHS

Henry Lane 3/6/1764
William Lane 10/15/1768
James Lane 10/7/1766
Joel Lane m. Mary Hinton in 1772
Nancy Lane 7/22/1773
Thomas Lane 9/12/1785
Mary Lane 1/1/1783
John Lane 3/6/1775
Dorothy Lane 12/13/1787
Martha Lane 2/19/1778
Joel Hinton Lane 10/11/1790
Elizabeth Lane 8/6/1780
Grizelle Lane 6/13/1793

CHARLES LANE'S BIBLE
Owner: Loula Kendall Rogers
Barnesville, Georgia

BIRTHS

Charles Lane 10/2/1756
Richard Lane 2/9/1759
Henry Lane 3/28/1760
Caroline Lane 5/26/1761
Rhoda Lane 5/21/1763
Patience Lane 3/8/1765
Jonathan Lane 4/3/1767
John Lane- Christmas Day
Simeon Lane 3/1011771
Rebecca Lane 3/5/1773
Joseph Lane 3/28/1775
Mary Lane 1/18/1777
Sarah Lane 1/18/1777
Winnefred Lane 10/11/1780

JONATHAN LANE BIBLE

Jonathan Lane 4/3/1767-3/12/1837 m. Ist Patience Rogers, 2nd, Polly Colley.

BIRTHS:

Theophilus Sterling Lane 10/1/1795
George W. Lane 6/14/1805
Richard A. Lane 11/2/1797
James M. Lane 12/22/1808
Mary R. Lane 11/25/1799
Edgar M. Lane 9/25/1811
Winnefred Anne Lane 3/21/1802
Hanson P. Lane 8/19/1814

CHESLEY JARNIGIN BIBLE

Chesley Jarnigin 11/21/1772-4/17/1826 Martha Jarnigan 2/16/1774-8/5/1843
        Child of above: Sarah Jarnigan 11/10/1796
Chesley Jarnigin, son of Thomas Jarnigin, to Martha Barton, 3/14/1793.
Dau of Rev. Isaac Barton. William H. Montgomery to Sarah Jarnigan, daughter of Chesley Jarnigan, 12/31/1818

HAMILTON KIMZEY BIBLE

John Kimzey b. 1/5/1800
Betty Ann Rabun b. 10/5/1799
John Kimzey m. Betty Ann Rabun 1819, Haywood Co., North Carolina

Hamilton Kimzey Bible continued...

BIRTHS of Children of John and Betty Ann Kimzey (b. Haywood Co., NC)

Hodge Rabun Kimzey 10/2/1820 -
Willis Jasper Kimzey 6/3/18)1
Nancy McClure Kimzey 6/3/1822
Elisha Lander Kimzey 1/27/1834

Thomas Judson Kimzey 5/14/1825
Aroninta Amanda Kimzey 2/25/1839

James Japthiah Kimzey 4/16/1827
Edith Louisa Kimzey 10/18/1841
William Calloway Kimzey 3/6/1829
Edith Louisa, daughter of Wills and Margaret Rabun, 1/6/1822
Hodge R. Kimzey m. Edith Rabun in Jones Valley, Jefferson Co., Ala. 11/16/1843.

BIRTHS of Children of H. R. and Edith Kimzey:

Herbert Clay Kimzey 11/4/1844 Jefferson Co., Aia;
Lucretia Moavia Kimzey 3/28/1847 Choctaw Co., Miss.
Bertha Lotitia Kimzey 6/4/1849 Choctaw Co., Miss.
Samuel Barrett Kimzey 3/16/1851 Macon Co., N. C.
Marshall Steuben Percival Kimzey 1/16/1854 Macon Co., N. C.- 1/8/1856, 8 days less than 2 yrs old;Son - stillborn 4/15/1856, bur. Beside his bro., N. S. Percivil 11/14/1855 H. R. Kimzey had his leg broken in winter of 1855 and 1856 Hubert, Lucretia, Bertha and Samuel, all had scarlet fever of which their little bro., Percival. died. Margaret Elizabeth, daughter of H. R. and Edith Rabun Kimzey, b.11/3/1838 Macon Co., N. C.

Hamilton Kimzey Bible continued...

Emma Iantha and Ella Samantha, daus., b. 4/23/1861, Macon Co.
Rodee Rabun Kimzey d. 7/17/1877, aged 58 yrs., 9 mos., 15 days, bur. near his own sons in Habersham Co., Ga.
Lucretia M. Meeks d. 1/2/1906, aged 59 yrs., 10 mos., 5 days
H. C. Kimzey d. 9/2/1906, aged 61 yrs.. 9 mos., 26 days
Samuel B. Kimzey d. 6/18/1907, aged 55 yrs., 7 mos., 2 days
Edith Rabun Kimzey d. 1/11/1913, aged 91 yrs., 5 days
Bertha L. Sellers d. 2/9/1924, aged 74 yrs., 8 mos., 5 days

ROBERT LUCIUS IVY BIBLE of Halifax County
Owner: Mrs. E. F. Barton
4224 Mitchell Rd., Waco, Texas

BIRTHS

R. N. W. Ivy 2/25/1799
John Ruffin Ivy 11/1834
Lucy L. Ivy 8/11/1809
Alfred Junius Ivy 9/6/1837
James H. Ivy 2/8/1825
Rebecca Elizabeth Ivy 2/10/1840
Sarah Jane Ivy 9/22/1831
Robert Lucius Ivy 2/7/1842
Lucy Ann Ivy 10/29/1832
Mary Frances Ivy 10/24/1845

MARRIAGES

Robert Ivy to Lou Barron 7/13/1865
Jeff C. Pierce to Minnie B. Ivy 10/9/1889
T. Beauford Ivy to Jennie L. Campbell 3/5/1890

Robert Lucius Ivy Bible continued...

Otto Joseph Kornik to Mary Ardelle Ivy 4/23/1902
W. Howell Wilson to Emma Elizabeth Ivy 10/7/1903
Lucille Alleen Ivy to Edward Raymond Callegos 6/17/1927
Roberta Lee Ivy to David Ogilvie Marshall --
Orman Jeff Pierce to Hazel (Mattie Sue) Hood ---
Maxine Ardelle VanKannon to Ernest Fred Barton 6/26/1943

BIRTHS

Robert Lucius Ivy 2/7/1842   Mary Louisa Ivy 1/23/1847

Their Children:

Minnie Barron Ivy 4/20/1866
Uzelle Karr Ivy 3/21/1884
Thomas Buford Ivy 1/28/1869
Fannie Myrtle Ivy 7/27/1886
Mary Ardell Ivy 6/15/1871
Orman Jeff Pierce 11/4/1890
Emma Elizabeth Ivy 6/26/1873
Maxine Ardelle Van Kannon
Alfred Monroe Ivy 3/9/1876 9/29/1917
Loua Aileen Ivy 12/12/1878
Robert Ernest Barton 2/17/1947
Roberta Lee Ivy 7/12/1881
Lucy Leora Barton 4/9/1952

DEATHS

R. N. W. Ivy 6/13/1854
Gene (Fowler) Ivy 2/10/1920
Mary N. Barron 3/20/1863

Robert Lucius Ivy Bible continued...

Max E. V. McKannon 2/7/1920
John T. Barron 12/2/1863
Myrtle Ivy McKannon 2/7/1920
Wallace Monroe Barron 6/24/1877
Edward Ramon Callegos 6/18/1928
Mary Louisa Ivy 8/5/1887
Alfred Monroe Ivy 5/1957
Jeff C. Pierce 6/21/1891
Minnie Barron Pierce 2/1/1958
Thomas Barron 1/8/1905
Mary Ardell Ivy (Kornik) Beauchamp 6/17/1958
R. L. Ivy 11/30/1933
Uiell K. Ivy 2/7/1920
Roberta Ivy Marshall 5/9/1964
Currie Ivy 2/8/1920
Emma Elizabeth Ivy Wilson 1/12/1968

S. J. DAWSON BIBLE
Owner: J. Hanna, Sr. 6450 Vernon Woods Drive, N. E.
Atlanta, Georgia

S. J. Dawson m. S. E. Doles at Abram Cores, Pitt Co., NC. 7/25/1867
S. J. Dawson, Pitt Co., N. C. 12/7/1846-1923 m. 7/25/1867
Sallie E. Dawson, Muscogee Co.. Ga. 3/2/1850-4/8/1900 m. 7/25/1867
E. C. Dawson, Pitt Co., N. C., 9/7/1868-12/2~/1895 m. 10/8/1890
Bulah May Dawson, Russel l Co Ala 5/25/1870-11/24/1894 m. 12/23/1891 W. M. Wilson, Union Spgs, Ala. 2/26/1866-

S. J. Dawson Bible continued...

7/5/1908 m. 12/23/1891

Isler Dawson Wilson, Union Springs, Ala. 11/15/1894-11/2/1959 m. 11/28/1915
Angeline Dawson, Lenoir Co., N. C. 8/12/1871-8/6/1925 m. 10/18/1890
Jessie Anne Dawson, Lenoir Co., N. C.. 2/4/1895-6/24/1935 m. 1920
Melvyn Kendrick Dawson, Russell Co., Ala. 12/15/1896 m. 9/8/1925
Emma Dawson,Bullock Co., 10/26/1898.. ;/12/1~20
--- Kenneth,Kinston, N. C. 1876-2/17/1918 m. 2/21/1896
Irene Wilson, N. Springs, Ala. 9/29/1897-20/ - m. 7/23/1912
Janet Eleanor Dawson, N. Springs, Ala. 6/1901-10/8/1903
Kenneth Dawson, N. Springs, Ala.,
Simelsun? Dawson, Columbus, Ga.
Lyra Field Wilson, Girard, Ala. 3/11/1898 m. 11/28/1915
Geneva Sansing Wilson, Newton, Miss. 3/12/1895 m. 6/16/1930
Elizabeth Undine Dawson, Columbus, Go. 11/15/1894-11/2/1959
Melvyn Hendrick Dawson, Jr., Columbus, Ga. 7/12/1926
Alice Nicholson Dawson 10/13/1930
Nathalie Ballard Dawson, wife of Ernest, Jr., 3/2/1905 m. 3/12/1920
Dau of Nathalie Margaret & Ernest Dawson, Jr., 8/15/1921 d.12/26/1940
Son of Ernest Calvert Dawson III 9/26/1924 m. 6/7/1950

JOHN OSBORN BIBLE

John Osborn 10/27/1770-11/2/1849, Ashville, NC m. 1790
Jane Claypool
Jane Claypool 2/18/1769-1834

BIRTHS of Their Children

Newman Osborn 2/9/1791 m. Elizabeth Jester
Margaret Osborn 9/3/1793 m. George Allen
Sarah Osborn 9/21/1794-9/1011816 m. Henry Hayes
Eleanor Osborn 4/23/1798-4/5/1866 m. Narhan Drake
Mary Osborn 4/23/1800-11/25/1866 m. William Heifren
Jeremiah Osborn 4/15/1802 m. 1/25/1829 Rebecca Fletcher

John Osborn 3/30/1804 (removed to Ill. where married)
Jonathan Osborn 11/9/1809 m. Harriet Grady 1/19/1832
Ann Osborn 11/3/1807 m. 12/20/1835 John G. Hightower
Jane Osborn 10/8/1813 m. 8/11/-- John Orr

JOSHUA WHITAKER, SR. BIBLE

Joshua Whitaker, Sr. 1/22/1735 Mary, wife of Joshua 10/30/1748
John Whitaker, eldest son of Joshua and Mary, 9/15/1765
Sarah Whitaker, eldest dau., 12/7/1767
Joshua Whitaker 6/9/1768

William Whitaker 11/22/1772
Mary Whitaker, 2nd dau., 1/3/1775
James Whitaker 4/3/1779

JOHN COFFIELD BIBLE

Owner: Mrs. Margaret White Evans Tyner, North Carolina

John Coffield, Sr., his Testament and Bible. 3/28/1813. This written by James Witheryton.

BIRTHS of Children of John and Sally Coffield

Henry Coffield 7/19.1810
Nancy Coffield 7/19/1817
Jeremiah Coffield 2/23/1812

BIRTHS of Children of John and Esther Coffield

William Coffield 10/5/1819
Elizabeth F. Coffield 11/27/1828
John Coffield 1/2/1821
Martha Ann Coffield 2/20/1832
Josiah Coffield 8/31/1823
Clarissa Coffield 10/17/1835
Allen Coffield -/1/1826
Margaret L. Coffield 2/12/1839
William Coffield, son of Josiah and Nancy, 11/23/1850

MARRIAGES

John Coffield to Esther Sanders 1/26/1819, daughter of Josiah Saunders

DEATHS

Esther Saunders Coffield 1867
John Coffield, son of Jeremiah and Sally Halsey Coffield

PHILEMON HAWKINS II

Philemon Hawkins II (son of Philemon Hawkins I of N. C., b. 12/3/1752 m. 8/31/1775 Lucy Hawkins.,his wife, 7/9/1759-9/29/1787

BIRTHS of Their Children

Eleanor Hawkins 6/23/1775 -
Philemon Hawkins 6/5/1789
William Hawkins 10/20/1777
Frank Hawkins 3/29/1791
Ann Hawkins 9/3/1779
George Washington Hawkins 10/20/1793

John D. Hawkins 4/15/1781
Lucinda Davis Ruffin Hawkins 6/26/1795
Delia Hawkins 10/16/1782
Sarah Hawkins 3/5/1784
Mildred B. Hawkins 12/13/1801
Joseph Hawkins 9/15/1785
Thomas P. Hawkins 8/29/1808

W. L. HALL BIBLE
Owner: Bryant S. Hall
304 Wilson Ave., Box 664 Kinston, North Carolina 28501

" Beulaville - W. L. Hall died at home of his niece, Mrs. F. E. Bass In Beulaville. He was 75 years old and had been in declining health for several weeks.

The funeral was conducted in the home by Rev. L. M. Holloway, assisted by a choir from the Baptist Church of which Mr. Hall was

W. L. Hall Bible continued...

a member. Interment was in the family cemetery near Hallsville. Mr. Hall is survived by three children, Mrs. R. C. Crew of Pleasant Hill M. J. Hall of Raleigh and B. S. Hall of Wilmington. He is also survived by a number of nieces and nephews."
Lola Tabitha Brinson m. Bryant Southerland Hall at Wilmington, N. C. 11/24/1920. Children:Martha Ann Hall, daughter of B. S. and Lola B. Hall, 2/24/1931 Winston-Salem, N. C.-2/24/1931
Continuation of Bryant S. Hall's Family (2nd marriage):
Dolly Mae Jones Hall 10/28/1906 Lenoir Co., N. C. m. Bryant S. Hall 9/24/1949 Kinston, N. C.Great grand-parents (Father's grandparents):
Father's Father- Solomon Hall 1831 Onslow Co., N. C.-1/17/1882
Father's Mother- Mary C. Hall 1841 Duplin Co., N. C.-1905 Duplin
Mother's Father- Isaac Sangerson b. & d. Duplin Co., N. C.
Mother's Mother-Sylvia Sangerson b. Duplin Co., N. C.-d Onslow
        Mother's Grandparents:
Father's Father- George Brinson d. Verona, N. C.
Father's Mother- Tabitha Ann Brinson d. Yerona, N. C.
Mother's Father- Henry Shepard d. Verona, N. C.
Mother's Mother- Matilda Shepard d. Verona, N. C.

        Grandparents:
William L. Hall 6/20/1860 Duplin Co., N. C.-3/24/1936
Mother- Anna Lee Hall 3/3/1870 Duplin Co., N. C.-2/17/1908
Father - John William Brinson 6/14/1848 Verona, N. C.-3/30/1933
Mother- Martha S. Brinson 4/12/1854 Verona, N. C.-11/20/1931

W. L. Hall Bible continued...

Parents:
Bryant S. Hall 9/28/1890 Catherine Lake, N. C.
Lola Hall 9/16/1894 Verona, N. C.-8/22/1849 Kinston, N. C.

DEATHS

Cratie Sandlin, Savannah, Ga. 2/12/71
Nora B. Sandlin (wife), Savannah, Ga. 6/29/70

Mamie G. Brinson 8/30/1986, bur. 9/1/76
Miriam Crew Clark, daughter of Clinton Richard and Ida Crew, 5/4/1972, bur. Spring Church Cemetery
John F. Brinson 3/16/1882-7/16/1951   New Bern, N. C.
Mamie G. Brinson 8/2/1889-8/30/1976 New Bern, N. C.
George H. Brinson 4/1960 Wilmington, N. C.
Lizzie Brinson
Ida Lee Crew 7/4/1966
Clinton Crew 4/12/1865 Pleasant Hill, N. C.-11/3/1970
Miriam Crew 5/4/1972 Spring Church, Goldsboro, N. C.
Eugene Boss Goldsboro, N. C.
Lucy Boss 4/18/62 Goldsboro, N. C.
E. Sandlin 1886-2/12/1971 Savannah, Ga.
Nora Sandlin 6/8/1888-6/29/1970 Savannah, Ga.
M. I. Hall 10/10/1954 Raleigh, N. C.
Miriam Hall 12/14/1967 Raleieh, N. C.

WILLIAM PEAKE I BIBLE
Owner: Miss Lula Peek Elberton, Georgia

William Peake I to Elizabeth Shockley 1776 in Virginia
William Peak II to Isabella Redmond 4/16/1812 Buncombe Co., N. C.

William Peake I Bible continued...

William Peek III to Julia Emaline Proffitt, daughter of Turner and Polly Proffitt, 8/14/1856, Yancy Co., N. C.

BIRTHS

William Peake I, 1/10/1755 Va William Peek II 3/19/1787 Va
William Peek III 8/18/1829 Buncombe Co., N. C.
Julia E. Peek 10/8/1835

DEATHS

William Peake I, 8/7/1843 in Buncombe Co., N. C.
Elizabeth Shockley Peake 5/3/1840
William Peak II 8/17/1867, aged 80 yrs., 5 mos., Hart Co., Ga.
Isabella Redmond Peak 6/16/1856 Buncombe Co., N. C.
William Peek III 8/27/1911 Hart Co., Ga.
Julia Proffitt Peak 5/2/1883 Hart Co., Ga.

ZACHARIAH EVANS BIBLE

Zachariah Evans to Elizabeth Coffield 3/8/1808
Edmund Brinkley to Susannah Evans 12/15/1825
Richard Jordan to Margaret Evans 5/1827

Zachariah Evans to Margaret Flury 2/19/1832
Zacharlah Evans to Nancy Goodwin 12/19/1833
Benjamin L. Evans to Clarissa Coffield 2/23/1858

BIRTHS

Zachariah Evans, son of Benjamin and Margaret, 11/25/1781
Elizabeth Coffield, daughter of Jeremiah and Sally, 9/28/1791

Zachariah Evans Bible continued...

BIRTHS of Children of Zachariah and Elizabeth Evans

Susannah Evans 7/13/1809, baptised by Rev. Richard Latemore
Margaret Evans 9/25/1810, baptised by Rev. Richard Latemore
Th. d. Evana 2/19/1812, baptised by Rev. Richard Latemore
Edwin Evans 1/14/1814, baptised by Rev. Richard Latemore
Zachariah Evans 7/2/1816, baptised by Rev. Benjamin Devany
Elizabeth M. Evans 11/12/1820, baptised by Rev. Benjamin Devany
Josiah Evans 4/25/1823, baptised by Rev. Benjamin Devany
Jeremiah Evans 1/7/1826, baptised by Rev. John Hess
John Wesley Evans 3/12/1828, baptised by Rev. Thomson Carard
Martha Eliza Evans, daughter of Zachariah and Margaret Evans, his 2d wife, 6/23/1833, bapt by Rev. The. Crowder, PE of Norfolk Dist.

BIRTHS of Children of Zachariah and Nancy Evans

George Bensen Evans 11/29/1834, baptised by Rev. George Nobly
James Hennery Evans 4/12/1836, baptised same day Mary J. Jordan, my grand-dau
Benjamin Lawrence Evans 4/19/1839, baptised by Rev. William Reed
Celey An Amelia Evans 9/10/1841, baptised by Rev. John M. White

DEATHS:

Elizabeth Evans 1/29/1830, 38 yrs, 4 mos, 2 days
Margaret Evans 9/1833, a little above 37 yrs.
Margaret Jordan 3/16/1832, aged 21 yrs., 6 mos.

Zachariah Evans Bible continued...

James Hennery Evans 9/1836, aged 5 mos.
George Benson Evans 7/1838, aged 4 yrs., 8 mos.
John Wesley Evans 8/16/1839, aged 11 yrs., 5 mos., 4 days
Celey An Amelea Evans 9/2/1845, aged 4 yrs.
Nancy Evans 11/6/1851, aged 50 yrs., 23 days
Zachariah Evans 10/15/1857, aged 75 yrs., 10 mos., 21 days
Benjamin L. Evans 5/19/1906, aged 68 yrs., 1 mo.
Clarissa Coffield Evans 10/17/1897, aged 62 yrs.

JOSEPH CRENCY BRADBURY BIBLE of Chowan Co.

Joseph C. Bradberry to Sarah Blount 3/22/1792
Edmund C. Bradberry, son of Joseph C. and Sarah, had Mary Elizabeth and Sarah. William Bradberry, son of Joseph and Sarah to Sarah Sutton Norcom 9/16/1822
Elizabeth Bradberry, dau of Jos. & Sarah to Silas Houghton 3/24/1821
John Nixon to Elizabeth Haughton 2/3/1834, James B. Thatch. wt.
Sarah Ann Bradberry, daughter of Jos C. &Sarah, to Lemuel B. Halsey 3/22/1825.
Richard R. Bradberry to Mary Leigh, daughter of James Leigh, Esq. And Mary, 11/14/1837
Elizabeth Ann Bradberry, daughter of William B. and Sarah S., to Joseph Thomas Waff 2/9/1847. Charles W. Bradberry, wit.
Alethia Bradberry, daughter of William and Sarah-Theodric Benjamin Blend 10/11/1870
Penelope Bradberry. daughter of William B. and Sarah S. to Frederick White 12/20/1870
Mary Bradberry, daughter of William B. and Sarah S., to Nathan L. Collins 5/4/1854.

Joseph Crency Bradbury Bible continued...

Mary S. Houghton, daughter of Silas H.& Elizabeth B. to John Roberts, 7/27/1841

BIRTHS:

Joseph C. Bradberry, son of Charles and Mary Ann, 1/5/1771
Sarah Blount, daughter of Edmund Blount and Mary, 7/13/1771
Their Children:
Charles Bradberry 12/21/1792
Elizabeth Bradberry 3/27/1804
Edmund B. Bradberry 9/20/1794
Sarah Ann Bradberry 6/7/1806
Charles Bradberry 1/13/1797

John Bradberry 12/26/1808
William R. Bradberry 8/12/1799
Richard Bradberry 6/13/1811
Mary B. Bradberry 12/11/1801
Edmund Blount, son of Charles Worth and Mary Clayton Blount 8/27/1745-2/26/1792 m. 2/26/1765 Mary Hoskins, daughter of William Hoskins and Sarah Whedbee, daughter of Richard Whedbee and Ist wife, Sarah Durant, who was daughter of John Durant and Sarah Jook who m. 4/9/1684. John Durant was son of George Durant and Ann Harwood who m. 1/4/1658 by Mr. David Lindsey. Charles Worth Blount 1721-1784 m. Mary Clayton 1744, daughter of Henry Clayton and Elizabeth Gale, daughter of Christopher
Gale and Sarah Laker, daughter of Benjamin Laker and Jane Day
Mary S.B. Houghton, daughter of Silas M. and Elizabeth, 9/27/1823

Joseph Crency Bradbury Bible continued...

James Edward Bradberry, son of Richard B. and Mary, 8/31/1841

Richard B. Bradberry, son of Richard B. and Mary, 3/20/1844

Elizabeth Ann Bradberry, daughter of William B. Bradberry and Sarah S. Norcom, 4/14/1827, Edenton, N. C.

Other children of William and Sarah Sutton Norcom Bradberry were:

Alethia, Penelope, Mary and William. Martha burned to death at Murfreesboro College, N. C. (Pasted in front of Bible: "Sergt. W. E. Bradberry, Co. F., Ilth N. C. Regt., 3rd Brigade, ist Div., 3rd, Corps, A.N.V. Dec. 6, 1864."

DEATHS:

Charles Bradberry 10/2/1795 John Bradberry 8/6/1814
Mary Blount Bradberry 7/6/1804 Charles Bradberry 1/2/1811
Edmund B. Bradberry 10/17/1824
Joseph C. Bradberry 4/6/1837, aged 66 yrs., 6 mos.
Sarah Bradberry 11/19/1843, aged 72 yrs., 4 mos., 6 days
Richard Bradberry 2/5/1844, aged 32 yrs., 8 mos.
William B. Bradberry 9/16/1872, aged 73 yrs., 1 mo., 4 days
Sarah S. Bradberry 5/9/1881, aged 76 yrs.
Elizabeth A. Bradberry Waff, wife of Joseph T. Waff, 3/26/1896, Gates Co., NC
Joseph T. Waff, son of Thomas E. S. and Mary Carpenter Waff, 6/9/1896. Gates Co., N. C.

Joseph Crency Bradbury Bible continued...

Thomas Edward Waff, son of Thomas E. S. And Mary Carpenter Waff, 6/9/1896, Gates Co., N. C.10/14/1892 aged 44 yrs., Brunswick, Ga., yellow fever
Caroline M. Rawls Waff, wife of Thomas E. Waff, 2/28/1924, aged 70 yrs., Athens, Ga.

Joseph Judson Waff, son of Joseph T. and Elizabeth Ann Bradberry Waff, 1/21/1891, aged 34 yrs, 10 mos. 16 days, McRae, Ga.
Sarah Sackie P. Waff, wife of Joseph ;udson Waff. 8/1932
William Bradberry Waff, son of Joseph T. Waff and Elizabeth Ann Bradberry, 1/6/1933, aged 79 yrs., Winton, N. C.
Sarah C. Warren, daughter of Joseph T. Waff and Elizabeth Ann Bradberry, Thomas Warren, her husbandEarnest L. Smith 10/26/1931, aged 68 yrs., Gates Co., N. C.

ALEXANDER McKIBBEN BIBLE
Owner: Mrs. Robert Clark, Macon, Ga.

BIRTHS

Alexander McKibben 7/22/1793
Hannah Moore 2/14/1798

Their Children:

Margaret McKibben 12/2/1818
Andrew Jackson McKibben 1/19/1826
John McKibben 4/5/1820
Adline Hannah McKibben 1/18/1832
James McKibben 4/5/1820
Nancy Emmerline McKibben 1/7/1834

Alexander McKibben Bible continued...

Thomas McKibben 3/14/1824
Minerva Ann McKibben 4/14/1836
   Clark McKibben 11/16/1829
   Elizabeth Baker McKibben 7/17/1839
Alexander McKibben 7/22/1793-1866 8. 1815 Mecklenburg Co., N. C., Hannah Moore 2/14/1798-1872
                Their Children:-
Clark McKibben 11/18/1829-10/6/1863 m. 9/14/1856 Henry Co., Ga.
Nancy Findley 5/6/1831-4/3/1862 John McKibben 1859-1894
Ida McKibben 3/26/1862 m. 1/7/1885 Meade LeSeuer Hendrick 7/14/1847-12/29/1898

THOMAS McKIBBEN BIBLE
Owner: Mrs. Morris Redman Jackson, Georgia

Thomas McKibben 2/26/1800-1/11/1881 m. 3/1/1825 Mecklenburg Co., N. C. Elizabeth Ward Duffey 8/1/1800-8/10/1859

                Children:

Margaret E. McKibben 2/24/1826-8/6/1914 m. 12/1/1844 Jefferson C. Thomason 4/24/1822-12/27/1893
Samuel McKibben 6/5/1827-11/14/1917 m. 4/4/1852 Mary Ann Harkness 5/11/1837-11/29/1927
Mary Bernice McKibben 1/25/1829-5/21/1903 m. W. P. Phillips
Sarah Jane McKibben 10/29/1830-2/11/1874 m. N. H. Woodward
Elizabeth Matilda McKibben 4/7/1832-5/4/1914 m. 2/6/1851 John Ridgeway

Thomas McKibben Bible continued...

Thomas A. McKibben 11/2/1834-3/21/1911 m. 11 29/1874 Lucy Emmerline Fuller
Martha A. McKibben 2/19/1837-5/4/1870 m. 4/16/1867 M. J. Cofer
Susannah McKibben 11/21/1838-12/21/1927 m. 1/19/1865 William J. Foster
Martin Van Buren McKibben 9/11/1840-9/7/1897 m. Janie Fletcher
J. F. McKibben 5/30/1842-4/12/1892
Hattie Clementine McKibben 8/14/1845-3/9/1920 m. Richard Merritt Fletcher
Thomas McKibben's 2nd wife was Penelope Foster

C. D. SHELNUTT BIBLE

William Charles Shelnutt 11/30/1821 N. C.-7/5/1890
Charlotte Huiet Black, his wife, 4/26/1838-12/10/1896

Children:

James Burket Shelnutt b. 11/14/1863 m. Juma Raegan b. 1/27/1870 m. 11/14/1888
Ernstus Lamar Shelnutt b. 11/26/1865 m. Tina Dean Stephenson 11/2/1910, b. 7/10/1888
Alice Rachael Shelnutt b. 10/26/1888 m. William Joseph Elder b. 7/18/1844 m. 12/5/1903-8. 4/12/1926

Calvin Doster Shelnutt b. 9/26/1868 m. Sallie Garter 11/10/1895
Mary Elizabeth Shelnutt 6/29/1873 m. William Mitchell 11/27/1892, b. 6/4/1871

C. D. Shelnutt Bible continued...

Sallie Queen Shelnutt b. 9/16/1875
Enoch Foster Shelnutt b. 9/14/1877. His wives. Fannie Langford b. 3/7/1881 m. 2/3/1904-d. 2nd wife, Anna Allen, b. 4/30/1882 m. 6/16/1918 m. 5/30/1928
William Charles Shelnutt b. 4/30/1880. His wife, Bettie Dickens b. 9/26/1884, m. 9/30/1908
Mother's Mother and Father:
Lemuel Black 12/9/1809-12/31/1859
Wife, Zillah Pass Black, 5/22/1813-3/10/1838

JAMES YEATES BIBLE
Owner: C. H. Yeates

MARRIAGES

James B. Yeates to Lucreria Johnson
Elizabeth Yeates, daughter of James B. and Lucretia, to James H Knight.
Jesse J. Yeates, son of James B. and Lucretia, to Maria E. Piper, daughter of George W. and James Y. Piper in Blountville, Tenn., 1849
George W. Piper and Jane Young Rutherford, daughter of Archibald Rutherford of Harrisonburg, Va.
James Scott to Martha Ann Res 1/16/1827
Lucretia Jane Yeates, daughter of James and Lucretia, to Hezekiah Revelle, 1851
James Y. Yeates, son of James B. and Lucretia, to Virginia Scott, daughter of James and Martha A. Scott, 1/8/1856, Baltimore, Md.

John Yeates Bible continued...

BIRTHS

James R. Yeates, son of Jesse, Hertford Co., N. C.
Lucretia Yeates, wife of James B.Yeates and dau of James Johnson Nansemond Co
George W. Piper In Warrenton, Va.
Jane Young Piper, wife of C. W. Piper and daughter of Archibald Rutherford, Harrisonburg, Va.
James Scott, son of James and Temperance, 8/24/1800, Hertford Co., N. C.
Martha Ann Scott, wife of James Scott & daughter of James Res 12/22/1805 Newton,NC
Jesse J. Yeates, son of James 8. and Lucretia, 5/29/1829,Hertford Co., N. C
Virginia Yeates, was 2nd wife of Jesse J. Yeates and daughter of = Martha Ann Scott, 8/21/1832 Murfreesboro, N. C.-9/4/1888
Jane Maria Yeates, daughter of Jesse J.and Maria E. Yeates,11/23/1849, Cedarville, Va
Archibald Piper Yeates, son of Jesse J.& Maria E.Yeates.8/1854, Harrisonville, NC

William Smith Yeates, res Jesse J. and Virginia Yeates,12/15/1856, Murfreesboro, NC
Charles Morris Yeates, son of Jesse J.&Virginia Yeates,4/21/1858, Murfreesboro, NC
Jim Yeates, son of Jesse J. Yeates of Virginia, 9/10/1859,Murfreesboro, N. C.
George Scott Yeates 7/1862
Virginia L. Yeates, daughter of Jesse J. and Virginia Yeates, 2/9/1870

John Yeates Bible continued...

DEATHS

James B. Yeates
Lucretia Yeates
George W. Piper
Jane Y. Piper
Maria E. Yeates 8/21/1854
Archie P. Yeates 9/1854
Virginia Scott, 2nd wife of Jesse J. Yeates, 9/4/1888

JOHN VERNER BIBLE

Rebecca DIckey 8/17/1774-6/30/1849
Rebecca Dickey, 2nd wife of John Verner, .. 7/18/1793
Jane Edmondson (d. 1792) m. 11/10/1785 John Verner (his Ist wife)

BIRTHS

John Verner 3/5/1763
Charles Verner 6/25/1801
Mary P. Verner 10/25/1786
Rebecca Verner 8/22/1774
David D. Verner 3/7/1804
Rebecca Verner 3/20/1805

William S. Verner 2/9/1788
Samuel Verner 7/10/1808
Anna Verner 2/4/1820
James Verner 3/25/1790
George Verner 12/2/1810
W. P. Verner 9/29/1815

John Verner Bible continued...

Nancy Verner 12/24/1794
Lemuel H. Verner 4/20/1813
Jane Verner 7/11/1796
John Augustus Verner 5/23/1799

DEATHS

Jane Verner, wife of John, 1/10/1792, 25 yrs. George W. Verner 9/18/1836, aged 26 yrs.

Nancy Verner 5/6/1798, aged 3 yrs., 4 mos. 10 days
John Augustus Verner 10/10/1822, aged 23 yrs.

MARRIAGES

John Verner to Jane Edmonson 11/10/1785

Ann Verner to M. S. Stribling 3/2/1843

Mary P. Verner to William Cocherham 12/12/1805
W. B. Verner to Elinor Cooper 9/7/1820
Jane Verner to Thomas Humphreys 4/23/1816
Charles Verner to Mary L. Davis 4/20/1824
George W. Verner to Harriet Harris 12/20/1833
Samuel Verner to Malinda Crawford 8/10/1832

Ebenezer Pettigrew Verner to Emma Foster 12/19/1843

TURNER C. PROFFITT BIBLE

Turner C. Proffitt m. Polly Wilson 3/26/1833

BIRTHS

Turner Calvin Profitt, son of John, 8/19/1796, Carter Co.,Tenn., Little Doe Creek
Polly Proffitt, wife of Turner C. Proffitt, and daughter of William Wilson, 5/6/1812, Buncombe Co., N. C., Bald Mountain Creek.
Children of Turner C. and Polly Proffitt:
Ira Jackson Proffitt 1/5/1834, Yancey Co., N. C. Bald Mtn Creek
Julia Emeline Proffitt 10/8/1835 Yancey Co., N. C. Bald Mtn Creek
Serephina Taylor Proffitt 8/21/1837 Yancey Co., N. C., Caney River
Marquis De Lafayette Proffitt 10/25/1838 Yancey Co., Caney River
Walghtstil Avery Proffitt 10/2/1841, Yancey Co., N. C.
Phebe Ann Proffitt 4/12/1844 Yancey Co., N. C., Caney River
John William Proffltt 6/26/1846 Yancey Co., N. C., Caney River
Landon Carter Halns Proffitt 3/31/1849 Buncombe Co., N. C.
Pulliam Pierce Proffitt 1/22/1852 Madison Co., N. C.
Martha Jane Proffitt 10/24/1857 Madison Co., N. C.

DEATHS

Turner Calvin Proffitt 4/13/1862, aged 65 yrs., 7 mos. 24 days
Mary Wilson Proffitt 6/29/1899, aged 87 yrs., 1 mos. ;3 days

ELISHA D. BRETT BIBLE

BIRTHS

Elisha D. Brett, son of James and Edith, 9/25/1800
Elizabeth Brett, daughter of Jacob Barrett and Mary, 10/2/1807

Children of Elisha D. and Elizabeth Brett:

James Patrick Brett 4/22/1828
Mary Elizabeth Brett 5/14/1844
George Augustus Brett 1/30/1831
Jacob Brett 5/4/1847
Pulaski Brett 10/31/1833
Elisha D. Brett 2/24/1850 Alice Virginia Brett 3/9/1853
Aurelius Brett 10/26/1835
Martha Odelia Brett 8/24/1838

MARRIAGES

Elisha D. Brett to Elizabeth Barrett. daughter of Jacob and Mary Barrett, 2/15/1827 by Rev. Exum Everett

DEATHS

Pulaski Brett, son of E. D. and Elizabeth, 7/11/1834, 8 mos., 11 days
Jacob Brett 10/4/1847, aged 5 mos.
James Patrick Brett 10/30/1847, 19 yrs, 7 mos.
Mary Elizabeth Brett 11/1/1847, aged 8 yrs., 7 days
Elisha D Brett, Jr., 7/3/1851, aged 1 yr., 4 mos., 9 days
Martha Odella Brett 9/8/1860, aged 22 yrs., 14 days
Aurelius Brett 5/3/1862
Allen Virginia Brett 8/24/1874, aged 21 yrs., 5 mos., 15 days

Elisha D. Brett, Sr., 11/16/1875, aged 75 yrs., 1 mo., 21 days, Funeral Serman by Rev. R. D. Savage
Elizabeth Brett, wid. of Elisha D., 5/20/1885, aged 77 yrs., 7 mos., 18 days. Funeral serman by Rev. C. W. Scarboro.

LEVI HARRELL BIBLE
Owner: Mrs. R. T. Ragan Eastman, Georgia

BIRTHS

Levi Harrell 9/16/1777
Elizabeth Holt, his wife, 10/16/1794

Their Children:

Isaac Harrell 1/13/1809
Levi Harrell Jr. 12/20/1825
William Harrell 7/27/1811
John W. Harrell 11/16/1827
Polly Harrell 4/5/1813
Nancy Harrell 1/13/1830
Lovett L. Harrell 3/6/1815
Katie Harrell 1/6/1832
Sara Harrell 3/4/1817
Needham Harrell 12/27/1833
Wright W. Harrell 2/11/1819
Joe Anna Harrell 12/24/1835
Samuel Harrell 4/13/1821
Edna Harrell 2/19/1838
Elizabeth Harrell 9/28/1823

REV. THOMAS BATTLE BIBLE
DAR Records, Ga. State Archives

BIRTHS

Rev. Thomas Battle 8/14/1786
Polly Baker Battle. his wife, 6/12/1792 m. 4/17/1808

Their Children:

Calvin Williams Battle 7/22/1812
Martha Elizabeth Battle 8/2/1814
Dr. Thomas William Battle 7/7/1816
Dr. Henry Luther Battle 6/16/1818
Judge Nicholas William Battle 5/11/1820
Mary Ann Battle 9/12/1821
Nancy Caroline Battle 3/26/1823
Josephine Harris Battle 7/20/1824
John William Battle 4/10/1826
James Branham Battle 9/2/1828
Antoinette Thomas Battle 2/19/1830
Robert Augustus Battle 2/10/1832
Louisa Marian Battle 8/26/1834

DEATHS

Nancy Caroline Battle 9/7/1850
Dr. Henry Luther Battle 4/30/1858
Robert Augustus Battle 12/18/1860
Rev. Thomas Battle 5/16/1883
Polly Baker Battle, wife of Rev. Thomas Battle, 4/26/1864
John William Battle 9/12/1890
Mary A. Battle Spear 5/25/1878
Calvin William Battle 3/11/1877

Rev. Thomas Battle continued...

Dr. Thomas W. Battle 6/17/1879
Louisa M. Battle Simmons 5/23/1895
Martha E. Battle Banks 8/14/1895
Judge Nicholas W. Battle 8/23/1905
James Branham Battle 11/15/1903
Antoinette T. Battle Leary 9/4/1920

Notes by Mrs. John Ponder, DAR, James Monroe Chapter, Forsyth, Ga.: "Capt. William Battle served in the Revolution. His name may be found upon the payroll at Kingston, N. C., dtd 10/1779, page 156
Capt. William Battle b. Halifax Co., N. C. 1758-d. Washington Co., N. C. 1802 m. 1785 Mary Ann Williams"

MARRIAGES of Children

Rev. Thomas Battle to Polly Bake?
Lawrence Battle to Martha Arrington

William Battle to Chloe Boddie
Betsy Battle to Nathan Boddie
Fred Battle to Temple Perry
Pattie Battle Ist to Gray Fort, 2nd to Col. Sharp
Larkin Battle to Sallie Sills

Alfred Battle to Melissa Bell
Mary Battle to Henry Collier, Governor of Alabama

GREEN HAYWOOD ALFORD BIBLE

BIRTHS

Green H. Alford 6/7/1820 Wake-Co., North Carolina
Rebecca Jones Alford, wife of Green H. Alford, 3/18/1822, Wake Co., NC

BIRTHS of Children of Green H. and Rebecca Alford

George Benton Alford 1/24/1845
Francis Adner Alford 3/9/1853
Andrew Jackson Alford 1/29/1847
Salina Blanche Alford 4/28/1857
Elizabeth Laland Alford 9/21/1848
William Leoria Haywood Alford 10/23/1863
Columbus Augustin Alford 2/8/1850

BIRTHS of the Godwin Family

Fernando Keith Godwin 11/9/1856 North Carolina
Carlton Haywood Godwin, son of Fernando K. Godwin and wife, Blanche Alford Godwin, 11/8/1880
Ellen Calvinda Godwin 11/15/1882
Columbus Barnes Godwin 4/14/1884
Rebecca Margarete Godwin 6/9/1886
Clair Alford Godwin 1/10/1896

MARRIAGES

Green H. Alford to Rebecca Jones /8/1844
Fernando Keith Godwin to Salina Blanch Alford 1/27/1880

Green Haywood Alford Bible continued...

DEATHS

Green Haywood Alford 12/13/1877 Charley E. J. Jones 7/18/1872
Mrs. Rebecca Jones Alford 8/6/1890

Ella Linyear Alford. daughter of G. A. Alford, 6/9/1856
Fernando Breitt Godwin 9/26/1818, Sylvester, Georgia

ISAAC HOLLAND BIBLE
Owner: Mrs. James J. Gilbert
1221 2nd Ave., Columbus, Ga.

BIRTHS

Isaac Holland 4/13/1770 m. 9/1/1790
Samuel Holland 6/21/1791
John Holland 5/12/1792
William Holland 8/3/1802
James Holland 12/27/1804
Orlando Holland 9/30/1806
Arestus Holland 4/9/1813
Amelia Holland (nee Brewington) 9/10/1772
Hetty Cole Holland 5/28/1793
Hannah Holland 8/16/1794
Nancy Holland 3/20/1799
Amelia Brewington Holland 11/7/1800
Elmina Holland 1/9/1809
Julia Ann 3/22/1811
Cynthia Holland 5/6/1816
Maria Louisa Holland 3/16/1839 Chambers Co., Ala. m. John Wesley Cargile Jr. b. 11/19/1833 Laurens Co., S. C.

JOHN H. CARRUTHERS BIBLE
DAR Records. Ga. State Archives

Sarah Carruthers 1800 Joseph Carruthers 5/8/1802

J. L. Carruthers 9/25/1803
Samuel Carruthers 7/25/1805
J. W. Carruthers 7/13/1807 m. Rachel Pue
Matilda Carruthers 7/10/1809 child 8/26/1811
Jane Carruthers 12/4/1814
Joseph Carruthers 5/8/1802
Della Carruthers 2/9/1817
Richard Carruthers 12/24/1819
Richard Carter Carruthers 12/25/1828

John and Rachel's children:

Sarah O. Carruthers 7/6/1834
Nancy J. Carruthers 5/26/1836
Hannah D. Carruthers 8/19/1839
J. W. Carruthers 1/1838-7/21/1861
Thomas Leith Carruthers 1/12/1843
Mary Carruthers 7/15/1844
Joseph Nelson Carruthers 7/19/1845
Cassie Carruthers 12/15/1848
Richard H. and Rachel H. Carruthers (twins) 5/5/1851
Thomas Leith Carruthers m. Mary Eleanor Deaton, 3/10/1848-1913, daughter of William and Mary Eleanor Peden Deaton
William Deaton 1812-1877 Hazelhurst, Mississippi
Mary Eleanor Peden 1826-1908 Hawkinsville, Georgia
Helen Carruthers. daughter of Thomas Leath and Mary E. Carruthers, b. 6/13/1876 Pulaski Co., Ga. m. 1898 Henry Hooker Sparrow

WILLIAM TURNER HURLEY BIBLE
Owner: Maggie Garrett Social Circle, Georgia

William Turner Hurley 1856-1915 m. 1875 Lillian Trogdon 1854-1931

Arthur Anthony Hurley 1878 Cedar Falls, North Caroline m. 1895 Maude Carolyn York b. 1878
Ernestine Hurley b. 6/21/1814

SAMUEL AND HANNAH JACKSON BIBLE of Stokes Co.
From: Rev. War Pension W5004

BIRTHS of Children of Samuel and Hannah Jackson

John Jackson 2/2/1783 –
Sarah Jackson
James Jackson 3/1/1785
Amos Jackson
Isaac Jackson
Joseph Jackson 10128/1801
Samuel Jackson
Hiram Jackson 10/28/1801

Note: Soldier applied for pension 3/15/1833 from Stokes Co., N.C., stating he was b. 1758 a few miles from Philadelphia, Pa. on Delaware River and while a child went with his parents to that part of Rowan Co. now called Davidson Co., N. C. He lived Surry Co., N. C., now called Stokes Co. Widow, Hannah Jackson, applied for pension 3/9/1939, stating husband d. 6/18/1834.

She was b. 1019/1764 and m. Samuel Jackson 1/23/1782 by Micajah Clark, J. P., Surry Co., N. C., and her maiden name was Hannah Gibson

DAVID AND REBECCA DURBOROW BIBLE

Bible in lawsuit-John Durborough Martha Polk v. Francis Hawks, exr of Mary Knox, Craven Co., 1825-1826

BIRTHS of Children of David and Rebecca Durborow

John Durborow 11/16/1771
Elizabeth Durborow 6/1/1778
Rebecca Durborow 3/19/1774
Rebecca Durborow 6/1/1778
James Durborow 9/9/1776
Martha Durborow 1/25/1781

Note: This leaf was shown to Ann Wales and testified to by her as an eye witness, Match 12, 1825. William Hall, Commissioner, This lawsuit states that Mary Knox d. 4/1822; her LWT left estate to bro., David Durborrow and his children and her sister, Martha and her children, all of Delaware. That David d. many yrs. before. Myer Cason stated that Rebecca Durborow d. 12/1805 leaving two children-David Durborow and Mary Knox (children of Hugh Durborow). This lawsuit should be examined for further data.

HAMILTON ALLEN BROWN BIBLE

Owner: Hugh Thomas Brown North, Wilksboro, North Carolina

Hamilton Allen Brown b. 9/25/1857 m. 4/29/1868 Amelia Seluia Gwyn b. 1/20/1846

BIRTHS

Hugh Thomas Brown 6/26/1871

Hamilton Allen Brown Bible continued....

John Brown 11/8/1880
Mary Lenoir Brown 11/18/1873
James B. Gordon Brown 12/2/1883
James Hamilton Brown 2/13/1876

DEATHS

Mary Seluia Brown 9/22/1877
Avery Lenoir Brown 1/9/1918
Colonel Hamilton Allen Brown 4/9/1917
Amelia Seluia Gwyn Brown 12/13/1926
James B. Gordon Brown 11/13/1926

STEPHEN MOORE BIBLE of Chatham Co., N. C.

Stephen Moore b. 1795 Person Co., NC-d. 4/9/1855 m. Elizabeth E. Dismukes 11/22/1815

BIRTHS

Their first son, Joseph W.,
Rachel Ann Moore 3/8/1829
11/14/1817-8/1/1827
Richard Romulous Moore 9/21/1829
Caroline Y. Moore 5/25/1819
Mary Elizabeth Moore 9/21/1831
Sarah Jane Moore 11/22/1820
Stephen Pleasant Moore 3/18/1834

Thomas Alexander Moore 8/1822-1823
John Waller Moore 6/17/1836
George Pinkney Moore 5/19/1824

Stephen Moore Bible continued...

Celia Martha Louisa Moore 11/18/1838
Elijah Ahraham Moore 11/3/1825

DEATHS

Celia M. L. Moore 7/19/1869 Rev. George E. Moore 7/23/1893
Mrs. E. E. Moore 8/16/1873, aged 80 yrs.
Stephen Pleasant Moore m. 1/12/1871 Samintha Poe. She was b. 7/29/1830.
Issue: John Romulus Moore b. 9/23/1874; Lucy Anne Moore b. 11/14/1876
John Romulus Moore m. 4/27/1904 Lily Eudora Murchison. She was b. 1/16/1877.
Issue: Julian Stephen Moore b. 7/16/1905 and Richard Murchison Moore b . 5/8/1911
Julian Stephen Moore m. 6/15/1931 Pauline Whitfield Gresham. She was b. 3/18/1910

JOHN MAY BIBLE of Rockingham Co., N. C.
DAR Records, Ga. State Archives

BIRTHS

John May 2/27/1757 Buckingham, Virginia
Elizabeth Hunter May, 4/21/1779, Bedford, now Campbell Co., Va.

BIRTHS

John Hunter May, their Iston, 7/5/1782 Guilford Co. (now Rockingham, N. C.)-12/10/1786

John May Bible continued...

Charles May 9/14/1784
Powhatan May 6/26/1795
Rook May 9/6/1787
John Wesley May Jr. 3/1011800
Alexander May 7/16/1790
James H. May 1/29/1802
Rachel McF. May 11/13/1792

Note: Tombstone inscription, Stoneville township, Rockingham Co.,N. C.: "Here in the mortsl part of John May, a Revolutionary Officer. He lived a Patriot and died a Christian. March 20th 1844, Born Feb. 27th, 1757."

MARY NEELY AND JOHN TAYLOR BIBLE
Owner: Mrs. W. F. Martin 2292 Nelson, Memphis, Tenn. 38104

Mary Neely, her Bible and age, b. 4/15/1785 John Taylor m. Mary Neely 9/29/1806

BIRTHS of Their Children

Jinsey Caroline Taylor 10/10/1807
Mary Neely Taylor 12/2/1817
Perry Campbell Taylor 5/15/1810
Edward M. Taylor 7/14/1819
Patsy Star Taylor 9/18/1812
Nancy Hannah Taylor 5/11/1823
James Lee Taylor 6/30/1815
John Marrion Taylor 3/12/1826
John Taylor d. 1/16/1830 (John and Mary bur. Steele Cr. Presby. Churchyard, Mecklenburg Co. (Jinsey Caroline d. 5/20/1846)

JOHN B. WEST BIBLE
DAR Records, Ga. State Archives

John B. West d. 182 m. 1817 Nancy Marinda Griggs 1802-1878

BIRTHS of Their Children

Celia West 1/25/1821 Runcombe Co., N. C.-d. Tenn.
John Henry West 10/18/1822 Buncombe Co., N. C.-d. 1874 California
M. Washington West 9/9/1825 Runcombe Co., N. C.-d. Dalton, Ga.
Phidiler Siler West 4/3/1827 Buncombe Co., N. C.-d. McGregor, Tx
Dr. Montreville West 5/10/1830 Buncoabe Co., N. C.-d. Woodlawn, Washington
Andrew Jnckson West 6/15/1832 Buncombe Co., N. C.-d. Turnerville, Ga. m. 11/29/1891
Sophronie Adaline West 10/1/1834 Buncombe Co., NC.-1877 Murry Co.Ga.
Margaret Ann West 9/8/1836 Buncombe Co., N. C.-d. Gilmer Co.. Ga.
Joseph Manson West 12/18/1842 Buncombe Co., N. C.-d. Cartersville, Ga.
Miriah Marinda West 7/23/1844 Buncomhe Co., N. C.-1922 Cartersville, Ga.

MARRIAGES of Above Children

Celina West to Mr. Creasman
John Henry West unmd
William Washington West to Caroline Roberts
Margaret Ann West unmd

John B. West Bible continued...

Phidiler Siler West to Amelia Milligan
Dr. Montreville West to Mary Cox, daughter of John Goolsby Cox
Andrew Jackson West to Leah King Osborn h. 4/3/1836,
daughter of Jonathan Osborn of Buncombe Co.. N. C.
Sophronia Adaline West to Nelson Trlplett
Joseph Manson West to Margaret Johnson
Mariah Marinda West to Alfred Smith

JOHN AND MARY FIELDS' BIBLE
From: Rev. War Pension

John Fields, Jr. b. 4/3/1752
Mary Gibson b. 12/24/1754 m. 12/4/1776 Guilford Co., N. C.

BIRTHS of Their Children

Anna Fields 10/6/1777 m. 12/17-- to Thomas Strong
Lydia Fields 5/27/1779 m. 12/11/1796 Charles Harris
Susan Fields 1/20/1785-8/20/1821 m. 3/14/1811 Robert Strong
Jeremiah Fields 2/20/1787 m. 10/31/1811 Jane Searla
Nathanihl Fields 5/5/1789
Lucy Fields 2/6/1792-11/3/1820 m. 1/21/1814 John Searls
John Fields 5/23/1794 m. 8/31/1811 Loneasy Gibson

Note: John Fields, Jr. applied for pension 1/15/1833, near Spring Garden, Rockingham Co., N. C., stating he was b. 4/3/1752 in Hanover Co., Va; went to Rowan Co., NC in 1765. Soldier d. 9/1/1835. Rockingham Co., NC, 11/28/1853 Richard H. Scales testified he was admr of Mary Fields, widow and pensioner. Mary Fields d. 10/24/1844, Rockingham Co., N. C. and left two surviving children: John and Jeremiah.

BENJAMIN CHASTAIN HOOPER BIBLE

Benjamin Chastain Hooper 12/5/1812-4/28/1962 m. Elizabeth Cathey 7/11/1815-8/17/1888, daughter of James Cathey 10/17/1784-5/27/1867 and wife, Sarah Bryson Hooper b. 9/28/1789. Thomas Jefferson Hooper, son of Benjamin Chastain Hooper and his wife, Elizabeth, b. Jackson Co., N. C. 11/1/l845- d.10/7/1921 m. 12/24/1865 Arminta Caroline Kimsey 9/22/1846-9/6/1874

BIRTHS of Children of Thomas Jefferson Hooper and Arminta

Caroline Kimsey Hooper
W. M. or William Hooper 11/21/1866 m. 1/7/1882 Emma Stuart Coffey
Violet Virginia Hooper 3/27/1869 m.. 3/27/1869 Warren Hedden

Georgia Ann Hooper 11/30/1871 m. 11/3011891 Colonel Bed Ledford
Olley Arminta Hooper 9/9/1872 m. 9/8/1887 David H. Prewett
Mary Caroline Hooper 9/1/1874 m. 5/28/1893 John H. Davis
William M. Hooper 11/21/1866 m. 1/7/1882 Emma Steward Coffey

BIRTHS of Children of William M. and Emma S. Hooper

Henry Oliver Hooper 10/27/1883-killed Near Murphy, N. C.
Oscar Lee Hooper 8/29/1885 m. Dorothy Annie Clare Grady West Rudisill
Wyly Ferdunan Hooper 11/18/1887 m. Bessie Jones
Mary Caroline Hooper 4/27/1890 m. Dock C. House
George Franklin Hooper 5/1/1892 m. 7/24/1929 Minnie Bell Luther
Catherine H. Hooper 5/1/1892, twin, d. at birth

Benjamin Chastain Hooper Bible continued...

John Struby Hooper 5/16/1894 m. Verner Kelly
Thomas Athan Hooper 9/28/1896 m. Clifford Bryan
Paul Lester Hooper 3/26/1898 d. a small boy
Ruby Hooper 1/21/1900 m. Fred Osborn Rowe
William Ray Hooper 3/11/1902 m. Grace Fain

BIRTHS of Children of Benjamin Chastain Hooper and Elizabeth

Martha Jane Hooper 7/3/1834
James Lafayette Hooper 3/22/1839
Mary Emmaline Hooper 11/4/1842
Sarah Hooper d. y.
Thomas Jefferson Hooper 11/1/1845-11/7/1921
Thomas Jefferson Hooper, 4th child of Benjamine Chastaine and Elizabeth Cathy Hooper m. Ist Arminta Caroline Kimsey, daughter of Rev. Eliza Kimsey and wife, Sarah (1846-1874), 2nd, Sarah Ellis. Children by 2nd Marriage:James Lafayette Hooper, Noah Hooper, Lizzie Hooper and Maggie Hooper James Cathy b. 10/17/1784, father of Elizabeth Cathy - d. 5/27/1867 m. Sarah Bryson 9/28/1789-5/10/1880

JAMES L. LANCASTER BIBLE of Edgecombe County

BIRTHS

James L. Lancaster 1/28/1810, Edgecombe Co., North Carolina
 Charity Lancaster 11/20/1804, Edgecombe Co., North Carolina.
         Their Children:
James Drew Lancaster 2/3/1828, Edgecombe Co.
Evelina Morgan Lizbeth Lancaster 11/14/1829. Edgecombe Co.
Anna Lucinda Maria Atkinson Lancaster 2/18/1832, Edgecombe Co.

James L. Lancaster Bible continued...

Sally Lancaster 4/28/1834, Talbot Co., Ga. Henry Lancaster 5/10/1836, Talbot Co., Ga.
Priscilla Lancaster 7/14/1838, Talbot Co., Ga.
Luizer Lancaster 10/2/1840, Carrsville, Bartow Co., Ga.

John Wesley Lancaster 9/11/1843, Carrsville, Barrow Co., Ga.
Charles Wesley Lancaster 4/20/1843, Talbot Co., Ga.

MARRIAGES

Charles W. Lancaster to Mary Ann Matilda Hand 7/30/1863
James Lupe Lancaster to Charity Lancaster 4/20/1827, Edgecombe Co., NC
Henry Lancaster to Fanny Hand 4/27/1863, Marion Co., Ga.
James M. Jordan to Louisa Lancaster 11/15/1858, Marion Co., Ga.
T. McCorkle to Louisa Lancaster Jordan 4/11/1866, Marion Co., Ga.
Jack Hagler to Priscilla Lancaster Hagler 9/27/1863, Marion Co., Ga.
John Densen to Priscilla Lancaster Hagler 9/27/1863 Marion Co., Ga.
George W. Hagler to Sarah Lancaster 11/28/1866, Marion Co., Ga.

DEATHS

John Wesley Lancaster 11/11/1813, Carrsville, Ga., aged 2 mos.
Charles Wesley Lancaster 10/31/1865, Marion Co., Ga., 20 yrs. 6 mos., 11 days
Charity Lancaster, wife of James, 8/31/1885, Marion Co. 80 yrs., 9 mos., 11 days

James L. Lancaster Bible continued...

James Drew Lancaster, oldest son of James. and Charity Lancaster, 7/22/1887, aged 59 yrs.. 5 mos., 19 days
James Lancaster 8/13/1895 Marion Co., Ga., aged 85 yrs., 6 mos., 16 days
Rosamond A. Lancaster Wadsworth-McGill 8/6/1907
Victor Wilson Lancaster 10/2/1907 Marion Co., Ga.
Henry Lancaster 12/23/1915 Marion Co.
Fanny Lancaster 7/19/1913 Marion Co., Ga.

   Grandchildren (Downs children)
Adrian Laverne Lancaster 9/14/1924
Dolly Lancaster 12/17/1926
   (Victor's children)
George Lancaster 11/1/1900 m. Annie May Webb of Adrain, Ga.
 (their child, Victor Lancaster, 3 yrs. old)
Clara Lancaster m. James Johnson (one child, a girl)
Luther Lancaster
Effie Lancaster m. Roy Johnson (one child. Lilius, 5 yrs. old)
Horace Lancaster m. Jewell Moore (one boy, John Wesley)
   (Ellery's children)
Bessie Lancaster b. 4/14/1896 m. Forest Anthony (one child, Ollida, 8 yrs. old)
Charles Wesley Lancaster 1/18/1898
Fred Lancaster b. 6/7/1900 m. Ist Della I,ocklier from Ala. (one child, Ellington Lancaster, 4 yrs. old), 2nd wife, Mildred Allen Eron Tennessee
John Willie Lancaster b. 9/16/1904 m. Mell Anthony (one child, girl, Jean, age 1 yr)
Ruth Lancaster b. 4/14/1909
Clyde Lancaster h. 6/6/1917
   (Isabell's children)
Carl Tillman Lawhorn b. 7/8/1900
Henry Roy Lawhorn b. 8/8/1902

James L. Lancaster Bible continued...

Carl Lawhorn m. Alice Roberts from Taylor Co., Ga.
Henry Lawhorn m. Bessie Clifton from Greene Co., Ga.
Maggie's children: Mary Jewell Harbuck - 16 yrs. old; Margaret Harbuck - 14 yrs. old

JANE C. ABERNATHY FITE BIBLE
History of Cass Co., Ga.

Abram Fite b. 12/11/1808
Jane C. Abernathy b. 7/15/1818 m. 11/14/1834

BIRTHS of Their Children

John C. Fite 3/5/1836 James A. Fite 4/19/1851
Mary Ann Fite 4/16/1838-6/15/1849
Washington S. Fite 4/19/1851
Lockey S. Fite 4/9/1840
David Fite 11/22/1853
Joseph H. Fite 3/7/1844
Christopher C. Fire 3/22/1856
Abram Marion Fite 8/11/1846
Laura I. Fite 7/8/1858
William C. Fite 11/30/1848
Jefferson D. Fite 12/23/1861

DEATHS

Jacob Fite 12/16/1846
James Barnes 4/30/1864
Joseph F. Farrar 9/10/1862
Abram Fite 4/30/1871
Lockey S. Fite Farrar 10/21/1862
Jane C. Abernathy Fite 11/18/1874

AARON DEVENY BIBLE

BIRTHS

Aaron Deveny 4/16/1747
Sarah Deveny, wife of Aaron, 10/26/1748

Their Children:

Robert Deveny 4/14/1773
Mary Deveny 3/26/1784
Margaret Deveny 10/29/1774
Sarah Deveny 2/24/1786
Ann Deveny 6/26/1776
Elizabeth Deveny 2/1/1788
Aaron Deveny 1/26/1778
Sarah Black Deveny 2/1/1791
Jane Deveny 11/1/1780
Susannah Grayson Deveny 5/25/1777
Rachel Deveny 3/7/1782
Aaron Deveny 7/5/1800

JAMES CLARK BIBLE of Orange County
Owner: Mrs. J. C. Greenfield, Jr., Atlanta, Ga.

James Clark 12/5/1762-3/17/1844
Ann Kerr 11/23/1763-1/22/1849 m. 5/5/1796

Their Children

Bethieh Clark 8 / 13/ 1 78 7- 2/11/1816
Archibald Clark 1/13/1789-6/22/1815
Agnes Clark 12/7/1790-
Stephen Clark 11/14/1792-9/22/1854

James Clark Bible continued...

Grace Clark 2/7/1797-8/8/1799
Sarah Clark 7/21/1799-
James Williamson Clark 2/17/1802-7/21/1860
Hannah Harriet Clark 4/14/1805-10/27/1890

Children of Bethieh Clark Lindsey

Lucretia R. Lindsey 3/11/1809
Sarah Lindsey 7/13/1821-
Ancennatus D. Lindsey 6/15/1810-
Nancy Lindsey d. 7/28/1831
Archibald Lindsey 10/1/1814-6/30/1862
Grace Lindsey 3/20/1820-2/29/1892
Hannah Harriet Clark m. 10/25/1832 David Dickie.

Their Children

Elizabeth A. P. Dickle 7/25/1834
John W. Dickie 1/2/1838-
James Brigham Dickie 4/2/1836-1/25/1864
Harriet N. Dickie 6/25/1841-
Laura Nebane Dickie 6/25/1850-5/4/1899

Among Other Grandchildren of James Clark and Ann Kerr

Elleanor H. Clark 9/12/1834-10/24/1836
James H. Clark 4/30/1836-5/1852
Samuel D. Clark 11/6/1837-10/1855
John H. Clark 2/22/1839-
Eliza Ann Clark 4/12/1841-7/3/1862
Eli T. Clark 11/9/1813-
William Rankin 7/30/1843-

James Clark Bible continued...

Stephen Taroy 3/30/1845-
G. L. Walker 6/1853-

HENRY COATE BIBLE
Vol. II, A Journal, etc. of George Fox

Collection of the Historical Commission NC Christian Missionary Convention
Mercy Willson b. 10/3/1785
Rebecca Willson, daughter of Robert and Mercy, b. 2/23/1793

BIRTHS of Children of Henry and Mary Coate

Lydia Coate 10/ 23/1793
Rhoda Coate 7/24/1801
Samuel Coate 7/8/1799
Isaac Coate 9/7/1795
Rachel Coate 11/6/1804
Esther Coate 12/21/1807
Mary Conte 6/28/1797

BIRTHS of Children of Henry and Rebecca Coate

Robert Coate 10/27~816
David M. Coate 7/9/1823
Henry W. Coate 9/16/1818
John H. Coate 9/24/1825

Caleb Coate 2/1/1821
Mary Davis, daughter of John and Lydia Davis, b. 10/26/1820

PRUDENCE GIBSON BIBLE
Owner: E. Eugene Dillon 104 S. "D" Street
Marion, Indiana 46952

Prudence Gibson 3/10/1760 N. C.-9/28/1835, Delaware Co.. Ind., at Abigail Gibson Taylor's, bur. Reese Cemetery, south of Muncie, Ind.

BIRTHS of Children of Garrett and Prudence Gibson

William Gibson 8/20/1779 Surry-Co., NC-9/23/1853 Muncie, Ind., m. Rachel Sarah DeWitt
Amelia Gibson 6/6/1786 Surry Co., N. C.-7/2/1841 Lawrence Co., Ind. m. 5/1/1801 Ashville, N. C., Isaac Williams, Jr. (Capt.)
Garrett Gibson 1787 Surry Co., N. C.-9/10/.1822 Greene Co. Ohio m. 9/20/1822 Greene Co., Ohio, Elizabeth Rhodes
Valentine Gibson 12/24/1787 Surry Co., N. C.-4/7/1845 Delaware Co., Ind., m. 1/31/1809 Jefferson Co., Tenn., Catharine Harrold
Bowater Porter Gibson 11/9/1793 N. C.-6/12/1869 Delaware Co., Ind. m. Mary Ann Rhodes
Robert Gibson 1804 E. Market, Jefferson Co., Tenn.-3/12/1858 m. 1st 11/13/1828 Randolph Co.. Ind., Sarah Heaton, 2nd, Nancy Davis, 3rd, Mary Brock Cheeseman Anna Gibson 9/12/1809 Jefferson Co., Tenn. m. 9/12/1809
Jefferson Co., Tenn., Jonathan Mills.   Susan Martha Gibson
Abigail Gibson m. Henry Taylor (d. 12/3/1860)
Celia Gibson m. William H. Brown

Sarah Gibson 1798 N. C. m. 6/10/1832 Delaware Co., Ind., Samuel Brown

JOSEPH CALLAWAY BIBLE of Rowan County

Joseph Callaway b. 9/21/1754 Halifax Co., Va. d. 6/12/1777
Sabrina Morgan

BIRTHS

Jesse Callaway 6/3/1796
Morgan Callaway 4/16/1831
Matilda N. Slough 3/20/1796
Sabrina Mildred Callaway 1/28/1834
Mary Ann Sharman 1/11/1834
Joshua Callaway 6/21/1836
Mary Smith Wootten 11/17/1805
Mary Ann Matilda Callaway 3/21/1839
Lydia B. Callaway 12/22/1819
Clarissa Elizabeth Callaway 11/18/1841
Frances Jemima Callaway 9/7/1825
Thomas Wootten Callaway 10/15/1828
John James Sharman Callaway 4/4/1844
Martha Sarah Callaway 2/2/1848
Nellie Jane Callaway 11/29/1858
Jesse Callaway 10/16/1850
Luke Henry Callaway 10/7/1860-7/18/1929
William Willls Callaway 3/12/1857
John Sharman 10/18/1799
John James Sharman, son of above, 10/6/1825
Joseph Samuel Callaway 9/20/1862 Mary Catharine Nansby? 9/18/1833

Woodson Kirby Callaway 6/18/1863
Wayland Callaway 8/30/1869
Ella Agnes Callaway 1/2/1868

Joseph Callaway Bible continued...

DEATHS

Joseph Callaway Sr. 11/13/1821
Mary Callaway 2/7/1826
Elizabeth Callaway 8/9/1822
Mary Ann Callaway 9/10/1826
Matilda K. Callaway 10/4/18--
Lydia B. Heard 8/18/1853
Frances Jemima Callaway 9/22/1829
John Sharman 9/12/1826
John James Sharman 11/10/1843
Joseph Morgan Callaway 11/9/1846, aged 63 yrs., 4 mos., 7 days
Martha Sarah Callaway 6/21/1848, aged 4 mos.
Thomas Wootten 8/14/1848
Lydia Boren 8/19/1832
Mary Smith Callaway 1/1855
Mary Catherine Callaway 1906
William Willis Callaway 10/19/1932

BRICE-NEWKIRK BIBLE of Duplin County
Owner: Harriet Newkirk Willard, North Carolina

BIRTHS

John Brice 1/3/1765
Joseph Brice 6/27/1769
George Brice 7/4/1768
Abraham Newkirk 6/15/1754
Ann Brosard, daughter of John and Ann Penny, 1/6/1716
Elizabeth Neson, daughter of Ann Brosard, 12/27/1742
Mary Ann Brosard, daughter of Peter Andrus and Ann Brosard, 11/21/1749

Brice-Newkirk Bible continued...

Peter Andrus Brosard, son of Peter Andrus & Ann Brosard, 11/20/1756-5/26/1773
Mary Ann Newkirk, wife of Abraham Newkirk, 11/21/1749

BIRTHS of Children of Abraham and Mary Ann Newkirk

Penny Newkirk 7/30/1785
Ann Jane Newkirk 5/5/1796

Mary Ann Newkirk 10/22/1787
Abraham Newkirk Jr. 2/20/1798
Rachel Newkirk 7/30/1767
Benjamin Rhodes Newkirk 4/3/1801
Joseph Newkirk 11/20/1791
Timothy Newkirk 11/20/1791
Jacob Felix Newkirk 8/26/1807
Bryan Newkirk 6/5/1794
Henry John Thomas Newkirk 6/12/1804

BIRTHS

John Brice 1/3/1765
Joseph Brice 6/27/1769
George Brice 6/4/1768
Abraham Newkirk 6/15/1754
Henry Newkirk. son of Tobias, 1/10/1750
Jacob Felix Newkirk 8/26/1807

Joseph and Timothy Newkirk 11/1791
Joseph Newkirk father of B. Newkirk and grandfather of J. H., T. E., J. B., C. Hettie, C.

CHARLES B. CRUTCHFIELD BIBLE Of Warren County
Owner: Mrs. Mildred T. Hope Shelbyville, Tennessee

BIRTHS

C. B. Crutchfield 6/15/1827
Anna Crutchfield 12/3/1858
Mrs. M. E. Crutchfield 6/6/1835
Marian Crutchfield 11/2/1832
Ida Crutchfleld 9/21/1853
Miss Jo Palmer 7/31/1837
Mrs. H. L. Crutchfield 9/12/1837
Mrs. E. H. Bumpass 1/16/1806
Mattie Crutchfield 8/28/1856
Charlie Wade Crutchfield, son of C. B. and H. L., 2/6/1860
James R. Wade, 3/16/1831, son of Mrs. E. M. Bumpass
Thomas, son of John Thomas ---- 12/23/1823
Thomas Crutchfield, son of Christie, 3/12/1812

BIRTHS of Children of C. B. and H.T. Crutchfield

Annabelle Crutchfield 3/9/1862- - - -
Jessie Thomas Crutchfield 2/6/1864
Johnnie Crutchfield 10/10/1866
James Porter Crutchfield 9/30/1869
Thomas Richard Crutchfield 5/4/1876
Unnamed son 9/9/1885, son of C. W. and M. G. Crutchfield
Hazel Crutchfield 4/5/1887, daughter of C. W. and M. G. Crutchfield
Helen Crutchfield, daughter of C. W. and M. G., 3/5/1890
Mrs. S. C. Crutchfield 6/15/1834

Charles B. Crutchfield Bible continued...

BIRTHS of Children of I. C. and Mattie Tharpe

Mary Love Tharpe 11/5/1875
Erin Tharpe, 8/27/1887 (dan)
John Crockett Tharpe 12/1/1877
Annie Blanton Tharpe 2/12/1890
Clifford Crutchfield Tharpe 8/7/1880
Robert Hamilton Tharpe 7/19/1893
Edith Lyle Tharpe 9/13/1882
Mildred Tharpe 3/15/1898
Charles Lueco Tharpe, 9/6/1884

DEATHS

Mrs. M E. Crutchfield, wife of C. B. C., 1/14/1854
Charles Crutchfield 6/17/1855, aged 80 yrs.
Anna Crutchfield, daughter of C. B. and H. L., 7/19/1859, aged 7 mos. 16 yrs
Mrs. E. Rumpuss 10/1/1862, aged 56 yrs.
Jessie Thomas Crutchfield, son of C.B. and H. L., 8/4/1864, age 5 mos. 27 days
Edith Lyle, daughter of J. C. and Mattie Tharpe, 10/7/1883
Mrs. H. L. Crutchfield, wife of C. B. Crutchfield, 2/15/1883, aged 45 yrs., 5 mos. 8 days

Jesse Thomas, son of John Thomas aged 60 yrs, 1 mo., 15 days
Infant son of C. W. and M. G. Crutchfield 9/13/1885
Thomas Crutchfield 5/22/1888, aged 76 yrs., 2 mos., 10 days
Mary Ida, wife of J. M. Humphreys, 11/15/1892, aged 39 yrs, 1 mo. 24 das
Sam Crutchfield 10/27/1898, aged 75 yrs., 5 mos.. 24 days

Charles B. Crutchfield Bible continued...

Mrs. Mattie Tharpe, wife of J. C., 7/11/1899
Charlie Blake Crutchfield 3/13/1906, aged 79 yrs.
Charlie Wade Crutchtield, son of C. and H. L., 11/2/1906, aged 46
Leila, wife of J. P. Crutchfield, 6/7/1915
Mildred Love Ivey, dau. of T. R.& Hope Crutchfield, 9/4/1931, Plainview, Tx, 33.
Novella Crutchfield, daughter of J. E. and Leila, 12/31/1901
James Fisher, son of J. P. and Leila Crutchfield, 9/8/1904
Alan Lasater, son of Novella C. and William Lasater, 9/11/1931
Mildred Love, daughter of T. R. and Hope Crutchfield, 4/18/1906

MARRIAGES

C.R Crutchfield-M.E.Van Dyke 10/13/1852 C R.Crutchfield-N L. Wade 6/12/1855
C. B. Crotchfield to S. C. Williams 9/21/1887
W. D. Looney to Johnnie Crutchfield, daughter of C. B. and N. L. 12/18/1889
Thomas R. Crutchfield to Hope D. Bomar 12/22/1897
John C. Tharpe to Mattie, daughter of C. and H. L. Crutchfield,11/24/1874
James M. Humphrey to Mary Ida, daughter of C. B. and H. L. Crutchfield, 3/9/1875
James P. Crawford to Anna Belle, daughter of C. B. and N. L. Crutchfleld, 2/8/1881.
C. W. Crutchfield to Mabel G. Scarborough 11/25/1884
James Porter Crutchfield to Leila Tedro 2/20/1900
Novella Crutchfield to William C. Lasater 12/24/1919
J. E. Crutchfield to Maude Waller 12/24/1919
James Fisher Crutchfield to Louise Travis 10/15/1933
James Porter Crutchfield, son of Blake and Love Wade

Charles B. Crutchfield Bible continued...

Crutchfield, 3/11/1952, aged 82 yrs.
Hazel Crutchfield Fields 2/14/1957
J. P. Crawford 2/27/1941, aged 84 yrs
W. D. Looney 2/14/1941, aged 75 yrs.
Anna Belle Crawford 7/3/1943, aged 81 yrs.

Johnnie Crutchfield Looney, wife of W. D. Looney, 12/22/1959

JESSE SWINSON BIBLE

Jesse Swinson Sr. 3/17/1759   Ann Swinson, Sr. 3/31/1762

Children of Ann (Winders) and Jesse Swinson, Sr.

Katherine Swinson 9/19/1784
Mary Swinson 7/28/1795
John Swinson 9/24/1793
Levi Swinson 2/28/1786
Edee Swinson 11/20/1797
Henry Swinson 4/21/1802
Austin Swinson 1/13/1788
Jesse Swinson Jr. 4/21/1800
Nancy Swinson 1/10/1792
Daniel Swinson 11/26/1789
James G. Swinson 7/10/1805

BIRTHS of Children of Elizabeth (Croom) and John Austin Swinson

Nancy Swinson 7/1/1817
T. A. Swinson 9/2/1818

Jesse Swinson Bible continued...

BIRTHS of Children of Teresa Ann and Jesse Swinson Jr.

John Austin Swinson 10/22/1839
Martha Swinson 8/2/1845
Teresa Ann Swinson 8/8/1842
Florence Victoria Swinson 9/20/1849

ANDREW McINTIRE BIBLE

Andrew McIntire 4/19/1775-2/12/1818
Nancy McIntire, his wife, 10/15/1776-12/7/1831.

BIRTHS of Their Children

Mary McIntire 10/5/1797-4/24/ 1875
Sarah McIntire 5/22/1799
James McIntire 2/1/1801
David McIntire 3/22/1803
Susan McIntire 10/10/1805
Andrew McIntire 3/25/1810
William Murdock McIntire 7/20/1808-5/29/1809
Elizabeth McIntire 5/4/1814-3/17/1885
Charles McIntire 2/10/1812-1/1/1887
Murdock McIntire 7/25/1816

Family of James McIntire (son of Andrew)

James McIntire 2/1/1801-96/1879 m. 7/18/1827 Julia Ann Williams 5/1/1810-12/21/1861
Susan Caroline McIntire 8/15/1828-1/30/1852, unmd.
Ann Eliza McIntire 5/20/1830-8/20/1850 m. 5/1/1849 Benja Franklin Grady.

Andrew McIntire Bible continued...

David Murdock McIntire 12/13/1831-6/11/1901 m. 10/7/1858 Eliza
Jane Chesnutt m. 2/25/1863 Teresa Ann Swinson
Margaret Matilda McIntire 5/23/1833-12/25/1837
James Harrison McIntire 11/9/1834-12/11/1837
Mary Ellen McIntire 9/10/1836-8/1/1867 m. 9/10/1854
Jonathan Chesnutt. He d. 3/4/1876. his 2nd wife was Eugenia
Hussey,cousin of his 1st wife and daughter of Susan Ann
(Stanley) Hussey,daughter of Mary (McIntire) and Redmond L.
Stanley
Thomas Henry Williams McIntire 6/3/1838-2/17/1905 m. 3/15/1864
William Charles McIntire 2/16/1840, stillborn. Hannah Caroline Elizabeth Hendry
Andrew Jas McIntire 8/13/1841-12/3/1893 m.12/22/1874 Susan J. Newell
Franklin Parish McIntire 4/30/1843-1/20/1906 m. 1/5/1870 Lucinda Wells
Gaston Calhoun McIntire 6/7/1845-8/17/1886 m. Lavinia Pierce Hendry 9/27/1876
Julia Sara McIntire 7/13/1847-9/29/1922 m. 6/17/1868 Dr. Amos J. Jones
Marion Bancroft McIntire 3/25/1849-8/7/1849
Laura Alvara McIntire 6/27/1852-9/4/1852. Josephine McIntire 7/6/1850, stillborn
Flavius Gustavus McIntire 3/12/1855, stillborn
James McIntire and his 2nd wife, Mary Emma Ellis, m. 12/2/1862.
She d. 5/13/1866, bur. churchyard of little Episcopal chapel within enclosure of "Airlee", near Wilmington, N. C.

Andrew McIntire Bible continued...

James McIntire and his 3rd wife, Margaret Alice Heath, m. 2/23/1868 in New Hanover Co., N. C. Children: Emma Agnes, Joseph Kinsey Lee, Susan Alice, Charlotte Davis and John Charles Hampton McIntire.

BIRTHS of Children of D. M. and T. A. McIntire

Lucille May McIntire 2/22/186r - -Clyde McIntire (dau.) 11/20/1873
Clarence Vivian McIntire 7/4/1868 Jesse Adrian McIntire 8/31/1877
Jesse Swinson to T. A. Swinson 16/22/1838
David M. McIntire to Teresa Ann Swinson 2/24/1863
Clarence V. McIntire to Laura Ann Bush 2/16/1891, Toomsboro, Ga.
Jesse Adrian McIntire to Verna Estell Carraway 12/10/1901, Mt Olive, NC

DEATHS

Jesse Swinson Sr. 4/17/1834
Nancy (Winders) Swinson 2/18/1837
Elizabeth(Croom)Swinson 8/19/1844
Nancy Swinson, daughter of John Austin Swinson, 8/24/1844
Teresa A. Swinson, wife of Jesse Swinson, 8/8/1861
John A. Swinson, son of Jesse and T. A. Swinson, 7/18/1862, Richmond, Va.
Jesse Swinson. Jr. 2/28/1864
Daniel Swinson. son of Ann (Windera) and Jesse Swinson Sr. 9/22/1864
Clyde Swinson, daughter of D. M. and T. A. Swinson, 7/9/1875
David McIntire 6/11/1901

Andrew McIntire Bible continued...

Ann Swinson McIntire 2/7/1922, Rocky Moune, North Carolina, aged 79 yrs, 6 mos.
Verna Estelle Carraway, wife of Jesse Adrian McIntire, 9/26/1916
Martha Swinson 12/9/1913 nt. Olive, North Carolina
Florence V. Swinson 12/19/1913 Mt. Olive, North Carolina

THOMAS ISBELL BIBLE

Thomas Isbell 6/27/1753 Albemarle Co., Virginia - 10/27/1819, son of James Isbell and wife, Frances Tompkins Livingston
Discretion Howard, his wife, b. 7/29/1764 Wilkes Co., N. C., m. 2/21/1782, daughter of Benjamin Howard and his wife, Prudence Satec Howard.

BIRTHS of Their Children

Prudence Isbell 1783 Wilkes Co., N. C. m. Ambrose Carlton
Benjamin Isbell m. 2/17/1818 Martha Parker
John Isbell 2/11/1788 Wilkes Co., N. C.
Frances Isbell 7/2/1791 Wilkes Co., N. C.-10123/1871 m. 9/25/1808 Micajah Ferguson
Livingston Isbell 4/15/1796 Wilkes Co., N. C. m. Mary Edwards
Elizabeth Isbell 11/1796 Wilkes Co.,NC.-7/19/1884 m. 10/11/1818 Nimrod Ferguson
Thomas Isbell, Jr. 1/29/1800 Wilkes Co., N. C. m. Lucinda Petty

Mary Isbell 12/21/1803 Wilkes Co., N. C.-1/6/1891 m. 8/16/1829 Joseph Tucker
James Isbell

BENJAMIN ISBELL of Wilkes Co., N. C.

Benjamin Isbell, son of Thomas Isbell and his wife, Discretion Howard, m. 2/17/1818 Martha Enrkes 4/6/1799 Wilkes Co., N. C.- 7/15/1840, bur. Isbelle Place, McMinn, Tennessee, daughter of Ambrose Parkes and his wife, Frances Isbell

BIRTHS of Their Children

Miriam Isbell 2/25/1819, Wilkes Co., N. CT - 1/9/1898 m. 5/28/1839 Matthew Jacob Turnley
Thomas Martin Isbell 3/3/1821, Wilkes Co., N. C. - 6/19/1859 m. 12/21/1943 Sarah Ann Terry
Frances Discretion Isbell 3/11/1823 McMinn, Tenn.-1/29/1886 m. 3/30/1852 John Hughes
Martha Ann Isbell 1/19/1825 McMinn, TN-4/27/1844 m. Robt Houston
Mary Louise Isbell 1/15/1827 McMinn, Tenn. m. 1/15/1844 Richard Franklin, Hampton,Tenn.-5/28/1864 m.
Sarah Elizabeth Isbell 9/29/1829 McMinn,12/26/1849 Judge Jesse Gaut

James Parker Isbell 7/20/1831 McMinn, Tenn.-4/19/1850
Benjamin Howard Isbell 7/1/1833 McMinn, Tenn.-9/8/1864
John Wallace Isbell 8/7/1835 McMinn, Tenn.-7/7/1864
Lucinda Missouri Isbell 7/4/1837 McMinn, Tenn.-4/25/1918 m. 7/9/1855 Robert Houson, McMinn Co.
Dennis Rowan Isbell 9/1/1839 McMinn, Tenn. m. 12/28/1871 Emma Callaway

MARY WILSON BROWN DICKINS' BIBLE

Robert Dickins of Person Co., North Carolina, b. in England (1748), d. 1804 Person Co.
Mary Brown, wife of Robert Dickins, d. 12/1809 Granville Co., N. C.
Jesse Dickins, eldest son of Robert and Mary Dickins, d. 1836, Person Co., N. C
Elizabeth Dickins, eldest daughter of above, b. N. C.-d. Virginia
Sally Dickins, daughter of above, b. b d. Person Co., N. C.
Samuel Dickins, son of above,1780 N.C.-7/21/1840 Madison Co., Tn, aged 60
Lucretia Dickins, daughter of above b. N. C., d. Greensboro, Ga.
Martha Dickins, daughter of above, Greene Co., Ga.
Parthenia Dickins, daughter of above, b. Person Co., N. C.
William Dickins, son of above, 9/27/1773 Person Co., N. C.-3/31/1945 Madison Co., Tenn.

Ann Dickins (Mrs. Martin), daughter of Samuel and Jane Dickins, b. Person Co., N. C.
Mary Hennon Brown Clack, only daughter of James and Sally Clack, b. 1808 Person Co., N. C.-d. Lincoln Co., Tenn.
Nancy Pulliam, daughter of John and Elizabeth, 4/22/1750 Granville Co., N. C.-11/29/1871 Panola Co., Miss. Children of William and Nancy Dickins:
Mary Wilson Brown Dickins 11/29/1811 Granville Co., N. C.-1825
Elizabeth Fisher Dickins 9/2/1813 Granville Co., NC-11/22/1844 Madison Co.
Lucretia Moore Dickins 8/28/1815 Granville Co., N. C.-7/10/1859 Phillips Co., Ark. (nee Hicks, E. R.)
William Barnett Pulliam Dickins 7/13/1818 Granville Co., N. C.-11/29/1866 Memphis

Mary Wilson Brown Dickins' Bible continued...

Nancy Pulliam Dickins 3/29/1820 Granville Co., N. C.-2/26/1883
John Robert Dickins 1/21/1822 Granville Co., N. C.-2/15/1887 Panola Co., Miss
Samuel Dickins 8/29/1824 Granville Co., N. C.-3/2/1867
Sally Clack Dickins 6/9/1827 Madison Co., Tenn.-9/11/1843 Fayette Co., Tenn.
Martha Dickins 4/23/1829 Madison Co., Tenn.-4/23/1829 Madison Co., Tenn
William Wilkins Hunt, son of William and E. F. Hunt 5/29/1831 Madison Co., Tenn.-6/19/1838 Madison Co., Tenn.

BIRTHS of Children of William and Harriet Dickins

Virginia- Dickins 12/1/1836 Madison Co., Tenn.-5/25/1857 Panola Co., Miss.
Ann Fisher Dickins 10/25/1838 Madison Co., Tenn.-11/20/1880 Memphis.
William Webb Dickins, only son, 4/28/1849 Panola Co., Miss.-4/20/1916 Batesville, Panola Co., Miss.
Sallie Rooker Dickins 1846 Panola Co., niss.-10/1855 Lafayette Co., Miss.
Roscoe Dickins, son of John and Mary Dickins, 5/22/1845 Madison Co., Tenn.-1/10/1874 Panola Co., Miss.

Mary Elizabeth Dickins, only daughter of Samuel and Virginia, 1847 Madison Co. TN

Sanford Wilbourn Dickins, eldest son of John and Fennie, 1858 Panola, MS 9/11/1862
Jessie Anne Belle Hicks, daughter of Jesse & Mary, 7/23/1835 Madison Co.TN.-2/29/1910

Mary Wilson Brown Dickins' Bible continued...

Imogene Hair Hicks, daughter of Jesse and Mary, 9/6/1848, Phillips Co., Ark.
William Dickins Hicks, son of Jesse and Mary, 7/25/1839 Madison Co.- 12/20/1871
Cornelia Octavia Hicks, daughter of Jesse and Mary, 2/25/1846 Phillips Co., AR
Elizabeth Wilkins Hunt, daughter of William and Elizabeth, 3/6/1834 Madison Co., TN
Robert Hunt, son of William and Elizabeth, 9/27/1836 Madison Co., Tenn.
Sallie Fisher Hunt, daughter of William and Elizabeth, 11/15/1843, Madison Co., Tenn.
Lucretia Moore Dickins Hicks, daughter of Edwin and Lucy, 5/13/1833 Madison Co., Tenn-1853 Phillips Co. Arkansas
Mary Elizabeth Hicks, Lucinda daughter of Edula and Lucy, 3/13/1831 Madison Co., Tenn. Her twin sister was Nancy Pulliam Hicks
Edwin Augustus Hicks, son of Edwin and Lucy, 7/24/1838 Madison Co., Tenn.

Emily Robert Blanch Hicks, daughter of Edwin and Lucy, 1847 Phillips
Lawrence Ewell Talbot, only son of James and Nancy, 1847 Jackson, TN-10/20/1919
Adah Della Talbot, only daughter of James and Nancy, b. Jackson, Tenn.
Robert Dickins to Mary Brown in Virginia (1766)
Jesse Dickins, son of Robert and Mary, in Person Co., N. C., Frances Moore, daughter of Stephen and Grizelda Moore
Elizabeth Dickins, daughter of Robert and Mary, in N. C., to Richard Bland

Mary Wilson Brown Dickins' Bible continued...

Sally Dickins. daughter of Robert and Mary, in N. C., to James Clack

Samuel Dickins, son of Robert and Mary, Ist in 1798 in Mecklenburg, Va. to Jane Vaughan, daughter of James Vaughan, 2nd. in Granville Co., N. C. to Frances Burton, daughter of Robert Burton.

Lucretia Dickins, daughter of Robert and Mary, Granville Co., N. C. to Thomas Moore

Martha Dickins, daughter of Robt and Mary, in Granville Co to Thomas Webb, son of William

Parthenia Dickins, dau of Robt & Mary, 1812 Granville Co., NC to Edward Danoho.

Mary Kennon Brown Clack, daughter of James and Sally, in 1822, Granville Co., N. C. to William F. Smith, son of James and Amy

William Dickins, son of Robert and Mary, 5/23/1810 in Granville Co., N. C. to Nancy Pulliam, daughter of John and Elizabeth Pulliam

Mary W.B. Dickins, dau. of William and Nancy, 8/3/1827 in Madison Co., Tenn. to Jesse H. Hicks, son of Daniel and Mary

Elizabeth Fisher Dickins, dau. of William and Nancy, 8/3/1830 Madison Co., Tenn. to William H. Hunt, son of Wilkins and Lucy

Lucretia Moore Dickins, dau. of William and Nancy, Madison Co., Tenn., 9/8/1831, to Edwin A. Hicks, son of Daniel and Mary

William Barnett Pulliam Dickins, son of William and Nancy, 10/27/1835 to Harriet Wilson Webb, daughter of William and Elizabeth Webb, Madison Co.

Nancy P. Dickins, daughter of William and Nancy, 1/16/1836 Madison Co to James Talbot

John Robert Dickins, son of William and Nancy, 1st 1842 Fayette Co., TN to Mary Hunt, daughter of Wilkins and Lucy Hunt

Samuel Dicksons, son of William and Nancy, 1842,Fayette Co. TN to Virginia Hunt, dau of Wilkins and Lucy Hunt

Mary Wilson Brown Dickins' Bible continued...

Sally Clark Dickins, dau of Wm & Nancy 12/1841-Avery Hunt, son of Wilkins and Lucy
John Robert Dickins, son of William and Nancy, 2nd, 11/29/1854 in Panola Co., Miss. to Fannie Wilbourn, daughter of Sanford and Nancy Virginia Dickins, dau. of William and Harriet, 1856 Panola Co., MS- James A. Hunt
Ann Fisher Dickins, dau of William and Harriet 1857 Panola Co., MS- Robt Abernathy
Jessie A. Hicks, daughter of Jesse and Mary, 7/22/1858 Rankln Co., Miss. to Benjamin T. Estes, son of William and Susan Bates
Elizabeth W. Hunt, daughter of William and Elizabeth, in Madison Co., Tenn. to Henry Glenn, son of James and Emily Glenn
Robert Hunt, son of William and Elizabeth, 1857 in Madison Co., Tenn. to Margaret Mathews, daughter of Edward Mathews
Lucretia Moore Dickins Hicks, dau. of Edwin and Lucy, 1851 in Phillips Co., Ark. to George W. Thompson. Mary Elizabeth Hicks, twin dau of Edwin and Lucy, Phillips Co. AR 1852 Wm Hutchinson
Nancy Pulliam Hicks, twin dau of Edwin & Lucy- Wm Burnett
Edwin Augustus Hicks, son of Edwin and Lucy in Phillips Co., Ark. to Elizabeth Nichols (Ist marriage)
Sallie Fisher Hunt, daughter of William and Elizabeth Hunt 3/1/1860 in Madison Co., Tenn. to James A. Hunt
Edward (George) Bruce b. Scotland-d. Granville Co., N. C.
Benjamin Pulliam, Sr. b. & d. Mecklenburg Co. Va.
Mary Bruce, daughter of Edward (George) Bruce, Granville Co., NC.
John Wilson of Mecklenburg Co., Va., b. England-d. Mecklenburg Co.
Mary Israel, wife of John Wilson, d. Mecklenburg Co., Va.
Elizabeth Wilson, eldest daughter of John and Mary, 5/1/1766 Mecklenburg Co., Va.-5/11/1824 Granville Co., N. C.

Mary Wilson Brown Dickins' Bible continued...

John Pulliam, Sr., eldest son of Benjamin and Mary, b. Mecklenburg Co., Va.-d. 12/11/1809 Granville Co., N. C.
John Bruce Pulliam, eldest son of John and Elizabeth, b. Granville Co., N. C.-d. 6/27/1837 East Tennessee
Burnett Pulliam, Jr., son of John and Elizabeth, b. Granville Co- d. 10/12/1807
Barnett Pulliam, Sr. d. 5/29/1813, Granville Co., N. C.
Mary Israel Pulliam, eldest daughter of John and Elizabeth, 4/21/--Granville Co.
Elizabeth Pulliam daughter of John and Elizabeth, 9/13/1792 Granville Co., NC
Harriet Wilson Webb (Mrs. Dickins), daughter of William and Elizabeth Webb, 5/3/1816 Granville Co. N. C.-6/21/1874 Hot Springs, Ark.
Lucy Wilson Pulliam, daughter of John and Elizabeth, b. Granville-d. Madison Co.
Martha Pulliam, daughter of John and Elizabeth, b. Granville Co., NC-d. Madison Co.
Harriet Wilson Pulliam, daughter of John &Elizabeth, b. Granville Co.-1847 MS
Mary Pulliam, only daughter of Benjamin and Mary, b. and d.Mecklenburg Co., Va.
Benjamin Pulliam, Jr., youngest son of Benjamin Sr., b Mecklenburg Co., Va..
Thomas Wilson, eldest son of John and Mary, b. Mecklenburg Co.-d. Richmond Co.
Harold Wilson, eldest son of Thomas and Elizabeth, b. Richmond Co. d. US Army
Thomas Wilson, Jr., son of Thomas and Elizabeth, b. & d. Richmond Co. VA

Mary Wilson Brown Dickins' Bible continued...

John Wilson Jr.. son of John and Mary, b. Mecklenburg Co., Va. d. Halifax Co.

Isabella Wilson, only daughter of John and Elizabeth, b. Mecklenburg Co., Va.

Miles Wilson, son of John James Wilson, son of John and Tabitha, b. Mecklenburg Co.,
Va.-d. 1832 Louisville, KY. Daniel Wilson, son of John, Hendersonville, KY
Tabitha Wilson, daughter of John & Tabitha,b. Mecklenburg Co.Va.-d. Hendersonville, KY
Euell Wilson, son of John and Tabitha, d. U. S. Navy
Lucy Wilson, daughter of John and Tabitha, b. Mecklenburg Co., Va.
Mary Wilson, daughter of John and Mary, b. Mecklenburg Co., Va.-d.Halifax Co., Va
Phoebe Eliam (Mrs. Collier), daughter of Mary Eliam, b. Halifax Co.,Va-d.1858, steamboat to TX
Nancy Wilson, daughter of John and Mary, b. Mecklenburg Co., Va.-d. Ohio
Mary Cheatham, daughter of Nancy, b. in Kentucky
Eliza Wilson (Mrs. Wingfield), daughter of Thomas and Elizabeth Wilson, b. Mecklenburg Co., Va.-d. New Orleans, La.
Mary Wilson (Mrs. Upshur), daughter of Thomas and Elizabeth Wilson,b. Mecklenburg Co., Va
Harriet Wilson (Mrs. Randolph), daughter of Thomas and Elizabeth Wilson, b. Mecklenburp, Co., Va.-d. Tuckahoe, the Randolph family near Richmond VA
Ann Wilson (Mrs. Upshur), daughter of Thomas and Lucinda Wilson, b.Richmond, Va.

Mary Wilson Brown Dickins' Bible continued...

Benjamin Pulliam, Mecklenburg Co., Va. Ist Mary Bruce, 2nd, Mrs. Hester

John Wilson, Mecklenburg Co., Va. Ist, Mary Israel, 2nd, Tabitha Cheatham

John Pulliam, Sr., son of Benjamin and Mary, in Mecklenburg Co., Va. to Elizabeth Wilson, daughter of John and Mary Wilson

John Pulliam. Jr., eldest son of John and Elizabeth, in Granville Co., N. C. to Temperance Norman, daughter of Thomas and Sallie Barnett Pulliam, Jr., son of John and Elizabeth, Granville Co., N. C. To Margaret

Margaret Norman, daughter of Thomas and Sallie Norman

Mary Pulliam, daughter of Benjamin and Mary, to Mr. Rose

Thomas Wilson, son of John and Mary, m. 1st in Mecklenburg Co., Va. to Elizabeth Vaughn, 2nd in Richmond, Va. to Lucinda Pope

John Wilson, Jr., son of John and Mary, in Halifax Co., Va. to Elizabeth Terry

Nancy Wilson, daughter of John and Mary, Ist in Mecklenburg Co., Va. to Mr. Cheatham, 2nd, in Kentucky to Mr. McCready

Mary Israel Pulliam, eldest daughter of John and Elizabeth, 10/1805 in Granville Co., N. C. to James Butler, son of Isaac and Mary

Elizabeth Pulliam, daughter of John and Elizabeth, 9/1813 Granville Co., NC to William Webb

Lucy Wilson Pulliam, daughter of John and Elizabeth Pulliam in Granville, N. C. to Portious Moore, son of Stephen and Grizelda

Martha Pulliam, daughter of John and Elizabeth, in Granville Co., N C. to Alfred Lane, son of James and Irene Lane Harriet Wilson Pulliam, daughter of John and Elizabeth, in Granville Co., N. C. to James Smith, son of James and Any Smith

Isabella Wilson, daughter of John and Elizabeth, in Halifax Co., Va. to Robert Nelson

Mary Wilson Brown Dickins' Bible continued...

Miles Wilson, son of John and Mary Wilson, in Mecklenburg Co., Va. to Margaret Fields
Daniel Wilson, son of John and Mary Wilson in Richmond, Va. to Henrietta Johnson
James Wilson, son of John and Mary, Richmond, Va. to Susan Pritcherd
Tabitha Wilson, daughter of John and Tabitha, in Mecklenburg Co., Va. to Obediah Smith

Lucy Wilson, daughter of John and Tabitha Wilson, in Mecklenburg Co., Va. to Bennett Marshall
Mary Wilson, daughter of John and Mary, in Mecklenburg Co., Va. to Mr. Eliam.

Footnotes by Harriet (Webb) Dickins

"Edward (George) Bruce was their father and Benjamin Pulliam and Mary Bruce were the parents of my husband's grandfather, John Pulliam, Sr., who inherited from his grandfather the family homestead in Granville Co., N. C. where the remains of both await the resurrection morn. April 28/62 /s/Harriet Dickins"

"Benjamin Pulliam and his wife, Mary Bruce, and John Wilson and his wife, Mary Israel, are all entombed in Blue Stone Church yard of Mecklenburg Co., Va."

"My husband's grandfather, John Pulliam, Sr. and his grandmother, Elizabeth Wilson and his Uncle Barnett Pulliam, Jr., all entombed In family burial ground of my husband's gg-grandfather, Edward (George) Bruce in Granville Co., N. C. /s/ Harriet Dickins" "Barnett Pulllam, Sr. survived his only brother. my husband's grandfather less than four years, he acted as

Mary Wilson Brown Dickins' Bible continued...

guardian to his brother's children until his death and then bequeathed to them.

BENJAMIN AND ELIZABETH DAVIS BIBLE
Of Chatham County From: Rev. War Pension W3783

Benjamin Davis m. Elizabeth Daniel 1/15/1786

BIRTHS

Nancy Davis 12/8/1786
Thomas B. Moon m. Emeliann Davis 8/12/1828, in 19th yr. of his age
Emeliann Moon
Jesse Benjamin Edmond Moon, son of Thomas B. and 1/6/1830-2/11/1930
William Francis Moon 12/17/1830
Woodson D. Moon 2/15/1833
Elizabeth Sarahan Moon 5/11/1835
Lydiann Haseltine Moon 8/7/1837
Rachel Rebeccah Moon 8/6/1841-8/25/1841
Elizabeth Daniel 3/16/1769
Benjamin Davis d. 2/1816 in Jefferson Co., Georgia

Note: Elizabeth Davis, widow, applied for pension 2/24/1845, Walton Co. Ga., will be aged 75 on 3/16/1845. She m. 1/15/1786 Benjamin Davis In Chatham Co., North Carolina (maiden name Elizabeth Daniel). Benlamin Davis d. 2/1816, Jefferson Co., Ga. They had 12 children, two of whom were: Nancy Davis b. 12/8/1786 and John R. Davis (aged 36 yrs. old In 1845, Walton Co., Ga.) Their youngest child was b. 10/11/1813

THOMAS AND ANNA DIXON BIBLE
From: Rev. War Pension W3963

"Thomas Dixon, his Book, bought with his money, price #1. S10, A. D. 1793"

BIRTHS

Thomas Dixon 8/1761
Peggy Dixon 1/16/1803
Ann Dixon 12/4/1771
Hannah Dixon 4/1/1805
Matty Dixon 1/27/1795
Betsy Dixon 7/22/1807
Mary Dixon 12/24/1796
John Dixon 9/13/1809
Anne Dixon 1/23/1799
Thomas Dixon 5/20/1813
James Dixon 1801
Edwin Reeves H. Dixon (grandchild) 6/6/1826

Note: Anna Dixon, widow, applied for pension 2/22/1839, Orange Co., N. C., stating she was b. 12/4/1771 and is widow of Thomas Dixon, 8/1761-4/9/1826. She m. Thomas Dixon 5/1793, Orange Co., N. C., by Rev. William Hodge. Her maiden name was Anna Turner.

ABRAHAM SUDDARTH BIBLE of Sumter
Owner: Mrs. Gamewell Houck, Lenoir, NC

Abraham Suddarth (father of children below) b. 12/28/1767, son of William and Margaret Suddarth
Martha Sumter, daughter of John Sumter, wife of Abraham

Abraham Suddarth Bible continued...

Abraham Suddarth, b. 2/17/1765
Abraham Suddarth m. Martha 2/16/1786.

BIRTHS of Their Children

William Suddarth 6/15/1787 -
Catherine Suddarth 5/11/1797
John Suddarth 4/8/1789
Nancy Suddarth 3/11/1799
James Suddarth 7/27/1790
Abraham Suddarth 6/15/1800
Emanuel Suddarth 10/11/1791-d.y.
Emanuel Suddarth 2/25/1802
Sallie Suddarth 7/27/1793
Thomas Suddarth 8/20/1805
Margaret Suddarth 7/18/1795
Myra Emily Suddarth 5/18/1809

DR. JAMES R. AND DORCAS ALEXANDER BIBLE

James Alexander m. Dorcas Garrison 11/26/1789 whose ages when added is 56 yrs. and 9 mos. What is the sum of each

BIRTHS

Silas Alexander 5/10/1791
Abigail Alexander 11/8/1799
Amanda Alexander 3/6/1793
Hannah Alexander 8/19/1801
Chas Garrison Alexander 8/27/1794
James Rankin Alexander 7/5/1803
Mary Sample Alexander 4/10/1796

Dr. James R. and Dorcas Alexander Bible continued....

John G. Alexander 3/2/1806
Mark Alexander 12/29/1797
Dorcas R. Alexander 12/28/1807

Note: Dr. James R. Alexander applied for pension 5/14/1833. Allen Co., Kentucky, stating he was b. 11/23/1756 In a house standing on the line dividing the states of Maryland and Pennsylvania. 3/22/1834 William Alexander, Mecklenburg Co., N. C. stated he was acquainted with Dr. James Alexander late of said co. Dorcas Alexander, widow, applied 5/9/1839, Allen Co., Kentucky, widow, stating her husband d. 3/11/1836 and that she .. him 11/26/1789 in Mecklenburg Co., N. C. 5/20/1839, Rockvllle. Park Co., Ind., Mark Garrison swore that Dr. James R. Alexander m. Dorcas Garrison In York Co., S. C. 11/26/1789.

EDWIN B. BRIDGERS BIBLE

Edwin B. Bridgers 10/1/1809-6/10/1863, son of William and Mary Bridgers, m. Mary Ann 3/8/1851
Mary Ann Bridgers, wife of Edwin B. Bridgers and daughter of Aaron Atkinson and Sally, his wife, 11/20/1820-4/27/1890

BIRTHS of Their Children

Wm Aaron Bridgers 2/3/1852 - James Franklin Bridgers 3/16/1853

JESSE CROOM BIBLE

BIRTHS of Children of Jesse Croom and Anne Grady, Ist wife
John Croom 1/25/1764
Zilpah Croom 3/3/4/1774
Lyddy Croom 2/6/1772
Mary Croom 9/8/1766
Ann Croom 1/22/1776
Abel Croom 1/20/1769
Elizabeth Croom 4/1/1779

BIRTHS of Children of Jesse Croom and Sarah Ramsey, 2nd wife
Jesse Croom 7/21/1784
Treacy Croom 8/6/1794
Lany Broom 1/28/1790
Major Croom 10/9/1785
Lott Croom 5/27/1797
Hardy Croom 8/18/1801
Wm R. Croom 8/24/1787
Nancy Croom 4/21/1799
Asceneth Croom 4/12/1792

EBENEZER AND MARY DICKEY BIBLE

BIRTHS of Children:
Elisha Dickey 10/20/1785
Grizilla Dickey 6/16/1797
James G. Dickey 2/15/1788
Levi Dickey 4/15/1799
Elizabeth Dickey 3/4/1790
Mary Dickey 5/20/1801
William Dickey 3/18/1792
John Dickey 7/13/1803
Dorcas Dickey 6/16/1793
Margeret Dickey 3/9/1805

Ebenezer and Mary Dickey Bible continued...

Ebenezer Dickey Jr. 4/15/1795 d.y.
Emily Dickey 8/24/1808
Note: Ebenezer Dickey applied for pension 9/4/1832, Simpson Co., Ky., was b. 11/1761 in Pa., lived Rowan Co., N. C. until 1787 when moved to Ky. Soldier d. 6/5/1840. Mary Dickey, widow, applied 12/4/1840, Simpson Co., Ky., was b. 12/22/1765 and m. Ebenezer Dickey 11/1783 or 1784, Rowen Co., N. C. Maiden Name, Mary Graham.

EBENEZER AND MARY DICKEY BIBLE

BIRTHS of Children

Joseph Walker 6/26/1791
Jonathan Walker 6/2/1805
William Walker 5/15/1792
Henry N. Walker 8/16/1807
Edward Walker Jr. 9/7/1795
Susanna Walker 11/5/1709
Martha Walker 11/9/1797
Margaret Walker 4/15/1812
John W. Walker 10/20/1801
Elizabeth Walker 5/30/1815
Samuel Walker 1/30/1802 or 1/31/1803

Note: Edward Walker applied for pension 4/25/1833, Clairborne Co., Tenn., was bb. 1756 N. C., lived Duplin Co. Jane Walker, widow, applied 5/19/1840, aged 69, Claiborne Co., Tenn. m. soldier 5/1/1790 Sullivan Co., Tenn, Richard Russel, Baptist minister. Her maiden name was Jane House, daughter of Frederick House of Hawkins Co., Tenn.

ENOCH NEWTON BIBLE

BIRTHS

Enoch F. Newton 1/27/1849-4/27/1927
Caldona Southerland, wife of Enoch F. Newton, 3/15/1858-7/30/1875
Sarah Margaret Carr 3/16/1851
James Ernest Newton 1/7/1878
Caldona Newton 7/28/1875-9/22/1875
Enoch Alton Newton 12/9/1891
Hiram Joseph Newton 12/13/1879-4/30/1881
Samuel William Newton 11/11/1883
Early Carr Newton 11/5/1881
Mary Ann Newton 2/26/1886
Katie Newton 11/30/1888
Enoch F. Newton to Caldona Southerland 5/7/1874
Enoch F. Newton and Sarah Margaret Carr 2/25/1877

James Ernest Newton and Mary Frances Newton 1/19/1901
Samuel William Newton and Nora Black Williams 11/25/1908
Mary Ann Newton and John Lester Williams 8/4/1909
Early Carr Newton and Emily Frances Wells 9/1912

RICHARD AND PENELOPE BRASWELL BIBLE

Richard Braswell 10/27/1781
Benjamin Braswell 6/28/1795
Delany Braswell 5/14/1782
Patty Braswell 9/19/--
Elizabeth Braswell (Dees) 7/22/1784
Bryant Braswell 10/22/1799
Burrell Braswell 11/30/1787

Richard and Penelope Braswell Bible continued...

Cullen Braswell 4/18/1801
Irvine Braswell 3/2/1790

Note: Richard Braswell applied for pension 10/11/1832, Anson Co., NC was b. 7/1755 Wayne Co., N. C. 7/25/1840 Penelope Braswell, age 79, applies, Anson Co., N. C. Husband d.8/20/1839. She m. 10/1780 Richard Braswell , by Burrell Morning in Wayne Co., N. C. Maiden name, Penelope Blow Matilda Jane, daughter of Cullen and Equela Braswell, b. 6/17/1838, reported that Penelope Braswell d. 8/30/1866. 8/15/1844 Lucresa Braswell, Anson Co., N. C. testified she knew Richard Braswell m. Penelope Blow 10/1780,Wayne Co.NC

GIDEON BYNUM BIBLE

Gideon Bynum, son of Benjamin and Judith of Pitt Co., N. C. 4/24/1785-6/14/1843 m. 2/14/1810 Sarah May, daughter of Benjamin May, Jr., 1/8/1794-7/29/1841.

BIRTHS of Their Children

Benjamin Bynum 2/3/1811-4/1876 m. 9]24/1837 Jedidah Pitt of Edgecome Co.
Fanny Bynum 2/13/1813-7/28/1885 m. 4/2/1829 Jacob S. Barnes
Priscilla D. Bynum 10/10/1815 m. 9/4/1838 John H. Dixon. He d. 11/15/1843
Margaret May Bynum 1/18/1818
Richard Allen Bynum 4/23/1820-9/23/1888 m. 10/3/1841 Mary Amanda Blow. She d. 3/13/1872,aged 56. Lizzie Blow Bynum, his 2d wife, d. 6/7/1888

Gideon Bynum Bible continued...

Tabitha Bynum 5/18/1822-1/28/1891. Gideon Bynum, Jr. 5/18/1824-7/11/1848
Susan Evans Bynum 11/22/1826 m. William Barrett, son of Josiah Barrett and wife, Selina May. John Turner Bynum 9/24/1829-11/16/1885
Joseph Nicholas Bynum 5/17/1832 m. 2/2/1860 Mary Alice Barrett, daughter of Josiah Barrett and wife, Selina May. She d. 2/19/1888, aged 54. 12/18/1888 he m. Margaret A. Sheppard Carolina J. Bynum 1/2/1835 m. Dr. Robert Williams King, son of John King & wife, Sallie Hines. he d. 1/19/1891 Benjamin May Sr. 3/17/1737-8/1808.
Mary Tyson, his wife, 4/6/1748-1/1800.

BIRTHS of Their Children:

James May 1/20/1784-7/25/1825 m. 2/12/1806 Harriet Williams, dau of Robert Williams and wife, Fannie Randolph of Pitt Co., N. C. She was b. 11/12/1786 and d. 12/22/1868. Their Son:James William May 7/24/1820- 5/21/1882 m. 6/25/1844 Tabitha Bynum daughter of Gideon Bynum and wife, Sallie May. She was b. 5/18/1822-d. 1/28/1891.

BIRTHS of Children of James U. and Tabitha May

John Edwin Benjamin May 3/19/1795-4/1884 m. 12/31/1873 Cornelia Joyner. Their dau., Ione Bynum May b. 11/2/1876 m. Travis Hooker
Susan Frances May 6/15/1855-10/6/1908 m. 3/9/1881 Thomas F. Hill. Her 2nd husband was Leon Albritton. James Oscar May 7/23/1849-1/8/1883
Adeline Gertrude May 11/19/1863-11/18/1901 m. 5/10/1882 Francis Marion Dupree. her 2nd husband wan Lorenzo DeVisconti. Her Son: Paul Clifford Dupree 7/29/1883-7/1911.

DUDLEY-EATON BIBLE

Children of Guilford and Anna Bland (Eaten) Dudley

Frances-Elizabeth 2/25/1785 Woodberry, seat of- Col. Benjamin Williams In Johnston Co., N. C.
Frances Bland 6/30/1786 Tweedside, near Fayetteville, N. C. m. 1/26/1815 Dr. Samuel Crockett of Franklin, Tenn.
Julia Ann Eaton 10/16/1788 Fayetteville, N. C. m. 9/11/1810 Dr. Elliott Hickman of Franklin, Tenn.
Theodoric Bland 5/5/1790 at Mill seat, near Fayetteville
Thomas Eaton 8/9/1792 Fayetteville, N. C.
Elizabeth Helen 3/18/1794 Fayetteville. N. C.
Sarah Bland 9/8/1796 on Appomattox River, Prince Edward Co., Va.
Guilford 1122/1799 Prince Edward Co., Va.
Judith Randolph 7/24/1800 Prince Edward Co. m. 5/23/1822 Nicholas I. Long of Maury Co., Tenn.
Caroline 4/28/1802 Cumberland Co., Va.
Virginia m. 8/27/1830 Thomas Woodson Cash, atty, Franklin, Tenn.
Mary Matilda Pugh m. 9/6/1830 James C. Hill of Franklin, Tenn.

JOHN AND ISABEL GRIDER BIBLE
From: Rev. War Pension W358

BIRTHS

John Grider 7/11/1755
Isabel Blair, wife, 12/13/1761
Barbara Grider 12/26/1781
Amos Grider 11/24/1792
James Grider 9/5/1783

John and Isabel Grider Bible continued...

Aaron Grider 1/5/1794
William Grider 5/3/1785
Silas Grider 12/1/1795
John Grider 6/13/1787
Sally Grider 6/9/1798
Moses Grider 11/1/1789
Joseph Grider 7/9/1801
Enos Grider 11/11/1791
Archibald Grider 3/17/1804

Note: 9/22/1853, Isabel Grider, widow, applied for pension, Henderson Co., Tenn., aged 93; she m. John Grider In 1781 by John Connolly, J. P. Her maiden name was Isabel Blair.

James CRUTHIS BIBLE
Of Randolph County
Owner: Mrs. R. T. Guthrle, Sr.
341 Center St, Apt. 3 Salt Lake City, Utah (1950)

James Cruthis 1780 Randolph Co., N. C.-3/22/1872 Sorento Bond, IL
His wife, Lydia Chamblis of Randolph Co., N. C.

BIRTHS of Their Children (all b. Randolph Co., N. C.)

Vincent Cruthis 10/18/1812-4/7/1899 m, 12/22/1832 Martha Williams
Nancy Cruthis 1816-1/20/1892 m. Nathan Willis
Sally Cruthis ---
Jane Cruthis ---
Henry Cruthis ---
Sarah Cruthis ---
John Cruthis ---

ROBERT SHEARER BIBLE
Owner: Mrs. Milton G. Shearer
301 E. College Ave., Lenoir, N. C.

Robert Shearer 7/24/1823-12/2/1895 m. 11/26/1854 Myra Emmaline Coffey 2/20/1836-3/30/1859
Wilborn Coffey b. 5/14/1807 and his wife, Sally, b. 5/1/1812
Milton Gordon Shearer 9/4/1855-1/18/1951 m. 9/25/1884 Mary Annie Elizabeth Estes. Her mother, Rebecca Estes, d. 12/31/1924
Jane Shearer 10/13/1858-11/3/1864

2/19/1860 Robert Shearer m. Martha Matilda Estes 10/11/1837-6/2/1917
Mary F. Shearer 10/31/1861-1/19/1937 m. 3/19/1889 Lee N. Perkins b. 11/3/1844
Myra Shearer 11/8/1863-12/2/1943 m. 7/24/1888 John G. Pulliam b. 8/27/1857

LEWIS AND ELIZABETH CARLTON BIBLE

Lewis Carlton, son of John and Elizabeth, h. 9/12/1758
Elizabeth Eve, daughter of John and Mary, b. 2/26/1762
Lewis Carlton m. Elizabeth Eve 1/18/1781

Their Children

Ambrose Carlton b. 12/30/1781,-Mary, Thomas, John, Lewis, David, Elizabeth, Nancy. William, Milly and Howard.

Note: Thomas Carlton, son of Lewis, applied for pension 1/31/1853, aged 65, Burke Co., N. C. His father, Lewis, d.

Lewis and Elizabeth Carlton Bible continued...

1/13/1827 Wilkes Co., N. C. and his mother, Eve, d. 10/21/1839 leaving following children: Polly Saxton, Elizabeth Hagler, Nancy Pearson, William Carlton, Milly Tucker and Thomas Carlton.

ROBERT FINDLAY SHEARER BIBLE

Robert Findlay Shearer b. 8/5/1768 m. 11/19/1789 Sary Kindall

BIRTHS of Their Children

Betsy Shearer 9/3/1790-6/23/1811 m. 1/22/1807 Joseph Green (Children: Sally Green b. 1/22/1808 and Robert Green b. 8/25/1810)

John Shearer 8/9/1792 m. 4/27/1815 Mary Green
Nancy Shearer 7/6/1794 m. 4/14/1814 Daniel Green (Children: Amy Green b. 4/3/1815 and Susana Green b. 3/4/1818)
Mary Shearer 1/16/1797 m. 8/18/1814 Richard Green (Child: Franky Green b. 7/17/1815)
Sally Shearer 3/24/1799 m. 9/11/1817 Gilbert Hedge
Fanny Shearer 4/19/1801 m. 7/1/1819 m. Joel Reese
William Shearer 3/3/1803 m. 4/9/1822 Anne Reese
Lucy Shearer 1/19/1806 m. 3/11/1824 John Norris
Thomas Shearer 8/10/1808 m. 1/15/1829 Patsy Earthing
Ann Shearer 9/26/1810 m. 3/8/1827 Henry Cook
Grace Shearer d. 10/17/1818

HARDY A. AND CHARITY POPE BIBLE

Hardy A. Pope b. 1/11/1782
Charity Pope, his wife, b. 11/13/1799 m. 3/4/1816

BIRTHS of Their Children

Henry T. Pope 2/27/1818
Susan Caroline Pope 1/20/1832
James W. Pope 8/11/1820
Alexander Pope 1/21/1834
John T. Pope 12/25/1821
Charity Lee Pope 1/1/1836
Mary Ann Pope 9/28/1827
Sarah Delilah Pope 5/9/1838
Elizabeth Pope 4/14/1830

DEATHS

Charity Pope 9/7/1848, aged 49 yrs.
Hardy A. Pope 5/16/1854

Note: Hardy A. Pope applied for bounty lands 1/7/1851, aged 70, Robeson Co., N. C. 2/12/1856 Henry T. Pope, gdn of Sarah D. Pope, minor child of Hardy A. Pope, deced, applied for same bounty lands for daughter.

JOSHUA L. HORN, JR. BIBLE

BIRTHS of Josiah Horn's Children

Priscilla Horn 11/12/1805
Mary Ann Horn 10/19/1810
Henry H. Horn 11/25/1807

Joshua L. Horn Bible continued...

Joshua Laurence Horn 11/2/1813
Abisha B. Horn 3/19/1809-d.y. Old Henry Thorpe h. 12/18/1760
Priscilla, his wife, b. 4/12/1765

BIRTHS of Children of Henry and Priscilla Thorpe

James Thorpe 12/1/1783
Henry Thorpe 9/5/1793-d.y.
Frances Thorpe 3/25/1785
Anselm Thorpe 1/6/1796
Jesse Thorpe 8/15/1786
Ann Thorpe 10/21/1797
Silvy Thorpe 5/9/1788
Henry Thorpe 3/7/1800
Ann Thorpe 12/10/1789-d.y.
Prissy Thorpe 11/23/1802
Phebe Thorpe 10/27/1791
Rebekah Thorpe 2/6/1807
Jacob G. Fort 7/17/1804-7/25/1828
Priscilla, daughter of Josiah and Frances Horn.

Children of Jacob G. and Priscilla Fort

Frances Fort 12/5/1823
Mary Elizabeth Fort 3/26/1829
Jacob C. Fort 6/24/1827

BIRTHS of Children of Reubin and Frances Bradley

Phebe Bradley 99/25/1817 -
Frances-Bradley 8/4/1820

Joshua L. Horn Bible continued...

Lucinda Bradley 5/23/1819
Anselm Bradley 6/22/1822

BIRTHS of Children of William J. and Lucinda Mercer

Sally Ann Mercer 9/I/1837 - Jesse-R. Mercer 2/10/1843

BIRTHS of Children of Joel Horn

Harris Horn 2/5/1778-
Rebecca Horn 3/18/1788
Howell Horn 11/1/1780
Mathew Horn 6/11/1792
Hardy Horn 12/24/1782
Etheldred Horn 11/27/1793
Milbrie Horn 2/14/1786

ROBERT AND LUCY HARRIS' BIBLE

BIRTHS of Children of Robert Harris and Lucy Stubblefield

Nancy Harris 1/4/1780
Thompason Harriss 12/21/1789
Robert Harris 12/2/1782
Susannah Harris 4/20/1792
Richard Harris 11/11/1785
Fanny Harris 3/16/1795
Elizabeth Harris 8/12/1787
John Harris 1/10/1798 Polly Harris 7/9/1800

Note: Lucy Harris applied for pension 2/1/1844, White Co., Ill., widow of Robert, res. of N. C. She was b. 11/17/1759 and m.

Robert and Lucy Harris' Bible continued...

Robert Harris 1/1779 in Gullford Co., N. C. by Rev. Thomas Mullins Her maiden name was Lucy Stubblefield, daughter of Dicky Stubblefield. Robert Harris d. 6/9/1806 Rockingham Co., N. C. Lucy Harris d. 4/16/1848 White Co., IL. leaving children: Nancy Trousdale, Robert Harris, Richard Harris, Susannah Taylor, Francis Taylor and Sally Trousdale

REUBEN ROGERS, SR. BIBLE

Reuben Rogers to Temperance James 12/15/1767
John Rogers.to Nancy Smith 1802
Reuben Rogers, Jr. to Elizabeth Emerson 8/3/1810
Joseph Rogers to Frances Gardner 1820
Michael Cody to Rebecca Rogers 1/18/1818
James W. Wellborn to Louisa A. Cody 5/9/1839
Marloo M. Cody to Rachel English 12/3/1839
M. D. Cody to Frances Carr 2/24/1852.
J. N. Cody to M. E. Cherry 1/16/1845
Reuben Rogers, Sr. b. 11/1/1735 Northampton Co., N. C.
    Temperance James b. 8/24/1751.

    BIRTHS of their Children:

John R. Rogers 4/23/1769
Reuben Rogers Jr. 9/10/1782
Collin Rogers 5/7/1790
Faith Rogers 5/19/1771
Joseph Rogers 2/9/1784
Abner Rogers 10/19/1798
Mary Rogers 10/28/1772
Rebecca Rogers 1/2/1786
Sarah Rogers 10/15/1794

Reuben Rogers, Jr. Bible continued...

Clara Rogers 8/11/1774
Pheby Rogers 11/5/1778
Temperance Rogers 10/21/1780
Nancy Rogers 3/1/1776
Asenath Rogers 11/11/1792

BIRTHS of Children of Nancy Rogers Saxon

Wiley Saxon 1/19/1814 -
Nancy Wilkinson Saxon 8/14/1804
Temperance Saxon 5/16/1800
Louisa Saxon 5/27/1807
Elizabeth Davis Saxon 3/18/1802
M. D. Cody 9/27/1824
Marian Cary 8/18/1822
Newton Cary 12/14/1824
Temperance Swain 10/4/1819
John Thomas Swain 4/3/1823
Stephen James Swain 12/25/1820
Josiah Thomas Darden 6/13/1824
Martha Ann Baker 2/26/1828
Temperance Sophronia Cody 10/30/1821
Marion M. Cody 12/3/1818
Jeptha M. Cody 1/15/1823
Louisa Amanda Cody 8/5/1820

DEATHS:

Temperance Rogers 4/9/1819
Louisa Amanda Welborn
Wiley Saxon 1/19/1814 10/26/1862
Missouri E. Cody 10/26/1849

Reuben Rogers, Jr. Bible continued...

Faith Darden 4/15/1810
Jeptha M. Cody 1/21/1864
Rebecca Cody 12/5/1851
M. D. Cody 1/25/1875
Michael Cody 3/8/1832

Temperance Sophronia Cody 9/20/1822

JOSHUA B. ANDERSON BIBLE

Joshua B. Anderson 10/5/1805-7/17/1877 m. 1/26/1836
Martha W. Sherman 10/18/1818-3/10/1887
James H. Anderson 12/5/1836-1/7/1910 m. 1st, 1/7/1880 Kitty Griffin, 2nd, Ella Patterson b. 1853. Mary E. Anderson 9/3/1838 m. 3/13/1854 Powell Ford.
Theopholis Sanders Anderson 11/13/1840-7/22/1903 m. 1/1/1867

Elizabeth J. Garrett 9/24/1842-6/30/1870
Mary Evaline Garrett 2/24/1844-8/22/1913- 12/21/1871
Elnora Anderson 2/24/1842- m. 1st, James Allan, 2nd, Powell Ford
Adelia Anderson 9/11/1844-.. Addison Rainey
Martha V. Anderson 3/7/1847-m. S. Bradford
Elmira J. Anderson 3/5/1850-6/17/1880 m. 4/18/1867
August L. Henley 9/27/1844-
Narcissa C. Anderson 10/4/1853-.. Ist Green Reynolds, 2nd, Frank Sutton
Susan R. Anderson 10/5/1855-1/3/1922 m. Ist, 2/24/1881 A. L. Henley who d. 10/16/1891 2/16/1898, W. J. Woodward
John M. Anderson 2/9/1857-1/22/1904 m. Willie Powell.
Nancy R. Anderson m. James Rutledge

Joshua B. Anderson Bible continued...

BIRTHS of Children of Theopholis Sanders Anderson

Floyd Augusta Anderson 12/3/1867-6/26/1903 m. Florence
Eustace Anderson 7/3/1873-7/6/1956 m. Caroline Woodward
Florence Elizabeth Anderson 10/23/1875 m. 7/6/1910
Lawrence Caswell Hamilton 5/15/1877-10/17/1960
John Preston Anderson 7/1/1878-9/4/1899
Ivan Anderson 6/17/1883-11/30/1957 m. Caroline
Ch of Eustace: Theopholis, Byron, Lawrence,Robt, Ruth, Wilson, Dorothy

JONAS STANHOPE CLONINGER

BIRTHS

Jonas S Cloninger 1/17/1841 ---Julius Johnson Cloninger 10/11/1861

Sarah A. E. Cloninger 9/20/1841, wife, Sarah Ann Elizaheth
Alburtus Hill Cloninger 12/9/1864   Edward Lee Cloninger 8/13/1867

Maggie Eva Cloninger 5/12/1870
Maynardie Peterson Cloninger 9/28/1872
Lawson Vance Cloninger 5/8/1875
David Melanchan Cloninger 10/28/1877
Sallie Isabella Cloninger 6/1/1882
Loy Odell Cloninger 3/17/1886
Moses Cloninger 4/8/1802
Lucinda 1/17/1841
Isabel Cloninger 2/22/1808
Laban Cloninger 12/8/1829

Jonas Stanhope Cloninger Bible continued...

Wiley W. M. Cloninger 8/10/1837
Lawson Cloninger 4/13/1826
Jonas Stanhope Cloninger
Sidney Cloninger 2/9/1828
Addelaide Cloninger 2/13/1844
Jonas S. Cloninger to Sarah A. E. Adderholt 10/1/1860 by Rev. J. R. Peterson.

DEATHS

Sallie Isabella Cloninger 2/18/1883
Julius Johnson Cloninger 2/23/1883
Maynardie Peterson Cloninger 7/16/1897
J. S. Cloninger 1924

Sarah Ann Elizabeth Cloninger 1923
Maggie Eva Stroupe Cloninger 4/12/1936
Dr. Lawson Vance Clonlnger 11/2/1928
D.M. Cloninger 11/1949
Alburtus Hill Cloninger 1938
Edward Lee Cloninger --
Loy Odell Clonineer --

WILLIAM PENN TAYLOR BIBLE
Of Louisburg, Franklin County
Owner: Miss Jessie T. Webb
1360 Harbert, Memphis, Tennessee

MARRIAGES

William P. Taylor to Rebecca 5/5/1813
William H. Foster to Ann Eliza 7/18/1833 at White Hall

William Penn Taylor Bible continued...

Moses F. Adamson to Mariah K. Taylor ---
William M. Ware to Martha H. 4/11/1840
Corydon Spencer to Mary R. 10/29/1840
Elizabeth Jane to R. B. Edwards 7/6/1853
Susannah F. Foster to John A. Ligon 11/15/1854

BIRTHS

Ann E. Taylor 3/6/1814
William F. Taylor 11/5/1825
Mariah K. Taylor 9/1/1815
Isaac H. Taylor 2/5/1828
John P. Taylor 5/111817
Rebecca R. Taylor 1/10/1830
Mary R. Taylor 1/8/1819
Willie P. Taylor 12/28/1831
Martha H. Taylor 3/26/1823
Elizabeth Jane Taylor 11/19/1834
Corydon Seth Spencer d. 10/8/1890
William P. Spencer d. 2/18/1905 at Ralelgh, North Carolina

BIRTHS

Eras Taylor Foster 4/16/1834
William H. Foster 6/4/1838
Susannah H. Foster 5/25/1836
William Penn Spencer 3/6/1844
Ann Elizabeth Spencer 8/17/1853
Mary H. Spencer 1/25/1850

William Penn Taylor Bible continued...

DEATHS

Patty Taylor 1/25/1835 at house of her son, W. P. Taylor in town of Louisburg, N. C.
Rebecca J. Taylor 5/8/1837. She was the wife of W. P. Taylor 24 yrs. and 3 days. She was the mother of ten living children at her death and had several to die quite young.
William P. Taylor 8/11/1838 at Wesley. Haywood Co.. Tennessee
Mariah K., daughter of William E. and Rebecca J. Taylor, 9/7/1841 at Wesley, Haywood Co., Tennessee.
Fras Taylor Foster 4/3/1835

ELISHA UZZEL BIBLE

Note: Elisha Uzzel m. Tabitha Boon.

BIRTHS -

Elisha Uzzel 1/29/1787
Tabitha Uzzel, wife of Elisha Uzzel, 8/30/1797.

Their Children:

James N. Uzzel 10/16/1917
Benjamin Edger Uzzel 1/9/1830
Rebecca Uzzel 10/29/1819
Martha Ellen Uzzel 2/14/1832
William D. Uzzel 10/24/1821
Peyton Randolph Uzzel 7/5/1834
Mary Ann Uzzel 7/21/1823
Luezer Elizabeth Uzzel 1/31/1837
Sarah Jone Uzzel 1/9/1826

Elisha Uzzel Bible continued...

Amanda Washington Uzzel 11/30/1839
Henry Thomas Uzzel 10/20/1827.

DEATHS:

Elisha Uzzel III 4/1867 in Franklin Co., N. C.
Tabitha Boon Uzzel 2/1863 in Franklin Co., N. C.
Benjamin Edgar Uzzel, son of Elisha and Tabitha, 5/16/1832

SAMUEL MAURICE WEBB BIBLE

James Webb, son of John and Amy Webb, 11/17/1779-8/3/1827 in Person Co., N. C.
James Webb son of John Webb and Ann Hunt Smith, daughter of James Smith, in Granville Co., N. C. 2/17/1803
Ann H. Smith, daughter of James and Amy Smith, b. Granville Co., N. C. 9/5/1784-d. Person Co., N. C. 8/18/1840
James Webb son of John Webb and Ann Hunt Smith, daughter of James Smith of Granville Co. N. C. 2117/1803
Alexander Smith Webb, sonof James Webb, b. in Person Co., N. C., 2/21/1804-d. Orange Co., N. C. 8/1849
Alexander Smith Webb m. Adeline Stanford in Person Co., N. C.

John P. (Pomfret) Webb, son of James Webb, b. Person Co., N. C. 1/17/1807, drowned at New Albany, Ind. 5/1846
John P. (Pomfret) Webb, son of James Webb and Melissa Daniel, daughter of Lewis Daniel. m. in Person Co., N. C.
James L. (Lewis) Webb, son of James Webb, b. Person Co., N. C., 6/20/1811-d. 2/10/1860, Memphis, Tenn.
James L. (Lewis) Webb, son of Jones Webb and Ariana Shepard, dau. of Thomas Shepard, m. in Person Co., N. C.

Samuel Maurice Webb Bible continued...

William H. (Henry) Webb, son of James Webb, b. Person Co., N. C. 2/23/1814-d. Nashville, Tenn. 12/1891
William H. (Henry) Webb m. Elizabeth Patillo In Granvllle Co., N. C. (later m. Margaret Kerr)
Mary A. (Ann) A. (Amy) Webb, daughter of James Webb, b. Person Co., N. C. 5/13/1817
Mary A. A. Webb m. John P. (Pomfret) Blackwell in Person Co., NC
Samuel H. (Maurice) Webb, son of James Webb, b. Person Co., N. C., baptised In Person Co., d. Raleigh, Tenn 7/21/1873.
Samuel M. Webb, son of James Webb and Elizabeth L. (Lucinda) Webb, daughter of Wm S. (Smith) Webb, m. in Williamson Co.,TN 9/8/1847

Robert C. (Clark) Webb, son of James, b. Person Co.NC 8/20/1824
Robert C. Webb m. Elizabeth Dortch in Fayette Co., Tenn. He m. 2nd, Mrs. Sue Webb Green, near Memphis, Tenn.
Thomas H. (Hunt) Webb, son of James Webb, b. Person Co., N. C. 3/5/1823-d. In Person Co. 4/20/1828
William S. (Smith) Webb, son of William Webb, b. in Greenville Co., N. C. 2/7/1776-d. 8/3/1866 in Williamson Co., Tenn.
William S. Webb, son of William Webb, m. Mildred A. Turner, dau. of Josiah Turner 3/4/1804 in Orange Co., N. C.

Mildred A. Wehb, daughter of Josiah Turner, b. Orange Co., N. C. 5/26/1780-d. Williamson Co., Tenn. 4/16/1830
Frances Y. (Young) Webb, daughter of Wm, b. in Orange Co.N.C. 10/8/1804
(James) G. Scales m. Frances Y. Webb, daughter of William Webb, 2/4/1819

Samuel Maurice Webb Bible continued...

James S. Webb, son of William Webb, b. Orange Co., N. C. 10/12/1805-d. in Williamson Co., Tenn.
James S. Webb, son of William Webb m. A. E. T. Ewing 9/18/1849
Mary E. Webb, daughter of William Webb, b. Williamson Co., Tenn. 12/27/1806-d. Maury Co., Tenn.
Mary E.Webb m. A. (Archie) P. Hughes 12/2/1824
Henry Y. Webb. son of Wm Webb, b. Williamson Co.7/23/1808-d. 10/9/1835
Henry Y. Webb, son of William Webb, m. Martha Jane Hughes 5/29/1834 in Williamson Co., Tenn.
Sallie Webb daughter of William Webb,4/27/1810-8/23/1834 b. Williamson Co., TN.
William Webb, son of Wm Webb, b. Williamson Co.12/15/1811-d. 1/16/1840

William Webb m. Mary M. Hughes 2/2/1837
Thomas E. Webb, son of William Webb,12/2/1813-7/10/1815
John R. Webb, son of William Webb, 9/4/1815-8/26/1836
Mildred A. Webb, daughter of William, b. Williamson Co., Tenn. 7/31/1818-d. Crawfordsville. Miss. 1871
Mildred A. Webb m. Nathaniel F. Scales 10/12/1837
Rachel M. (Martin) Webb, daughter of William Webb. b. 2/7/1820
James S. Orvie m. Rachel M. Webb, daughter of William S. Webb, 2/28/1844
Samuel (Smith) Webb, son of William Webb,6/30/1822-1863 Williamson Co

Samuel (Smith) Webb, son of William S. Webb, m. Adalaide Battle, daughter of William Battle, 4/18/1849 In DavIdaon Co., Tenn.

Samuel Maurice Webb Bible continued...

Josiah T. Webb, son of William Webb, b. Williamson Co 7/19/1824

Josiah T. Webb m. Margaret I. Gilleland 12/30/1845
Elizabeth I. (Lucinda) Webb, daughter of William S. Webb, b. 12/20/1826 in Williamson Co., Tenn.-d. Memphis. Tenn. 6/12/1872
S. M. (Samuel Maurice) Webb, son of James Webb. m. Elizabeth L. Webb, daughter of William S. Webb, 9/8/1847 in Williamson Co., Tenn.
William Smith Webb, son of S. M. and E. L. Wehb, b. Williamson Co., Tenn. 6/3/1848-d. Fayette Co., Tenn. 8/15/1848

N. (Nathaniel) Macon Webb, son of S. H. and E. L. Webb, b. Memphls, Tenn. 6/10/1849, baptised 3/11/1860 by Rev. R. C. Grundy-d. 10/13/1878, Memphis, Tenn.
James Henry Wehb, son of S. M. and E. L. Webb, b. Memphis, Tenn. 6/17/1851, baptised 3/11/1860 by R. C. Grundy-d. 10/22/1886 Glendale MS Robert Maurice Webb, son of S. M. and E. L. Webb, b. 8/3/1853 in Williamson Co., Tenn., baptised 3/11/1860-d. 8/2/1872 Crittenden Co. AR.

Walter Webb, son of S. M. and E. L. Webb, b. 11/16/1856 Memphis, Tenn., baptised 3/11/1860 by R. C. Grundy-d. 6/24/1917 Memphis
Paul Webb, son of S. M. and E. L. Webb, b. Memphis, Tenn. 7/16/1859, baptised 3/11/1860 by R. C. Crundy-d. 11/19/1941 Memphis.
Paul Webb, son of S. M. and E. L. Webb, m. Tempe Taylor, daughter of Fanny L. Taylor and Wiley P. Taylor, 2/16/1904, in Memphis, Tn.

Samuel Maurice Webb Bible continued...

Lizzie Sue Webb, daughter of S. M. and E. L. Webb, b. 2/26/1862 in Memphis, Tenn., bapt.by Mr. Doak in 1864-d. 2/25/1944, Miami, FL
Henry H. Maury, (should be Hal Hancock) son of Abram Maury and Lizzie Sue Webb, daughter of S. M. and E. L. Webb, m. Shelby Co.TN 10/20/1885
Lewis Percy Webb son of S. M. and E. L. Webb, b. Memphis, Tenn.
1/31/1866-d. 7/15/1886, Memphis, Tenn.
Tempe Taylor, dau of Wiley P. and Frances Lenow Taylor, b. 12/23/1872 in Haywood Co., Tenn.-d. 12/18/1957, Memphis, Tenn.
Jessie Taylor Webb, daughter of Paul Webb and Tempe Taler, b. 3/3/1905 In Memphis, Tenn., baptised at Central Methodist Church

JAMES PORTER BIBLE

BIRTHS

James Porter 3/7/1777
Catharine Porter 1/22/1783

Their Children:

Andrew Porter 6/9/1802
Mary Porter 5/4/1815
Sarah C. Porter 11/25/1804-2/12/1860
James Porter 9/4/1818
Jane N. Porter 11/28/1806
John Porter 5/7/1820
Elizabeth Porter 1/22/1810

James Porter Bible continued...

John J. Porter 8/1/1822
Robert H. Porter 11/22/1811
Leroy Porter 6/7/1824
William Porter 1/5/1813
Susan Porter 7/17/1826

SAMUEL CHANCY BIBLE

Samuel Chancy, son of John and Sarah, 5/24/1821

BIRTHS

Samuel Chancy, son of John and Sarah, 1/27/1798
Julian Chancy, wife of above Samuel, 3/13/1801
Mary Ann Chancy 3/27/1822
John James Chancy 3/5/1834
Eliza Elizabeth Chancy 12/8/1823
Samuel Jackson Chancy 3/15/1836
Sarah Jane Chancy 1/27/1826
Julian Rebecca Chancy 3/27/1838
Lucy Mariah Chancy 11/9/1827
Frances Caroline Chancy
Nancy Dandridge Chancy 4/17/1830 5/8/1840
William Henry Chancy 2/28/1832

JOSEPH HENRY BIBLE

Joseph Henry d. 9/14/1814 Orange Co., Ind. Wife, Mary Shearer b. 1756 m. 1/1/1781 in Lincoln Co., N. C.

BIRTHS of Children, Lincoln Co., N. C.

Mathew Henry 6/1783
William Henry 10/25/1794
Polly Henry 8/2/1805
Nancy Henry 8/21/1785
Hugh Henry 1/5/1796
Hugh Henry 2/7/1798
Philip Henry 12/6/1787
Malcolm Henry 12/1/1810
Hannah Henry 6/26/1792
Sally Henry 6/6/1790
Joseph Henry 5/12/1801

Note: Mary Henry, wid. applied for pension. Joseph's brothers, John and Moses Henry, were killed in Battle of Kings Mountain His sister, Hannah.

Hamilton b. 1754 (still living in 1836). Mary lst applied 7/1/1844 from Carroll Co., Ark. In 1845 she was in Johnson Co., Mo. 2/7/1846 she was in Washington Co., Ind. 9/6/1951 she was in Taney Co., Miss with son, Malcolm who had moved there in 1848.

JOSEPH HENRY BIBLE

Joseph Henry b. 1765 Lincoln Co., N. C.-d. 9/22/1816 Buncombe Co., N. C. Wife, Mary McCashland (or McCasland) b. 1772-d. 5/8/1848 Buncombe Co., N. C. m. 5/17/1792 Lincoln Co., N. C.

BIRTHS of Children

John Henry 11/13/1793
William Henry 6/12/1803
Joseph Henry 8/28/1796
Farmer Henry 5/27/1806-6/3/1808
Nancey Henry 11/14/1798
Alexander Henry 1809 James Henry 1/24/1801

Note: Nancey, James and Alexander survived their mother. Alexander appointed 3/1852, Buncombe Co., N. C. to admr est. of his mother, Mary Henry. Nancey Henry m. William Cudger

NEILL CHANCY BIBLE

Neill Chancy to Elizabeth Baldwin 8/25/1836
Elizabeth Chancy to Calvin McFarlin 8/20/1860
Stephen L. Chancy to Frances Anthony 12/29/1869
Frances Ann Chauncy, wife of Stephen Loyd Chauncy - sons Stephen
Loyd Chauncy and Samuel Bogue Chauncey, d. 1/2/1902 (diff. sp.)

Neill Chancy Bible continued...

BIRTHS

Neill Chancy 5/7/1808
Mary Baldwin 10/15/1816
Elizabeth Baldwin 1/14/1809
Frances Ann Chauncy, wife of Stephen Loyd Chauncy, and Bone Stephen Loyd Sr. and Samuel Bogue Chauncey, d. 1/2/1902
James Chancy 7/25/1837
Penelopy Chancy 5/22/1845
Mary Ann Chancy 7/2/1839
Charles Chancy 2/25/1847
July Ann Chancy 10/29/1840
Frances Ann Chancy 2/17/1850
Elizabeth Chancy 6/29/1842
Sally Columbia McFarland 11/9/1861
Neill Chancy 12/24/1843

DEATHS:

James Chancy 9/6/1837
July Ann Chancy 6/29/1855
Neill Chancy 7/13/1864
James Baldwin 2/16/1852
Mary Ann Chancy 12/11/1858
Calvin P. McFarland 4/28/1862, aged 30 yrs., 10 mos., 18 days

JAMES HENRY BIBLE

James Henry b. 1753 Cumberland Co., Pa.-d. 2/20/1841. Wife, Elizabeth Russell, b. 1761 m. 5/11/1780.

BIRTHS of Children

William Henry 4/4/1781
Mathew Henry 4/6/1792
Jane (Jennie) Henry 5/20/1782
Polly Henry 8/29/1794
Hannah Henry 1/20/1783
Enos Henry 9/9/1796
James Henry 3/21/1788
John Henry 10 11/1798
Elizabeth Henry 3/2/1790
Resign Henry 8/15/1800
Eliza Russell 11/27/1810
Nancy Smith 11 13/1812
John Garson 12/21/1815
Betsey Caroline 11/3/1815
James Henry Newton 10/22/1817
Joseph Harvey 5/17/1819-12/11/1819
E. W. Harvey 4/9/1821
Jane Henry b. Lincoln Co., N. C. m. 2/15/1810 James Mitchell (b. 11/9/1780)

James Henry applied for pension 6/25/1833 from Lincoln Co., N. C. Widow, Elizabeth Henry's pension approved 8/28/1848 while residing Marshall Co., Tenn.

NATHANIEL BROCK of Rowan County

BIRTHS

Nathaniel Brock 2/3/1757-1818;-F. Huddlestone 1778
Mary Huddlestone 6/1/1753-1785
Sarah Eaten 5/3/1755-1851
Frances Brock 9/27/1779-1817 m. 1814 J. McDonald
Enoch Brock 9/611782 m. Sarah Ethredee in 1804
Amy Brock 10/22/1786 m. W. Taylor in 1805
Polly Brock 11/24/1788 m. P. Sainer in 1823
Joshua Brock 10/29/1790
Caleb Brock 1/6/1793 m. 1820 H. F. Jones

Moses Brock 9/12/1795
Benjamin Brock 9/12/1797 m. R. Y. Kimbro
William Brock 8/1/1799 m. 1823 F. S. Chaffin
Elizabeth Brock 5/29/1801 m. 1823 L. Ward
Penny Brock 4/10/1806 m. T. Smoot
Noah Brock 7/14/1803
Sally S. Brock 3/26/1814-1818

THOMAS MAXWELL BROCK BIBLE

James Nathaniel Brock 12/6/1810-6/18/1886 m. 10/2/1834 Mary Maria Maxwell
Mary Maria Maxwell 1/8/1814-4/7/1849, aged 35 yrs., 3 mos., bur. Liberty Graveyard In Davie Co., N. C. (formerly Rowan Co.)

Children:

John William Clark Brock 10/27/1835-d. in prison at Point Lookout 7/19/1864

Thomas Maxwell Brock Bible continued...

Enoch Nathaniel Brock 6/18/1837-d. of typhoid fever 1861, bur. beside his mother in Liberty Graveyard.

Thomas Maxwell Brock b. 4/30/1839 m. Beulah Cornelia Brunt 3/19/1866 at home of per parent., William and Elizabeth Lindsey (Lunn) Brunt, near Farmington, in Davie Co., N. C.
Sarah Elizabeth Brock b. 10/18/1840-d. Texas, near Clarendon
James Victor Brock 12/20/1842-2/14/1870, aged 27 yrs., 1 mo., 4 days at Union Springs, Alabama
Mary Maria Brock 6/9/1845-10/5/1846, aged 1 yr., 3 mos., 26 days

    Children of Thomas Maxwell Brock and Beulah Cornelia Brunt

Victor Ximona Brock 8/23/1867-7/27/1905, bur. Farmington graveyard
Mary Elizabeth Brock b. 10/19/1869 m. Thomas Joseph Conrad 2/19/1896
James William Brock b. 7/30/1873 m. Agnes Martha Hubert 5/11/1904
Edgar Huddleston Brock 3/27/1876-2/5/1904, bur. In Summit Lake Cemetery, Minnesota, m. Mabel Wilcox 3/28/1902 and had Edgar Lee Brock b. 8/22/1903
Moses Maxwell Brock b. 5/25/1876
Lee Franklin Brock b. 7/5/1880
Ora Brunt Brock b. 7/16/1882

    Children of Thomas Joseph Conrad and Mary Elizabeth Brock Conrad
Winton Brock Conrad b.-1896 Beulah Eliza Conrad b. 4/7/1899
Thomas Joseph Conrad 3/25/1902-11/14/1903
Richard Max Conrad b. 6/20/1904

JOHN McDONALD BIBLE

John McDonald 7/24/1791, Fayetteville, N. C.
Elijah Ann McDonald 4/29/1817
Emaline McDonald 10/24/1819, Hillsborough Point, Fayetteville
Carmon McDonald 2/25/1821, Fayetteville, N. C.
Margaret McDonald 9/22/1822, Fayetteville, N. C.
Charles Morris McDonald 11/22/1823, Fayetteville, N. C.
Catherine McDonald 8/13/1825, Rockingham, N. C.
Helen McDonald 11/24/1827, Cheraw
John McDonald 7/9/1829, Cheraw
Philip McDonald 6/6/1832, Covington, La.
Samuel Perkins 10/23/1818, Wilkes Co., Ga.
Catherine Perkins 10/11/1849, Wilcox Co., Ala.
Jenny Perkins 5/11/1856
Helen McDonald m. E. Perkins 4/29/1846, New Orleans

LEWIS BLEDSOE BIBLE

BIRTHS

Lewis Bledsoe 12/15/1756 Sandy Creek, Bute Co., N. C.-d. Granville Co., N. C. 6/24/1833 m. Penny Moore b. 2/6/1766, in Granville Co., N. C. 12/5/1780.

BIRTHS of Their Children

Yancey Bledsoe 11/30/1781 - Beckey Bledsoe 5/1/1795

Jincey Bledsoe 4/7/1784
Thurza Bledsoe 12/31/1798
Terrel Bledsoe 5/12/1786
Washington Bledsoe 12/21/1801
Cechoniah Blednoe 7/31/1788

Lewis Bledsoe Bible continued...

Alice Bledsoe 6/4/1804
Mahala Bledsoe 9/30/1790
Allanda Bledsoe 1/13/1806
Elkins Bledsoe 2/15/1793

Note: Lewis Bledsoe was carried to Wake Co., N. C. when an infant, in 1810 or 1811 removed to Granville Co., N. C. where applied for pension 2/5/1833. Fanny Bledsoe, widow, applied for pension 11/8/1836, Granville Co. (alive in 1852)

JACOB BROWN BIBLE

BIRTHS

Jacob Brown 8/3/1761 on Jumping Creek, near Columbia, S. C., son of Jacob Brown (12/11/1736-6/28/1785) and wife, Ruth (8/14/1740-10/8/1810).
Jacob Brown m. 3/9/1786 in Washington Co., N. C., Elizabeth Bird, b. 1/28/1769. He d. 8/21, 8/23 or 8/28/1838 (all dates shown in pension).

BIRTHS of Children of Jacob and Elizabeth Brown

Ruth Brown 10/10/1787
Rebecca Brown 2/8/1799
William Brown 10/9/1789
Bird Brown 10/20/1801
Thomas J. Brown 9/15/179-
Jacob Keen Brown 1/28/1804
Sarah Brown -/4/1794-3/25/1797
Malinda Brown 1/5/1807
Mary Brown 11/5/1796

Jacob Brown Bible continued...

BIRTHS

Jacob Logan, son of J. K. Brown, 818/1829 in Scott Co.. Va.
Matthew Moore Brown 8/7/1830
Lewisah Gains Brown 4/7/1832
Their mother d. 4/27/1832

RICHARD CAMPBELL BIBLE
From: Rev. War Pension

BIRTHS

Richard Campbell 3/20/1755, d. 6/13/1844, Hickman Co., Tenn.

BIRTHS of Children of Richard Campbell and wife, Susannah

Mary Campbell 2/28/1783   Jane Campbell 3/19/1785
Richard Campbell m. Rachel 10/1789 in Rockinghum.Co., N. C.

BIRTHS of Children of Richard and Rachel Campbell

Hiram Campbell 4/11/1790
Richard Campbell 4/3011797
Smithey Campbell 12/16/1791
William Campbell 7/11/1799
John Campbell 8/9/1793
Wiley Campbell 12/28/1804
Elizabeth Campbell 8/27/17--
Tubal Campbell ---

Richard Campbell Bible continued...

Note: Soldier enlisted from Montgomery Co., N. C., applied for pension 7/11/1833, Perry Co., Tenn. Rachel, widow, applied for Pension 10/1849, aged 80 yrs., Perry Co., Tenn.

WILLIAM BROCKETT BIBLE
From: Rev. War Pension W24665

BIRTHS

William Brockett 6/26/1748
James Brockett 2/21/1790/1
John Brockett 2/4/1778
Thomas I. Brockett 7/21/1792/3
Benjamin Brockett 4/18/1775
Mary and Betsy Brockett 8/15/1795
Jesse Brockett 8/9/1777

Patsey Brockett 10/25/1797
William Brockett, Jr. 3/24/1782/3
David Taler Brockett 12/12/179-
Elisha Brockett 11/9/1786
Fanney Brockett 10/21/1813
Frederick Brockett 1/7/1788/9
Marget Brocket 1/11/1794
Merada Brocket 10/24/1813
Benjamin Brockett m. 11/19/1809, aged 31 his wife 22 yrs.
Minerva? Brocket m. 12/23/1830, aged 22 yrs,
Marada Brocket m. 6/21/1832, aged 22 yrs, 9 mos., - days.

Note: Widow, Patsey Brockett, applied for pension 6/18/1839, aged 88 yrs., White Co., Illinois. She m. William Brockett 10/1/1771 at Newbern, North Carolina. Husband d. 5/3/1821.

INDEX

ABBOTT: Dorothy D., 26

ABERCROMBIE: Cynthia, 123; Elizabeth, 123(2); Isabella, 123(2); James, 123(3); Margaret, 123(2); Mary, 123; Rebecca, 123(2); Susannah, 123(2)

ABERNATHY: Jane C., 519; Robert, 540

ACKER: Elizabeth, 202; Ella, 263, 264(2); H. H., 263, 264; Mary C., 263,264; P. B., 263; Sue, 263; William, 264; William H., 263; Willie, 263

ADAMS: Abigail, 369; Alfred, 369; Alford, 368; Alfred, 369; Benjamin Franklin, 287; Charley Gillum, 287; Charlie, 368; Clotilda, 445; George, 286, 287; James Nealy, 286; Jesse Arrington, 287; John, 286, 445; John Arch, 286; John McLeod, 368; John Wisdom, 286; Katie, 368; Leonard Hamilton, 287; Lucinda Holland, 287; Margaret Susan, 287; Martha Newberry, 287; Mary Ella, 368(2), 369; Mary Jane, 368, 369(2); Mary Retincey, 287; Maude Eliza, 368; Minnie S., 236; Minnie Savannah, 236; Nancy Olive, 286; Nattie, 368; Nettie, 369; Nona Bell, 369; Nona Belle,368; Olive, 286; Olive Welch, 287; Robert, Rev., 239; Samuel David, 368,369(3); Sarah, 286; Sarah Elizabeth, 287; Sarah Proctor, 287; Thomas Alfred, 368, 369; Walter Brannon, 368; Walter Branson, 369; William Sims,287; Winston, 369; Zachariah Taylor, 287

ADAMSON: Moses F., 566

ADDERHOLT: Sarah A. E., 565

ADDINGTON: Delilah, 365(2); Mary, 365; William, 365

AIKIN: Margaret, 172

ALBRITTON: Leon, 553

ALEWINE: Sara Hamilton, 232

ALEXANDER: Abigail, 547; Amanda, 547; Annie, 401; Charles Garrison, 547; Dorcas, 547, 548; Dorcas R., 548; Hannah, 547; Hugh C., 197; James R., 547, 548; James Rankin, 547; John G., 548; Julius H., 20, 328; Mark, 548;Martha, 96; Martha Isabella, 30; Mary Sample, 547; Miss, 225; Ruth, 362; Sarah Harriet, 30; Silas, 547; William, 450, 548
ALEXANDER, REV. MR.: Minnie S., 236

ALFORD: Andrew Jackson, 505; Columbus Augustin, 505; Elizabeth Laland, 505; Ella Linyear, 506; Francis Adner, 505; G. A., 506; George Benton, 505; Green H., 505; Green Haywood, 505, 506; Rebecca Jones, 505, 506; Salina Blanche, 505; William Leoria Haywood, 505

ALLAN: H. A., 399; James, 563

ALLEN: Arva, 260; Bannister, 260; Caroline Elizabeth, 71(2), 72, 73; Charlotte, 260; Garrett, 323; James Owen III, 323; John Showell, 71, 73,260; Leroy, 260; Mary, 167; Nancy, 260; Renee, 323; Ruth Linton, 71, 73;Sally, 150; Thompson, 260

ALLISON: Catherine, 113; Hugh, 113(2); Margaret, 113; Martha, 113; Mary, 427; Robert, 113(2); Robert Turner, 113; Robert Turner, Dr., 113; Sarah, 113; Sarah Turner, 113; Thomas, 113(2)

ALMON: Bonnie Lee, 26

ALSTON: Sarah, 228

AMAZI: Julius, 229; Sylvanun, 229

ANDERSON: Ada Hamlin, 300; Adelia, 563; Amos, 358; Baylis E., 358; Benjamin, 357; Beriman D., 358; Byron, 564; Caroline, 564; Catherine, 251; David, 358; David C., 223; Dennis, 224; Dorothy, 564; Edmond W.,

(Anderson continued...)

223; Elizabeth, 223, 358; Elmira J., 563; Elnora, 563; Elvira Eugenia, 300; Eustace, 564(2); Florence Elizabeth, 564; Florence Eustace, 564; Floyd Augusta, 564; George, 306, 358; Harriet, 223; Isaac, 357; Ivan, 564; James, 223, 358(2), 359; James Edward, 299; James H., 563; Jannet, 358; Jasper V., 223; Jinny A., 224; John, 6, 223(2), 336, 357(2), 358; John Bonjon, 299; John F., 223; John J. Coker, Mrs., 298; John M., 563; John Preston, 564; Joshua B., 563, 564; Josiah Eldridg, 223; Lawrence, 564; Marey, 358; Margaret, 5, 6, 336; Mariah, 223; Martha, 223; Martha V., 563; Mary E., 563; Mary Valira, 299; Merium, 358(2); Moses, 223; Nancy R., 563; Narcissa C., 563; Oliver, 358; Robert, 358, 564; Robert B., 358; Ruth, 564; Samuel, 358; Sarah, 358; Summerfield, 358; Susan ., 563; Theopholis, 564; Theopholis Sanders, 563, 564; Thomas Hamlin, 8; Thomas W., 250, 251; William, 358; William C., 223; William Norris, 300; William P., 358; Wilson, 564

ANDREWS: Elizabeth, 123

ANGEL: John, 303

ANIL: Francis Permelia, 262, 267

ANTHONY: Forest, 518; Frances, 575; Mell, 518; Ollida, 518

APPLEBY: T., 40

ARDIS: Polly, 245; Sarah, 245

ARLEDGE: Annie Dorcas, 156; Elsworth Nun, 156; Etelka, 156; Glenn, 156; H. P., 156; Harriet, 156; Horace Volney, 156; Israel, 156; Israel Clement, 156; Jennie Grace, 156

ARLEGE: Clementine, 387; J. B., Rev., 387

ARMESBURY: Sarah, 53

ARMSTRONG: Alice, 370; Annie, 370; Barbara, 371; Dawson T., 370; Edward, 370(4), 371; Edward Hall, 370; Huldah, 370; Isham, 370; John, 371; Martha Ann, 370; Martha Jane, 370; Mary, 370(2); Mary Eliza, 371; Pauline, 370; Richard James, 370; Samuel Horton, 370(2); Sarah Isabella, 370; Sarah, 370; T. J., 370(2), 371; Thomas J., 371; Thomas James, 370(3), 371; William Freeman, 370(2); Wilson Alderman, 370(2)

ARNOLD: Alston, 251, 252; Ann H., 312; Ann Hendricks, 251, 252(2); Benjamin, 251, 252(2); Benjamin Jr., 251; Benjamin Sr., 251; Charity, 251, 252; Edmund, 251; Edward, 251; Hendricks, 251, 252; John, 252; Kezziah Camp, 251; Malinda, 252(2); Martin, 251, 252; Sarah, 252(2); Temperance, 251; Temperance H., 312; Temperance Hamilton, 252(2); Thomas, 251, 252; William, 251; Winifred Washington, 252(2)

ARRINGTON: Martha, 504

ARTERBERY: Benjamin F., 405; Benjamin H., 405; Elizabeth, 405; Lucinda B., 405; Martha R., 405; Mary L., 405; Moses A., 405; Nancy A., 405; Thomas, 405; William F., 405; Wilson C., 405

ASBELL: Mary Thomas Evens, 473

ASBERRY: Daniel, Jr., 25

ASH: Alexander Fleming, 227; Dovey, 227; Elijah McWhorter, 227; Elizabeth, 227; Isabella F., 227; James, 227; Jennet, 227; John, 227; Mary Hunter, 227; Rachel, 227; Robert Rutherford, 227; William, 227; William Jr., 227

ATKINS: Sarah, 145; Statia, 356(2)

ATKINSON: Aaron, 548; Mary Ann, 548; Sally, 548

AULD: Josiah Freeman, 285

AUSTIN: John, 530; Thelma, 424

AVERY: Luvena, 145; Selina, 474

AYCOCK: Lois Johnson, 226

AYRES: Elizabeth, 464

BAILEY: Alfred, 383; Amelia T., 384; Arthur A., 384; Baylus C., 384; E. Thurlo, 384; Elizbeth, 401; Emma L., 384; John T., 384; Loretta, 384; Marinthis L., 383; Mary C., 384; Mattie B., 384; Minnie M., 384; Nancy, 383; Nancy E., 384; Nancy P., 383; Pat, 25; Rosa A., 384; Susan B., 383; Theodocia Eu, 384

BAKER: Alice, 209; Alice Reedy, 448; Anna E., 448; Anna Mariah, 356; Charles Edward, 448; Charles Keyser, 448; Edward B., 356; Edward Bonneace, 356; Felix Walker, 448(2); German, 448, 449; German, Jr., 448; Hannah, 350; Henry Roland, 448; James Denton, 448; Jane, 110; Jim Ella, 449; John, 209, 356; John G., 356; Joseph, 355, 356; Lois, 355; Martha,224; Martha Ann, 562; Mary, 208, 356; Mary Elizabeth, 355, 448; Mary Etta, 448; Mary N., 195, 268; Polly 504, Rebecca Bowen, 448; Reese Henderson, 448; Richard, 208; Robert L., 356; Robert Little, 356; Samuel, 284; Sarah,209; Thomas Jefferson, 356; William DeKay, 448; William N., 356; William Rucker, 448

BALDRIDGE: Catherine, 463; Daniel, 463; Hugh, 463; James A. J., 463; John, 463; Lucinda, 463; Nancy S., 463; Polly, 463; Robert, 463(2); Sarah, 463; Sarah J., 463; Wilson, 463

BALDWIN: Elizabeth, 575, 576; James, 576

BALE: Amanda, 253; Caroline Emeline, 253; James Alfred, 253; John, 253; Matilda Moore, 253

BALL: Beaufort Watts, 309; E., 359; Elan Sophia, 262; Elias, 350, 359; Elizabeth, 266, 275; Ella Sophia, 267; Fanny, 266, 275; Florence C., 262,267; Francis Parmely, 275; Harris, 266, 275; Huldah, 262, 266, 267;

(Ball continued...)

Huldey, 266; Huldy, 275; Jeremiah, 266, 275; Jesse, 266, 275; John, 266(3), 275, 309; John Minyard, 262, 267; Lydia, 359(2); Martin, 262, 267, 275; Martin M., 266; Mary, 266; Mary Driscilla, 266; Mary Priscilla, 275; Mattie I., 262, 267; Minyard, 266, 275; Nancy, 266, 275; S. M., 274; Sally, 266, 275; Samuel, 262, 267; Samuel H., 266; Sarah, 266; Simeon, 275; Simeon P., 262, 266, 267; Stephen, 266, 275; Walter Jeremiah, 262, 267

BALLENDER: James Alexander, 285

BALLENTINE: Jo, 192

BAMER: Genny, 87; Jane, 88

BANKS: Martha E. Battle, 504

BARGER: Rebecca, 68

BARKER: Joseph Sanford, 349

BARKSDALE: Adelaide M., 296; Elihu, 226

BARNES: Aaron, 410; Alfie, 412; Ann, 410, 411; Arch, 411; Bennett, 412; Berry, 410; Blount, 410; Carolina, 410; Clary, 410; Dina, 410; Eacy, 410; Fanney, 411; Feriby, 410; Florence, 412; Frances, 411, 412; Frank, 410; George, 410(2), 411; George Washington, 412; Gerret, 410; Giles, 411;Hannah, 411; Harriet, 411; Harry, 411; Hector, 411; Henry, 412; Isaac,411; Jacob S., 552; James, 519; Jane, 411(2); Jarmon, 411; Joe, 411, 412; John, 412; Jones, 410; Joshua, 412; Julia, 410; Laura, 412; Lewis, 410; Louisa, 412; Lucy, 412; Mariah, 411(2); Mariam, 411; Marina, 410; Martha, 412; Martha Frances, 412; Mary, 410, 411; Mary Elizabeth, 412; Mike, 411; Mima, 410; Ned, 411; Pen, 410; Peter, 410; Prissy, 412(2); Rebecca, 410; Rosa, 412; Rose, 411; Sam, 410; Sam Perry, 412; Sarah, 412; Sary, 410; Sherod, 410(2); Sylva, 412; Tom,

(Barnes continued...)

411; Toney, 412; Venas, 410; Warren, 411; Washington, 412; William, 412; William Henry, 412

BARNETT: A. Evin, 47; Addie, 46; Agnes, 65; Anna, 46; Anner May, 47; Emma, 47; Florence, 46; Florence Eller, 47; Hannah, 187; Jesse C., 47; John, 46(2), 47; Lorene, 54, 64; Lorene B., 57, 385; Peter, 46; Ray, 46; Will, 47; Willie, 46; Willie E., 47

BARNHILL: Calvin, 378; Eliza, 378(2); Elizabeth, 378; Ellen, 378; James, 377, 378; John, 378; Nancy, 377; Robert, 377; Susan, 377, 378; William, 377

BARR: Joseph William, 453; Moses L., 451; Nancy, 453; Retina Ann, 453

BARRETT: Elizabeth, 501; Jacob, 501; Josiah, 553; Mary, 501; Mary Alice, 553

BARRON: A. I., 344; Archibald, 343; Archibel, 343; Barron, 343; Benjamin Glenmore, 167; Eliza, 343, 344; Elmer, 344; Fannie, 343; Fannie Stewart, 343; Glenmore Benjamin, 169; Jane, 228, 229(2), 343; John, 344; John Pressley, 167; Lou, 479; Lucy Anna Bynum, 169; Mary A., 344; Mary E., 344; Mary L., 343; Mary Locke, 167; Mary N., 343, 344, 480; Philo Conner, 167; Preston DeKalb, 167; Rachel, 230; Rebecca A. E., 343; S. D., 343; S. L., 343(2); Samuel Preston, 167; Thomas, 343(2), 344, 481(2); Thomas A., 343; W. H., 344; W. I., 343; W. M., 343; Wallace Monroe, 481; William, 343

BARROW: Thomas, 454

BARRY: Aletha Keziah, 26, 27; Richard, 28

BARTON: E. F., Mrs., 479; Eliza E. A., 168; Ellen Elizabeth, 409; Ernest Fred, 480; Glenmore B., 167; Isaac, Rev., 477; J. T., 344; Jesse Hix, 168; John G., 167; Lucy Leora, 480; Margaret, 343; Martha, 477;

(Barton continued...)

Mary Locke, 168; Philo Conner, 168; Robert Ernest, 480; Rutherford, Rev., 409; S. D., 167, 168; William, 344

BASKIN: Isabella, 244, 304

BASS: E. R., 333; Emie V., 332; Emmie, 333; Emmie Inez, 333; Emmie V., 332; F. E., Mrs., 485; Gretchen, 333; Henry, Rev., 240; J. L., 332, 333; Natalie, 333(2); Richard, Dr., 119; Sallie G., 333; W. L., 333; William Leonidas, 333

BATES: Barbara Christine, 86; Emily, 171; Susan, 540; William, 540

BATTE: Edward L., 206; James Henry, 206; John W., 205

BATTLE: Alfred, 504; Antoinette Thomas, 503(2); Betsy, 504; Calvin William, 503; Calvin Williams, 503; Fred, 504; Henry Luther, 503(2); James Branham, 504; John Branham, 503; John William, 503; Joseph Harris, 503; Larkin, 504; Lawrence, 504; Louisa Marian, 503; Martha Elizabeth, 503; Mary, 504; Mary Ann, 503; Nancy Caroline, 503(2); Nicholas W., 504; Nicholas William, 503; Pattie, 504; Polly Baker, 503(2); Robert Augustus, 503(2); Thomas W., 504, 506; Thomas William, 503; Thomas, Rev., 503(2),504; William, 570; William, Capt., 504

BATTS: Joseph, Capt., 413; Mary, 413

BAXTER: Andrew, 169; Cynthia, 169; Eli H., 169; James, 169; John H., 169; Mary, 169; Richard, 169; Thomas N., 169

BAYLING: Catherine, 129; John, 129

BEAIRD: Frank, Mrs., 138

BEAN: Elizabeth, 444

BEARD: Rodney, 323

BEARDEN: William E., 332(2)

BEATTY: Mary, 278

BEAUCHAMP: Mary Ardell Ivy, 481

BEAUFORD: T., 479

BECHMANN: John, Rev., 351

BELCHER: Arrela T., 105, 159; Arrelia T., 106; Arrella T., 158; Carrie T., 105, 106, 158, 159; Elias, 105, 106(2), 158, 159(2),160; John, 160; Johnie, 105, 158; Joseph Elias, 105, 158; Koa Delia, 106; Mary E., 105, 158; Polly Ann, 106; Pollyann, 159; Posey, 105, 106, 158, 160; Roa Delia,105, 159; Roa Della, 158; Tennessee, 105, 106, 158, 159; Thomas, 105, 158

BELL: B. E., Mrs., 244; Eliza Jane, 354; Elvira, 216; Martha, 78; Melissa, 504; Minnie, 515

BELLING: Abigail, 252

BELLINGER: Rev., 74, 75

BELLS: Rev., 168

BELOTTE: Jacob, 254; Sarah, 256

BERNARD: Annie, 63

BETHSON: Elizabeth, 296

BIRD: Elizabeth, 581

BIRT: Lucy, 246

BISHOP: Albertha, 45; Alburpha, 43; Beauford G., 46; Carrie, 106; Cleveland, 44; Edith Abigail, 43; Elijah Defate, 43; Elijah I., 46; Eliza, 44; Eliza Jane, 43; Eliza L., 43; Evie, 43; H. J., 43, 44(2), 45, 46; Helen, 294; Henry, 45(2); Henry Jeff, 43, 46; Henry Jefferson, 43, 45, 46; Henry Simpson, 43, 45; Isaac Newron, 43; James Alms, 44; James E., 46; Jane N., 46; Jesse Lee, 44; Jo Parris, 182; John Jeff, 43; L. J.,44; Liza Jane, 45; M. L., 44; Martha E., 43; Martha J., 45; Mary, 43, 45; Mary E., 43; Mary Elizabeth, 44-46; Marzie Lee Nora, 43; Polly Ann C., 105, 106; Pollyann C., 158; Susan, 38; Talithalums, 44; Tex Anner, 38; Tusarah, 43, 45

BLACK: Catherine, 392; Catherine Mary, 391; Charles, 391; D. L., 168; Docia T., 391; Elizabeth, 165, 383, 391; Elma Bynum, 169; Flora A., 391(2); Isador, 391; Isodor Eugenia, 392; Isodor Eugenia Priscilla, 392; J., 392; J. S., 391; James, 391; James S., 392; James Solomon, 391; Jane H., 326; John J., 391(3), 392; Lemuel, 496; Malinda Jerusia, 391; Martha Frances Sardenia, 392; Mary Ann, 391; N., 392; Nancy, 392; Nancy J., 392; S. Victoria, 392; Samuel Thomas, 391; Sophia, 168; Susana, 391(2); Susanah Victoria, 391; Thomas P., 391; Vincent, 391; Wade Will, 391; William, 57, 95, 391; William M., 391; Zillah Pass, 496

BLACKSTOCK: Clara, 216; Daniel, 216(2); Effie, 216; Elizabeth, 216(2); Elvira, 216; Fannie, 215; Floyd, 216; Francis, 216; Henry, 216; James, 215, 216(2); John, 216; John L., 216(2); K., 215; Kennie, 216; Kindred, 216; Kindrid, 215, 216; Leroy, 216; Lizzie Mae, 216; Loucinda, 215; Lucinda, 216; Marah, 215; Martha, 216; Nancy, 215, 216; Nola, 216; Ona, 216; Susan, 215; Susana, 215; William, 215; William B., 215

BLACKWELL: John P., 568; Josiah, 123; Michael J., 339; Richard, 123; Samuel J., 262, 267

BLAIR: Drury, 385; Isabel, 555; James, 385; James J., 385; John F., 385; Polly, 385

BLAND: Anna, 554; Frances, 554; James, 402; Richard, 538; Theodoric, 554(2); Theodric Benjamin, 490

BLANTON: Agness Alene, 425; Andrew Pinky, 425; Axem Fready, 425; Carl Green, 425; Flora Lenora, 425; Greenberry, 425; Huston Lee, 425; Ida May, 425; Ira Bull, 425; Jacob Deva, 425; James Ody, 425; Kenon Shilet, 425;Maria E., 426; Mary, 425; Mendel Cletous, 425; Viola Lorene, 425

BLASSINGAME: Easley, 290; Elizabeth, 290; James, 290; Nancy, 290; Obedience, 290; Polly Ann, 290; Robert Easley, 290; Samuel Easley, 290; Thomas, 290(2)

BLEDSOE: Alice, 581; Allanda, 581; Beckey, 580; Cechoniah, 580; Elkins, 581; Fanny, 581; Jincey, 580; Lewis, 580, 581; Mahala, 581; Terrel, 580; Thurza, 580; Washington, 580; Yancey, 580

BLIZZARD: Ellie E., 81; S. E., 82

BLOUNT: Charles Worth, 491; Edmund, 491; Elizabeth, 472; James, Capt., 458; John, 458; Martha, 458; Mary, 491; Mary Clayton, 491

BLOW: Mary Amanda, 552; Penelope, 552

BLYTHE: James, Rev., 387

BLYTHEWOOD: D., Rev., 177

BOBBINS: Mary An, 400

BODDIE: Basheba, 433; Bennett, 433; Elijah, 433; Elizabeth, 433; George, 433; Mary, 433; Mourning, 433; Nathan, 433, 504; Temperance, 433

BOGGS: Eliza Ann, 48

BOLT: Pheobe, 307

BOMAR: Barbery A., 109; Francis C., 109; Hope, 529

BOND: Ann Eliza, 389; Baker, 470; Charles Stanhope, 389; Edm., 467; Edmund, 470; Elizabeth, 468, 470; Guy Hamilton, 389; James, 467, 469, 470(2); James McCarver, 389; Lewis Baker, 468; Lizzie Kate, 389; Mahaly, 389; Mary, 467, 469; Mary Adah, 389; Mary Bell, 389; Nancy, 468; Richard, 468, 469; S. F., 389; Sorento, 555; Stephen Findley, 389; Stephen Homer, 389; Thomas, 285; W. E., Mrs., 467; William Leon, 389; Winefred, 468

BONELL: Anthony, 170

BONNELL: Rebecca, 170

BONNER: Ann L., 49; Eliza Ann, 48; Elizabeth Boggs, 50; Irvine H., 48; John L., 48; Mary C., 48; Oliver Y., 48; Rebecca Jane, 50; T. J., Rev., 48, 49

BOOKER: Nancy, 385

BOOKOUT: Faster, 162; Joycy, 415

BOON: Tabitha, 567

BOONE: Anna, 353; Cinthia Ann, 353; Daidamia, 353; Daniel, 353; Higgason Grubbs, 353; Ira, 352; Isaiah, 353; Levi, 353; Lucy, 353; Nancy, 353; Polly, 353; Samuel, 353(2); Squire, 352; Suire, 353; Susanna, 353; Thomas, 352

BORDEN: N., 40

BOREN: Lydia, 525

BOSS: Eugene, 487; Lucy, 487

BOSTICK: J., Rev., 282; Raymond, Mrs., 389

BOSWELL: Ethel I., 230; Mary, 427(2)

BOTHWELL: Ann Milledge, 320; James T., 320

BOUNDS: Lou, 340, 341

BOUNETHEAU: Anne, 197; Peter, 197

BOURDEAUX: Alice, 371

BOURQUIN: John Lewis, 12, 298; Margaret, 12, 298; Sophia, 12, 298

BOWEN: Rev. Mr., 350(2)

BOWERS: William, 111

BOWES: Francis, 13; Rachel, 13

BOYD: Charles M., 264; Eleanor, 125; Hugh M., 351; Joseph, 4; Keziah, 351; Nancy, 351; Rev.,298; Robert C.,108;Sarah Jane,451; William,351-2

BOYKIN: Burwell, 14, 17; Edward, 14; John, 17; Mary, 14; Sally, 14; Sally Wyly, 17(2); Thomas Lang, 17(3); William Hamilton, 17

BOYLSTON: Polly, 252

BRADBERRY: Alethia, 490(2), 491; Charles, 491(3), 492; Charles W., 490; Edmund B., 491, 492; Edmund C., 490; Elizabeth, 490, 491; Elizabeth A., 492; Elizabeth Ann, 490, 491; James Edward, 491; John, 491,492; Joseph,490; Joseph C., 490-492; Martha, 491; Mary, 490, 491(2); Mary Ann, 491; Mary B., 491(2); Mary Blount, 492; Penelope, 490,491; Richard, 491, 492; Richard B., 491; Richard R., 490; Sarah,490(2),492; Sarah Ann, 491;Sarah S., 490, 492; W. E., Sergt., 491; William, 490, 491; William B., 490(3), 491(2), 492; William R., 491

BRADBURY: Joseph Crency, 490, 491(2)

BRADFORD: Anna Maria, 7, 337(3); Anne Maria, 7; Elizabeth, 474; Frances, 303; Hariot, 303; John, 474; John Mitchell, 303; John S., 7(3), 337;Mary, 303, 304; Middleton, 303; Nancy, 474; Nathaniel, 304; Robert Rivets, 303; S., 563; Susan, 303; Vermeille, 7(2), 337; William, 474; William Wade, 303; Winfret, 303

BRADLEY: Anselm, 560; Frances, 559; George Walton, 443; John, Sr., 443; Lucinda, 560; Minnie, 54; Phebe, 559; Sarah, 443

BRADWELL: Alexander Moultry, 194; Alexander Mountry, 268; Annie Campbell,194; Daniel, 194-196, 268, 269; Eleanor Jane, 194; Elenor Jane Gordon, 268; Emily Angeline, 194, 268; Francis Orland, 195, 269; Herbert Burr, 269; Herbert Durr, 195; Irene Gordon, 195(2), 269; Isaac Gordon, 194,268; James Sumter, 194-196, 268, 269; Leila Ramelle, 196, 269; Leiler Remelle, 195; Lelle Ramelle, 195; Louis Philip Taylor, 196, 268(2); Louis Phillip Taylor, 194; Louise Philip Taylor, 269; Marion Gordon, 195,269(2); Mary Catharine, 194, 268; Mary Catherine, 269; Matilda Caroline, 194, 268; Thomas, 194(2), 195(3), 196, 268, 269; Thomas Maclon, 194;Thomas Marion, 268

BRAMLETT: Malinda, 266

BRANCH: Willis, 446

BRANNEN: Allie Gertrude, 33

BRANNON: Alice Belle, 70; Daisy Rosalie, 70; Francis Marion, 70; James Bruce, 70; John Benjamin, 70; John Wesley Lee, 70; Joseph Monroe, 70; Lois Alice, 70; Mildred Arlivia, 70; O. Murray, 70; Robert Columbus, 70; William Manson, 70(2)

BRASWELL: Benjamin, 551; Bryant, 551; Burrel, 551; Cullen, 552; Delany, 551; Elizabeth, 551; Irvine, 552; Lucresa, 552; Molly, 171; Patty, 551; Penelope, 551, 552; Richard, 551

BRETT: Alice Virginia, 501(2); Allen Virginia, 501; Aurelius, 501; E. D.,501; Edith, 501; Elisha D., 501; Elisha D., Jr., 501; Elisha D., Sr., 502; Elizabeth, 501(3), 502; Jacob, 501; James, 501; James Patrick, 501; Martha Odella, 501; Mary Elizabeth, 501; Pulaski, 501

BRICE: Adolphus L., 109; D. M., 109(2); George, 403, 525, 526; John, 403,525, 526; Joseph, 403, 525, 526; Mary C., 109

BRIDGERS: Edwin B., 548; James Franklin; Mary, 548; Mary Ann, 548 William Aaron, 548

BRIDGES: Harriet Adeline, 383

BRINKLEY: Mary, 35

BRINSON: Asa, 430; Charles, 429(2), 430, 431; Daniel, 430(2); Elizabeth, 429-431; George, 486; George H., 487; James, 430; John, 431; John L., 429-431; John Smith, 431; John William, 486; Lizzie, 487; Lovenia, 431; Mamie G., 487(3); Martha, 486; Martha S., 486; Mary, 430; Mary Smith, 429; Mathew, 430; Meaty, Mrs., 430; Nora, 429; Persia, 430; Sarah L., 429; Silas, 430; Smith, 430; Stativa,430; Susannah Slade, 429

BRISTER: Benjamin, 23; Calvin, 23; Calvin, Mrs., 23; Dolly Louise, 24; Eunice Thompson, 22; Jane, 24; Vinson Vastine, 24

BRITTON: Julia Johnson, 81; Mary, 335

BROCK: Amy, 578; Benjamin, 578; Caleb, 578; Edgar Huddleston, 579; Edgar Lee, 579; Elizabeth, 578; Ella Angeline, 204; Enoch, 578; Enoch Nathaniel, 579; Frances, 578; James Nathaniel, 578; James Victor, 579; James William, 579; John William Clark, 578; John, Mrs., 193; Joshua,

(Brock continued...)

578; Lee Franklin, 579; Mary, 239; Mary Elizabeth, 579; Mary Maria, 579; Moses, 578; Moses Maxwell, 579; Nathaniel, 578; Noah, 578; Ora Brunt, 579; Penny, 578; Polly, 578; Sally S., 578; Sarah Elizabeth, 579; Thomas Maxwell, 578, 579(2); Victor Ximona, 579; William, 578

BROCKETT: Benjamin, 583(2); Betsy, 583; David Taler, 583; Elisha, 583; Fanney, 583; Frederick, 583; James, 583; Jesse, 583; John, 583; Marada, 583; Marget, 583; Mary, 583; Merada, 583; Minerva, 583; Patsey, 583(2); Thomas I., 583; William, 583(2); William, Jr., 583

BROGDON: Addie Inez, 339, 341; Alice Cornelia, 339; Anna L., 339; Anna Leonora, 339; Bertha Lawrence, 340; Cecil Eugene, 340, 341; Elizabeth P., 338; Esther Lillian, 340(2); George Albertus, 340, 341; Harriet Elizabeth, 340(3); Harriet Rebecca, 339; Jake, 339, 341; jane Adelaide, 339; Joel Davis, 338; Joel Edwin, 340(2), 341; Joel Thomas, 339; John B., 339; John Bagnal, 338, 340, 341; John Bagnall, 340; John Ingram, 339(2), 340; John R., 339; Julius Leon, 340(2), 341; Malle Demetrius, 338; Margaret Eudora, 339; Mary Amanda, 339; Sally Melvina, 339; Samuel McDonald, 340; Sue, 340(2); Susan Frances, 339; Susie, 341; William Graham, 339, 340; William Turner, 339

BROOKER: Clem M., 221

BROOKS: Betsy, 352; Elisha, 352; Frank, Mrs., 382; Jane Washington, 312; Joe H., 382; John Wesley, 352; Jordan, 472; Lavina, 352; Matilda, 352; Nancy, 352; Obediah, 352; Stanmore, 352; William Butler Brooks, 352

BROSARD: Ann, 403(4), 525(2), 526; Mary Ann, 403, 525; Peter Andrus, 403(2), 525, 526

BROWN: A., 220; Abigail, 52; Alexander, 473; Allen, 474; Amelia Selina Gwyn, 474; Amelia Selucia Gwyn, 510; Ann, 473; Avery Lenoir, 510; B. L., 399; Badger L., 398; Bird, 581; Caroline Matilda, 198; Dempsey, 398; Eliza Florence, 53; Elizabeth, 97(2), 398, 473; Ellen Ann, 52; George E., 398; George W., 364; Hamilton, 474(3); Hamilton Allen, 474, 509, 510; Hamilton Allen, Col., 474, 510; Hamilton, Major, 474; Hannah, 52; Hannah E., 53(2), 54; Henry, 398; Hugh, 474; Hugh Thomas, 474, 509(2); Hugh Thomas, Capt., 474; J. K., 582; Jacob, 581, 582; Jacob Keen, 581; Jacob Roberts, 198; James, 201, 247, 398, 473; James B. Gordon, 510(2); James Chambers, 97; James Hamilton, 510; Jane, 366; Jane Amanda, 364; John,473, 474(2), 510; John Alonzo, 97; John Henry, 399; John Logan, 582;Joseph, 52(3); Laura Iantha Medora, 97; Lewisah Gains, 582; Malinda, 581;Margaret, 474; Margaret Eugenia, 97; Mary, 52(3), 399, 538, 581; Mary Ann Maria, 398; Mary Elizabeth, 96; Mary Lenoir, 474, 510(2); Mary Selucia,510; Matthew Moore, 582; Michael, 398; Michael James, 399; Moses, 52-54; Moses S., 53, 54; Moses, Jr., 52; Nancy, 398; Rebecca, 398, 581; Ruth, 581(2); S. G., 96; Samuel, 523; Samuel G., 96, 97; Samuel Sesostris, 97; Sarah, 581; Sarah J., 333; Sophia Adalaide, 97; Sophie, 52; Susannah, 52; Susannah M., 52; Thomas, 474; Thomas J., 581; William, 473, 581; Zora B.,398
BROWNING: Jane, 116; Lula B., 323

BRUCE: Edward, 540, 544(2); Elizabeth, 355; Laura Mickey Joanna, 70; Mary, 540, 543, 544

BRUISTER: Thomas J., 22

BRYAN: Brown, 282, 283(3); Dorcas, 224; Elizabeth, 359; H. F., 282; John, 359(2), 360; Julia B., 282(2); Julia Brown, 282; L. M., 282; Lucille Van Cleve Smith, 282; Lula Martha, 282; Lydia Ball Simons, 360; Maria Louisa, 282; Maria Louisa Sparks, 282; Mary Frances, 282(3), Rose; Robert Francis, 283; Rosa Jane, 282; S. F., 282, 283; T. H., 282; T. M., 283; Thomas A., 283; Thomas M., 282; Thomas Marion, 282; William D., 283;William Drayton, 282; William Thomas, 282; Willie Thomas, 282

BRYANT: Solomon, 22

BRYSON: Rachel, 444; Sarah, 516

BUCHANAN: Anna, 231; Annie, 427(2), 428; Arthur, 427, 428; Benedictor, 427;Benjamin, 231, 232; Clement, 428; Elizabeth, 428; Elizabeth Jones, 428;George, 232; George B., 428; Isabella, 427; James, 232, 427(2); Jessie, 232; John, 428; John Wood, 232; Joseph Alexander, 428; Leonard, 428; Lewis, 428; Mary Boswell, 427; Mary Elizabeth, 232; Mary J., 428; Micajah, 232; Nancy, 428; Patsy, 428; Ruth, 428; Sally, 428; Sara, 232; Silas Brooks, 232; Susannah, 232; Thomason, 232; William, 231, 427(2), 428

BUCKHEISTER: Annie Nation, 4; Edward Hampton, 4; J. B., 4; John Bellinger Sr., 3, 4; John Benson, 4; Mary Bellinger, 4; Sallie Elliott, 4; Warren David, 4

BUFF: Pascal D., 312

BUFFINGTON: Joseph, 224; Mary, 224, 225; Mary Few, 224

BULL: Elizabeth Frances, 281; Izard Wittie, 281; Jessie Daisy, 281; Lula Rebecca, 281(2); Minnie Gertrude, 281(2); William H., 281; William Henry,281; William James, 281(2)

BUMPASS: E. H., Mrs., 527; E. M., Mrs., 527

BUNCH: Americus, 446; Andrew Jackson, 447; Benjamin Franklin, 447; Elijah, 446; Gilbert H., 446; Jacob, 446; Jacob K., 446, 447; John, 447; Margaret Melissa,447; Mary Jane, 447; Thomas Jefferson, 446;W., 68

BUNN: Essie, 412

BURCH: David, Capt., 209; Emily G., 454

BURDEN: Drucilla, 276; James, 277; Lathy, 277; Lucinda, 277; Mary, 276; Milly, 277; Nancy, 277; Sarah, 277; Sisley, 277; Thomas, 276, 277; Thomas Liles, 276; William, 276, 277(3)

BURDINE: Margaret, 104; Margaret Turner, 104

BURGESS: J. G., 207

BURNAM: Hannah, 100

BURNETT: James A., 332; John H., 331, 332; Mary J., 332; Mary Jane, 332; Naomi, 432; Susan A., 332; Susan F., 332; Susie F., 332; W. C., 332; William C., 331

BURT: James, 245; Nancy, 245

BURTON: Frances, 539; Mary Ann, 125; Robert, 539

BUSBY: Thomson, 24

BUSH: John P., 215; Laura Ann, 533

BUTLER: Ann, 286; Francis, 286; James, 543; Mary, 285, 286; Nancy, 352

BUTTS: C. B., 168

BYERS: Adam Meek, 96; Benjamin, 96; Edward, 96; Elizabeth, 96(2), 97(2); George A., 119; Henry, 237; Ison Davis, 96; James C., 96; Joseph, 237; Joseph Alexander, 96; Margaret, 237(2); Martha Adalina, 96; Mary Margaret, 96; Robert, 237(2); Samuel Baldwin, 96; Susanna, 237; Susannah Sr. 238, 237; William Walton, 96

BYNUM: Benjamin, 552(2); C. L., Mrs., 169; Carolina J., 553; Cynthia L., 168; E. J., 168; Elma, 168; Fanny, 552; Florida, 168(2); Gideon, 552, 553(2); Gideon, Jr., 553; James, 168(2), 169(2); James May, 553; John Turner, 553; Judith, 552; L. A., 167, 168; L. S., 168; Leon Sumpter, 169; Lizzie Blow, 552; Margaret May, 552; Mary S., 168; Mary

(Bynum continued...)

Sophia, 169; Priscilla D., 552; Richard Allen, 552; Susan Evans, 553; Tabitha, 553(2)

CADDIN: Catherine, 129; J. W., 129; James Jackson, 129; John Wesley, 129; Nancy Ann Dora, 129(2), 130; Nelson Edward, 129; Redmon, 129; Redmond Ausley, 129; Richard David, 130

CAIN: Martha Allison, 113

CALDWELL: Andrew P., 108, 109; Elender, 360; George, 360; J. C., 109; Jane, 360; John, 360; John C., 108, 109; Joshua, 360; Laney, 108, 109; Laney A., 108; Margaret Cameron, 360; Margaret M., 108; Mary C., 108; Rachel, 199; Samuel, 199; Samuel A., 108; Samuel P., 109; Sarah A., 108; W. A., 108, 109; Wiley, 360; William, 109

CALHOUN: Francis Sullivan, 313

CALISTA: Russell, 229

CALLAWAY: Clarissa Elizabeth, 524; Elizabeth, 525; Ella Agnes, 524; Emma 535; Frances Jemima, 524, 525; Jane, 524; Jesse, 524(2); John James Sharman, 524; Joseph, 524, 525; Joseph Morgan, 525; Joseph Samuel, 524; Joseph, Sr., 525; Joshua, 524; Luke Henry, 524; Lydia B., 524; Martha Sarah, 524, 525; Mary, 525; Mary Ann, 525; Mary Ann Matilda, 524; Mary Catherine, 525; Mary Smith, 525; Matilda K., 525; Morgan, 524; Sabrina Mildred, 524; Thomas Wootten, 524; Wayland, 524; William Willis, 524, 525; Woodson Kirby, 524

CALLEGOS: Edmond Ramon, 481; Edward Raymond, 480

CAMERON: Roger, 325

CAMP: Benjamin, 252; Kezziah, 252

CAMPBELL: Annia Eleanor, 268; Annie Eleanor, 195; Catherine, 77; Elizabeth 582; Elizabeth Mary Ann, 449; Hiram, 582; Jane, 582; Jennie L., 479;John, 582; Mary, 582; Mary Ellison, 8; Nancy, 21(2); Rev., 201; Richard,582, 583(2); Rob., Rev., 247; Smithey, 582; Susannah, 582; Tubal, 582;Wiley, 582; William, 582

CAMUS: Elizabeth, 273

CANDY: Harriet, 183

CANNON: Alsey, 302; Amelia M., 247; Amelia Melvina, 247; Angeline, 315(2); Ann S., 248; Augustus D., 249; Augustus Devan, 248; Augustus Swan, 201; David, 302; Elizabeth, 200(2), 248; Elizabeth Jane, 247, 314, 315(2); George Dallas, 314, 315; George James, 200, 248; George Speake, 302, 315;George Speaks, Col., 314; Henry, 201, 247, 248; Hezekiah S., 302; Hugh E., 200, 247, 248; Isaac, 302; Isaac Pennington, 302; Jane, 200; John J.,201, 247, 249; John Julius, 201, 248(2); Louisa A., 247; Louisa Adaline, 247; Martha Ann, 315(2); Mary, 200, 247, 248, 302; Mary Ervin, 247, 249;Mary Louisa, 314, 315; Richard, 439; Richard Speake, 302, 315; Robert Augustus, 200, 248; Robert Rasha, 247; S. A., 247; S. S., 308; Samuel,248, 302; Sarah, 200, 248, 302, 315; Sarah A., 315; Sarah Abigail, 315; Sarah Ann, 200, 201, 247-249; Sarah Smith, 314; Susan Morville, 201; Susan N., 201; Susan Speake, 308; Susanna M., 247; Susanna Monselle, 248; Susanna W., 201; Susanna Williams, 247; Susanna Wilson, 200, 248; Susannah W., 247; William, 302; William H., 201, 247(2), 248; William H.Sr., 201; William Henry, 247; William Henry Sr., 201; William Henry, Sr., 200; William Smith, 315(2); William, Col., 448

CANTEY: John M., 260; Sarah, 12

CAPERS: Samuel M., Rev., 240

CAPPS: Elizabeth, 387

CARAWAY: Arthur, 346

CARDWELL: David, 131; David Edward, 131; David, 131; Edward David 131; Edward Frances; Livingston, 131; Edward Josephine Randolph, 131; Edward Sinton, 131; Edward, Dr., 130, 131; Jane Sinton, 131; Thomas Davant, 131; Virginia Cook, 131

CARGILE: John Wesley, Jr., 506

CARL: Sarah Margaret, 551

CARLISLE: Agnes, 121; Ann, 121; Frances, 121, 122; Francis, Lt., 121; H. A., 326; Isaac, 121; James, 121(2), 122; John, 121; Margaret, 121(2),122; Martha, 121; Robert E., 121; Samuel, 121; William, 121

CARLTON: Ambrose, 534, 556; David, 556; Elizabeth, 556(2), 557; Elizabeth Eve, 556; Eve, 557; Howard, 556; John, 556(2); Lewis, 556(3), 557; Mary,556(2); Milly, 556; Nancy, 556; Thomas, 556(3), 557; William, 556, 557

CARMICHAEL: C. T., Mrs., 381

CARPENTER: Abner Franklin, 422; Asbury, 203; Benjamin, 219; Benjamin F., 219; Nancy, 383

CARR: Frances, 561

CARRAWAY: Verna Estell, 533; Verna Estelle, 534
CARROLL: Elizabeth, 361; Henry, 361; Isabella, 361; Je-et, 361; John, 361; Joseph, 360; Samuel, 360(2); Sarah, 361

CARRUTHERS: Cassie, 507; Della, 507; Hannah D., 507; Helen, 507; J. L., 507; J. W., 507(2); Jane, 507; John, 507; John H., 507; Joseph, 507(2); Joseph Nelson, 507; Mary, 507; Mary E., 507; Matilda, 507; Nancy J., 507; Rachel, 507; Rachel H., 507; Richard, 507; Richard Carter, 507; Richard H., 507; Samuel, 507; Sarah, 507; Sarah O., 507; Thomas Leith, 507(2)

CARSON: Charles Edward, 390(2); Elizabeth S., 390; Elmina, 390; James, 390(2); John, 390(4); John E., 390; Mary, 390(3); Mary Hennery, 390; Robert, 390; Robert S., 390; Sarah Isabella, 390(2); Selena, 390; Selina, 390; Thomas, 390; William Carson, 390

CARTER: Abbott, 428; Adam D., 133, 134; Albert Freeman, 429; Alice Loring, 429; Anna D., 133; Annie Bessie, 52; Conrad, 133, 134; Elizabeth, 133; Elmer Abbott, 429(2); Gardiner Fieoths, 429; George Friend, 429; J.William, 133; J. Williams, 133; J. Williams Jr., 133; Jacob, 133, 134; Jacob H. A., 133; Leonard David, 133; Lewis, 133, 134; Lucy, 133; Lula, 133; Margaret, 134; Margaret O., 133; Mattie S., 133; N. Lula, 133; Pauline Augusta, 429(2); Ronald St. Clair, 133; Thomas, 133, 134; W. C., 133; Wilhelmenia King, 133; William D., 429; William Sr., 134

CASEY: Ira, 135

CASH: Thomas Woodson, 554

CASON: Myer, 509(2)

CASSANDRA: Frances, 69

CASTLEN: Sarah, 132

CASTLES: Warren P., 190

CATER: Caroline, 251; Catherine, 251; Catherine Johnson, 250; Charles F., 250; Irvin, 250; Margaret Elizabeth, 251; Richard, 250; Samuel F., 250; Sarah May, 250; William Francis, 251

CATHERINE: Samuel, 580

CATHEY: James, 515

CATHY: Elizabeth, 516; James, 516

CATONNET: Georgianna, 324

CAVE: William Henry, 22

CHAFFIN: F. S., 578

CHAMBERS: Mary, 96

CHAMBLIS: Lydia, 555

CHAMBLY: Elizabeth, 37

CHANCY: Charles, 576; Eliza Elizabeth, 573; Elizabeth, 575, 576; Frances Ann, 575, 576; Frances Ann Mary B, 576; Frances Caroline, 573; James, 576(2); John, 573; John James, 573; Julian, 573; Julian Rebecca, 573; July Ann, 576; Loyd, 575; Lucy Mariah, 573; Mary Ann, 573, 576; Nancy Dandridge, 573; Neill, 575, 576(2); Penelope, 576; Samuel, 573; Samuel Bogue, 575, 576; Samuel Jackson, 573; Sarah, 573; Sarah Jane, 573; Stephen L., 575; Stephen Loyd, 575, 576; Stephen Loyd, Sr., 576; William Henry, 573

CHAPLIN: Eliza, 75, 76; John, 76; Mary, 76

CHAPMAN: M. E., 44

CHAPPELL: Hicks, 361(2); Howell, 361; John Joel, 361; Joseph Henry, 361; Nancy, 183; Polly Ellen, 361; Robert, 361; William, 361

CHARLTON: Mary, 310; Sallie, 313

CHARMAYNE: Franie, 166

CHASE: Abner, 52, 53; Mary, 52, 53

CHATWORTHY: Thomas J., 203; Thomas John Sr., 204

CHEATHAM: Mary, 542; Nancy, 542; Tabitha, 543

CHEESEMAN: Mary, 523

CHERRY: E. Pugh, Rev., 201; George, 201, 248; John, 450; M. E., 561; Susannah, 201, 248

CHESNUTT: Jane, 532

CHESTNUT: Harriet, 13; James, 12(2), 13, 14; John, 12, 13; John, Col., 12; Margaret Rebecca, 13; Mary, 5, 12; Rebecca, 13; Sally, 12; Sarah, 13

CHESTNUTT: Jonathan, 532

CHEWNING: William F., 399

CHIAM: Elisha W., 381

CHILDRESS: Agnes, 451

CHILDS: Alice, 260, 261; David Augustus, 260; Eben Allston, 261; Edith, 260, 261; Elizabeth, 260, 261; Ellen, 260(2); Ellen Hoke, 261; Eugenia T., 260; Eugenia Talley, 261; Hoke, 261; John Eben, 261; Lucy, 447; Lysander D., 260; Lysander D. Jr., 260; Lysander O., 261; Lysanders D. Childs Jr., 261; Mary T., 260; Mary Thomas, 261; Nancy, 260; Nannie, 261;Robert G., 260; Robert Gibbes, 261; Susan Emily, 128; William Gibbes, 261; William Guion, 260, 261

CHILTON: Sally Winefred, 406; William, 405

CHIPLEY: Mary Jane, 219

CHISM: Elisha W., 381

CHISOLM: Ellen Louisa, 75

CHISUM: C. A., 74; M. E., 74

CHOICE: Ann, 139; Aralintha, 139; Cyrus, 139; Jefferson, 139; John, 139, 140; Josiah, 139; Mary, 138-140; Sophia, 139; Tully, 139; William, 138-140

CHRISTOPHER: James, 42; Leander J. C., 41; Leander M., 42; Marget N. E., 41; Marget Nancy Elizabeth, 42

CHURCH: A. R. P., 264; Alonzo, 249

CLACK: James, 536, 539; Mary Henson Brown, 536; Mary Kennon Brown, 539; Sally, 536, 539

CLARDY: Catherine, 306

CLARK: Agnes, 520; Albert, 291; Archibald, 520; Avalin, 291; Bethieh, 520; C. J., 290; Catherine Me., 371; Cinthia M., 371; Cinthia Mourning, 372; D. A., 372; D. Alexander, 372; David Alexander, 371; Diedmiah B., 371(2); E. L., 157; Eli T., 521; Elijah, 362; Elijah C., 362; Eliza Ann, 521; Eliza M., 291; Elleanor H., 521; Elmira, 291; Elvica A., 291; Emily J., 291; Floyd, 23; Grace, 521; H. I., 291; Hannah Harriet, 521; Harriet, 291; Harry J., Mrs., 365; Henry, 397; Henry T., 291; Hugh, 371; Hugh McCrainey, 371; James, 520-522; James A., 362; James Crawford, 371, 372; James H., 521; James Williamson, 521; Joel E., 372; Joel Erwin, 371; John, 271(2), 290, 444; John H., 521; John P., 291; Joseph 362; Josiah G., 362; Julia P., 291; Louise, 234; Margaret, 362; Martha S., 291; Marthy Jane, 371; Mary, 362; Mary E., 23; Mary L., 291; Mary Stuart, 371; Matilda, 291; Micajah, 508(2); Miriam Crew, 487(2); Mollie, 23; Mourning, 372; Nancy A., 291; Oliver, 271(2); Rebecca T., 362; Robert U., 291; Ruth, 362; Ruth Goodson, 271; Samuel D., 521; Sarah, 463; Sarah Anne Margaret, 371; Sarah C., 78; Sevier, 271(2); Stephen, 520; Susanah, 362; Susanna, 397; Thomas E., 291; William, 271(2); William A., 362; William Rankin, 521

CLARKE: James L., 450; Micajah, 438(2); Polly, 260

CLASTRIER: Sarah, 366

CLAY: Archer, 408(2); Charity H., 408; Docie W., 408; Elizabeth, 408; Jesse, 408; John W., 408; Maria A., 408; Mary Ann, 408; Sarah B., 408; Teresa, 232

CLAYPOOL: Jane, 439, 483

CLAYTON: Ann R., 184; Ann Rebecca, 184; Charles Polk, 184; Edward, 184; Elizabeth, 372; Florence, 184; Frances Temperance, 184; Henry, 491; James, 184; Mary, 184; Rachel, 184; William Herbert, 184

CLEAVLAND: M. V., 356

CLEGG: Emily I., 151

CLEMENT: Nancy, 203

CLEMENTS: Arrenia, 377; Elizabeth, 377; William, 377; Woodson, 377

CLIBURN: Susannah, 114

CLIFTON: Bessie, 519

CLINE: John, 164

CLINKSCALE: Ellen, 312; Ophelia, 264

CLINKSCALES: Elvira S., 156

CLINTON: Edward B., 96; Joseph B., 96

CLONINGER: Addelaide, 565; Alburtus Hill, 564, 565; D. M., 565; David Melanchan, 564; Edward Lee, 564(2), 565; Isabel, 564; J. S., 565; James Stanhope, 565; Jonas, 564; Jonas S., 564, 565; Julius Johnson, 564, 565;Laban, 564; Lawson, 565; Lawson Vance, 564, 565; Loy Odell, 564,

(Cloninger continued...)

565;Lucinda, 564; Maggie Eva, 564; Maggie Eva Stroupe, 565(2); Maynardie Peterson, 564, 565; Moses, 564; Sallie Isabella, 564, 565; Sarah A. E.,564; Sarah Ann Elizabeth, 564(2); Sarah ANn Elizabeth, 565; Sidney, 565; Wiley W> M., 565

CLYMPH: Martha, 217

COATE: Caleb, 522; David M., 522; Esther, 522; Henry, 522; Henry W., 522; Isaac, 522; John H., 522; Lydia, 522; Mary, 522; Rachel, 522; Rhoda, 522;Robert, 522; Samuel, 522

COBB: Amanda, 139; Ann, 138, 139; Areldia Ann, 233; John D., 139, 140; Josiah, 139; Lovicy, 139; Mary, 140; Mary H., 139; Nancy, 140; Ophelia, 233; R. S., 233; Ransom H., 139(2); Ransom M., 140; Samuel, 139-141, 233; Sarah, 140; Thomas J., 139; Tulley, 139; William Alfred, Rev., 467; William C., 139, 141

COBIA: Ann, 86; Ann M., 86; Anne Flutter, 86; Christiana Elizabeth, 86; Daniel, 86; Elizabeth, 86; Francis, 86; Francis J., 86; Francis Joseph, Col., 86; Henry, 86; John, 86; Mary, 86(2); Sarah, 86; William Henry, 86

COCHERHAM: William, 499

CODY: Jeptha, 563; Jeptha M., 562; Louisa A., 561; Louisa Amanda, 562; M.D., 562, 563; Marian, 562; Marian M., 562; Michael, 563; Missouri E., 562; Nancy, 391, 392; Newton, 562; Rebecca, 563; Temperance Sophronia, 562, 563

COFER: M. J., 495

COFFEY: Myra Emmaline, 556; Sally, 556; Wilborn, 556

COFFIELD: Allen, 484; Clarissa, 484, 488; Elizabeth, 488(3); Elizabeth F., 484; Esther, 484; Esther Saunders, 484; Henry, 484; Jeremiah, 484, 488;John, 484(2); John, Sr., 484; Josiah, 484(2); Margaret L., 484; Martha Ann, 484; Nancy, 484(2); Sally, 484, 488(3); Sally Halsey, 484; William, 484(2)

COHEN: Moses H., 318

COKER: John J., 300

COLBERT: Henry, 243

COLCOCK: Adelaide H., 296; Sarah Rebecca, 297; W. F., 296, 297

COLE: L. S., 386; Martha, 376

COLEMAN: Julius C., 356; Robert P., 276

COLLEY: Polly, 477

COLLIER: George W., 265; Henry, 504; Phoebe Eliam, 542

COLLINS: Ailsey, 154; Alice, 100; Ann, 100, 154; Barbara, 321; Eleanor, 320; Elizabeth, 101; Etheldred, 101; George W., 321(2), 322; Hanah, 100;Hannah, 100, 154(2); Henry, 100, 101, 154; James Furse, 321; James Richardson, 101; Joseph, 100, 154; Joseph Jr., 101; Joshua, 101; Joshua Greenberry, 101; Laura Elizabeth, 146; Lemuel P., 101; Lucinda, 101; Martha, 321; Mary, 101; Moses, 100, 101(2), 154; Moses, Jr., 100; Nathan L., 490; Rebecca, 100, 154; Robert H., 58(2); S. D., Jr., 100; Sarah,100, 154; Seaborn, 101, 154; Seaborn Davis, 101; St., 321; Susan Ann, 321, 322; Susannah, 100, 154; Wiley Harris, 101

COLTON: Caroline H. E. Smith, 199

CONGER: Abbe J., 464; Abijah, 464; Anne, 464; Betsey, 464; Betsy, 464; Cyntha, 464; David, 464; Delia, 464; Emily, 464; John, 464; Phebe, 464;

(Conger continued...)

Polly, 464; Sally, 464; Stephen, 464(2), 465; Zenas, 464(2)

CONNELER: Jane, 112

CONNELL: Simon, 201

CONNER: Thompson, 315

CONNETT: Simon, 247

CONNOLLY: John, 555(2)

CONRAD: Beulah Eliza, 579; Elizabeth Brock, 579; Mary, 579; Richard Max,579; Thomas Joseph, 579(3); Winton Brock, 579

CONWELL: Joseph, 102; Leodicia, 102; Sophia Goodwin, 102(2)

COOK: Adah, 409; Amy Leona, 409; Ann Martha, 132; Benjamin, 239; Charles,132; Edward, 132(2); Edward Bocksins, 132; Eliza, 142; Elizabeth, 409;Elizabeth Darrans, 132; Elizabeth H., 241(2), 242; Elizabeth Rabb, 408;Elizabeth T., 408; Ella Newton, 409; Ellen, 409; Emily Jane, 132;Francis, 237(2), 239-242; Francis Asbury, 240, 241; Francis I., 237, 239; Francis, Rev., 237, 242; Henry Massey, 240, 242; Henry S., 239(2); Isaac, 239; J. O. A., 240; Jacob, 408; Jacob N., 408, 409; Jacob Newton, 408;James, 237; James A., 409; James L., 408; James Osgood Andrew, 241;Jemima, 240; Jemima S., 239; Jesse, 408; John E. Laughton Francis, 132; John Ellison, 240(2); John F., 408; John Henry, 132; John J., 237; John Ligon, 130, 132; John, Capt., 286; Julia, 240; Julia Blending, 241; M. M., 241; Margaret J., 240; Margaret Jane, 241; Margaret M., 242; Margaret Milligan, 240, 242; Maria Virginia, 132; Martha P., 408; Mary, 238; Mary I., 409; Mary Susan, 132; Naomi, 409; Oliver, 132; Robert, 239; Robert Dunlap, 241, 242; Samuel, 237, 239; Samuel K., 240; Samuel Kennedy, 241; Sarah, 132, 225; Sarah Ann, 132;

(Cook continued...)

Sarah Jane, 240(2), 241; Sarah Jemima,239; Sarah Jemima Flake, 240; Sarah Jemimah Flake, 241; Susan E., 240;Susan Elizabeth, 240, 241(2); Susannah, 73; William, 237, 240; William Francis, 240(2); William Prosser, 132; William Sr., 237, 239(2); William Thomas, 240, 241; Winfield Leonard Davis, 241, 242

COON: Casper, 107; Elizabeth, 107; George, 99; Lewis, 107; Sarah Elizabeth, 99; William, 99

COOPER: Annie Belle Frye, 58; Elinor, 499; Elmer Reid, 59; Eugene Clarence,59; J. P., 59; John L., 58; John L., Sr., 58; John Pinkney, 58; Leon, 59;Lillie Grace, 59; Martha Sue Scruggs, 134; Myrtle Sarah, 59; Ruth Kathryn, 59; Sarah, 215; Thelma Aline, 59; Walter P., 58; Walter Plural, 59; William S., 417

COPE: Alma, 111

COPELAND: Mary, 206; Sarah, 212

CORARD: Rev. Thomson, 489

CORBIN: Caroline, 37; Elizabeth, 37; Ilender, 37(2); Lucious, 37; Murray Susanah, 36; Samuel, 36, 37; Samuel P., 36(2); Samuel Senn, 37; Susanah, 37; William P., 37

CORDOZO: Aaron, 318; David, 318(2); David N., 318; Frances, 318; Isaac N., 318; Jacob, 318; Judith, 318; Leah, 318; Rachel, 318(2); Sarah, 318; Seixas Leah, 318

CORE: Malinda, 215

COSKREY: Christine, 230

COUCH: Erma Martin, 171; Pertima, 8

COUNTS: David, 108

COVINGTON: Rebecca, 444

COWAN: Thomas L., 375

COWLING: S. B., 184

COX: Abner, 197; Ally, 376; Ann Eliza, 264, 265; Benjamin, 375(2), 376; Benjamin L., \, 265; Benjamin Lee, 264; Cary Spencer, 264; Catherine, 13(2); Charles C., 375, 376; Daniel, 376; David, 375(2), 376; David, Jr., 376; David, Sr., 376; Elizabeth, 14; Emery Taylor, 265; Ephraim, 375,376; Esther, 13(2), 14; Esther, Mrs., 13; Frances E., 264; Frederick Ezell, 375; Hattie Graham, 264, 265; Israel, 375(3); J. Polk, 204; John, 13(2), 14; John Goolsby, 514(4); John Rowes, 14; Joseph Edward, 265; Joseph Elvira, 203; Joseph Elvire, 203; Mark, 375; Martha, 376(2); Martha Griggs, 264, 265; Mary, 12, 14(2), 375(2), 376, 441, 514; Mary Mildred,265; Moses, 375; Orren D. Rountree, 264; Phebe, 375; Rachel, 13; Reuben, 203; Samuel K., Rev., 366; Sarah, 14; Susannah, 375(2); William, 13, 375,376; Willis C., 265; Winnie, 59

CRABBE: Charles H., 471

CRADDOCK: Charity, 1, 2; Clementine, 2; Cornelius, 1; Daniel Cargill, 1; David, 1; Elizabeth, 2; James J., 2; John, 1, 2(3); John J., 2; John P., 2; Mary S., 2; Salley, 1; Salley C., 2; Sarah Rebecca, 2

CRAIG: A. F., 29; Agnes, 28, 29; Agnes Greer, 32; Aletha Keziah, 32; Aletha Keziah Barry, 28(2); Alexander, 29; Alexander Franklin, 32; Alonzo Franklin, 26, 27; Amelia, 32; Billie Gene, 26, 28(2); Bonnie Lee, 27; Bruam Leotj, 28; Camille P., 28; Charles Michael, 26, 27; Charles W., 28; Charles Weldon, 26, 27; Dorothy, 28; Frances Elizabeth Smith, 29; FrancesSmith, 27; Ida Stribling, 27, 29; James D., 28, 29, 32(2); James G., 29, 32; James Leroy, 26, 27; Jessie W., 28; John Almon, 27; John Almon, Dr.,26; John Andrew Knox, 26, 27; John B., 26, 27; John Kerr, 26; John Kerr,27; John Kerr, 28(2), 29(2), 32; John R.,

(Craig continued...)

26; John Stribline, 26; John Stribling, 27, 31; Margaret Elizabeth, 26, 27; Margaret Lucinda, 29, 32; Martha Amanda, 29; Mary Cordelia, 26, 27; Mary Cordella, 28; Mary Matilda, 29(2), 32; Michael Lynn, 28; Minnie Alice, 28; Nancy Amanda, 27, 28; Richard, 28; Richard A. B., 27; Richard Albert, 27; Richard Albert Barry, 26, 29, 32; Richard William, 26, 28, 29; Rosanna Alice, 27; Stuart Hoffman, 28(2); Thomas Clarkston, 28, 32; Travis Stribling, 28; William A., 29; William Alexander, 32; William Alexander Greer, 29; William Luther, 27

CRAIN: Isaac, 35; James, 34; Mary, 34, 35; Sarah, 34; Stephen, 34, 35(2); William, 34

CRAWFORD: Anna Belle, 530; J. P., 530; James P., 529; Malinda, 499

CREASMAN: Celina, 513(2)

CREIGHTON: R. L., Mrs., 356

CREW: Clinton, 487; Ida Lee, 487; Miriam, 487; R. C., Mrs., 486(2)

CROCKER: Arthur, 155; Betsey, 155; Dorcas, 155; James, 155; James Arthur, 155; John, 155; Nancy, 155; Patsey, 155; Polley, 155; Rhoda, 155; Solomon, 155; Susannah, 155(2); William, 155

CROCKETT: Agness, 433; Margaret A. W., 178; Samuel, 554; William, 433, 434

CROMLEY: Anne, 88; Catey, 88; Christly, 88; Irah, 87; James, 87; James R., 87; John, 87, 88; John B., 88; Margaret, 88; Samuel, 87; Sarah, 88; William, 88

CRONICK: Mary Ann, 151

CROOM: Abel, 549; Ann, 549; Asceneth, 549; Elizabeth, 530, 533, 549; Hardy, 549; Jesse, 549(3); John, 549; Lott, 549; Lucy, 549; Major, 549; Mary,549; Nancy, 549(2); Treacy, 549; William R., 549; Zilpah, 549

CROSBY: Bettie N., 157; Charity, 188; David, 157; William H., 112

CROUCH: Polly, 245

CROWDER: Mary, 162; The., Rev., 489

CROWE: Rachel, 431(2)

CRUDUPS: Mary, 60

CRUMB: Nancy, 143

CRUMP: Reuben D., 356

CRUMPTON: Thurston, 188

CRUTCHFIELD: Anna, 527, 528; Anna Belle, 529; Annabelle, 527; C. B., 527(2), 528(2); C. R., 529; C. W., 527-529; Charles, 528; Charles B., 527-530; Charlie Blake, 529; Charlie Wade, 527, 529; Christie, 527; H. L., 527, 528; H. L., Mrs., 527, 528; Hazel, 527; Helen, 527; Hope, 529; Ida, 527; J. E., 529; J. P., 529; James Fisher, 529; James Porter, 527, 529(2); Jessie Thomas, 527, 528; Johnnie, 527, 529, 530; Leila, 529; M. E., Mrs., 527, 528; M. G., 527, 528; Marian, 527; Mary Ida, 529; Mattie, 527; Mildred Love, 529; Novella, 529(2); S. C., Mrs., 527; Sam, 528; T.R., 529; Thomas, 527, 528; Thomas R., 529; Thomas Richard, 527

CRUTHIS: Henry, 555; James, 555; Jane, 555; John, 555; Nancy, 555; Sally,555; Sarah, 555; Vincent, 555

CUDGER: William, 575

CUIGNARD: Caroline E., 260

CULLER: George Harmon II, 324

CUNNINGHAM: Caty, 61; Frances, 20; Mary, 62

CURETON: Sarah Moon, 312

CURRY: Mary, 380; Rebecca M., 344

CURTIS: James W., 369; Robert Kent, 369

CURTISI: Mary Jane Katie Adams, 369

DALCHO: Rev. Mr., 350

DALLAS: Andrew S. J., 385; Cora Ellis, 384; Francis Smith, 385; Henrietta, 385; James, 385; James J., 384(3), 385; Mary D., 384; Mary J., 385; Milton K., 385; Polly, 385; Robert W., 385; Sarah S., 384, 385; Thomas G., 384

DALTON: Matilda, 386; Roy, 388

DANIEL: A. Montague, 214; Charles, 214; Charlotte Stith, 214(2); Eliz. Anderson, 214; Elizabeth, 545(2); Ellyson Anderson, 214; Fannie Nelson, 214; James B., 215; Jane Anderson, 214; Jane Mickelborough, 214; Jesse, 214; John, 214; Jones, 568; Lewis, 568(2); Matilda A., 214; Melissa, 568; Milburry Serena, 172; Pleasant, 214

DANIELL: Alfred, 431; Catharine F., 432; Clarissa, 431; Deaton, 431; Eleanor, 431; Elizabeth, 432; George, 432; George L., 432; Green B., 432;Isaac, 432; James, 432; Jeremiah M., 431; John S., 432; Josiah, 431;Martha Ann, 432; Mary, 431, 432; Masters H., 431; Moses, 431; Naomi, 432; Nathaniel, 432; Olive Ann, 432; Ollive, 431; Pinkney Y., 432; R. G., 431; Rachel, 431(2); Rebecca, 432; Robert, 431(3), 432; Robert P., 432; Sarah, 432; Stephen, 431; Susannah, 431; Thomas, 432; William, 431(2); William P., 432

DANIELS: Dr., 461

DANSBY: Daniel, 188

DARDEN: Faith, 563; Josiah Thomas, 562

DARRONS: Ann, 130(2), 132; Elizabeth Otey, 130, 132; John, 130, 132; Mary,130

DARWIN: Mollie, 265; Rachel, 229

DASHWOOD: Eleanor, 287

DAUGE: Margaret W., 445

DAVENPORT: Sarah, 125

DAVIDSON: Eliza, 50; Mary S., 51; Robert, 48; Walker Y., 48

DAVIS: Amanda, 339; Amelia, 351; Ann Elizabeth, 191; Anne Elizabeth, 191; Annie, 234; Benjamin, 545(2); Bettie Gamble, 191; Catherine Ireson,351(2); Elizabeth, 203, 458, 545; Elizabeth P., 339; Emeliann, 545(2); Esther Eliza, 191; Esther Monford, 190; Frances, 350(2); Henry Jefferson, 190, 191(2); Horace, 110; J. M., 351; J. U., Rev., 152; J. W., Rev.,152; James, 192; James Marcus, 110; John, 522; John Maynard, 350, 351; John R., 545; Joshua, 190, 191; Lydia, 522; M. E., 351; Malcolm, 236;Martha Lucinda, 191(2); Mary, 522; Mary A. G., 191; Mary L., 499; Nancy, 523, 545(2); Robert C., 29; S. W., 339; Sarah, 29; Sarah Elizabeth, 191;Thomas Allen, 191; William, 191; William Benson, 24; William Booker Wright, 191; Zentippe, 191

DAWSON: Alice Nicholson, 482; Angeline, 482; Bulah May, 481; Carolina, 350; Caroline, 350; Catherine Cordes, 350; E. C., 481; Elizabeth Undine, 482; Ellen, 350; Emma, 482; Ernest Calvert III, 482; Ernest, Jr., 482; Janet Eleanor, 482; Jessie Anne, 482; Joanna, 349, 350; John

(Dawson continued...)

Cordes, 350; Kenneth, 482; Melvin Kendrick, 482; Melvyn Hendrick, Jr., 482; Nathalie Ballard, 482; Nathalie Margaret, 482; S. J., 481, 482; Sallie E., 481;Samuel Prioleau, 350; Simelsun, 482; William, 349, 350; William Alfred, 350

DAY: Jane, 491

DE BARDOT: Antoinette Genevive, 273

DE BAROTTE: Marguerite, 273

DEAL: Augustus Moore, 97; Samuel Myers, 97

DEAN: Tina, 495

DEAS: James, Col., 13; Margaret, Mrs., 12

DEATHERAGE: Ursula, 227

DEATON: Mary Eleanor, 507(2); William, 507

DEGRFFENREID: Mary, 227

DELLINGER: Barbara Jezebel, 422; Bettie, 422; Cleveland Odell, 422; Franklin P., 422; James Buran, 422; Joseph, 422; Lillen Florence, 422; Lucy Clementine, 422; Marcius Wesley, 422; Margaret Sarah Elizabeth, 422;Mary Ann, 422; Violet Rebena, 422; Violet Robene, 422

DELOACH: Redic L., 33(2)

DELOATCH: Simon Rebecker, 461

DELONG: Nancy, 274

DEMOSS: Ellen, 228

DENDY: Bob, 230; Bobby Gerald, 231; Earline Lancaster, 39; Eugene Leonard, 231; Harvey Eugene, 231; Isabel, 236; Jan Clyde, 231(2); Leonard Latharo, 230, 231; Martha Ann, 231; Minnie A., 231; Nathaniel Walker, 230; Roscoe, 216

DENNIS: Cathrine G., 82; Katherine Martin, 236; Pearl, 236

DERDEN: Amy Lizabeth, 110; Andrew Jackson, 110; Dorothy, 110, 111; Elijah B., 110; Elijah Dobbit, 110; George W., 110(2); George Washington, 110; J. W., 110; James Patterson, 110; John M., 110; John Marcus, 110, 111;Mark, 110, 111; Martha Harris, 110; Mary Emma, 110; Matilda, 110; Sarah A., 110; Sarah Ann, 110; Temperance Hill, 110

DEVANE: Benjamin, 463; Burrell, 458(2); Clause Lee, 463; Cornelia, 457; Cornelia Dickson, 457, 458; Elizabeth, 457; Franklin, 457; Franklin E., 463; George Albert, Sr., 463; Ireton C., 457; James, 457; James Dickson, 458(2); James Stewart, 457, 458; John, Jr., 463; John, Sr., 463; Margaret, 457; Margaret Dennell, 458; Margaret Fennell, 457; Mary Jane, 457; Patrick Stewart, 457; Rufus, 457; Stewart, 457; Stuart James, 458(2)

DEVANE: Thomas, 402

DEVANE: Thomas, 457(2), 463; Thomas, Sr., 457; William King, 457

DEVANY: Benjamin, Rev., 489

DEVENY: Aaron, 520(2); Ann, 520; Elizabeth, 520; Jane, 520; Margaret, 520; Mary, 520; Rachel, 520(2); Robert, 520; Sarah, 520(2); Sarah Black, 520;Susannah Grayson, 520

DEVISCONTI: Lorenzo, 553

DEWITT: Rachel Sarah, 523

DIAMOND: Anna, 181

DICKENS: Bettie, 496

DICKENSON: George, 60; Jacob, 60(2)

DICKEY: Dorcas, 549; Ebenezer, 549, 550; Ebenezer, Jr., 550; Elisha, 549;Elizabeth, 549; Emily, 550; George, 363; Grizilla, 549; James G., 549;John, 549; Levi, 549; Margaret, 549; Mary, 549(2), 550(2); Nancy, 363; Rebecca, 498; William, 549

DICKINS: Ann, 536; Ann Fisher, 537, 540; Elizabeth, 538; Elizabeth Fisher, 536, 539; Harriet, 537, 540(2), 544; Jane, 536; Jesse, 536, 538; John,537(2); John Robert, 537, 539, 540; Lucretia, 536, 539; Lucretia Moore,536, 539; Martha, 536, 537; Mary, 536-539; Mary Brown Wilkins, 537; Mary Elizabeth, 537; Mary W. B., 539; Mary Wilson, 541(2); Mary Wilson Brown,536(2), 538-540, 542-545; Nancy, 536, 539, 540; Nancy P., 539; Nancy Pulliam, 537; Nancy Virginia, 540; Parthenia, 536, 539; Pennie, 537;Robert, 536, 538(2), 539; Roscoe, 537; Sallie Rooker, 537; Sally, 536,539; Sally Clack, 537, 540; Samuel, 536(2), 537(2), 539(2); Sanford, 540;Sanford Wilbourn, 537; Thomas Webb, 539; Virginia, 537(2); W. B., Mrs.,539; William, 536(2), 537, 538, 539(3), 540(2); William Barnett Pulliam, 536, 539; William Webb, 537

DICKLE: Elizabeth A. P., 521; Harriet N., 521; James Brigham, 521; James W., 521(2); Laura Debane, 521

DICKSON: Addie C., 257; Annie, 256; Christine Jones, 256; Elizabeth, 256; Elizabeth Eugena, 256; Elizabeth Eugenia, 254; Elsie J., 255; Evelyn,119; Florence Scott, 254, 255; Henry Franks, 254-256; Inez Sadler, 256;James Remey, 254; Jane Eliza, 254, 256; John, 253(2), 256; John Calhoun, 256; John Franks, 254; John Miller, 254, 256; Lucius Clark, 254, 256; Martha Eula, 254; Mary Montgomery, 254(2); Mary Scott, 256; Michael, 254;Michael C., 257; Michael Calvin, 256(2); Michael, Rev., 256; Nancy Eugenia, 256, 257; Nancy S., 255; Nancy Y., 254; Sarah, 254(2); Sarah Ann, 254; Sarah Antoinette, 254, 255; Thomas,

(Dickson continued…)

253(2), 254(2), 255, 257(2), 259; Thomas E., 255; Thomas Eugene, 253-257; Thomas Paul, 256; William Scott, 256

DICKSON (COLORED): Augusta, 258; Albert, 257; Allen, 259; Anderson, 258; Andy, 258; Angerona, 258; Ann, 257; Banister, 257; Brena, 258; Caroline, 258; Catherine, 257; Cecelia, 258; Cornelius, 258; Cubit, 258; Dallas, 258; Edmon, 258; Eliza, 258; Ellen, 258; Elmirah, 257; Emily, 258; Esther, 259; Fanny, 259; Ferasure, 259; Ferry, 258; Frances, 258; Franks, 258; Garison, 258; George, 259; Hariet, 258; Henrietta, 259; Holacy, 259; Isaac, 258; Jackson, 258; James, 259; Jane, 258; Jerry, 259; John, 257; Johneston, 257; Joseph, 258; Joseph Linton, 259; Lizzie, 259; Louise, 259; Lucinda, 258; Lucy, 259; Major Randal, 258; Martha, 259; Mary, 257; Miles, 258; Nancy, 257; Nannie, 259; Napoleon, 259; Oliver, 258; Peter, 259; Robert, 259; Rutter, 259; Sally, 258; Sam, 258; Sophia, 259; Stephny, 257; Susan, 258; Tolivar, 259

DICKY: Sarah, 200

DILLARD: Mary Benson, 3, 4

DISMUKES: Elizabeth E., 510(2)

DIXON: Ann, 546; Anna, 546; Anne, 546; Betsy, 546; Edwin Reeves H., 546; Hannah, 546; James, 546; John, 546; John H., 552; Mary, 546; Matty, 546; Oliver, Mrs., 429; Peggy, 546; Rebekah, 11, 298; Thomas, 546(2); William H., 54

DOAK: Mr., 572

DOBBINS: Lennie, 165, 383

DODGEN: Bernice, 235, 236; F. J., 236; Fred, 235(2), 236; George Washington, 236; Jack, 235; Jack Allen, 236; William Anderson, 235

DOLES: S. E., 481

DOLSHEIMER: A., 390

DONALDSON: Rebecca, 471

DONALY: Eliza, 84

DONOHO: Edward, 539

DORTCH: Elizabeth, 568

DOUGHTY: Martha, 349; Rebecca Cheppelle, 349

DOVE: Elder, 423

DOWDLE: Eleanor, 122; Elenor, 283; Robert, 122, 283

DRAKE: Florence Sue, 264; Thomas Franklin, 264

DRAYTON: Eliea Elliott, 210; Mary, 296

DRINAN: Mary M., 454

DUDLEY: Anne Faust, 185(2); Florence Doling, 185; Frank Gordon, 185; Guilford, 554; Herberta, 185, 186; I. N., 185; John Augustus, 186(3); Julia Myrtle, 186; T. N., 186(2); Willa Pierce, 185; Willie Nell, 185, 186

DUFFEY: Elizabeth Ward, 494

DUKE: Charles H., Duke, 198; M. E., 207

DUKES: Elizabeth, 62

DUNBAR: Eleanor Smith, 319; Finklin, 319; Francis, 319; Francis, Major, 319; George Robinson, 319; George Robison, 319; Lucy, 319; Lucy Eleanor, 320; Mary Pickling, 319
DUNKLIN: Angie, 185; Angie L., 185; Angie R., 186; Ann Rebecca, 186; Anne, 184(2); C. P., 184; Charles, 185; Charles Elbert, 185; Charles P., 184,186; Charles Raymond, 185, 186; Claudia, 185; E. C. Sr., 185; Edward,185; Edward C., 184; Edward Clayton, 185; Florence, 184(2); Frances Temperance, 186; Freeman Hardy, 185; J. W., 186; James Herbert, 185; James W., 184; James W. Jr., 186; Joseph, 311; Mary, 311, 312; Mary Paisley, 185, 186; Oscar Leonard, 185; Rebecca Clayton, 185; Washington,184; William, 184, 185; William Herbert, 186; Willie Clayton, 185

DUPREE: Francis Marion, 553; Paul Clifford, 553

DURANT: Ann, 372(2), 373; Elizabeth, 373; George, 372(3), 373; Hagar, 372;John, 372(2), 491; Mary, 373(2); Sarah, 372, 373(2), 491

DURBIN: Sarah, 447

DURBOROUGH: John, 509

DURBOROW: David, 509; Elizabeth, 509; James, 509; John, 509(2); Martha, 509(2); Rebecca, 509(2)

DURHAM: Anna Sinton, 131; Edward Francis Marion, 131; Frank M., 131(2)

DURKIN: Keziah, 377

DURR: Catharine, 194, 196, 268, 269

DURRENCE: Debbie Ions, 33

DWIGHT: L. A., Mrs., 129; Sarah Jane, 129; William, 129
E.: Samuel, 580

EARLEY: George Lee, 386; L. O., 386; R. W., 386; Robert W., 386; Temperance 386

EARTHLING: Patsy, 557

EATON: Julia Ann, 554; Theodoric, 554; Thomas, 554

EBORN: Arcadia, 454; Benjamin F., 449, 451(2); Eliza, 454; Eliza Ann, 449; Eliza Ann Louise, 449; F. Arcadia, 454; Harriet Ann Elizabeth,449; Harriette Ann Elizabeth, 450; Henry, 449(2); John, 449, 454; John Robert, 449(2), 451; Lucille Eliza, 449, 451(2); Lydia Olive, 449(2); Martha Ann, 450; Mary Ann, 454; Nancy Olive, 454; Robert, 454; Robert Boyd, 454; Thaddeus Caleb, 449, 450(2); Theodore, 449; William Benjamin, 449

EDDINS: Edgar Freeman, 440; Sarah Virginia Palmer, 441

EDGAR: J. B., Rev., 211

EDMONDSON: Jane, 498, 499

EDWARDS: Betty, 120; Elizabeth, 187; Henrietta, 120; James, 121; John, 120(2); Joseph, 120(2), 121; Martin, 120; Mary, 120, 534; Nancy Berry, 131; Polley, 120; R. B., 566; Sally, 120; Sanford, 121; Sarah, 120; Thomas, 120, 121; William, 120(2)

EGGER: Alexander Ramsey, 65; Andrew, 64, 65; Ann, 64; Ann Hubbard, 64; Elizabeth Orr, 64; John, 65; Lemuel William, 65; Lovice, 65; Mary, 64, 65; Moses Bond, 64; Rhoda, 65; Sally, 65; Ursley Holland, 64

EHNEY: George Marion, 342; Jacob H., 342; Jacob Preston, 342; Mary Ann, 342; Stacy Houser, 342; Talula Emma, 342; William, 342

EIGELBERGER: George Michael, 107; Mary, 107; Rosinn Cathrina, 107(2)

EIGLEBERGER: George, 107; Rosen Catharine, 107

ELAM: Mary, 544

ELDER: William Joseph, 495

ELENOR: William Gillilah, 284

ELGIN: Margaret, 11

ELIAM: Mary, 542; Phoebe, 542

ELLINGTON: Edward, Rev., 359

ELLIOTT: Sarah H., 249

ELLIS: Augusta Fair, 357; Augusta P., 357; Enoch, 357; Enoch, Rev., 356; Frances Louise, 356; George Dyer, 357; Little Ednie, 356; Lizzie Ednie, 357; Martha Ann H., 356; Martha Ann Hicks, 357; Mary Adaline, 357(2); Mary Adeline, 357; Mary Ann, 233; Mary Emma, 532; Nora B., 357; Nora Bell, 357; Phebie Caroline F., 356; R. A., 357; Roda, 357; Rosa Amanda, 356; Sarah Malinda, 356, 357; Statia, 357

ELLISON: Jane, 37; John, 237, 240; Margaret Milligan, 239; Susannah, 240; W. H., Rev., 240, 241

ELMORE: Sophia, 192

EMERSON: Elizabeth, 561

EMERY: Cecil B., Jr., 59; Cecil Bernard, 59; Gwendolyn, 59; Kimberly Diane, 59; Paul James, 59

EMORY: Faye Berry, 155

ENGLISH: Rachel, 561; William, 188

ENRKES: Martha, 535

EPPS: Daniel, 272, 273; Elizabeth A., 273; Francs H., 272; Frank, 272; George J. T., 273(2); Harriet M., 273; Harriet W., 273; James N., 273; John, 273; Laura H. W., 273; Louis T., 272; Louisa H. W., 273; Mary, 273;Peter G., 273; Samuel M., \, 272; Sarah Ann, 273; Susannah E., 273; Susannah H., 273; Susannah M., 273; William, 272

ERVIN: Sara S., 310; W. S., 271

ERWIN: George, Mrs., 71

ESPY: Elizabeth, 444

ESTES: Benjamin T., 540; Martha Matilda, 556; Mary Annie Elizabeth, 556; Rebecca, 556

ETCHERSON: Easter, 419

ETCHISON: Walter, 420

ETHOFFER: Joseph Edward, 388

ETHREDEE: Sarah, 578

EVANS: Benjamin J., 490; Benjamin L., 488; Benjamin Lawrence, 489; C., 76;Celey An Amelea, 490; Celey An Amelia, 489(2); Clarissa Coffield, 490; Edwin, 489; Elizabeth, 104, 489; Elizabeth M., 489; Ellen Margaret, 366;George Benson, 489, 490; Isaac, 104; James Henery, 490; James Hennery,489; Jeremiah, 489; John Wesley, 489, 490; Josiah, 489; Margaret, 488,489(2); Martha Eliza, 489; Nancy, 489, 490; Susanna, 488; Susannah, 488,489; Th., 489; Unity, 103(2), 104; Zachariah, 488, 489(2), 490

EVE: Elizabeth, 556

EVERETT: Exum, Rev., 501(2)

EVERITT: David K. F., 370; David Kendrick Futch, 371; Mary Elizabeth, 370

EWAN: Caroline V., 78; William I., 78

EZELL: Frederick, 376; Mary, 376

EZZARD: William, 399

FALLAS: Ann, 360; Elizabeth, 360; Ellender, 360

FANNING: Elizabeth, 431

FARIS: Dorcas, 91; Elizabeth, 91; Isabella, 91; James, 91; Margaret, 91; Rachel, 91; Robert, 91(2); Sarah, 91

FARR: Wilhelmena, 9

FARRAR: Joseph F., 519; Lockey S. Fite, 519

FELDER: Katherine Greer, 25

FERGUSON: A., 230; Betty, 192; Joel, 313(2); Micajah, 534; Nimrod, 534

FEWELL: Alexander, 344; Margaret, 344

FIELD: Frederick T., 236

FIELDS: Anna, 514; Celia, 102; Hazel Crutchfield, 530; Jeremiah, 514(3);John, 514(3); John, Jr., 514(5); Lucy, 514; Lydia, 514; Margaret, 544; Mary, 514(2); Nathaniel, 514; Susan, 514

FIGGINS: Miss, 387

FILPUT: Thomas Sr., 320

FINDLEY: Nancy, 494

FINLEY: Martha, 68

FINNEY: Henry, 278; Nancy, 278

FISCHARDE: Nancy Y., 79

FISHER: Ann, 470; Martha Elizabeth, 470; Martha, 470; Oscar, 470; Thomas Edwin, 470; Turner, 470; Turner Franklin, 470; William, 470

FITE: Abram, 519; Abram Marion, 519; Christopher C., 519; David, 519; Jacob, 519; Jane Abernathy, 519; Jefferson D., 519; John C., 519; Joseph H., 519; Laura I., 519; Lockey S., 519; Mary Ann, 519; Washington S.,519; William C., 519

FITZPATRICK: Elizabeth, 471

FLAKE: Jemima, 237

FLEMING: Anne, 227; Barbara Atlas, 79(2); Belinda Catherine, 78, 79; George Marvin, 78; James S., 227; Jonathan, 79; Mary Emily, 79(2); Rebecca W.,79; Samuel Mathew, 78; Sarah Jane, 79; Sary Jane, 79; W. A., 79(2); Warren S., 204; William Anderson, 79

FLETCHER: Effy, 225; Janie, 495; Richard Merritt, 495; Rudolph, Mrs., 51

FLURY: Margaret, 488

FOGARTY: Pamela C., 199

FOGG: J. D., 448

FONTS: Irvie R., Mrs., 217

FOOTE: Mary Elizabeth, 401

FORBES: Mary H., 410(2)

FORD: Powell, 563(2)

FORE: Jane, 60

FOREMAN: Arcadia Foreman, 449; Joshua, 449; Rebecca, 449

FOREST: Wake, 401

FORREST: Benjamine Stoddard, 471

FORT: Anne, 60; Frances, 559; Jacob C., 559; Jacob G., 559; Mary Elizabeth, 559; Priscilla, 559; Sarah, 60

FOSTER: Alma Janett, 465; Annie Cader, 11; C. S., 10; C. T., 11; Dora, 400; Dwight C., 464, 465; Edward, 465; Elijah, 11; Emma, 499(2); Eras Taylor, 566; Eva P., 165; Harrison, 281; Hawkins, 10; J. R., 10; J. T., 11; Jesse C., 11; Lucretia Angeline, 280; Lydia, 464, 465(2); M. A., 10; M. P., 10; Malinda, 499; Mary, 465; Mary Grisby, 196; Penelope, 495; Rebecca Weyman, 349; Ruth B., 465; Samuel W., 464; Susannah F., 566; Susannah H., 566; Theodore, 464; W. C., 10; William H., 565, 566; William J., 495; Zach B., 11

FOSTERS: Mrs., 210

FOWLER: Sophia, 140; Willis, 345

FOX: Amelia, 325; Ann, 324, 325(2); Benjamin, 324-326; Catherine, 325; David, 324, 325; Elizabeth, 324, 325(2); George, 325(2); James, 324; Jane, 325; John, 324; Jonathan, 325; Joseph, 324; Margaret, 324; Mary, 324-326; Richard, 324; William, 324

FRANCIS: Mary Ann, 69

FRANKLIN: Richard, 535

FRANKS: Elizabeth, 253

FRASER: Clara Isabella, 274; Jane Barton, 366; John, 274

FREDERICK: Charles, Rev. Mr., 209

FREEMAN: Arabella Myriam, 128; Aveline Augusta, 128; Betty Baulden, 126; David, 151(2); Duffie, 383; Edith Arabella, 126; Elmira Amanda, 126;, 126; Eugenia Frances, 128; Henry, 126; Jacob Elbert, 151; James Albert, 151; James Hiram, 128; John, 126; John Forsythe Smith, 128; John Fraser, 151; John Holland, 128; Martha Ann, 128; Martha Jane, 371; Martha Lelia, 128; Mary Elizabeth, 128, 151; Nancy W., 126; Nannie A., 128;Permelia 126;Polly T., 126; Roberson, 126, 128; Roberson Camilla, 128; Sarah E., 128;Susan Alice, 128; Thomas Edwin, 128; Townsend, 168; William Henry, 128; Willie, 383; Winfield, 128

FREER: Claudia, 288; Edward, 288; Margaret, 288

FRENCH: Eleanor Jane, 301; Elizabeth R., 301; James, 300, 301; Joseph Taylor, 301; Lafford Berry, 301; Lewis P., 300; Love Ann, 300; Moses T.,300; Ruth Sylvania, 301; Sallie, 300; William Doss, 301

FREZIL: Marie, 292

FRIERSON: James F., 5; James J., 5, 6, 336; James Julian, 6, 7(2), 336, 337; John F., 7; John J., 6, 7(3), 335-337; John N., 7, 337; John Napoleon, 6, 336; Julia F., 7(3), 336, 337; Julia P., 6; Julia Vaughan, 6(2), 336; Mary Chestnut, 14, 336; Mary Chestnut Grant, 7, 337; Minnie C., 5, 6, 336; William Grant, 6, 336

FRIPP: A. L., 74; Alice Louisa, 75; Amelia, 76; Charles Benjamin, 75; D. P., 74; Daniel Perry, 74; E. L., 75; Edgar Walter, 74; Eliza, 76(2); Eliza Emily, 74; Ella Rosalee, 75; Ella Rosalie, 74; Ellen Louisa, 74; Florence Amanda, 74-76; Isabella Phoebe, 74; John, 76; John E., 74,

(Fripp continued...)

75(2); John Edwin, 76; John Ervin, 75; Julian Jenkins, 74; Martha M., 75; Martha S., 75; Martha Sarah, 75; Mary Emily, 76; Mary Rosa, 74-76; Paul, 76(2); Robert Lee, 75; Thomas, 75; Thomas Benjamin, 76; Thomas Screven, 74; William, 76; William Augustus, 76; William B., 75(2), 76(2); William P., 74, 75(2)

FROST: Rev. Mr., 349

FRYE: Annie Belle, 59; John Pinkney, 58

FUDGE: Margaret, 293

FULLER: Diane, 388; Edward, 388; Edward J., 388; Lillian, 388; Lucy Emmerline, 495; Marian, 431; Robert C., 388

FUNICELLA: Debra, 26; Toni, Dr., 26

FURSE: Edward, 320; James, 320-322; Julia A., 320; Lovisa Robison, 320; Martha, 321; Robert Thompson, 180; Stephen S., 180; Stephen Smith, 178; Susan Ann, 321

FUTRAL: Jenny, 353

GAILLARD: Bartholomew, 348, 349; David, 348; E., Mrs., 348; Elizabeth, 348,349; Ellinor Serre, 348; Henrietta, 349; Henrietta Catherine, 348; James,348; John, 348(2), 349; John E., 348; Peter, 348(2), 349(2); Samuel, 348; Serre, 348; Theo., 348; Theodore, 348, 349; Thomas, 348

GAILLERD: Abram, 296; Anna, 296; Theodora O., 296

GAINES: Elizabeth, 307; Margaret C., 447(2); Peggy C., 447

GALE: Christopher, 491; Elizabeth, 491

GALPHIN: Sarah, 320

GAMBRELL: James, 203(2); Matthew, 203

GANN: Frank Floyd, 103

GARDNER: Frances, 561

GARNETT: James G., 178

GARRETT: Ambrose, 274, 275; Edward, 275; Elizabeth, 275; Elizabeth J., 563; Frances, 274; Joseph Martin, 274; Manervy, 275; Mary, 116; Mary Evaline, 563(2); Nicholas, 275; Reuben, 275

GARRIS: Andrew J., 461; George W., 461; Harriet An, 461; Henry P., 461; John W., 461(2); L. B., 461; Levenia An, 461; Louisa, 461; Mary, 461; Mary J., 461; Mitchell James Henry, 461; Rebecca, 461; S. B., 461; Sally, 461; Sarah R., 461; Simon Rebecker, 461; Wade H., 461; Wade N., 461; Willie R., 461

GARRISON: Dorcas, 547; Mark, 548

GARRISS: Ann, 462; Anny Thomas, 460; Daniel Webster, 462; Elizabeth Frances, 460; F., 462; Frances, 460; George Washington, 462; Harriet T., 460; Hawkins, 462; John W., 462(2); John Whitfield, 460; L. C., 460, 462; Lender, 462; Levenia An, 460; Littlebury, 460; M. L., 462; Margaret, 462; Margaret B., 462; Mary, 462; Mary Jane, 460(2); Mary Turner, 462; N. L., 462; Patrick Henry, 460; Salley, 460; Sarah An Rebecker, 460; Sidney, 462; Wade, 460, 461; Wade H., 460; Wade H. D. Dallas, 462; William S., 460

GARSON: John, 577

GARTER: Sallie, 495

GARVEY: Michael, 12, 298

GASTON: Alexander, 20, 327; Anne, 328; James, 327; Jane, 20; John, 20; William, 20, 328

GAUT: Jesse, Judge, 535

GEES: Solomon, 284

GEORGE: Robert, 72

GIBBES: Alice E., 260(2), 261; Elizabeth Mason, 261; Mary E., 260; R. W.,261; Rev. Mr., 350

GIBBS: James, 116

GIBSON: Abigail, 523; Amelia, 523; Anna, 523; Bowater Porter, 523; Celia, 523; Garrett, 523; Gladys, 364; Hannah, 508(2); Loneasy, 514; Mary, 514(4); Prudence, 523; Robert, 523; Sarah, 523; Susan Martha, 523; Valentine, 523; William, 523

GILBERT: James J., Mrs., 506; Lucy Jerusha, 322

GILBREATH: P. W., J. P., 146

GILDER: Lucinda Jane, 298

GILES: Hattie M., 332

GILFILLIAN: R. A., 230

GILKERSON: Annie Adelaide, 255

GILL: Mary, 35

GILLAM: David H., Jr., 323; David H., Mrs., 322; Edith Elaine, 323; Kenneth David, 323

GILLELAND: Margaret I., 570

GILLESPIE: John, 117(2); Mary Ann, 117(2); Mary Anna, 119

GILLETT: Elijah, 322

GILLIAM: Sarah, 326

GILLISON: Anna, 296; Berry, 296; Berry Pitman, 296; David William, 296; Elizabeth, 296; Joseph, 296; Mary, 296; Molsey, 296; Rebecca, 296; Sarah, 296; Susannah, 296; Thomas Charles, 296

GILLUM: William, 448

GILMER: Robert A., 285

GINN: Cherry, 111; Dorcas, 111; Mary, 112; Miles, 112; Sary Ann, 111; W.M., 111

GIRADEAU: J. L., Rev., 262, 267

GIRARDEAU: Catharine, 290; Claude Hearne, 288; Claudia Hearne, 288, 289; Claudia Mary, 288; Edward Feer, 288; Edward Freer, 288(2), 289; Edward Hearne, 288, 289; Eleanor D., 289(2); Emily Margaret, 288; Emmie, 289, 290; Evelyn Lee, 289; Hannah Moore, 288, 289; Isaac, 287, 289; J. B., 289, 290; J. L., Rev., 287; John, 287(2), 289(2), 290; John Bohun, 287, 288(3), 289(2), 290; John L., 288; Pierre, 290; Richard Bohun, 289; Sarah DuPre, 288; Susan King, 288; Thomas Hamlin, 288, 289; Thomas Jefferson, 288; William Richmond, 288

GIST: Addie Eloise, 160; Alice Victoria, 160(2); Annie Bell, 160; Carrie Clementina, 161; Clarence Calhoun, 161(2); David C., 160, 161; David Jesse, 161; E. Jones, 161; Ellen Douglas, 161; Inez, 160; Laura Lavinia, 161; Lavinia Katherine, 160; Lillian Estelle, 160(2); Mary Elizabeth, 160, 161; Richard Valerius, 161; Sadie Isabel, 161; Thomas Monroe, 160; Vivian, 160; W. H., 160; William Henry, 161

GIVENS: John, 85

GLASCOW: Martha Ann, 315; Spencer L., 315(2)

GLAZE: Martha, 451

GLAZIER: Elizabeth E., 187(2); Elizabeth Edwards, 187; John, Capt., 186,187(2); Mary, 187; Nancy, 187(2); Rebecca, 187(2); Renthea, 187, 188

GLEASON: Anna Milnor, 279; Elizabeth, 279; Frances Parker, 279; Harris Hall, 279(2); Henry, 279; Henry Bull, 279; John Cleaveland, 279; Mary Dick, 279; Sarah Potter, 279

GLEN: A. J., 82, 84; Ellie E., 82

GLENN: Emily, 540; Henry, 540; James, 540

GLOVER: Allen A., 277(2); Caroline N. Finney, 278; Elizabeth, 277; Henry W., 278; John Jackson, 278; John T., 277(2); Julius Jefferson, 278;Julius N., 277; Nancy A. E., 278; Nathaniel Seth, 277, 278; Temperance Mary J., 278; Temperance Towles, 277; W. P., 277; Washington Pierce, 278; Wiley, 277(2)

GODWIN: Blanche Alford, 505; Carlton Haywood, 505; Clair Alford, 505; Columbus Augustin, 505; Columbus Barnes, 505; Ellen Calvinda, 505; Fernando, 506; Fernando Keith, 505; Rebecca Margarete, 505; Salina Blanch, 505

GOFF: E. Byrd, 322

GOLDING: Anthony, 198; Anthony Foster, 198; Caroline Matilda E., 199; Christina Neely, 198, 199; Clementina Brown, 198(2); Henry Laurens, 198, 199; Isabella, 199; John Brown, 198, 199; John Reid, 198, 199(2); Marquis Lafayette, 198, 199; Nancy Campbell, 198, 199; Pamela

(Golding continued...)

Cunningham, 199;Rachel, 199; Robert Cunningham, 199; Sallie Morgan, 198, 199; Thomas Wadsworth, 199; Thomas Willis, 198, 199

GOODBREAD: Catherine, 443; Phillip, Sr., 443; Sarah, 443

GOODGOIN: J. W., Capt., 312

GOODWIN: Mary, 271; Nancy, 488

GOODWYN: Robert Morris, 472

GORDEN: Anny, 26

GORDON: Alexander, 224; Alonzo, 225; Buffington, 225; Charles, 224; Clarissa Few, 225; Elizabeth, 224, 225; Few, 225(2), 226; George Aston, 224; Georgianna, 226; Harvey, 474; James, 97, 225; James B., 474; James M., 225; Jane McCutchen, 268, 269; Jane McCutcheon, 195; John, 226; John Few, 224; John Fletcher, 225; Joseph Roy, 224; Marquis de Lafayette, 225;Mary, 225; Mary B., 225; Missouri, 226; Nathaniel, 474(2); Samuel, 224;Sarah, 199; Sarah Cook, 225; Thomas, 224, 226; Thomas Few, 225; Thomas J., 225; William, 224; William M., 225

GORE: Albert, 176; Albert Jr., 177; Bessie Ledford, 177; Georgia, 176; Julia, 176; Mile Corbitt, 177; Milton Burr, 177; Thurber, 177; Victoria,176; Virginia, 177; William Henry, 176; William Irdell, 177; William Iredell, 176, 177

GORTENY: David, 303

GOTUE: Jane, 325

GOULDING: E. R., Col., 153

GOURDIN: Elizabeth, 349; Ellinor, 349; Hamilton Courturier, 349; Henrietta,349; Hester, 349; Peter Gaillard, 349; Robert Marion, 349; Samuel Thomas,349; Theodore, 349; Theodore Lewis, 349

GRADY: Anne, 549; Benja. Franklin, 531; Harriet, 440; Harriett Sammons, 441

GRAHAM: Eliza Carey Smith, 320; M., 320; Mary, 550(2)

GRAMBRELL: Matthew, 203

GRANT: Minnie C., 5, 336

GRAY: Alonza William, 436(2); Emiline, 436; Emily A., 437; Emily Ann, 437;Emma Jane, 437(2); Francis Ve, 436; Harriet, 437; Henry Childs, 437;Jessica, 436; Joseph G., 437; Joseph Gates, 437; Mrs., 232; Tereno Erastus, 436, 437; William, 436, 437

GREEN: Amy, \, 557; Byron Bonapart, 445; Clotilda, 445; Daniel, 557; DeWitt Oscar, 445(2); Elizabeth, 215; Franky, 557; Jane, 445; Joseph, 557; Julia Jane, 445; Lucy, 265; Mary, 557; Napoleon B., 445(2); Richard, 557(2); Robert, 557; Sally, 557; Susana, 557; Tillie, 165, 383; Turner L., 265; William, 445

GREENE: Ellen E., 427; George W., 427; J. W., 427; Jefferson, 427; Martha Jane Rollins, 427; Noah J., 427; Rebecca A., 427(2)

GREENFIELD: J. C., Mrs., 520

GREER: Amos, 24; Bennett, 22; Chaney, 23; Charles, 23; D. C., 25; Dolly Jane, 25; Ella Agnes, 159; Ellen Thompson, 22; Floyd, 23; George C., 23(2); Isaiah, 22; J. Wallace, 22; Jesse, 22; Jim, 23; John A., 24, 25; Margaret Jones, 25; Martha Davis, 26; Monroe, 23; Ray, 22; Roy, 22; Sallie, 23(2)

GREESON: Lillie, 153

GREGG: Walter, Mrs., 200; William Pinkney, 155

GREGORY: Arrelia T., 106, 159; Bobby E., 105, 159; Garibaldi, 105, 106, 158, 159; J. A., 105, 158; J. C., 158; James A., 106, 159; James Donald,105, 159; Juda Caroline, 106; Jude Caroline, 159; Mary Lillian, 106, 160; Michael David, 105, 159; Minnie Hettie Lee, 105, 158; Ottis Grady, 105,106, 158; Ottis Grady Jr., 105, 158; Ottis Grady Sr., 106, 160; Ottis Grady, Jr., 106; Ottis Gregory, 106; Ottiss Grady Jr., 159; Paul Franklin, 105, 159; Paul James, 105, 106, 158, 159; Rolin Montague, 159;Rowland Montague, 105, 106(2), 158; Sarah Frances, 106; Sarah Francis,105, 158, 159; Wells Belcher, 158

GRESHAM: Pauline Whitfield, 511

GRIDER: Aaron, 555; Amos, 554; Archibald, 555; Barbara, 554; Enos, 555; Isabel, 554, 555; James, 554; John, 554, 555(2); Joseph, 555; Moses, 555; Sally, 555; Silas, 555; William, 555

GRIER: Agnes, 29; Ann, 58; Ebenezer, 58; Elizabeth, 58; George Benjamin,58; James Martha, 57; Judith, 58; Mary Jane, 58; Samuel, 57, 58; Samuel,Jr., 58; Thomas William, 58

GRIFFIN: Elizabeth, 474; James, 474; Joshua, 474; Kitty, 563; Moselle M., 195, 196, 268, 269(2); Noah, 474; Rhoda, 474; Shadrack, 474; Solomon, 474; Thomas, 474

GRIGG: Alonso Roland, 155; Burton Crage, 155; Cynthia Lenorah, 154; Eslcy Vann, 155; James Hilliard, 154, 155; Joseph Jonah, 155; Lily Cornelia,155; Marinda Leonria, 155; Tanso, 155; Thomas Clingman, 155; William Pinkney, 155(2); Williard Sisero, 155

GRIGGS: Nancy Marinda, 513

GRIMES: Letitia, 450(2)

GRIMLING: George H., 445

GRIZEL: Sarah, 447

GRUBBS: Anna, 353

GRUNDY: R. C., 570; R. C., Rev., 570

GUESS: Ollion, 22

GUIGNARD: Caroline E., 261

GULLATTE: Mary T., 265

GUNNELS: Charles O., 382; E. N., 382; Electra, 382; Estella, 382; G. M., 382; Mary E., 382; Olivia Ware, 382

GUTHRIE: R. T., Mrs., 555

GUY: George W., 26; Sue Alma, 270; Victoria Greer, 25

GUYTON: Aaron, 148, 149; Amos Charles, 294; Augusta Helen, 294; Charles, 294; E. H., 82; Elizabeth, 149, 294; Emma Saxton, 294; H. E., Mrs., 84; Hannah, 149, 294; Jane, 149(2); John, 294(2); Joseph, 149, 294; Judith, 294; Julia Elmira, 294; Katherine, 149; Margaret, 149; Margaret Love, 294; Margaret V., 149; Mary, 148, 294; Mary Elizabeth, 294; Moses, 294; N. H., 82; Robert, 148; Sarah, 294; Sarah Caroline, 294; Tabitha, 294; Tabitha Jane, 294

GWATHMEY: Ellen Joel, 455; H. B., 456; Humphrey Brooke, 454; William Gaston, 455

GWYN: Amelia, 474; Amelia Seluia, 509(2); Caroline, 474; James, 474; James, Jr., 474; James, Sr., 474; Lorenzo, 474; Peyton, 474; Richard Ransom, 474(2); Sarah, 474(3)

HABERSHAM: Alexander Wylly, 250; Annie Righton, 249; Barnard Elliott, 250; Catherine Esther, 250; Edward M., 249; Francis Bolton, 250; James,

(Habersham continued...)

250;John Bolton, 250; Richard U., 250; Richard W., 249; Richard Wiley, 250; Sarah Georgia, 250; Stephen Elliott, 250
HACKETT: Augustus Griffin, 237(2); Edgar Sheppard, 237; Isabel Wright, 236; Lillie Fuller, 236, 237; Mary Isabel Dendy, 237; Minnie S., 237; W. J., 236; W. W., 236; William J., 237; William Julian, 236, 237; William Wright, 237(2)

HAGLER: Denson, John; Elizabeth, 557; George W., 517; Hagler, Geo.; Jack,517

HAILE: Mary, 298(2)

HALE: Rev., 75

HALEY: Clarence Trenton, 370; Mary Ella Adams, 369

HALFACRE: Elizabeth Heneretta, 298

HALL: Ann Lee, 486(2); B. S., 486(2); Bryant S., 485-487; Dolly Mae Jones,486; J. L., Rev., 153; Jane, 118; John, 474; Lola, 486, 487; M. I., 487(2); M. J., 486; Martha Ann, 486; Mary C., 486; Melona, 22; Miriam,487(2); Nancy, 474; Priscilla, 474; Robert, Rev., 20; Solomon, 486; W. L., 485-487; Whitman C., Rev., 240; William, 509(2); William L., 486

HALLUM: R. A. R., 172

HALSEY: Lemuel B., 490(2)

HAMILINE: Elizabeth, 419

HAMILTON: Gen., 83; Horace, 67; Lawrence Caswell, 564; Thomas, 252

HAMITER: David, 183

HAMLIN: Ann Cobia, 262, 267; Harriet Moore, 262, 267; James Hibben, 262,267; John, 262(2), 267; Nicholas Cobia, 262, 267; Penelope Sarah, 262,267; Philip Moore, 262, 267; Sarah P., 288; Thomas, 262, 267

HAMMOND: Mary C., 263

HAMMONDS: Richmond, 227

HAMRICK: A., 423; A. L., 423, 424(2); Abbie D., 423; Abbie Dean, 424; Amelia, 424; Billy, 383; E. E., 423; E. O., 423; Ellie, 424; Ezra C., 425; Francis Ann, 425; G. E., 423; G. P., Mrs., 162; Grove, 424; Grove Cleveland, 425; Isom Clinton, 425; James W., 425; Johnie, 423; Johnnie, 424; M. C., 425, 426; M. L., 423(2), 424; M. S., 423; M. T., 423; Martin Colver, 425; Martin Luther, 424; Mary Susan, 424; Mattie Priscilla, 425; Myrtle, 165; N. C., 423, 424; N. O., 423; N. S., 423; Oaky, 424; Ockie, 424; Ollie, 423; Oma Jane, 423; R. Z., 423; Sarah Ann, 383; Siley C., 424; Susan E., 424; Susan Faye Webb, 424; Thomas Frank, 425; W. C., 423,426; W. O., 423; W. W., 426(2); William Edgar, 426

HANCOCK: Harriet, 344; Henry, 286

HAND: Fanny, 517; Mary Ann Matilda, 517

HANDY ALTINA: Sarah Rebecca Ann, 51

HANEY: Betheney, 400; Celia, 400; Drusilla, 400; Elizabeth, 400; John, 400; Lidemia, 400; Mary, 400; Nancy, 400; Rebecca, 400; Robert, 400(2), 401;Salley, 400; Syntha, 400; Thomas B., 400; Timothy, 400(2); Washington,400; William, 400

HANKINSON: Robert, 320

HANNA: J., Sr., 481

HANNAN: Elizabeth, 192

HANSON: Emma, 265

HARBIN: A. C., 419; Allen C., 419(2), 420; Caswell, 419; Commodore E., 420; Cosmodore P., 419; Easter, 419(2), 420; Elizabeth, 419(2); Frances, 419;Jackson, 419(2); Lydia, 419; Matilda A., 419; Matilda A. H., 420; Nancy, 419; Sarah A. M., 419; Walter, 419(3), 420

HARBUCK: Maggie, 519; Margaret, 519; Mary Jewell, 519

HARD: J. S., Rev., 233

HARDEN: Correy Allice, 233; Frances Elizabeth, 233; Francis, 233; Mary Amedia, 233, 234(4); Mary Ann Price Sharpe, 232; Nancy Ann, 233; Thomas Jefferson, 233(2); William, 232; William LaFayette, 232

HARDIN: Clarissa, 225; Henry, Lt., 225

HARDING: Charles T., 452; Joseph, 453; Joseph Sr., 453; Julia, 452; Mary,452; Retina, 453

HARDY: Alice E., 184; Elizabeth, 272(2); Elizabeth L., 272; Henrietta Marie, 272; Martha, 272(2); Mary, 272(2); Mary A., 184; Samuel, 272; Susannah, 272(2)

HARKNESS: Mary Ann, 494

HARMON: A. H., 163; A. P., 163; B. B. C. E., 163; C. M., 163; C. N., 164; D. R. L., 164; G. A., 163; J. H., 163; Jacob, 163; M. G., 163, 164; M.R., 163; N. R., 162-164; R. I., 163; S. C., 163

HARPER: Susan, 377

HARRELL: Altina Jane, 51, 52; Edna, 502; Eliza Elizabeth, 51; Elizabeth, 502; Handy Altina, 52; Harriett Laura Tabitha, 52(2); Hartwell Spain, 51; Isaac, 502; James Lewis, 283; Joe Anna, 502; John,

(Harrell continued)...

51; John Henry, 52; John Pembroke, 461; John Riley, 51; John W., 502; Katie, 502; L. E. Maud, 51; Levi, 502; Levi, Jr., 502; Liley Hay, 52; Lovett L., 502; Marthy Mazell, 51; Mary Elender, 52; Mary Elenor, 51; Maxie Alexander, 52(2); Nancy, 502; Nancy Henraetter, 51; Nancy Henrietta, 52; Needham, 502; Pauld Wade, 462; Polly, 502; Roxalaney Jane, 52; Sallie John, 462; Samuel, 502; Sara, 502; Sarah, 51; Sarah Rebecca Ann, 51(2); Silas Tafford, 52(2); William, 51(2), 52(2), 502; William Edward, 52(2); William Osker, 52; Wright W., 502; Zedun Beatrice, 51

HARRIET: Mary A., 111

HARRIS: Alford, 413; Ann, 20; Ann L., 20(2), 327; Charles, 514; Daniel, 413; Elizabeth, 20(2), 560; Fanny, 560; George W., 413; Harriet, 499; Harry, 413; James, 20; Jane, 20, 328; John, 20(3), 327, 328, 560; Lucy, 560, 561(2); Mariah, 413; Nancy, 560; Pennina, 413; Polly, 560; Richard, 560, 561; Robert, 560(2), 561(2); Robert, Col., 20; Susannah, 560; T. A., 20; Thomason, 560; Turner, 413; Wiley, 20

HARRIS (COLORED): Amey, 328; Charles, 328; John, 328; Juda, 328; M., 328; Mary, 328; Nelson, 328; Sam, 328

HARRISON: Benjamin, 204, 205; E. W., 205; Edmund, 205; Heartwell, 204, 205; James Henry, 204; John, 204(2); L. C., Rev., 241; Mary, 204, 205; Nancy, 204; Polly, 204; Steuart, 205

HARROLD: Catharine, 523

HART: O. Frank, 260; Oliver, Rev., 209

HARTMOUTH: James H., 450

HARVEY: E. W., 577; Joseph, 577; Robert, 276; Thomas, 49, 50

HARWOOD: Ann, 491

HASELWOOD: Dorcas, 62(2); Lancaster, 62(2)

HASSELTINE: Martha Ann, 69

HATCHER: Rhesa, 101

HAUN: Elizabeth, 99

HAUPT: Eliza Bolles, 146

HAUSIHL: Johann Adam, 107

HAWKINS: Ann, 485; Delia, 485; Eleanor, 485; Frank, 485; George Washington, 485; John D., 485; Joseph, 485; Lucinda Davis Ruffin, 485; Lucy, 485; Mildred B., 485; Philemon, 485; Philemon I, 485; Philemon II, 485; Sarah, 485(2); Thomas P., 485; William, 485

HAWKS: Francis, 509

HAYNES: R. W., 82, 83

HAYWOOD: Benjamin Sherwood, 396; Marshall DeLancey, 475

HEAD: Joseph C., 265

HEARD: Jane M., 114, 345

HEATH: Margaret Alice, 533

HEATON: Sarah, 523

HECTOR: Patty, 225

HEDGES: Susie Edna, 33; W. W., Rev., 156

HEDING: Rachel, 439

HEDLESTON: Allie, 34; Allis, 33; Ann Agnes, 33; Ann Susannah, 34; Annie Gertrude, 33; Edna Mae, 33, 34; Elizabeth, 33; Ernestine Sutton, 33; Glendine Elizabeth, 33, 34; Herbert Nathaniel, 34(2); Jane P., 32; Jefferson Davis, 33; John James, 32, 33; John Presley, 33(2); Maggie Lou, 33, 34; Mary Agnes, 33; Mattie Lou, 34; Nettie Lou, 34; Samuel, 34; Samuel Barlow, 33(2), 34; Sarah Jane, 32; Susie, 34; Susie Edna, 34; W. D., 32-34; William Barlow, 32, 33; William C., 33, 34; William Charles, 33; William Davis, 33(3), 34; Willie Barlow, 34; Willie C., 34

HEFFNER: Louise Brown, 154

HELEN: Elizabeth, 554

HEMPHILL: Emma Katharine, 94

HENDERSON: Billy, 387; Calder Mastin, 125; Drury Hampton, 125; Franky, 448; Gabriel Pinson, 125; Hugh Lee, 125; James, 125; James C., 125; James N., 48; Jasper, 387; John H., 125; Joseph, 448(2); Kate, 189; Lucinda, 125; Nancy, 125; Rebecca, 125; Ruth, 125; William F., 125

HENDREN: A. G., 395; Andrew G., 394(2); Charles Bradford, 394; Clyde Elizabeth, 395; Della May, 395; Effie Leola, 394; Freda Emily, 395; I. L., Mrs., 282; Jesse, 394; Jesse Van Dora, 395; L. H., 395; Louisa Jane, 394; Luther, 395(2); Mable Rebecca, 395; Mary Elizabeth, 394, 395(2); Noami, 394; Pearl Eugenia, 394; Rebecca E., 395(2); Rebecca Emily, 394; Rufus Luther, 394; Russell Blaine, 395; Theodosia Marie, 394; William Rufus, 394

HENDRICK: Meade LeSeuer, 494

HENDRIX: Madison, 145

HENDRY: Hannah Carolina, 532(2); Lavinia Pierce, 532

HENLEY: A. L., 563; August L., 563

HENRY: Alexander, 575; Betsey Caroline, 577; Catherine Allison, 113; Celia, 102; Celia Fields, 102; Eliza, 577; Elizabeth, 577; Enos, 577; Farmer, 575; Hamilton, 574; Hannah, 574, 577; Hugh, 574; James, 575, 577(3); Jane, 102, 577(2); Joel, 102; John, 574, 575, 577; Joseph, 574(2), 575(2), 577; Liza, 102; Loucey, 102; Lydia, 102; Malcolm, 574(2); Margaret Allison, 113; Mary, 102, 574; Mathew, 574, 577; Moses, 574(2); Mutual, 102; Nancey, 102, 575; Nancy, 574; Peninah, 353; Philip, 574; Polly, 574, 577; Resign, 577; Robert, 102(2); Sally, 574; Temperance, 102; Theophilus, 102; William, 574, 575, 577; William Henry, 102

HENSON: Aaron, 467; Absalom, 467; Alton, 467; Charlotte, 467; Daniel, 467; Emma, 47; Lloyd, 467; Wiley, 467

HERBEMONT: Alexander, 274(2); Alexander Jr., 274; Clara Isabella, 274(2); Elizabeth, 274; George, 274; Martha, 274; Nicholas, 274; Nicholas Michel Laurent, 274; Victoire, 274

HERBERMONT: Andre, 273; Claire, 273; George Laurent, 273; Michael, 273; Michel, 273

HERDING: Nancy, 451

HEREFORD: Brook Gwathmey, 456; Ellen, 456; Howell, 456; Mary Mason Bronaugh, 456; Robert A., 454; Robert Jr., 456; Virginia, 456

HERNDON: G. P., Jr., 466

HERRION: Anna, 303; James, 303

HESS: John, Revolutionary, 489

HETHERINGTON: Jane, 359

HETZLER: Neal, Mrs., 399

HEUGHTON: Silas, 490

HICKMAN: Elliott, 554; Julia Ann, 554; Phariby, 24

HICKS: Alexander, 378; Anna, 378; Cornelia Octavia, 538; Daniel, 539; David W., 378; Edula, 538; Edwin, 538, 540(2); Edwin A., 539; Edwin Augustus, 538, 540; Elizabeth, 378; Elizabeth Jane, 365; Emily Robert Blanch, 538; Fanney, 378; Galen, Revolutionary, 249; Hardy D., 365; Harvy K., 365; Imogene Hair, 538; James, 364, 365; James Tu, 365; Jesse, 537, 538, 540; Jesse H., 539; Jessie A., 540; Jessie Anne Belle, 537; John, 378(3); John D., 365; Jonathan, 364; Joseph, 378; Larkin W., 378; Lucinda, 538; Lucretia Moore Dickins, 538, 540; Lucy, 538(2), 540(2); Martha, 365; Martha E., 365; Mary, 537-540; Mary A. D., 365; Mary Elizabeth, 538, 540; Nancy, 364; Nancy Pulliam, 538, 540; Naomi, 365; Polley, 378; Sarcy, 378; William Dickins, 538; William Nu, 365

HIERS: Cornelia Ellot, 170; Joseph Abraham, 170; Julia Elizabeth, 170; W. H., 170(2); Wade Hampton, 170; William Abraham, 170

HIGGINS: Eliza Ann, 156; J. S., 156(2); John Butler, 156; Martha S., 21;Theodocia Leah, 156; Yates, 156

HIGH: Agnes, 466, 467; Alsey, 466, 467; Amelia M., 466; Amelia Mitchel, 466; Candes Scriven, 466; Delilah Hawkins, 466; Elizabeth, 408(2); Elizabeth Ann, 466; Fanney Martin, 466; John Terrell, 466(2), 467; Margaret M. C., 109; Martin, 466; Patsey Brandy, 466; Ruth Terrell, 466; Scriven, 466; Solomon, 466; Thomas P., 109

HIGHTOWER: John G., 440

HILEY: Anderson Jacob, 214; Ann Elizabeth, 214; Ann Sophia, 213; Anna Sophia, 213; Barbary, 213; Cathrine, 213; Elia, 213; Elizabeth, 213; Frances Emma, 213; James Samuel, 214; John, 213; John Thomas, 214; Lavinia Adelaide, 214; Martha Sophia, 214; Mary Caroline, 214; Mary H.,

(Hiley continued...)

214; Mary Magdalene, 213; Nancy, 213; Rebecca Caroline, 214; Roland, 213,214; Thomas, 213; William, 214

HILL: Charlie, 424(2); Dorothy, 110; Elizabeth H., 329; James C., 554; Lucius, Mrs., 458; Octavia Hamrick, 424; Sarah, 116; Susannah Parham, 433; Thomas, 284; Thomas F., 553

HILLEY: Calista Alberta, 265

HILLIARD: Eugenia B., 394; Genie, 395; James, 433

HILLS: Abigail, 52; Mary N., 59, 60

HINES: Sallie, 553

HINTON: Martha, 475; William H., 400; William W., 400(2)

HISAW: Mary B., 225

HOBBS: Sarah, 446; Thomas, 446

HODGE: Gilbert, 557; William, Revolutionary, 546

HODGES: Ann, 236; Sallie, 215

HOFFMAN DI CURTONI: Camille Pruett, 26

HOKE: Nancy Harriet, 260; Nannie H., 261

HOLCOMB: Ann Fallas, 360; Isaac, 360

HOLCOMBE: A. S., Dr., 68; Alva J., 67; Darius, 67; Darius J., 68; Eudocia, 68(2); Frances Cassandra, 69; Frances H. S. M., 68; Harmon C., 67, 68; Harriet N., 69; Hosea H., 67(2), 68, 69; John B., 68; John R., 68; Leah, 306(2), 307; Martha R., 67, 68; Nancy, 69; Nancy E., 69; Rebecca Jones, 68; Tartan, 67; Tarton P., 68; Teresa, 67, 68; Thomas M., 68, 69; Thomas N., 69; W. H., 68; William, 68; William Henry, 69

HOLLAND: Amelia, 506; Amelia Brewington, 506; Arestus, 506; Cynthia, 506; Elmina, 506; Emma Cooper, 58; Hannah, 506; Hetty Cole, 506; Isaac, 402, 506; James, 506; Jane E., 9; John, 506; Julia Ann, 506; Margaret, 402; Maria Louisa, 506; Mathew, 402; Matilda, 402; Nancy, 506; Orlando, 506; Samuel, 506; Susannah, 402; William, 402, 506

HOLLEY: John, 188; Mary, 189; Nathaniel, 187

HOLLINGSHEAD: Revolutionary Mr., 210

HOLLINGSWORTH: Anny, 403; Elizabeth, 403(2); Eve, 403; Jenny, 403; Mary, 347; Polly, 403; Zedebee, 403

HOLLIS: Isabella, 444

HOLLOWAY: L. M., Revolutionary, 485

HOLMES: Joseph, Revolutionary, 286

HOLT: Elizabeth, 502; Leah Elizabeth, 307; Mary, 126; Pheby Caroline, 307; Temperance, 407; W. F., 306

HOME: Pauline, 165

HONOUR: John M., 366

HOOD: Hazel, 480

HOOKER: Travis, 553

HOONER: Millie, 271

HOOPER: Arminta, 515; Benjamin Chastain, 515(2), 516; Carolina Kimsey, 515; Catharine H., 515; Elizabeth, 515(2), 516; Elizabeth Cathy, 516(2); Emma S., 515; George Franklin, 515; Georgia Ann, 515; Henry Oliver, 515; James Lafayette, 516(2); John Struby, 516; Lizzie, 516; Maggie, 516(2); Martha Jane, 516; Mary Caroline, 515(2); Mary Emmaline, 516; Noah, 516; Olley Arminta, 515; Oscar Lee, 515; Paul Lester, 516; Sarah, 516; Sophia, 176; Sophia Cynthia, 177; Thomas Athan, 516; Thomas Jefferson, 515(2), 516; Violet Virginia, 515; W. M., 515; William, 515(2); William M., 515; William Ray, 516; Wyly Ferdinand, 515

HOPE: Adam, 228; Agnes, 229, 230; Catherine, 228; Celena Mary Ellen, 229; Clarence Bland, 265; Ellen D., 230; Ellen DeMoss, 229; Ethel, 265(2); Hugh Washington, 229, 265; Isaac, 228; Isaac Meek, 229; J. Albertus, 229; J. W. P., 230; J. William Preston, 229; James, 228(2), 229; James Lindsay, 265; Jane Amanda, 229; Jane Maddison, 229; John, 228; Julius A., 230; Lucinda Powell, 229; Mary Darvin, 265; Mary Darwin, 228; Pamela, 229, 230; R. L., 230; Robert Peyton, 229; Syntha, 229; William Asbury, 265

HOPKINS: Martha J., 266

HORN: Abisha B., 559; Alice, 139; Alice S., 140; Etheldred, 560; Frances, 559; Hardy, 560; Harris, 560; Henry H., 558; Howell, 560; Joel, 560; Joshua L., 559, 560; Joshua L., Jr., 558; Joshua Laurence, 559; Mary, 61; Mary Ann, 558; Mathew, 560; Milbrie, 560; Priscilla, 61, 558, 559(2); Rebecca, 560; William, 61

HORNE: Margaret, 134

HORRALL: Eliza L., 296

HOSKINS: Fanny Reed, 470; Harriette N., 464; Mary, 470, 491; Richard, 470; William, 491

HOTLEY: Frances A., 420

HOUCK: Gamewell, Mrs., 546

HOUGHTON: Elizabeth, 490, 491; Elizabeth B., 491; Mary S., 491; S. B., 491; Silas H., 491; Silas M., 491

HOUSE: Dock C., 515; Frederick, 550; Jane, 550

HOUSEAL: Johann Adam, 107, 108; John Adam, 108; John Bernard, 178; Margaretha, 177; Mary Elizabeth, 107, 108; Mary Magdalene, 108; Rose Cathrine, 108

HOUSTON: Robert, 535

HOWARD: Benjamin, 534; Charles B., 247; Discretion, 534, 535; George, 129; John, 293(2); Marion, 128, 129; Prudence Satec, 534; Roberta, 293; Spencer Claborn, 129; Tallulah Bell, 294; William Sanders Jr., 293; William Sanders Sr., 293

HOYT: Mary Abbie, 53

HUBERT: Agnes Martha, 579

HUDDLESTON: Ellis Fleming, 281

HUDDLESTONE: F., 578

HUET: Annette, 215

HUFF: Augustus, 312

HUGHES: Herman, 236; Jack, 236; John, 535; Mary M., 570

HUGHEY: C. H., 38; Charles Hebron, 38; Harland, 38; John, 37, 38; L. G., 38; Livingston Green, 38; Martha Jane, 38; Mary, 38; Maryan, 37, 38; Milly M., 38; Nancy, 38; Rebecca, 38; Susan, 38; William, 38

HUGHLETT: Ann, 404-406; Charles, 310; Elizabeth, 404, 405(2); Eunice B., 404; James, 310; John, 404, 405; Margaret, 310(2); Mary, 404, 405; Mary Tate, 406; Owen, 310; Peter Morgan, 404-406; Pleasant, 310; Robert, 404; Sally Winefred, 405; Sally Winifred, 404; Thomas Tate, 404; Thopmas Tate, 405; William, 404, 406; William Hardy, 404; William M., 405; William T., 405; William Thrift, 404; William Thrist, 405

HUGHS: Lucinda Jane, 451

HUGUEIN: Abram, 296

HUGUENIN: Abraham, 297; Abraham, Capt., 297; Abram, 296, 297; Adelaide, 297; Anna, 296; Anna Maria, 297; Anna Serena, 297; Cornelius, 297; Cornelius M., 296; Cornelius Macdonough, 297; Emaline Lucia, 297; Emmaline L., 296; J. G., 296, 297; Julia Theodora, 297(2); Julius, 297; Julius G., 296; Julius Gillison, 297; Lawrence A., 297; Louisiana, 297; Sarah, 297; Sarah Rebecca, 297; Theodora O., 297; Thomas E., 297

HUMBERT: Harriet G., 312(2)

HUMPHREY: James M., 529

HUMPHREYS: J. M., 528; Mary Ida, 528; Thomas, 499

HUMPHRIES: David, Rev., 298

HUNT: Amanda Hall, 22; E. F., 537; Elizabeth, 538, 540(3); Elizabeth Wilkins, 538; James A., 540; Lucy, 539; Mary, 539; Robert, 540; Sallie Fisher, 538, 540; Virginia, 539; Wilizabeth W., 540; Wilkins, 539; William, 68, 537, 538, 540(3); William H., 539; William Wilkins, 537(2)

HUNTER: Humphrey, 192; Mary Louise, 167; Ruth T., 467; William, 285

HURDLE: Kedar, 446; Nancy, 446(2)

HURLEY: Arthur Anthony, 508; Ernestine, 508; William Turner, 508

HUSSEY: Eugenia, 532; Susan Ann Stanley, 532

HUTCHERSON: Ambrose, 264; William Robert Christoph., 43

HUTCHINS: Claude, 265; Mary Lalagi, 265

HUTCHINSON: William, 540; William Franklin, 220

HUTCHISON: Bessie May, 222(2); Dolpheus, 221; Dolpheus S., 222; Dolpheus Sophia, 221; Irvin, 220; Jefferson, 218; Jefferson Davis, 219(2); John Maxamilian, 218; John Maxamillian, 219; Joseph F., 218, 222; Joseph Fletcher, 218, 219, 221, 223; Joseph Wesley, 222; Lucy Elizabeth, 222; Lydia, 220; M. A., 219; Martha Eliddier, 221; Martha L., 219; Martha Lydia, 218; Mary A., 219; Mary Ann, 218(2), 219; Mary C., 222; Mary Cathron, 222; Mary Christianah, 221; Mary E., 222; Mary Elizabeth, 222; Rebecca F., 218; Rebecca Frances, 218; Samuel Peter, 221; Sarah E., 219; Sarah Elizabeth, 218; Sarah Jane Elizabeth, 221; Sonora B., 219; Sonora Benicia, 218; W. F., 219; W. P., 217; William C., 219; William Carvosson, 218, 219; William F., 217, 218; William Franklin, 218(2), 219; William R., 222(2); William Richard, 221, 223; William Vearl, 222, 223; Willie Geneva, 222

ILERAN: Rev. Dr., 74

INABINET: Adria R., 322; Alva Juanita, 323; Barbara Lynn, 323; Earl Alva, 323; Earle A., 323; Emanuel P., 323; Harriett Stick, 323; J. H. Kennerly, 322; J. Preston, 322; James Henry, 324; James Henry Mallard, 322, 323; James Mallard, Jr., 324; John O. R., 322; Marion Durham, 323; Mark Kennerly, 324; Mary Cordelia, 324; Mary E., 322; Nancy Carole, 323; Pamela Durr, 324; Pearl Edith, 323; Sarah Frances, 323; William L., 322

INABNIT: Ann Caroline, 341, 342; Ann M., 342(2); Anna M., 342; Anna Matilda, 341; Derrell G. W., 342; Derrell George Washington, 341; Drucilla Colson, 341; Elizabeth, 342; Elkanah Emory, 342; Emery E., 342; Frank H., 341; Hilliard Jacob Malachi, 341, 342; J. H. Mallard, 342; Jacob, 341, 342; James Henry Mallard, 342; Jane, 342; Jane Rebecca, 341; Malinda Emily, 342; Mary, 341; Rachel Olivia, 341; Sarah Elizabeth, 341

INGRAM: Ely, 271

INMAN: Edith, 176

IRVINE: Mary S., 48

IRWIN: Cecile Henry, 157; James, 432; Robert, Rev., 48

ISBELL: Benjamin, 534, 535; Benjamin Howard, 535; Dennis Rowan, 535; Discretion, 535; Elizabeth, 534; Frances, 534, 535; Frances Discretion, 535; James, 534(2); James Parker, 535; John, 534; John Wallace, 535; Livingston, 534; Lucinda Missouri, 535(2); Martha Ann, 535; Mary, 534; Mary Louise, 535; Miriam, 535; Prudence, 534; Sarah Elizabeth, 535; Thomas, 534, 535; Thomas Martin, 535; Thomas, Jr., 534

ISRAEL: Mary, 540, 543

IVY: Alfred Junius, 479; Alfred Monroe, 480, 481(2); Currie, 481; Emma Elizabeth, 480(2); Fannie Myrtle, 480; Gene, 480; Iola, 344; James H., 479; Loua Aileen, 480; Lucille Alleen, 480; Lucy Ann, 479; Lucy L., 479; Mary Ardell, 480; Mary Ardelle, 480; Mary Frances, 479; Mary L., 344; Mary Louisa, 480, 481; Minnie B., 479; Minnie Barron, 480; R. L., 481; R. N. W., 479, 480; Rebecca Elizabeth, 479; Robert, 479; Robert Lee, 480; Robert Lucius, 479(2), 480(2); Roberta Lee, 480; Sarah Jane, 479; Thomas Buford, 480; Uiell K., 481; Uzelle Karr, 480

JACKS: N. G., Rev., 234

JACKSON: Alfonses A., 92; Alphonso, 92; Amos, 508; Ann E., 326; Anne Eliza Fox, 325; Betsy Faris, 92; Casey, 68; Cassandra, 67; Dorcas, 92; Dorcas A., 92; Eliza Fox, 326; Eupheny A., 92; George T., 325; George Twiggs, 325; Hannah, 508(4); Hiram, 508; Isaac, 508; J. Frank, Rev., 153; James, 508; James F., 91, 92; Joannah, 92; Joannah A., 92; Johannah, 471(2);John, 508; John F., 92; John K., 325; Joseph, 508; Joseph Hillhouse, 92; Margret Minerva, 92; Mary Ann, 326; Robert, 92; Samuel, 325, 508(3); Sarah, 508; William, 92(2), 325(2), 326

JACKSON (COLORED): Charles Columbus, 93; Curtis, 93; Elizabeth, 93; Jane,93; Lucy, 93; Luis, 93; Lyda, 92; Marchel, 93; Martha, 93; Moses, 93; Prince, 92; Sara, 93; Suzanna, 93

JAGGERS: Susanna, 183
JAMES: A. A., Rev., 95; Aaron, 76; Albert Franklin, 39; Alfred Javan, 39; Benjamin, 76; Charles, 39(2); Drury, 345; Edgar Boyt, 345; Ela A., 345; Elizabeth, 345; Georgia A., 345; H. G., 345; Hannah, 76; J. F., 345;John, 345; John Luther, 39; Jonathan, 76; Joseph, 77; Joseph F., 345; Kitty, 39; L. A., 345; Lucinda, 345; Manervy Adaline, 39; Martha, 76,345; Mary, 76, 77, 344; Mary E., 345; Milas Milford, 39; Morgan, 76, 77; Nancy, 344; Rebecca, 345; Reuben, 39; Reuben Joseph, 39(2); Reuben, Sr., 39; Samuel, 9; Sarah, 345; Sarah C., 345; Susannah. 345; Temperance, 561;Thomas, 76, 345; Walker Manning, 39; William, 344; William Lancaster, 39

JAMESON: M., Rev., 235

JARNIGIN: Chesley, 477; Martha, 477; Sarah, 477; Thomas, 477

JARRELL: W. L., 276

JELKS: J. T., 240

JENKINS: Cecil Ross, 164; Dorothy Irene, 164; Elender, 1; Isabella Phebe, 75; James, 164; Lewis, 367; Lewis Harris, 367; Mary C., 367; Rev. Mr., 349; Shadrick Jr., 1

JENNINGS: John, 272

JENNY: Samuel, 580

JESTER: Abner, 280(2); Allie Mae, 281(2); Benjamin, 280; Henry, 280; James, 280; Jane, 281; John, \, 280; Levi, 280(2); Levi Dickey, 280; Mary, 280;Mary Jane, 280; Nancy, 280; Rayannah Frazier, 280; Razannah, 280; Rosa,281; Rosa Lee, 281; Sara, 280; William, 280

JETERS: Armentia, 206; E. A., 212; G., 206; George W., 212; Polly, 206

JEWELL: Gabriel, 123

JOHNS: Harvy, 405

JOHNSON: Ahah, 243; Annie Bell, 387; Arthur L., Mrs., 428, 436(2); Bailey Meredith, 386, 387; Bertie, 21; C. O., Rev., 241; Cary, 270; Charlton, 310; Clayborn, 310; Elizabeth, 388(2); Elizabeth G., 243; Elizabeth P., 428; Elizabeth Phillips, 429; Evelyn, 388; Fannie E., 243; Fannie Emma, 243; Frances E., 215; Gideon, 227; Gideon Jr., 227; Golet C., 387; Greene Berry, 243; Greene P., 243; Henrietta, 544(2); Hewlett, 310; Isham, 416(2); Isham Peter, 415; James, 497, 518; James Anderson, 452; Jane, 232, 472; Jared Smith, 315; Jesse Lawrence, 416; Jessie Lawrence, 416; John H., 243(2); John P., Jr., 387; John Patterson, 387; John S., 386-389; John William, 226; L. B., 285; Laussie Emmeline, 243; Lawrence, 416(3); Leaner, 388; Leonard, 386; Leussie E., 243; Lilly, 388; Louise, 243(2); Lucretia, 270; Lucretia Davenport, 243; Lucy A., 243; Luticia Wells, 226; Maggie T., 103; Margaret, 310(2), 514(4); Margaret M., 415, 416; Martha A. M., 416; Martha Ann Lisa, 416; Martha Ann Melissa, 416(2);Martin Ann, 243; Mary, 387; Mary A., 416; Mary Ann, 416(2); Mary Charlton, 311; Mary DeGraffenreid, 228; Mary F., 243; Mary Frances, 243; Mary Louisa, 315(2); Mary Phillips, 428, 429; Mary Virginia Conley, 416; Michael, 428, 429; Moses, 310; N. C. Betty, 387; Nancy Ann, 443; Nelle May, 388; Neucie, 416; Neucie Sylvania, 416; Ola Kathleen, 387; Oleve, 388; Rachel, 452; Rev. Mr., 74; Rezina, 452; Roy, 518; Saloma Loma,

(Johnson continued...)

388; Samuel Henry, 416(2); Sara, 310; Sarah Alston, 228; Sarah J., 243; Sarah Jane, 243; Stephen, 310; Susan W., 471; Telutha, 21; Thomas, 415, 416; Thomas B., Rev., 416; Thomas Bradley, 416; Thomas Bradley, Rev., 415,416; Thomas Furman, 388; W. D., 226; William F., 243; William Floyd, 243; William Luther, 388; William Weakley, 227, 228; William Weakley Jr., 228

JOHNSTON: Adds, 270; Annalisa, 142; Cary, 271; Daniel, 141, 142; Daniel J., 142, 143; Eliza, 142; Elizabeth, 447; Elizabeth S., 142; H. R., 141; Hannah, 142; Hannah Irena, 142, 143; Henderson R., 142; J. D., 142; J. Gillian, 270; James D., 142; James J., 142; John, 448(2); John Chew, 447; John S., 387; Joseph P., 142; Joseph R., 143; Larkin, 447; Margaret Elizabeth, 143; Margareta, 143; Margarett, 141; Margarett G., 141; Mariah W., 142; Martha Clemmit, 271; Mary M., 143; Mary T., 141; Myra, 142; Nathan, 447; Omy L., 143; R. C., 141, 142(3); Reuben J. D., 143; Sarah, 142; Sarah L., 143; Thomas, 447; William, 142, 447

JOHNTON: Johnson, 447(2)

JOLLY: Joseph A., 247; Rhoda, 399

JONES: Amanda, 25, 444; Amelia Mitchel, 467; Amos J., 532; Andrew V., 25;Andrew Vastine, 24; Bennet, 25; Bessie, 515; Candus Riley, 232; Carol David, 294; Charley E. J., 506; Daniel Asbury, 23, 24; Dolly, 24, 25;Drucilla, 23, 24; E. E., Rev., 167; Elizabeth, 24(2), 427; Elizabeth P.,460; Emily, 24, 25; F. J., 399; George K., 460; Graham Sue Vinson, 25; Granny Pat, 24; H. F., 578; James William, 24, 25; Jane, 25; John Pride, 466; Margaret, 24(2), 215; Martha Ann, 24; Mary Ann Eugenia, 161; Mary Elsie, 255; Mary G., 291; Nancy, 25(2); Neil Robert, 294; O. J., Rev., 167; Phebe, 24; Pheby, 24; Polly K., 460; Rebecca, 68, 69, 505(2); Rebecca K., 460; Remedy, 444; Robert Smith, 466, 467; Sally A. C., 460; Sinthy, 23, 24; Tignal, 466(2), 467; Vincent, 24; Vincent Sr., 22, 24; Vincent, Sr., 26; Vinson, 25; Vinson Grier, 25; Vinson, Sr., 25; Virginia Key, 294; W. B., 126; William Andrew, 25; William J., 400;

William S., 459; Winkler R., 466; Zachariah, 24(2), 25

JOOK: George, 491; Sarah, 491

JORDAN: Britain, 407; Burrel, 406; Burwell, 407; George, 406, 407; Green H., 407; James M., 517; John, 406, 407(2); John B., 449; Margaret Ann, 449; Mary, 406, 407, 461; Mary J., 489; Patience, 407; Priscella, 407; Wineford, 406, 407

JOYNER: Amy, 460

JULIEN: Elizabeth, 103; Jense, 103; Jesse, 104; Mary, 103; Peter, 103; Precious, 103; Ruth, 103; Susannah, 103

JULIUS LEON: Harriet Elizabeth, 340

JUMPER: Henry Etta Oswalt, 19

KEELER: Barley G., 54; Josephine, 54

KEITH: Calhoun William, 299; Elizabeth Mary, 300; Elliott Monroe, 298, 300; Flora Cornelia, 299; J. S., Rev. Dr., 210; Mary Sue, 95; Virginia Elvira, 299

KELL: J. E., 230

KELLINGER: John, 467

KELSICK: John R., 473; Levina, 473; William, 473; Wo;;oa,, 473

KEMP: Margaret M., 415

KENDRICKS: Annie Noon Turner, 65

KENNEDY: Agness, 157; Alexander, 379; Andrew, 379(2); Ann, 157; Arthur, 379; Betsy, 379; Catherine, 157; Catrin, 157; Esther, 379; George, 157; Ginsey, 379; Hope, 157; James, 158; Janet, 158; John, 157(2), 192; John Foster, 157; Major, 157, 158; Margaret, 157; Mary, 158; Mary Ann K., 157; Nancy, 379; Peggy, 379; Polly, 379; Richard, 157; Robert, 158; Warren, 450; Wil., 157; William H., Rev., 240

KERCE: Mary, 218; Mary C., 222; Mary Cathron, 221; Sarah A., 222

KERR: Ann, 521; D. E., Mrs., 334; D. F., 334; Elizabeth Jane, 334; Fanny Drucilla, 334; Henry Richard, 334; James, 334; James Harold, 334(2); John R., 334; John Robert, 334; William, 334(3); William M., 334; William Mobley, 334

KEY: Georgia Walker, 294; John Robert, 294; Vivian, 294

KEYSER: Mary, 448

KIMBALL: Caleb, 52; Hannah, 52; Mary, 52

KIMBRO: R. Y., 578

KIMBROUGH: Amy, 460; Ann, 459; Anna, 459; Anne, 459; Catey, 459; Catherine, 459; George, 459; George Markadule, 460; Goldman, 459; James Gibson, 460; John, 460(2); John Anderson Young, 460; John William, 459; Lewis William, 460; Marmaduke, 459; Mary, 459(2); Orinon, 459; Ormon, 459; Ormon Harison, 460; Rebecca, 459; Sarah, 459; William Nathaniel, 460

KIMSEY: Arminta Carolina, 515; Bertha Lotitia, 478; Edith, 478; H. R., 478; Herbert Clay, 478; Lucretia Moavia, 478; Marshall Steuben Percival, 478(2); Mim Louisa, 364; Samuel Barrett, 478

KIMZEY: Aroninta Amanda, 478; Bertha, 478; Betty Ann, 478; Edith Louisa, 478; Edith Rabun, 478, 479; Elisha Lander, 478; Ella Samantha, 479; Emma Iantha, 479; H. C., 479; H. R., 478; Hamilton, 477-479; Hodge

(Kimzey continued...)

R., 478; Hodge Rabun, 478; Hubert, 478; James Japthiah, 478; John, 477, 478; Lucretia, 478; Margaret Elizabeth, 478; Nancy McClure, 478; Percival, 478; Rodee Rabun, 479; Samuel, 478; Samuel B., 479; Thomas Judson, 478; William Calloway, 478(2); Willis Jasper, 478

KIND: J. H., 230

KINDALL: Sary, 557

KING: B. F., 230; Fannie, 21; John, 553; Malissa, 188; N. W., 230; Robert Williams, 553; Sarah Elizabeth, 451; Thomas G., 243; W. C., Miss, 133

KINNETT: Donovan DeWitt, 236, 237; I. H., Mrs., 236; Mary Isabel, 236

KIRK: Douglas Earl, 183

KIRKLAND: Alie, 235; M. A., 234

KIRKPATRICK: M. R., Rev., 264

KNIGHT: James H., 496

KNOTTS: Frank L., 322; William R., 322

KNOX: Mary, 509

KOBB: Mary Ann, 171

KORNIK: Otto Joseph, 480

LA HATTE: Russell, 229

LAFAR: Margaret Will Seyle, 147; Sanford Branch, 146; Sanford Branch, Mrs., 148

LAFITTE: Mary, 320

LAFITTS: John H., 319

LAIRD: Mary, 169
LAKER: Benjamin, 491; Sarah, 491

LAMB: Emma Victoria, 104; Mary, 115, 116; Unity, 104(2); William, 104

LAMBRIGHT: James, 321

LANCASTER: Absalom, 39; Adrian Laverne, 518; Anna Lucinda Maria, 516; Bessie, 518; Charity, 516-518; Charles W., 517; Charles Wesley, 517, 518; Clara, 518; Clyde, 518; Dolly, 518; Effie, 518; Ellery, 518; Ellington, 518; Evelina Morgan Lizabeth, 516; Fanny, 518; Fred, 518; George, 518; Henry, 517; Horace, 518; Isabell, 518; James, 518; James Drew, 516, 518; James L., 516-519; James Lupe, 517; John Wesley, 517, 518; John Willie, 518; Louisa, 517; Luizer, 517; Luther, 518; Mildred Allen, 518; Nancy, 39; Priscilla, 517; Rosamond A., 518; Ruth, 518; Sally, 517; Sarah, 517; Sarah N., 61; Victor, 518; Victor Wilson, 518

LANE: Adelia M., 400; Adelia Manerva, 399; Alfred, 543; Almeda M., 400; Almeda Malvina, 399; Caroline, 475; Charles, 475; Clorena Winaford, 399; Dorothy, 475; Edgar M., 477; Elizabeth, 473, 475; Elizabeth Francina, 399; Emily Ann, 399; George W., 477; Grizelle, 475; Hanson P., 477; Henry, 475; Irene, 543; James, 475, 543; James M., 477; Jesse, 399; Joel, 475; Joel Hinton, 475; John, 475(2); Jonathan, 475, 477; Joseph, 475; Jula A., 400; Julia Artimissa, 399; Martha, 475; Mary, 475(2); Mary R., 477; Nancy, 475; Patience, 475; Rebecca, 475; Rhoda, 475; Rhoda C., 400; Rhoda Caroline, 399; Rhoda Jolly, 399; Richard, 475; Richard A., 477; Rosanah, 473; Sarah, 475; Sarah Sophia, 399; Sharlotte, 400; Sharlotte Ann, 399; Simeon, 475; Theophilus Sterling,

(Lane continued...)

477; Thomas, 475; William, 473, 475; William Robertson, 399; Winnefred, 475; Winnefred Anne, 477

LANG: Chestnut, 17; Duncan McRae, 14, 15, 17(3); Edward Brevard, 16, 17; Elizabeth, 15; Flora McRae, 16, 17(2); Hannah, 15; Harriet McRae, 17; Honoria Logan Lang, 17; James Wilson, 15; John, 14, 15; John C., 17; John Chestnut, 16, 17; Louisa Salmond, 17; Lucius Bellenger, 17; Marrier McRae, 16, 17; Mary, 14, 15(2), 17; Mary Chestnut, 16, 17(2); Mary McRae, 14; Obadiah, 14; Sally Wyly, 15, 17; Samuel Logan, 14, 17(2); Samuel Wyly, 15; Septimus, 16, 17(2); Theodore, 16, 17(2); Thomas, 14(2), 15(2), 16, 17(2); William, 15(2), 16(2), 17(3); William Wyly, 15

LANGFORD: Alexander, Mrs., 151; Fannie, 496; Mary Elizabeth Freeman, 151

LANIER: Edith, 450; Harriette A., 450(2); Leucy, 450; Lothenis, 450; Louisa P., 449, 450(2); Lovinda R., 450; Lowenda R., 450; Lucille Eliza, 449; Lydia, 450; Lydia L., 450; Martha, 450; Martha A., 450(2); Martha H., 450; Robert, 450; Robert F., 450; Robert, Sr., 450; William, 450; William A., 450

LARIENE: Catherine, 290

LARIMORE: Bessie Alma, 22; Capers Elmo, 22; Charles, 22; Charles Keen, 21; Collin, 21(2); Collin Larimore, 21; Eliza, 21(2); Elsie Lorine, 22; Leon Grady, 22; Lila Mona, 22; Mary, 22; Mary Louise, 22; Mary Rebecca Rodgers, 21, 22; Rufus Maxey, 22; Simeon Giles, 22

LARK: Ann, 321

LASATER: William C., 529

LATEMORE: Richard, Rev., 489

LATIMER: James M., 313; Mary Sullivan, 314

LATSON: Ruth Gissell, 90

LAWHORN: Carl, 519; Carl Tillman, 518; Henry, 519; Henry Roy, 518

LAWRENCE: Bertha Irene, 341; Ethel, 341

LEAGUE: Anna, 126; Archer, 126; Benjamin, 126; Berry, 126; Candace, 126; Casnader, 126; Drusilla, 126; Edward, 126; Elijah, 126; Elisha, 126; Elizabeth, 126; George, 126; George B., 126; Harriett, 126; Isham, 126; James, 126; Jane P., 126; Joab, 126; Joel, 126; Joshua, 126(2); Lucy, 126; Mary, 126(3); Nancy, 126; Nathan, 126; Oney, 126; Rachel, 126; Robert, 126; Sallie, 126; Usilla, 126; William, 126

LEARY: Antoinette T. Battle, 504

LEDBETTER: Alfred Webb, 444; Elizabeth, 444; Isaac, 443, 444(2); James, 444; Jonathan, 444; Martha Heath Ann, 444; Mary, 443; Nancy, 444; Richard, 443, 444; Silas, 444

LEE: Aron Bridges, 165, 383; Elizabeth, 98; Evie, 165, 383; Gardiner, 98; George, 421; Hatcher, 165, 383; Jesse, 402; John, 98; Roy, 165; William O., 383; William Wallace, 383

LEGARE: Ed Mortimer, 242; Elizabeth Hammett, 242(2); Isaac II, 242; Isaac III, 242; James, 288; Mary, 242; Thomas Isaac P., 242

LEGER: Abigail, 244

LEGGETT: Emily Frances, 89

LEIGH: James, 490(2); Mary, 490(2)

LEMAND: Eugene, 230

LENOIR: Amelia, 474(2); Isaac, 116; James, 474; James Middleton, 116; Jane,116; Martha, 116(2), 474(2); Sarah, 116(2), 118; William Vance, 116

LEOPOLD: Abigail, 368

LESLIE: Jane, 20(2); Thomas, 20

LETTON: Anna Maria, 471; Martha, 470(2); Mary Willett, 471; Michael, 471
LEVY: Frances, 318; Olivia, 318; Sarah, 318

LEWIS: Abigail, 381; Andrew J., 382; Ann, 381(2), 382; Augustus Dana, 456; Bette, 456(2); Betty Washington, 454, 455; Dewey, 388; Eliza M., 456; Elizabeth, 381; Ellen, 455; Ellen Joel, 454, 455; Frances Fielding, 454,455; George, 388, 454, 455, 456(2); George Baylis, 456; Harold, 456; Henry Daingerfield, 455; Howell, 454, 455; Howell, Sr., 456; Jane, 455; Janette, 456; John E., 454; John Edward, 455; Lawrence, 455(2); Lewellen, 381; Lotspeich, 381, 382; Margaret, 77; Martha, 381, 382; Martha E., 454; Martial B., 381; Mary, 176; Mary Ball, 455; Milton, 381; Robert Pollard,455, 456; Samuel, 77; Synthia, 381; Virginia, 454, 455; Vivian Ella, 90; William, 381, 382; William E., 381; William F., 381

LEYSATH: Rebecca, 322

LIGON: John A., 566

LILES: Abraham, 181; Amanda K., 182; Daniel H., 181; George W., 182; John, 182; Judith M., 182; Micah, 182; Milly, 277; Nancy Howard, 182; Narcissa, 181; Obediah, 182; Samuel, 181(2), 182; Susannah, 181, 182; Telitha O.J., 181; William M., 181

LINDSAY: Clarissa Moore, 94; Johnie E. A., 94; Philip W., 94; Phillip Williams, 94

LINDSEY: Ancennatus D., 521; Archibald, 521; David, 491; Grace, 521; Lucretia R., 521; Nancy, 521; Sarah, 521

LINTON: Esquire Samuel, 72; Ruth, 72

LITCHFIELD: Rachel Ann, 176, 177; Y. L. B., 176

LITTLE: Louis G., 449

LITTLEJOHN: Forest, 64
LIVINGSTON: Frances Tompkins, 534

LOCKET: John M., 124

LOCKLIER: Della, 518

LODGE: Sarah, 474

LOFTIS: C. V., 327; Elizabeth M., 326; H. A., 327; Hutson, 326; James T., 326; James W., 327; Jane M., 326; John L., 327; Luther B., 327; Maggie B., 327; Mary M., 327; Mattie M., 327; Sarah Gilliam, 327; Sarah R. E., 327; William P., 326

LOGAN: Mary Honoria, 14, 17; Nonorin, 17; Thomas, 145

LOKEY: Burt C., 140; Early, 140; Early W. H., 141(2); Eliza A., 141; Emily C., 141; Emily Mae, 140; Mackey, 140; Mary E. S., 140; Mary M., 140; Sallie, 140; Samuel B., 140; Shepie A., 140; Sheppie A., 139; Thalia B., 141; Thalia Bradley, 141; Wade, 140; Wade H., 139; William Earley, 140; William Emley, 139

LOLLEY: Tom, Mrs., 367

LONG: Ann, 302(2); David, 1; Elizabeth, 302; Ezekiel, 302, 303; George, 302, 303; Henry, 302; James, 302, 303; John A., 303; John Anderson, 302; Margaret, 302; Margery, 302, 303; Mary, 302; Mathew, 302, 303; Nicholas I., 554; William, 1, 302, 303

LOOKADOO: G. W., 423

LOONEY: W. D., 529, 530

LOOP: Magdelene, 376

LOPP: Catherine, 376; David, 376(2); Elizabeth, 376; Jacob, 376(3); John, 376; Mary, 376(3); Susannah, 376

LORD: Harriet, 349; Sarah A., 225

LOVE: D. K., 184; Jutson, 129; Mary Ann, 294

LOVELL: Alfred L., 456; Alfred Lewis, 455; Howell Lewis, 455; Joel, Mrs., 456; Joseph, 454; Joseph, Col., 456; Richard Channing, 455

LOVERN: Eliza, 276

LOVETT: Berrien M., 170; Candace, 170(2); Elizabeth, 170; John Forbes, 170; Louisiana, 170; Mary McKinny, 170; Nancy, 170(2); Rebecca, 170; Thomas F., 170(2); Thomas F. Jr., 170; Thomas Fenns Sr., 170; William Henry, 170

LOWE: Carrie Roberta, 166; Dudley Thomas, 166; William Boyce, 166

LOYD: Anne, 233

LUCAS: Alfred, 317; Amanda Emily, 317; Charles D., 316(2); Charles Daniel, 317; Dorcas, 316; Eddie R., 333; Edward P., 332, 333; Elizabeth, 316; Elizabeth Jane, 316, 317; Emmie V., 332, 333; Holley Elizabeth, 317; James T., 317; Jane Caroline, 316; Jennie Ann, 317;

(Lucas continued...)

Jeritta H., 317; Jesse Ludlen, 317; John, 316(3); John Hasten, 317; John Marion, 317(2); John Thomas, 317; Lorenzo, 316, 317; Louisa, 317; Manervey Rosan, 317; Margaret, 316(3); Margret An Feline, 317; Marthy Allis, 317; Mary, 316(3), 317; Mary Jane, 316; Maryan Frances, 317; Monica, 317; Murray L., 317; Nancy B., 316(2); Purvey F., 317; S. J., Mrs., 333; Sarah Frances, 317; Sarah J., 332(2); Silas Watts, 317; Silas W., 317; Thomas, 316;Uriah, 316; William, 316; William James, 316; William Marion, 317

LUCINDA: Russell, 229

LYLE: Cemira Carolina, 97; James, 97; Martha Adaline, 97; Mary Margaret, 96; Paralee Pennsylvania, 97

LYNCH: Dr., 366

LYNES: Ann, 82, 83; Annie B., 82; Betsy, 81; Cathrine G., 83; Christiana, 83, 84; Conner, 83; E. H., 82; E;ozabetj, 84; Eliza, 83(4); Elizabeth H., 83; Emely, 83; George, 81, 82(2), 83, 84(2); George J., 83; J. H., 82,84; Lency, 81; Martha Ann, 84; Richard, 82; Samuel, 82, 84; San, 81; Sarah J., 84; Toney, 81

LYNTHYCUM: Daniel, 396; Frances, 396

MCADAMS: Dolly, 68; Susan, 68

MCARTHUR: Selena, 63

MCBEE: Ida Blanche, 230

MCBRAYER: Sarah, 145

MCCALF: Jen, 388

MCCALL: Juanite, 323

MCCANTS: Alexander Nathaniel, 72; Allen Gautier, 71; Amanda Louisa, 71; Beuna Vista, 72; Elizabeth Gautier, 71; James, 72; Jane, 71-73; John James Clay, 71; Lois Anna, 71; Nathaniel, 71, 72; Pristine Cherokee Taylor, 71; Robert George Alexander, 71; Robert James Pembroke, 71(2), 73(2); Samuel Inman, 71, 72(2)

MCCARVER: Anne, 389; C. C., 389; M. Kate, 389; William Pitt, 389

MCCASHLAND: Mary, 575

MCCASKILL: Alexander, 80(2), 81; Catharine, 81; Catherine, 80; Daniel, 80; Florah, 80; John, 77, 80, 81(2); Margaret, 77, 80, 81; Mary, 80(2); Murdoch, 80

MCCASLAND: Mary, 575

MCCLENDON: Anderson, 143; Burrell, 143; Elizabeth, 143; Ellender I., 143; James, 143; John, 143; Joseph, 24; Judy Lee, 143; Lewis, 143; Mary, 143; Nancy Mariam, 143; Patsey, 143; Phebe, 25; Sarah, 143; Susan, 143; William, 143

MCCLINTOCK: John, 172, 173; Mary, 173

MCCOLGAN: Anna, 406; James, Col., 405, 406

MCCOMB: Polly Greer, 26

MCCONKEY: Mary, 260
MCCONNELL: Joseph T., 400

MCCORKLE: T., 517

MCCOULTER: Jesse, 69

MCCOY: Maryan Nancy, 316

MCCRACKEN: Elizabeth, 227; Mary F., 48

MCCRARY: Joseph, Rev., 49

MCCRAW: Elizabeth, 405; Polly, 405

MCCULLOGH: Mary, 385

MCCURDY: Margaret, 148, 149

MCCUTCHEN: H. G., 174

MCDANIEL: Biddy S., 423; J. B., 423(2); Pinson, 123

MCDAVID: Mary, 252

MCDONALD: Carmon, 580; Catherine, 580; Charles Morris, 580; Elijah Ann, 580; Emaline, 580; Helen, 580(2); J., 578; John, 580; Margaret, 580; Mary, 139; Philip, 580; Susan Rebecca, 339(2)

MCDONOUGH: Davis, 229

MCDOWAL: Rev. Dr., 279

MCDOWELL: Benjamin, 335; Daniel, 335; David, 57, 95; Elizabeth, 334, 335; Francis, 335; George B., 335; Georgia Ann, 335; Henry, 57, 95; J. T., Mrs., 334; James Talbert, 335; Jane, 473, 474; Joe J., 332; John, 56, 57, 335; John, Jr., 57, 95; John, Sr., 57, 95; Kitish, 335; Lucintha, 335; Mary, 57, 95; Savannah, 335; Shennel, 335; William, 334; William E., 285; William H., 220; Wister, 335

MCEACHERN: Linda Faye, 324; Peggy Marian, 324; William J. T., 323

MCELKERAN: O., Rev., 76

MCELLERAN: D., Rev., 75

MCELRATH: James Matthew, 91; John, 91; John Augustus, 91; Margaret Lula, 91; Nancy Jane, 91; William Joseph, 91; Wilmath C., 91

MCELROY: James D., 255; Martha Ellen, 255(2); Mary H., 255; Mary M. Dickson, 256; Samuel M., 255; Samuel R., 255, 256; Sarah Antoinette, 255; William H., 255

MCELVAIN: Alexander, 5; Elizabeth, 5; George, 4; James, 5; John, 4, 5; Jule Ann, 5; Mary, 5; Polly, 5; Sarah, 5; William, 5
MCELWEE: Abner, 85; Ann, 85; Dan, 85; Elizabeth, 85; James, 85; Rhoda, 85; Ross, 85

MCFADDIN: Eudora, 340

MCFALL: Aletha Caroline, 284, 285; Anna Warnock, 284, 285; Elenor Frances, 285(2); John, 284; John Carter, 285; John Cater, 284; Julia Emily, 285(2); Margaret Jane, 284, 285; Martha Cornelia, 285(2); Mary Elizabeth, 284, 285; Rachel Amanda, 284, 285; Rebecca Ann, 284, 285; Samuel, 284; Samuel Newton Whitmill, 284, 285; Samuel R., 284; Samuel Robertson, 284, 285; Sarah Cinderella, 284, 285

MCFARLAND: Calvin P., 576; Sally Columbia, 576

MCFARLIN: Calvin, 575

MCGILL: Amanda M., 207, 208; Burr, 202; Drucilla, 207, 208; Elizabeth, 202; Elizabeth Amelia, 206, 207; Emma Mary, 421; Hugh, 199, 200, 202; James, 200; Jane Caroline, 207(2); Jean, 200, 202; Jennet Louisa, 207(2); John, 200, 202; John Sanders, 207; Martha, 202; Martha Emeline, 207, 208; Mary,200, 202; Mary Ann, 208; Mary Ann Sanders, 207(2); Mary McCottry, 207(2); Minto Witherspoon, 207, 208; Roger, 200, 202, 206; Samuel, 200, 202, 206; Samuel D., 202; Samuel Davis, 206, 207(2), 208; Samuel Gadsdon, 208; Samuel Goadsden, 207; Sarah, 200; Sidney Spencer, 207(2); Wadsworth, 518;William Wilson, 207, 208

MCILVAIN: Sarah, 4

MCINTIRE: Andrew, 531(2), 532-534; Andrew James, 532; Ann Eliza, 531; Ann Swinson, 534(2); Charles, 531; Charlotte Davis, 533; Clarence Vivian,533; Clyde, 533; D. M., 533; David, 531, 533; David Murdock, 532; Elizabeth, 531; Emma Agnes, 533; Flavius Gustavus, 532; Franklin Parish,532; Gaston Calhoun, 532; James, 531, 532(2), 533; James Harrison, 532; Jesse Adrian, 533, 534; John Charles Hampton, 533; Joseph Kinsey Lee, 533; Josephine, 532; Julia Sara, 532; Laura Alvara, 532; Lucille May, 533; Margaret Matilda, 532; Marion Bancroft, 532; Mary, 531, 532; Mary Ellen, 532; Murdock, 531; Nancy, 531; Sarah, 531; Susan, 531; Susan Alice, 533; Susan Caroline, 531; T. A., 533; Thomas Henry Williams, 532; William Charles, 532; William Murdock, 531

MCIVER: Malcolm, 418

MACIVOR: Hazel Arnold, 120

MCKANNON: Max E. V., 481; Myrtle Ivy, 481

MCKENZIE: Joseph, 138

MCKIBBEN: Adline Hannah, 493; Alexander, 493, 494; Andew Jackson, 493; Clark, 494(2); Elizabeth Baker, 494; Elizabeth Matilda, 494; Hattie Clementine, 495; Ida, 494; J. F., 495; James, 493; John, 451, 493, 494; Margaret, 493; Margaret E., 494; Martha A., 495; Martin Van Buren, 495; Mary, 454; Mary Bernice, 494; Minerva Ann, 494; Nancy Emmerline, 493; Robert Emmet, 453; Samuel, 494; Sarah Jane, 494; Susannah, 495; Thomas, 494(2), 495; Thomas A., 495

MCKIBBIN: Rezina Jane, 453; Robert Emmet, 453

MCKINLEY: Archibald Carlisle, 278; Elizabeth Montgomery, 278; Enter Barksdale, 278; Guy, 278(2); James Betty, 278; Jane Moseley, 279; John Wilson, 278; Mary Ansley, 278; Robert Mecklin, 279; William, 278; William Harris, 279

MCKINNEY: Biddy S., 423, 424; H. A., 423; Martha A., 423; Willis A., 423,424

MCKITTRICK: James, 270

MCLAWS: Elizabeth V., 297; Harold Lamar, 90; James, 297

MCLEAN: Anna Saloma, 395(2)

MACLEAN: Eliza, 454

MCLEAN: Ernest Sherwood, 395; Jesse Ezra, 395(2)

MCLEOD: Elizabeth, 472; Murdock B., 472; Norman, 472(2); Norman William, 472; Sarah, 368

MCLURE: Alexa Wylie, 131(2)

MCMEANS: Jesse, 360; M., 360

MCMILLAN: Ark Malcolm, 393; Edward, 393(2); Henry, 393; Jane, 394; Jason,394; Joanna, 393; Joanna Jacobs, 393; John, 393; Joseph, 393; Josiah, 393; Malcolm, 393, 394; Robert, 393; William, 394

MCMILLIAN: Jean, 117

MCMORINE: Jacob, 446; John, 445(2), 446(2); Martha, 445, 446

MCNAIR: Ada Leala, 327(2); Arthur Murray, 327; George W., 327(2)

MCNEESE: Robert, 150; Sally, 150

MCNORINE: Marion, 445

MCRAE: Duncan, 12, 17(2); Mary, 17(3); Moses Bransom, 368; Moses Branson, 369; Sarah McLeod, 369

MCTYER: Sarah Ann, 201, 247(2)

MCWHIRTER: Lester, 64; Martha Susan Ann, 61

MADDEN: Huldah, 266

MADDOX: E. C., 433; Francis, 434

MAGID: Louis Morris, 249

MAHAFFEY: L. T., 312

MAHAN: Seneca, 436(2)

MAHONY: W. H., Rev., 339

MALLON: Laura McClain, 330(2)

MALONE: Fowler Reed, 448(2); German Clyde, 448; Joseph H., 448

MALTBIE: Kate, 225

MANN: Louise, 341; Malissa M., 416; William H., 416

MANNO: Jane, 366

MANSE: Pres., 167

MARCUM: Rebecca F., 218

MARION: Elizabeth Mary Wickham, 100; John Samuel, 100; Louisa Charlotte, 100; Nathaniel, 100; Nathaniel Peter, 100

MARLOW: Elizabeth, 243

MARSHALL: Bennett, 544; David Ogilvie, 480; P. B., 448; Roberta Ivy, 481

MARTIN: Abraham, 226; Absalom, 174; Agnes, 466; Albert, 171; Allen Hansford, 235; Andrew, 438; Archibald, 438; Benjamin, 173, 174; Benjamin Martin, 171; Bernice Leora, 235; Bernice Leoria, 235; Cary Idorah, 176; Daniel, 173, 174(2); David, 172(5), 173(3), 174; Doris, 236; Edward, 172; Eliza Rebiah, 174; Elizabeth, 171(2), 173-175, 437; Elizabeth R., 172; Elizabeth Reed, 172; Francis Marion, 171; George, 437; George, Capt., 252; Georgia Anner Zilpha Jane, 176; Ginney, 437(2); Henry, 171; Henry Benjamin, 176; Herusha, 174; James, 172(2), 173, 174, 437, 438(2); James M., 174; James, Sr., 438; Jane Ropers, 171; Janet Scott, 116; Jean Meek, 172; Jerusha Licuzen, 173; Joab, 174, 175; Joannah, 174; Joel, 174; Joel Josiah, 173; John, 172, 174(2), 437(2), 438; John Christian, 171(2); John H., 173; John Theodore Brunson, 174; Johnie Herbet, 234; Johnnie, 234; Johnnie Herbert Jr., 235; Joseph, 173(2), 174(4), 175, 434(2), 435(2), 437; Joseph Frankling, 176; Josiah, 174(2), 175(3); Katherine Virginia, 235; Louise, 235; Louts Fountain, 176; Lovice, 174; Margaret, 172(3), 173(3); Mariah, 171; Martin, 173; Mary, 172(2); Mary Coalman, 437; Mary Margaret, 171; Micajah, 438; Mourning, 435(2); Nancey, 438; Nancy, 173, 174(2), 227, 438; Nancy A., 183(2); Newton Claudius, 176; Nicholas, 171; Parley S., 175; Patsy, 434, 435; Rachel, 438; Rebecca, 173, 438; Rebeccah, 172(2); Robert, 172(2), 173; Sabra, 175; Sabra A., 175; Sabre, 174; Salley, 438; Samuel, 175; Samuel Newton, 226; Samuel Wilborn, 176; Sarah, 175, 261, 266, 275; Shug, 176(2); Stephen, 434; Susanna, 435(2); Syrene B., 175; Thirsa Ann, 171; Thomas, 174(3), 175(2), 435, 437; Thomas Sr., 175; Tinney, 175; Toliver Hison, 176; Valentine, 174, 175; W. E. Sr., 235; W. F., Mrs., 512; W. N., 235; William, 174, 438; William A., 173(2); William Aiken, 172; William

(Martin continued...)

Elbert, 235; William Elbert Jr., 235; William Gilliam, 437; William Jerryl, 176; Zachariah, 438; Zadeyadlin, 173

MARY ELIZABETH: Sarah Tucker, 209

MASON: Eliza Myers, 104; Malinda, 253; William, 253

MASSEY: Elizabeth Heath, 239

MATHEW: Rev. Philip, 75

MATHEWES: John Raven, 249; Martha I., 249

MATHEWS: Edward, 540; Margaret, 540; P., Rev., 76

MATTHEWS: Susannah, 123; Willis O., Rev., 240

MATTISON: Abner, 203; Ann Paralee, 204; Anna Mariah, 203; Benjamin Newton, 204; Daniel, 203; Elizabeth, 203; Gabriel Walter, 204; James, 202, 203; James Jr., 203; James Lawrence, 204; Lettice N., 203; Lettice Nicoll, 203; Mahala, 203; Malinda, 202; Margaret Elizabeth, 203; Mary, 203(2); Mary F., 204; Presley, 202; Savanna Eudora, 204; Urius J., 203; Urius Jackson, 203; William, 196, 202, 204; William Robert, 204; Wyatt, 203; Wyatt Maulding, 204

MAULDIN: John, 197

MAULDING: Benjamin, 203; Sarah, 203

MAURY: Abram, 572; Henry H., 572

MAXWELL: Mary Maria, 578; Thomas Kees, 114, 345, 346

MAY: Adeline Gertrude, 553(2); Alexander, 512; Benjamin, Jr., 552; Benjamin, Sr., 553; Charles, 512; Dorethea Ann, 226; Eliza Rebecca, 226; Elizabeth Hunter, 511; Hundy, 244; Ione Bynum, 553; James Franklin Elmore, 226; James H., 512; James Oscar, 553(2); James U., 553; James William, 553; John, 245, 511, 512; John Edwin, 553; John Hunter, 511; John Perry, 226; John Wesley, Jr., 512; Martha Catherine, 226; Mary, 101; Powhatan, 512; Rachel McF., 512; Rook, 512; Sally, 553; Sarah, 552(2);Susan Frances, 553; Tabitha, 553; Thomas Jefferson, 226; William, 187, 245; William F., 226

MAYBRY: Elizabeth, 405

MAYER: J. Benedict, 107(2)

MAYES: Edward, 227; Mary M., 56

MAYFIELD: Jack, 46; Patti, 46

MAYHEW: Charity, 138; Matilda, 138
MAYNEW: Rezen, 138

MAYS: Thomas, 227

MEADOR: Bernal M., 98

MEAL: Martha Ann Greer, 23

MEANS: Polly, 379

MEDLIN: James C., 282

MEEKS: Lucretia M., 479

MEGS: John, 98

MELTON: Isaac D., 356

MENDEZ: Abraham, 318

MERCER: Jess R., 560; Lucinda, 560; Sally Ann, 560; William J., 560

MERCY: Mary Ann, 304

MICHAUX: Mary Alice, 341

MIDDLEBROOKS: James, 278

MILLER: Albus, 47; Andrew, 472; Andrew William, 472; Charles Christian, 323; Charles Worth, 472; Cora Antonia, 395; D. H., 56, 95; David H., 57, 95; E. M., Mrs., 472; Edward B., 365; Edward Jonathan Meyer, 249; Edward R., 366(2); Eliza, 196; Elizabeth, 47, 472(2); Emily Jones, 249(2); Emma 365, 366; Emma P., 365, 366; Francis, 365; Francis C., 366; Hannah Elizabeth, 57, 95; Hannibal Edger, 395; J. Claudius, 366; Jacob, 365,366(2); Jacob C., 365, 366; Jacob, Sr., 365; James, 472; James Anderson, 197; James Arthur, 323; Jane, 197; Jane L., 365, 366; Jerome, 47; Jerome A., 47; John, 47; John Bounetheau, 198; John David, 197(2), 198(2); John W., 365; John William, 366; John, Capt., 294; John, Rev., 49; Jonas T., 47; Jones T., 57; Judith, 197; Laura A., 365, 366; Margaret C., 365, 366; Margaret Smith, 249; Maria Juliana, 198; Marry, 472; Mary, 47(2), 307; Mary Clayton, 472; Mary Dorcas, 95; Mary Dorcus, 57; Mary F., 146; Mary M., 57, 95; Mary Magdalene Grimball, 197; Mary Mahala, 47; Peter Bounetheau, 197; Rachel Alexander, 198; Rebecca, 47; Richard Cauley, 472;Samuel D., 366; Samuel N., 365; Samuel Stuit, 197; Sarah Clastrier, 366(2); Sarah E., 365; Selena, 47; Stella Augusta Miller, 395; Stephen H., 365, 366; Stephen N., 366; Thomas R., 47; W. H., Rev., 189; William, 47

MILLHOUSE: Dinah, 14, 15

MILLIGAN: Amelia, 514(2); Elizabeth, 237; Jane, 237; Joseph, 237; Joseph, 237; Margaret, 237(2); Mary Byers, 237; Rachel, 237; Robert, 237; Susannah, 237

MILLS: Alexander Feagon, 35; John, 35(2); Jonathan, 523; Laurens T., 208; Mary, 35; Mary N., 41; Rev. Mr., 350; Robert, 35; Thomas Sumter, 35; William Wilson, 211

MILNOR: Elizabeth P., 279; Elizabeth Paul, 279

MINTON: David Hampton, 144; Edward Priestly, 144; Francis Marion, 144; Hannah E., 144; Harriett Good, 144; James Madison, 144; John M., 144; Joseph Alphred, 144; Martha Miles, 144; Mary, 144(2); Mary Ann, 144; Nancy Jane, 144; Rebeccah L., 144(2); Reuben R., 144; Sarah Ann, 144; Sarah Matilda, 144; Sidney R., 144; Silvanus, 144; Silvanus Moody, 144; Thomas Allen, 144

MITCHELL: Anderson, 379; Ann, 87, 380; Clarence, 59; Cornelia Ann, 408; David, 379(2), 380; Eli, 89; Elizabeth, 305, 380; Ephraim, 196; Francis, 379; Greenberry, 305; Helena, 89; Herberta, 186; J. B., 87; James, 87, 577; Jane, 305, 379; Jesse, 305; John, 87(2), 379; John B., 87; John Wesley, 89; Lani, 87; Lewis, 305; Margaret, 87(3); Martha Me. G., 87; Mary, 87(2), 303, 305; Mary Ann, 89; Morris, 305; Nancy, 305(2), 306; Polly, 305; Rebecca, 305; Richard, 305; Robert, 305, 379; Samuel, 379; Sara, 87; Solomon, 305, 306; Stephen, 305; Susa, 89; Susannah, 305; Taner, 306; William, 87, 379, 380, 495(2); William W., 89; William Wells, 89; William Wilson, 87; Zachariah, 89

MOATS: Alice Elizabeth, 270; Ann H., 270, 271; Arthur, 270; Cary J., 270; Charlie H., 270, 271; David, 270, 271; Davis, 269; Henrietta, 270(3); Henry, 270; Henry J., 270; Jennie W., 270; Martha Ann, 271; Martha Ann Goggins, 270; Martha Clemmit, 270, 271; Martha Lou, 270; William, 269; William B., 270(2)

MOBLEY: Dulcena Frances, 334

MODRELL: Rev., 48

MOLES: Tabitha, 245

MOLMEN: Susan Ligan, 171(2)

MONCRIEF: Mary Eliza, 351

MONFORD: Ann Johnson, 190; Esther, 190(2); John, 190

MONROE: Robert S., 356

MONTGOMERY: Isabella, 191; James, 188; Jonathan, 30; Mary, 30; Robert Davis, 29; Sarah, 30; William H., 477

MOODY: T. D., Rev., 21

MOON: Agnes M., 65; Ann, 374; Carey, 375; Daniel, 374; Edom, 375; Elinder Angaline, 65; Elizabeth, 374(2), 375; Elizabeth Sarahan, 545; Emeliann, 545; Frances Jane, 65; Grace, 374; James, 374; James Randal, 65; Jemmy, 374; Jesse, 374, 375; Jesse Benjamin Edmond, 545; John, 374(4), 375; John P., 65, 66; John Walker, 65; Johnney, 374; Joseph, 374(5); Lawrence, 374; Leucrecher, 374, 375; Louisa Jones, 65; Lydiann Hazeltine, 545; Malinda Caroline, 65, 66; Mary, 374(2); Narcissa, 65; Rachel, 374; Rachel Rebeccah, 545; Rebecca, 66; Rebecca Adaline, 65; Samuel, 374; Sara, 375; Sary, 374; Sintha, 65; Susan Elizabeth, 65; Thomas, 374(2), 375; Thomas B., 545; Thomas Henry, 65, 66; William, 374(2); William Francis, 545; William H., 65; William Henry, 66; Woodson D., 545

MOOR: John, 137

MOORE: Alice, 324; Ann, 350(5); Caroline Y., 510; Celia M. L., 511; Celia Martha Louisa, 511; Charles McMorine, 445; Clarissa, 94; Cynthia L., 168; E. E., Mrs., 511; Edward Martin, 445; Elijah Abraham, 511; Elizabeth, 29; Elizabeth Marion, 94(2); Estelle, 341; Frances, 538; George E., Rev., 511; George I., 371; Grizelda, 538, 543; Hannah, 493, 494; Huldah, 371; J. P., 94; J. W., 94; James, 168, 445; Jamie, 94; Jewell, 518; John Edwin Augustus, 94; John G., 30; John M., 94; John Romulus, 511; John Waller, 510(2); Joicey, 263, 264; Julian Stephen,

681

(Moore continued...)

511(2); Lemuel C., 445, 446; Lemuel, Jr., 445(2); Lucinda, 125; Margaret, 30; Margaret W., 445, 446; Marion, 446; Mary, 267; Mary Elizabeth, 510; Nadaline Marion, 94; Nation, 446(2); Penny, 580; Phillip, 267; Portious, 543; Rachel Ann, 510; Richard Murchison, 511; Richard Romulous, 510; Samuel, 313; Sarah Jane, 510; Sophia, 168; Stephen, 510(2), 511, 538, 543; Stephen Pleasant, 510, 511(2); Thomas, 539; Thomas Alexander, 510

MOREHOUSE: Betsy, 464(2)

MORELAND: Nancy L., 68; Thomas, 69

MORGAN: Clara Blackstock, 215; Margaret, 142

MORREAU: Charles Frederick, Rev., 209

MORRIS: Carolyn Gladys, 265; Frederick Keating Jr., 265; Gladys Endell D., 265; John, 233; Keating, 265; Mary, 136, 144; P. K., Mrs., 265; William, 330

MORROW: Debra Key, 59; U. C., Mrs., 338

MOSELEY: Addie Harriet, 212; Amelia, 205, 206; Augustus, 205; Carrie T., 212; Charlotte I., 212; Dandridge, 205; Daniel, 205, 206, 211-213; Daniel Eugene, 212; Hampton, 205, 206, 212(2); Harriett, 205; Jessie Eva, 212; John, 205; Julia C., 212; Julia Carlisle, 212; Katie Louis, 212; Lucy Elizabeth, 129; Lurena, 211; Lurene, 212; Luriah, 212, 213; Mary, 205; Mary G., 129; Mildred, 205; Olivia, 212; Sallie, 211; Sally, 206(2); Samuel, 212; Sarah, 211, 212; Sarah Elizabeth, 212; Thomas, 206; Thomas P. J. M., 213; Thomas P. Martin, 212; Thomas R., 205; Wade, 206; Wade C., 211-213

MOZELL: Martha, 52

MULDOW: Ann, 201

MULDROW: Ann, 247; Simon C., 247

MULL: Catherine, 467; John, 467(2)

MULLINS: Thomas, Rev., 561

MUNDINE: Rhoda D., 68

MURCHISON: Alexander, 77, 80; Catherine, 81; Christian Eliza, 81; Colin Campbell, 78; Daniel, 77(2), 80, 81; Daniel Peter Columbus, 80; Isabel, 81; Isabella, 77; John, 77; John E., 78; John Wesley, 81; Kenneth, 77; Lily Eudora, 511; Margaret, 77(2), 80(2), 81; Margaret Jane, 80; Margaret McCaskill, 80; Mary, 77, 80, 81; Nancy, 77; Regina Catherine, 78; S. P., 80, 81(2); Samuel, 77; Sarah Isabel, 80, 81; Susan Colin Campbell, 78

MURFF: Caroline Gaines, 192; Caty C., 192; Elizabeth, 193; Elizabeth Martha Manson, 193; Helena, 193; Malachi Andrew, 193; Malinda, 192; Margaret, 193; Minus Hillery, 193; Randolph S., 192, 193(2); Uriah Hilton, 193; Waldemar, 193; Washington, 193; Wylly, 192

MURPHY: A. J., 207; Abner J., 382; Adella Ware, 382; George W., 382; Rachel M., 382

MURRAY: Elizabeth, 217; J. Scott, Rev., 157; John, 217(2); Samuel John, 217

MYERS: Eliza Eveline, 104; Elizabeth, 103; George, 103; Isaac Newton, 104; Isabel, 104; Isable W., 103; J. D., 104; John, 103(2), 104; John David,103(2), 104(3); John, Jr., 104; Margaret Caroline, 104; Marget T., 103;Mary Ann E., 103; Mary Elizabeth, 104; Molly, 103; Pearl Ethel, 103(2); Sarah, 103; Sarah Ann I., 104(2); Sarah Ann Isabellah, 104; Unity, 104;Yates C., 103

MYRES: George, 102; Isabel, 102; John, 102; William F., 102

NAIL: Elder J. P., 367(2)

NALMS: Hiram, 145

NANSBY: Mary Catharine, 524

NAPIER: Leroy W., 400(2)

NARCUM: Henry, 218

NASH: John B., 419; W. B., 420; Wylie B., 419

NAYER: Eve Margreta, 107; Johan Benedict, 107

NEELAND: M. M., 230

NEELY: Christini, 198; Mary, 343, 512(2)
NELSON: Charlotte Stith, 214; D. M., 31; Daniel, 30, 31; Daniel M., 30, 31; Daniel Milbourn, 29(2), 30, 32; Eliza J., 215; Elizabeth, 30, 31(2), 217; Frances E. B., 215; Hannah, 30; Hannah Harriet, 29, 30; Harvey G., 215; Ida M., 31; Ida Martin Stribling, 26, 31; James, 30; James Alex, 30, 31; James Calvin G., 31; James H., 31; James Moore, 30; Jesse Daniel, 215; John Calvin Greer, 32; John Nesbet, 30; John Nesbit, 30; John Nesbit, 31; Jonathan A., 30; Jonathan Alex, 30; L. M., 31; Margaret, 30, 31; Margaret Asenath, 30; Margaret Aseneth, 29; Martha, 30; Martha M., 30; Martha Malinda, 30; Mary Lucinda, 31(2); Mary M., \, 28, 30, 31(2); Mary Matilda Craig, 32; R. W., 31; Robert, 29, 30(2), 31(2), 32, 215, 543; Robert Miriam, 31; Robert Thomas, 30(2); Robert Watt, 31(2); Sarah, 30; William A., 30; William Alvah, 29, 30; William H., 214

NESON: Elizabeth, 403, 525

NEVILLE: John Coleman, 285

NEVIS: John, 419

NEWBURY: W., 54

NEWCOMB: Lois, 445(2)

NEWELL: Sarah J., 532

NEWKIRK: Abraham, 403, 404(2), 525, 526(2); Abraham, Jr., 526; Ann Jane, 404, 526; B., 526; Benjamin Rhodes, 404, 526; Bryan, 404, 526; C., 526; C. Hettie, 526; Henry, 404, 526; Henry John Thomas, 404, 526; J. B., 526; J. H., 526; Jacob Felix, 404, 526(2); Joseph, 404, 526(2); Mary Ann, 403, 404, 526(2); Penny, 404, 526; Rachel, 404, 526; T. E., 526; Timothy, 404, 526(2); Tobias, 404, 526

NEWMAN: Ann, 483; Eleanor, 483; Jane, 483(2); Jeremiah, 483; John, 483; Jonathan, 483; Jose Alphonse, 389; Margaret, 483; Martha, 321; Mary, 483; Sarah, 483

NEWTON: Caldona, 551; Early Carr, 551(2); Enoch, 551; Enoch Alton, 551; Enoch F., 551; Hiram Joseph, 551; Isaac, 402; James Ernest, 551(2); James Henry, 577; Katie, 551; Margaret, 227; Mary, 407; Mary Ann, 551(2); Mary Frances, 551; Samuel William, 551; Samuel Wilson, 551

NICHOLS: Archibald, 377; Arrenia, 377; Baldy, 377; Dudley, 377; Elizabeth, 540; Evelina, 465; Lucco, 377; Samuel, 464(2), 465; Susan Ann, 377; W. Nichols, 377

NICHOLSON: Wright, 335

NIX: Elijah, 44(2), 45(2); Elijah D., 45; Martha, 44; N. A., 44, 45

NIXON: John, 490; Sarah, 432

NOBLE: Adolphus Avery, 145; Avery, 145; Bennett, 145; Betsy, 145; Claudie Bentley Madison, 145; Eliza, 145; Ellen E. J., 145; Francis Elizabeth,145; John, 146; John Baptist Noble, 145; John Camp, 145; John, Rev., 145; Madison, 146; Nancy, 145; Patsy, 145; Robert H., 146; Robert, Mrs., 145;Rufus Bennett, 145; Sarah J. P., 145; William, 145(2); William Jr., 145

NOBLY: George, Rev., 489

NOLEN: John, 38; Sally, 38

NORCOM: Sarah Sutton, 490

NORCUM: Sarah S., 491

NORMAN: Catherine, 171; Margaret, 543; Matilda, 116; Sallie, 543; Temperance, 543; Thomas, 543

NORRIS: Baxter Andrew, 263; Eugenia Rachel, 298; F. M., 263; Fanny Claudia, 300; Francis Reuben, 263; Frank M., 264; Guy H., 263; Guy Hammond Jr., 264; Guy Hammond Jr., 263; Hansford, 2; James Gilder, 299; James Rufus, 263; John, 557; John Ewing, 263; John Thompson, 298, 299; John Thompson Jr., 300; Johnny, 2; Leila Jane, 300; Lucinda, 300; Mamie, 264; Mamie M., 263; Marion F., 263; Mary, 284; Mary Cornelia, 263; Mary Rebecca, 298, 299; Mary Tabitha, 299; Ophelia C., 263; Pearl S., 263; Rachel, 263; Rachel Eugenia, 299; Sue C., 264; Wade Benjamin, 263; William, 2; William Calhoun, 298(2), 299, 300; William Calhoun Jr., 299; Wilson Abney, 300

NORTH: Ann, 73, 74; Edward, 73, 74, 209, 210; Edward Washington, 209, 210; Elizabeth, 73; George T., 209; George Tucker, 209; John, 73; John Laurens, 209, 210; Joshua, 73, 74; Mary E., 210; Mary Elizabeth, 210(2); Richard Baker, 209; Sarah, 209, 210; Sarah Tucker, 209; Susannah, 73; William, 73, 74

NORTON: Samuel E., Rev., 366

NUNELEE: J. D., 367; John A., 367; John Thomas Bartow, 367; Loucinda, 367; Mary A., 367; Mary C., 367; R. C., 367; S. E., 367; S. M., 367; Thomas Bartow, 367; W. F., 367; Walter F., 367; William D., 367

NUNNELEE: Bryant Hubbard, 368; John Ervin, 368; Mary Sarah, 368; William Asa, 368

NYFONG: Emily, 376; Magdalene, 376(2)

OBANION: Elizabeth, 451

OCAIN: Mrs., 37

O'DANIEL: William, 123

O'DELL: Edith, 156

O'DELT: Edith, 156

ODOM: E. N., 219; Ebenezer, 218

O'HAGAN: Harriet Shuler, 90

OLIFF: Elizabeth, 472; John Shears, 472; Mary, 472; Susannah, 472

OLIVE: Benjamin F., 450; Luella Eliza, 450; Lydia, 450

OLLIFF: Benjamin Shears, 471; John Shears, 471; Joseph, 471

O'NEAL: Amanda, 141; George A. M., 141; Joseph Early, 141; Mary E., 141

ORR: John, 440

ORVIE: James S., 570

OSBORN: Ailsey Gober Leah King, 441(2); Ann, 440; Champion, 439; Eleanor, 439; Fannie Powell John G., 441; Harriet Elizabeth, 442; Henry Grady, 441; Jane, 439, 440, 483; Jeremiah, 439; Jessie, 439; John, 439(4), 440, 441, 483; John Humphrey George, 442; Jonathan, 440, 441(2), 514(2); Joshua Caleb, 441, 442; Leah King, 514(2); Margaret, 438; Mary, 439(2); Mary Jane, 442; Nancy, 439; Newman, 438; Powell John Griffin, 441(2); Rebecca, 439; Ruth, 439; Samuel, 439; Sarah, 439

OSTERVALD: J. F., 291

OSWALT: Cedecte Luany, 18; Cedicia L. E., 18; Draden Brooks, 18; Emanuel, 18; Ernest A., 18; Euhema Lewis, 18; Euphemia, 18; Franklin W., 18; Henry Etter, 18; Ianth M., 18; Ianth Minerva, 18; James Boyd, 18, 19; L. B., 18; Nancy Luezer, 18; Reuhama, 18; Samuel Frederick, 18; Sarah E., 18, 19; Sary Edney, 18; Wade Franklin, 19; Zebulan Zenoah, 18

OTEY: Elizabeth, 130

OTWELL: Alexander B., 66; Amelia C., 66; Charles G., 66; George H., 66; John C., 66, 67; John H., 66, 67; Mary J., 66; Mathew C., 66; Obad. J., 67; Obed. J., 66; Sally, 67; Sarah, 66; Sarah El, 66; Watson T., 66; William W., 66, 67

OUTS: Core, 156

OUZTS: Elizabeth, 335

OVERTON: Rev., 282

OWEN: Elias Keith, 176; Fred Elias, 176; Julia Gore, 177; Red Elias, 177

OWENS: Andrew, 426; Caroline, 426; Elizabeth, 426; Ella Virginia, 26; Frances E., 426; Isom W., 426; Mary E., 426; Mary Eloise, 21; Sarah J., 426; Wiley D., 426

PACE: Americus Martial, 246(2); Catherine, 245(2), 246; Clement, 245, 246;Elkana, 245; Elkanah, 246; Elkanah Stephen Olin, 246; Harmon, 388(2); James, 246, 325; John, 245(2), 388; Lucy, 245(2); Lucy May, 245; Mary Havilah M., 246; Nancy, 245, 246(2); Polly, 244, 245; Rose, 389; Stephen, 245, 246(2); Susan, 246; William, 244, 245, 246(2); William Henry, 246;Willie, 389

PADDOCK: Eudora Lucy Thompson Bass, 118; Sarah Josephine Thompson, 118

PADGETT: Anna, 181; B. B., 181; Elijah, 181; Elizabeth, 181(2); Henry, 181; Ira, 181; James, 181; Levina, 181; Martha, 181; Wiley, 181; William, 181(2)

PAGAN: Alexander, 35; Mary, 35

PAGE: Alin E., 41; Elizabeth Emaline, 42; Rebecca A., 42

PAISLEY: Mary, 186

PALMER: Addie, 440; Addie Reed, 441; Charley Reny, 442; E. L., 442; Edward P. Smith, 442; Elizabeth, 443(2); Ella L., 443; Freddie Lee, 442, 443; G., 443; George, 440; George D., 440; George D., Jr., 440; George Daniel,440, 441; Hannah B., 443; Hannah R., 441; James, 442, 443; James Daniel, 442; James E., 440; James Edwin, 440; Jo, 527; Julia A., 440, 441; Lucy,442, 443; Margaret, 443; Martha, 442, 443; Martha Gertrude, 440, 441; Marthen, 442; Mary, 442; Mary Adelaide, 440; Sarah Virginia, 440(2); Seardl, 443; Serbeana, 443; Serbeann, 443; Thomas A., 440; Thomas Augustus, 440, 441; Thomas J., 440, 441; V. W., 196; W. P., 442, 443; W. P., Jr., 443; W. W., 195, 268, 269; Wilbur Lucius, 442; William, 442,443; William J. Love, 442; William P., 440, 441; Willie Eugene, 442

PAPER: Jane Y., 498

PARAMORE: Arthur Franklin, 195

PARKE: C. H., Mrs., 129

PARKER: Ashford, 1; Elender, 1, 2; Elizabeth, 1(2); Ezra, 464(2); Helen M., 465; Helen May, 465; James Harvey, 407, 408; James William Fletcher, 408;Jane Caroline, 210; Joe, 407; Joseph, 1, 2, 407; Martha, 534; Mary, 1; Mary Jane, 408; Orin Ezra, 465; Rom B., Sr., 407; Sam Watts, 408; William, 1(2); William Rebecca, 408

PARKES: Ambrose, 535

PARKS: Susan, 290

PARLIER: Rebecca Emily, 394

PARRIS: Ada Lee, 165; Carrie T. Belcher G., 106; Carrie T. Belcher Gregory,160

PASSMORE: Arthur Francis, 268

PATRICK: J. H., 119; Sarah Josephine Thompson, 119; Thomas J., 119

PATTERSON: Butler, 156; Catherine, 146; Ella, 563; Ellen Price, 451; Sarah, 330

PATTON: Thomas, 192

PAULK: Martha, 123

PAWLEY: Ann Shova, 247

PEAKE: Elizabeth Shockley, 488; Isabella Redmond, 488; Julia E., 488; Julia Proffitt, 488; William I, 487, 488(3); William II, 487, 488; William III, 488

PEAL: Daniel Merry, 58; John Henry, 58; Mary Prudence, 58

PEARCE: Edith, 449, 450; Elizabeth, 450, 451(2); Lazarus, 450, 451; Rev. Mr., 211; Rhody, 451

PEARSON: George Butler, 286; Isaac Kirkland, 286; Joel Erskine, 286; John, 285; John Weston, 286; Martha, 286; Martha Christian, 286; Mary Ann, 285, 286; Nancy, 557; Philip, 286; Philip Edward, 286; Philip Peter, 285; Rachel, 286; Robert Raiford, 286

PEDEN: Elizabeth, 173; J. T., 172(2); Jean, 172; Mary Eleanor, 507

PEGUES: Annie Louisa, 282; Annie Louise, 283; Francis Henry, 283; J. F., 282

PENDER: John, 413; Nancy, 413; Paul, 413; Solomon, 413

PENDER (COLORED): Abby, 414; Adaline, 415; Agnes, 414; Amanda, 414; Anna, 414; Betty, 414; Bunny, 415; Charles, 414, 415; Dallas, 413; Daniel, 415; Deborah, 415; Dicey, 414; Dick, 414, 415; Dinah, 413, 415; Elijah, 414; Eliza, 414; Fanny, 414; Frank, 413; George, 415; Hannah, 414(2); Harriet, 414, 415; Henry, 414; Hilliard, 415; Ilander, 413; Isaac, 413; Jane, 413;Joe, 414; John, 414; Julia, 414(2); Julius, 415; Kitty, 414; Lasarus,415; Lewis, 413; Maria, 414; Marina, 414; Martha, 414; Mary, 414; Mary Baly, 415; Matthew, 415; Mike, 414; Monroe, 414; Nancy, 414; Ned, 414; Patty, 414; Peter, 413; Rachel, 413; Richmond, 415; Robert, 414; Sucky, 415; Tom, 415; Turner, 415; William, 414; Willis, 415; Winney, 414

PENNINGTON: E. I., 281; Mary Lundy, 401

PENNY: Ann, \, 403, 525; Ann Brosard, 525; John, 403, 525; Rachel, 379

PERCIVAL: N. S., 478

PERDUE: Jefferson, 218; Jefferson D., 218; Joseph Walter, 218; Mittie A., 218, 219; Thomas Ardus, 218

PERKINS: C. M., Capt., 312; Hood Dennis, 22; Joseph, 454; Lee N., 556; Samuel, 580

PERRY: Charley Wesley, 420; Cleo Clifford, 420; Earl Franklin, 420; Eddie Pendleton, 420; Elsie Marie, 420; Ethel Motley, 420; Eunice Lee, 420; Frances, 420; Jeremiah, 399; Jeremiah, Col., 433; John W., Jr., 420; John Wesley, Jr., 420; John, Capt., 433; Joshua, 433; Maude Ellen, 420; Nellie May, 420; Roy Arnold, 420; Temple, 504; Willie, 420

PETERSON: J. R., Rev., 565

PETTY: Lucinda, 534; Mary, 367; Thelma Aline, 59

PHIFER: C. M., 332

PHILLIP: Elizabeth, 212; George, 212

PHILLIPS: Elizabeth Carolina, 17; H. L., 16, 17(2); Honoria Logan, 17; Honoria Logan Lang, 17; Jacob, 112; L. B., 16, 17(2); Logan Lang, 17; Lucius Bellenger, 14(2), 17; Mary, 112; Mary Chestnut, 16, 17(2); W. P., 494; William Francis, 17, 18

PHILPOT: Emily, 220; Joseph, 220

PHILSON: Thomas, 75; Thomas A., 76

PHINAZEE: William Harrison, 281

PICKENS: Sallie B., 145

PICKETT: John Birdsey, 285

PIERCE: Berta D., 184; Edna Faust, 185; F. D., 186; Florence, 185; Florence D., 186; Grisselda P., 26; Herberta, 185; James Augustus, 185, 186; Jeff C., 479; Mary Camilla, 185; Maude, 185; Minnie Barron, 481; Orman Jeff, 480; W. H., 186; W. Harry, 185; William H., 186

PIERSON: Jennie F., 9

PIKE: P. H., 39

PILLSBURY: Samuel, 52(2)

PINSON: Edith, 123; Elihu, 125; Elizabeth Sullivan, 313; Lucinda, 125

PIPER: George W., 496, 497; James Y., 496; John, 472(2); Mary E., 496

PITT: Jedidah, 552

PIX: Kathleen, 167

PLAYER: Mary, 242

POE: Samantha, 511(2)

POLK: Martha, 509

POLLARD: Ellen, 454(2); Robert, 456

PONDER: John, Mrs., 504

POOL: Betsey, 301; Fariba, 467; Gabriel, 301; James, 301(2); John, 301; Polley, 301; Rebekah, 301; Salley, 301; Ursula, 301; William, 301

POPE: Alexander, 558; Charity, 558; Charity Lee, 558; Elijah, 61; Elizabeth, 61, 558; Hardy A., 558; Henry, 61; Henry T., 558(2); Jacob, 61; James W., 558; John T., 558; Martha, 183; Mary, 61; Mary Ann, 558; Mourning, 61; Sarah Delilah, 558; Solomon, 61; Susan Caroline, 558; Susannah, 61

PORTER: Alexander, Rev., 48; Andrew, 572; Baziel Smith, 193; Caroline, 344; Catharine, 572; Elizabeth, 193, 572; Hugh, 193; J. V., 357; James, 194,572(2), 573; Jane N., 572; Job, 194; John, 193, 572; John J., 573;

(Porter continued...)

Joseph, 193; Keziah, 352; Leroy, 573; Lida, 1; Martha, 194; Mary, 572; Mary Ann, 194; Mikel Grimes, 1; Phillip, 193, 194; Rebecca, 193; Robert H., 573; Sarah Ann, 1; Sarah C., 572; Susan, 573; Thomas, 194; Thomas D., 406; Thomas D., Rev., 405; William, 193, 573

POWELL: Albert Crenshaw, 120; Allan, 225; Almon, 225; Britain, 401; Britain Devan, 402; Carrie Jones, 119; Clara Travis, 120; Elijah, 401; Elisha, 402; Emma Christian, 120; Isaac, 402; Jacob, 402; James Abercrombie, 120; James Moore, 119; Jolcey, 402; Josie Arvie, 120; Lavinia, 225; Lucinda, 230; Marion Granville, 119; Mary, 402(2); Mary Eugene, 119; Mary Eugenia Thompson, 118; Mary Eugenie Thompson, 116; Mary Jane, 154; Mike, Mrs., 291; Milly, 401, 402(2); Minnie Jackson, 120; Polly, 402; W. P., 119; W.P., Dr., 118; Walter Tabb, 120; William Edward, 119; Willie, 563

PRESSLEY: L. E., 207; Leon, Rev., 167; Rev., 167

PRESSLY: David, Rev., 49; James P., Rev., 48

PRICE: Mae Greer, 23; Quincy, 232

PRIESTLY: Ann Iserbeller, 338; Edward Leonadas, 338; Eliza Ann Ragsdale, 338; Frances Montgomery, 338; Harriet Chapel, 338; James Polk, 338; James, Sr., 338; Louisa Josephine, 338; Martha Elizabeth, 338; Mary Eliza, 338; Samuel Baxter, 338; William Pylander, 338

PRINCE: Catharine, 78; Cuetan W., 79; Edward, 78, 79; George W., 78; Hudson, 78; Hugh M., 79; Jonathan, 78; Jonathan, Jr., 78, 79; Margaret L., 78; Melba, 79; Milly, 78, 79; Rebecca, 78; Rebecca W., 79; William, 78

PRITCHERD: Susan, 544

PRITCHETT: Thomas W., 243

PROCTOR: Susan, 188; Theodore C., 340(2)

PROFFITT: Ira Jackson, 500; John, 500; John William, 500; Julia Emeline,500; Landon Carter Halns, 500; Marquis de Lafayette, 500; Martha Jane,500; Mary Wilson, 500(2); Phebe Ann, 500; Polly, 500(2); Pulliam Pierce, 500; Serephina Taylor, 500; Turner C., 500(2); Turner Calvin, 500; Walghstil Avery, 500(2)

PROSSER: Ann, 130; Elizabeth, 130; George, 130; John, 130; Mary, 130; Otey,130; Rebecca, 130; Susan, 130; William, 130

PROVENCE: Lily, 190

PRUETT: John, 442; Keziah, 442

PUGH: Hill, 554; Mary Matilda, 554

PULLER: Celia, 125

PULLIAM: Barnett, Jr., 544; Barnett, Sr., 541, 544; Benjamin, 541, 543, 544; Benjamin, Jr., 541; Benjamin, Sr., 540, 541; Burnett, Jr., 541; Elizabeth, 541, 543; Harriet Wilson, 541, 543; John, 543; John Bruce, 541; John G., 556; John, Jr., 543; John, Sr., 541, 543, 544(2); Lucy Wilson, 541; Martha, 541, 543; Mary, 541(2); Mary Israel, 541; Nancy, 539; Sallie Barnett, 543

PURCEL: Robert, Rev., 359

PURCELL: Henry, Rev., 209

PURSE: Anne Ellen, 178

PURTLE: Thomas, 69; Thomas Jefferson, 69(2)

PUTNAM: E. E., 42

PYLES: Nancy Rosamond, 196

QUAILS: Janie, 144

QUILLIAN: Eliza, 220; Eliza Hutchinson, 221; Hardy H., 220; I. W., 220; Lewis, 221; Mary, 220; Mary Day, 221; Milligan P., 221

RABB: Calvin, 188, 190; Charles K., 189, 190; Charles Kincaid, 189(2); Edwin Belzer, 189; Elizabeth E., 188; Elizabeth Edwards, 188; Hannah, 190(2); Harriet, 188; Harriett, 188; Horace, 189; James, 187, 190; James Bell, 188; James Kincaid, 189; James Kincaid Watts, 189; Jessie Mary, 189; Joel, 188; John, 187-190; John Bell, 190; John Glazier, 188(2), 189,190; Kate Henderson, 189; Lily Provence, 189; Louise, 188; Martha C., 188(2); Mary E., 188; Nina, 189, 190; Patience, 188(2); Renthea Glazier, 190; Robert, 188(2); Sarah A., 188(2); Thomas U., 188; Virginia, 189; William, 188, 190; William Clarence, 189(2)

RABUN: Betty Ann, 477(2); Edith, 478; Edith Louisa, 478; Margaret, 478

RAEGAN: Juma, 495

RAGAN: R. T., Mrs., 502

RAGSDALE: James H., 273(2); John H., 272, 273; John W., 272; Martha, 273; Mary C. C., 273; Peter, 313; Samuel N., 272; Susannah, 273; William M.,272

RAIFORD: Cooper, 23; Martha, 285; Mary, 285; Philip, 285

RAINES: Arkansas, 41; Christopher C., 41(2); Clerinda P., 41; Frank C., 46; Frank Coleman, 42; J. E., 41, 42; J. J., 42; James, 41-43; James E., 41,42; James F., 41; James Joseph, 42, 43; James W., 42; John T., 41, 42; Joseph, 42; Joseph R., 41, 42; Margaret, 41; Marget, 42; Marget Allis, 42; Marget N. E., 41; Marget Nancy Elizabeth, 42; Mary, 42; Mary M., 41; N. W., 42; Nathaniel W., 41; Nellie J., 42; Rebecca, 41;

(Raines continued...)

Rebecca A., 41; Robert C., 41(2); S. J., 41; Sarah J., 42; Viny Sary Ann, 42; Walter, 41,42; William, 41(2), 42

RAINEY: Addison, 563

RALEY: Ida Jane, 367; Mary Ella Adams, 369

RALL: Mary, 456

RAMSEY: Annie Lee, 235; Carrie Elizabeth, 235; Effie Meal, 235; James Conrad, 164; Janetta Montgomery, 254; Katie Bell, 235; Sarah, 549; Tom, 164

RANDOLPH: Arcadia Foreman, 449; Elizabeth, 449; Fannie, 553; Harriet Wilson, 542; Jesse, 449, 450; John, 449(2), 450; Judith, 554

RASKIN: William, Jr., 244

RATCLIFF: Ann, 372; John, 372; Thomas, 372

RATHBONE: Dean, 91

RAVANNA: Sarah M., 129(4)

RAWLS: Rose Cathrine, 108

RAY: Adah Delilah, 115; Ambrose, 115, 116; Carrolton, 115, 116; Elijah, 115; Homer Thomas, 115; Hosea, 115, 116; Hosea Holcomb, 115; Irena, 115,116; Jane, 115; Jesse, 115, 116; Judith, 116; Robert, 115(2), 116; Spencer, 115; Thomas, 116; William H., 115; William Martindale, 115; Willis, 115

REAVIS: Rhoda, 362

REDMOND: Isabella, 487

REECE: Benjamin, 11, 298; Joel, 557; Mary, 11, 298; Rebekah, 11, 298

REED: Abel, 330; Ann, 373; Asa, 330; Charlotte, 330; Christian, 372, 373; Daniel, 330, 331; Daniel R., 331; Elizabeth, 304; Fanny, 470; Frances, 330, 373; Francis, 331(2); George, 304; Isabella, 304(2), 305; Jesse, 330; Jessee, 331; John L., 331; Joseph, 304, 305, 373; Joseph Jr., 304; Joshua, 331; Keziah, 331; Kezziah, 331; Leasy, 331; Levi, 331; Lorrah, 331; Margaret, 304; Mary, 304, 330, 372(2), 373; Milford, 331(2); Nancy O., 331; Penelope, 373; Rebecca, 330, 331(2), 373(2); Rose, 304; Samuel, 304; Sarah, 331; Sarah Hargrove, 304; Silas, 331; Susannah, 331; Thomas Baskin, 304;William, 330, 331, 373(2); William B., 331; William, Rev., 489; Wilson Francis, 373

REEDER: Helen, 59

REES: Emma, 336; Julia V., 5, 336; Julia Vaughan, 6, 337; Maria Ford, 6, 337; Mary Margaret, 6, 7, 337(2); Vermeille, 6, 7, 336, 337; Wentworth,337; Wentworth F., 5-7, 336

REESE: Anne, 557

REEVES: Bessie, 45; Malcolm Hardy, 23, 26; Mary J., 142; W. Linus, 26

REID: Alexander, 244; Ann, 244; Elizabeth, 293; George, Capt., 244; Hugh, 244; Isabella, 198, 292; John, 284; Joseph, 244, 292, 293; Joseph Jr., 292; Margaret, 292; Mary, 293; Rose, 292; Ross, \, 244; Samuel, 244, 293; Sara Hartgrove, 293; Thomas Baskin, 292

REIGEL: Jack, 260

RENARD: Francis Henry, 283; Joseph F., 282; Julia, 283

RES: Martha Ann, 496

REVELLE: Hezekiah, 496

REVENEL: Daniel, 349; James, 349

REYNOLDS: Green, 563; Mark, 5

RHEA: Esther, 379

RHODES: Elizabeth, 523; Jenelle, 388; Jesse, 388(2); John, 388; Mary Ann,523(2); Melvin, 388; Viola, 388(3)

RICE: Washington, 98

RICHARD: Richard Lawson, 135

RICHARDS: Ann, 470; J. G., Rev., 249

RICHARDSON: Charles Y., 146; Eliza, 21(2); H. D., 110; Sarah, 110; Sarah Ann, 111; Susannah Wesner Seyle, 147

RIDGEWAY: John, 494

RIDLEHUBER: Elizabeth, 108

RIGGS: John R., 356

RIGHTON: Jane, 197

RILEY: Altina J., 52; Anne, 88(2); Ira Draton, 52; James H., 88; John, 88(2); Lamar, 87; Rachel, 88; Rebecca, 52, 88; Rosa Anna, 88; Sarah, 52,88(2), 89; Susan C., 88(2); William, 87; William F., 88; William Jasper,52

RIVERS: Ashley Grey, 90; Benjamin Lafayette, 90; Brandwell Cozart, 90; Emily F., 89; Evora Janet, 90; John Randolph, 90; Lacurkias, 90; Mabel,

(Rivers continued...)

90; Mamie, 90; Mary Elender, 151; Sopha Neal, 90; Sophia Serfaniel, 90; Tresse Al Wilder, 90; William George, Jr., 89, 90; William Sinclair, 90

RIVES: Angie E., 184

ROBERSON: Toll, 388

ROBERT: Myrtle Andrew, 447

ROBERTS: Adeal Kremlin, 222; Alice, 519; Bavarian Kabira, 222; Carolina, 513; Fabian Malone, 222; John, 491; Joy Olmutz, 222; Khiron Euca, 222; Mary Christian, 223

ROBERTSON: Daniel, 219; Henry P. F., 390

ROBESON: Anna, 418; Chloe, 418; Cloanna, 418; Harmon, 418; Henry, 418(2); James, 418(2); John, 418; Luke, 418; Martha, 418(2); Mary, 418; Milley, 418(2); Noah, 418(2)

ROBINSON: Allen, 472; Allen Y., 435; Ann Eliza, 48; Anne Videtto, 294; Clack, 435, 436(2); David U., 260; David U. Jr., 261; David W., Mrs., 273; David Wallace, Mrs., 260; Edith Courtenay, 261; Eleanor, 435; Eleanor A., 436; Elian A., 49; Eliza A., 49, 50; Eliza Ann, 49; Elizabeth, 48; Elizabeth Boggs, 48; Guy Hartwell, 259; Henry Allen, 294(2); Henry Burton, 261; J. D., 230; James, 48(2), 49(2), 50, 51; James P., 48; James Pressley, 51; James Pressly, 49; Jesse, 467; John, 50; John Burrell, 436; John Lee, 49; Keziah, 188; Lucy R., 435; Lula, 322; Margaret Joel, 49,50; Martha Campbell, 50; Martha Virginia S., 436; Mary C., 435, 436; Mary Carolina Ann, 436; Mary Susannah, 48, 49; Noll Sharp, 259; Pearl Edith Drucilla, 323; Pearle E., 323; Rebecca Jane, 48; Rowena T. F., 435; Sallie H., 48; Samuel, 49, 50; Sarah Ann, 435; Sarah Hope, 49; Susan, 259; Susanne, 237; Tom H., 48; V. W., Rev., 241; Virginia, 436; William, 48(2); William Childs, 260; William E., 435; William Wire Bonner, 48; William Wirt Bonner, 49, 51

ROBISON: Elizabeth, 319

ROCHESTER: Sallie, 8

ROCKETT: James, 68; Mary T., 68

RODDY: Marcus, 52

RODGERS: Christopher, 209

ROGERS: Abner, 561; Asenath, 562; Clara, 562; Collin, 561; Eli Oscar, 21(2); Faith, 561; Fannie B., 21(2); J.V., 21; James Thomas, 21(2); Jeremiah Foster, 21(2); John, 561; John R., 561; Joseph, 561(2); Lillie Johnston, 141; Loula Kendall, 475; Mary, 561; Mary Rebecca, 21(3); Nancy, 562; Nancy Campbell, 21; Patience, 477; Pheby, 562; Rebecca, 561(2); Reuben, Jr., 561(2), 562, 563; Reuben, Sr., 561(2); Robert Simeon, 21(2); Sarah, 561; Temperance, 562(2); William Capers, 21(2); Willis, 21(2)

ROLLINS: D. O., 427; Doctor O., 426; George W., 427; James J. E., 426; John E., 426; Jonas, 426, 427; Julian, 427; L. M., 427; Lawson R., 427; Malley, 426; Martha Jane, 426, 427; Mary, 426; Mary A., 426; Noah J., 426; O. D., 426; Rebecca, 426; T. J., Rev., 44

ROQUEMORE: Lafayette F., 243

ROSE: Ann, 396; Anthony U., Rev., 210; Asa, 396; Benjamin, 396; Elizabeth,396; John, 396(3); Milley, 396; Nancy, 396(2); Patience, 396; Rachel,396; Sterling, 396; Thomas, 396; William, 396

ROSS: A. M., 162; Ada Maude Matina, 163; Annie Louise, 163; Belle, 164; Catherine, 191, 192; E. J., 161; Easter L., 162; Eliza, 162, 163; Forest,164; Fred Ramsey, 163, 164; George, 192; George A., 162; George Sr., 191; George Jr., 192; Isabella Montgomery, 192; James, 192; James Harlan, 163, 164; Jane, 192; John, 192(2); John Lester Crowell, 163; Julia Ann, 162,163; Lettie Ula Belle, 163; Margaret, 191, 192; Margaret

(Ross continued...)

C., 162; Margaret Caroline, 162; Maryland Jane, 191; Mattie Ruth, 163, 164; Moses,162(2); Moses C., 161(2), 162(2); N. W., 164; Noah V., 162; Noah W., 162; Noah Webb, 161, 164; Osborne, 162(2); Perry, 162, 163; Rachel, 162, 163; Rebecca, 192(2); Reuben Jacob Forest, 163

ROUGH: Christian C., 84

ROWE: Jane, 276

ROWELL: Tamp, 111

ROWIE: Malor John, 244

RUCKER: Catharine, 438(2); David, 37; George, 438; Hannah Mary O., 37; Margaret, 37(2); Nancy, 438; R. D., 37; Wesley Asbury, 37

RUDISELL: Dorothy Annie Clare Grady, 515(2)

RUDOLPH: Kate, 221

RUFF: David Franklin, 217; Francis M., 217; George W. C., 217; Henry F. Benson, 217; John, 217; John Holmes, 218; John Lemuel, 217; Martha, 217; Mary Ann, 217, 218(2), 220; Samuel A. Coke, 218; Sarah Victoria, 217;Thomas J., 218

RUKENBAKER: Dibbie, 168; Lillie Mary Locke, 168

RUMPASS: E., Mrs., 528

RUSH: L. K., Mrs., 390

RUSSEL: Richard, 550

RUSSELL: A. Phiny, 363; Albert Burton, 363; Aminta Martha, 364; Aminta Matilda, 363; Andrew, 363; Andrew Dacia, 363; Andrew Davis, 363; Carl Ferris, 364; Carrie Virginia, 364; D. C., 364; Eli Morrison, 97; Eliza, 577; Ellen, 363; Esteline Mary, 363; George W., 255, 363; George, Jr., 362; George, Sr., 362; Hannah Adaline, 363; James Frank, 364; Jane Amanda, 363; John, 362, 363; John Burton, 363, 364; John H., 364; John Harrison, 363; John, Sr., 364; Loucinda, 363; Maggie Seavina, 363; Martha, 363; Martha Wood, 364; Mira Louisa, 363; Nancy, 363, 364(2); Oily Haseltine, 363; Samantha, 363; Sarah Ada, 97

RUTHERFORD: Archibald, 496; Jane Young, 496

RUTLEDGE: Francis F., Rev., 350; James, 563

SABDERS: Samuel, 112

SAIN: Jacob, 419(2); Lydia, 419

SAINER: P., 578

SALKINS: Susan, 54

SALMOND: Louisa, 14

SAMS: Frances, 260

SANDERS: Ann, 201, 247; Anna E., 82; Annie Elizabeth, 82; Esther, 484; Jordan, 247; Jordon, 201; Josiah, 484; Martha Jane, 434; Mary, 112; Mary Ann, 206; Polly, 225

SANDLIN: Cratie, 487; E., 487; Nora, 487; Nora B., 487

SANGERSON: Isaac, 486(2); Sylvia, 486

SATCHWELL: Arcadia F. E., 454

SAVAGE: R. D., Rev., 502

SAWYER: Martha, 445

SAXON: Alexander, 150; Allen, 150; Charles, 150; Clarissa, 150; David, 150; Elizabeth Davis, 562; Harriette, 150; Hugh, 150; Joshua, 150; Lewis, 150(2); Louisa, 150, 562; Lydall P., 150; Nancy Rogers, 562; Nancy Wilkinson, 562; Polly, 150; Sally, 150; Samuel, 150; Susannah, 150;Tabitha, 150, 294; Temperance, 562; Wiley, 562(2)

SAXTON: Polly, 557

SCALES: James G., 568; Nathaniel F., 570; Richard H., 514

SCARBORO: C. W., Rev., 502

SCARBOROUGH: Elizabeth, 322; Mabel G., 529

SCHELL: Catherine, 467

SCHMIDT: Mae Greer Smith, 23

SCHWARTZ: Henry Garad, 261

SCILLMAN: Eliza, 145

SCOTT: J. T., 207; James, 496, 497; Martha A., 496; Mary C., 408(2); Mary Miller, 257(2); Mary Sullivan, 313; Nancy Young, 254, 257(2); Rebecca M., 408; Robert, 313; Temperance, 497; Thomas, 196; Virginia, 496, 498;William, 257

SCRUGGS: Beulah, 134; Charles G., 134; Francis, 135; Franklin, 135; Glenn Allen, 135; Hazel Eliz, 135; Hazel Elizabeth, 135; James Frederick, 135; John Goldwire, 134, 135; Kate Young, 135; Lilly, 134; Margaret, 134, 135; Margaret Horne, 135; Martha Sue, 135; Ralph Leon,

(Scruggs continued...)

135; Richard, 134; Richard Harriet, 134; Richard Lawson, 135(2); Susan E., 134; Thomas Sutton, 134; William Richard, 135(2)

SEABROOK: Pinckney, 260

SEARLS: Jane, 514; John, 514

SEAWRIGHT: Eleanor Ann, 197; James, 37; John, 37
SEAY: Belcon, 44; Belton, 45; Bertha Lee, 45; Cleveland Columbus P., 45; Dean, 46; Dean Durant, 44; Elizabeth, 44; Eunice, 45, 46; Mary Abigail, 44; Mary Elizabeth, 45; Mattie Kate, 44, 45; Robert Clee, 45; Robert Elbe, 44; Sarah Maria, 91; W. D., 44; William Cleveland, 45

SEIZAS: Abraham Mendex, 318; Benjamin, 318; David Cordozo, 318; James Madison, 318; Miriam, 318; Virginia Zipporah, 318

SELF: G. M., 424(2); George M., 423

SELLERS: Bertha L., 479

SELY: Sarah, 330

SEWELL: Frank L., 119

SEYLE: Eliza Bolles, 147; John Frederick, 146(2); John Henry, 146; Laura Collins, 147; Margaret Will, 147; Maria Edgerton, 147(2); Mary F. Miller, 147; Mary Lavinder, 146, 147; Rebecca Eliza, 147; Samuel Henry, 147; Savannah John Frederick, 147; Susannah U., 146; Susannah Wesner, 147; William J., 146(2); William Jackson, 147

SEYMOUR: Alma Janette, 465; Alma Jannett, 464; Betsy, 465; Claudius B., 464, 465; Cornelia, 464, 465; Evelina, 464(2); Frances D., 464; Francis D., 465; Ira, 465; Ira, Jr., 464; Joseph W., 464(2), 465; Ruth B., 464, 465; Uranie Smith, 465

SHANKS: Eleanor, 300

SHANNON: Ann, 398; James, 398

SHARMAN: John, 524; John James, 524, 525
SHARP: Alice, 233, 234; Col., 504; Elizabeth, 233; G. W., 233, 234; John H., 233; Johnie, 233, 234; Tyler Edward, 234

SHARPE: Anni, 235(2); Annie, 234; Annie Davis, 234; C. W., 234; Eddie Lee, 234; Erma Beatrice, 234; G. W., 234; George, 235; John H., 235; John Hansford, 232; Mary Ann, 232; Opelia, 232

SHATANA: James Pritchard, 42

SHAW: Caroline, 306; Pleasant, 306

SHEARER: Amy Green, 557; Ann, 557; Betsy, 557; Fanny, 557; Franky, 557; Grace, 557; Jane, 556; John, 557; Lucy, 557; Mary, 557, 574; Mary F., 556; Milton G., Mrs., 556; Milton Gordon, 556; Myra, 556; Nancy, 557; Robert, 555, 556(2); Robert Findlay, 557; Sally, 557; Thomas, 557; William, 557

SHELL: Sarah Jane, 226

SHELNUTT: Alice Rachel, 495; C. D., 495, 496; Calvin, 495; Doster, 495; Enoch Foster, 496(2); Ernstus Lamar, 495; James Burket, 495; Mary Elizabeth, 495; Sallie Queen, 496; William Charles, 496; William Clarkes, 495

SHEPARD: Ariana, 568; Henry, 486; Matilda, 486(2); Thomas, 568(2)

SHERBERT: Callie B., 46

SHERMAN: Martha W., 563

SHERWOOD: Daniel, 396(2)

SHIPP: Thomas, 438

SHOCKLEY: Elizabeth, 487

SHOUSE: Christennah, 405

SHRADER: George Washington, 452; Henry H., 452; Isaac Chancery, 452; Jackson Van Buren, 452; James Asa Clark, 452; John W., 452; Katharine, 452, 453; Mary A. R., 452; Rachel, 452, 453; Thomas W., 452

SHROPSHIRE: Naomi, 253

SHUFFIELD: Barbara, 370

SILLS: Abigail, 114, 345; Benjamin, 346; Benjamin Sills, 114; Elizabeth, 114, 345; James Monroe, 114, 345; Jane, 114; Jane H., 114; Jane M., 346(2); John, 114, 346; Nancy, 114, 346; Samuel Joseph, 114, 345; Samuel Joseph Jr., 114; Samuel Joseph, Jr., 346; Tabitha, 114, 346; Thomas Kees, 114

SIMMONS: Benjamin, 401; Benjamin Franklin, 401; Calvin Jones, 401; Joseph B., 306; Joseph Pleasant, 307; Lockey, 401; Louisa M., 504; Mahala, 307; Marcus De Lafayette, 243; Nancy Ann, 401; Walter Alexander, 401; William Gaston, 401

SIMMS: John, 306

SIMONS: B., 359; Catherine, 359; Edward, 359; Edward Ball, 359; Lydia, 359; Lydia Ball, 359(2); Rev. Mr., 350

SIMPSON: Charles U., 308; Edward E., 308; Edward Eugene, 306; James, 306; James W., 308; John W., 308; Leah E., 308; Samuel, 8, 9; Sarah Walker, 308; William H., 308

SIMS: Rebecca S., 82

SINTON: Anna Cook, 131, 132; David Cardwell Samuel, 132; Edward, 132; Rebecca C., 132; Samuel, 132; Sarah Elizabeth, 132; William, 132

SITTON: Ambrose, 444

SKINNER: Harriet, 473; Harvey, 473; Levina, 473; William H., 473

SLATTER: Solomon, 458; Solomon, Jr., 458

SLAUGHTER: Susan, 244

SLIGH: Mary Magdalena, 108; Robert Creswell, 108; Solomon, 108

SLIGHT: Robert Creswell, 107; Texana C., 315; William C., 315

SLOAN: R. F., Rev., 152

SMALL: D., 467, 469; David, 467, 470; David A., 469; Edmond B., 469; Edmund B., 469; Jane E., 469(3); Martha, 467, 469; Mary F. Frances, 469(2); Richard H., 469(2); Richard T., 469; Thomas M., 469, 470; William B.,469(2)

SMITH: Abraham, 149; Alfred, 514(2); Alice Elliott Drayton, 211; Amy, 568;Ann, 112; Ann H., 568; Ann Hunt, 568; Ann Millege, 320; Ann Vince, 319; Anne Adair, 276; Any, 543; Barbara Scriven, 320; Beatrice Ann, 230; Benjamin, 210; Benjamin C., 182; Benjamin Savage, 211(2); Catherine Barnes, 319; Charles B., 112; Charles H., 112; Charlie M., 182; David, 276; David H., 39; Dill, Capt., 434; Dorcas, 398; Douglas, Jr., 204; Edward, 210; Edward Darrell, 210; Edward Stewart, 434; Eleanor, 321; Eliza Carey, 320; Eliza J., 182; Eliza Jane, 210; Elizabeth, 276, 320,321, 390; Elizabeth Sarah Vinson, 211; Emily Hayne, 211; Emma Lovenia, 182; Frances Elizabeth, 26; Francis Lee, 433; George H., 112; Harriett, 323; Henrietta, 321; Hugh A., 276; Hughy, 276; Isaac, Rev., 239; J. L., 434; Jacob A., 111, 112; James, 80, 543, 568(3); James Franklin, 182; James H., 240; James Vince, 319, 321; Jane, 276; Jane M., 173; John, 133,283, 390, 434; John Laurens North,
(Smith continued...)

211; John M., 434; John Miles, 433; Joseph, 320; Joseph E., 182; Julia Arabella, 320; Katherine, 149; Laura, 133; Lauvern, 407; Lettice Wyatt, 203; Lovisa Robison, 320; Lucretia, 112; Lucy Eleanor, 319; Lula C., 182; Lula Jane, 433; Manning, Mrs., 10; Margaret, 276; Margaret Palestine, 183; Martha, 283, 319, 320; Martha A. V., 282, 283; Martha Ann, 433; Martha J., 434; Martha Jane Saunders, 433; Martha Rebecca Elizabeth, 182; Mary, 193; Mary A., 276; Mary E., 112; Mary Eliza North, 211; Mary Elizabeth, 210; Mary Frances, 182; Mary Louisa, 320; McMichael Lafayette, 434; Nancy, 276, 561, 577; Nancy Annah, 182; Nancy C., 183; Nancy Caroline, 182; Nancy Peer, 183; Nimrod, 203; O. K., 182; Obediah, 544; Owen K., 183; P. L., 434; Patsy, 432; Piasl Calvin, 112; Richardson, Capt., 434(2); Robert, 209, 276; Robert Wilson, 276; Robert, Rev., 359; Robert, Rev. Mr., 209; Rosannah, 276; Sanders E., 434; Sanders Egleston, 433; Sara, 210; Sarah, 112, 313, 315, 321, 433; Sarah Edith Ann, 211; Sarah Elizabeth, 319; Sarah Emiline, 182; Sarah North, 210; Stephen, 320; Stephen, Jr., 319(2), 320, 321(2), 322; Stephen, Sr., 321; Susan George, 320; Tennessee Arkansas, 58; Thomas B., 320; Thomas Barnaparte, 319; Urias H., 112; Urias M., 112; Valeria Elmer, 133; W. T., Rev., 230; William, 203, 276, 413; William C., 210; William Cuttine, 211; William D., 111, 112; William F., 539; William P., 182, 183; Wilson, 276

SMOOT: T., 578

SNIDER: Earl H., 10; Earl McKinney, 9; Jane E., 9, 10; Mary Louise, 9, 10; W. J., 9; Wilhelmena Farr, 9; Wilhelmina Farr, 10; William Farr, 9, 10; William J., 9; William Judson, 9, 10

SNOWDEN: L. J., 207

SOLEBY: Madeline, 159

SOLESBEE: Irene Allison, 159

SOMMERS: Susannah, 209

SORRELS: Emily, 24; Jane, 23

SOUTHERLAND: Anne, 203; Caldona, 551
SPARKS: Benjamin, 396; Rachel, 396(2); William, 396(2)

SPARROW: Henry Hooker, 507(2)

SPEAR: Mary A., 503(2)

SPEARMAN: Angeline, 315; C. W. I., 315; Frank, 270

SPEIGHT: Lucille H., 473

SPELL: Eva Lavon, 90

SPENCER: Ann Elizabeth, 566; Corydon, 566; Corydon Seth, 566; Mary H., 566; William P., 566; William Penn, 566

SPRING: Mary E., 260

SPRINGER: William Green, 169(2)

STANDIN: Penelope, 473

STANFORD: Adeline, 568(2); William, 472

STANLEY: Mary, 532; Redmond L., 532

STARK: Mary King, 203

STATON: Adlyn, 388; Alice, 388; Eveline, 387(2), 388, 389; Jesse, 389; Loma, 388; Margie, 389; Melvina, 389; Mont, 388; Thomas, 387(2); U. Grant, 389

STEEL: Grizzell, 20; Hannah, 363

STEELE: Antoinette, 256; Betty Washington, 455; Howell Lewis, 455; James, 257; James T., 255; Lowell Lewis, 456; Martha Ellen, 455; Robert, 454; Robert M., Jr., 456; Robert McAney, 455; Sarah Antoinette, 255-257; Thomas, 256; William, 455

STELLE: Rebecca, 381

STEPHENS: Amanda, 418; Annie Cader, 11; Betty, 417; D., 418; David Augustus, 418; Elijah, 11; Ella Cornelia, 418; Enoch, 10; Floziel, 417; Hardy, 417; Hardy Henry, 418(2); Jemima, 417; John, 10(2), 11(3), 417; John W., 418; Joseph A. McArthur, 418; M. A., 418; Margaret, 10; Martha Ann, 418(2); Martha Ann Thames, 418; Mary, 418; Mary Eliza, 418; Nancy, 10; Rebecca, 432; Reubin, 10; Robert, 10; Sabra Underwood, 418; Sallie, 106, 159; Sarah, 10(2), 11(3); Sarah D., 418; W. D., 418(3); William Ann, 418; Willoughby D., 418

STEPHENSON: Abigale K., 386; Ann, 3; Darkus M., 93; David L., 386; Edward M., 385; Eleaner, 93; Eleanor, 93; Elizabeth, 3; Elizabeth C., 93; Finis E., 3; Hamilton, 385; Hedge L., 3; Hugh W., 3(2); James G., 93(2); James H., 386; Jane, 93, 386; John, 93(2); John C., 3; John H., 93; Marey, 93; Margaret, 3; Mary Elizabeth, 386; Nancy Ann Catherine, 233; Pleasant W., 3; Polly M., 3; Robert B., 93; Robert S., 385; Salley, 460; Sallie R., 3; Samuel E., 386; Samuel T., 93, 386; Watson W., 3; William J., 386

STEPPE: Allen Hansford, 236; Katherine Martin, 236

STERLING: Alexander, 132

STEVENS: Allred W., 146; Drusella, 417; Hardy, 417; James, 417; John, 417(2); Mary, 417(3); Mary Lavinder Seyle, 147; Sabre, 417; Sally, 417; Sarah, 372; Surthoma, 417; Tistoni, 417; William, 417; Willoughby, 417; Zelphia, 417

STEVENSON: Clyde Thomas, 234; George Washington, 234; Jane, 229; Martha, 234; Nancy Ann Catherine, 234; Robert, 229

STEWART: C. B., 312; J. T., 253; Marjorie Haley, 368; Nellie H., 457

STIRMAN: Jane Caroline, 280

STIVENDER: Margaret, 37

STOCKTON: Harriet Chestnut, 12

STOKES: Benjamin, 330; Elizabeth, 330; John W., 330; Priscilla, 330; Priscilla Stokes, 330; Stephen, Major, 330; Thomas, 330; William, 330
STOL: Mary, 208
STOLL: Catherine, 298; David, 11, 12, 298; David Dixon, 12(2), 298; Elizabeth, 298; Gabriel, 298; Jacob, 298; John Lewis Bourquin, 298; Louis Bourquin, 298; Rebekah, 11, 12; Susannah, 11, 12, 298(2); Susannah Garvey, 298

STONE: C. H., 20; Reba Gladys, 90

STOREY: William D., 392

STOVER: Susannah, 329

STRANGE: Calvina, 152; Martha, 227

STREADWICK: Stella, 388

STREDSON: T. B., 235

STREPPE: Katherine Martin, 234

STRIBLING: Clayton, 36(2); Elisabeth Henderson, 36; Fanny Martin, 36; Ida, 31; John Beckham, 36; Lucy, 36; M. S., 499; Mary Leak, 36; Molly, 36(2); Nancy Kinchelow, 36; Samuel Henderson, 36; Thomas, 36

STRICKLAND: U. H., Rev., 9

STROBEL: Arthur Merkley, 351; Cordelia, 351; Eliza, 351; Martin, 351; Mary Eliza, 351; R. H., 351(2)

STROBIA: Francis Richard, 130

STRONG: John, 514; Robert, 514(2); Thomas, 514

STROUD: A. Phiny, 363; Adam, 98; Caty, 98; Clarissa, 99; E., 99; Elizabeth, 98, 99; Emma Line, 99; Isom, 98; James, 98(4), 99(2); James Chant, 99; Jesse, 98; John, 98, 99; John Haun, 98; Joseph, 98; Joshua, 98, 99;Margaret, 99; Mary, 98; Montgomery, 98, 99; Nancy Tiphena, 363; Patty, 98; Rebekah, 98; Robert Hardin, 99(2); Susanah, 99; William, 98, 99(2)

STROUP: Catherine, 392

STROUSE: Mooney Alphonso, 33

STUBBLEFIELD: Dicky, 561; Lucy, 560, 561

STUDATERT: Lyda Carter, 261

SUBER: Mary, 232

SUDDARTH: Abraham, 546, 547; Catherine, 547; Emanuel, 547; James, 547; John, 547; Margaret, 546, 547; Martha, 547; Myra Emily, 547; Nancy, 547; Sallie, 547; Thomas, 547; William, 546, 547

SULLIVAN: Addie J., 312; Adelaide, 311; Anna Belle Freeman, 126; Benjamin,311; Charles, 310, 313; Charles M., 312; Charles P., 313, 314; Charles Pascal, 311; Charles Pinckney, 310; Charles Pleasant, 311; Charly, 311, 313; Clarissa, 311; Claudia C., 312; Claudia Caroline, 311; Clayborne, 310; Dunklin, 313; Dunklin, Judge, 314; Elizabeth, 310; Fannie A., 312;Felicia, 312; Frances, 310; Frances Elizabeth, 311;

(Sullivan continued...)

George W., 312, 314; George Washington, 310; Harriett Humbert, 314; Hewlett, 310(2), 314;Hewlett, Capt., 313, 314; Hughlett, 311-313; J. D., 312; James, 313; James M., 310; James N., 314; Jane, 310; Jane Washington Brooks, 313; Jefferson, 310, 314; John, 252, 312; John C., 310, 312, 313; John Dunklin, 311; John Hewlett, 311; Joseph, 252, 311; Joseph O., 312; Joseph P., 311, 314; Joseph Pinckney, 313; Keziah, 311; M. Hettie, 312(2); Mary,310(2), 311, 313, 314; Mary Anne, 311; Mary Charlton, 310, 313; Mary Dunklin, 310, 313; Mary Henrietta, 311; Mary Mayberry, 314; Milton A.,311; Milton A., Capt., 314; Moses, 311, 313; Owen, 310, 312; Pleasant, 310; Sallie C., 312; Sarah Cureton, 311; Sarah Mimms, 313; Sarah Rutledge Cureton, 314; T. Jeff, 314(2); T. Jefferson, 312, 314; Temperance, 311, 314; Thomas J., 312(2), 314; Thomas Jefferson, 311(2); William, 251; William D., Capt., 314; William Dunklin, 311; William, Capt., 312

SUMMER: John Adam, 107; Maria Margreta, 107; Marie Magadalena, 107

SUMMEROW: Henry, 467

SUMMERS: Anna Maria, 471(3); Benjamin, 471; Benjamine, 471; Caleb Letton,471; J. H., Mrs., 471; John Adam, 171; John Letton, 471; Leah, 471; Letton, 471; Mary Letton, 471; Michael S., 471; Rheubin, 471

SUMMEY: Matilda, 386

SUMNER: Thomas E., 406(2)

SUMTER: John, 546; Martha, 546

SUSAN E.: Richard Lawson, 135

SUTTLE: Mary D., 384

SUTTON: Joseph, 373

SWAIN: Amelia, 453; John Thomas, 562; Joseph, 454; Stephen James, 562; Temperance, 562

SWANCY: Martha, 361

SWANEY: Eleanor, 136; Nathaniel, 136; Robert, 136

SWANSEY: Martha, 361

SWEAT: Murry J., 219

SWINSON: Ann, 530; Ann, Sr., 530; Austin, 530; Clyde, 533; D. M., 533; Daniel, 530, 533; Edee, 530; Elizabeth Croom, 533; Florence V., 534; Florence Victoria, 531; Henry, 530; James G., 530; Jesse, 530, 531, 533; Jesse Jr., 531; Jesse, Jr., 530, 533; Jesse, Sr., 530, 533; John, 530,533; John Austin, 531, 533; Katherine, 530; Levi, 530; Martha, 531, 534; Mary, 530; Nancy, 530(2), 533; Nancy Winders, 533; T. A., 530, 533(2); Teresa, 532; Teresa A., 533; Teresa Ann, 531(2), 533

SWORDS: Andrew, 136; Dorcas, 136; Eleanor, 136; Eleanor Swaney, 137(2); Elizabeth, 136; Esther, 136; Isabella, 136; James Swaney, 136, 137; John,136; John Sr., 136, 137; Jonathan, 136; Robert, 136; Ruthy, 136; William, 136

SYLVIA: Annie V., 82

SYMMES: Elizabeth, 203

TABB: Mary Elizabeth, 117, 118

TACKY: Elizabeth, 152

TALBIRD: Mary, 178, 180

TALBOT: Adah Della, 538; James, 539; James and Nancy, 538; Lawrence Ewell, 538

TALER: George, 78

TALLEY: Alex, 392; Ann, 393; Berry, Sr., 392; Charles B., 393; Elizabeth P., 393; James K., 393; John W., 393; Nancy P., 393; Polly, 393; Polly P., 392; Rebecca A., 393; Sarah D., 393; Wiley M., 393; William A., 393; Winnie S., 393

TALTON: Nannie Florence, 146

TAROY: Stephen, 522

TARVER: Clyde, 449

TATE: Cicero, 424; Mary, 404, 405; Oaky R. Hamrick, 424

TAYLOR: Abigail, 523; Abigail Gibson, 523; Ada P., 164; Alexander Miller, 472; Alfred Blevins, 400; Ann E., 566; Ann Eliza, 565; Cornelius Ware, 382; Edward M., 512; Elizabeth, 433; Elizabeth Jane, 566(2); Fanny L., 570; Frances Lenow, 572; Francis, 561; Hannah Steel, 363; Henry, 523; Isaac H., 566; James Lee, 512; Jinsey Caroline, 512; John, 13(2), 512(4); John Marrion, 512; John P., 566; Joshua, 363; Mariah K., 566(2); Mariak K., 567(2); Martha H., 566; Mary Neely, 512; Mary R., 566(2); Nancy Curry, 72; Nancy Hannah, 512; Patsy Star, 512; Patty, 567; Perry Campbell, 512; Pristine Cherokee, 72; Rebecca, 565; Rebecca J., 567; Rebecca R., 566; Robert Thomas, 400; Susannah, 561; Tempe, 570; Tom P., 400; W., 578; Wiley P., 570; William, 472; William A., 419; William B., 400; William F., 566; William P., 565, 567(2); William Penn, 565-567; William, Major, 286; Willie P., 566

TEAGUE: Agnes, 172

TEBEAU: L. C., Revolutionary, 82

TEDRO: Leila, 529

TEEL: John, 181

TELFORD: George, 284

TEMPLETON: William, 172

TERRY: Anna, 329; Elizabeth, 329, 543(2); John, 329(2), 330; Joseph Minter,329; Mariah, 329(2); Rowland, 329; Sarah, 330; Sarah Ann, 535; Stephen,329, 330; Stephen D., 329; Stephen, Major, 329; William, 329

TEUSCHER: Russell Henry, 90

THAMES: John, 417; Martha Ann, 417, 418; Nancy, 417; Polly, 417(2); Sarah, 417; Sarah Rebecca, 417

THARPE: Annie Blanton, 528; Charles Lucco, 528; Clifford Crutchfield, 528; Edith Lyle, 528; Erin, 528; J. C., 528; John C., 529; John Crockett, 528;Mattie, 528, 529; Mildred, 528; Robert Hamilton, 528

THATCH: James B., 490(2)

THIGPEN: Pernetta, 413

THOMAS: Ann, 292; Ary Matilda, 409; Carnelia Jane, 347; Charity, 60; Christian, 60; David Harry, 347; Elizabeth, 60, 346, 347; Etienne, 291; George Augustus, 347; Jacob, 60; James, 292, 346; James Clothier, 347; Jeane, 292; Jesse, 528; John, 60, 292, 347, 527, 528; John Clothier, 346;Joseph, 60(2), 346; Joseph D., 347; Josiah, 346; Louis, 227; Margery, 303; Marry, 347; Martha, 60; Martha Ann, 347; Mary, 60, 292, 346(3); Micajah, 60; Mourning, 60; Narcissa Elizabeth, 347(2); Phil, 346; Philip, 347; Robert, 347; Samuel Joseph, 292; Sarah, 346, 347; Stephen, 292(2), 347; Susannah, 60, 346, 347; Susanne, 292; T. H., 346; Thomas, 77, 527; Tristram, 346, 347; Tristram H., 347; William, 346

THOMASON: Jefferson C., 494

THOMPSON: A. J., 117; Albert Crenshaw, 117, 118; Andrew Jackson, 116(2),118, 119; Anna Lillia, 117-119; Beulah, 221; David, 116(2), 118(2); David Lyon, 177; Elizabeth, 305; Elvira, 298; Eudora Lucy, 117, 119; Frank Lenoir, 117-119; George W., 540; Gideon Phillips, 117; Jackson, 117; James Middleton Lenoir, 118; Jane, 183; Jane Gillespie, 117, 119; John, 298(2), 300; John Tabb, 117, 118; Lucinda S., 151; Maria, 119; Mary, 300; Mary Anna, 117; Mary Anna Gillespie, 118; Mary Elizabeth, 117; Mary Elizabeth Tabb, 118; Mary Eugenia, 118, 119; Melville Edward, 117, 118; R. A., 119; Robert Andrew, 117-119; Sarah Josephine, 117, 119; Sarah Lenoir, 116, 118; Shirley C., 37; Sillar, 23; Susan Fly, 117, 119; Vida, 23; Walter Jackson, 118, 119; William Vance, 116, 118

THOMSON: Addie, 178; Anna Margaretta, 178; Anne Margaretta, 179; Bernard Helchlor, 179; Bernard Melchior, 180; C. M., 178, 180(4); C. N., 180; Caroline, 244; Christianna B., 179; Christianna Crawford, 179, 180; Christianna H., 178; Christianna M., 178; Christianna Margaretta, 180; D. L., 180(2); David L., 178, 179; David Loyd, 178; David Lyon, 177, 179, 180(2); E. I., 180; Eliza, 169; Elspeth, 178(2); Elspeth Lyon, 179; Emilie A. Thomson, 179; Euphremia J., 179; F. John Houseal, 180; James, 178-180; James C., 179; John, 178; John Houseal, 179; John Mouseal, 178; Margaret Crockett, 179; Margaret W., 179; Mary, 178; Mary Talbird, 179; Robert, 178-180; Robert R., 179; William, 178-180

THORN: Ann, 293; Charnel Hightower, 294

THORNTON: Biddy, 447; Wiley, 447

THORPE: Ann, 559(2); Anselm, 559; Frances, 559; Henry, 559(3); James, 559; Jesse, 559; Phebe, 559; Prissy, 559; Rebekah, 559(2); Silvy, 559

THREEWITS: Dewellen, 361; Elizabeth, 361

TIERE: Mary, 252

TINNON: Alutia Ware, 382; M. Octavia, 382, 383

TIPPIN: George, 303; Mary, 303

TITSHAW: Anderson Harrison, 151; Ara Frances, 153; Carl Shaw, 153; Columbus, 152; Cornella A., 152; Elizabeth, 151; Emma Cintha, 152; Erie Sampson, 153; Ezra Tyler, 153; Fannie Melissa, 153(2); Grady Wilson, 153;Isaac E., 152; James Omer, 153; James T., 153(2); James Tyler, 153(2); John Sampson, 151; John Stephen, 151; John Wilson, 152; L. V. C., 152; L. W. C., 153; L. Wilson, 153; Lewis Columbus, 153; Lucinda, 153; Manley, 152; Manley H., 152; Mary, 152(2); Maude Myrtle, 153; Meley, 152; Niles, 151; Rosina, 152; S. W., 152; Sampson, 153(2); Serena, 153; Serena Pirkle, 152; Sheriff, 152; Stephen Jr., 151, 152(2); Wilson, 151, 152

TODD: Adam, 284

TOMLIN: Julius S., 357(2)

TONEY: Susana, 100

TOOMER: Elizabeth Mary, 356

TORBET: Francis James, 276

TORRENCE: Viola, 389

TOWLES: John Jr., 278; John Sr., 278; William, 277

TOWNSEND: Thomas, 202

TRAVIS: Louise, 529

TRAYLOR: John R., 119

TRAYWICK: J. B., 312

TRESCOTT: Edward, 209

TRICE: Emmie, 288

TRIMMER: Betty, 271

TRIPLETT: John Goolsby, 514; Nelson, 514

TROGDON: Lillian, 508

TROLINGER: John H., 43; Julie, 44; Nancy Terlula, 44; William, 43

TROUSDALE: Nancy, 561; Sally, 561

TUCKER: Joseph, 534; Milly, 557(2); Reuben, Revolutionary, 240; Sarah, 210; Sarah Tucker, 209

TUGGLE: Sarah Jane, 152

TULLIS: W. F., Revolutionary, 146

TURNER: Elizabeth, 471; Josiah, 568; Sarah, 113

TURNLEY: Matthew Jacob, 535

TUTEN: J. W., 111

TYNER: Margaret White Evans, 484

TYSON: Mary, 553

ULMER: Ann Susannah, 33

UNDERWOOD: Sally, 447

UPSHUR: Ann Wilson, 542

URQUHART: Ann, 326; James B., 260

URSHEL: Mary, 107

UTLEY: P. M., Mrs., 401

UZZEL: Amanda Washington, 568; Benjamin Edgar, 568; Elisha, 567, 568(2);Henry Thomas, 568; James N., 567; Luezer Elizabeth, 567; Martha Ellen, 567; Mary Ann, 567; Peyton Randolph, 567; Rebecca, 567; Sarah Jane, 567; Tabitha, 568; Tabitha Boon, 568; William D., 567

VAN DYKE: M. E., 529

VAN KANNON: Maxine Ardelle, 480(2)

VANDERSLICE: Frances Anne, 228

VARIEN: Harriet Elizabeth, 57

VAUGHAN: Elizabeth, 6, 336; Henry, 5, 6(2), 7, 335, 336(4), 337; Henry, Jr., 5-7, 335-337; Henry, Sr., 6, 336, 337; James, 539; Jane, 539; John Anderson, 6, 336; Julia F., 5, 335; Julia Finetta, 6, 336; Margaret, 6, 7, 337; Marlene, 166; Mary Margaret, 6, 7, 337; Vermeille, 5-7, 336(2); Willis L., 382

VAUGHN: Henry, Jr., 6, 7; L. E., 165; Marjorie White, 165; Willis L., 381

VENABLES: Betsey, 380; Jesse, 380; John, 380(2), 381; Malcolm, 380; Margaret, 380; Mary, 380; Rebecca, 380; Richard, 380, 381; Sally, 380; Ursuly, 381; William, 380, 381

VERDERY: Benjamin F., 326

VERNER: Ann, 499; Anna, 498; Charles, 498, 499; Davis D., 498; Ebenezer Pettigrew, 499; George, 498; George W., 499(2); James, 498; Jane 499 (2);John, 498, 499(2); John Augustus, 499(2); Lemuel H., 499; Mary P., 498, 499; Nancy, 499(2); Rebecca, 498(2); Samuel, 498, 499; W. B., 499; W. P.,498; William S., 498

VIDETTO: Robert James, 293, 294; Roberta Howard, 293

VINCE: Joseph, Capt., 319, 320; Judith, 319; Lucy, 319

WADDELL: Tommy, 59

WADE: Arthur W., 323; Blake, 529; Love, 529; Mary Beth, 323; N. L., 529; William, 304

WADSWORTH: Rosamond A. Lancaster, 518

WAFF: Caroline M. Rawls, 493; Elizabeth Ann, 493(2); Elizabeth Ann Bradberry, 493; Joseph, 493; Joseph Judson, 493; Joseph T., 492, 493(2); Joseph Thomas, 490; Mary Carpenter, 492, 493; Sarah Sackie P., 493; Thomas E. S., 492, 493; Thomas Edward, 493

WAGGONER: Magdelene, 376

WALDRIP: Broadus Ezell, 9; Ellin Davis, 8; Henry Jefferson, 8; James Albert, 8(2); Jesse Taylor, 8; John Landrum, 8; Margaret Elizabeth, 8; Mary E., 9; Mary Pertima, 8; Pernecia Victoria, 9; Pertima, 8; Sallie Rochester, 8; Samuel James, 8(2), 9; Thomas Brook, 8

WALKER: Berriman, 306, 307; Edward, Jr., 550; Elizabeth, 306, 550; Frances, 388; G. L., 522; Georgia V., 293; Henry N., 550; James, 306(2), 307(3); James, Revolutionary, 178; John, 306(2), 307, 308; John H., 307; John W., 550;Jonathan, 550; Joseph, 550; Joseph, Revolutionary, 76; Leah, 307, 308; M. M., 230; Mahala, 306, 307; Margaret, 550; Martha, 550; Mary, 306, 307(2); Mary Jefferson, 189; Minnie Almedia, 230; Moses H., 307; N. H., 344; Nancy Caroline, 307(2); Nathaniel, 231; Nathaniel Jr., 230,

(Walker continued...)

231; Nathaniel Sr., 230; Phebe, 306, 307; Samuel, 550; Sarah, 306, 307; Susanna, 550; Thomas,Revolutionary, 234; William, 550; William, Revolutionary, 217

WALL: L. R., 427; Margaret, 427

WALLACE: H. A., 138; Marshall Perkins, 165

WALLERN: F. J., 107; Frederic Joseph, 107; Frederick, Revolutionary, 108

WALLING: Hay B., 82; J. Florrie, 82; W. H., 81
WALLIS: General, 377

WALSH: Annie, 322; Thomas P., 322

WALTERS: Elbert Franklin, 128; George Franklin, 128; Martha Frances, 128

WALTON: Margaret Ann, 180; Robert, Mrs., 319

WARD: Carolina, 181; L., 578; Simeon, 181

WARE: Adeline, 354; Angelina, 354; Elizabeth, 381; Erasmus, 382; Francis Asbury, 354; George W., 382; Hugh Bell, 354; Martha Watt, 354; Priscilla, 354; Sarah Aedy, 354; Thomas, 183; Thomas Cooke, 354; Virginia, 382; William, 354; William F., 566; William Thomas, 354

WARNOCK: Anna, 284(2); Annie, 122; Betsy, 122; Eleanor, 122(2); Elizabeth, 122, 284; Fanny, 122; Frances, 284; James, 122, 284; Jane, 122, 284;John, 122(2), 283, 284; Margaret, 122, 284; Mary, 122, 284(2); Rebecca, 284(2); Robert, 122, 284

WARREN: Sarah C., 493; Thomas, 493

WASHBURN: Rubin, 143

WATERS: A. B., 242

WATKIN: Mary V., 219

WATKINS: Amanda, 130; Carrie, 255; Lewis, 353; Othello J., 353; Sarah J., 353; William N., 353

WATSON: Revolutionary Mr., 167

WATT: Revolutionary, 178(2)

WATTS: A. K., 309; Arah Newberry, 309; Arrah, 312; Braxton, 309; Charles,183(2); Cornelia, 309; Eliza Henrietta, 309; Eliza Kynnion, 309; Elvira, 309; Hugh Bell John, 183; Isabella, 195, 268; J. V., 309; James Dunklin,309; John, 309; John Pollard, 309; John William, 309; Laurens Hayne, 309;Louisa, 309; Lucy Nancy, 309; Martha, 183; Martin Jane, 183; Nancy Ann Kincaid Margaret, 183; Nancy Dendy, 308; Nancy Kincaid, 188(3); Narcissa, 309; Peggy, 309; Phoebe Augusta, 309; Rhoda Belle, 309; Richard, 309; S.C., 308; Susan Young, 309; Thomas, 183; W. D., 308, 309; William, 183(2),309; William Augustus, 309; William Dendy, 308; William Hills, 309; William O., 308

WAY: Elizabeth F., 281

WEATHERLEY: A. H., 451, 453; Agnes, 453(3); Amelia, 453(2); Charles Holland, 453; Elizabeth, 453; F. A., 453(2); Isaac J., 453; J. A., 453; James, 453; James A., 451, 453; Jesse R., 453; John Benjamin, 453; John P., 453; Joseph H., 453; Joseph Morgan, 453; Joseph, Sr., 453; Julia Ann Levinia, 453; Martha, 453; Mary Eliza, 453; Thomas Jefferson, 453

WEATHERLY: Asa A., 452; Benjamin Franklin, 451; Elizabeth, 451, 452; F. A., 451; Francis A., 452; Frankling, 452; Isaac J., 452; James A., 452; Jesse R., 451, 452; John P., 452; Joseph, 451, 452(2); Joseph P., Jr., 451;Mary F., 451, 452; Nancy, 451, 452; William N., 452

WEBB: Alexander Smith, 568; Amy, 568(3); Ann, 568; Annie May, 518; E. L.,570(2), 572(2); Elizabeth, 539, 541; Elizabeth L., 568, 570; Frances Y., 568(2); Harriet Wilson, 539, 541; Henry Y., 570; Isabell, 80; James,568(3); James Henry, 570; James L., 568; James S., 570; Jessie T., 565; Jessie Taylor, 572; John, 568(2); John P., 568; John R., 570; Lewis Percy, 572; Lizzie Sue, 572(2); Louis, 366; Mary E., 570; Mildred, 568; Mildred A., 570; Nathaniel Macon, 570; Paul, 570; R. A., Revolutionary, 289; Rachel M., 570(2); Robert C., 568; Robert Maurice, 570; S. H., 570; S.M., 570, 572(4); Sallie, 570; Samuel, 80; Samuel Maurice, 568, 570, 572; Samuel Smith, 570; Sarah DuPre, 289(2); Sarah Elizabeth, 289; Susan, 424; Tempe, 572; Thomas H., 568; Walter, 570; William, 539, 541, 568, 570(2); William S., 568(2)

WEDDINGTON: Zeno, 244

WELBORN: Louisa Amanda, 562

WELDON: Liser Jane, 175

WELLS: Emily Frances, 551; Frank A., 341; Lucinda, 532; Rebecca, 125; Sarah Cook Gordon, 226

WERNER: Julia, 157

WESBURY: Elizabeth, 202

WESNER: Frederick, 148; Henry Philip, 148; Margaret, 148; Mary Susannah,148; Seyle Barbery, 148(2)

WEST: Andrew Jackson, 441, 513, 514; Annie Bernard, 64; Ben, \, 270; Benjamin T., 62; Bryan Cornelius, 61; Carrie, 62; Cassander, 62; Celia, 513; Celina, 513; Charles Marion, 63; Charles N., 61; Charles Nation, 64; Charles Norris, 63; Charlie Norris, 64; Cora, 62; Elizabeth, 62, 458; Francis, 62; Isaac, 62, 63; Isabel, 63; Jasper, 62, 63; John B., 441,513(2); John Henry, 513; John Littlejohn, 61-63; John Littlejoun, 64;Joseph Manson, 513, 514; Landy Porter, 63; Lety, 62; Lula, 61; Lula Adella, 64; M. Washington, 513; Margaret Ann, 513(2); Mariah Marinda, 514; Martha Susan Ann, 63, 64; Mesina, 62; Mirian Marinda, 513; Mitchell, 63(2); Montreville, 514; Nancy, 62; Phidiler Siler, 514; Phidiler West, 513; Polly, 63; Rachel, 61, 62; Rhoda, 62; Rhoday, 63; Sarah Nettie L.,64; Seborn, 63(2); Selena, 62; Solomon, 62; Sophonie Adaline, 513; Sophronia Adaline, 514; T. J., 63; Thomas, 458; Thomas Jefferson, 62;William, 62, 63; William C., 61, 63; William Carroll, 63, 64; William Carson, 63(2); William Perrian, 64; William Washington, 513

WESTCOAT: Mary, 287

WESTMORELAND: J. R., 260

WHEDBEE: Richard, 491; Sarah, 491; William, 491

WHEELER: Benjamin, 397; Henry, 397; Isaac, 397; James, 397; John, 397(2);Mary Ann, 397; Matilda, 397; Polly, 397; Sally, 397; Serena Pirkle, 152;Susan, 397

WHETSTONE: Pearlie, 322

WHILDON: Martha, 242

WHITAKER: James, 483; Jessie J., 265; John, 483; Joshua, Sr., 483; Mary, 483(2); Sarah, 483; William, 483

WHITE: Benjamin, 56; Betty Lee, 166; Bishop, 350; Boyce, 165, 166; Calvin A., 56; Carrie, 165; Carrie Ruth, 166; Charles, 56(2); Elizabeth, 56;Eunice B., 405; Eva Foster, 166; Eva P., 166; Evelyn, 59; Frederick, 490(2); Hazel Lorene, 166(2); J. S., Revolutionary, 168; James Darby, 341(2); James U., 56; Jane, 54; Jessie T., 56; John, 54; John M., Revolutionary, 489; Lewis R., 56; Marian Elizabeth, 166; Marjorie, 165; Marjorie Ethel, 166; Mary, 54, 165, 166; Mary Anne, 166; Mildred, 165; Mildred M., 56; Nancy N., 56; Paley D., 56; Paul, 165; Phyllis, 165(2); Ralph, 165; Robert, 54(2); Robert E., 56; Robert, Jr., 56; Stephen, 54; Susan, 54; Susan C., 56; Susannah, 242; Thomas T., 56; Tillman, 56; W. F., 165, 166; Wallace Franklin, 166; Will, 166; William, 54; William Boyce, 166(2); William F., 166; William H., 44

WHITENER: Abram, 467; Barbara, 467; Catherine, 467; Daniel, 467; Elizabeth, 467; Henry, Capt., 467; Henry, Sr., 467; Mary Ann, 467; Molly, 467

WHITESIDE: John, Sr., 362; Mary Underwood, 362

WHITESIDES: E., 230

WHITFIELD: Elizabeth, 82

WHITMAN: Margaret, 87

WHITMEL: Mary, 458; Thomas, Col., 458

WHITSON: Evelyn, 90

WHITTEN: Reuben, 171

WIDEMAN: Dr., 167

WIGFALL: Revolutionary, 74

WILBOURN: Fannie, 540

WILBUR: Jennie Higgins, 156

WILCOX: Mabel, 579

WILDER: R. H., Mrs., 332

WILEY: Abener, 397; Alfred, 398; Ann, 398; Elizabeth Mary, 20, 328; Isaiah, 397; James, 20(3), 327; Jane Ann, 20; Mary, 169; Samuel, 398; Shannon, 397; William, 397(2)

WILEY (COLORED): Anney, 20; Charles, 19; John, 20; Juda, 20; M., 20; Mary, 20; Nelson, 19; Sam, 19

WILFONG: Elizabeth, 467

WILKERSON: Jessie, 26

WILKIE: Grace M., 384

WILKINS: John J., 152; John Julian, 282; Lucille, 282; S. B., Revolutionary, 282; Samuel M., 152; W. B., 282(2)

WILLARD: Harriet Newkirk, 525; William B., Revolutionary, 321

WILLIAM: Jeremiah, 100

WILLIAM OSKER: Sarah Rebecca Ann, 51

WILLIAMS: Aaron, 123, 124; Andrew L., 216; Benjamin, Col., 554; Eleanor, 124; Eleika, 156; Elzey, 124; Esther, 123(2); Etelka, 156; Harriet, 553; Henry, 125; Isaac, Jr., Capt., 523; J. Adeline, 94; James R., 123, 124; Jane, 124; John, 123, 124; John Lester, 551; Joseph Absalom, 171; Joyce,61; Julia Ann, 531; Lightfoot, 467; Lucy, 433; Margaret, 123; Marget,124; Martha, 555; Mary Ann, 504; Moses, 123, 124(2); Nancy, 63; Naomi,124; Naomi L., 124; Nora Black, 551; Rebekah, 124; Robert, 553; Robert Anderson, 228; S. C., 529; Sarah, 124; Susanna, 124; Walter, Mrs., 408;William, 124

WILLIAMSON: John R., 83

WILLINGHAM: R. J., Dr., 220

WILLIS: Emily, 54; Nathan, 555; Susana, 100; William, 100

WILLSON: Horace, 471; Mercy, 522; Rebecca, 522; Rpbert, 522

WILSON: A. J., 282; Alexander, 152; Ann, 542; Daniel, 544; Eliza, 542; Elizabeth, 15, 405, 406, 540, 542(2), 543(2), 544; Emma Elizabeth Ivy, 481; Euell, 542; Geneva Sansing, 482; Harold, 541; Harriet, 542; Irene, 482; Isabella, 542, 543; Isler Dawson, 482; J. W., Revolutionary, 321; James, 544; James Jennings, 319; John, 540, 541, 542(2), 543(2), 544; John James, 542; John, Jr., 542; Joseph, 15; Leon, Mrs., 260; Lucinda, 542; Lucy, 542, 544; Lyra Field, 482; M. M., 481; Magnolia Ramsey, 156; Mary, 540, 541, 542(2), 544(2); Mary Rosa, 282; Miles, 542, 544; Nancy, 542; Samuel, Gen., 405, 406; Sarah Elizabeth, 320; Stephen Mazyck, 211; Tabitha, 542,544(2); Thomas, 541, 542(2); Thomas F., 405; Thomas, Jr., 541; W. Howell, 480; William, 500(2)

WIMBERLY: George, 60; Mourning, 60

WINDERS: Ann, 530; Nancy, 533

WINGO: Eunice, 46

WISE: Isaiah, 276

WITHERS: Josephine Randolph, 131

WITTE: Ernest M., Mrs., 279

WOLF: Ann Mary, 342

WOLFE: A. Ere, 421; Ann Mary, 341; Emma, 221; Jacob, 421; Jefferson Beauregard, 421(2); John C., 421; Larance Marchel, 421; Marshall L., Jr.,421; Mary L., 421; Mary P., 421; N. E., 421; Nancy, 421; Nancy Ellen,421; P. L., 421; Phebe L., 421; Phoebe L., 421; Sanford Robert, 421(2);Sarah Jane, 421(2); Sary G. Jane, 421; W. C., 421; William C., 421;William Cathey, 421; William Ivey, 421

WOOD: Aaron, 137, 138; Achsah, 138; Ann, 40; Anne E., 191; Barzilia, 137; Candis, 137; Charity, 40; Daniel, 40; Dorotha, 137; Elizabeth, 40(2),137, 355; Elizabeth Nash, 40; Fanney, 137; Gracy, 355; Henry, 39, 40(2); Isham, 40(2); J. Terry, 40; James, 40; James Edmund, 355(2); Jesse, 191; John, 40, 355(2); Joseph, 137; Keziah, 355; Lotty, 40; M. A., 139; Mahala, 40; Martha, 138; Martha Josephine, 191; Martha O., 40; Mary, 40; Mary A. G., 191; Matilda, 138; Matthew, 137; Nancy, 354, 355; Nancy Jane Dink, 353; Patsey Ruckner, 354; Patsy, 137; Patsy Bush, 355; Rebecca, 137, 355; Rezen, 137; Robert, 355; Robertson, 355; Salley Anderson, 355;Stephen, 137; Stony, 355; Thomas Jefferson, 191; William, 354; William Bush, 355; Zentippe, 191

WOODSON: Jane, 252

WOODWARD: Caroline, 564; N. H., 494; W. J., 563

WOOTTEN: Mary Smith, 524; Thomas, 525

WORTHAM: Benjamin, 171

WRIGHT: Eliza Jane, 417; Elizabeth, 171; H. Grady, Mrs., 334; J. T., 417;William Harrison, 171

WYATT: Edna Esther, 196; Eliah, 196; Elias Key Harriet, 197; Elijah, 197; Eliza, 196; James, 202; James Foster, 196; Malinda, 197; Mary, 183;Mildred Lunni, 197; Redmond Grisby, 196; Susan Cecile, 197; William, 196; William Newton, 196; Willie, 196

WYLIE: M. L., 230; William, 351

WYLLY: Samuel, 14

WYLY: Dinah, 14; John, 15; Robert, 15(2); Sally, 14, 15; Sam, 14; Samuel,15; William, 15

YARBOROUGH: Arthur, 187; Elizabeth E., 187

YEAGER: Emaline, 68

YEATES: Archibald Piper, 497; Archie P., 498; Charles Morris, 497; Elizabeth, 496; George Scott, 497; James, 496; James B., 496(3), 497(2),498; James Y., 496; Jane Maria, 497; Jesse, 497; Jesse J., 497, 498; Jim, 497; John, 497(2); Lucretia, 496(2), 497, 498; Lucretia Jane, 496(2);Maria E., 498; Virginia, 497; Virginia L., 497; William Smith, 497(2)

YORK: Maude Carolyn, 508

YOUNG: Anna Elizabeth, 448; E. D., Mrs., 197; Eleanor, 435; John, 98; John Prewit, 98; Molly, 104; Raney, 98; S. C., 308; Susan C., 308

YOUNGE: Rachel, 286

Other books by Jeannette Holland Austin:
1860 Paulding County, Georgia Census
Alabama Bible Records
DeKalb County, Georgia Probate Records
*Fayette County, Georgia Probate Records: Volume II
Annual Returns, Inventories, Sales, Bonds, 1845-1897*
Georgia Bible Records, Supplement, 1772-1940
Georgia Obituaries, 1740-1935
Georgia Obituaries, 1905-1910
Jackson County, Georgia Tombstones
Jeannette Holland Austin and Dorothy Holland Herring
Masters of the Low Country: A History of the Georgia Colony
North Carolina–South Carolina Bible Records
The Georgians Database: Genealogical Notes
Virginia Bible Records

www.ingramcontent.com/pod-product-compliance
Lightning Source LLC
Chambersburg PA
CBHW070903300426
44113CB00008B/922